THE AFRICAN ORIGIN OF MODERN JUDAISM:

FROM HEBREWS TO JEWS

THE AFRICAN ORIGIN
OF MODERN JUDAISM:
FROM HEBREWS
TO JEWS

JOSÉ V. MALCIOLN

Africa World Press, Inc.

P.O. Box 1892

Trenton, NJ 08607

P.O. Box 48

Asmara, ERITREA

Africa World Press, Inc.

P.O. Box 1892
Trenton, NJ 08607

P.O. Box 48
Asmara, ERITREA

Book and Cover design: Jonathan Gullery

Library of Congress Cataloging-in-Publication Data

Malcioln, José V.
   The african origin of modern Judaism : from Hebrews to Jews / José V. Malcioln.
     p.   cm.
   Includes bibliographical references and index.
   ISBN 0-86543-371-2. -- ISBN 0-86543-372-0 (pbk. : alk. paper)
    1. Jews--History--Miscellanea. 2. Blacks--History--Miscellanea.
   3. Blacks--Relations with Jews. I. Title.
   DS118.M253   1996
   909'.04924--dc20
                                       96-33719
                                           CIP

This book is composed in Bookman and Copperplate

CONTENTS

INTRODUCTION

Some historians blinded by prejudice, racial myth, and ethnicity, have proved their ignorance of history by the inaccuracies they write about Africa and Africans.

One writer quoted as an authoritative statement of unquestionable merit a pseudo-historic statement that said ". . . a wholly spurious history was foisted on the black man in over compensation for his comparatively recent arrival in the stage of history."[1] This statement and so many other distortions of facts have been published that dissemination of African History should be the responsibility of persons concerned with truth rather than the self-gratifying occupation of those burdened with prejudice.

Ethnocentrism and xenophobia are forms of prejudice which cause certain scholars to become blind to historical facts or inclined to falsify them deliberately. These weaknesses often degenerate to viciousness. When prejudiced writers become vicious, it is easy, perhaps gratifying, for them to present Africans as backward people or members of naked tribes dancing and living in the jungle.

We might then ask: Weren't all people naked at one time or another? Then we must state: Historians and anthropologists have found no conclusive evidence to prove otherwise! Furthermore, there is no evidence to support any theory that the so-called white race has evolved more than any other. Nevertheless, some European writers, and their American counterparts ignore that fact.

The history of Africa in its pristine or near-pristine form has been transmitted to its oppressed peoples through records, oral traditions, tribal customs, and relics passed down from one generation to the next. Some of it has been inaccessible to Europeans. It does not mean that the tradition of passing accurate data or family recollections is exclusive. It does mean that the history pertaining to the earliest state or time is not always accessible to all people who wish to tell the truth using evidence presented without deliberate omissions. African history recorded by Africans in Africa is sought even less by prejudiced historians who do not seek or wish to know the facts.

The history of Africa is the legacy and knowledge acquired by the heir of its past generations. In addition to this inheritance are the innate and environmental naturalness the individual acquires from his ancestors. Consequently, his development and behavior follow the path that his heritage has traced for him. One must understand how spiritual ideas, religious preference, idealistic or rationalistic elaborations began in an epoch whose records were lost, but which have continued to be transmitted nevertheless from generation to generation to become deeply rooted in many minds.

African history shows that many distortions have been published. Moses of Egypt, northeast Africa, was made "white," and Abraham is often depicted with pale skin, and described as "Semitic but of European origin." In the midst of the confusion, however, the media did admit in a movie *Entebbe*—about the Israeli invasion of Uganda—that they were both black. Hanibal de la Barca, a North African, Socrates, a Greek of non-Greek origin, and the Great Yeshua (Jesus), a descendant of Naphtali, the sixth son of Jacob, are also painted with pale faces.[2] Nevertheless, Godfrey Higgins proved that they were black. The fact that these leaders came from Africa where the sun is very hot, causing melanin to be abundant in the pigmentation of persons born and raised in that environment, is omitted from the information disseminated by self-proclaimed scholars. How did these researched and studied Africans become Caucasians?

These leaders became Caucasians when Africa lost its power and Europeans began writing the continent's history and publishing its accomplishments as European cultural developments. The contributions of these leaders were then offered with present distortions and past omissions. Overlooking certain important facts about African cultural and scientific developments was the much-needed element in the transformation process of justifying ethnic, social, and economic prejudice.

J.A. Rogers, an on-the-spot reporter who saw the transformations after undertaking extensive research, began writing true African history to contradict distortions he encountered. In response to European accounts, he said, "They wrote books glorifying themselves and minimizing the achievements of other races." Rogers also noted, "Race prejudice sprang out from the writings of Europeans."[3]

Since most historians are Caucasians, and being pale-faced is supposed to be a badge of honor, European writers and their American counterparts support their undeserved pride with ancestor-worship based on the biased transformations. European ethnocentrism is understandable. It is unacceptable, however, to true scholars who have visited the areas and gathered their own evidence. Unbiased historians like Doris Lessing and some others feel that "the single biggest hang-up Europe has got" is that it is "almost impossible for anyone in the West not to see the West as the God-given gift to the world."[4]

European and African, as well as other writers who profess undistorted evidence as gathered, serve notice: History's fiction writers will be compelled to realize that they are suddenly dealing with an awakening humanity not only conscious of its history but capable of writing it.

The presentation of historical developments from strictly European points of view, ignoring African cultural and technological contributions, is analogous to ignoring the fact that while some African tribes wore flowing robes and ate cooked meat, most European clans were still eating raw meat and living in caves without clothing. Presentations blinded by prejudice are ethnically offensive, moraly disturbing, and psychologically abrasive to Africans and persons of African origin.

Rogers (1880–1966), an historian of world renown, also affirmed, "our ancestors were the originators of great civilizations both inside and outside Africa long before Europe appeared on the map. African History is what the race has thought, felt, and accomplished."*

Africa is a vast continent of 11,700,000 square miles. It is "four times the size of the United States, and the whole of Europe, India, China, and the United States could be held within its borders."[5] African history encompasses a gigantic land mass inhabited by diversified tribes, nations and admixtures with different customs and lifestyles. Most of these variables existed before its recorded history became known to foreigners, and long before the European invasions. Any attempt to present world history with segments of linguistic, anthropologic, demographic, or other progress of mankind must therefore show Africa on the vertical as well as the horizontal charts with lines of progressive developments originating through and developing by all races: How the people spoke, what they looked like, where they came from, how, why, and when they came to be what they are today?

This historical study will show vertically the contributions made before and after certain periods of Jewish dispersion from Africa. It will also deal with simultaneous occurrences in the periods discussed, and show the areas inhabited inside, and outside the continent. We will prove that amalgamation, mutation, and even transformation can change people.

When studies overlook the cultural and material contributions of any ethnic group that inhabited an area, particularly an oppressed group, they manifest justification for existent prejudices and unwarranted oppression. Those studies show indifference to the susceptibilities of the group oppressed and exploited, causing some of its members to feel inferior. But isn't that their primary purpose?

Distorted histories also repudiate debts owed to the oppressed group for its contributions to the advancement of all mankind.[6]

Historians blinded by prejudice are fond of writing African history. They unscrupulously refer to Africa as the Dark Continent. Any traveler, white or black, knows that Darkness is in the North! All Worshipful Masters are in the East, and we seek *light* in the East. The darkness was in Europe until approximately the year 7 B.C. Ethiopia had already been founded in 6280 B.C., by Cush. One European scholar attested to the truth when he wrote:

> The records left by Europeans do not commence till the latter part of the fourteenth century, and none of them have left any account on any statements that may have been made to them by the people as to their past history. Very little is known, therefore, about the origin of these tribes, and such accounts as have been handed down and are current among them at the present are purely traditionary.[7]

Walton Claridge was one white scholar who presented his findings without bias. He studied many African tribes, and reinforced his arguments with facts. Claridge pointed out that although the Gold Coast African seldom migrated, he made long journeys for the purpose of trade and may have stayed away from his home for years. But, he stressed, "they always return to their original home." A good historian, he concluded with unbiased judgment of the evidence amassed. Claridge wrote that the better-class, from whom his traditionary accounts of past events were obtained, belonged to families which had their homes in the same place from time immemorial. His final statement was:

> Among such a people, tradition has a far greater value than among less settled races, for places and natural objects connected with their past history are constantly before their eyes, and assist in preserving the story from generation to generation.

FROM AFRICA TO EUROPE

One might ask: What relationship exists between Africa and the Hebrews or Jews? The answer is not simple, but the facts are clear and simple. Hebrews were first, and they came out of Canaan; they are associated with the land *Cana*. Jews were second, and are mainly identified with Europe and the converts gathered there through the *Diaspora*. The people and languages were Semitic. Semites do not come out of European admixtures or origins. Europe was not a recognized cultural entity during the days of Hebrew prominence, or even in the days of Muhammad.[8]

What was Canaan then is now called *Eretz Israel* (Land of Israel). The Bible (a very good book of reference) states clearly that Jacob built an altar in the city of Luz "which is in the land of Canaan, that is Bethel (Beth–el)." After Jacob was blessed by the Almighty, "God said unto him, Thy name is Jacob: thy name shall be called no more Jacob, but Israel shall be thy name."[9] Israel is in northeast Africa. Any person who has visited Israel, crossed into Egypt, then on to the Sudan, will recognize that conspicuous fact.

In order to better acquaint those interested in all monotheistic religions that originated in the same region with an understanding of their ancient beginnings and ancestral ties, the facts have been gathered and presented herein with a minimal amount of personal comments or opinions. The history is merely presented as it relates to the common origin of the Hebrew, and other religions, as derived from the common origin of man, without self-serving revisions like those of European historians.

Consequently, this book is prepared with two groups of readers in mind. The first, college and university educators and students who deliberately misinform others, and the second, citizens of all countries and religions who might espouse distortions inadvertently, and are honestly seeking scientific guidance through truth, to improve inter-group relations everywhere.

This book will also attempt to correct as many false historical pronouncements as possible. It will show—as most Hebrews and Jews already know—that Hebrews and Hebraism originated in Africa and not in Europe. It will even show monotheism originating in Africa before Arian pagans recognized that concept.

All findings presented in this work are carefully documented. If my effort shows the slightest difference with proper sources in some of its minor details, that fault will be due to human fallibility rather than advantageous purpose or deceptive intent. It is with the hope of avoiding inconsistencies that the major facts are selected and presented with a consistent determination to present a study beyond scrutiny or contradictions of any significance.

The presentation of diverse facts and views herein are not intended to discredit Zionists or Europeans. Neither is it intended to apologize for expressing those facts that had to be expressed with frankness which might distress selfish and prejudiced groups that have nurtured myths of racial superiority for generations.

This simply means that Africans must be heard also. It is their duty to show through their history why descendents of Africans from Patagonia, Canada, the Caribbean, England, and elsewhere, are attempting no longer to be "tired of living and afraid of dying," as the American composer wrote for them. "We are tired of abuses, and will die if we have to, but not alone!"

Furthermore, with oppressed Europeans and Euro-Americans also protesting their controlled existence while resounding their vulnerability to nuclear plants around the world, Africans are awakening and are no longer satisfied with merely clapping their hands, stomping their feet, and singing "We Shall Overcome." Many Africans are willing to join any group struggling for freedom of expression to obtain knowledge, self-determination, and mutual respect through equal opportunity. Ethnic identity based on color without merit is unimportant. The most important objective sought is sincere intent and purpose in the concerted effort of creating a better world for all mankind, where its space and wealth will be equitably shared, without the many being crowded, abused, and exploited by the selfish few.

NOTES

1. Craenum Berger. *Black Jews in America* (New York: Federation of Jewish Philanthropies, 1978), p. 54.
2. Colerus, the historian, said that Socrates had dark skin, unruly hair and beard. And the Greeks said that Kristos had "wooly hair and skin like unburnished brass." Godfrey Higgins. *Anacalypsis* (England, F.S.A.F.R. Asiat. Soc. F.R. Ast. Soc. of Skellow Grange near Doncaster, 1833). Vol. I. p. 138.
3. J.A. Rogers. *The Real Facts About Ethiopia* (London, England: The African Publication Society, 1981), p.1.
4. Doris Lessing. "On Feminism, Communism and 'Space Fiction'" New York Times Magazine/ July 25, 1982.
5. Stanlake Samkange. *African Saga* (New York: Abingdon Press, 1971). J. R. Rogers. *World's Great Men of Color*. New York: McMillan, 1972.
6. Lerone Bennett, Jr. *Before the Mayflower*. (Baltimore:Penguin Books, 1966). Thaddeus Stevens proposed a measure authorizing the President to set aside lots of 40 acres to compensate freedmen after slavery in "the land of the free." Stevens, Thaddeus: 1792–1868. Radical Republican Congressional leader during Reconstruction. Admitted to the Maryland bar, he moved to Pennsylvania. Proposed to give each freedman 40 acres of land. The New Encyclopaedia Britannica. 1987: Vol. 11. p. 261.
7 Constantine François de Chessebeux Volney (France *Voyage in Syria et en Egpyt*)
8. Joseph J. Williams, S. J. Williams S. J. *Hebrewisms in West Africa From Nile to Niger With the Jews* (New York: Bible Tannem Booksellers and Publishers, Inc. 1967), p. 30.
9. Genesis 35:10: The name Israel means "He who strives with God."

CHAPTER I

FROM HEBREWS TO JEWS

The history of the Jews is the history of the Hebrews. It is also a history interwoven with religion. The story of the Jews is based on the history and religion of the Hebrews. Neither can be related without mention or support of the other. James Parkes said, "The history of the Jews is not the history of a 'race'; for Jews were not of pure stock at the beginning of their story, and in their dispersion their borrowings have been physical as well as intellectual and spiritual."[1]

Not only did the Jews borrow in their dispersion, they borrowed before. Even their Ten Commandments were borrowed from the *147 Negative Confessions* written by Africans 4100 B.C.E., as we intend to show and explain later.[2]

Who are the Jews and what is their proper place in history? The Jews are descendants of the Hebrews! The Italians did not exist before the Romans or the Greeks before the Hellenes; so the proper place of the Jews is after the Hebrews. The Jews are a people so named after their return as refugees to the "Land of Judea" from their Babylonian captivity. The original people who left Chaldea and came to Canaan to preach monotheism were called Hebrews.

The king of Judah was Ahaz, son of Jotham. He ruled from ca.735-to ca.720 B.C.E. His kingdom had been attacked by Israel and Syria. Finding himself overwhelmed by his enemies, Ahaz robbed the Temple of part of its gold and silver and sent it to Tiglath—Pileser, king of Assyria, to purchase his friendship and assistance, promising Ahaz, besides, to become his vassal and to pay him tribute. The King of Assyria, finding so favorable an opportunity of adding Syria and Palestine to his empire, readily accepted the proposal. Centuries later, after the Assyrian annexation, Babylon captured and ruled Judea, under Nebuchadnezzar.

From 597 to 596 B.C.E. we see the Kingdom of Judah conquered by Babylon, the Temple of Jerusalem destroyed, and the Hebrews dispersed along with the Jews. This period is known as the Babylonian Captivity, and mourned as punishment for the Tower of Babel. When the Babylonian captivity ended, with Babylon crushed in turn by the vast Persian Empire of Cyrus II (558–529 B.C.E.), the Jews were permitted to return to Palestine. Some returned to Jerusalem to rebuild the Temple in 538 B.C.E., but many of them chose to remain in Babylon.

Solomon Reinach says of those who returned: "The name 'Jews' applied to any people is posterior to the exile . . . Strictly speaking, it means the region to the west of Jordan and to the south of Samaria . . . those who inhabited Judeah."[3]

Then who are the Hebrews? The Hebrews were Babylonians! They came from Babylonia to Canaan. They crossed the river Jordan to reach Canaan. Where is Babylonia? Babylonia is between the Tigris and the Euphrates rivers—near Canaan. Canaan, now called Palestine or Israel, is in northeast Africa. It is not in Asia as some European and American cartographers conveniently put it.[4]

The name Palestine comes from the Latin *Palestina*. That name properly denotes the land of the Philistines, and was first applied to the hinterlands by the Greeks. The present Palestine was named Palestinian Syria in classical antiquity, the latter component being omitted in due course. It is considered possible that the name *Palestina* was imposed by the Romans on the former Judea, to discourage Judaization. The frontiers of Palestine, as determined in the Bible, are approximately: the Mediterranean Sea to the west; the Syrian Desert to the east; and bordered on the south by the the Brook of Egypt—Wadi El-Arish. Her boundary with Egypt is on the southwest. From there one may travel north to Ethiopia or the area now called Sudan on the new maps.

When the Hebrews came to this land from Babylon they called it *Eretz Cana*, Land of Canaan. The Zionists later called it *Eretz Israel*, Land of Israel. These Babylonians who became Hebrews or Canaanites were descendants of Nimrod, a black son of Ham. They arrived with Abraham, the *rosh aboth*, or patriarch and founder of the Hebrew colony.

Abraham came from Ur in the Chaldea. His father's name was Terah. Abraham, like the Ethiopians and Arabians, was a native of the territory where Nimrod, the first king of Shinar or Babylonia and Mesopotamia, reigned. He built the city of Erech—Iraq today—visited by Abraham and other Semites.[5]

Abraham's countrymen were Bedouins. These Babylonians worshipped the sun, djinns, spirits, fetishes, totems, and idols. They celebrated ritualistic festivals, practiced magic, and prayed or shouted to Baal, Sabaoth, Theraphim, and other gods.

Reinach also stated, "The Hebrews made their first appearance in History as nomads." Abraham, their patriarch, is said to have crossed the Jordan every Friday night—the Sabbath eve—to preach monotheism to the people of Canaan. Abraham taught the Canaanites exaltation of the Supreme God above all other gods. His proclamation was *Shema Israel Adenai Elohenu Adenai Ehad!* It meant: Hear O Israel, the Lord our God is One! The Lord is One!

Abraham professed visions from the Almighty who changed his name to Abram, as it is written in the Torah. After making several trips across the Jordan river into Canaan (Israel), the Canaanites began to call Abraham and his relatives and followers "Habiru, Habiru!" It meant: people from across the river. Reinach stated that they were also called "Hibri," meaning immigrants from the other side of the Jordan or Euphrates rivers. For the natives of Canaan, the name Hibri meant, in their language akin to Hebrew, "people from beyond."

In any case, the thoroughly researched etymological and historical derivation of the word is established. Its translation became Hebrew (in English), Hebreo (in Spanish), Ebreo (in Italian), Hebreu (in French), and Hivrit (in Hebrew).

Ish Kishor Sulamith (1948) described Abraham and the Hebrews as nomadic Bedouins who lived in tents, and roamed the desert: "4,000 years ago the Hebrews pitched their tents in Canaan." They seem to have finally settled in Canaan after migrating to the east, south, southwest, and west. Reinach dated their settlement at approximately 2100 B.C. He quoted Genesis 14, and other data, and placed Abraham in the reign of a king named Amraphel, possibly identified with Hammurabi, who reigned in Babylon during that period.[6]

Reinach's 1929 work shows a slight difference from other historians' date of 1775 B.C.E. The Bible gives no precise date. It merely states that "Terah begat Abraham . . . Now the Lord had said unto Abram, get thee out of thy country, and from thy father's house, unto a land that I will show thee. And I will make of thee a great nation."

Abraham was said to be seventy-five years of age when he left Haran for Canaan. Be that as it may, we should be more concerned with his "ethnic stock at the beginning of their story," as Parkes put it. Was Abraham Ethiopic, Semitic, or Asiatic? Were the Canaanites in fact Ethiopic or Asiatic? Is there any linguistic proof of their racial origin? The Bible, translated into many languages and revised in many ways to suit different purposes, gives no precise data or evidence on which one might erect resistant pillars under a temple of unquestionable proof. Nevertheless, the Arabs document these facts, supported by Josephus Flavius and other historians of that time.

They state, "the forefathers of Ibrahiym lived in the 'CUSH' (Sudan or Africa), then migrated to Ur Chaldees. Therefore, his forefathers were called 'Cushites', which was part of his inheritance."[7] In Hebrew Cush means dark-faced, and in Arabic it means black.

Josephus, whose Hebrew name was Yoseph ben Mattityahu ha–Cohen, ca.38–ca.100 C.E., was a Palestinian of rabbinical descendance. He was considered an expert in political affairs. The Revolutionary government sent him against Rome at Galilee. When the Romans attacked Galilee in 67 C.E. and besieged it, Josephus went over to them, and abandoned the Jews. Josephus took notes at the time, and preserved one of the most accurate accounts of the wars with Rome, the people and places. He recorded that the children of Ham possessed the land from Syria to Amanus. "The Hamitic people were in Syria as overlords."[8] His text described the Syrians as an "originally Hamitic tribe." Josephus inferred that if they were not black at their beginning, Abraham and the rest of the people from the area became black, curly-haired, and Hamitic through infusion or amalgamation with the Cushites and other descendants of Ham. And the children of Ham possessed the mountains of Albanus, controlled everything even its seacoasts as far as the ocean, and kept it for quite some time. Josephus drew attention to the fact that some of the names of places he mentioned have vanished and others have been changed. This made it difficult for some of them to be discovered in modern times; yet there are a few which have kept their names; for of the four sons of Ham, time has not affected the name of Cush. Josephus impartially declared that while theocracy was developing in that area, the other descendants of Cush were migrating from Gaza to Egypt. The Encyclopaedia Britannica surreptitiously or inadvertently declares, "The people involved seemed to have been of Caucasian race."[9]

Evidence gathered by Josephus, Godfrey Higgins, the Ansaru Allah Community writers, and other recognized researchers contradict the obvious distortions published by *The Encyclopaedia Britannica*.

The Ansaru researchers describe Abraham in more detail. They mention his three wives: Sarah, Hagar and Keturah. From their sons, Ishmael, Isaac, and Midian, came the Twelve Tribes of Ishmael—Arabians, Twelve Tribes of Israel—Hebrews, the Edomites (descendants of Esau), and the Midianites, whose eponym was a son of Abraham and who were the first people to use the camel.[10]

ABRAHAM VISITS EGYPT

During the middle of the second millennium B.C.E. a series of droughts beset the areas in geographical positions on the Mediterranean seacoast between Asia and Africa. With Canaan between the river valleys of the Nile and the Euphrates, it was easy for Abraham to travel from Ur to Palestine, Syria, Egypt, and Arabia. During one of his visits to Egypt, Abraham met Imhopteh the architect (also known as Inhotep and Aesculapius), who was more prominent as a physician than as an architect. Imhopteh was the high priest of Egypt and a student of the Pharoah Zozer, who had him build the first Step Pyramid at Saqqara. Hearing of Abraham's encounter with the Pharoah, Imhopteh went to visit him. The Moslems declare that they prayed and fasted forty days and forty nights.

In any event, it is during this visit that the two high priests discussed the uncleanliness of the animal-like people from behind the rock, and the Caucasoid Mountains. Abraham is said to have informed Imhopteh of the people and asked how to deal with their strange curse. The Egyptian is said to have smiled because he was familiar with these people. He then explained to the patriarch that their curse was a disease called baras, meaning leprosy.[11] Imhopteh described the mountain people as soulless, heartless, hemophiliacs who ate anything, including an animal called *khinzir* that they had hybridized from rodents. They were carnivorous, preferring bloody carcasses rotting in their midst. As a result, they contracted the leprosy that plagued them and caused famine. Their cohabitation during menstruation added to their unhealthful conditions, and they cohabited with jackals and sheep, ate raw flesh, and did not bury their dead. Imhopteh said these people had attempted to come down to live in Egypt. They had sought to cleanse themselves and be raised from the dead level on which they lived. However, they had failed to remain in Egypt long enough to receive knowledge of hygiene and proper diet because their diseased bodies could not resist the heat of the valleys.

Reinach relates Manetho's account of the expulsion of the lepers among the people of the Exodus. Manetho (circa 300 B.C.E.) was an Egyptian historian and a priest at Heliopolis under Ptolemy I and II. Manetho, like the Ansaru researchers, agrees that these lepers were not "Asiatic Black men, but Caucus-Asians, who had been cursed." Their bodies were like dead carcasses . . . and they were called "Deteriorating Blacks."[12]

The consumption of raw meat with blood is prohibited by a Hebrew law *Kashrut* (from Hebrew *kasher,*meaning fit). It was obviously promulgated to avoid cannibalism as well as the barbarism practiced by the Caucasians. In regard to their bestiality, Graves and Patai give scientific rationalizations for their acts. They explain:

> Primeval man was considered by the Babylonians to have been androgynous . . . .The tradition that man's first sexual intercourse was with animals, not women, may be due to the widely spread practice of bestiality among herdsmen of the Middle East, which

is still condoned by custom, although figuring three times in the Pentatouch as a capital crime. In the Akkadian Gilgamesh Epic, Enkidu is said to have lived with gazelles and jostled other wild beasts at the watering place.[13]

AMORITES: SONS OF CANAAN

The Bible clearly states: Canaan begat Si-don, his firstborn, and Heth, and the Jebusite, and the Amorite, and the Girgasite. The Bible has three important parts. It can always be depended on as a source of reference in one of three literary phases. It contains their myths, history, and our history. The King James version states that there was a flood which destroyed all but eight living souls. They emerged from the Ark on a mountain peak called Ararat, Eastern Turkey.[14]

The pious Moslems proclaim that after the flood, Noah planted grapes in his vineyard. Having no idea of the intoxicating effects of the juice pressed from the grapes, he drank of this beverage and became intoxicated. Noah was uncovered within his tent. Ham, Noah's middle son and the father of Canaan, is said to have seen the nakedness of his father, called his brothers Shem and Japheth, and discussed their father's helplessness with them. When Noah awoke, he is supposed to have cursed Ham for his indiscretion. "Cursed be Canaan; a servant of servants shall he be unto his brethren." This curse also caused Ham's son to be cursed with leprosy. It is said to have been inherited by the Amorites, Horites, Canaanites, Hittites, and others, who became the progenitors of Caucasoid people.[15]

With the sin of Ham falling on his descendants, Isaac called Jacob before he died, gave him the birthright, and said unto him, "Thou shalt not take a wife of the daughters of Canaan." This command was probably given, because the Almighty had given Terah—father of Abraham—a command to cleanse and cure the lepers of the mountain. Once they were cleansed, they could be civilized and redeemed, even brought down to the valley.

Terah had become frightened, and lost faith in God when his food and water finished. Then there was no cultivation or provision for potable water nearby. So Terah panicked upon realizing the danger of being isolated in an area surrounded by savage lepers and tried to hide.

Terah decided to go higher up into the mountains during the night. But he was seized by lepers. Seeing that he was black, smooth-skinned and healthy, the lepers contaminated him.[16]

Isa Muhammad quotes Ezekiel 16:2-4 : "Thus saith the Lord God unto Jerusalem; Thy birth and thy nativity is of the land of Canaan; thy father was an Amorite, and thy mother an Hittite, in the day thou wast born thy navel was not cut, neither wast thou washed in water

. . . He adds: "Because Canaan was an albino he lacked normal eye coloring which caused his eyes to be weak and sensitive to direct sunlight. This is why his sister (who was black) and his descendants (who inherited this trait) sought refuge in the mountains, where the light was dim." Muhammad also elaborated on how the lepers were adaptable to the cold climate of the mountains "because it stopped the leprosy from spreading." He further stated, "The blood of an albino does not contain the necessary salt for reproduction." Many of them must receive blood transfusions at birth, and some throughout their entire lives. Muhammad felt that it was due to those circumstances that the Amorite came down from the Caucasus to mate with the Nubian woman. "She had the proper blood for reproduction and would not bear the full curse of leprosy."[17]

One factor was overlooked by Muhammad. He did not mention that no white woman can produce a black child! Her offspring from a black mate is always a mulatto or pale-faced half-breed, regardless of how black the husband might be! Only a black or an Indian woman can produce a likeness of her mate be he black, mulatto, oriental, or white.

Muhammad gave illustrations of "mankind's fascination with the idea of having sexual intercourse with other animals (especially the dog)." He reinforced this observation with evidence of "French poodles, Great Danes, and Doberman pinschers walking the streets with their female masters." The illustrations, in Muhammad's work, show the abominable act of bestiality which he proclaimed is practiced with gorillas, bulls, bears, and horses. [18]

While studying gorillas, we encounter an eminent scholar, Gordon Allport who wrote about facial features of blacks often mistakingly classified as seeming similar to the ape, while the whites are the ones who definitely have thin lips like most of the apes, plentiful body hair and white skin. Even the great apes—when their hair is lifted up—have a lighter skin color than the African, much closer in resemblance to the skin of the European.[19] Michael Bradley also wrote that Caucasians are of Neanderthal origin: "and carried off other women than their own."

The Europeans did live in caves during the period when some parts of Africa had paved streets and houses made of stone. Europeans in Spain still live in caves.

Basil Davidson presents a different but related argument. He says:

> Those old Cro-Magnon Europeans and "Caucasoids" who came into North Africa some 12,000 years ago were quite surely far from blonde, and any notion that they were European in any sense of the word must be completely dismissed. What one needs to hold

in mind is the gradual crystallization of a few main stocks out of an extremely complex process of natural selection through tens of thousands of years this process being itself the sequence to another and immensely longer period of selection among a range of hominids who were not apes, but who were not full fledged men either.[20]

After reading these studies with different but related approaches to the same question we return to James Parke's remark that "The History of the Jews is not the history of a 'race'; for Jews were not of pure stock at the beginning of their story, and in their dispersion their borrowings have been physical as well as intellectual and spiritual." What does Parkes mean by pure stock ? What does he mean by their borrowings being physical? These pivotal questions were left partially unanswered by him, forcing us to turn elsewhere. In our search we found another exegete or seminarian.

Clarke Jenkins said: the "White man's historical beginnings," in the book of history opens on a page where lines, "contain records of villages, towns, and cities around 2500 B.C.E." This researcher seemed to base most of his findings on history deciphered by keys found in the Bible. Nevertheless, his exegetic treatment of the subject might be accorded validity on the basis of his training in interpretation of the "Book of books." Furthermore, even Parkes agrees that the history of the Jews is one interwoven with religion, and one cannot deal with it justly without, at least, referring to the religious threads which make up its fabric.

Jenkins describes residential areas as being built with walls to keep out intruders and wild animals. He later quotes Leviticus 13 as his source for the information concerning leprous conditions that plagued certain persons whom others considered unclean. These persons with the "blight disease of leprosy," according to him, were put outside the walls as outcasts or untouchables.

The curse of leprosy was even put on Miriam when she criticized Moses, her brother who married the "Ethiopian woman of Abraham's seed [with] rich black oily skin . . . a bearer of fine health and strength."[21]

These outcasts are said to have increased abundantly and attempted to invade the villages and towns in search of nourishment and protection from the wild beasts and inclement weather. "The heads of tribes, and leaders of the villages and towns, often made aggressive and defensive forays [sic] against these increasing hordes of—outcast lepers—driving them hundreds of miles away, into surrounding hills and caves." Jenkins also mentioned the lepers' fear of the heat of the sun's rays: explaining that they had to hide under trees during the day, dig holes in the mountains or live in natural caves. They "were driven northward into a region with mountain ranges called the Caucasian Mountains."

Jenkins concludes, "The period allotted in history, from 1200 B.C. [approximates] the total number of years that the many families, tribes and divisions of people" acquired different names "according to published histories such as Caucasians, Gauls, Goths, Druids, Franks, Anglos, Saxons, Jutes, Celts, etc."

The Bible shows the "stock" beginning with Adam and Eve. Cain, their first born, murders his brother Abel, gets cursed and banished to the area of Nod, east of Eden: "Cain went out from the presence of the Lord, and dwelt in the land of Nod east of Eden. And Cain knew his wife; and she conceived and bore Enoch."[22]

If we could agree on nothing else we might agree on one fact: history is mixed with mythology, and it is sometimes difficult to determine which is which. If Cain did have a wife—and he must have had someone to beget Enoch and the other people who populated that area—from where did Cain's wife come? Adam and Eve, Cain and Abel were supposed to be the only persons on earth with reason at that time! Did Cain meet some hominids, or did he meet hairy apes or other primates? Is that the reason why so-called Caucasians have hairy bodies, flat buttock-less bottoms, thick ankles, and the blue, green, or pale brown eyes of the beasts?

Muhammad emphasizes that there were two Canaans afterwards. There was one in the Caucasus Mountains, and the other in Palestine. He further declares that "Ibrahiym (Arabian name for Abraham) [saw] much disease in the land of Canaan, for the Canaanites were in the land and with them was the leprosy." Abraham is said to have cleansed the lepers, since his father, Terah, had failed to fulfill God's command. After the lepers were restored to an almost healthy condition, they were formed in packs, and brought down, and shipped out. They migrated to parts of Arabia and North Africa. This migration probably accounts for the misnomer Berber. Muhammad continues:

> Therefore, the Paleman began to lose the power to reproduce, because the salt in his body had reached a dangerous minimum. So they had to kidnap the Nubian women in order to have sexual relations and reproduce offsprings that would not bear the full effect of leprosy . . . The pictures that you see of the Cave men with their clubs in one hand and a woman in the other, is a symbol of this fact . . . The result of this "amalgamation" (rape) produced a being, dark in complexion, but with straight dog-like hair having the *nature* of an Amorite.[23]

Many lepers established cities in the lands adjacent to and around Haran, a trading town in northwest Mesopotamia, named after the brother of Abraham, the father of Lot. Those cities were ruled by a Nubian named Nimrod, a son of Cush.

Nimrod had governed his subjects well, until he was tempted by Satan. Influenced by the devil, Nimrod began a life of unrighteousness. His arrogance caused him to feel as mighty as a god—the beginning of his undoing. He considered expansion. But to accomplish his aim he needed more inhabitants to populate his kingdom of "Babel, Erech, Ac-cad, and Cal-neh, in the land of Shinar" Gen.10: 8–10. Therefore, "He welcomed all persons of the descendants of Canaan," promising them that he would cure the unhealthy ones if they would worship and adore him.

Nimrod then erected an empire state building—the Tower of Babel. It towered over all other structures on earth. He wished to prove that there was no one higher than he.

When Abraham arrived in Babylon, he saw Nimrod governing the Amorites whom he had healed and redeemed. He soon learned that Nimrod had duped them into believing that he was deified. Abraham had to prove to the people that they were misled. To expose Nimrod, he quickly challenged the mighty one to make the sun rise in the west. Only the Creator was supposed to have that power. Nimrod decided to make the sun rise in the west instead of the east, but the lepers did not know that he could not perform that feat. The next morning, after Abraham's arrival, the patriarch faced the east as the sun rose. He prayed while Nimrod summoned his best magicians and sorcerers, among whom was the great Merlin. Nimrod's wizards tried every trick they knew, but the sun continued to rise in the east.

The lepers then grabbed Nimrod, crucified him, and left him on a cross for three days [24] Koran 2:258.

Abraham was now free to continue his mission of curing the Amorites of their infectious disease, today called Hansen's disease. The Canaanites lacked melanin, the high concentration of black pigment caused by the sun's rays in the skin or absorbtion from sunlight for long periods of time. It has affected their descendants up to this day; that is why some people sit in the sun for hours trying to get what they call a tan.

NOTES

1. Frederick M. Schweitzer. *A History of the Jews* (New York: The Macmillan Co. 1971). p.27.
2. Yosef A.A. Ben Jochannan. *Tutankhamun's African Roots Haley, et.al., Overlooked:* (New York: Alkebu-Lan Publishers, Inc. 1979).
3. Salomon Reinach. Orpheus: *A History of Religions* (New York, N.Y. Liveright Inc. 1929). p.182.

4. Cecil Roth. *Standard Jewish Encyclopedia* (New York: Doubleday 1959) pp. 974-975.
5. The people of Iraq are original Semites—for whatever that pseudo-linguistic term means. Like the people of Palestine, Ethiopia, Egypt, and Arabia, there are no blond-haired, blue-eyed people (with the exception of hybrids) among them. Semites are not Europeans, and Europeans are not Semites. One cannot be both.
6. The Code of this well known king was '... discovered at Susa in our times." See *The New Columbia Encyclopedia*. (New York: Columbia Univ. Press, 1975).
7. Ansaru Allah Community News. "Forgotten Tribe of Kedar" (New York, 716 Bushwick Avenue, Brooklyn, 11221). p.27.
8. Josephus Flavius. *The Works of Josephus* (Hartford, Connecticut: S.S. Scranton Co. 1917).
9. *Encyclopedia Britannica* (Chicago: 1966). Volume 4. p.726.
10. Josephus Flavius. *The Works of Josephus* Antiquities of the Jews and a History of the Jewish Wars, etc. (Hartford, Connecticut: S.S. Scranton Co. 1917). Godfrey Higgins. *Anacalypsis* (England, F.S.A., F.R. Asiat. Soc., F.R. Ast. Soc., of Skellow Grange near Doncaster, 1833) Vol.I.
11. *Ansaru Allah Community Press* (Bushwick Avenue, Brooklyn, N.Y. 11221. 1930). pp. 36-38. Yosef ben-Jochannan. *Black Man of the Nile* (New York: Alkebu—Lan Books, 1970). p.91.
12. Salmon Reinach. *Orpheus: A History of Religions* (New York, Liveright Inc. 1929). Isa Muhammad. *Ancient Egypt and the Pharaohs* (New York: Ansaru Allah Community Press, 1930). The Gideons. *Holy Bible* (Nashville, Tennesee: Gideons International, 1971 Edition). Leviticus 13.
13. Robert Graves and Raphael Patai. *Hebrew Myths:* The Book of Genesis (New York: McGraw—Hill Book Company, 1964). p.67.
14. *Encyclopedia Britannica*
15. Genesis 9: 20–26 Genesis 28: 1
16. Holy Quran 9:114
17. Isa Muhammad. *Ancient Egypt and the Pyramids* (New York: Ansaru Press (1930). p.15.
18. Isa Muhammad. p.15.
19. Gordon W. Allport. *The Nature of Prejudice* (New York: Doubleday & Company, 1958).
20. Basil Davidson. *Africa In History:* (New York: Macmillan 1974). p.12.
21. Clarke Jenkins. *The Black Hebrews of the Seed of Abraham—Isaac and Jacob* (Michigan: Jenkins Press, 1969). p.70.
22. In the Ethiopian *Book of Adam,* the invention of musical instruments is attributed to Jubal, and of edged brass and iron to his brother Tubal Cain.
23. Isa Muhammad. *Forgotten Tribe of Kedar* (New York: Ansaru Allah Press, 1980). Genesis 14: 13.
24. Isa Muhammad. *Forgotten Tribe of Kedar.* p.37.

CHAPTER 2

SONS OF HAM

The Canaanites were called *Habiru*, an Amharic word used by Ethiopians—a Semitic people. This name forces us to seek sociolinguistic evidence to prove from whence it came, the people it named, and their progenitors.[1] Who were the ancestors of these people? We begin by tracng their communal development and their language. Knowing our history through oral tradition, as it relates to Europeans, we try to make comparisons between what our progenitors told us and what the Europeans write. We find many distortions printed by historians and archaeologists who do not accurately interpret the paintings or hieroglyphics. Furthermore, we North Africans know that our history written in Semitic languages, such as Ge'ez, Amharic, Hebrew, and Arabic, in that order, are often conveniently misunderstood by most of the western world. We are not interested in discussing hieroglyphics here, but it is important to note that some Europeans consider this art form a "spoken language". They sometimes pretend they even know all its secrets. But the writings in tombs, crypts, and other areas are merely a form of art the Egyptians adopted to record important events occurring during battles and the like within certain periods. Many mysteries have been kept—and handed down—orally. Outsiders will never inherit them.

The historians, archaeologists, and pseudo-Egyptologists have located some manuscripts, and inscriptions on stones, as well as the Dead Sea Scrolls and other ancient writings. Godfrey Higgins says of the distorters:

> I sometimes find myself qualified to teach those by whom I was at first very willing to be taught, but whom I do not always find disposed to learn, nor to be untaught the nonsense which they learned in their youth.[2]

All of the findings related to the origin of mankind, proclaimed to have been deciphered, and decoded by these scientists, have been documented with dates before Europe evolved from savagery. Some were written as late as 49 B.C.E., when Julius Caesar visited what is now England, and found the naked clans there using runes.

Higgins sought the story of Noah and his sons, Ham and his sons. He traveled widely and received information firsthand. He described them, and even the Christ, as black. His works were never supported by the London Museum or any other promoters of academic research, because of his straight-forward reporting of facts.

Historian James Parkes, who wrote of Canaan, places its "geographical position on the Mediterranean seacoast between Asia and Africa, between the river valleys of the Nile and the Euphrates."[3] Parkes, however, omitted another important river, the Tigris that also flows there. Babylon and Canaan are on the border of the Tigris and Euphrates rivers.

Canaan was called Cana which meant "Land of Purple," another ancient name given to this important strip of land. A rich purple dye was extracted from murex mollusks which inhabited its nearby waters. This commodity was quite valuable in ancient times. The name *phonix*, meaning purple, was translated by the Greek visitors as Phoenicia (Proverbs 31:22 and Isaiah 23:8). The Canaanites were purveyors of purple dyes.

With Babylon and Canaan established as cities on the banks of the Tigris, Nile and Euphrates rivers, we are forced to investigate the language spoken in those communities. The sociolinguistic network of the Canaanites and their progenitors determined their origin. It also explained who they were before, and after, Nimrod built the Tower of Babel, and the multilingual experience occurred. To reach conclusions, however, we must bear in mind that places and languages were named after persons of importance. That factor brings us to the etymological root of Tigris. Its stem gives us Tigre, the name of a province in Ethiopia, on the Eritrea border. Tigrinya is one of the three important languages evolved from Ge'ez. It is a living language of the Hamitic people (also known as Cushitic). These people spoke: (1) Bedawiye, (2) Agaw, (3) Sidama, consisting of approximately thirty-eight languages, and (4) other separate but related language systems as well. When the Semitic people came to them with a South Arabian speech system, Ge'ez developed. It was also called Ethiopic. Ge'ez was the national language until political upheavals and military defeat brought about gradual sociolinguistic —living together and speaking alike—changes. As a result, Tigrinya, Tigre, and Amharic developed.[4]

With the unraveling of this part of the sociolinguistic knot, we leave linguisitics or language, for a brief moment and move on to the other parts of that study. The anthropological trees and the societal or sociological branches now produce the leaves that complete the hypothesis.

We flash back to the soil. Noah is the soil. He had three sons: Ham, Shem, and Japheth, although the order of their birth is disputed. They were the roots. Ham, the most important of the three, had four sons. They were Cush, his firstborn (also known as Kush or Koch), Phut, Mesraim, and Cana (or Canaan). Cush settled in the land called Ethiopia, "Aethiopia," to Homer the Greek who thought the people there had "burned faces," and described them as "the furthest of mankind." Ethiopia was the kingdom of the Cushites.[5]

Kings came from surrounding areas to pay tribute to the Negus or King of kings. Even the Carthaginians came to trade their goods for Cushite gold. Cush was the father of Nimrod, Seba, Havilah, Ramah, and Sabtecha. He was also the grandfather of Dedan and Sheba, people with burnt faces. The name of Cush stretched far and wide. It can be traced to different places he and his sons occupied during their migratory courses.

Cush dwelt in Babylonia for quite some time during which Nimrod laid the foundation of the great city of Babylon. Nimrod was a Cushite!

Phut settled in an African country south of Cush. It is now called Libya (Genesis 10:6, Chronicles: 1:8). He was the second son of Ham.

Mesraim dwelt in the land now called Egypt. The Arabs call it Misr or Mesre, and the Egyptians Mesri: (Genesis 10:6,13).

Canaan, the fourth son of Ham, "occupied the lands of Phoenicia and Palestine," (Genesis: 9:18,22, 10:13, or. Exodus 15:15). Palestine is now called Eretz, or Medina, Israel, Land or State of Israel.[6]

NOTES

1. Habiru translates to "Nomad people from the other side."
2. Godfrey Higgins. *Anacalypsis* (England, F.S.A.F.R. Asiat. Soc., F.R. Ast. Soc. of Skellow Grange near Doncaster, 1833). Vol I. p. 138.
3. James Parkes. *Whose Land?* A History of the Peoples of Palestine (England: Oxford University Press, 1970). p. 9
4. Ethiopian Ministry of Education at *Addis Ababa*—a name meaning "New Flower."
5. *Encyclopedia Britannica* (Chicago: 1966). p. 790. Vol. 8.
6. William Smith. *Smith's Bible Dictionary* (New York; Doubleday 1966). p.76.

CHAPTER 3

SONS OF SHEM AND JAPHETH

The Semitic people and languages are believed to be descended from Shem, the first son of Noah. They dwelled in western Africa. During the time of Nimrod's rule, they worshipped *Adoshem*, which meant *O Shem*. Today Hebrews and Jews call the Almighty *HaShem*, meaning the Name, for no one truly knows His Name.

The offshoot of their languages consists of two main branches, according to Von Schlözer.[1] They are north Semitic and south Semitic. The third branch is called east Semitic. The south Semitic cuneiform writing was used by the Akkadians, the first people to use it in written form. The north Semitic language has two main branches: Canaanite and Aramaic. The offshoots of the Canaanite branch are Early Hebrew and Phoenician.

Semitic Languages

East Semitic

Akkadian
Babylonian
Assyrian

Canaan or Amorite Group

Phoenetic
Ugaritic-
Hebraic
Moabitic
Punic-Carthaginian

North Semitic
Aramaic
Talmudic language
of the Babylonians
Mandean
Aramaic—western inscription
Toraic Aramaic

South Semitic
Arabic-Northern inscription

Arabic-Modern dialects

Classical antiquity

Palestinian Jewish and
Gentile Aramaic [Southern]
Paletene   Minean and Sabean
Nabatean-Southwest Asia[2]   Ethiopic-Ge'ez

Aramaic was commonly spoken in northern Africa, along with other
Semitic tongues, during biblical times. Another popular language
used in those areas was Punic. A sociolinguistic observation (social
interaction and language use) unfolds the comparison between the
Punic words for new city, *Kart Hadash*, and the Hebrew words *Iyr
Hadash*. The word *hadash*, the name of Carthage, means "new" in
both Semitic languages.

SONS OF JAPHETH

We now come to the supposed second son of Noah, by birth. The
description of the sons of Noah should lead us to the origin of the celebrated term "Chosen people." We have read how Ham was cursed,
and Shem and Japheth were blessed.

Japheth—according to the Pentateuch (or five) Books of Moses in
the Torah: Genesis, Exodus, Leviticus, Numbers, Deuteronomy,
Joshua—was the second son of Noah. "The sons of Japhets; Gomer,
and Magog, and Mã-daî, and Ja-vãn, and Tubal, and Meshech, and
Ti-ras. And the sons of Gomer; Ash-ké-naz, and Ri-phath, and Te-
gar mãh" Genesis (10:2-3).[3] The twenty-seventh verse of the Ninth
Chapter of Genesis proclaims: "God shall enlarge Japheth and he
shall dwell in the tents of Shem; and Canaan shall be his servant."
The Encyclopedia Britannica: Volume 12, page 965, (1966), states,"
tents of Shem; and let Canaan be his slave."[4] The distortions continued "the passage thus indicated friendly relations between the
descendants of Japheth and the Semites."

The encyclopedia writers and editors did not mention the
Hamites. Nevertheless, the Hamitic people have not only dwelled in
the tents of Shem and Japheth, they have dwelt in many other tents.
In the Bible we read that "Cush begat Nimrod: he began to be a mighty
one in the earth . . . Canaan begat Sideon his first born." What we
do not read is "The Phoenicians are Sidonians. The modern name of
Sidon is Saida. It was destroyed in 351 B.C.E. by Jezebel, a Phoenician
princess, who was the daughter of Ethobal, Zidonian king and former priest of Astarte." Jezebel introduced Baal cultism into Israel and
Samaria. She wined and dined 450 prophets of Baal and 400 of
Astarte while she slew all the Lord's Prophets she could lay hands on
(1 Kings: 16:31-32, 18:19). This African woman was no one's slave.

Many writers do not know the origin and the extent of slavery. As
a result, they often pretend that it is endemic to Africans. Slavery

extended from Africa to Europe, and white slavery still exists. Those distorters of historical data, who also omit certain facts, force us to prematurely bring the reader to the soil that was cultivated to hold the roots of ancient civilizations which bore the fruits of sciences and arts, and the branches from which they came.

NOTES

1. August Ludvig Von Schlözer, *Ludvig Ernst* (Germany: Göttinen, Van der Hock-Ruprecht, 1787).
2. Ethiopian Ministry of Education text, Addis Ababa, Ethiopia, 1989.
3. The word Ashkenaz means German. It designates the Jews of Europe. Ashkenazim (plural)
4. The words: slave and salavic, came from Slavonia, Serbia, Croatia, where the Russians enslaved the peasantry. Today, peasants can still be seen wearing burlap bags for shoes in mid-winter, at Yugoslavia, Bulgaria, and elsewhere.

CHAPTER 4

SONS OF CUSH

The sons of Cush were called Cushites. They were the first people to originate the gods of ancient mythology. They were also the first people to build shrines and temples—long before the Egyptians. The Cushites were the first to establish a priesthood, formulate religious creeds, and idolatrous ceremonies. They created the concepts that opened legendary paths along the celebrated avenues of traditions; and transported culture through those avenues to the heathen nations of Asia, Europe, America, and Australia—in that exact order.[1]

Cush founded a land now called Ethiopia. According to the reliable sources, Ethiopia or Cush was founded in 6280 B.C.E. That date is approximately three times as long as the period from the birth of Jesus to the present, or a total of 8,200 years.

Cush had two capitals. They were Napata and Meroe, whose mighty ruins are evidence after all these centuries. One part of Cush is now called Anglo-Egyptian Sudan. The other is extended to the southeast on the Red Sea. In ancient history, Cush included not only Africa but Southern Asia as far as India, according to Herotodus (525-484 B.C.E.).[2] Africans or so-called "Negro" peoples predominated then in Asia Minor where Nimrod, a son of Cush, was founder of the Assyrian Empire. Africans inhabited Southern Arabia, Southern India, Siam, Australia, and the islands of the Pacific. They still exist, and the Moros of the Philippines and other areas, will so attest.

J.A. Rogers, addressed the matter in these terms, "Professor Dorsey, one of the foremost and most realistic of the modern anthropologists says, "Wherever the Indian Ocean touches land it finds dark-skinned people with strong developed jaws, relatively long arms, and kinky or frizzly hair."[3]

The Cushites, fathers of all these black people laid the foundation on which the great poets of Greece and Rome built their monumental literary and scientific colossus and colosseum. The more celebrated Cushite kings were usually deified after death, and sometimes metamorphosed to be identified with stars and constellations perpetually gazed upon and adored.

Commenting on one of these kings, Thomas Conant, the American Bible scholar and editor, stated that Nimrod is identical with Orion of Greek mythology. He said "Nimrod was the mighty hunter (and also king) commemorated by the constellation of that name." He meant Orion.

Perhaps the reader is now beginning to understand why the Greeks often visited Africa when she abounded in glory, and referred to the Cushites as gods.

Another explorer and recorder of history was the Englishman G.A. Hoskins. He made expeditions through Ethiopia in 1884–1885. Hoskins reported: "In this remarkable country we behold the earliest efforts of human science and ingenuity . . .by my own observation, this was the land whence the arts and learning of Egypt, and ultimately Greece and Rome, derived their origin."[4] Hoskins also recorded data on the first pyramids built by man. He visited the tomb of the great Taharka Melek Cush, and stated most emphatically that the Egyptians learned geometry from the Cushites.[5] Hoskins made drawings of the pyramids at Meroe, took measurements, and made maps that were tested for accuracy. Signor Rossellini visited Ethiopia and declared that the masonry on Taharka's tomb showed excellent workmanship. These historians visited Meroe at different times, but they both agreed on the inscription found in Hebrew on the great ruler's tomb. According to them it read: "Taharka Melek Cush." *Melek*, means king in Hebrew!

Herotodus and Champollion (the former a Greek and the latter a Frenchman), both eminent scholars of different epochs with credence in cathedratic circles throughout the world, agree that Ethiopian culture developed long before Europe evolved from savagery to civilization. They also agree that when the Greeks were teaching their Roman masters what they had learned from Africa, the Romans kept using the knowledge to conquer the world. However, the Romans were never able to conquer Ethiopia, even though they conquered Jerusalem a few times.[6]

A Brief History of Ethiopia

In ancient times, the Africans were proud and mighty, and mighty proud. As early as 1270 B.C.E., Memmon, king of Ethiopia, left Susa, his capital in Persia, with an army of 200,000 men. These troops were "half white, half black," and they were taken to aid his uncle, King Priam, in the famous Trojan War.[7]

In 981 B.C.E. Makeda, Queen of Sheba, visited King Solomon of Judea. Their son Menelik ascended the throne of Ethiopia in 955 B.C.E. In 944 B.C.E. Zera, King of Ethiopia, invaded Egypt and Palestine with an army of one million troops (according to the Bible) and was repulsed through disease and the armies of Asa, King of Judea.

In the years that followed, Thodorus Siculus (fl. 60-30 B.C.E.), a Greek historian, wrote *The Library of History*. He stated therein:

> It is from the Ethiopians that the Egyptians learned to honour their kings as gods, to bury their dead with so much pomp; and their sculpture and their writing (hieroglyphics) had their origin in Ethiopia.

In the year 30 B.C.E. The Romans invaded Ethiopia and destroyed the capital Napata before they withdrew. Ten years later, in 20 B.C.E., Queen Candace III, ruler of Ethiopia invaded Egypt with its Roman governor who had destroyed Napata and pillaged Thebes.[8]

Homer (circa eigth century B.C.E.) stated: "In Ethiopia where history tells us gold was once so plentiful," it was not difficult for him to appreciate, and testify to the celebrity of the great Ethiopian oracle from whence the "Hercules clearing the earth of monsters were partly derived from Ethiopia, together with the worship of divinity." Homer was so impressed by the cultural advancement of the Ethiopians that he also said and wrote "the furthest of mankind; the gods go to their banquets and probably the sun sets in their country." He called them *Aethiopes*, which meant burnt faces.

Homer agreed with Diodurus Siculus, who had said before he did, that the Chaldeans were a group of learned men resembling the priests of Egypt, "(both of the same race) . . . The Cushite Ethiopians were the absolute governing class in politics. They commanded the armies and held the offices of state. From them came the royal families of Babylon."[9]

In 70 A.C.E. Queen Candace III established Christianity at her capital Axum and Ethiopia became, according to Rogers, "the first Christian nation. In the same year Juda, the eunuch of Candace, was baptized by the Apostle Philip."

About 341 A.C.E. Christianity was said to have been restored in Ethiopia by Abraha and Saint Frumentius.

Around 524 A.C.E., the Ethiopians invaded Arabia and captured Yemen from the Hebrews. Forty–five years later, in 569 A.C.E. they attacked Mecca and were repulsed. That encounter kindled an almost interminable war which lasted more than a thousand years.

In 601 A.C.E., the Ethiopians were forced back across the Red Sea by the Moslems. That disaster cost Ethiopia to lose all of her coastline to the sons of Islam. [Note: All dates now: After the Christian Era or A.D.]

In 937 Judith, Queen of the Falashas, or black Jews , seized the Ethiopian throne and governed all territories for forty years.

In 977 Tekla Haimanot, an Ethiopian saint, overthrew the

Falashim and restored the dynasty of Solomon and the Queen of Sheba, which had become Christian.

In 1192 King Lalibala of Ethiopia built the famous rock temples of Lasta, and invaded Arabia.

In the year 1434 King Zara Jacob sent his envoys to the Council of Ferrara, Florence, Italy.

In 1442 Pedro de Covilham, an envoy of King John II of Portugal, visited King Eskender II of Ethiopia.

In 1529 the centuries-old war between Ethiopia and Islam continued. The renowned and feared Moslem general, Mohammed-Gerad, invaded Ethiopia. The Ethiopians were assisted by the Portuguese; together, they routed the Moslems and killed Mohammed-Gerad.

In 1649 King Fasildas of Ethiopia turned around and drove the Portuguese from Ethiopia.[10]

By 1843 Sahle-Selassie, "the Great," signed a treaty with France.

In 1867 Britain sent an army with many troops to invade Ethiopia and free white missionaries.

In 1889 The Mahdists (Arabic for he who is divinely guided in Sunni Islam) invaded Ethiopia with forty thousand troops. They were repulsed and terribly slaughtered by King John. To add to the woes of the Mahdists, Muhammad Ahmad, who had declared himself the Mahdi, met his final defeat at the hands of Kitchener's army at Omdurman giving Britain control of the Sudan. That defeat practically ended 1,100 years of Muhammadan attempts to seize Ethiopia.

In 1896 Menelik defeated the Italians at Adowa. Although Menelik had one-third of his army away for the holiday, he used mountain passes unknown to the Italians, surrounded them, speared them like sheep, and set them to flight leaving over twelve thousand dead.[11]

CUSH-NUBIA

Before Nubia was known in the United States, Arthur Schomburg read a paper before a 1913 summer class of teachers at Pennsylvania's Cheney Institute. This unsupported historian was pleading to have African history taught in colleges and schools throughout the United States where only "Negro History" was known. The paper stated:

> J. Ludolph's "History of Aethiopia" was written in Latin and Coptic and published in four folio volumes from 1681-1694 . . .Ludolph received great assistance from the Amharic Patriarch . . . Ludolph in his description of the Patriarch says he had "curly hair like other Aethiopians" . . . Many Abyssinians have curly hair as the famous Abbas Gregorius whose handsome likeness I have before me.[12]

The curly-haired Cushites, or Nubians, built one of the greatest civilizations man has ever known.

King Piankhi (ca. 741–715 B.C.E.) under his son-in-law Sabacon was also victorious at Memphis. The great Taharka, or Tirhaquah in the Bible, was related to Piankhi. He was a nephew of Sabacon. Taharka Melek Cush extended Ethiopian power as far as Assyria, and showed world dominance until he was defeated by the Assyrians and forced to retreat up the Nile to his original Ethiopian domains.

The Cushites ruled Egypt for about one hundred years until the Assyrians—descendants of Nimrod the mighty hunter—invaded Ethiopia with superior weapons made of iron. The Nubian weapons of copper and bronze were ineffective against this firm unyielding implement.

The Cushites were driven out of Egypt, back to Nubia. They moved their capital from Napata to Meroe further south along the Nile River. Cushite civilization flourished even more. Both timber and iron were to be found in abundance at Meroe. It became a great ironworking center.[13]

By 328 B.C.E. Cushitic hieroglyphics (picture writing) was in popular use. It was followed by an alphabet and script, all Cushitic.

The Cushites changed their ram gods in 225 B.C.E. to a lion god never seen before. They also raised another animal to a position of prominence, but for a different reason. It was the elephant, now brought into battle to trample the enemy and pull down his battlements.

The Cushites sailed to Arabia, India, China, and even Rome. In turn, foreign merchants went to the Cushite capital to trade their wares.

In 1947 some Europeans built and sailed an Inca-type balsa-log raft called *Kon-Tiki*. They traveled from South America across the Pacific to find out if the West had contributed to early Polynesian culture. In 1969, after the Polynesians shouted *"Tiki-Kon, Tiki-Kon,"* to the boats, the mariners built a papyrus-reed boat similar to those the Cushites had used. They called her Ra I after the Egyptian sun-god Amon. "I sailed her from Africa into the western Atlantic where I had to abandon her when the reed bundles came apart," said the navigator. A year later he set sail with Ra II, an improved version, He "made the trans-Atlantic voyage from Africa to Barbados, proving that ancient man could have done the same."[14]

By the year 300 A.C.E. Axum, a nearby empire replaced Cush as the major trade center. At that time the nomads began abandoning their tents, and huts, like the people of today, and rushed to live in the city. They preferred the new houses built of mortar and bricks. These newcomers adopted Kushitic customs and crafts. They also became part of the Christian kingdoms in Ancient Nubia. Christian Nubia remained under that religious influence for twelve hundred years before it fell to Moslem rule.[15]

"The History of this country," says Ladislas Farago, "is really a history of its Church, which was converted to Christianity in the fourth century A.D. Till then it had been half pagan, half Jewish," Farago, like Rogers, and other sources cited, wrote: "At one time Mohammedans and another time a Jewish dynasty were able to conquer the land, but the power of the Coptic Church always dominated in the end."[16]

LAND OF A MIXTURE OF PEOPLE

Physical law holds that opposite poles attract, The same holds for people. Once the Nubians traveled to other lands wearing as much gold jewelry as they did, people of paler skin began to visit Cush to trade.

With the conversion of the highland Ethiopians to Coptic Christianity during the fourth century, the Moslem invasion of the sixteenth century under Mohammed-Gerad, and the continuous migrations of different nomadic people since ancient times, the cultural and ethnic composition of Ethiopia-Cush-Nubia became like the incohesive melting pot of the United States. There were people there from many parts of the world. The great difference was that in Nubia people actually interacted instead of simply tolerating one another. They melted like cheese which clings to spaghetti. People did not discriminate against one another under false pretenses, like the tossed salad of the United States where each person, or vegetable, is united but separate, maintaining its own identity and flavor, despite the expected ethnic amalgamation to produce a palatable native American.

Foreigners came into Cush and saw the many products and novelties. An unusual sight was the Nubian woman in her splendor and beauty. She was beautiful to admire as she approached, irresistable to behold when she passed and gracefully displayed her protruding buttocks. The Nubian woman did not require a crinoline petticoat or a hoop-skirt with a wire cage to attract a man of good taste. And when the foreigners discovered that it was not necessary to put a pillow under her to obtain the peristaltic movements so gratifying in harmonious sexual relations, they sought her favors or took her by force.

As a result, there are fifty or more tribal groups with separate customs and looks. There are also about fifty languages spoken, and four times as many dialects. The Amhara-Tigre people of the Ethiopian plateau have been culturally and politically dominant for two thousand years. This group consists of approximately 30-35 percent of the country's population, and are predominantly Ethiopian Orthodox Christians.[17]

The numerically dominant Galla people—approximately forty percent of the total population of the center and south—have considerably increased their participation in politics in recent times, and have begun to challenge traditional Amhara-Tigre dominance. In regard to religious practices, the Galla participate in three principal forms: Christianity, Islam, and different forms of paganism.

Among the Somali people of the east and southeast, about ten percent of the population are Moslems or pagans. The others are Christians. The Sidama in the southwest have about nine percent who are Moslems or Pagans and the Shankella in the west six percent. They are both predominantly pagan.

The Amhara-Tigre groups are descendants of Semitic peoples who came into Ethiopia and were called Falashas. Sommer discovers them coming into Ethiopia long ago (tenth through seventh century B.C.E.) from southern Arabia. He states, "the Galla, Sidama, and Agau groups are descendants of even earlier inhabitants, the Cushites."

The Amhara-Tigre group has governed and controlled the economic and cultural development of the country. They have collectively and scornfully forced the wooly-haired, darker-skinned groups, pejoratively called Shankella, into slavery by keeping them ignorant. The Amhara-Tigre are now producing this holocaust at a tremendous cost in life and culture to the Falashim, or black Hebrews, of pure stock.[18]

LANGUAGES SPOKEN IN ETHIOPIA

Ethiopian languages belong to three linguistic families: Semitic, Cushitic, and Niletic.[19]

The original language group of Ethiopia was Cushitic. It was not until the first millenium B.C.E. that the Semitic people, called Habasat, entered Ethiopia from southern Arabia. These Semitic people brought their language, but sociolinguistic interaction combined it with Ethiopic or Cushitic to form Semitic-Ethiopic. Since the indigenous language group of Ethiopia was Cushitic, there was a very strong influence of Cushitic on the phonology, morphology, syntax and vocabulary of Semitic-Ethiopic. Consequently, the Semitic-Ethiopic languages became Ge'ez, Tigre, Tigrina, Amharic, Argoba, Harari, Gurage, and Gafat.[20]

The South Semitic alphabet was used for Epigraphic South Arabic communication, and for the North Arabic inscriptions of Thamudenic, Lihyanite, and Safaitic. The South Arabic alphabet crossed into Ethiopia during the last millenium B.C.E. also. This alphabet is consonantal, but the Ethiopic alphabet is syllabic. A single symbol is used for the consonant and vowel together (see Tables 1 and 2 for word chart on commonly used words of related languages and groups).

Table 1.
Semitic Languages [Compared to English]

English	Akkadian	Hebrew	Aramaic	Ugaritic	Ethiopic	Arabic
brother	ahu	'ah	'ahã	ah	'eh	'ah
master	belu	ba'al	ba'la	b'l	bã'el	ba'l
dog	kalbu	kelab	kalbã	klb	kalb	kalb
fly	zumbu	zebub	dabbãbã		zemb (Amharic)	dubãb
seed	zeru	zera'	zar'a	dr'	zare'	
head	resu	ro(')s	resã	ris	re'es	ra's
eye	enu	'ayin	'ayna	'n	'ayn	'ayn
tongue	lisãnu	lason	lissãnã	lsn	lesãn	lisãn
tooth	sinnu	sen	s nãnã		senn	sinn
sky	samu	sãma-yim	s mayya	sm(y)m	samay	samã'
night	l lãtu	laylã	lelyã	LL	lelit	layla
water	mu	mayyã	mayyã	my	mãy	mã'
house	b tu	bayı	baytã	bt	bet	bayt
peace	salãmu	sãlom	s lãma	slm	salãm	salãm
name	sumu	sem	s mã	sm	sem	ism

Table 2.
Cushitic Languages of the Northeast
The Hamitic (Cushitic) people of northeast Africa spoke:
(1) Bedawiye;
(2) the Agaw group;
(3)   the Sidama group, consisting of:
    (a)   Sidamo, Darasa, Hadya, Kambatta, Alaba
    (b)   Wolamo, Gofa, Kullo, Konta, Zala, Kuera
        or Koyra (Baditu), Kucha, Gamo;
    (c)   Chara;
    (d)   Basketo, Zaysse, Doko;
    (e)   the Gongo group including Kafa, Shinasha, Mao;
    (f)   the Gimira group including Gimira,
        Maji (Mazhi), Nao;
    (g)   Yamma or Janjero;
(4) the separate but related language systems: Galla,
    Somali and Saho-Afar.

The South Arabian Semitic speech was brought in by migrants and influenced by the Cushitic to become Geez (Ge'ez). Ethiopic was the national language until sociolinguistic changes, through gradual influence and socio-political upheavals, caused its decline. The change resulted in the evolvement of three important languages in the linguistic network: Tigrinya and Tigre, spoken in the north, and Amharic spoken by about 40 percent of the people south of the Tigrinyal language area. Tigrinya, nonetheless, is comparatively related to Ge'ez, and is in fact rather close. Amharic is unrelated. The role of Ge'ez can be regarded as the language of scholarly and ecclesiastical pursuits. It is also used as a status symbol linguistically and socially speaking. Ge'ez is accorded national recognition in this country of high illiteracy and unequal opportunities, however, its legal status or official recognition is limited. Ge'ez is used mostly by monks who read history, documents, manuscripts, scriptures, and records of ancient times. Few young Ethiopians know Ge'ez. Most of the people who speak, read, and write it are scholars of some caliber.

Because of the limited fluency in Ge'ez, many Hebrew and Jewish scholars have refused to read the records of Hebrew religious and ethnic origins held by the Ethiopian Falashas in Gondar and in other parts of the country. Addressing that question, Ephraim Isaacs, an Ethiopian Hebrew who speaks, reads, and writes eight languages and teaches African-American studies at Harvard University, stated in 1973 at a meeting of the Synagogue Council of America held at Congregation Shearith Israel in New York City: "The world is raving about the Dead Sea Scrolls while the Ark of the Covenant and myriads of old original Hebrew manuscripts are rotting in Ethiopia."

Semitic Amharic has been the official language of Ethiopia, dating from the 14th[21] century. It was originally spoken in the province of Amhara. It has been greatly modified by the Cushitic influence. It uses the Ethiopic syllabary with additional signs. Amharic has seven forms representing a consonant followed by different vowels. The syntax and vocabulary are strongly influenced by Cushitic language systems, especially Galla and Sidamo.

Amharic is spoken by three to five million people as the modern official and literary language in a population of twenty million. It is not unusual to hear members of the intelligentsia and officialdom use Amharic and English interchangeably, while Arabic and Italian might also be heard on a lesser scale.

Amharic has thirty-three consonants, or consonantal sounds, each of which may be combined with any of its vowels. To print a page of a book in Amharic 7 x 23, or 161 different types are required, instead of the forty types which would be ordinarily sufficient in an alphabetical typesetting method. This is truly a Semitic language.

Amharic embraces all religions, social systems, and other facets of Ethiopian culture. It relates to tangible and secular things. Ge'ez, on the other hand, is used mostly in legal matters of the Coptic Church, and the Sabean writings in the old Hebrew, and other texts copied by the Europeans.[22] Nevertheless, some languages are unknown to them.

As late as February 15, 1834, a Nubian dialect different from Kenous, spoken above the first cataract, was spoken at Korosko in the Nubian desert. These two linguistic systems were separated by the districts of Wady el Elayat er Wasi el Arabi, which divided these two Nubian tribes.[23]

FROM CHALDEA TO ETHIOPIA

It is difficult to research and present facts about the Falashas before dealing with the Chaldeans. After all, the Chaldeans were unquestionably in existence before the Falashim, Sepharadim, and Ashkenazim. Noah, the first Patriarch after the Flood, was a Chaldean. He is supposed to have built the Ark that is legendarily recognized as the cradle of man after the Deluge.

Some scientists recently cooperated with the movie industry and produced a motion picture concerning an ark found in the East. Whether the planks taken from that wooden vessel to be processed in laboratories for authenticity were part of Noah's Ark is irrelevant to this study. What is significant, however, is the fact that Noah was recorded as a Chaldean. His descendant Abraham was also said to be a Chaldean from Ur. On that much information there is widespread agreement.[24]

There also is general agreement that the Babylonian story of a flood is older than the story of Noah's flood. The Babylonian story of deluge, and the epic of Gilgamesh (studied by many in freshmen history classes), can be seen in cuneiform tablets in the British Museum in London. They mention the deity as God-One. These tablets describing the epic of the Babylonian deluge date back to 1900 B.C.E. Their heir was Utnapishtim.[25] The Hebrew story in Genesis, Chapters one through seven, give no dates. The coming of a Messiah was also written on Babylonian tablets before 2000 B.C.E. And Abraham, patriarch of the Hebrews and Moslems, was supposedly not existent until the Thirteenth Egyptian Dynasty (ca.1789 B.C.E.)

These cuneiform tablets of Babylonia show how its people worshipped planets and demons, and practiced witchcraft and magic. These customs were distinctly Hamitic.

Abraham, a Hamite, was chosen by the Almighty to come out of Haran—a name similar to the province Harrar in Ethiopia—after leaving his birthplace Ur. The purpose was to save the Canaanites, who worshipped idols, magic, and the like. All people in the vicinity imitated the Chaldeans. Babylon was the international leader, like the United States today.

Even Europe, which did not come into existence, or history, until 2000 B.C.E.,[26] adopted witchcraft, magic, demons, superstitions, and metaphysics from Babylonia.

But despite their pagan religious practices, the Babylonians recognized the unity of the seven planets and the sun as being under one supernatural force whom they addressed as God-One, meaning one God omnipotent, omniscient, omni-present. The number one to be above all other gods.[27]

Even Greece and later Rome, according to Seneca, considered the Babylonians' theory of comets "as exact and intelligent as that of modern 'scientists' (sic)." The ancient calculations of the lunar eclipse cited by Ptolemy (ca. A.D. 150) are only slightly different from most modern calculations.

Another researcher, Drusilla Houston, tells us:

> The earliest civilization of Babylonia was coexistent with the earlier civilization of the Upper Nile, and the Babylonian script went back to 6000 B.C. Houston cited Rawlinson's mention of a Cushite inscription of 3200 B.C. It informs us: Havelah son of Cush peopled the region where the Tigris and Euphrates unite. We know that the Hebrews while in captivity in Babylon secured the authentic genealogies of the first children of men. We would believe that the Babylonians could not have given them incorrect information as to their origin.

The Babylonians equatorial coordinate system measured exactly the same (38,600 km.) as we calculate today with modern computers and instruments. As early as 2200 B.C.E., the Babylonians had already named their twelve months of thirty days each, after the signs of the Zodiac developed by the Cushites before them. Babylonian discovery of the solar circuit dates back to 2234 B.C.E. And the duo-decimal system is also credited to Babylonian ingenuity—according to documents in the British Museum. And, of course, their Code of Hammurabi, (1792–1750 B.C.E.), is very well known.

This Babylonian Code of Laws carved on a diorite tablet of 3,600 lines, written in cuneiform, is considered one of the greatest laws of ancient times. It was found at Susa, an ancient city of Persia, and is now in Paris at the Louvre, the national museum.

Hammurabi is identified with Nimrod, builder of the famous Tower of Babel (Genesis 11:1-4); which is presently identified with a temple tower in Babylon called *Etemenanki*. They both built towers to show majesty.

These Babylonians, Chaldeans, Chayas, Casdim or Cushites, as they were variously called, were the superior and ruling caste of all Ethiopian colonies.

Dionysius of Hallicarnassus (30-38 B.C.) stated that the Chaldeans were the most ancient and early constituted settlers of any people in that area of northeast Africa, recently named, the Middle East. Dionysius emphasized how the Chaldeans did not migrate at the general dispersion. They moved to Egypt westward and eastward to the Ganges. These were the Akkadians of Chaldea, who looked to the southwest of the Caspian for the cradle of their race.

Diodorus also spoke of their great reputation in astronomy and other sciences. It was customary for the Chaldeans to spend most of their time in philosophic meditation. Studying was a family tradition. And the Scriptures speak of them as the "Wise men of the East." Sons were taught by their fathers and other elders. Babylonian cities were popularly spoken about as regions replete with libraries, temples, and schools. Almanacs, clay coffins, ceramics, and art treasures were made there.

The Babylonian tablets reveal history of an original race of black men from the region called Admi. Their influence spread through the area to such an extent that even as late as the first century B.C.E., Adiabene, an ancient district in northern Mesopotamia became an independent kingdom whose queen Helena converted to the Hebrew religion with her sons kings Monobaz II and Izates I. This family supported the Hebrews against the Romans, and was later buried in the Tombs of Kings at Jerusalem (ca. 30 C.E.).[28] The Babylonian tablets were similar to the Cushitic form of preserving inscriptions.

THE CUSHITES

The Cushites descended from Cush. The black, and dark-skinned people of Eretz Israel call every black person who visits that land "Cushi", a diminutive of Cush.[29]

Drusilla Houston researched the area and its people of antiquity most thoroughly. She concluded: "The pictures on the Egyptian monuments reveal that Ethiopians were the builders of the first pyramids. They, not the Egyptians, were the mastercraftsmen of the earlier ages. The first courses of the pyramids were built of Ethiopian stone."

The Cushites built temples that stretched as far as the first cataract. Among them we find the ancient town of Mahendi, whose tunnel galleries were later imitated and erected in Crete. Dakka with its immense gateways was erected by the Cushites. The temples of Dakka and Dabod were built by King Ergamenes of Ethiopia. Houston also said that some "Egyptologists try to identify these relics as Egyptian, but they are definitely Cushitic. Even Rameses II, surnamed 'The Great', because he preferred size to quality, could not compare his work to the brilliantly painted and sculptured stones used in the temples of Dakka and Dabod."

Hoskins himself considered the temples at Meroe, capital of Cush, and the pyramids of Gizeh magnificent and wonderful Cushitic architectural accomplishments. He supported his convictions with these words:

> According to Heeren, Champollion, Rossellini and other eminent
> inquirers, whose judgement was confirmed by my own observa-
> tions. . . . In this remarkable country we behold the earliest efforts
> of human science and ingenuity.

Hoskins, an Englishman who visited Ethiopia and delivered on-the-spot reporting, was eager to share his findings with the world, and to promote truth rather than foster bigotry. To support his conclusions, Hoskins cited Signor Rossellini, who translated the inscription on Taharka's tomb. It read "Taharka Melek Cush," which means in Hebrew: Taharka Cushite king. Taharka was a pharoah of Egypt who ruled over both Upper and Lower Egypt simultaneously. He is mentioned in the Bible (2 Kings 19:9) as "Taharka, king of the Ethiopians."

Davidson contributes more clarification by stating Herodotus' clear view of world history when the Greek reported his travels through Monomotapa, later called Africa. Herodotus is quoted as having said in 450 B.C.E., "Egypt's cultural origins lay in continental Africa." On the subject of circumcision Davidson remarked, "as between the Egyptians and the Ethiopians I should not like to say which learned from the other." In regard to racial phenomena, he declared: "the popular use of the term 'white' as attributed to the North African Nile Valley and other people (as of the term 'black' to others), is merely a latter day mystification of the racialist sort."[30] Davidson was simply showing how the whitening of certain Africans is a fabrication with ulterior motives. Color distinction is a part of ethnocentricity and justifies unwarranted abuse and infringement of the right of others.

Certain historians, like their fellow usurpers, consider that if the gold of South Africa, the uranium and copper of Zambia, and other metals elsewhere, can be stolen from Africa's subsoil without compunctions in Europeans' minds, or physical resistance by Africans; then why not steal Africa's history as well? After all, Africans have no ancient past. And furthermore, these Europeans reason, we write both world history and African history; the Africans will never know the difference.

But we Africans do know the difference. Africans are not all born or educated in any one particular region or one language. Some of us speak many languages. Let us take a moment to clarify those hypothetical charges before we continue with the numerous accomplishments of the Cushites.

Abraham Maslow (1954) and Michael Bradley (1992) explain how and why "The white race rampaged through the world killing and conquering." Maslow described a hierarchy of needs in his work on the psychopathogenic relations of man. He explained his theory in these terms: "Man," said Maslow, a professor at City College in New York, "needs his food, raiment, and shelter." After obtaining these basic needs, he steals or accumulates whatever he is able from other men. Then man requests safekeeping for his stolen or accumulated wealth.[31] He buys locks, builds safes and banks, puts up fences or moves to suburbia for security, where he joins a club, lodge or society for status, puts up signs, and segregates those men he exploited or robbed. With accumulated wealth, man inherits leisure time at the expense of those persons he exploited or exploits. With free time, man seeks prestige through culture—which is merely one's way of life. He then associates with someone more cultured than he. Soon, that person's culture becomes his own. The Americans did it to the English; the Romans did it to the Greeks, who did it to the Africans. The cause and effect was presented by another Caucasian in a different manner.

Michael Bradley stated: "Occasionally, Western authors have been truly serious and, rarely, truly informed . . . It is as if we are searching for insight but not searching too well for fear of what we may discover about ourselves."[32] The discovery might well be, as Ruth Benedict has stated, that we all came from one common origin—the black man.[33]

In analyzing evidence of the origin of man and its relationship to Africa and antiquity, we find Boyce Rensenberger stating in the New York Times:

> Evidence of the oldest recognizable monarchy in human history, preceding the rise of the earliest Egyptian Kings by several generations, has been discovered in artifacts from ancient Nubia in Africa.[34]

Rensenberger showed without a doubt that as far as we know to date Ancient Nubian artifacts yield evidence of the earliest monarchy in human history having existed in Nubia. His conclusion verifies and supports our presentation of facts and evidence that African civilization existed before European days or Arabian nights. This was Rensenberger's second find.

Rensenberger's first find was announced just before anthropologist Mary Leakey publicized "Two sets of footprints made 3.6 million years ago in Africa, are now definitely known to have been made by direct ancestors of man."[35] These findings of man's earliest development in Africa, especially Ethiopia, our area of primary focus, lead us back to the Cushites.

Davidson shows Africa's advancement from the Stone Age to the Iron Age. The earliest written records recording these facts are said to have been produced by the scribes of the Pharoahs of Egypt, the Phoenicians of Carthage, and the Sabeans of Ethiopia.

The use of iron reached the Nile about the same time as its use began circulating through non-Mediterranean Europe. Bronze was the popular metal of manufactured armament in Egypt when the Assyrians arrived and invaded the land in 666 B.C.E. Prior to that date the Hyksos (or Shepherd Kings) had also invaded Egypt with superior weaponry (1720 B.C.E. and 1710 B.C.E.)—15–18 dynasties. However, the Hyksos were absorbed by the Egyptians who had a much superior culture than their invaders. Early Iron Age relics and oral tradition transmitted to us by our progenitors testify that Phoenician seamen and travelers took iron into other parts of Africa. At another source of commerce, the Nile was busy with traffic and so was the great desert *Saqqara*, now called the Sahara.[36] Ships and caravans headed to the mass of land known today as East Africa, located at one-third of the equator's surface and two-thirds below, bordered by Ethiopia and Sudan to the north.

East Africa transmitted African culture and civilization all the way across the continent and to southern Africa. Here at Monomotapa, linguistically derived from *Mwana-mtapa*, which follows our ancestral tradition of naming the land after a ruler or king, we find Kilwa. It was the busiest metropolis trafficking in ivory and gold. Kilwa was situated near Engaruka on the scorching hillside of the Rift Valley, not far south of the Kenya-Tanzania border.[37] The Rift Valley is a depression in the earth. It begins in Israel in the Jordan Valley of the Near East, crosses the Red Sea through Kenya and Tanzania.

The reader may now determine if these names sound Asiatic and whether Israel is still in northeast Africa, or placed in Asia because of the Suez Canal, politics or socioeconomic advantage.

The Cushites were not only scientific and artistic, they were also quite religious. Their pyramids, crypts, temples, and burial sites, even in Egypt, contain religious and astronomic significance and shapes.

Archaeologists have found in the monastery of Abou Hornis—according to Masoudi and Al Kadhi—a papyrus with Coptic characters. It reads: "On the walls are written the mysteries of science, astronomy, geometry, physics and a lot of precious knowledge to be read by all those who understand our writing."[38] Scholars have also found "in Upper Egypt there were pictured black priests who were conferring upon red Egyptians, the instruments and symbols of priesthood."[39]

James Henry Breasted was amazed when he entered the antechamber of a Pharoah's tomb filled with wealth and splendor of the imperial age of Egypt. This scholar stated with enthusiam, " it is an astonishing revelation of the beauty and refinement of Egyptian art—beyond anything I had imagined. That first room of the tomb had statues, caskets, chests, beds, chairs, and chariots all beautifully carved and decorated." Breasted continued his praises, saying, "On the lid of one chest were hunting scenes. The beauty and minuteness of the details of the painting excels the finest Chinese and Japanese art."[40] This archaeologist was among the first visitors to enter this tomb following Howard Carter who had searched for it about thirty years. Carter found it after diligent effort in 1922.

It was the tomb of the son of Amenophis, born ca. 1350 B.C.E. and universally known as Tut-ankh-amen. This pharoah's tomb was discovered in the Valley of Tombs, where it was the only tomb that had not been disturbed. This valley is about five miles from modern Thebes. The tombs of the other pharoahs of the Eighteenth, Nineteenth, and Twentieth Dynasties had all been plundered. This tomb was visited in 1981 by students, professors, and tourists from Africa, Japan, the United States, Spain, England, and France. We saw none of the items mentioned by Breasted in it. There was only the mummy. Even though there was not much to see in the tomb, other historical paintings and reliefs revealed information concerning symbols, and religious precepts about Tut-ankh-amen's predecessors.[41] Those relics inform us that Pharoah Amenophis IV, better known as Akhenaton the Heretic King (1300 B.C.E.) reigned more than four hundred years before the Hebrew King David was born.

Akhenaton (1372-1354 B.C.E.), also known as Ikhnaton, king of the two lands, married the black princess Nefertiti, also known as Nefertari and Nefruari, who was famous for her dusky charms, wealth and accomplishments. Akhenaton—meaning in Egyptian Aton is satisfied—abandoned polytheism to embrace monotheism. He held that the sun, named Aton, was god, and god alone. Akhenaton defaced all monuments to the god Amon. The marriage of pharoahs to black princesses was to establish claim of descent from the black god Amen-Ra, whom the ancients represented as God.

The earliest recordings of monotheistic religious beliefs show— even in the Memphite Drama on a slab of basalt made by an Ethiopian king—great similarity to the Hebrew and Christian texts. These writings were inscribed four hundred years before the Hebrew Scriptures, and were first adopted by the Ethiopian Coptic Church. These records show on paper, and most especially on the walls of monuments in Egypt, how the Christ story was copied from the story of Horus. The Hebrew Ten Commandments, copied from the *147 Negative Confessions*, were written after 2000 B.C.E.—"Between the years 700 B.C. and 500 B.C." The Confessions were written in Africa ca.4100 B.C.E.[42]

We will cite some of these negative obligations for comparison. The reader will determine, through the evidence, whether or not the Ten Commandments were copied from them. Compare:

African—Negative Confession against stealing:

"I have not committed theft."

Hebrew—[Fifth] Commandment:

"Thou shalt not steal."

African—"I have not uttered falsehood."

Hebrew—Leviticus 19:11 in the Bible was also copied:

"Ye shall not steal neither deal falsely, neither lie to one another."

African—"I have not defiled the wife of any man."

Hebrew—"Thou shalt not commit adultery."

After the exegetic Fourteenth Commandment, we shall try just one more for comparison of sound and similarity.

African—"I have not slain man or woman."

Hebrew—"Thou shalt not kill."

The *Mitzvot lo tasseh* or Negative Commandments in the Torah of the Hebrews is used by Catholics, White Anglo-Saxon Protestants' (WASPS)—who hate non-whites, and non-Protestants—Bible, and the Holy Koran. These testaments are all byproducts of the *147 Negative Confessions* first used in the Holy of Holies in Egypt. These laws were circulated in Africa several years before the birth of Jesus, and long before he became condemned by a pretentious Jewish Sanhedrin, fearful of him, and a sadistic Roman military force, thirsty for excitement through torture.

The Bible story originated in Ethiopia and was popularized in Egypt, as we have shown and will attempt to reinforce with more evidence. When many foreigners, including Herodotus and Aristotle, came to Egypt to marvel at the painted story on the walls, the Egyptian population was black.

The Hebrews copied the Bible story and adapted it to their Scriptures. The Christians copied it, and still worship the African god to whom it was dedicated. At the end of most prayers they hallow his name by saying "amen"! Amen-Ra was an African god. The Psalms of David were written by Akhenaton before David's grandmother, Ruth was born.

Ruth was a Moabite who adopted the Hebrew faith. This simple woman who cast her lot with the Hebrew people gave us the writer of the Psalms, from whose house the Redeemer of Israel would one day emerge to spread God's light over the earth. Ruth's grandson was David, unquestionably from a black-skinned tribe. Ruth's famous passage is known to all Bible students. It is unmatched for devotion and unselfishness. It reads:

Entreat me not to leave thee, and to return from following thee; for whither thou goest, I will go; and where thou lodgest, I will lodge; thy people shall be my people, and thy God my God; where thou diest, I will die, and there will I be buried; the Lord do so to me, and more also, if aught but death part thee and me.

— Ruth I:16,17

Cushite accomplishments were innumerable. Apart from the Bible story copied from them, some mention might be made regarding the origin of philosophy. We will not deal with that branch of the humanities as yet, but let it be sufficient to say, at this moment, however, that Thales of Miletus was not the first philosopher, as we learned in Spanish and English college courses, and philosophy did not originate in Greece.

Might our Hebrew progenitors have broken the Fifteenth Commandment when they copied the Cushite accomplishments? The Holy Commandment states most emphatically "Thou shalt not steal"! By copying the *Negative Confessions* and not giving the Gentiles credit for their efforts, was there an act of plagiarism committed by the Hebrews? Might they have stolen other treasures as well? Could this be the reason for the verse, "And the Lord hardened the heart of Phâraoh king of Egypt, and he pursued after the children of Israel being poor enough to force Jacob's sons to travel to Egypt for Pharoah's grain."

Egypt had plenty of food stored in her granaries. Ethiopia furnished the perfumes of the world. The Cushites worshipped their deities with golden and silver vessels, well gilded, richly ornamented vestments, precious stones, and other offerings unheard of and unseen in some parts of Europe at that time. Ethiopian substances for incense were distributed and consumed from Meroe to Memphis, the temptations were great. The Hebrews burned Ethiopian incense. The Greeks emulated them, and the Romans followed.

The first three popes used incense and the Roman Catholic Church imitated the Apostolic order, and continues to do so up to this day. Ethiopia's spices were used to embalm the dead. She had fountains with the odor of violets, and her prisoners were fettered with chains of gold.

Herodotus (son of Lyxes, ca.484-420 B.C.E.) described the Ethiopians as people eating boiled meats, roasted foods and fish, while drinking milk. At that time, European clans were still eating raw meat, running around half naked and living in caves.[43] Herodotus wrote:

> Ethiopia had a skill in embalming superior to Egypt. The Ethiopians' mummies could be seen all around and they were preserved in columns of transparent glass. The Egyptians' mummies could be seen from the front. In the sepulchres the corpses were covered with plaster on which were printed lifelike portraits of the deceased.

The sun shone on Ethiopia's soil and it yielded two or more crops per year when her rivers overflowed. Her sons and daughters wore flowing robes, gold, and other precious jewelry about them, governed kingdoms, and cooked their food, while the Caucasians lived in caves like they still do in Spain to this day. Those are some of the historic reasons why the Negus of Ethiopia is called "King of kings!" Ethiopia had the first kingdoms on this planet. She was so great many historians wrote about her at different periods. Among them was Charles Rollin.

Rollin (1729) expostulated with pseudo-historians and concluded his argument in this manner:

> Historians are unanimously agreed that Menes was the first king of Egypt. . . He is the same with Misraim, son of Cham. . . Cham was the second son of Noah. . . After the Tower of Babel they dispersed themselves into different countries, Cham retired to Africa. . . He had four children. They were Chus, Mesraim [whom the Arabians call up to this day Mesre], Phut and Canaan. The son named Chus settled in Ethiopia, Mesraim in Egypt, Phut in Libya and Canaan in Palestine.

In his "Bible Dictionary," William Smith wrote historical explanations for the places named after the fathers and founders of biblical times.

> Canaan 1. The fourth son of Ham (Genesis 10:6; 1 Chronicles 1:8), whose descendants occupied the lands of Phoenicia and much of Palestine (Genesis 9:18, 22, 10:13; 1 Chronicles 1:13).

> 2. The land inhabited in early biblical times by the Canaanites, being mostly Palestine between the Jordan and the Mediterranean and Syria or Phoenicia (Exodus 15:15).

> Cush 1. Son of Ham and grandson of Noah (Genesis 10:6-8; 1 Chronicles 8:10).

> Misraim.. . .one of the sons of Ham in Genesis 10:6,13. . . the usual Hebrew term for Egypt.

> Phut, Put the third name in the list of the sons of Ham (Genesis 10:6; 1 Chronicles 1:8), elsewhere applied to an African country of people. . .Some scholars have located Phut south of Cush.

> Ham 1. One of Noah's sons (Genesis 5:32, 6:10) The biblical Hamites ranged from the Canaanites and Phut (Libya).[44]

Smith's work was based on biblical accounts to a great extent. The Bible is considered, however, one of the oldest books of history. Like these chapters cited, we find other mention of the Cushites, or Ethiopians, in the Bible. We read, "Thus saith the Lord, the Labour of Egypt, and merchandise of Ethiopia and of the Sabeans men of stature, shall come over unto thee" (Isaiah 43:3, 45:14). In the book of Judges III, 8th verse we read, " the anger of the Lord was hot against Israel, and he sold them into the hand of Cushan-rishathaim King of Mesopotamia: and the children served Cushan-rishathaim eight years."[45] In the book of Jeremiah 46:9, there is more data mentioning these descendants of Ham. "Come up, ye horses and rage, ye Chariots; and let the mighty men come forth; the Ethiopians and the Libyans that handle the shield; and the Libyans that handle the bow."

The Bible relates epics of war and warfare. It is not a history of slaves or servants—hand-clapping or fearful. It is a history of warriors, but battles fought to prevent suppression, to foster self-determination, and to maintain survival. It stresses watchfulness and prayerfulness, which is why Hebrews do not pray on bended knees with their eyes closed. Even the Jews were wont to pray with their toes prepared to run if necessary. The Ethiopians or other Africans who allowed the missionaries to encourage them to pray on bended knees, with their eyes closed, often reopened them to find themselves surrounded by cruel slavers brandishing guns, whips, chains, and staves, and set to march them onto slave ships bound for hell instead of heaven.

The reader must have noticed how the English and other historians, who actually visited Ethiopia recorded their information with less prejudice and more truth and scholarly effort. Unlike many Americans (sometimes descendants of cowboys and gangsters or mafiosos seeking literary popularity and social acceptance at other's expense), these scholars visit the market places of Cairo, Aswan, Tel Aviv, Benghazi, Addis Ababa, and other African metropolises. They cannot be identified with pseudohistorians who sit in the Rameses Hilton, Sheraton or other American oases and determine through interviews with indigenous servants what actually takes place in the desert or interior of a country. Those real scholars who visit the Bedouins and the man on the street observe that most of them are blacks or mulattoes.[46]

The recently built Aswan Dam covers some historic statues with flat noses and other African features; nevertheless, almost any Egyptian guide will take a visitor up the Nile to see numerous black people at Aswan. One has to mention only one word, "Nubian." The blacks will proudly step forward and say, "Me Nubian, original Egyptian!" And even if the half-breeds glance at him or smile derisively, they'll never contradict him. The honest ones might even add, "He pure, not mixed-up foreigner."

These Nubians know more about the Nile, its sources and original inhabitants, than the Europeans and their American descendants who visit parts of Africa for brief periods, then write books as authorities on African history. Such writers often fool themselves, and those who accredit them into thinking Africans reveal all our secrets and history to them in spite of their discrimination against us.

The Nubians relate how civilization came from Ethiopia, gradually winding its way, like the Nile, through the valley onto the shores of the Mediterranean. Guiseppe Sergi supports their argument with documented proof. Sergi assures us that, "The primitive populations of Europe originated in Africa and the Basin if the Mediterranean was the chief center of movement when the African migrations reached the center and north of Europe."[47]

A television series of the United States Army in Korea called "M*A*S*H" showed a white corporal Klinger becoming ill with a type of anemia supposedly endemic to blacks and Asians. When Hawkeye, the doctor, investigated this phenomenon, he discovered that the disease was common among whites who hail from the Mediterranean area. They are carriers of the same genetic trait as the Africans and Asians similarly affected. Over two million Greek Americans, as well as Syrians, Israelis, and others of Mediterranean, African and Asian ancestry, are carriers of the genetic traits of Cooley's anemia, according to the U.S. Public Health Department.

The Nubians, and certain diligent historians, inform us why Amenophis I, son of Ashmes and Nefertari carried on Ethiopian wars when Ethiopia was breaking away from Egypt. His son Thotmes I is said to have subjugated Phoenicia and Syria. They claim that this ruler was so powerful, his daughter Hatasu considered herself daughter of Amen and his incarnation. Thotmes' name was also pointed out at Karnak and Meroe. He is seen on the walls at Karnak making offerings before sixty-one of his ancestors.

Houston felt that the recordings of these previous monarchs could give posterity some idea of the many Ethiopians who sat upon Egypt's throne. She also noticed an astonishing resemblance among the artworks from the Fourth, Twelfth, and the Eighteenth Dynasties. These great dynasties, she assured, were purely Ethiopian and proved Cushite superiority in culture, politics, and religion in Egypt. "When they are out of power," says Houston, "her culture always declined."[48]

> The engravings on the walls and stelae depict Thotmes III as an unquestionably great Pharoah. And the Nubians claim that during his reign of some fifty-four years, he covered the area with monuments and commerce. Treasures are said to have flowed into Egypt, and Thebes became the capital of the world. Thotmes III built a considerable navy which controlled the Mediterranean, and was absolutely supreme upon its waters.[49]

Thotmes called himself the Royal Son of the Land in the South. Due to his pride in that land, he erected more edifices in Nubia than any other ruler. Thotmes III was considered a worshipper of the gods from the south, and appears showing his return from expeditions to Asia. Like Alexander the Great who followed him, the walls, cartouches, and stelae of Karnak and Aswan reveal carved names of 628 vanquished nations. Among them are Syria, Mesopotamia, Arabia,

Armenia, as part of the Nubian kingdom. A portion of the Temple at Karnak was also built by Thotmes III. Tribute and taxes were paid to him by Palestine, Phoenicia, and northern Syria. And he received homage from kings of Cush, Punt, Assyria and Chaldea.

Petrie, after a find of the upper portion of a figure from the ruling class, agreed through extensive research, that what's "On the chest is the cartouche of Tahutmes III (ca.1450 B.C.) . . . one of the chief figures in the Punt pictures on the temple of Deir-el-Bahri." [50]

Readers might ask (especially North American blacks who are psychologically programmed to an inferiority complex and unexposed to African history before the 1960s): If Africans were so great, how is it they are so backward or underdeveloped today? The answer is simple, yet difficult to relay to a mind brought up to believe in racial superiority based on color acceptance, or another mind psychologically subjected through dehumanization until it has surrendered and become psychologically ambivalent. However, let us say civilizations fall in proportion to others that rise. We will treat fallen Ethiopia, Greece, Rome, and falling England more extensively under Commensalism.—(people living side by side without exploiting one another.)

For convincing proof of the greatness of Ethiopia for historians and persons interested in historical evidence, a stelae can be seen in the British Museum that shows the fleet of Cambyses of Persia being destroyed by Ethiopians on the Nile, and his fleet in flight, forcing his land troops eventually to succumb to starvation.

Well-informed readers and historians of high calibre all know well why among the monuments erected to the pharoahs there also were pyramids erected to the queens of the Nile.

The first of the Ethiopian queens was Queen Hatshepsut, who ruled with Thotmes III (1486-1468) in the Eighteenth Dynasty.[51] This daughter of Thotmes I managed to rule Egypt by making more accurate judgments and administrative decisions than her husband Thotmes II. After his death, she took possession of the throne as regent to her son Thotmos III. Her regency was recorded as peaceful and successful. Queen Hatshepsut is said to have renewed mining excavations at Sinai between the Mediterranean and the Red Sea. She is credited with building the famous temple at Deir-el-Bahari in West Thebes or Luxor. Queen Hatshepsut died in 1468 B.C.E. She is still revered and considered remarkable due to her insight, ability, and determination to execute her ideas.

The second queen was Queen Metuma who reigned about 1400 B.C.E. This queen was the mother of Amenhotep III (called Amenophis) by the Greeks. Amenhotep is the Memnon who came to the rescue of Troy in the Iliad, where he is called "black prince."[52]

There were other queens such as Tiyi and Amenhotep III (1405-1370); Nefertiti or Nefertari: (1370-1352), and Cleopatra, the daughter of the mulatto Pharoah Ptolemy XIII who was named "Neus Dionysius" by the Greeks. Our line of queens is extended by those named "Candace," in the Bible and elsewhere. They ruled over an Ethiopian kingdom which included Yemen and Abyssinia. Their commercial and administrative centers extended as far as Meroe, where these queens buried their dead.

Queen Ashotep was the Nubian mother of Asmes, who routed the Shepherd Hyksos from Egypt. This mulatto king was born in Thebes. He is mentioned in history by the Greeks as "Amiosis", who ruled north and south. Queen Ashotep's jewels have been on exhibit at the Nubian Museum of the Cairo Museum.

The marriage of quadroon and octoroon pharoahs to black princesses was common. Social intercourse was similar to the experience of princesses in Hawaii, and other original people like native Americans.[53] The woman was actually or usually the royal descendant of a king or chief. The explorer or invader was in most cases a nonentity, social outcast, or a peasant. Some were outright criminals escaping justice. Determination to maintain the surname of a worthy ancestor explains why the boy carries his mother's name, in many cases, and a widow clings to her deceased husband's name if it is a name of distinction. She will invariably sign with *viuda de* at the end, meaning in Spanish, "widow of," unless her father's name was a name more widely recognized. This tradition prevails even in North Africa, Spain and Hispanic America.

Queen Taitu was King Menelik's II wife, and a great warrior was she. This queen led her own troops to battle against the Italians at Adowa in 1896. Queen Taitu encouraged her Ethiopian troops to exert their best effort in out doing a woman. They did! The Italians were put to flight after losing two generals, twelve thousand dead, all their supplies and seven thousand captured. Menelik II and Queen Taitu lost between three thousand and five thousand troops.

The Ethiopian woman has been accustomed to marching into battle with her husband. If he fell in action, she fought more fiercely to avenge his death. J.A. Rogers said,"Europeans sometimes kill themselves rather than fall into the hands of an African woman."

In 937 A.C.E. Queen Judith of the Falashas (a people misnamed "Black Jews") soon seized the throne skillfully, and remained Queen of Ethiopia for forty years.

THE PYRAMIDS

All histories of social interaction among different peoples in a given area contain explanations of languages, politics, religions, industrial development, and even socioeconomic values of the groups studied. When a study is prepared without a predisposition toward a certain group or groups, it will definitely show one ethnic group exploited by another or even members of its own group. Scholarly studies will also reveal that every square foot of habitable land contains the remains of someone long deceased. Those studies will also produce evidence of a group or subgroups that had been enslaved at one time or another, if not by their own ethnic group, then by some other. It is with these hypotheses in mind we intend to contradict fallacies popularized as historical facts.

It is easy to tell many lies if one can reinforce them with a few truths. But prejudice, vanity and ethnocentrism supported by economic power and military might defeated Hitler despite his ego, and his superior race, conceived through lies.

Races are not intellectually superior, regardless of how many millions of dollars are granted to A.R. Jensen to prove that theory.[54] To support truth and discredit falsehood, the Peruvian philosopher Manuel Gonzalez Prada said, "There are no longer superior races, only superior individuals, each man with his own intellectual capacity."

These statements lead us to the task of exposing false information which was not based on scholarly effort or diligent researching for validation, but hastily accepted as fact. This propaganda seems intended to sway judgment of audiences sympathetic to ancestor worship, promote prejudice against economically poorer ethnic groups, underestimation of certain peoples' awareness, of self-conceived racial superiority.

The information repudiated is a deplorably untrue statement made by the Prime Minister of Medina Israel in a tabloid of considerable circulation and reputation—*The New York Post*. On November 11, 1977, that paper published reasons for Prime Minister Menachem Begin saying to United States congressmen, "I only hope if I come to Cairo he would receive me hospitably. If he gives me a chance to have a glimpse of the pyramids—which our forefathers helped to construct and for which we don't ask any compensation—I shall be very grateful." The comment inferred request for hospitable treatment from Anwar-el Sadat, who was then president of Egypt. Any statement regarding Jews having assisted in building pyramids is inconsistent with facts and dates. Begin was either possessed by preposterousness, fallaciousness, or ignorance.

The first Hebrews of recognition became historically significant as a tribe or organized monotheistic group about 1100 B.C.E. The first king of Israel was Saul, the son of Kish of the tribe of Benjamin.

Salomon Reinach says:

Authentic history begins for the Israelites with the constitution of Saul's monarchy (c. 1100 B.C.). All that precedes this—the Deluge, the dispersal of mankind, Abraham, Jacob, Joseph, the captivity in Egypt, Moses, Joshua, the conquest of Canaan—is more or less mythical; but this mythology interwoven with historical traditions, and the proportion of these becomes considerable from the date of the Exodus of the Hebrews out of Egypt.[55]

The Babylonian Deluge dates back to 1900 B.C.E. Abraham, the patriarch of the Hebrews and Moslems, was not born until (ca. 1789 B.C.E.) the Thirteenth Egyptian Dynasty.

Hebrew enslavement did not begin until ca.1625–1571 B.C. The Egyptian pyramids were built beginning with the Third Dynasty and ending with the Sixth Dynasty, from ca.2700 to 2300 B.C.E. Egyptian chronology places dates of erection between 2700 and 3100 B.C.E.[56] The astronomic data provided at the entrance of the Great Pyramid indicates 2592 to 2654 B.C.E.

Therefore, with the data presented, it is more than impossible for someone born in Poland in 1913, like Begin, to have had ancestors who built pyramids in Egypt. There were no Hebrews during the period, and therefore no Jews!

Rash statements such as Begin's are not only misleading, but discrediting to the speaker and publisher who might have unscrupulously printed information without researching facts for accuracy and validity, or simply attempted to propagate new untruths about "old facts." The statement discredited here is mainly written in journals by so-called archaeologists and historians popularizing a new science named "Egyptology"!

The pyramids built for the kings and queens of Africa are more than most Europeans realize. Karl Richard Lepsius accounted for about seventy-seven. The real amount is eighty or more, when those of Meroe are included. These pyramids are all situated along the left bank of the Nile River. Some of them are isolated, others are scattered along the valley within an area of forty kilometers. Europeans claim that their primary purpose was entombment. Africans learned they were for astronomical observations, predictions of future events, and recording those past. The pyramids have openings on each landing. They face the sun at an angle which provides enough light to illuminate the entire chamber. Each pyramid is built with a rectangular base supporting four sloping triangularly shaped sides meeting at an apex. Each opening is approximately one square foot.

The first pyramids were built at Meroe, in Ethiopia, over 6,000 years ago. At that time Egypt was considered Northern Ethiopia. The largest of these is the pyramid of King Taharka at Nuri.[57] The largest of those in Egypt is the pyramid of Keops, (also known as Cheops, Khufu, Konfu or Krefen) and Mycerinus (or Menkaure), second in size.

The Cushites taught the Egyptians to build these remarkable, tangible and durable structures. They were not built by Europeans or men from outer space. And they were not built by Asians. Construction on the later-built pyramids began during the Third Dynasty and ended during the Sixth Dynasty, ca.2700 to 2300 B.C.E. Over the centuries, the pyramids, especially Cheops's, have contained highly mysterious and scientific secrets.[58]

In the eastern pyramid of Cheops the celestial sphere and the figures representing stars and planets were drawn before Europe existed as a continent of any cultural or civilized account. As a matter of fact, at Abu Simbel, near the bottom of the murals, there are four figures representing the continents (what Darwin, the Nazis, and Coon preferred to call "races") as the ancients saw them in their travels.[59] The tallest person is a black male, fully robed, including head covering, and bejeweled. He represented Africa, as it was explained by Ben-Jochannan. The person to his left is a brown-skinned man, representing Asia, but not quite as tall as the first. The third character is a reddish-brown man, a little shorter than the other two, representing Arabia. Each of these representatives is fully dressed, in his regional attire, from head to feet. Off to the side, apart from the others, is a little man, smaller than all of the others. He is pale-white, naked and bareheaded, with an animal skin around his shoulders. This man represented underdeveloped Europe.

In addition to the paintings of the cosmic forces, there are other mysteries that are not scientifically divulged. Tradition tells us, nonetheless, that in one of the unknown areas of the pyramidal passages there is an unexposed system of passages. One of these causeways contains the formula with essential laws and elements for inventing electricity through extraction from the atmosphere. The data disclosed by the initiated and most wise of the ancient people contain the variables for proving their hypotheses.

Another chamber encloses the secret of the secrets concerning disintegration of matter, secretly known as the philosophic stone of contemporary times. The concealed information predicts events that are now occurring, and others coming to pass.

In terms of less hypothetical and secretive revelations, we can almost divulge that a hidden area in the antechamber mentioned above, presently covered and purposely made invisible, contains and conceals the underground passage that led the ancients to the Nile directly from the pyramid of Cheops.

In terms of astronomical observations, George Barbarin stated that Mahmoud-Bey—an Egyptian expert in astronomy—estimated that Cheops was built five thousand two hundred years ago. It was a specially selected period. At that time, the rays of Sirius (the Dog Star or brightest star in the sky) reached the height of its powerful illumination and was falling perpendicularly on the meridional face of the pyramid.

Unlike Lepsius, the German Medicua, his colleague saw more than met the average eye. Medicua said he saw in the pyramids an immortality of the human soul.[60] These scholars did not concentrate their investigations on the secondary pyramids near Abousyr, Sakharah, Dachour, Maranyeh and Meidoun. Their interest, says Barbarin, was centered on the village of Gizeh and its surroundings commonly called the area of the "Great Pyramids."[61]

The Pyramid of Cheops is usually of greater interest to most students and scholars, and therefore receives more scrutiny. Its Horizontal Passage has also revealed having the same section as the Ascending Passage. Nevertheless, its height seems to be lesser than the former. In the last meters traversed, there is a descending stair where the stone floor inclines. Its passage leads, after thirty-eight meters, to the Queen's Chamber, which measures 5.23 x 5,76 meters.[62] The Horizontal Passage and the Queen's Chamber symbolize the era of Spiritual Rebirth, and the arrival of the "True Light to the East" during the "Last Days of the Law."

These steps, beginning at the intersection of the Entrance Passage and the Descending Passage, have a measurement of 1,06 meters at its midsection. Ascending a slope of forty meters, it joins with the beginning of the Great Gallery on the same axis, at the beginning of the Horizontal Passage.

Symbolism of the two Ascending Passages is interpreted as "Double Chambers of the Truth." The first Ascending Passage is merely called "Chamber of the Truth in the Shadow" in the "Book of the Dead." The architectural symbolism, however, has been interpreted as a narrow, low passage. Barbarin was observant enough to notice how although this passage has the same section as the Descending Passage, one can walk through it more comfortably.

The History of the Pyramids, and their mysteries, could occupy volumes. So let the mysteries divulged, and the limited measurements provided, suffice for the present. Many kings and queens have not been mentioned because of the same enormity of the task. Their histories would also require volumes. However, the writer has tried to compensate by adding the Chronology (of 11 into 11) which is recorded in the Pyramid of the Great Cheops.

This table is merely an attempt to present the numerological relationship of mathematical computations, and one of the countries mentioned by the ancients. In this case it is France, the national environment of the observer, which has been given the honor.

Table of 11 Predictions and 8 Surprises

Year	Event
1804:	Advent of the First Empire.
1815:	Fall of Napoleon I.
1826:	Reign of Nicholas I of Russia.
1837:	England begins freedom of slaves in her colonies.

1848:   The February Revolution.
1859:   John Brown is feared then hanged.
1870:   The Franco-German War—Rome is taken from
             France.
1881:   Czar Alexander II of Russia is assassinated.
1892:   Wilhelmina reigns in Holland.
1903:   U.S. helps Panama become independent from the
             Canal.
1914:   World War I, predicted as "The Great War."
1925:   Hindenburg becomes president of Germany.
1936:   The date of the Pyramid (by archeologists seeking
             the entrance to the King's Chamber).
1947:   Partition of Palestine into Jewish and Arab states.
             Arabs reject!
1958:   Egyptian President Nasir becomes head of
             United Arab Republic.
1969:   Astronaut Neil Armstrong first man to walk on the
             moon.
1980:   Egypt and Israel exchange first ambassadors.
1991:   Russian World communism amazingly collapsed.
2002:   Beginning of the millenium in 2001.

The number six stamped on the measurements of the Pyramid of
Cheops, is copied by the popes and worn on their miter as 666.[63]
This number was the unit of the inch and its sexagesimal multiples.
"The first multiple is the foot, twelve inches (2"x6"); and after this the
rises are 18"(3"x6"), 24"(4"x6"), 30"(5"x6"), and 36"(6"x6") or 6"= the
yard."[64]

    E.W. Bullinger himself declared that these measurements corre-
spond with the first division of time spaces which measure man's six
days of labor divided into the day of twelve hours 2x6, and the night
2x6. The months also are composed of 2x6 (two semesters), and the
minutes and seconds as well: 6x10 = 60.

THE FALASHAS

The Falashim are direct descendants of Cush. We will reinforce this
declaration with historical facts and biblical testimonies rather than
ethnocentrism or subtle distortions.

    The Ethiopians and Southern Arabians descended from Cush.
Abraham converted the people of Canaan during a period when
Babylonia, Ethiopia, and Arabia were ruled by Africans.[65]
Nebuchadnezzar was the famous king of that era; certainly his name
or any of the names of these places does not sound European Asiatic.

    The people converted (including Abraham himself), went to Egypt,
in Africa, abandoning Palestine and looking farther south. When they
reached Ethiopia, the Egyptians and other Africans called them

"Falashim," meaning strangers or foreigners. This name is a Semitic name; words ending in im to form a plural are from the Semitic linguistic repertoire.

Williams reports:

> By two routes Hebraic culture may have penetrated to West Africa from the north, across the desert wastes; and from the east, along the general line of traffic that skirts the great tropical forests. The possibility of its introduction by sea is so remote that it may for the present at least be disregarded.

These followers of Abraham, converted from sun worshipping Chaldeans to monotheistic or one-god worshipping had become "Habiru." Their escape from famine and pestilence—in Canaan and Babylon—to Egypt had now caused them to become Falashas or strangers in another land.

Their adjustment in the land makes it apparent that Abraham spoke Aramaic and whatever Cushitic languages and dialects existed before Hebrew and Arabic. With this sociolinguistic fact in mind we should be able to see through the veil or etymological origin of so-called Semitic languages and people.

The word *fallasa* (in Ge'ez) means to emigrate. These immigrants established the first Hebrew religious kingdom in a land where all of the people looked alike. There were no major groups; the new caucasoid psychological term "race" did not exist. Bradley says, of this pseudolinguistic term that it seemed incongruous to even enter a discussion of the origin of the word race, which most scientists agree does not exist in any functional, evolutionary sense or even in a concrete classificatory sense."[66] Since the term "stranger" is not the best-liked term for Hebrews or any other sojourner in a strange land, the Hebrews used the Cushitic equivalent to *fallasa*. They called themselves *kayla*, for those persons insisting upon making them feel strange. To persons sympathetic or empathetic toward their religion, among themselves they used the words *Beta Israel*. These two words could not reflect "conversion" even in the mind of the most rabid racist or Zionist because they translate from Hebrew as "House of Israel." It might be interesting to point out that only the Falashas and the Cochin Jews of India legitimately classify themselves as Beta Israel (translated House of Israel).

These clarifications are stated to build our story on hard facts with documented validity. They are not based on his-story for heritage seeking, latifundist claims or racist denunciations. They follow unbiased reports with no self-serving purpose or expansionist intent.

In a letter dated February 9, 1973, Rabbi Ovadia Yossef, the Sephardi Chief Rabbi of Israel, gave a rabbinical ruling that the "Falashas of Ethiopia are Jews and he has accepted their claim that they are the descendants of the tribe of Dan." Rabbi Yossef said he had come to the "conclusion that the Falashas are descendants of the Tribes of Israel who went southwards to Ethiopia, and there is no doubt that the above sages who established that they 'the Falashas' are of the tribe of Dan, investigated and inquired and reached the conclusion on the basis of the most reliable witnesses and evidence."[67]

Some hard-hearted Zionists still insisted that in order to invoke the law of return, like the Russian Jews and others, the Falashim should be converted, like Sammy Davis, to be covered by the Spirit of Torah and *halacha*, the Written Law and the Oral Law, without restrictions. But European descendants of converts cannot legitimize the Falashas. Falashim conversion from sun-and-idol worshipping Chaldeans to monotheistic worshippers made them "Habiru."

Their escape to Egypt from pestilence and famine in Canaan and Babylon caused them to become *Falashim*. When they settled in Ethiopia that region was named Land of the Ten Tribes.[68] When they began using the writings copied from the drawings of the pharoahs in Ta-Merry, Qamt, Kimit, Sais, Mizraim, better known as Egypt, they developed a linguistic repertoire or list of words. These words were easier and fewer than the Cushitic language. This laconic language they called by their given name "Habiru" or "Ivrit." With their new language, similar to Aramaic and Punic—both Semitic languages—they wrote a book between 700 B.C.E. and 500 B.C.E.

Several men able to read and translate the Egyptian hieroglyphics and the Ethiopic alphabet began writing contemporary history. Some copied the predictions of the sages from the walls of tombs, shrines, obelisks, and pyramids. Others wrote prophecies and laws. These writers were called prophets. Their collection of short and long stories copied from Egyptians and Babylonians was called the Bible in modern times. Before that, a part of it was called *Torah*. Their compilation of history, myths, predictions, laws, and admonitions became chapters or "books." In the books there was covered history: Deutoronomy 1:4, "After he had slain Sihon the king of the Amorhites," myth: Genesis 4:20, "Adam called his wife's name Eve," prediction: Joshua 1:5, "There shall not any man be able to stand before thee all the days of thy life," law: Leviticus 19:13 "Thou shalt not defraud thy neighbor." These epics and tales interwoven with history produced hope through the Supreme Force, or Being, omnipotent and omnificent. A religion was created with a One-God force to be feared. This force was mightier than the sun, he was the Father of all men; protecting his followers from the evil forces, negative spiritual influences, and from physical harm. "Though I walk through the shadow of death, I will fear no evil." Thus, the Falashas became known as "the People of the Book."

The People of the Book were immigrants in the vast Kingdom of

Ethiopia, which spread from Egypt to Yemen. Josephus said of that kingdom with the only Lion of Judah, King of kings: Abraham contrived to acquire land for his sons and grandsons by Keturah, in colonies that "they took possession of troglodytes, and the country of Arabia the Happy as far as it reaches unto the Red Sea."[69] Josephus associated Arabia with Ophren, son of Madian, who made war against Libya, and took it, and his grandchildren when they inhabited it, called it from his name, Africa."

Houston's findings corroborated that Arabia was part of Ethiopia's territorial domain in ancient times:

> At the time that Ethiopians began to show power as monarchs of Egypt about 3000 to 3500 B.C. the western part of Arabia was divided into two powerful kingdoms. In those days the princes of Arabia belonged to the descendants of the Cushites, who ruled Yemen for thousands of years. Zohak, celebrated in Iranian history, was one of these famous "Cushitic" rulers.

Strabo, Pliny, Diodorus, and Ptolemy tell about Yemen's high civilization, art, wealth, commerce in silk and products of India, and treasures of Africa.[70]

The kings of Yemen were so interrelated with the kings of Ethiopia they claimed descent from Khatan. Houston says these ancient Yemenite monarchs were so dark-skinned and proud of their African origin that they gloried in being called Khatan and Himyar "the dusky, a name denoting African origin whose rulers were called 'Tobba' of Hamitic etymology." In reference to the Cushites from whom the Yemenites, Falashas, and other Ethiopic people descended, Houston added: "Yemen bore considerable resemblance to the Nile Valley . . . Arabia, Egypt, Chaldea and India were colonies of the Cushite empire." The conquest of Sargon 3800 B.C.E. was of "African Arabs" and he was said to have been of the same race. These African Arabs are recorded as having formed a ring around the deserts of Arabia inhabited by the half-breeds or paler-skin Arabs who spoke a language akin to Syriac and Hebrew.

Houston pointed out that historians who "speak of the Semitic conquest of Babylon as early as 4500 B.C.E. is erroneous unless they explain that these Arabians were Cushite Arabians, another division of the race of the black Sumerians."[71]

Houston would be amazed to learn how Ashkenazi and Sephardic Zionists are now disclaiming the religious heritage of the Falashas.[72] The Moslems support her, nonetheless, with the Bible and their Koran. They state: "When Bilal (HWON) came he brought with him the clear Tawraah (Old Testament). The Bible that most people read now is a tampered version." The Moslems also insist that the words are lost in translations. That fact is known to all scholars who read and write any language considered second to English, as the native tongue. With other languages it is an unavoidable linguistic phenomenon due to the fact some words are not translatable. With English it is even worse because many English writers distort facts, even when idiomatic equivalents are available. The Moslems state:

> The distortions of facts ". . . came about when the children of Israel fell into captivity under Nebuchadnezzar. After Nebuchadnezzar, the Israelites fell into the hands of Cyrus, who gave the command for the rebuilding of Sulaymaan's (Solomon's) temple. Now these Israa'iylites finally left Babylon, but they no longer were the true Israa'iylites because after one hundred thirty six years passed their seed became mixed and diluted. The Amorite had already destroyed the versions of the Bible that the Israa'iylites had. It was only the so-called learnt Pharisees who kept the law committed to memory. But the tribe of Judah who went South to Ethiopia had the true Scriptures or Tawraah. It was the seven thousand of the tribe of Judah who kept the law of the Tawraah pure. They took it up to Ethiopia and put it on a high mountain and only the Priest of the Falashans (tribe of Judah) was able to climb the mountain to get it.[73]

Wolf Leslau stated "Very few of the western scholars who have dealt with the problem of the Falashas are of the opinion that they are ethnically Jews." In the first place, Leslau was correct in stressing western scholars' fallibilities. Nevertheless, eastern scholars, and even some westerners know better methods of seeking facts and reporting them. Leslau omitted two key words which should have preceded the adjective western. He should have written *so-called* western scholars. In the second place, the word "problem" when applied to the Falashas is offensive to Africans. It has a connotation of racial superiority on the part of the classifier.[74] This term was used by the Gestapo when Hitler demanded a solution to the Jewish people's "problem" existence in Europe during World War II.[75] In regard to whether the Falashas are ethnically Jews, let us cite Adolphe Joseph Reinach—an Egyptologist.

In 1915-1916, Reinach made a most startling proclamation to the white-minded world. He declared that not only were the Egyptians of African origin but, "the human races of Europe, Asia and Africa, are descended from a single family, whose original seat was on the shores of Equatorial Africa."[76] Thirty years later the University of Pennsylvania reported a remarkable find during a successful archaeological expedition. The university claimed this discovery would radically change popular opinion concerning the historical and ethnological origin of man. Fellows at the University of Pennsylvania notified scholars the world over that due to evidence gathered they had concluded, "Negro art is primarily original and that civilization probably had its rise in the great lake regions of the African continent." *The New York Times* of October 1, 1991, stated: "Proponents say the genetic path back to Africa is clearer than ever in new study."

To add insult to distortion of facts or lack of information, Leslau added "we know of the existence of a Jewish community in Elephantine in the fifth century B.C.—or the Jews of Yemen may have sent forth missionaries who converted these Africans to Judaism." Any student of the history of religions knows that the term Judaism comes from Judah, whose kings displayed the lion on their thrones, emblems, and reliefs. The British copied it, for there are no lions in Britain. The term "Lion of Judah" was used by his Majesty the Negus of Ethiopia, who kept a live lion for a pet at his side to continue this African tradition. The Yemenite and Babylonian kings— descendants of Africans who sent them the lions— also depict lions as a symbol of power. Are there any lions in Europe? If there aren't any, then ask yourself: Why is the lion with a golden crown on its head the visible symbol on all legitimate Torahs, mantles, and Ark covers used throughout the Hebrew communities of the world?

There are three Falasha tribes of record. One group lived in Gondar near the city. This group's exposure to so-called modern civilization, caucasoid mores or lack thereof, and pragmatic materialism affected them. Their environmental corruption, as a tribe, and conformity to certain western values caused them to be spoken of locally pejoratively. This Gondar group was also ostracized by the other two groups, to some extent.

The second group of *Beta Israel* was assisted by some Israelis and Zionists from time to time; one significant gift being a hospital erected for the Falashas through joint efforts of the European and Hebrew tribes.

The third component of *Beta Israel* feels like the ostracized first group. Both think the second group, which receives European assistance, is exploited and untraditionally subservient. That second group is reported on in newspapers worldwide, invited to television talk shows, and are featured in slide pictures at temples where funds are collected for them. These, and all Falashas, are officially accepted as Jews (without conversion) during the fundraising. The famous slogan used is "Save Falasha Jewry!" Millions of dollars are collected from well-meaning Jews, and a few gentiles. These large sums enable fundraisers, coordinators, and executives to be well-salaried. Only a token handful of the proceeds actually goes to the Falashas, and a hand-picked jeepfull of Falashas is sent to Israel, under the Law of Return, now and again.

Traditionally, Falasha acceptance of foreign aid, especially from Ethiopians of other religious preferences and also Europeans trying to force them into conversion, is unpardonable.

The third group lives in isolation. The members live in large stone-and-mud huts. They have the original scriptures of the Hebrew religion written in Ge'ez. These Falashas also have the original Ten Commandments buried at Axum in Ethiopia.

The *Kebra Nagast*,which contains the names of the princes, temples, provinces and churches of Ethiopia, tells how Menelik inherited the Ark. A son of the Queen of Sheba and Solomon of Israel, Menelik's mentor Azariah, the high priest, "gave the carpenter the measurements which were the same as those of the Ark of the Covenant. . . .The night before they were to depart [from Jerusalem], Azariah took the raft in every way like the Ark, went to the temple and stole the sanctuary, the angel of the Lord opening the doors for him." Solomon had offered his son Menelik the throne of Judah, but Menelik refused the throne and begged to be allowed to return to Ethiopia. Solomon received a dream advising him to comply, so he annointed Menelik, and called him David, because they were from the House of David. The day after the anointment, Solomon gave his son the outer covering of the Ark as a going-away present. "The young kid [Menelik] rejoiced with the gift. Then Menelik and the nobles set out for Ethiopia with a caravan. When they reached Egypt the sons of the nobles of Israel revealed to Menelik how they had stolen the Ark and brought it with them. After a few days, Solomon missed his son and went to the Ark to pray. He discovered that it was gone. King Solomon pursued his son and the nobles through Egypt, where the Egyptians informed him that the Ethiopians had already passed there many days before. He started to continue farther, but was comforted upon learning through a vision from the Lord that the Lady of Zion was at peace with his firstborn son. Solomon returned to Jerusalem."

The Ark was then buried at Axum, about one hundred seventy miles from Adulis, the famous port of the Red Sea. Through that port, Axum contacted the countries of the Orient. It is also there at Axum where the Bible was translated from Greek into Ge'ez, after African civilizations declined, and the Greeks had become civilized.

Sankange informs us, "when the Bible was translated from Greek into one of the country's native languages called Ge'ez, the translators used the name Ethiopia in place of Axum." As a result, the desendants of Axum became known as Ethiopians. But Axum had been the capital of the entire Ethiopian Empire from the first to the eighth centuries A.C.E. And the Ark of the Covenant, brought from Jerusalem, was placed in the Church of Saint Mary of Zion, where Ethiopia's emperors were crowned, and huge obelisks were carved with history dating from pre-Christian times, and even pre-Hebrew times.[77]

In 1941 the Negus officially decreed that the entire area—and remnants of the kingdom extended from Yemen to the Red Sea in ancient times—be called Ethiopia.[78]

The Falashas were caught in this web. Nevertheless, as the People of the Book, their traditions and high moral standards steeped in deep orthodox convictions made some of them have compunctions about dishonesty and hypocrisy. Consequently, they accepted no handouts for relinquishing their principles, or conversion for authenticity. As a result, they lived in dire poverty.

The family unit is most important among Falashas. An extended family might also be included; it is usually composed of orphans. Family units live, work and play together. Female members of the groups are isolated during their menstrual cycle—a custom unheard of among Europeans and their descendants. The law against sleeping with an unclean woman is clearly stated in Micah and Isaiah: "Wash you, make you clean; put away the evil doings before mine eyes." The Falashim observe the laws to the extent that no woman is allowed to sleep in the same hut with neighbors, let alone her husband, until she has ceased her cycle. Until then she is forced to live outside the community. In the case of childbirth, she is isolated for nine days. This separation prevents intercourse during menstruation —a strictly forbidden act under Hebrew laws and customs.

It is said that intercourse during menstruation was practiced in the Caucasian mountains. That practice helped to cause leprosy, and albino reproduction, which led to varied types of anemia persistent among Europeans and other people of color who amalgamated with them, up to this day.

Falasha families practice dietary and hygiene laws according to Torah. They do not recognize the Talmud or the Kabbala. Whatsoever goeth upon its paws is considered unclean, and he that beareth the carcass of them is unclean until the evening, and is expected to wash his clothes. Plants have unconsecrated fruits and vegetables, unless the edibles are forbidden for three years after the tree or root was planted, and during the fourth year when the harvest is dedicated to the Almighty. After those years one might eat thereof because some fruits have fallen, rotted, and revitalized the earth.[79]

Falasha families observe all Hebrew holidays and Holy days except Hanukkah, the mythological story of lights, and Purim, the festival of lots centered around Persian Jewry.

The existence of these tribes was known to Africans from ancient times. They were not "discovered" by Europeans, or anyone else. Europeans have a great penchant for discovering people and lands already inhabited before their arrival. The Falashim (called Falashas in English), came to Ethiopia—a land eight times the size of New York State—with their religion and rituals long, long ago. They lived apart from their people in the area.[80] They recognized the Sabbath more rigidly than those who wished to convert them, and practiced their own prayers and customs exercised by the elders, and transmitted to the young through oral tradition. They pray in Ge'ez, but in some of their prayers, however, "one still finds passages in Guarenya, the Cushitic language previously used by the Falashas."[81]

The first widely reported information concerning their religious practices and unpopular customs were recorded by a Jewish traveler of the ninth century named Eldad Haddani. Haddani noticed how these people looked exactly like other Ethiopians but had different customs, to the extent of seeming strange to their neighbors. A Sephardi Benjamin from Tudela, Spain, also visited the Falashim in 1165. Benjamin also visited the Khazar notables in Constantinople and Alexandria. He even visited Jews in China. Benjamin noticed and recorded that unlike Falashim, the Khazars were obviously non-Semitic. He explained his meeting with the Khazars in the East, but they spoke differently, were dressed differently from Hebrew people, and had different customs.[82]

In 1870 a French Jew named Joseph Halevy visited the Falashas. He was studying the languages of the various African tribes when he met this unusual group observing Hebrew customs and religious practices. The Falashas informed Halevy that they were the only Hebrews left in the world.[83] They had not come in contact with any other Hebrews or Jews for centuries. The Falashim's Torah was written in Ge'ez. This sociolinguistic find was announced by Halevy as the "discovery of the Falashas." Halevy had not researched his findings thoroughly, and probably had not even heard of Benjamin of Tudela. Halevy, like Christopher Columbus who met Indians and Africans in America when other Africans steered him here, was anxious to claim fame as a discoverer. Halevy had not read or heard of other persons who had been in touch with the Falashas before he met them.

Another effort which attempted to make Halevy a discoverer was the *Jewish Week—American Examiner* of January 14, 1979. It announced on its second page:

> There has been a great deal of academic discussion over the years as to the true origins of the Falashas and the authenticity of their "Jewishness." Both of Israel's present chief rabbis, Ashkenazi Chief Rabbi Ovadia Yosef, have ruled that Falashas are Jews who should nevertheless undergo a symbolic conversion ceremony.[84]

Even to suggest Falasha conversion is impudent, and inconsistent with the Hebrew Law of Return. Other Jews, especially Russian Jews in particular, are not subjected to conversion. That unfairness is Zionist-racist insensitivity clearly unveiled. If anyone is lacking "Jewishness" he is unquestionably of that impure stock Parkes mentions.

Most European Jews are unquestionably descendants of converts. It is therefore advantageous to the neo-Zionists to claim reli-gious godlike authority in the legitimacy of Beta Israelites whose her-itage they have usurped. The suggestion of Falasha conversion is again inconsistent with Hebrew tradition because it is interwoven into the fabric called Judaism. Even the patriarch Abraham was con-verted. There is hardly an ethnic group that does not contain at least a minority of Hebrew or Jewish adherents or followers of the religious tenets.

Salo W. Baron says even "a large number of former Phoenicians and Carthaginians had joined the Jewish community via conver-sion."[85]

JEWISHNESS

Even the sound of the term "Jewishness" is obnoxious. It has patron-izing as well as obsequious connotations. In this particular case, it is euphemistic and much more pseudolinguistic than "Semitic," another meaningless word. How does one authenticate Jewishness? How does one recognize a Jewish Semite? One might say the authen-ticity of Hebrews, Jews, or Gentiles can only be determined through religious practices. The difference or degree of "Jewishness" calcula-ble among Hebrews and Edomites, Jews and Goyim, is merely one of individual responsibility. An Edomite may claim to be Jewish while he eats bacon, pork sausages, cheats in business, and worships money instead of Hashem (God).[86] This same Germanic or Russianic descendant of converts will often be the claimant of godly authority to authenticate other people who usually respect the laws, and wor-ship God more faithfully and honestly than he. Nevertheless, his material and political power, and his added military might, afford him the authority to force defenseless people suffering starvation and other hardships to succumb for survival to his dictates. After all, sur-vival is of primary importance in these times when power is the only reality, and spirituality and religiousness are actually losing ground to materiality, and constantly reinforced with modern technology.

The authenticity of Falashas through "Jewishness" cannot be truthfully, honestly discussed without an overall introduction to the Jews, their origin, definition of Jewishness, and an accurate analy-sis of their definition related to ethnicity or identity.

The same demand should be made concerning authenticated "Semiticness." Who is a Semite? Are the Palestinians Semites? Are the Ethiopians, Arabs, Lebanese, Libyans, and other people of that area Semites? This term is pseudolinguistic. It could well be a term adopted by certain people for political, economic and even religious advantages. The term as an ethnic stamp is so vague that even its origin is unrelated to it. The etymological root shows the term evolving from Latin *semita* to Spanish *semita* meaning footpath.[87] This term now legitimized advantageously is really a "footpath" toward special considerations, pity and empathy while enmasking expansionism through violence; acts which disturb many Jews even more than some Gentiles.

On the other hand, "blackness" is feared by racists who popularize the term "nigger" throughout the United States. The term nigger,which originally meant a person of low moral standards and behavior in English, *regardless of color or racial orgin*, is now pejoratively used to designate only people of color. The American dictionaries have changed the meaning to such an extent that North American blacks use it to refer to themselves, and find it incomprehensible that other blacks resent the term and seldom use it for endearment or identity. The baseness implied by the term has become so psychologically internalized by Negroes (not blacks) that it actually influences the bad behavior externalized by American people of color, and the self-hatred they have been programmed to perpetuate. The term nigger has conditioned the North Americans to psychological ambivalence with such success, that a college-educated comedian of color, who is a firm believer in human progress, went as far as to say on worldwide television that "nigger" was a term of endearment when used among blacks in the United States. He did not know that foreign blacks in many countries would not attack a white person for addressing them with that term, but would and do openly resent it from black persons ignorant enough to use it. For that reason many Africans and Latin Americans avoid relationships with those confused blacks, and even prefer association with other races. The term nigger as applied to persons of any color or racial origin is one implying gross disrespect and scorn. The acceptance of the term camouflaged with explanations of the term originating in or from the word "Niger" must be unacceptable to blacks. Whites stopped calling themselves "honkies" once they found out honky tonk was no longer used to imply partying or a social club, but was cut to honky meaning "white nigger." Any black who uses the term "nigger" to another is sycophantic or has psychologically surrendered to social programming.

Here is one case among many that point out the facts. The racists of Hollywood made a motion picture showing a Jew who doggedly pursued the blood-thirsty Nazis who murdered Jews during World War II. When the Nazi—played by Gregory Peck—caught up with the Jew he wanted to kill, the Jew said we are not concerned with Nazis here, the niggers are the ones we are worried about.[88]

Regardless of our ethnic identity or religious persuasions, we must be reminded that some people read the Bible and the Torah without the keys to interpretation of their parables. Many persons still pray with their eyes closed, expecting to go to heaven, while others rob them blindly and make heaven with their money right here on earth. This exploitation is accomplished mainly through the "inferiorization" process. The exploiter superiorizes himself by stereotyping or categorizing the exploited, robbing him of his cultural heritage, its richness and values. The ends are achieved through transferring facts, changing names of locations, racial origins, and data pertaining to areas, demographic changes and the peoples involved. The conditioning process also has other ways of programming thoughtless masses who keep their ears plugged with earphones full of music, or their eyes glued to television propaganda. One of the principal conditioning methods is to appropriate funds to miseducate and trap gullible people with poor speaking habits, poor self-images, lack of self-respect (particularly for their women), and tendencies to imitate the ways of their oppressors. Once a people allow themselves to be inferiorized to the extent or level of psychological acceptance of conditions forced upon them, it becomes easy for the mentally incompetent and academically inadequate (who usually accept policemen and sanitation jobs, and Ku Klux Klan affiliation requiring no artisan skills or professional ability) to pretend ethnic superiority merely on the basis of color or group identity. The pretenders of pale-face superiority then refuse equal opportunities, unsegregated housing, social privileges, and basic human rights to the majority whom they treat as inferiors. In many cases, the bigots or racists are less academically prepared or skillfully qualified than those persons they discriminate against. But it is only in the United States of North America, Britain, South Africa, and Argentina, as well as a few other so-called "free world" countries which disregard human rights, does social classification of white being right without insight become acceptable as a way of life. In the more socially advanced countries such as France and Sweden, where the progenitors of the nationals were not mostly peasants, mafiosos, gangsters, highwaymen, and criminals from Europe, policemen and sanitation men are considered handlers of garbage, and they are not paid higher wages than teachers and college professors.[89]

In the more advanced Latin American countries and the West Indies, where some educated and respectable explorers landed and conquered, individual superiority is based on professional titles. This social status, or *roce social* as it is called, rejects individuals whose occupations do not require more than basic intelligence, but, who still pretend to be acceptable as important cultural contributors. Only an administrator of the health department or an investigator of the police department is considered a person of social importance or accomplishment.

Among Jews and Hebrews education is a most important factor in childhood needs for proper upbringing. To allow a child to grow up illiterate is a sin. Among North American blacks, and none other, it is quite noticeable that ignorance is tolerated with benign acceptance. Any fool can simply turn his collar around, call himself a preacher, and become economically independent overnight. The penchant for permissiveness toward ignorance has also caused the Jews to discriminate against blacks and to pretend that the Ethiopians, and other conscious blacks are unidentifiable with Negroes who call themselves niggers and "motherf____rs." Self-disrespect has also caused foreigners, from wherever, who visit the United States to become amazed at the manner in which the Negro denigrates himself as an incestuous beast when the whites know that only the slave master slept with the slave and her offspring—his daughter—to make her a mother producing more chattel to enrich him. Incest was one of the first acts outlawed by African family planners, especially Falasha elders.

But in countries where cowboys shoot presidents with whom they disagree, kidnap legislators and execute them at will, exploit educators, abuse executive privileges and plunder national reserves, citizens acquiesce and allow pretentiousness to become the order of the day.

In many countries we find oppressed groups resigned to acceptance of inferiorization as a matter of survival or opportunity to obtain material gains and special privileges they feel will allow them upward mobility through equalization or acceptance by whites. Others attempt to whiten themselves or pass for white. But obsequiousness only makes them Uncle Toms and Aunt Jemimas. It also affects them and their future generations. Money alone will not change the status of any individual or group discriminated against. Only education, even without money, will change their lot. Sammy Davis proved that money alone was not enough.

Davis joined a white congregation, never visited a black congregation in Harlem where he was raised and praised, and was continuously promoted by bigots as the ideal "black Jew," with obvious ridicule whenever conversion of Falashas or other Hebrews was discussed.

Jews have learned throughout the ages that money cannot educate anyone incapable of learning. As a medium of exchange, it can be taken away, exhausted, or mismanaged. But an educated person is capable of earning money in more than one country. And an educated poor person will survive even among the wealthy. But an uneducated poor is even more disadvantaged than the uneducated rich. He has no skills the rich will buy.

Joshua A. Fishman stated, "It is a characteristic of the newly rich to supply their own ancestry." This acquisition of wealth enabling false creation of worthy ancestry to justify self-imposed creation of worthy ancestry through falsehood is the basic reason for cowboys, gangsters, and highwaymen to often state that the Egyptians were white, or the Cushites were Caucasians, and therefore Ethiopians must be classified as members of a white race. Fishman also pointed out why persons who manufacture respectable ancestry will be concerned with standard speech in preference to other varieties. For example, societal belief about language associates language with occupation, social class and behavior. The dialect spoken by a group can help to feed stereotyping. If a group " from region A comes to be a large portion of the poor, the disliked, and the illiterate in region B, then their speech variety (dialect A) will come to stand for lower social status (educationally, occupationally) than will dialect B."[90]

In an American play called "Purlie Victorious" the black people were encouraged to "Be proud of your southern dialect." These Negroes showed unawareness of the immigrants who themselves used to shout different, low dialectal forms of English in past decades: "ten cents a pound a tomat" (while pushing a hand cart), "fresh green a vegetable," or the ones who pulled a cart picking up old rags and newspapers as they shouted "be vise don't you,"and asked, "vas is das?" while insisting upon their offspring learning to progressively speak the standard dialect, or high language variety (linguistically speaking), rather than the low varieties called southern black English. The Purlie Victorious group "A" ignores the fact that the former peddlers and rag pickers, when accosted with snide remarks concerning their present or former occupations, proudly allude to their progressiveness by saying, "I might be a rag picker, but do you know my son the doctor?" Or those who ask "do you know my son the politician or the lawyer?" These are factors observed by the racists for patronage or justification of stereotyping minorities. However, some blacks born and educated in the North still insist upon speaking worse English than their counterparts from the cotton fields or cabbage farms of the South. Their excuse is refusal to speak the slave master's language. But their excuse is not valid, for they can speak no other language well. The smart people of the Harlems are aware that Africans, Latin Americans, and other dark-skinned people in the United States speak standard English as well as their regional dialect. The foreign-born minorities and the smart Americans are aware that those who speak well, perform their occupations and professions with excellence, and will be in demand—through requests by Third World countries—as ambassadors of Britain and the United States in the near future. And the Jews who helped to keep the Blacks economically and academically ignorant will feel the repercussions because regardless of how mighty she becomes, Israel is surrounded by African countries.

The demand by Third World countries to negotiate with dark-skinned Africans rather than pale-skinned Europeans (who have to sun and paint themselves to have some color and cannot be trusted) will be the order of the day. Khomeini of Iran and Khadafi of Libya proved that. Furthermore, people are becoming quite disgusted with being discriminated against in their own countries. And in order to survive without a constant threat of nuclear sabotage by poor blacks and underprivileged whites around the world, nations will recognize that resisting force and deal more equitably in the distribution of world resources and equal opportunities in the pursuit of individual independence.

In many countries, especially South Africa, where Jews have huge interests in diamond markets, money-lending, and other monopolies, black people have become placated with their grievous conditions and compensated with deliberate mediocrity in their performances or achievements. Many of them seeing so few possibilities of receiving adequate compensation for their efforts have despaired, and even lost faith in government and democracy. Narcosis and dipsomania have become their ill fortune. These addicts and alcoholics have had their decadent psychophysical conditions met by their governments with benign neglect. Their situation has been overshadowed by the greed of their politicians. But will any nation that has allowed alcohol and drug abuse, racial discrimination, and general inequality of opportunities, flourish and survive despite the inevitable consequences of this malaise? Can the Jews who support these injustices continue to call in Ha-shem (God) to bless them?[91]

In the United States of North America in particular, many Jews who have acquired a certain amount of economic power—Ashkenazim and Sephardim—have turned toward discrimination against those American blacks using dialect A, even if they are of the Hebrew persuasion, of African or Falashim descent. But regardless of how bleached the Jews become their Gentile counterparts still consider them strange, of impure stock, and guilty of the unforgiveable sin. We read these condemnations in many works about racial purity and superiority.

Eugen Rosenstock-Huessy remarks: "Among the pagans as with the Jews, everyone aspires to be founder, father, owner, testator, ancestor, guardian, master. Each one rules over a bit of the world." Huessy followed with explanations of the pagans' cries among their tribes, a cry that proclaimed them "Sprung from Zeus, nobly born."

As for the Jews, Huessy pointed out more weaknesses on their part. His argument proved how Zionists have actually gone from conceivable religious modesty to inconceivable cleverness and militaristic ruthlessness. Their pompousness had to be condemned by good Hebrews and Jews because we, like almost everyone else, know how people tend to judge all members of a group by the actions of a few or a majority—which in this case happens to be a few. Huessy, a Christian, reinforced his argument by saying:

That new humanity from universal need and sin, that ever newly born *corpus christianum* of all men of good will—that being called out from all people—is something of which she knows nothing. She knows an original union in blood, that of the chosen people, but no final becoming united of all the children of the Father. The Jews have the saying that one day all people will come to Jerusalem to pray, and they always crucify again the one who came to make the word true. In appearance they wait upon the word of the Lord, but they have grown through and through so far away from revelation that they do everything they can to hinder its reality. With all the power of their own promises. They are the image on earth, the Lucifier, the highest of the angels, elect of God, who wanted to keep God's gift for himself as a dominion in his own right, and fell. So Israel stands upon its own inalienable right. This naive way of thinking that one has won inalienable rights in perpetuity against God, which by nature remain for posterity as properties inherited by bequest, is the relic of blind antiquity in Judaism.[92]

These truths are also the properties of several true Hebrews and Jews who are Israel's conscience. We are concerned with her soul and therefore clamor for her guilt to be recognized, a political purge brought about to regain her soul through recognition of the injustices perpetrated by a handful of fanatic racist Zionists and her Law of Return which has not been made available to all of her sons and daughters.

If Israel is to be a moral symbol of man's humanity to man, and cause compunctions for injustices, she should carry the torch of peace. Israel should be the torch of illumination for this world in its quest for peace and universal brotherhood. She should be like a light unto the universe, for light penetrates all areas where it is focused. "It overcomes, and thereby shows what it is."

Cush was great and it fell, Babylon, Greece and Rome declined and Great Britain is rapidly deteriorating as an empire. The United States has selfish magnates manufacturing products with built-in obsolescence, cancerous additives in foods and beverages, air, soil and water pollution, in addition to dissatisfied citizens who no longer have any patriotism or civic interest in the electoral process. Others demand equal rights and opportunities or promise to see the country blow up, even if they have to go with it. The times are more crucial for Israel and the United States than some comfortably wealthy people realize. Statutes and laws must be enforced if civil rights mandates are to be meaningful in Israel and the United States.

The United States, which sets precedents, must decide whether the country will survive based on its Constitution, with its promises of "liberty and justice for all," or perish because of a few (or many) bigots, some wearing white sheets, teasing blacks with false genetic hypotheses, terrorizing and harassing minorities with police brutality and murder incorporated.[93]

Omission of injustices, and distortions of facts have made it convenient for whites to pretend to be superior to the point of determining who are inferior, and what characteristics determine ethnic classification. The ulterior motive behind that process is justification of the oppressed becoming oppressor. But inferiorization was also practiced by the Germans when they considered the Romans as inferiors, after the Romans had "civilized them." They later scorned and treated the Italians with disdain—even though they were allies during World War II. The Italians, in turn, dyed their hair blond and married blonds to appease their inferiority complex. The Jews oppressed by the Romans before and later massacred by the Germans in World War II, intermarried with Romans and Germans to appease their inferiority complex. With that purpose accomplished, they decided to become the greatest oppressors of the Palestinians, Hebrews and blacks, even in Israel. Their Jewishness has made Zionism synonymous with ungodliness!

The Roman writer said the Jews, during Roman times, " are gaining so much ground that they find followers in all countries, and thus the defeated have imposed their law upon the victors." But Jews later lost ground, and will lose again if they do not mend their evil ways. The meek will inherit the earth, and the powerful will always be challenged by an equally powerful opposite force pulling in the opposite direction.

Since Jews are not a race, and Jewishness is not an attribute, one must determine that categorization of Jewishness through its entire promulgated definition. The questions then become: What is a Jew? Who is a Jew? What is Jewishness? Perhaps eliciting answers with questions in the Socratic manner might help. Among Hebrews we say "Always answer a question with a more difficult question!"

First, is a Jew "a person born of a Jewish mother or a person reaffirming his Judaism before a Bet Din, (a Jewish court of religious elders)"? (Article II, Section 1, of the Constitution drawn October 1969 by a now non-existent group of Jewish leaders). Second, who is a Jew? is answered by the first Hebrews and Abraham. We might add: A Jew is a convert, or by birth, a member of a group practicing an ancient religion, united for self-protection through affirmative action with guaranteed economic potential, military might, and political power. Third, is Jewish identity bestowed by God, or by self-appointed patrons and donors of Jewishness?

Jewishness must be defined as individual exercise of a personal God-given right to choose one's religious preference, and to select the

God one chooses without recriminations.

Jewishness is also the individual's right to worship the God of his choice in spirit and in truth, realizing that one owes no explanation of one's preference, deeds, and atonement for one's faults to no one but one's self, and his or her God.

Jewishness is the exercise of goodwill, honest dealing with Gentiles and Jews alike with malice toward none.

The Zionists and their American supporters must realize that man creates God out of himself and his intrahuman mind. Man also creates group identity out of his own mind. Man by definition knows absolutely nothing about God, therefore, it is selfish and impudent for any particular group to be the receiver and possessor of the knowledge and blessing which God has of Himself bestowed upon all men. Consequently, people must realize that Jewishness and/or Jewish identity extends beyond themselves and their criterian of "God" or man's "chosen."

This treatment of those questions presented bring us to the polemic root of this matter. How would Abraham, who was among the first Hebrews, be classified at the Bet Din's altar in these times? Certainly, some persons would classify him a Black Jew. This fact can be judged through experience and observation. It is common knowledge that North Americans have a strong penchant for labeling people and places. They made Panama Canal workers "Gold" and "Silver" employees, called blacks "colored" in the United States—not withstanding the fact that if you line up ten whites on a train, each one has a different complexion, causing you to wonder who is really colored. And they classify dark-skinned people of any religious persuasion other than worshippers of a white Christ, "black Moslem, black Jew, and the like.[94]

Abraham was named a Hebrew because of his religious preference, very unorthodox beliefs, according to the religious practices. His color had no bearing on the name given to him and his people. If his monotheistic (One-God) religion did not exist, he would not have been psychologically distinguished as being different from the other people of Canaan or Babylon, actually Lebanon today. Abraham's physical characteristics were the same as those of other black people in the region. After he began practicing Hebrew monotheistic teachings, this preacher and his followers became characterized as people with a different pattern of behavior or religious practices. These Hebrews worshipped on the Sabbath, and said praises to one God, Yahweh, Adonai, Elohim, Jehovah YHVH (the Tetragrammation or *Shem ha-Mephorash*) the particular name of the God of Israel which occurs in the Bible almost 7,000 times. Abraham's wife was Sarah, mother of Isaac. His other wife, or concubine, was Hagar, a black Egyptian woman, and his third wife was Keturah.

Abraham was a Hebrew priest in touch with black Egyptian priests, according to Egyptian records and the Holy Koran. This premise forces us to trace their language usage for more conclusive sociological evidence to validate historical claims and original Jewish identity. Let us then seek to establish the languages spoken by people called Hebrews during the Babylonian period. Who were these people, and who was Abraam or Abraham, and what was the language variety spoken by his tribe? The evidence gathered shows these Semites were people who spoke an Ethiopic language. The language was called Cushitic. It was the root of Aramaic, Hebrew, and Arabic.

The language had an alphabet composed of *Alf, Bet, Gemal, Dam, Dent,* etc. From that language root we get the Hebrew *Aleph, Beth, Teth, Gimmel, Daleth,* etc. For the Arabic language version we find *Alef, Ba, Jim, Dal,* etc.

Then came the Greeks who continually visited Africa to obtain cultural development Europeans pretend originated in Greece. They adopted the Cushitic alphabet and made: *Alpha, Beta, Gamma, Delta* on to *Omega.* The barbaric Romans, educated by their Greek slaves, learned the Greek alphabet which they translated into *A, B, Ce, D,* etc.[95] The Roman missionaries later taught the English savages (whom Julius Caesar had seen naked in Britain in 49 B.C.E.). Thus the Cushitic alphabet reached the British alphabet to become A, B, C, D, etc., as we know it.[96]

Since there is a direct connection between the ethnic identity (group) and language code (everyday speech) in the network of human interactivity, we must consider the correlation between ethnicity and language variety.

With the language sector of Jewishness identified, we shall proceed to complete the historical section of Jewishness as it relates to the Falashas. We shall also attempt to determine why the Patriarch was of unquestionable African origin.

The Hebrews of Ethiopia relate that after Manasseh, King of Judah, captured Jerusalem and destroyed all its monuments, he led away priests and prophets. They made it obvious that there were two kingdoms: the kingdom of Israel and the kingdom of Judah. The Falashim further stated how Manasseh took "precious stones that Solomon had made for it, 'Zion' and took captive its men and animals." The Jews, according to them, were warlike and plunderous. Their aggressiveness caused many Hebrews to flee Zion. Before Abraham received orders from Ha-Shem to go to Mizraim (Egypt) his handmaid Hagar substituted for his wife Sarah in compliance with conjugal obligations because Sarah was barren, and could not reproduce. This arrangement enabled Hagar to become pregnant with a descendant from Ham. Hagar bore a son named Ishmael. Ishmael was Abraham's first born son. "And Ishmael his son was thirteen years old when he was circumcised, and Ishmael, in the flesh of his foreskin. In the self same day was Abraham circumcised, and Ishmael his son."[97]

Graves and Patai relate how although one hundred and thirty-seven years of age, Abraham with locks white as wool, married Keturah. Some writers claim that Keturah was a nickname for Hagar. "Others say that Abraham chose Keturah, a descendant of Japheth, so that he might have posterity in the female line from each of Noah's sons: Hagar being descended from Ham, and Sarah from Shem."[98]

Abraham's sons by Keturah are said to have been: Zimram, Jokshan (the father of Dedan and Sheba), Medan, Midian, Ishbak, and Shuah. These sons received gifts from Abraham before they left to go eastward, unto the east country. They are supposed to have taken "possession of many lands, including Trogloditis and the Red Sea shores of Arabia Felix," Graves and Patai point out that distant nations now claim descent from Abraham, through those descendants, even the Spartans of Greece.[99] Among the children of Dedan were those called Asshurites, who founded Assyria; the Letushites; and the Leumites. Midian's sons were Ephah and Epher, Hanoch, Abida and Eldah.

With the intent of diminishing prejudices based on Jewishness, this chapter has been purposely extended to encompass as many roots as possible. These genealogical trees should show origins of all people, and their beginnings or introductions to the various religious customs transmitted and adopted from one generation to the next. The facts are gathered and documented without psychological or analytical treatment. There are no ulterior motives involved other than to eliminate prejudice and arrogance and to lay the foundation for mutual respect among worshippers of all religious persuasions or beliefs. The facts found in numerous reports are presented to allow the reader to form an individual judgment or opinion based on conclusiveness of the evidence. Validity of that evidence, and all findings which compile these anecdotal reports, is also left to the reader's conclusions.

Negro baiters constantly fan the flames of racial hatred with hostility and create vengeance thereby. Their reward will most likely be their consumption, and that of many innocent well meaning persons, by an international uncontrollable conflagration ignited through their efforts. They fan the flames of hatred and rekindle remorse in those persons they label as Black Jews, others they call "Black Muslims," Negroes from "Negroland," and even those they refer to as "you people!" They refuse to conceive of people as people. In most cases, the ones who are most inclined to perpetuate negro baiting are descendants of Africans advertently or inadvertently. The racists pretend that some continent exists where the black man has not shed his blood, inhabited, or slept with the women. They read well-written histories of mankind, and yet fail to recognize the fact that there is hardly a white woman who has not wished to sleep with at least one black man to fulfill the dimorphic dream. These bigots whose feeling of superiority is the fallacy of their vanity are consistent with Caucasoid sexual maladaptation. They blind themselves to the fact that among human beings, unlike poles are attracted to each other; although there might seem to be some difference in the light, there is no difference at night. This fact was proven in South Africa, England and the southern bastion of prejudice in the United States even during slavery.

Lerone Bennett cites the case of Elizabeth, who was " delivered of a mulatto child, and now is so bold as to say it was begotten by a negro man slave." Another case among several documented by Bennett shows a prominent planter's wife sleeping with a slave and enjoying his affection as well as the dimorphic challenge imposed.[100]

These and other innumerable intrahuman experiences prove why the clamor for proving Jewishness, applied strictly to persons of African origin, is not only absurd, but totally irrelevant in classification of persons practicing Judaism. All original Hebrews and Jews, Semites and Berbers, Arabs and Moors either had dark skin or were black. Those who became palefaced were the result of an Asian-African, African-European, or Eurasian admixture begun in Babylonian times and continued with Ghengis Khan, Alexander the Great, Scipius Africanus, and other conquerors like the Great Hanibal de la Barca. The Latins referred to these labeled persons as the result of *mutatis mutandis*.[101]

These offspring of various admixtures can be easily detected through the lack of melanin in their skin. When they are pale enough to classify themselves as white, the octoroon, quadroon or mulatto becomes freckled when burnt by the sun. These hybrids also wrinkle on their necks, wrists, and mouths by the time they reach age fifty. And regardless of how pale they might appear, the skin behind their ears is usually darker.

In order to escape African or Asian identity through mutation or amalgamation, these racists solicit funds from Jewish philantrophies to write books denegrating blacks. One of these libelous books is titled *Black Jews in America*. Another diatribe on black Hebrews is Israel Gerber's *The Heritage Seekers: Black Jews in Search of Identity*.

These disseminators of North American-Zionist racist propaganda would certainly be among the first defenders of the victims of the African Holocaust. They would point out the hatefulness of Nazi racial propaganda. But they would totally ignore the "hell of a cost" that blacks suffered during the unforgivable African slave trade in which Gentiles, Arabs and Jews participated. Hitler unjustifiably murdered approximately six million Jews and Gentiles. The slavers murdered, mistreated, mutilated, enslaved, lynched, and still exploit over six billion blacks, and other people of color. The disseminators would also point out the massacres of the inquisitions, but they, as a God-chosen people, have never condemned their participation in black enslavement documented by Jewish writers in the "Grandees," Indian and African slavery, not to mention Europeans, in "Economic History of the Jews."

People live interracially in all of the American mainland and the Caribbean. They call themselves Catholics, Panamanians, Puerto Ricans, Dominicans, and the like. As soon as the North Americans visit or "discover" them labeling begins. They become "black" this or that. To the Gringo, if they are born in South Africa, they are called "Black Africans" by the Boers. In North Africa they are called Berbers, Blue people, Negro Africans, Bedouins in Israel, and the like. However, there are no Black Europeans, even if African descendants have been born in England over two generations.

The propagators of racial hatred would probably pretend that Nazi hatred was not provoked directly or indirectly by their arrogance and selfishness, which gave validity to the predictions of the *Protocals of the Elders of Zion*.[102] Nevertheless, they expose themselves as propagators of two principal aims. (The author considers this book a fabrication. No hard evidence was found to support its claims.)

These aims seem to be:

> to divert prejudice from themselves (not anti-semitism, Europeans are not Semites; they cannot be both Semites and Europeans); to foment distraction and cause racial and ethnic confusion among right extremist groups such as the American and other Nazi Party elements, Ku Klux Klan psychopaths, insecure and incompetent whites afraid of the black man's natural physical and mental ability.

The disseminators of the kind of hate we condemned in the Nazis also suppress facts that would credit blacks with credit due to them, and instead speak of them pejoratively and emphasize fabricated stories to prove *non-Jewishness*. These racists have put on the robes of the oppressors they condemn while their oppression is being reemphasized to arouse public sympathy. But even though oppression is not endemic to any particular group, it has plagued humanity throughout the history of the European "discoveries." But incompassion has also caused despots often to fall harder than their predecessors and those persons they oppress; "for vengeance is mine sayeth the Lord; and retribution is sure!"

Why do some people insist on Jewishness from others. During the 1950s when most of the world was anxiously considering the establishment of a Jewish homeland, founded on the precepts of peacefulness, friendliness, and strength, very few persons expected

hostility and bigotry to emanate from such a moral state particularly when its people pretended to base its existence on their religious
consciousness, longing for compassion and empathy. But studies of
Nazi concentration camps have shown "identification with one's
oppressors was a form of adjustment" by Nazi victims. These studies also showed that when "pecked at by those higher in pecking
order, one may, like a fowl. . . peck at those seen as weaker and lower
than oneself or as threatening."[103]

Hitler had demanded "Aryanness" from the victims of Nazism.
These victims and their descendants are now demanding Jewishness
from other members of their own religion. When the designators of
authentic Jewishness encounter criticism of any kind, be it from
Hebrews, Lebanese, Palestinians, or other original Semites, they hurriedly activate their "Great Power" with the cry "anti-Semite" or "anti-
Semitism." They accept no disagreements with their war-mongering
policies, even though they are supported by American tax dollars paid
into the U.S.Teasury by contributors of other religious beliefs.

When Jewish settlers arrived in northeast Africa from Nazi
Germany and elsewhere, Gamal Abd-an-Nasir had a premonition that
they would be as ruthless as their former oppressors. He told the
Zionists, in speeches and on Egyptian television, "You will never be
able to live here in peace, because you left here black, and now you
have returned white. We cannot accept you"! Nasir also referred to
the Zionists as "the imposter."[104] A Jewish woman read the statements and declared Nasir an anti-Semite.

His statements seem to be reiterated through Palestinian self-
determination with use of arms. Counteraction to terrorism with terrorism, and an aggressive policy lined with genocidal elimination is
dangerous. Even a rat will eventually fight back, especially when
forced into a corner. Territorial expansionism without just compensation is also dangerous. And the chastisement of Israeli and
American leaders who disagree with warmongering and jingoistic tactics is frightening. Particularly when one objectively and unbiasedly
considers a handful of Europeans on African soil, eventually ending
up sitting in the sun trying to become dark and inconspicuous enough
to survive among Africans, when all dark-skinned people decide to
unite and reclaim their land and heritage.

It is incumbent on those who respect human rights to stress—
when discussing the history and identity of Jews—that an undeniable African origin exists in all Jews of unquestionable Jewish or
Semitic heritage. It is also very practical and beneficial to encourage
friendliness among all Israelites regardless of outward appearance or
skin color. That friendly relationship should be built with the stones
of mutual respect, cemented with mortar of equal recognition from
mixed sand of varied ethnic origins molded into one solid wall of reli-

gious identity. Only such a determination would revive the old battle cry *Kal Israel Chaverim*, all Israel are brothers. Nondiscriminatory practices would also secure Jewish or Israeli survival, especially in Africa.

No one can dispute that, when we raise the status of one group within a family and lower that of another, we diminish the well-being of the family as a whole, especially when it is surrounded by enemies. Equalizing—improving one group's circumstances without decreasing the other's welfare—strengthens both groups.[105]

To discredit the Falashas is to discredit all Israel. The History of the Jews shows without doubt and through documented evidence that the Hebrew monotheistic concept originated with the African Falashim, who were called Sabeans, and not with the Ashkenazim in Europe. The Falasha kingdom was the first Hebrew kingdom established after the diaspora. It is from Africa that Judaism emanated and flowed into all directions reaching Europe, a continent only 2,000 years old in recorded histories.[106]

TABLE OF THE 70 FAMILIES AFTER THE FLOOD: GENESIS CHAPTER 10

NOAH

JAPHETH	SHEM	HAM
Aryan Branch of Speech: Indo European	Semitic Branch of Speech: Asiatic	Hamitic Branch: African-Asian
1. GOMER: Galatians, Gauls, Celts of Western Europe	1. ELAM: East of Mesopotamia	1. CUSH: Ethiopians in Eastern Africa and Arabia
2. ASHKENAZ: Southeast of Black Sea	2. ASSHUR: Assyrians	2. SEBA: Mer'o-e in Eastern Africa
3. RIPHATH: Paphlagonians, Europe Northwest of Black Sea	3. ARPACHSHAD: Early Chaldeans	3. HAVILAH: In Yemen and Southern Arabia
4. TOGARMAH: Armenians	4. SHELAH: Toward Mesopotamia	4. SABATH: In Southern Arabia
5. MAGOG: Scythians, Tartars of Northeastern Europe and Central Asia	5. EBER: In Mesopotamia	5. RAAMAH in Southern Arabia
6. MADAI: Medes, South of the Caspian Sea	6. PELEG: Pre-Hebrews	6. SHEBA: In Southwestern Arabia
7. JAVAN: Ionians, Greeks of Southeastern Europe	7. JOKTAN: An Arabian Tribe	7. DEDAN: In Southern Arabia
8. ELISHAH: Near Cilicia in Asia Minor	8. ALMODAD	8. SABTECA: In Southern Arabia (Nimrod)
9. TARSHISH: Pre-Spanish in Southwestern Europe	9. SHELEPH	9. MIZRAIM: Egyptians
10. HAZARMAVETH	10. KITTIM: Cyprus	10. LUDIM: In Northern Africa
11. DODANIM (RODANIM): Isle of Rhodes and Aegean Isles	11. JERAH	11. ANAMIN: In Egypt
12. TUBAL: Tibareni, in Asia Minor	12. HADORAM	12. LEHABIM: Libyan
13. MESHECH: Cappadocians, later the Muscovites of Russia	13. UZAL	13. NAPHTUHIM: In Northern Egypt
14. TIRAS: Thracians, Southeastern Europe	14. DIKLAH	14. PATHRUSHIM: In Upper Egypt
	15. OBAL	15. CASLUHIM: Between Canaan and Egypt
	16. PHILISTINES: Coast of Palestine	16. ABIMAEL
	17. CAPHTORIM: Cretans, Copts	17. SHEBA
	18. OPHIR	18. PUT: In Eastern Africa
	19. HAVILA	19. CANAAN: Eastern Mediterranean Coast
	20. JOBAB	20. SIDON: Phoenicians
	21. HETH: Hitttites	21. LUD: Lydians of Asia Minor
	22. ARAM: Arameans, Syrians	22. JEBUSITES: Jerusalem
	23. UZ: In Northern Arabia	23. AMORITE: Palestine
	24. HUL: Near Armenia	24. GIRGASHITE: Palestine
	25. GETHER: East of the Jordan	25. HIVITE: Central Palestine
	26. MASH: East of Syro-Arabian Desert	

A more annotated lineage of the families is given by Dr. Perry. It shows:

NOAH

HAM

SONS OF HAM

CUSH MEZRAIM PHUT CANAAN

SONS OF CUSH (Ethiopians and South Arabians descended from Cush).

1. SHEBA (Founder of Meroe the ancient capital of Ethiopia).
2. HAVILAH (Hauloteens of South Arabia)
3. SABTAH (South Arabia) 4. RAAMAH 5. NIMROD (First king of Shinar Raamah father of Sheban and Dedan or Babylon and Mesopotamia).

SONS OF MEZRAIM (Egyptians)

1. LUDIM 2. ANANIM (African nations)
3. LEHABIM or LUBIM (Lybians) 4. NAPHTURIM (Between Egypt and Asia).
5. PATHRUSIM (Pathrures, a part of Egypt). (Nubia ancient part of Egypt).
6. CASLUHIM (Colchians—"Out of whom came (1) Philistim—the Philistines, (2) Caphtorim—the Cretans".

   PHUT (The Mauritanians or Moors)

   CANAAN (From whom descended the original inhabitants of Palestine which included Lebanon: (1) Sidonians or Phoenicians; (2) The Hethites; (3) The Jebusites, in and around Jerusalem; (4) The Amorites, east and west of the Dead Sea; (5) The Girgasites; (6) The Hivites, at the foot of Hermon; (7) The Arkites, at the foot of Lebanon; (8) The Sinites, in the region of Lebanon; (9) The Arvadites, on the Phoenician coast; (10) The Zemarites, of the Phoenician city Simyra; and (11) The Hamathites, of Epiphania, on the Orontes.

   The borders of Canaan extended from Sidon, "as thou comest to Gerar unto Gaza; as thou goest unto Sodom and Gomorrah, and Admah and Zeboim, even unto Laska."

   These explanations from Genesis,Tenth Chapter, verses fourteenth through nineteenth also cover large portions of this genealogical tree and its roots. Perry did not mention the Sabeans of Ethiopia, descendants of Sabtah (sab' ta), third son of Cush from whom came the tribe Sabeah (Chronicles 1:9). It is important to know exactly from whence came the Sabeans. The Encyclopedia Judaica states that Sabea is a country in South Arabia. The Falashim state that Sabea was once a part of the Ethiopian kingdom.

   In 1941 Abraham N. Poliak, an eminent Jewish scholar, born in Kiev in 1910, arrived in Palestine with his family determined to make a valuable contribution to Eretz Israel. Poliak was appointed professor of Medieval Jewish History at Tel Aviv University. He had read

the true history of the origins and amalgamations of the original
Hebrews and other tribes who lived in that area after the Flood.
Qualified, secure, honest, and dignified as a scholar pursuing evi-
dence to publish truth, Poliak read the books in Sabean, Cushitic,
Aramaic, Arabic, and Hebrew. He then began publishing his findings
in many books. In 1941, Professor Poliak wrote a book titled *The
Khazar Conversion to Judaism!* His work appeared in a Hebrew pub-
lication called *Zion*.

The article was a bombshell which shook the Zionist pillars of the
structure referred to as Jewishness. Professor Poliak's book,
Khazaria, became even more controversial. It is said to be almost
unavailable at this time. *Khazaria* was published in Tel Aviv 1944,
and like *"Khazar Conversion* it unveiled those who pretend to have
the authority to decide who are Jews and who are not Jews. The book
proved that the Hasidim and other Europeans were, in fact, converts
who could not genuinely shout any famous cry of "anti-Semitism"
because they were not Semites or of that origin. Poliak was hated and
ostracized for this exposure of false identity. He did not write his story
(history) the way other so-called scholars often make it relate to their
needs, prejudices, and purposes. Poliak did not offer the facts in the
normal European, American or Zionist manner of presenting historical data. His style was not of the biased genre commonly used when
non-Caucasians are represented. The Zionists could not find any
blaming of the victims, or misstatements that they could quote as
facts. The anti-defamation leagues could not appreciate his unselfishness, but could not label him anti-anyone or anti-anything. Poliak
was more educated, honest and sincere than the bigots promising
brotherhood under very false pretenses. They even call other Jews
"anti-Semitic" when the latter expose them.

Abraham Polisk read and wrote pristine Hebrew. He was not interested in using his deserved Semitic heritage for political or personal
ends. But the Encyclopedias omit him and mention the impostor
Halevy instead.

We find Joseph Halevy (1827-1917) recorded as a "French Semitic
Scholar" ordained by the society of *impostors uber alles*. This deceiver lauded in the Jewish Encyclopedia of 1959 was praised as follows:

> He taught at schools of the Alliance Israelite Universelle in Turkey
> and Rumania and in 1868, went at the request of the Alliance to
> Ethiopia where he visited the Falashas. Subsequently, the Academic
> des Inscriptions et Belles Lettres sent him to Yemen where, disguised
> as a native rabbi, he succeeded in collecting 686 Sabean inscriptions
> (1869-70). He was appointed professor of Ethiopic studies at the Ecole
> des Hautes Etudes of Paris in 1879. He wrote many works in Semitic
> philology, epigraphy, archeology, and biblical exegesis. 8.p.826.

The writers and editors of the Encyclopedia admitted that Halevy "disguised as a native" obtained Sabean inscriptions for knowledge of Semitic customs and religious teachings under false pretense. There is another form of deception practiced by authentic Zionists. This dishonesty proves that Ethiopian and Yemenite documents on liturgy, ritual, and Semitic culture was urgently needed for general instruction of converts from Europe and surrounding regions aspiring to practice the Hebrew religion. The question to ask is: Why would Europeans go to Ethiopia and Yemen to procure documents and customs of Hebrews if they in fact were original family members of Hebrew tribes so recognized after the Flood?

In all human relations, whether it be familial, ethnic, or international, "the engendering power of expectancy," says Allport, "is enormous." We find such expectancy of more authenticated Jewishness in *The Heritage Seekers*. The author, who without any doubt would claim that Hitler was cruel to other human beings, lynched the black Hebrew community with his literary talent. The author of *Heritage Seekers* would probably cry anti-Semitic to anyone who calls him a Zionist racist or pointed out the fact that his effort was intended to discredit Africans despite the fact that Jews were among the slave traders responsible for death, dehumanization, and cultural dispossession of Falasha educational development. Nevertheless, he patronizingly stated in his cathecism on acceptance, "you can be accepted under the Law of Return. All you need do is authenticate or substantiate your Jewishness."[107] He did not even take into consideration psychological premises that "an outsider welcomed into our group is likely to make a solid contribution and not from defensive layers alone."

By writing this book, Gerber made it obvious that he had never heard Ben Gurion state that the Yemenites, Falashas, Moroccans, and other dark-skinned Jews were needed in young Israel because European-Jewish blood was diluted through intergroup marriages and possibilities of incestuousness. Ben Gurion also pointed out that many of the Europeans were effete and myopic because of inbreeding.

Anyone who has visited Ethiopia, Egypt, and Yemen, or read any of Josephus' writings knows that Saba was the name of the oldest son of Cush, and one of the names of ancient Egypt. Part of that land is now called Pathrures or ancient Nubia. The people here, in modern-day Aswan, are mostly of pure African stock. Furthermore, there were no Europeans in Africa when Saba was an African nation. Genesis 10:7 and Chronicles 1:9 attest to that fact, although the names Seba and Saba are used interchangeably. How then will Europeans, who have usurped African land, authenticate Jewishness when they barely escaped "authenticated Aryanism" by Hitler and his

Nazis just decades ago?

If their argument is based on their religious laws, they must then admit that religion, in its true sense, is not mere adherence to man-made dogma, rituals, or false testimonies. Authenticators have to also recognize that true religion is based on the creed or testiminies of faith. In addition, all legitimate religions are more than a tradition that one adopts and calls one's own, particularly to the exclusion of other persons considered of a different race.

The history of any people shapes its character as well as the people's behavior or character shapes their history. Zionist's referral to Africans, in Africa or abroad, as heritage seekers reminds one of Hitler's insensitivity to German Jews who justifiably preferred to stay in Germany as *"Luftmenschen"*. By that Hitler meant that all Jews were vagabonds who lived by their wits rather than venture abroad. Anyone who lived in Germany or visited that "Fatherland" had to have observed that Hitler's generalization was stereotypical and irresponsibly made.

Irresponsible Jewish writers who hatefully insist upon ridiculing persons of color should therefore pause and reflect on their times of persecuted existence, and what their future might engender. For social climate is often a result of a tone set by persecutors who seek scapegoats and end up being sheep without realizing that the same knife which sticks the goat also sticks the sheep when the time of slaughtering arrives.

The Goyim read Jewish histories, and make their judgments as well. In England Reverend A.H. Sayce declared that the Hebrews, not Jews, first made their appearance thusly:

> Abram went down into Egypt to sojourn there. When he entered the country the civilization and monarchy of Egypt were already very old. The pyramids had been built hundreds of years before, and the origin of the Sphinx was already a mystery. Even the great obelisk of Heliopolis, which is still the object of an afternoon drive to the tourist at Cairo, had long been standing in front of the temple of the Sun-god.[108]

Another writer, John H. Clarke, stated:

> The early, and present, relationship of Jews to African people is beclouded by the often told, and exaggerated story of four-hundred years of Jewish persecution in Egypt, and the eventual Exodus, both of which is probably the creation of a brilliant and highly imaginative Jewish fiction writer.[109]

These reporters who have gone to visit Egypt—this writer included—searched the site where Hebrews were supposed to have made bricks with mortar and straw. But there were only massive stones, and sand in the area.

It might also be important to mention how among the families after the Flood, certain writers feel that the exploitation of blacks, and other minorities continually disrespected by Jewish writers, and others, is a direct attempt to inferiorize the minorities. Minority members even feel that the continued cry of "Hitler murdered six million Jews in gas chambers" is an exaggeration of the facts, and omits the Gentiles that were included. Furthermore, the continued harping on Jewish tragedies beclouds their denial of civil rights to other minorities, and allows Jews to condemn everyone, including honest Jews abused or exploited by them. The minute someone complains, he or she is promptly labeled anti-Semitic even if the person is a non-Zionist Jew. The continued harping to exact empathy and pity for Hebrew enslavement in Egypt (Exodus 1:14) does not receive the same pejorative treatment meted out to black enslavement throughout the world. When black slavery is mentioned by Jews and others it is always presented as if the victims were to be blamed for their own enslavement. For example, Albert Einstein or terrorist Menachem Begin are never mentioned as descendants of former slaves. When George Washington Carver and Ralph Bunche are written about, they always receive the added epithet, "descendants of former slaves."

Prichard addresses the questions in this manner "The history of the Jews, Blacks, and slavery has been cleverly and insidiously suppressed for many years. It is this author's contention that the Jews' grand strategy has been to use Blacks as their major tool in their quest for world power and domination . . . . This has been accomplished through their programmatic use and manipulation of the Negro Zionists who have pursued a policy of racial integration which very few Blacks wanted".[110] Prichard certainly addresses statements of Jewish liberals who keep writing about backs intermarrying with Jews to be classified as Jews. Jewish Liberals with a capital "L" are mentally developed enough to understand that people intermarry when they are spiritually, sexually, and idealistically attracted to each other regardless of shape, size, height, color, race, or even religious persuasion. Hebrews married Egyptians, Greeks married Romans, Spaniards married Indians, Germans married Britons, and Americans marry Asians, a people whom they not too long ago denigrated as undesirable aliens excluded from permanent residence status under laws of the United States Immigration and Naturalization Service.

While digressing for a brief comment on Jewish claim to African history, and their inferiorization of minorities for their superiorization as "Chosen people," it might be necessary to refer to the Book that they wrote, or claim to have written, authenticating that claim. It is the Bible which states, "Are ye not as children of the Ethiopians unto me, o children of Israel? saith the Lord. Have I not brought up

Israel out of the land of Egypt? and the Philistines from Caphtor, and the Syrians from Kir?" And in the Book written by Christians of Greek, Hebrew, and Roman origin or prophets, we read (with malice toward none), "I know thy works, and tribulations, and poverty (but thou art rich), and I know the blasphemy of them which say they are Jews, and are not, but are the synagogue of Satan."

The name synagogue comes from the Greek *synagoga*. It was the place where the Greeks gathered to teach Hebrew and the Torah to converts. They called their students "proselytes of the gate."

The Book of Revelation adds: "Behold, I will make them of the synagogue of Satan, which they say are Jews, and are not, but do lie; behold, I will make them to come and worship before thy feet, and to know that I have loved thee".[111]

NOTES:

1.   Rufus L. Perry. *The Cushite or the Descendants of Ham* (Massachusetts: Wiley & Co., 1893).

2.   Herodous, *The Histories.*

3.   J. A. Rogers: *World's Great Men of Color.*

4.   G.A. Hoskins. *Travels in Ethiopia, Above the Second Cataract of the Nile;* Exhibiting the State of that Country, And its Various Inhabitants, Under the Dominion of Mohammed Ali: And Illustrating The Antiquities, Arts, and History of the Ancient Kingdom of Meroe (London: Rees, Ormae, Brown, Green & Longman, 1835).

5.   Melek in Hebrew means King. There was no Greek, or other European language on the Cushite's tomb.

6.   G.A. Hoskins. *Travels in Ethiopia, Above the Second Cataract of the Nile.* (London: Rees, Ormee, Brown. Green, & Longman, 1835).

7.   J.A. Rogers. *The Real Facts About Ethiopia* (London: African Publication Society. Reprinted 1981).

8.   E.A.W. Budge. *The History of Ethiopia* (London, 1928), 2 Vols. Drusilla Dunjee Houston. *Wonderful Ethiopians of the Ancient Cushite Empire* (Oklahoma: Universal Publishing Co. 1926, Book 1,. pp. 52-53.
     G.A. Reisner. *Excavations at Nuria—The Kings of Ethiopia* (Mass. Harvard African Studies, 1923).
     G.A. Reisner. *The Pyramids of Meroe and the Candaces of Ethiopia* (Massachusetts: Museum of Fine Arts. Bull, April, 1923).
     J.A. Rogers. *The Real Facts About Ethiopia* (London: African Publication Society. Reprinted 1981).

9.   Drusilla Dunjee Houston. *Wonderful Ethiopians of the Ancient Cushite Empire* (Oklahoma: Universal Publishing Company 1926). *Encyclopaedia Britannica.* (Chicago, 1966). Volume 8.

10.   J.A. Rogers. *The Real Facts About Ethiopia*
11.   J.A. Rogers. *The Real Facts About Ethiopia*
12.   Arthur A. Schomburg, a Puerto Rican of color (with a Sephardic name), was the Secretary of the African (Negro) Society for Historical Research. A public library now stands in his honor—due to the efforts of former Senator State Von Luther of New York, and others. The Schomburg Center for Research in Black Culture is located at 515 Lenox Avenue, New York City.
13.   Chancellor Williams. *The Destruction of Black Civilization: Great Issues of a Race From 4500 B.C. to 2,000 A.D.* (Chicago: Third World Press, 1976).
14.   *National Geographic Magazine*, December 1978.
15.   Robert Fitzgerald. *Golden Legacy*: Illustrated History Magazine (New York: Fitzgerald Publishing Co. Inc., 1972).
16.   Ladislas Farago. *Abyssinia on the Eve* (New York: Putnam's Sons, 1935).
17.   John W. Sommer. *Focus Ethiopia* (New York: American Geographical Society, 1965). Vol. XV, No.8, April.
18.   *The Jewish Week-American Examiner* Week of January 14,1979. p.2.
      Undercurrent. Newsletter of Temple Mount Horeb (Black Hebrew community of Queens, N. Y.). Vol. 10, No. 1
19.   *History of Ethiopian People and Languages*: Imperial Library, Addis Ababa, 1950 (Ethiopia: Translated by Haila Shanquella from Ge'ez).
      Wolf Leslau. An Annotated Bibliography of the Semitic Languages of Ethiopia (London: Mouton and Company, 1965).
20.   *Encyclopaedia Britannica* (1966). p.789 Vol. 1.
21.   *Encyclopaedia Britannica* Vol. 1., 15th edition, p. 339.
22.   Frederick Bodner. *The Loom of Language* (New York: Norton, 1944).
      History of Ethiopian Peoples and Languages: Imperial Library Addis Ababa, 1950 (Ethiopian Translated by Haila Shanquella from Ge'ez).
      Ralph Uwechue, Editor in Chief. *Africa*, an International Business, and Political Monthly. (London: Africa Journal Ltd. April, 1975).
23.   G.A. Hoskins, Esq. *Travels in Ethiopia* p.15.
24.   Jack Grimm, Texas oil millionaire, financed the Noah's Ark expedition in which he personally took part. Grimm is a geologist.
      Summer Spectator (New York: Columbia University Newspaper, July 9, 1980).
25.   William L. Langer. *An Encyclopaedia of World History* Boston: Houghton Mifflin, 1968). pp. 38-41.
      Robert Graves and Raphael Patai. *Hebrew Myths: The Book of Genesis* (New York: McGraw-Hill, 1964). pp.108,109,120. 121-122.
26.   The Greeks left Asia 2,000 B.C., Encylopedia Britannica, 13th Edition, 1966.
27.   Diodorus Siculus, The Library of History (Cambridge: Loeb C.H. Oldfather, 1933) 12 vols.
28.   Flavius Josephus. The Works of Josephus , pp.600-601

29.   Cushi is a patronymic term denoting Ethiopians as descendants of Cush, the son of Ham, in Hebrew.

30.   Basil Davidson. *Africa in History* (New York: Macmillan, 1974). p.12.

31.   Abraham Maslow. *Psychology A Scientific Study of Man.* (California: Brooks/Cole Publishing Company, Inc. 1970). p.219.
Michael Bradley, *Chosen People from the Caucasus* (Third World Press, 1992). p. 2.

32.   Michael Bradley. *The Iceman Inheritance* (New York: Warner, 1981). *Chosen People of the Caucasus,* (Third World Press: 1994).

33.   Ruth Fulton Benedict. *Race Science and Politics* (New York: American Anthropological Association, 1947).

34.   Boyce Rensenberger. "Ancient Nubian Artifacts Yield Evidence of Earliest Monarchy": *The New York Times.* March 1, 1979. pp. A1-A16 Col.3.

35.   Mary Leakey *Daily News* (New York: March 22, 1976). p.14.

36.   The Egyptians emphasize the English redundance by stating Saqqara means in itself Great desert.

37.   Albert C. Nevins. *Away to East Africa* (New York: Dodd Mead, 1959), p.48.

38.   Georges Babarin. *Le Secret de la grande pyramide* (Barcelona: Editions Adyar/Fingraf, S.A. Translated to Spanish *Los Secretos de la Gran Piramide* by Sofía Noguera, and translated to English by José V. Malcioln, 1977 & 1982).

39.   Houston. *Wonderful Ethiopians.*

40.   James Henry Breasted, *History of Egypt,* 1905.

41.   James Henry Breasted. *Ancient Records of Egypt 1927,* 5 Vols. *History of Egypt* 1906. *Ancient Times* 1916. President of the American Society (archaeologist).

42.   Yosef ben-Jochannan. *A Chronology of the Bible, Challenge to the Standard Version* (New York: Alkebu-lan Books Assn., 1973).

43.   Barry Fell. *America B.C.* (New York: Simon and Schuster, 1976), p.112.
Colin Turnbull. The Lonely African (1963). p.40.

44.   William Smith.,*Bible Dictionary,* based on the Dead Sea Scrolls (New York: Doubleday, 1966). pp.68, 76, 300.

45.   The name Cushan-rishathaim is Aramaic-Hebrew. It is not translated in the Septuagint or Vulgate versions of the Bible, but its etymological interpretation means the ungodly Ethiopian.

46.   Eye witnesses accounts: experienced by students, professors, and the author on the spot, 1949, and 1981.

47.   Guiseppe Sergi. *The Mediterranean Race,* a study of the origin of the European peoples (New York: Scribner & Sons, 1901).

48.   Houston. *Wonderful Ethiopians*

49.   *Ibid,* p.100.

50.   Joseph S. Williams S.J. *Hebrewisms of West Africa* (New York: Bible and Tanen, 1976). p.176.
Sir Flanders (William Matthew) Petrie (1853-1942) *History, Archeology and Christian Humanism,* 1964.

51. *The New Columbia Encyclopaedia.*
52. Homer. *The Iliad,* Britannica Book #4.
53. The Africans and Indians are called *lampiños* in Spanish. The term connotes hairless, not descended from the caveman and the apes.
54. A.R Jensen., "How Much Can We Boost I.Q. and Scholastic Achievement?" Harvard Educational Review, Vol.39, No.1, 1969. This "social scientist" proposed a genetic and racial difference in average intelligence. . . His theory was discredited by other studies proving "there is no significantly or innately determined mental superiority attributable to any particular race."
55. Salomon Reinach. *Orpheus A History of Religions* (New York: Horace Liveright, translated from French by F. Simmonds, 1930). p. 182.
56. Georges Barbarin. *Los Secretos de la Gran Piramide* (Barcelona, 1977).
57. Chancellor Williams. *The Destruction of Black Civilization: Great Issues of a Race From 4500 B.C. to 2000 A.D.* (Chicago: Third World Press, 1976). p.132.
58. Georges Barbarin. *Los Secretos de la Gran Piramide* (Barcelona: Editions Adyar... Original title *Le Secret de la Gran Pyramide.* Translated by Sofía Noguera to Spanish, José Malcioln to English. 1977-1982).
59. Karl Richard Lepsius. *Denkmaler aus Ägypten and und Äthiopian— Monuments From Egypt and Ethiopia* (1849-59), 12 Vols. Charles Robert Darwin. *Origin of Species. . . The Descent of Man* (1871). C.S. Coon. *The Origin of Races* (New York: Knopf, 1968).
60. Karl Richard Lipsins. *Egyptian Chronology,* 1849.
61. Georges Barbarin. *Los Secretos de la Gran Pirámide* (Barcelona: Editions Adyar, 1977).
62. *Ibid.* p. 17.
63. Georges Barbarin. *Los Secretos de la Gran Pirámide* (Barcelona, Spain: Editions Adyar/Fingraf, S.A. Translated to Spanish from the original French *Le Secret de la grande pyramide.* by Sofia Noguera. Translated to English by José V. Malcioln. 1977 & 1982). pp. 239-240.
64. E.W. Bullinger. *Number in Scriptures* (Michigan: Kregel Publications, 1981). pp.150-151. Genesis 6: 12, 13, 17. These verses together, "concerning violence and corruption, add 13320 (666x 20)."
65. Joseph S. Williams S.J. *Hebrewisms of West Africa* (p.159.
66. Michael Bradley. *The Iceman Inheritance.*
67. From a Special Correspondent. *London Jewish Chronicle*: April 1973. Rabbi Yossef's letter was published with his seal.
68. Yosef ben-Jochannan. *A Chronology of the Bible* (New York: Alkebu-lan Books Associates, 1973), p.4.
69. Rufus L. Perry. *The Cushite or the Descendants of Ham* (Massachusetts: Wiley & Co., 1893). Flavius Josephus. *The Works of Josephus Antiquities of the Jews*

(Connecticut: S.S. Scranton Company, 1917) lib. 1, cap.15.

70. Rufus L. Perry. The Cushite or the Descendants of Ham
     Houston. *Wonderful Ethiopians.* p.120.

71. Houston. *Wonderful Ethiopians.*

72. *Ibid.*

73. Muhammad. *Ansaru Allah Community Press* (Bushwick Avenue
     Brooklyn, New York 11221. June 10, 1981), Edition 97.

74. Wolf Leslau. *Falasha Antology The Black Jews of Ethiopia* (New
     York: Schocken Books—Translated from Ethiopic sources, 1951),
     p.63.

75. Edward Crankshaw. *Gestapo* (New York: Pyramid Books-Viking
     Press, 1957).

76. Adolphe Joseph Reinach. *La question cretoise vue de Crete:?*(Paris:
     Librairie P. Geunther., 1916) , p. 142.

77. Stanlake Samkange. *African Saga* a brief introduction to African
     history (Nashville, New York: Abingdon Press, 1971). pp. 82-83.

78. The Axumites were originally called *Solomonids*, because they were
     related to Solomon. See Chancellor Williams. *The Destruction of
     Black Civilization* (Chicago: Third World Press, 1976,) p.149.

79. John Cook. *Diet and Your Religion* (California: Woodbridge Press
     Publishing Company. 1976).

80. Wolf Leslau. *Falasha Antology The Black Jews of Ethiopia* (1951).

81. John H. Tobe. *Provoker* (Canada: Volume 18. September-October,
     1978).

82. Arthur Koestler. *Thirteenth Tribe* (New York: Random House, 1976).

83. *The Jewish Week-American Examiner* (New York, Week of January
     14, 1979). p.2.

84. *Ibid.*

85. Salo W. Baron, Arcadius Kahan & Others, edited by Nachum Gross
     Economic History of the Jews (Jerusalem: Keter Publishing House
     Ltd. 1976).

86. God: (have explained that a Hebrew is a person who is descended
     from people originally of Israel, unquestionably of Jacob. Those
     descended from Esau are Edomites, with non-European origin. The
     name Jew of popular use connotes identification with Judea. See
     Chapter 5.

87. sêmita: feminine noun= a narrow path, footpath, footway—
     Cassell's Latin Dictionary.

88. This despicable statement was made in words to that effect in a
     picture called *Boys from Brazil.*

89. White Americans who lived in Norway and Sweden were overheard
     complaining that even after having lived in those countries for over
     ten years, they were socially ostracised and commonly called
     descendants of cowboys and gangsters.

90. Joshua A. Fishman. *The Sociology of Language* (Massachusetts:
     Yeshiva University) (Massachusetts: Newbury House Publishers.
     1972), p. 16.

91. Salo W. Baron, Arcadius Kahan & Others, edited by Nachun Gross.
     Economic History of the Jews (Jerusalem: Keter Publishing House

Ltd. 1975).

92. Eugen Rosenstock-Huessy. *Judaism Despite Christianity* (New York: Schocken Books, 1969). pp. 124-125.

93. Three policemen brutally beat Mexican and drown him in Houston. *Diario la Prensa*, Wednesday 29, 1978... East side policeman revealed misconduct and crimes of fellow officers: *New York Times* 7-3-77. "Dead Detective's Note Deplores Racism" *New York Times* 12-23-78. Tornsney and other white sadistic cops shoot defenseless Blacks for target practice. *New York Times* 12-2-77. *New York Times*, 2-17-93: Rodney King was brutally beaten on March 3, 1991, by four white police officers. King, who was lying on the ground during the beating, was stopped for speeding. The whole brutal incident was videotaped by a bystander with a video camera.

94. The Japanese and Chinese worship Shinto and Buddha who look Asiatic. The Indians and Hindus worship Krishna, who is black like they are. The Klu Klux Klan worships a paleface Jesus with blond hair. The blacks and Latins expect the white Jesus to help them against his white Klu Klux Klan and their burning crosses.

95. Ethiopian Ministry of Education. *Origin of Languages of Ethiopia* (Addis Ababa, Ethiopia, 1920).
    E. Glyn Lewis. *Bilingual Education An International Sociological Perspective* (Middle Road, Rowley, Massachusetts: Newbury House Publishers, Inc., 1976). "It is not surprising that Paulinus, the grandson of Ausonius, brought up by Greek slaves, is reputed to have been able to read Homer and Plato when he was only five years of age. And there must have been many children like Fulgentius, in Africa, who acquired a perfect Greek accent".

96. John Samuel Kenyon. *American Pronunciation* (Ann Arbor, Michigan: George Wake Publishing Company, 1962), pp. 18-19... Caesar insisted that the Angles, Saxons, and Jutes running around the British Isles naked, with painted bodies, and iron torques around their necks, be taught to read, write, and record their history. He called them "Britons" when he saw the primitive script they were using called "runes" around 49 B.C.E. It was not until the Sixth Century B.C.E. that those clans actually learned to read and write a language instead of the ideographic dialect they were wont to use.

97. Genesis 18:25-26

98. Genesis 25:1-24.

99. Robert Graves and Raphael Patai. *Hebrew Myths: The Book of Genesis* (New York: Mc Graw-Hill Book Company, 1966). p.179.

100. Lerone Bennett, Jr. *Before the Mayflower* A History of the Negro in America 161901964 (Chicago: Johnson Publishing Company, 1966), 255-273.

101. *Mutatis mutandis:* [Results of the] necessary changes having been made.

102. *The Protocals of the Learned Elders of Zion* (Kuwait: Al Assyria Printing Press, 1979). p.54. (A Moslem Press). We must compel the

government of the goyim to take action in the direction favoured by our widely-conceived plan, already approaching the desired consumation, by what we shall represent as public opinion, secretly prompted by us through the means of the so-called "Great Power"—the Press, which with a few exceptions that may be disregarded, is already entirely in our hands... if we allow the possible of a general rising against us we shall respond with the guns of America or China or Japan.

Goyim: means Gentiles or non-Jewish nationals. everywhere.

103. Gordon W. Allport. *The Nature of Prejudice* (Massachusetts: Addison-Weslry Publishing Company, 1954), pp. 152-153.
104. José V. Malcioln. *How the Hebrews Became Jews* (New York: Universal Brotherhood Publishers, 1978). pp.26-27.
105. *Ibid.*
106. Koestler. *The Thirteenth Tribe* , pp.3 4, 180-214.
107. Israel J. Gerber. *The Heritage Seekers* (New York: Jonathan David Publishers, Inc., 1977).
108. A.H. Sayce. *Sermons* (London, England: Rivington, Percival and Co., 1876), pp. 1-5
109. John Henrik Clarke. *Blacks and Jews* (Chicago, Black Books Bulletin: The Institute of Positive Education, 1978).
110. William Prichard. *Blacks, Jews, And Negro Zionists: A Crisis In Negro Leadership.* Black Books Bulletin (Chicago, 1978).
111. Revelation 2:9, 3:9.

CHAPTER 5

ALL HEBREWS ARE JEWS, ALL JEWS ARE NOT HEBREWS

As we have seen, the Jewish migrations and intermittent return to Eastern or Western Europe during the seventeenth and nineteenth centuries did not continue in a continuous stream or even flow. The refugees shuttled back and forth. Their migrations were also blocked time and again by political dams which enabled Jewish traffic to increase or diminish according to the ebb of the political tide. Their mobility also depended on the forcefulness of a ruler's determination in a given area.

While the Sephardim and Ashkenazim moved back and forth, the Falashim remained stagnated in Ethiopia. After the great dispersal from the homeland, the Sephardim took two main directions. Some headed toward the Mediterranean and nearby countries or protectorates, Italy, the Balkans, and Turkey. Other groups moved toward southern France, the Netherlands, Germany and England.

In the case of the Ashkenazim or lighter-skinned Jews, bearing hardly any resemblance to Hebrews by this time, the migrations went on to Western Germany, with some groups continuing on to Austria, through, and to, Bohemia, Hungary, Poland, Lithuania, Belorussia, and the Ukraine. Eastern and Northern Germany were said to have been preferred by Austrian, Bohemian, and Western Germany's Jews readmitted.[1]

The first huge waves of eastward migrations occurred about the middle of the seventeenth century when Chmielnicki rebelled against the Polish nobility. This hetman attacked Poles and Jews alike in the Ukraine and behind the Whisper Falls. Subsequent Swedish and Russian invasions of Poland occurred and those wars were followed by economic decline.

These events and others caused the gushing tide of Jewish refugees to flow into Western Germany and the Netherlands.

From the middle of the eighteenth century, the flow of Central and European Jews seeking refuge in Western Europe was continuous, but in a trickle rather than a surge. The tidal waves went to North and South America instead. A historian stated, "migration stream from Europe during the one hundred years preceding World War II accounted for approximately four million individuals, of which over 70% went to the United States." The other Jews were divided into about 10% to South America, the same amout to Palestine, and the balance to Canada, South Africa, Australia, and other smaller countries. The agricultural settlements of Argentina and Palestine are said to have been the outstanding contributors of funds donated for migrations.[2]

THE NETHERLANDS

One of the important countries where Jews and Hebrews settled was Holland. Following Columbus' expedition—after he had followed the route taken by Abu-bari II of Mali in 1310—were the Dutch explorers.[3] They spread out across the Atlantic, founding settlements and colonies in North and South America, the Caribbean Islands, Africa, and the Orient. The Sephardic Jews accompanied the Dutch explorers as their brokers, accountants, and middlemen. In Aruba, Curacao, and Surinam, the Dutch West Indies settlements were founded. In Curacao, the Dutch-colonized West Indies, there is still the oldest Jewish cemetery and temple built by the Sephardim in 1732.

David Nassay had been granted a charter to encourage a Jewish settlement there back in 1652. Refugees had arrived from Brazil in 1654, when a congregation was formed, and its little wooden synagogue built.[4]

The people of the Netherlands were supposedly the most cultured in Europe during the sixteenth and seventeenth centuries. They had waged a long heroic battle for freedom of religion defying Spain, which was the world power of that epoch. It was therefore natural that the Marranos of Spain would want to flee to the Netherlands. In 1579, the seven United Provinces of the Netherlands freed themselves from Spanish rule, after Spain had just absorbed Portugal through force of arms. Spain's war against the English and the Dutch decreased Portugal's fame as world trade center of exports and imports, causing accountants and merchants to be in demand in the Netherlands and its territories.

Despite the thousands of Jews who had escaped to Africa, Italy, Turkey, and the New World during the sixteenth and seventeenth centuries because of the inquisitions, there were still numerous converted and non-converted Marranos in Spain and Portugal. These descendants of new Christians were watching and praying for an opportunity to renounce their positions and religion as soon as their prayers were answered by the Almighty. They eagerly awaited news and opportunities regarding placements elsewhere.

In 1590 a vessel slipped out of Portugal with some of these passengers who had lasted through faith. They were grandchildren of those Jews who had been forcibly baptized in the Christian faith. The ship was stopped by a British battleship engaged in capturing ships of the Portugese registry or Spanish possessions. The English captain was a duke who fell in love with one of his passengers, María Nûnes. The Duke thought, it is said, that María was from a family of Portugese grandees and he wanted to marry her. He did not know he had fallen in love with a secret Jewess. To his amazement, she rejected his suit because she was determined not to marry a Christian.

Maria was taken to London with the rest of the captives. Her beauty, which had caused the captain's infatuation, now stirred such attention and admiration in London that Queen Elizabeth I expressed desire to meet her. When María was brought before the Queen, her majesty was so impressed by the beauty of the young Marrano that she invited her to ride by her side through the streets in an open carriage. María had not forgotten her objective, however, and pleaded to the Queen for permission to continue on her journey to the Netherlands. She later asked that her fellow passengers be permitted to continue on as well. María's supplications were heeded, and the entire group reached Amsterdam where they recaptured their religious heritage in a free country.

Before these children, their parents, and Maria came to Amsterdam, there had been no sugar production in Europe, and hardly any consumption during the Middle Ages. But Africans had been using sugar cane syrup in coffee grown in Kaffa, Ethiopia, and mixing sugar with milk. Milk was also used to cook meat for certain tribes.[5] Jewish commercial insight had caused sugar to travel from North Africa to Spain, then to be produced in Egypt, Sicily, Palestine, Syria, and Crete for consumption in advanced European metropolises. Many Jewish merchants made sugar and Sukkari (a syrup-like sweetener), common names in Jewish circles throughout the North African regions of Egypt, Algiers, and other parts of Morocco.

The Sephardim of Madeira, the Azores, Cape Verde, and other Portuguese territories, took sugar cane saplings to Brazil where they began organizing plantations maintained through forced labor from Africa. Duarte Coelho Pereira contracted several Jewish technicians to process cane syrup, and to operate and maintain the sugar mills of Brazil. The Ximenes family controlled the clearinghouse, or

European sugar exchange, in Lisbon. They imported the merchandise from the Brazilian mills, then exported it to northwestern European countries demanding that commodity. Antwerp, Belgium, was a stock supplier, and later Amsterdam became the clearinghouse.

This newfound homeland and sugar trade center in Amsterdam emerged as leader in the 1620s. It played its part later on when Jews engaged in the African slave trade triangle. Ships sailed from there, and Newport, Rhode Island, in the United States, to the west coast of Africa loaded with hogsheads of rum to be traded for slaves later carried to the West Indies—partly Dutch—where those slaves would in turn be traded for sugar to be transported back to Amsterdam and Newport.[6]

Stephen Birmingham was sure to point out: "The Episcopal Church itself owned a plantation in Barbados." What he did not point out, and should be mentioned, are Hebrew laws against slavery. Talmudic laws (Sha'arei Zidek, fol. 25 a , attributed to Amram Gaon), and the slave trade of Christians from Slavonic countries to manpower-hungry Middle East and Moslem Spain. Even the Jewish or Hebrew law which makes detailed provisions for circumcision and specifically stipulates humane treatment of slaves and their release after six years (and in some cases seven) was ignored. The avaricious holy men obeyed it not. They were too busy worshipping their newfound god—money.

Prominent Jewish slavers were Jacob Rodriguez Rivera and Jacob Lopez Rivera of Newport; Hyman Levy, Alexander Lindo, David Henriques of Jamaica, and many others. In Jamaica and the United States there was no limit to the amount of slaves a trader could own. However, in Barbados there was a limit to the amount of slaves a Jew could own. Another nasty business in which Jews were engaged for quick profit was castration of slaves to create eunuchs, sexual contact with female slaves, and purchases of emaciated and ailing slaves whom they would fatten up and cure for return to the auction block the following year. Since the eunuchs were popularly used for homosexuality, plying them to that trade was an even greater sin than sleeping with the female slaves.

Jewish traders engaging in slavery and other enterprises from northern France, southern Morocco, on to India and China, were called Rhadamites.[7] Their coordination and cooperation with the Dutch helped them infiltrate Latin America as well.

The religious tolerance of Holland's Dutch citizens was known to travelers around the globe. As a result, Jews flocked to Amsterdam in such numbers that by 1608 there were already over 100 families there with permanent residence as their intent.[8]

Then came the Thirty Years War (1618–1648) between France,

Sweden, Denmark, England, and the United Provinces against the Holy Roman Empire. Since the war was fought mainly on German soil, a significant number of Jewish immigrants escaped to Holland requesting refuge from German hostilities and economic chaos. These were the German Ashkenazim—an admixture of German, Slavic, Turkish, and other origins. Many of them, or at least some of them, could very well have been offsprings of the Mongols who had invaded Germany, raping and breeding the progenitors of Hitler's pure Aryan stock. After all, his fantasy of Teutonic superiority totally overlooked the Mongol invasion of 1241.[9]

The Ashkenazim were not as rich as the Sephardim during the Dutch period. Therefore, they could not own as much property and sugar refineries in Amsterdam plantations in Dutch Brazil. Ten of the 166 *engenhos*, or plantations, in Brazil belonged to known Jews. The other plantations were owned, according to the records, by Marranos from Spain and Portugal who pretended to be Christians. As soon as Brazil came under Portuguese rule in the seventeenth century, many of the Marranos left Amsterdam for Surinam, Dutch West Indies, Barbados, Curacao, Martinique, and Jamaica, British West Indies, at that time. They became financiers, brokers, importers, and exporters in sugar and slaves.

Benjamin d'Acosta introduced sugar mills to Martinique in 1655. He had nine hundred Jewish workers with him, who were expelled in 1683. Aaron de Pass, of Natal, took the sugar trade to South Africa in the 1840s.

At the beginning of the seventeenth century, Marranos in Hamburg, Germany, began competing with their coreligionists in Amsterdam. Because of this Hamburg competition, and the persecution of Jews in Brazil, sugar lost its position as king of the industries there. By the first half of the eighteenth century, London began squeezing out Amsterdam from the position as world center of the sugar trade.

By this time the British had abolished the slave trade in 1833. But the Boers were emerging as the "Coloured people" of the Cape of Good Hope, a mixture of, Boer, and Hottentot ancestry, in South Africa.[10]

With the coming of the Jews to this area, the General Mining and Finance Corporation was set up by Hamiton Ehrlick and Turk in South Africa. This enterprise was financed by the Barnato brothers. Industrial banks were organized by Moses Montefiore with the Anglo-American Corporation connected to the diamond and finance corporation of A. Dunkelsbueler, established by Ernest Oppenheimer. Another mixture of mention is one that took in biblical times but bore some similarity. The more forceful and aggressive rules and exploits, the more tolerant group.

GERMANY

From ancient times it was prohibited to intermarry with certain people who engaged in abnormal or sinful behavior. Such people were
the Moabites who descended from Lot. The Moabites practiced
sodomy and lesbianism openly. Nevertheless, Solomon married
women who descended from Moab, Ammon, Edom, Sidon, and even
Hitites. Of these admixtures came a palefaced follower of the Hebrew-
Mosaic religion commonly called Edomite or Ashkenazim.

Since the language and customs of a people can be acquired by
another people of a completely different origin, we cannot speak of
Ashkenazis, Khazars, or Edomites as being of Semitic origin.
Furthermore, the most elementarily prepared scholars consider a
group's name also identifies their speech, culture, physical appearance and earliest habitat.

At the same time, one must also consider that no ethnic group
in history has remained totally unchanged, even if the rate and degree
of change varied. As a result, we find Hebrews and Jews having come
from Ethiopia, as Falashas, nearest to Canaan, Tamil and Cochin of
India, also Semitic, Chinese of Kowloon and Kai-Fengfu, in Central
China, the Sephardim of Spain, Portugal, Latin America, and the West
Indies, the Ashkenazim of Europe, and last but not least, the Khazars
of a Turkish origin. Of all these tribal groups, the Ashkenazim and
Khazars are the least identifiable with any language or physical characteristics considered Semitic. On the contrary, there is document-
ed proof of unquestionable sources to show their conversion to
Hebrew or Judaic religious practices.

Hebrew and Jewish migrations, or Diasporas, were so numerous, and from so many different countries at so many different time
periods, that it would be extremely difficult for one writer—without
a grant affording him to employ assistants—to engage in no other
task than the completion of this manuscript. Only with such assistance could the author have been able to complete this monumental
presentation in precise chronological order, and without flashbacks,
especially on conversions to Judaism.

The reader is therefore asked to consider those variables when
attempting to recognize such insignificance from a critical point of view.

The Khazars—with whom we will deal more thoroughly in a separate chapter—were of Turkish-Caucasoid origin.[11] Germany, Poland
and Russia are replete with descendants of these people whose forefathers converted to Judaism for political expediency rather than
because of religious fervor. The Khazars did not speak Hebrew during the time of their conversion. They visited the Turks requesting to
be taught Hebrew. The Turks advised them to visit the Greeks
because they did not know the language either. The Khazars also

learned from the Turks how much the Greeks had visited Africa to obtain knowledge of Hebrew studies or means of meeting someone imparting those studies elsewhere. The Greeks, who had been visiting and studying in Africa, and transporting information to Greece, taught the Khazars Hebrew and Torah in a religious school called *synagoga*.[12]

The Khazars, had their state between the Caucasus, the Volga, and the Don. Their Khagan, or leader, was Bulan who converted to Judaism about 740 A.C.E. From the reign of Obadiah up to the last ruler, Joseph, none but a few in religion was permitted to ascend their throne.

With those semi-barbaric people becoming a part of the Ashkenazi tribe, one became aware of the causes for the Hasidim rejecting the establishment of an Israeli state without the coming of the Messiah, and their continuous disruption of Israeli affairs. It also explains Jews' insistence upon legitimization of Jewish hereditary claims. And most of all their charges of illegitimacy as a screen to conceal their lack of such originality.

Karl Kautsky, without even mentioning the converted Khazars, declared: "A mixed race from the very start, the Jews, in the course of their migrations, have come into contact with a great succession of new races and theirs has become more and more mixed."[13] He also commented, "the Jews proved to be by no means uniform in their physical characteristics, and the great majority appeared to be of a different type from that found among other Semitic-speaking people."

Eugene Pittard expressed this view: "I do not know what specialists think about the influence that may be attributed to the Jewish people in the general history of the Oriental peoples. It seems to me that if we take into consideration the two kingdoms of Judah and Israel only, the influence would appear to be a small one." A little later the same author points out a fact repetitiously dealt with in this paper. Pittard ascribes heterogeneity to Jews, declaring, "The Jews belong to a religious and social community to which, in every period, individuals of different races have attached themselves. These Judaized people have come from every kind of ethnic stratum, such as the Falashas of Abyssinia and the Germans of Germanic type; or the Tamils—Black Jews—of India, and the Khazars, who are supposed to be of Turki race."

Griffith Taylor, in his turn, comes to very much the same conclusion. He wrote: "There is of course little relationship between the original Semitic Jews of Syria and the Russian Jew of Poland and the vicinity." In support of their arguments, we also find anthropological finds, and claims.[14]

Ripley explained that their physical diversity is due mainly to conversion or proselytizing movements among the Southern Russians.

He affirms that "Jews are not a race, but only people. . . In long headed Africa they were dolichocephals, in brachycephalic Piedmont they
were quite like the Italians of Turin, and all over Slavic Europe no
distinction between Jew and Christian existed."

In addition to these factors, environmental influence has to be
considered in relation to ethnic homogeneity. Kautsky argued: "It is
only in the ghetto, in a condition of compulsory exclusion from their
environment, and under political pressure, deprived of their rights
and surrounded by hostility, that the Jews can maintain themselves
among other peoples. They will dissolve, unite with their environment
and disappear where the Jew is regarded as a free man and as an
equal."[15] This statement can be easily supported with documented
evidence of Jews intermarrying with non-Jews. Assimilation can also
become inevitable through language adaptation. When the artificial
restriction of a ghetto does not exist, the younger generation speaks
the language of the indiginous population, and is usually regarded
as a native.

Flavius Josephus was accepted as a Roman, despite his dark
skin, Disraeli became Prime Minister of England, and Mendes,
France, Pierre was a statesman in Blum's government in France—to
mention a few. Acculturation, amalgamation, and miscegenation has
caused the Hebrew or Jew to generally approximate the physical and
other characteristics of the Gentile or other people with whom he
interacts.

Judging from the evidence presented, one might very well consider the sociolinguistic factors governing human behavior were very
well covered although language was not extensively emphasized. But
Max L. Margolis and other researchers did take that factor into consideration. Margolis and Marx remarked: "Often the language of one
people is acquired by another of a totally different stock. When, therefore, we speak of Semites, we have in mind solely their speech and
culture, not the form of the skull or facial expression."[16] Other linguistic studies show where early language use within a particular
community always found uniformity in surrounding and even outlying areas. It is only after the passing of time that a language plurality emerges.

The Cushitic language, as previously shown, bears witness to her
position as the early language of so-called Semitic people, even though
her origin might have been laid by some other language originating
in Africa or Asia. Nevertheless, there can be no doubt that plurality
of Hebrew, Aramaic, and Arabic did emerge from that etymological
source. Cushitic was undoubtedly the mother of Greek—learned in
Ethiopia—turned into Latin, and combined to become parents of
many words used in the English language.

Hebrew became mixed with German to form Yiddish. Many Jews,

including the converted Khazars, used Yiddish as part of their Jewish identity. Their language usage enabled them to become accepted as Jews, just as the Bedouins of Arabia, whom Sargon added to the mixture of races which were in Sumaria, and intermarried with the remnants of Israel in 715 B.C.E.

Stanley A. Cook said, "and their descendants might in time be regarded as truly remnants of Israel, even as the semi-Ediomite clans that entered Judah were reckoned as Israelites." Similar ethnic infusions and diffusions took place in other areas simultaneously.[17]

We find that while Spanish Jewry, for example, was on the decline, German Jewry was also running low. Even the Khazar kingdom, which was defeated by the Moscovite Russians, had started taking many converted Jews within its ranks, especially in Kiev. Those Jews were said to be waning in Torah educational development because of their lack of knowledge or inclination toward the humanities. It was said that in all probability, it was because of their Khazar origin that they lacked zeal for learning. They did not feel comfortable with the Tartar invasions of the area now called the Ukraine, so many of the Jews, preponderantly Ashkenazim, fled to the new state being formed as Poland. Along with those refugees were quite a few German settlers infiltrating their ranks, as they all sneaked into Poland. Some of the Germans were nobles, and they soon organized themselves into bands of marauders under the guise of Crusaders. These German nobles pretended to arduously pursue pagans, while they were actually usurping Slavic land by killing the owners. After enough Slavic land had been usufructed, the Slavs were either absorbed or driven farther east. "That is how Prussia came into being."[18]

The Germans organized guilds to monopolize artisanship, control apprenticeship, and limit competition among craftsmen. Jews found themselves excluded from farming, limited in trades, and even in trading. Their only avenues to the storehouse of wealth were through tax-farming collection or commerce. However, during the same period that the Iron Chancellor Otto Von Bismarck of Prussia (1815–1898) fought for Jewish rights in the Balkans, an unprecedented change reverberated through his efforts. Jews received some alleviation from prejudices in Germany as well.

Prussian chancellor of the German Empire from 1871 to 1890, Bismark fomented anger and prejudice against the Jews, despite his intent to unify Germany. Nevertheless, Bismarck was the Prussian nationalist who did eventually unify Germany.

Bismarck had been made Chancellor by William I (1797–1888) emperor of Germany from 1871 to 1888, and King of Prussia. During the Prussian uprising of 1848 William fled for his life to England. When the revolution was quelled in 1849, he returned, commanded troops that crushed the republican insurrection in Baden, and appointed Bismarck prime minister in 1862.

There had been fifteen years of liberal tolerance under William I. But the Emperor was really, like most liberals today, a liberal with a little "l". During those years there had been a Social Democratic party of Marxist socialist disciples. They preached the doctrine of Karl Marx, the Messiah of Socialist Dialectism, or Dialectical materialism. This Jew (1818–1883) was a leader.

Karl Heinrich Marx, whose parents denounced Judaism and became Christians before he was baptized, headed the Working Men's Association founded by Ferdinand Lasalle (1825–1864), also of Jewish origin. They were live products of the Khazaric, Slavic, Turkish, Teutonic admixtures with even Magyars, commonly called Ashkenazim or European Jews, in present-day Germany and elsewhere. The sons of these descendants of Japheth are now found in the religion of Shem disclaiming and discrediting the sons of Ham.

The Ashkenazim are determined to disinherit the sons of Ham by selecting preferred Israelites for return to the land they have acquired through treaties that the landowners and others who remained on the land did not even sign. The "unselected" people, were often not even allowed to sit at the bargaining tables where their fate was being discussed. The Ashkenazim comprise the largest element of non-Semitic Zionists in Israel and in other parts of the world. It is they whom Koestler calls "The Thirteenth Tribe."

Koestler explains how the ancient Hebrews started their migratory treks, due to diasporas, long before the destruction of Jerusalem. Their treks before the Christian Era, a "mile apart" from the Turko-Khazar tribes on the Volga, add more evidence to the fact that they could not be related to the Semitic tribes from the Jordan. The two river banks were too far apart, the languages too unrelated, and the culture too incomparable. The Babylonians or Hebrews came from the East; the Khazars or Zhids (Jews) came from the West.[19]

Another factor to be considered in the search for identity of originality and conversion is behavior. Ancient history shows it is quite true that the Roman of yesteryears is not comparable to the Italian of recent years. The former was brave and honorable, the latter incomparable. We would then ask: How did the Romans become Italians, and act the cowardly way they acted in world wars of the recent decades? The next question would be: How did the Hebrews become Jews? We know that the Romans employed mercenaries who no longer have the Roman esprit de corps. We also know that the converted Khazars no longer have the devotion to honesty, justice, and fraternity which Moises Maimonides, Jose Ben Halafta, and Abraham preached.

Is it because these Ashkenazim are mainly offshoots of Khazaric tribes why their behavioral patterns show so much inhumanity? They avariciously exploit Hebrews and Goyim alike; refuse to sit down and bargain in the rights and lands of others under their jurisdiction; resort to indiscriminate slaughtering of women and children, with and without provocation, while praying for God's mercy but showing none to others! Is it possible that the Ashkenazim, and the Sephardim who join them, are merely using religion pretentiously? Perhaps they are seeking political advantages and other expediencies such as continued United States economic aid, world sympathy, military adventure to test armament, and the like.

Koestler mentions these people as "believers in the dogma of the 'Chosen Race'." Koestler, himself a Hungarian, seemed to feel strongly that even though Professor Poliak proved before the Holocaust that Khazar Jewry was the nucleus of the majority of Jewish settlements in Eastern Europe, some persons still dispute the facts. Poliak is said to have also proved that the descendants of the Khazar settlements, "those who stayed where they were, those who emigrated to the United States and to other countries, and those who went to Israel—constitute now the large majority of world Jewry."

We must then investigate these people through their history. Their origins, as cause, might reflect their behavior, as effect! These present-day Jews of Eastern European and Teutonic appearance are said to have really been of Khazar rather than German origin. Koestler says, with firm conviction that the Jewish community was rather insignificant before the First Crusade, and even smaller after the slaughtering of innocent persons in the name of the Cross. He further assured us that east of the Rhine, in central and northern Germany, "there were as yet no Jewish communities at all, and none for a long time to come." Investigations also prove that traditional publications by Jewish historians stating that the Crusades of 1096 forced a mass-migration of German Jews into Poland "is simply a legend—or rather an ad hoc hypothesis invented because, as they know little of Khazar history, they could see no other way to account for the emergence, out of nowhere, as this unprecedented concentration of Jews in Eastern Europe."[20]

KHAZAR CONVERSION

We have all read or heard about the "Lost Tribes of Israel;" supposedly found among Native Americans, the Eskimos, West Africans, and just about anyone who practices a religion similar to the Hebrew religion, uses Hebrew characters for writing, and prays in Hebrew. However, very few people have heard about or sought to popularize their knowledge of the found tribe—a most startling but true discovery, and a most discomforting fact. This part of Jewish History is often distorted or totally emitted, *his story* is told.

The Khazars were an ancient Turkish people who appeared in Transcaucasia in the second century A.C.E. Before they evolved to sovereignty, their kingdom was under a protectorate, and they existed as vassals of the so-called Turkish Kingdom, which did not last very long.

The Khazars were interconnected through a confederation of tribes controlled by the Khagan or leader. They became powerful after settling in the lower Volga River region. The Khazar Empire expanded when it became strong enough to overpower other smaller Turkish tribes in the seventh century. They enjoyed invading surrounding areas.

Khazaria extended from the northern shores of the Black Sea (during the eighth to tenth centuries) and the Caspian Sea to the Urals, and as far westward as Kiev or what is now called southern Russia. The capital of Khazaria was Ityl, situated at the mouth of the Volga.[21]

The Khazars conquered the Volga Bulgars and the Crimean peninsula. The eastern Slavs were then forced to pay them tribute while they warred against Arabs, Persians, and Armenians. In the tenth century, the Khazars entered into friendly relations with the Byzantine Empire, which attempted to use them against the Arabs. By their interaction with the native Slavic people from the 600s, this belligerent tribe of half-Mongolian people, similar to modern-day Turks, had begun to be realized as a relatively civilized people. During his exile, Justinian II had spent several years with these Khazars, and in 704 he had even married the sister of the Khagan. It is in this same tenth century, however, that the Khazar Empire fell. It met defeat when Sviatoslav, duke of Kiev, defeated its army in 965.[22]

Having mentioned cause and effect, while other writers stressed origin and Jewishness, it becomes necessary to investigate European Jewry more analytically and critically. Some writers have even condemned Africans and their descendants as "heritage seekers", while others have reported, "the bulk of modern Jewry is not of Palestinian, but of Caucasian origin."[23] The Columbia Encyclopedia states, "The Khazars (or Chazars) are believed by some to have been the ancestors of many East European Jews."

Before forming our own conclusions, however, it might do us some judgmental service to seek enlightment through a synopsis of the Khazars behavior and customs, before their mass conversion. We read that a delegation of Islamic persons was sent from the civilized court of the Caliph al-Muktadir to visit the barbarous tribes of the North. These eastern ambassadors traveled from Baghdad through Persia, and Bukhara, to the Volga and Kana, inhabited by the Bulgars.

The Bulgar king had permitted the Caliph to convert his people to Islam. In return, the Caliph would build the Bulgar kingdom a fortress which would resist Khazar incursions and devastation of his land if he refused to continue paying tribute to the Khazar king.

The Caliph's ambassadors took a scribe with them to serve as translator and interpreter. This scribe was none other than the famous Moslem recorder Ahmad ibn-Fadlam ibn-al-Abbas, ibn-Rassis, ibn, Hammad. Ahmad wrote what he saw in the strange land of the Turks, Khazars, Rus, Bulgars, Bashkirs, and others.

Ahmad related the religion of these groups as a form of Shamanism based on the belief that the visible world is pervaded by invisible forces or spirits affecting the lives of the living. Ahmad was also amazed and ashamed of the manner in which Turkish-Bulgar women wore no veils in the presence of men or strangers in social gatherings and did not mind undressing or dressing in public places. He became even more embarrassed when on one occasion a nomadic woman opened her legs at court "uncovered her private parts and scratched them, and we all saw it." Ahmad and his delegation were so ruffled, after having had an eyeful, they covered their faces and said "May God forgive me." The woman's husband laughed and said to the interpreter, sensibly and confidently: "Tell them we uncover it in your presence so that you may see and restrain yourselves, but it cannot be attained. This is better than when it is covered up and yet attainable." The husband was confident his wife would not commit adultery, because if she did, and got caught, the adulterer would be tied to two branches of a tree brought together and then suddenly released to snap and rip him in half, from his crotch upward. No mention was made of the guilty woman's fate. However, another group of Volga Bulgars later confirmed that Bulgar-female adulteresses were also ripped apart when caught.

Homosexuality, commonly practiced in Islamic-controlled countries, was disdained by these Turkish tribes. It was considered a great sin. Nevertheless, a seducer of a beardless youth only paid the inconvenient fine of four hundred head of sheep, but did not lose his own head when caught.

These Volga Bulgars were called Ghuzz, but considered almost indistinguishable from the other Turkish tribes. Their uncleanliness surprised their visitors from Baghdad, where baths were regularly taken. These Bulgars were not in the habit of washing themselves after defecating, urinating, or eating. More astonishing was their manner of attending routine duties after cohabitation or menstruation. Their unsanitary habits forced the scribe to record: "They refuse to have anything to do with water particularly in the winter." Surprises never ceased. Ahmad received a great one when the Ghuzz commander-in-chief took off his expensive regal overcoat to try on a new coat the visitors had brought him as a present. "They saw that his under-clothes were 'fraying apart from dirt, for it is their custom never to take off the garment they wear close to their bodies until it disintegrates'."

A similar Turkish tribe called the Bashkirs used to shave their beards to get rid of some of their lice. But while they encountered a scurrying louse here or there, the shaver would nab him and eat him. This tribe also searched their garments for lice which sheltered in the pleats. When they found them, they would crack them in their teeth, like the apes do in zoos. When Ahmad gaped at this incredible sight, the snacker remarked to him: "They are delicious."

Apart from these bizarre patterns of behavior among the Turkish tribes, the Arabs experienced many cases of human sacrifices. They saw the Turks punish murderers with brutal forms of capital punishment, and torture victims selected to appease Bashkir gods of the phallus cult, which worshipped a wooden penis. There were another twelve gods worshipped by these tribes. These dieties reigned over rain, wind, summer, winter, night, day, the figure of a horse, etc.

Those Bulgars of the Volga mistrusted intelligent members of their community. It paid to be ignorant, or at least pretend to be. Any man who achieved progress through mental alertness, empirical awareness of giftedness, would soon find himself seized and hanged from the nearest tree. He would be left there to rot away while the ancestors came to take his soul to heaven. His fellow Bulgars thought that high achievers were better suited to serve God in heaven than their countrymen here on lowly earth. Their criterion has been analyzed by some scholars of Eastern and Western psychology as a psycho-political defense against militant non-conformist or innovative implementation of ideas rising above the status quo of routine brutality and uncleanliness, as the Bulgar way of life.

The principal reason for the Bulgars overtures to the Caliph and anxiety to become Moslems was fear. They feared the Khazars, as stated before, and sought a strong ally the Khazars would respect.

Ever since the first twenty years of the prophet Ali Muhammad's recognition as a military force, Islamic hordes had overrun Persia, Syria, Mesopotamia, and Egypt. They had encircled the Byzantine center with Colishis, a part of modern day Turkey.[24] The Moslems looked at Turkey from the Mediterranean to the Caucasus mountains and the southern shores of the Caspian Sea. But the Caucasus was an impregnable obstacle fortified with savage, skillful horsemen and composed of ferociously trained fighting hordes.

The pass of Dariel gorge (Razbek pass in modern times) called *Bab al Abwab*, or Gate of Gates, was just that. It was a bottleneck that had to be transited to reach the Caucasus. It was treacherous, and therefore advantageous to the Khazars. They and other tribes had been funneling through the pass to raid countries to the south, and retreat without being pursued.

But the Arabs broke through those portals, advanced far into Khazaria, and attempted to capture Balanjar, the nearest Khazar town. They were repulsed by the fierce Khazars in 652, with four thousand Arabs slain along with their commanding officer Abd-al-Rabiah, whose remaining troops retreated in disorder. It took the Islamic forces thirty or more years to regroup, rearm, and return for another attempt at invading Khazar fortified territory. The Arabs concentrated on Byzantium during their years of recess, laying siege to Constantinople by land and sea. Some historians feel that if the Arabs had rounded the Black Sea simultaneously, the Roman Empire would have lost its military might, political and spiritual influence, and Islam might have become the religion of present-day Christian domains.

The wars seesawed year after year with Arab attacks through the pass and Khazar counterattacks in the opposite direction, until the eighth century when the Khazars became strong enough to get the edge.

The eighth century in which, despite the backwardness of other Bulgar tribes, the people of Khazaria were evolving from barbarism to a higher form of human behavior. Their city of Ityl was now a commercial capital transited by Jewish merchants in their yarmelkes and turbans, Christians with their customs, and Moslems with their colorful costumes and turbans, while the Colchians, dressed in their fezzes and balloon pants, traded in slaves, flax, linen, pitch, wax, furs, gold, and agricultural products.[25] The merchandise and customs of these visitors all seemed superior to those of the Khazars. Therefore, cultural influences took effect on the urban population, and by the eighth century their king, or Khagan, became civilized enough to decide paganism should no longer be the national religion. There was also a matter of political influence to be considered.

The Khagan wished to adopt a monotheistic religion but could not determine which one would best suit his purposes. Byzantine merchants of the Eastern Roman Church encouraged the Khazars to adopt Christianity, and join the Crusades against non-Christian infidels. The Persians urged the Khagan to join Islam and put to shame the believers cruelty for the sake of the cross. But both of these religions were practiced by mighty conquering kingdoms, with ideological doctrines attached to a balance of power achieveable with any added force or alliance. Each religious body argued that God was on its side. Most Khazars were ignorant of whose side God was really on, so some joined the Christians, and another small number joined the Moslems.

The Khagan and his ruling class were clear on the issue. He and the top echelon knew the military power of the Caliph of Baghdad. If they chose Islam, they would be subjugated by the Caliphate according to the Islamic laws. If the Khazars chose Christianity, they would be equally subjugated by the Roman Emperor and dominated by his laws through the cross. So the majority of Khazar pagans followed their leader and the nobility, who selected Judaism to avoid subordination. These Pagans converted for convenience; they were not interested in the promises of being on God's side. They wanted to be on the side of a religious group which posed a threat, through force of arms, or political power, and through religious persuasion.

The Khazars had been observing the three religious groups for over a century before reaching their decision. And just as the Caliph had been sending delegates to acquaint them with paradise in the Koran, and the Christians had been sending missionaries to send them to heaven through the Testaments, they had been sending Khazar emissaries to Turkey and Greece. They had even sent scouts to Baghdad and Palestine to seek persons with knowledge of Hebrew rituals, customs, and language.

In adapting to their politically motivated conversion, most Khazars were willing to accept circumcision, but they were not willing to abide by all of the rigid laws of Torah. The Khagan himself did not conform to all of the teachings or force his subjects to do so. Most of the communities continued pagan worship and idolatry.

When travelers began spreading the word about a Jewish kingdom called Khazaria, Jews became curious and eager to find out if such a place actually existed. Steeped in a religious tradition that stressed hope for a land of one's own: *Le-shanah ha-bah bi-Yrushalayim* (next year in Jerusalem) they soon began treks to Khazaria. Furthermore, there were persecutions in Byzantium and in Arab-controlled territories, which forced them to migrate. Another cause for alarm was the fear of the Arab trafficking in white slaves.

The Arabs bought and enslaved women in the countries they conquered. They also raped or lived with others. This amalgamation with the Circassians, in particular, accounts for the halfbreed offspring or pale faced Arabs, who could also be called mulattoes. Those descendants of Arabs and their slaves could also be called non-Semitic or non-descendants of Shem. But the coreligionists, like the Africans, do not practice the master versus slave hatred practiced by Europeans. To Africans, a slave is not chattel, and might become a leader if worthy, since they too are all sons of Allah.

Ityl, the Khazar capital, was built on the Volga Delta with mostly round-shaped tents, wooden structures similar to those in Russia, and round houses plastered with mud. There were very few houses built of mortar and brick. They did not have the knowledge of masonry or the abundance of fine stones like Egypt in the East. So, streets were unpaved, and cabins were made of logs. The Khazars also knew very little about the square. They liked the round shape. They decorated their saddles with circles and even wore round hats trimmed with fur to keep their heads warm. Their hats were called *streimel*. They can be seen on the heads of the Khazars, now called Hasidim.

These descendants of the Khazar people, and the royal family of their kingdom, have given us proof, based on the evidence confirming their conversion, of traditionally accepted stories, contrary to European and "all-American" writers. They approved that Judaism is not a racial identity (race), but a religion. Judaism, like other major religions, is a part of a whole, or an aspect of a culture. It differs from most religions, however, because its adherents are associated with the culture of a community which, in spite of dispersions and persecutions, has managed to retain most of its original beliefs.

NOTES

1. Salo W. Baron, Arcadins Kahan & others: edited by Nachun Gross, *Economic History of the Jews* (New York: Schocken Books, 1976), pp. 60-61.
2. Salo W. Baron & Others. *Economic History of the Jews* (New York: Schocken Books, 1976). pp. 92-94.
3. van Van Sertima. *They Came Before Columbus:* (New York: Random House, 1976). Africans had already arrived in Panama by 1310.
4. This little temple was visited by the author and his wife Benedicta Malcioln accompanied by a representative of B'nai B'rith in 1975.
5. Oral traditional transfer, Sabean records of Ethiopia, and the Genizah records of Cairo at the Cairo Museum.
6. Stephen Birmingham. *The Grandees: America's Sephardic Elite* (New York: Harper & Row, 1971).
7. Rhadamites: Rhadamanthus was a son of Zeus and Europa. He became a famous judge of the underworld after his death.
8. *The Grandees: America's Sephardic Elite.*
9. The New Columbia Encyclopaedia Koestler. *Thirteenth Tribe* p. 148.
10. R. Oliver & J.D. Fage. *A Short History of Africa* (Middlesex,England: Penguin Books, African Library. 1960).
11. Griffith Taylor. *Environment and Race* (London: Oxford, 1927), p. 184.
12. *Synagoga*: a Greek word meaning"assembly" (in Hebrew *bet keneset*), a place where the Greeks taught the Jews Hebrew and prayers.
13. Williams, *Hebrewisms of West Africa* (New York: Biblo and Tannen, 1967), p. 147.
14. Taylor. *Environment and Race* p. 184.
15. Karl Kautsky, *Foundations of Christianity* (New York: 1925). Are the Jews a Race? (New York: 1926).
16. Max L. Margolis and Alexander Marx, *A History of the Jewish People* (New York: Jewish Publication Society of America, 1973).
17. Stanley A. Cook. *Israel and Totenism* (Philadelphia: Jewish Quarterly Review. Volume 14. 1923).
18. Solomon Graysel. *A History of the Jews* (Philadelphia, Penn.: The Jewish Publication Society of America, 1947).
19. Arthur Koestler. *The Thirteenth Tribe* (New York: Random House, 1967).

20. Arthur Koestler. *The Thirteenth Tribe* (New York: Random House, 1967), pp. 164–170.
21. The Encyclopaedia Britannica states that their origin is unknown. ". . . the Khazars were in fact direct descendants of the Sabirs." (1966) vol. 13. p. 239.
22. Israel Gerber. *The Heritage Seekers Black Jews in Search of Identity* (New York: Jonathan David Publishers, 1977).
23. Arthur Koestler. *The Thirteenth Tribe* p. 94
24. It might interest the reader to know that an Arab geographer said that there were two kinds of Khazars who did not resemble the Turks. "They are black-haired, and of two kinds, one called the Kara-Khazars, "Black Khazars' who are swarthy, verging on deep black as if they were a kind of Indian, and a white kind 'Ak-Khazars', who are strikingly handsome." Arthur Koestler, *Thirteenth Tribe*. p. 20.
25. The Colchians might have been the Kara Khazars. The *Encyclopaedia Britannica* (1966) vol. 6. states, "Some ancient writers describe the Colchians as dark and wooly-haired, and akin to the Egyptians. . . elsewhere they are depicted as yellow, fat and lazy." Herodotus. *The Histories* (Great Britain: The Chaucer Press Ltd. 1982) p. 167.
   Herodotus said it was in no way surprising to see blacks in that area with "black skins and wooly hair [not that that amounts to much, as other nations have the same], and more especially, on the fact the Colchians, the Egyptians, and the Ethiopians are the only races which from ancient times have practiced circumcision."

CHAPTER 6

JUDAISM IN EUROPE

In the beginning of European recognition, and man's consciousness of that continent's existence, the Greeks got credit for civilizing the world, the Romans for conquering it, and the Africans were discredited for letting it slip away from them. As a result, the Greeks became the world's teachers after receiving the knowledge from the Africans.

Therefore, Jewish history is usually based on the *diasporas*, a Greek word meaning "dispersion." This word is often cited when reference is made to Jewish migrations and settlements outside of Palestine. The history of such Jewish settlements and experiences are dated from the period of the First Temple, 480 B.C.E. Those records of kings contain the most important facts reckoned with when discussing the overthrowing of the Kingdom of Judah. These diasporas occurred during the sixth century B.C.E., in 70 a.c.e., and in 1492 when the major diasporas caused by the Spanish Inquisition took place. The British libeling of Jewish landowners and property lords, for acquisition of their property holdings and investments, also occurred during this period. Despite these abuses, many of these exiled Jews did not return to Palestine when subsequent opportunities were made available. Some adjusted to their new homelands and adopted the customs while others could not forget the horrors and oppressions previously experienced, but still returned to retest the sugar-coated offers of redress extended by the new Babylonian conqueror. Some Jewish refugees remained in Egypt, while many dispersed themselves throughout the 127 provinces of the Persian Empire. Quite a few Jews traveled to Asia Minor and Greece, with some reaching as far as Rome.

Prior to these events, the Greeks had also played important parts in the history or story of Judah ha-Makbee (c. 175-164 B.C.E.), also known as Judah the Maccabee, who was called "Judah the Hammer." During his time, Israel was conquered by the Greeks and quite a few Jews adopted the ways of their conquerors and even emulated them. These Jews spoke Greek, wore broad Greek hats, and long Greek mantles. They worshipped Greek gods, and tried to convince other Jews that the Greek gods were more interesting than Jehovah. The true Hebrews despised these "Greekfied" Jews who were neither Jews nor Greeks. One of these "Greekfied" Jews invaded Jerusalem with his followers and made proclamations. He massacred the protectors of the Temple, went in, stole all the Holy treasures, and enslaved surviving inhabitants. The Sabbath could no longer be observed, feast days were ignored, and Greek holidays replaced Jewish holy days and holidays. The penalty of death was imposed on anyone who possessed a scroll of the Torah. The Temple was transformed into an altar of Jupiter, whom the Greeks called Zeus.[1]

The sacreligious practices were unacceptable to a priestly orthodox old man named Mattathias. This rabbi called upon all faithful Jews to join him in organizing an insurgent group. Mattathias, his five sons, and followers fled to the mountains to discuss strategy and action. His son Judah was unusually stronger than his brothers. When this young man swung a sword, it would strike his victim with the force of a hammer hitting an anvil. When Mattathias died, Judah became the leader of the insurgent Jews. He trained his army well, and made them build up their endurance and fierceness for combat.

When Judah felt that his insurgents were ready, he led them into battle against the superior forces of the Greeks. Judah and his men were successful in their first encounter against the better organized Greek army. His men gained courage from this experience and later engaged the crack troops of the feared Greek general Gorgias, while Gorgias was out searching for the Jewish camp to take them by surprise, and demolish their bivouac. Then he awaited Gorgias' return in camouflaged surroundings. This ruse resulted in the liquidation of Gorgias' army.[2] Heavy casualties and loss of glory made the Greek King Antiochus so angry that he sent new generals and fresh troops to attack Judah. But the "Hammer" defeated them also.

The Jews then headed toward Jerusalem, where they recaptured the Holy City from the Greeks and their sympathizers, cleansed the area, rebuilt its walls, and erected a new altar dedicated to the Almighty. The warriors relit the lamps in the Holy of Holies, and proclaimed that this rededication should be celebrated every year thereafter as the Feast of Lights known as Hanukkah.

The next Greek king to ascend that throne was Eupator. He yielded to Jewish demands for independence in statehood of Judea, and religious worship.[3]

Another famous Greek ruler, who affected Jewish existence, was none other than Alexander the Great (356-323 B.C.E.), born at Pella in Macedonia. This conqueror overthrew the Persian empire, and carried Macedonian armies into India. Alexander laid the foundations for the Hellenistic world of territorial kingdoms and so-called Hellenistic culture, which Jews imitated. He received his education in philosophy and medicine from Aristotle when he was 13 to 16 years old. Alexander—who raided African libraries at Alexandria, Egypt— felt that non-Greeks should be treated as slaves. In line with that view, Alexander also conquered and unified the entire East Mediterranean area. But civilizations rise and yet fall, in order that others might fall and also rise; Alexander did not reign forever, and the Romans later conquered most of his Greek territories. Palestine was a Greek-dominated area, and the Jews soon gravitated toward the conquering Roman forces.

Some Jews went to Spain, northern France, the Rhineland, and along the coast of North Africa. Most of these Jews communicated in Greek or Latin; they had begun to forget Hebrew and Aramaic.

By the time the Islamic conquests erupted and later subsided (sixth and seventh centuries A.C.E.), a large Jewish settlement had been founded in that part of Babylonia today called Iraq. The Middle Ages also found a considerable number of them residing in the Greco-Roman Mediterranean, and others resettling in northern and western Europe.

Persecutions and expulsions of the later Middle Ages caused many Jews even to gravitate toward eastern Europe, mainly Poland and Turkey. Their "exile" was no longer golah, it was a voluntary decentralization or *tephutzot*.[4]

The first Jews that settled in ancient Rome, around the second century B.C.E., were part of the Diaspora which entailed their dispersal to every niche of the Mediterranean during the next hundred years. They were so scattered that the authors of the *Sybylline Oracles*[5] exclaimed, "Israel, every land is filled with thee, and every sea"! Their numbers increased during the years that Romans hastily carried on wars through the ravaged Middle East like tornadoes. Thousands of Jews were taken to Rome, and other parts of the peninsula, as booty.

Despite several confrontations with the Romans, those Jewish populations still experienced a tolerant existence, similar to that of blacks in the United States, land of the free and home of the slave, during the 1920s. Nevertheless, a decree of expulsion was due to the corrupt cult of "Jupiter Sabazius," and its practices. In 19 A.C.E., the cult was reactivated, and led to deportation of four thousand Jews who were sent to Sardinia. In 49-50 A.C.E., another decree provoked by the first imposition of Christian religious doctrine on Jews came into law. However, it was not rigorously enforced. As a result, the Jews were granted general privileges which allowed them to group themselves into communities for protection and interaction, as well as to exercise their religious preference.

Their conditions saw a turn for the worse when Christianity became more popular and powerful. Both Christian emperors and Church hierarchy attempted to convert Jews. Failing in that attempt, the rulers relegated the Jews to second-class citizenship. The Jews were offered the right to an inviolable area of religious beliefs and practices and the exercise of their individual right, but only in exchange for their submission to severe restrictions, taxations, and other unfair burdens.

It was recorded that the most important document relating to their circumstances at that time was the papal bull "Sicut Iudaesis" of Gregory the Great (540-604). As Pope of Rome, Gregory attacked Donatism—challenging purity—in Africa, and Simony (the buying or selling of sacred things) in Gaul; Gregory I also attacked secularies and enforced papal supremacy, establishing the temporal position of Pope.

Among the Jews of Rome, the most distinguished members of their community were Cecilius of Galatte (Sicily), famous for his Greek writings fifty years preceding the Christian era (only the titles exist today), the well known and feared Flavius Josephus (a Roman citizen who dared tell the truth about Jewish antiquity and its African origin) who wrote *Wars of the Jews, Antiquities of the Jews,* and *Flavius Josephus against Apion.*

JEWS IN ITALY DURING MIDDLE AGES AND RENAISSANCE

During the Middle Ages, and the first centuries following the year 1000, most Jews were located in southern Italy and Sicily, near Africa. By the thirteenth century they were present in all regions of Italy, with many of them migrating from Germany and France. That Jewish migration continued into later centuries, with some more groups from Germany going mostly to Portugal, Spain, Africa, and the Near East.

By the sixteenth century, the Jews of southern Italy were migrating to the north or dispersing to the Turkish Ottoman Empire.

A Sephardic Jew named Benjamin of Tudela, from Navarre, a region of northeast Spain, and southwest France, believed to be the first Jew to reach Spain, included some experiences in a log found with his itinerary. In that documented compilation, Tudela explained his trip around the world. He recorded how his arrival and sojourn in Italy acquainted him with 35 to 40,000 Jews there. Sixty families were settled north of Rome, and two hundred were in Rome itself. The rest of the Jews were in southern Italy and Sicily. These Jews, he declared, were second-class Roman citizens subject to discrimination, limited freedom in business, and the professions. They were considered barbarians according to Roman concept and laws.

Three intermittent attempts were made with more and more pressure exerted to convert them to Christianity. The conversion—according to papal bulls of Gregory the Great, Calixtus, et al.—was not to be carried out by physical force. They were only supposed to be pressured into considering becoming law-abiding Christian-Jews. Those who refused were not allowed to own property or use Christians as servants or hired hands. Jews were forced to wear an identifiable patch, on their clothing, distinguishing them from Christians. They were only permitted to practice medicine because it was more costly, time-consuming and difficult to complete, and were barred from all other professions. No Jew was allowed to marry a Christian. It was prohibited by written law.

The end of the fifteenth century saw Jewish freedom diminishing at even a more rapid pace. In 1492 they were expelled from Spain and England. In 1511 on to 1545, the "Chosen People" were expelled from Sardinia, Sicily, and the Kingdom of Naples.

In the sixteenth century, the Counter-Reformation came about, and the papacy adopted repressive measures for Jews. These measures included designated residential areas for non-Christians, called "ghettoes."[6] The first ghetto was built in Venice between 1516-1517. The idea of establishing segregated residential areas for Jews had been mentioned emphatically in earlier Church legislation dating back to the Latera Councils of 1179 and 1215. That legislation prohibited Jews from living with Christians, either together or in close proximity. The laws just had not been enforced in earlier times.

From the fifteenth century, the Friars in Italy had begun exerting pressure for the effective segregation of Jews. And in 1555, Pope Paul IV in his bull *cum nimis absurdum,* ordered that Jews in the Papal States should be forced to live apart from Christians. To enforce the laws, every gate of the first Ghetto of Venice was locked at night. The study of Talmud and Torah was banned, and heavy taxes were imposed on all Jews. Their conditions, in terms of rights and privileges, continued to deteriorate.

During 1569 Jews were expelled from all cities of the Papal States, with the exception of Rome and Ancona. Their survival was better in Mantua, the Duchy of Este, Venice, Tuscany, and especially the city of Leghorn where the Grand Dukes of Tuscany granted them special privileges. In this desert of uncertainty, Leghorn became an oasis. It attracted a large influx of Jews from elsewhere.

By the close of the eighteenth century, Italy saw a Napoleonic incursion and invasion which was enough to inspire a liberalization movement; Jews were less restricted. Then their freedom was interrupted for a short period which lasted until 1815. After that, the restrictions were eased and freedom restored to some extent in the Kingdom of Sardinia. Freedom gradually permeated other Italian states, as soon as they became part of the Kingdom of Italy, which was constitutionally established in 1861—during the struggles of Garibaldi.

From then on, the centuries leading up to the final decline of the Roman Empire, through 1870, the emancipation of Jews living in Rome improved progressively through quotas. This improvement came as a consequence of continued deterioration of political power and military might throughout the Papal States. Jewish conditions, with only a very few exceptions, improved steadily. It was better for Jews in Italy, than for those living in any other European country. Restrictions and prejudices diminished progressively one family after another, and co-existence with Gentiles prevailed. When this Gentile deliverance arrived, the Jewish population was approximately forty to fifty persons of varied ages and occupations.

NINETEENTH AND TWENTIETH CENTURY ITALY

Although Italian Jews were the last Jews to obtain equal rights in Europe, they have made great progress from 1861 to the present. Some Italians feel that Jews in Italy are among the most respected people in the world.

After obtaining the right to move about freely, Jews first settled in the capitals of the various Italian cities. Later on, many Jewish families moved into Rome and Milan, where they participated in all phases of Italian life. Jews joined the Italian armed forces, and fifteen of them became generals during World War I; and three became admirals in the Navy. Jewish generals Guiseppe Ottolenghi and Pugliese were instructors of late King Vittirio Emanuele III. Many Jews were deputies in the Italian Parliament and Cabinet. Others were ministers, such as Luigi Luzzalti (1841–1927) who was reelected a few times, and was even premier (1910–11). There was even a Jewish treasurer. Among Italian officials were prominent Jews like Modigliani and Claudio Treves of the *Socialista* party.

From 1930 to 1931, legislation was promulgated to encourage Jewish leadership. Among politicians taking advantage of these opportunities were Angelo Sacerdoti, Abgelo Seremi, Mario Falco, and others. The Jewish community was reorganized and centralized as a political entity. Jews were so integrated into Italian life that Italians boasted that even under Fascist rule there was no "Jewish problem," per se, as late as 1936. Three Jews even died supporting Fascist ideals, and two hundred thirty of them were actively involved in the March on Rome. "Margherita Sarfatti, who was a valuable assistant and biographer of Mussolini, was Jewish."[7] Guido Jung, a minister during the Fascist era, also was Jewish.

Nevertheless—like the North American blacks who watched Fascism gain momentum, erasing their civil rights gains of previous years—Jews watched Hitler gaining power in 1938. The Jews made minor protests, like the blacks now protest the marches of the Ku Klux Klan. But Germany's silent majority was against them.

Scarcity of jobs and slow political gains made the insecure Italians prejudice. Italian newspapers and businessmen, as well as professionals and artisans, began a campaign of discrimination against Jews. To make matters worse, Italy's Axis ally Germany began exerting pressure on Italian officials and the populace. Italian ethical and judicial principles did not engender discrimination against race or religion, therefore, the wartime laws decreed in principle were not rigorously applied against the Jews up to 1938. But the Germans were overpowering allies, and although Il Duce prided himself in stating that his official policy was free from anti-Jewish sentiments, the Germans pressed the issue of the "Jewish problem."

Jews continued to participate in general Italian life and business as usual. Dr. Aldo Finsi, who had taken part in Mussolini's March on Rome, was now Assistant Minister of the Interior, and Eldorado Polacco was General Secretary of the Fascist Party in Brindisi. But Jews in high government positions, such as: Guido Jung, Finance Minister from 1932 to 1935, Ludovico Mortara, Lord Chief Justice and First President of the Court of Appeals, and others, began to worry.

The law of 1930 regarding Jewish communities, had established representative communal authority under Jewish leadership. Seremi, Falco, Sacerdoti, and others, had received enough autonomy to tax their communities, collect charitable contributions for religious and needy purposes. A national organization of Jewish philanthropies and intergroup affairs was also established, with a central office in Rome. Every Jew by birth or conversion was automatically considered part of the Jewish community. But now the Fascists had changed that policy.

Mussolini issued anti-Jewish legislation, similar to the Nuremburg Laws. There was a "Jewish problem" whether the Italians acknowledged it or not. In this crucial year (1938), approximately 5,000of the 60,000 Jewish permanent or other residents of Italy managed to escape. About 2,000 thousand of the others either converted to Christianity or became absorbed outside of the Jewish community. Of those loyal to the faith, 1,000 were massacred, and 75,000 were deported to concentration camps in Germany.[8] Many Italians empathized with the Jews and helped some to escape to France, Yugoslavia, Greece and to the United States. The Jews in high official positions who were coveted by their Italian countrymen, were not that fortunate. Many of them, confident in legal due process but insecure in their citizenship, lost their lives. These died without knowing that a Jew is the only national who is identified internationally by his religion rather than his nationality. Among the innocents lost in World War II were the writer Leone Ginzburg, and the politicians Eugenio Colorni and Eugenio Curiel.

After the war many important Jews were reinstated or reactivated. Umberto Terracini became deputy and president of the Constitutional Assembly, Professore Guido Castelnuovo became president of the Academia del Lincei, and General Giorgio Liuzzi was chief of staff in the Armed Forces.

Throughout this century, Jews have been making outstanding contributions in all areas of Italian national development. The Italian Jews declared, nonetheless, that there has been more integration and assimilation of Jews in Italy than any other country, except France and Greece, at varied times. The most progressive Jews of Italy, during the twentieth century were Enzo Sereni, Labor Zionist; Umberto Cassuto, biblical scholar; and the writers Umberto Saba (of only one Jewish parent), Sabatino Lopez, Italo Evevo; and Carlo Levi, writer and poet. One really famous Jew was Amadeo Modigliani (painter and sculptor of long-necked subjects). Bruno Levi was an architect; Professore Arnoldo Momigliano, historian; Graziadio Isaia and Ascoli, linguists; Tullio Levi Civita and Guido Castelnuovo, mathematicians. Arturo Castigliani, professor of music and history, had such colleagues as Alberto Franchetti and Mario Castelnuovo in music; Achille Loria, Gino Luzzato, and Cesare Vivante were economists.[9]

HEBREWS AND ROMANS

The history of Hebrews and Romans is easier to determine than the question of the chicken and the egg. With facts and dates, we do know how the Hebrews became Jews, and the Romans became Italians.

After the Greeks learned religion and philosophy from Africa, they Hellenized it. The Greeks took Ethiopian gods like Ammon, worshipped at Ethiopia's ancient capital Meroe, and in Thebes, Egypt, and Libya. They called Ammon "Zeus." The Romans later called him Jupiter.

Herodotus, Plutarch, and Diodorus all declare that Osiris left Ethiopia, invaded and civilized Egypt, placed his sister and spouse Isis on the throne with Hermes to assist her and administrate government, while Hercules was put in command of the troops. The Greeks made Hermes their messenger, and the Romans called him Mercury.

The people whom the Hebrews called Cushites and the Greeks called Ethiopians were named by the former because they descended from Cush and the latter because of their beautiful skin color.

The Ethiopian Queen Cambyses, ruler of the Cushites (525 B.C.E.), subjugated Egypt during the reign of the shepherd kings called Hyksos.

In 334 Alexander the Great took over Persia's empire. His objective, as stated before, was to make all conquered nations adopt and maintain the same culture, or a Greek-and-Oriental fusion. Alexander built Alexandria at Egypt, and other new cities as well. He also restored the old cities. Alexandria was so beautiful and important that the Romans later built a city like it. They named theirs *Alessandria fra Torino e Geneva.*[10]

Alexander had confidence in the Jews as economic catalysts. He was not fearful of them as an enterprising people, and therefore made them contribute rather than repress or restrict them. Alexander refused to conscript Jews as soldiers so as not to violate their Sabbath. But as soon as he died those policies changed. Wars broke out among his generals seeking control and territorial expansion.

Ptolemy took Egypt and Seleucus Nicator took the conquered lands of Asia. Palestine was the battleground for those wars. It was important to Ptolemy and Seleucus to get Palestine. Ptolemy got Palestine, and Seleucus desisted from further battles. However, Seleucus' descendants were more persistent than he. They never gave up their claim to the land, and a vendetta ensued for generations. The Jews, and Hebrews, were caught in the middle. They became living targets when Ptolemy's soldiers found no resistance from them when they were attacked on the Sabbath. Ptolemy's soldiers began referring to the Hebrews and Jews as foolish people who would not defend themselves if it were Saturday.

The Jews then moved from Palestine westward rather than return to Babylonia in the East. They settled along the coasts of the Mediterranean, on the Greek Island, and the coasts of the Black Sea. At that point, their western Diaspora began. Many Hebrews were among these people from Judea. Far away from Hebrew traditions and language these hybridized Canaanites began to study Greek, and act like Greeks. The Jews had left home speaking Hebrew and Aramaic, but by the third generation they had intermingled with the charming Greek women and men to such an extent that they were unable to read or write Hebrew. In order to keep their Hebrew language and traditions alive, the converts, children of the Hellenized Jews, and the remnants of original Hebrews attended Greek *synagogas* to study Hebrew, Torah, and the teachings of Israel and Judea, and Edom which had now become popular.

Toynbee explains, "Though there is no surviving record of the origin of the institution of synagogues, it can be inferred that it dates back to the Age of Babylonian captivity. It can also be inferred that it was introduced into the Jewish community in Palestine from the Diaspora."[11]

Judea, the smaller of the two principal Hebrew Kingdoms, had come to an end in 585 B.C.E. This catastrophe probably made the

Jews decide to come to Alexandria rather than return to ruin and desolation in Judea. Coming westward to Alexandria, they later engaged in commerce with Roman-Byzantium. They became shipowners, silk manufacturers, and expert goldsmiths. Some were doctors. Quite a few Jews held important positions in southern Italy, around Apulia and Calabria, where the natives were dark-skinned. Many Jews became date growers in Sicily, while others plowed the fields as farmers, and a small number occupied themselves with trade. Most of these Jews became Hellenized, Romanized, or a combination.

Alexandria under the Romans was not the same as it had been under the Greeks. There were mean and lean years with more sad than glad times.

After the death of Tiberius Julius Caesar Augustus (42 B.C.E.–14 A.C.E.), Judea had a king once more. Julius Agrippa, grandson of Herod and his Hasmonean wife Marianne, was appointed by Tiberius' successor Emperor Caius Caesar Germanicus (emperor from 37–41 A.C.E.), popularly known as "Caligula."[12] Agrippa had been imprisoned for comparing Tiberius to Caligula. As a reward for adulation, Caligula made Agrippa the king of Judea.

When the news reached Judea, there was jubilation and hope for better years. Caligula had appointed a pro-Jewish ruler, and it must have been with good intent. No one expected that he was merely paying a debt to a believer in his authority.

Agrippa departed for Judea by way of Egypt, encountering strong anti-Jewish sentiment in Alexandria. There had been continued clashes between the Greeks and Jews; and Caligula's selection of Agrippa was considered pro-Jewish. This appointment caused the rich Jews to be attacked during the month of August in 38 A.C.E. The rioting began shortly after Agrippa's arrival in Alexandria, and the Jews extended a most cordial welcome to him. Their rousing cheers promptly activated reaction by two municipal employees named Isidorus and Lampon.

Apion was a popular Roman orator and writer of those times. He was considered a philosopher by some pagans, and a charlatan by others. In any case, he was a popular personality. Apion spread rumors against the Jews, inciting the pagans and other Gentiles to attack them. While the rioters read and listened to Apion's accusations, Isidorus and Lampon, two "intriguers, demagogues, slanderers, and brigands with the pen," as Philo described them, set up a convention in the Gymnasium.

Isidorus and Lampon gathered a huge crowd with a promise of entertainment. Verses were read discrediting Jews before the feature presentation. It was a short play depicting Agrippa as a nitwit. The actor was none other than the town's biggest clown and bum,

Karabas. This derelict innocently appeared on stage as "King of the Jews." He was crowned with reeds of papyrus and robed with a torn blanket thrown around his shoulders for a royal cape or robe. A whip was placed in his hand to represent a scepter. Some boys were placed beside him, with long sticks, as his royal guard. The crowd shouted hail *Marin*, meaning "Lord" in Syrian.[13] When the agitators felt that the mob had reached the boiling point, they opened the doors of the Gymnasium and the crowd burst out into the streets, spilling toward the suburbs. The rioters attacked the luxurious homes of isolated rich Jews.

Over four hundred of them were robbed, and their homes stripped of valuable, transitable property. But the Jews were not as defenseless as the rioters had imagined. They retaliated with arms, as they had done before, and defended themselves well. It seems that previous Jewish defense in the main premises had shown enough resistance, thereby causing the mob to resort to the suburbs for easy pickings. The rich Jews knew that it might not be advantageous to seek more revenge at that time, so they sought redress through due process of law. They sent a delegation to Rome. Josephus states that Philo was their representative. The Alexandrian pagans sent their delegation with deputized Apion and Lampon, a chief instigator of the rioting, and Isidorus, his counterpart.

The opposition received immediate attention, but the Jewish representatives were forced to wait for a long time. Apion addressed the Roman emperor as a god whose statue was refused a place in the Temple of the Jews in the winter of 39. He stressed how the Jews had refused to allow a statue of Caligula to be erected in the Temple of Jerusalem, the summer of 40.

Caligula granted the Jews a hearing after their long waiting period. He had the envoys of both sides walk behind him until they reached a villa on the outskirts of Rome. He walked through the garden of the villa inspecting newly planned buildings and gardens. The plaintiffs and respondents patiently followed him. Caligula would intermittently interrupt his audience to issue orders about changes in construction and landscaping. In the meantime, impatience mounted in the petitioners like anxiety in horses chafing at their bridles and champing at their bits before a race. Suddenly the Jews were allowed to greet Caligula. With unexpected impetus, he shouted, "So you are the blasphemers who are unwilling to acknowledge me as a god." The Jews responded with vague explanations of sacrifices and prayers made for the welfare of the Emperor and the Roman Empire in the Temple at Jerusalem. Caligula replied, "All very well. But you sacrifice for my welfare, not to me myself." He walked a few steps farther and made another sudden stop. Then he asked the Jews, "Why do you refuse to eat pork?" The Jews gave some more vague answers and tried to explain their grievances. Caligula paid them very little attention. Caligula asked Philo a few more unimportant questions, but before Philo could answer them, he shifted back to talking about his architecture and its environment. After a few more steps, Caligula asked in an angry outburst, "I want to know what rights you possess and what kind of political constitution you have?" The Jews mumbled they had no political power or constitution. They were summarily dismissed.

The Jews were left no other choice than to accept their dismissal as a rebuff. That assumption was soon confirmed when they received word, before their departure to Alexandria, that Caligula had ordered his statue erected in the Temple at Jerusalem. The Jews left shortly after and Caligula remarked to his servants and admirers, "These men are not so much guilty as to be pitied, for they do not believe in my divinity."

The Jews had tried to tell him how they had been beaten, some of their coreligionists stoned, their ships burned, others who had their homes set afire and were forced to flee back into their burning homes rather than to be stoned, beaten or shot to death. They had also wanted to tell Caligula how Avillius Flaccus, the Roman Governor of Alexandria, had even fettered 38 Jewish elders who were members of the Jewish Council. These highly respected members of the community had been humiliated before their Greek attackers. But Caligula had not listened, so the Jews returned to Alexandria and bided their time for revenge.

The pagans were expecting a vendetta, so they also kept alert. They had dragged statues of Caligula into the synagogues, and they knew their disgusting acts would be unforgivable. One group of pagans had also dragged a two-wheel carriage into the main synagogue.

In the spring of 40 A.C.E., Petronius had arrived in Ptolemais, ancient Accho, near the border of Judea with two legions. Caligula had ordered him to slaughter the Jewish insurrectionists that Agrippa was trying to save. The Jews had met Petronius and beseeched him to take pity on them and to avoid unnecessary bloodshed. They did not intend to be measured without defending themselves as best they could. Petronius was not too eager to force their hand, so he continued his march on to Tiberias, the capital of Galilee. Thousands of Jews met Petronius there also. After listening to their pleas and warnings, he wrote to Caligula explaining the gravity of the situation and the explosiveness that could probably be contained with a slight change of heart on the Emperor's part. Agrippa had also returned to Rome and hurriedly approached the Emperor on the same issue. Having listened to Agrippa's petition on the Jews' behalf, Caligula agreed to rescind his orders—but probably considered that by then

Petronius had perhaps slaughtered many of the Jews. Much to the Emperor's surprise, and the Jews' momentary disadvantage, Petronius' letter arrived on the same day—just a few hours later. This communication disturbed Caligula to such an extent that in a burst of anger he dictated a letter sent to Petronius ordering the commander to commit suicide and leave his troops to a subaltern. To the good fortune of everyone concerned, however, a storm delayed the ship carrying Caligula's letter of self-sacrifice. When the ship of bad tidings finally reached port, and the Emperor's letter reached Petronius' hands, it was already popular knowledge that Caligula had been assassinated by a tribune of the Praetorian Guard, at the Palatine games, on January 24, 41 A.C.E.

Before Caligula died, however, he performed a deed which favored the Jews by circumstance. Avillius Flaccus, who felt insecure after Tiberius' death, had tried to gain admiration or appreciation from Caligula by encouraging rioters to place the mad emperor's statue in synagogues. His scourging of Jewish elders, tormenting and abusing of Jews in the Jewish quarter was not overlooked by his victims nor was it compensated by his divine emperor. Flaccus was ordered arrested instead, and banished to an Aegean island. Caligula did not trust him.

With the divine emperor dead, the Jews suddenly picked up arms. They distributed weapons from their hidden arsenal, and made gang war an even contest of the one-sided surprise attacks the pagans had been inflicting upon them.

Claudius I (Tiberius Claudius Drusus Nero Germanicus), 10 B.C.E.–54 A.C.E., was the son of Nero Claudius Drusus Germanicus, which made him the nephew of Tiberius. When Caligula was murdered, he was sent for to ascend to the throne. He could not be located. When the soldiers finally found Claudius, he was discovered hiding behind a curtain in the palace, trembling with fear. Claudius knew that the throne was the undoing of whomever sat on it, so he did not want it. But the soldiers knew he was no political threat, so they dragged him forward, and the Praetorians proclaimed him emperor.

With Claudius on the throne, as new emperor of the Caesars, many senators became jealous. To counteract their conspiracies, Claudius supported the military forces. He appointed Agrippa, who had supported him, to be king of the entire kingdom that Herod I had once ruled.

Agrippa had helped Claudius I by rallying undecided senators to vote for Claudius. Many senators were reconsidering restoration of the republic after Caligula's reign with divine power. Agrippa was therefore capable of counseling Claudius on restoration of Jewish civil rights in Alexandria. As a result, the Jews recovered their com-

munal autonomy, religious freedom, and authority to keep Roman
idols and statues out of their Temple at Jerusalem, and the synagogues in Alexandria.

After removing the soldiers who had witnessed Jewish persecution and assaults without upholding the law, Claudius I issued a
decree against such indifference. He stated that "the nation of the
Jews be not deprived of their rights and privileges . . . but that these
rights and privileges which they formerly enjoyed . . . be preserved to
them, and that they may continue in their own customs." In order to
maintain a balance of responsibility, Claudius added, "And I charge
both parties to take very great care that no troubles may arise after
the promulgation of this edict."[14]

Jewish existence under Claudius I was far better than Jewish
survival under Caligula. Claudius mandated punishment for the instigators of Jew baiting and harassment which continually caused
unprovoked attacks on Alexandria's Jewish inhabitants. Insidious
Isidorus and Lampon were tried for demagoguery and incitement of
rioting, and libel in the emperor's presence. Both men were sentenced
to death and executed forthwith. Claudius felt that the Hebrews and
Jews should freely exercise their God-given and natural rights to
maintain and practice their ancient tradition without fear or inter-
ference. He sent out an edict to all Roman provinces proclaiming:

> I think it just in no Grecian City should the Jews be deprived of
> such rights and privileges as they enjoyed under the great
> Augustus. It will, therefore, be fit to permit the Jews, who are in
> all the world under us, to keep their ancient customs without being
> hindered. And I charge them to use this my kindness to them with
> moderation, and not show a contempt for the observances of other
> nations, but to keep their own laws only.

This edict was ordered posted in all public places and on walls,
"in such a place whence it may be plainly read from the ground."

Claudius I was more decisive than many thought he would be.
He was as just, nonetheless, as they might have anticipated. But the
animosity, loathesomeness, and rage had become so intense among
Jews and Gentiles, Claudius had to send to the president of Egypt to
order a ceasefire between them. He also notified King Herod and King
Agrippa at Alexandria: "Alexandrians . . . have obtained from their
kings equal privileges with them, as is evident by the records that are
in their possession, and the edicts themselves."

Claudius was so satisfied with Agrippa's cooperation, he promoted
his friend and servant to a higher military rank and political honor.
Claudius also gave Agrippa a gold chain equal in weight to the iron
chain Agrippa had worn during his imprisonment by Tiberius.

Josephus informed us Agrippa performed all his divine worship, then removed Theophilus, the son of Ananaus, from the position of high priest. The priesthood was subsequently bestowed on Simon, the son of Boethus, son-in-law of King Herod.

After Agrippa settled the dispute concerning the high priesthood, he showed gratitude to the residents of Jerusalem by discontinuing real estate taxes. Shortly thereafter, the young men of Doris carried a statue of Caesar into a Jewish synagogue and erected it there. When Agrippa heard of this insolence and defiance of the emperor's edicts, he went to Petronius and complained. Petronius was president of Syria. He immediately notified the people of Doris why punishment would be meted out to persons who had disobeyed Claudius' orders and had offended the Jews.

Agrippa built a splendid theatre and other buildings, performed several acts of kindness for all citizens, and continued to protect the Jews. Since good things and good people do not last long, he died after moving to Tiberias. From Judea, Cesarea, and elsewhere, came lamentations for this just ruler who died from a severe pain in his belly at the age of 54.

Claudius was not far behind his friend on the voyage from which no traveler has returned. He was allegedly poisoned by his wife Agrippina the Younger (A.C.E. 16–59) daughter of Agrippina the elder, a sister of Caligula, and mother of Nero. After encouraging Claudius to marry her and adopt Nero as heir to the throne, in place of his own son Britannicus, she is said to have ended Claudius's days in 54 A.C.E.[15]

With Claudius and Agrippa dead, Israel and Judah's children were once again vulnerable to persecutions. They were now ruled by Roman procurators, similar to military regimes of today. When Claudius received word of King Agrippa's untimely death, he tried to protect the Jews by appointing Agrippa's son, Marcus Julius Agrippa, king of Judea. But the lad was only seventeen years of age and the elder members of his tribune did not approve. They argued that Judea was a trouble spot and the youthful Agrippa would be too inexperienced to handle troubleshooting there. An older statesman was appointed procurator and the area of his control extended to include Galilee in the north and Perasa in the south, along with Judea and Samaria of old.

THE PROCURATORS

The reader may ask: why is this history told in such great detail? The answer might well be: To have you read more than a succession of facts, dates, and events! Details help one discover hidden motives, and puts one in a frame of mind where while reading, hidden motives or causes for certain unusual effects might be discovered, and thereby relate one result to another, rather than having to assume or take some incident for granted. Lack of details has, in some cases, caused not only readers but writers to misinterpret narrations or to presumptuously state errors as facts.

The procurators were despotic, self-centered, and disinterested in Jews, or even civil rights. They were tough, pragmatic, military rulers concerned with procuring and amassing wealth from the provinces they were sent to govern. The procurators considered Jews insignificant as Roman citizens, but productive as sources of revenue.

Judea and its surroundings were far away from Rome, and Jewish tradition was equally far different from Roman customs and concern. During the reign of the last five procurators, there was an uprising which warrants some attention. It was the first really big confrontation between Jews and Gentiles, and it began under procurator Cumanus.

On the day of Passover (Pesach) when flocks of Jews, Hebrews, and other pilgrims poured into Jerusalem, the Holy City, a bloody massacre occurred. Some details will show how it could have been avoided. Cumanus wanted to show his military prowess with mass control. He placed a subaltern to guard between the columns of the Temple, outside the Tower of Antonia. This guard was a short distance from the columns of Boaz and Jachin. The sentinel was ordered to survey the multitude and detect any suspicious individuals or groups among the worshippers. The appearance of Romans in and about the Temple's surroundings and grounds caused concern among some Jews, and anger among others. To add to Cumanus' poor judgment and bad taste, an unusual incident occurred. The Jews had already felt their privacy invaded, and their right of sanctuary violated. Their anger was ignited when, "Suddenly one of the soldiers pulled up his garment, crouched down indecently, and presented his breech to the Jews." After showing the crowd his buttocks, the soldier produced flatus, according to Josephus, "a sound such as might be expected."

The Jews became infuriated and insulted. They demanded an apology from the legionnaire, and his punishment from Cumanus. They referred to his act as sacrilegious. Instead of redressing their grievance, Cumanus sent out more troops. The sight of troops in battle gear frightened the crowd, and panic among the worshippers turned into a stampede. Thousands of people were trampled to death or injured trying to escape through the narrow passages and streets from what they thought had been an attack. The day of a Seder, a Passover feast, was transformed into a day of mourning. "The whole nation and every family lamented."

On another occasion, a Roman soldier on a raid party house to house could not resist temptation and the search for weapons turned into a confiscation of valuables. The Jewish residents were tolerant until he pushed them too far. The soldier's mistake was to tear up a Torah scroll and throw it into the fire. The Torah burned from the intensity of the heat, and the people's wrath was aflame. Josephus narrates, "Hereupon, the Jews were in great disorder, as if their whole country were in flames."

The Jews ran to Cumanus pleading to have this soldier punished for his terrible affrontery to God, his law, and his people. Cumanus ordered the man executed. It was not long, however, before he avenged the soldier's sacrifice. The Samaritans were accused of murdering a Jewish pilgrim attending the Feast of Tabernacles. Cumanus was petitioned to bring the suspects to trial. He ignored the charges. The Jews decided to resort to gun law once more. They went home, passed out their weapons, and went forward to avenge their own cause.

They were led by Eleazar ben Dineus, a robber who burglarized many Samaritan villages and lived in a mountain hideout. Some of his followers slew quite a few Samaritans at will, and escaped punishment. So they began to become bolder and bolder. These Galileans did not know that the Samaritans had bribed Cumanus, and he was setting a trap for their enemies from Galilee. Furthermore, Cumanus was angry with the Galileans because when they had taken the law into their own hands after the Passover confrontation, some of them had "robbed Stephanus, a servant of Caesar, as he was journeying, and plundered him of all that he had with him." That robbery had been the cause of the house-to-house search.

Cumanus mobilized the band of Sebaste[16] with four regiments of infantry troops. He led these well-armed men against the poorly prepared Jews, slew many of them, and captured quite a few whom he kept alive as an example.

The religious Jews went into penitence (shiva)[17] using sackcloth and ashes. They considered the possible burning of their Temple, and the enslavement of their families and themselves. So they promised to lay down their arms, and live peacefully thereafter. The decent people dispersed, and returned to their homes and their obligations while the robbers went up to their mountain retreats.

But the leader of the Samaritans was determined to get more revenge. He appealed to Umidius Quadrantus, the president of Syria, who was sojourning in Tyre. After the hearings in Rome, Cumanus had succeeded Petronius, and now Quadrantus was president of Syria. He listened to the Samaritans' accusation of the Jews having set their villages afire, and robbing them. They also stated that in suffering at the hands of the Jews, abuse had been committed against them, but much greater abuse and disrespect had been shown against the Romans. The Jews defended themselves and accusations went back and forth. Uncertainty of guilt and the necessity to gather evidence forced Quadrantus to visit Judea personally for an on-the-spot judgment. Cumanus and the leader of the Samaritans were sent to Rome for the trial. Young Agrippa rallied to the cause of the Jews, and earnestly pleaded to Agrippina to persuade Claudius—her husband—to blame the Samaritans for the unrest. Claudius heeded!

When Nero came to power, however, Azzius, king of Emesa died, and his brother Soemus succeeded him in ruling his kingdom. Aristobulus, the son of Herod, king of Chalcis, became king of the Lesser Armenia under Nero. Young Agrippa was given part of Galilee, Tiberias, and Tarichae. The Jews under his rule behaved worse and worse. They took advantage of his kindness toward them. The Jews infested the country with robberies and forgeries.

Antonius Felix succeeded Cumanus who was sent into exile. Felix speedily chased and caught many of the robbers and quite a few of the impostors. He even caught Eleazar, whom he fooled by promising him amnesty if he would surrender. When he caught him, he bound him and sent him to Rome.

There was a high priest by the name of Jonathan. As head of Jewish affairs, Jonathan kept demanding more and more equal opportunities and due process of law for his people. Felix complied until he was disgusted with Jonathan. He decided to subtly have the high priest eliminated. Jonathan did not know and felt especially privileged because he had requested from Rome that Felix be sent to Jerusalem as procurator. Without warning, Felix contracted one of Jonathan's friends, Doras, to fulfill the assassination of the high priest.

Doras subcontracted the elimination to a murder incorporated association which went up to Jerusalem disguised as worshippers. They had daggers hidden under their robes. While they mingled with the crowd, concealed weapons were drawn, and the victim was stabbed. As Jonathan fell, the murderers dispersed. These "Sicarii" received other contracts. As popular hit men, they struck targets, enemies, and pursuers even in the Temple.[18]

The Sicarii became so popular and fearless that they inveigled other zealots to follow them in their pursuits, and to their refuge in the hills. In the wilderness, the bandits pretended that God was guiding them, and He would show His manifestations through signs their multitudes would see. Their fervent believers would even be able to perform miracles.

In the meantime, an Egyptian Jew came to Jerusalem proclaiming to be a prophet. He encouraged the multitudes to follow him because through his powers the Holy City of Jerusalem could be liberated from Roman control. With faith, a group could march up to the Holy City, and the walls would miraculously crumble as they approached. Many decent people and even intelligent ones believed him. There was the usual hope mixed with fear that he might be the

Messiah expected in troubled times, finally arrived unrecognized.

But Felix was sure that he was another opportunist. He sent the Romans after the hypocrites. The guards brought them back from the hills, and Felix punished them. The walls never crumbled, but the Egyptian did manage to escape. This Messiah had 400 of the Jews slain, and 200 taken alive, but made no attempt to save them, and fled back to his country as fast as he could.

It was not too long before the instigators reactivated. They urged the Jewish settlements to attack the Romans once more. When certain prudent communities refused, the militants "set fire to their villages and plundered them." Such abuses caused the Jews of Cesarea and their Syrian neighbors to have continuous quarrels about rights and privileges. "The Jews claimed the pre-eminence, because Herod their king was the builder of Cesarea, and because he was by birth a Jew." The Syrians accepted Herod's birthright, but insisted that Cesarea was originally called Strato's Tower, and that "then there was not one Jewish inhabitant." When the residents of the country heard of these disagreements, they punished ringleaders of both sides. The disturbances abated for a while. "But the Jewish citizens depending on their wealth, despising the Syrians reproached them again, and hoped to provoke them by such reproaches." The Syrians, though poorer in material wealth, valued themselves highly and equally as human beings.

The Romans stationed there were said also to have been residents of Cesarea. So they took sides with the Syrians, and went against the pompous Jews. With this coalition, a balance of power developed against the Jews. This united front of Syrians and Romans reproached the Jews, who insulted them in return. One insult led to another, until cursing degenerated into stone-throwing. Since the Romans had weapons, it would be supposed that the Jews ended up being on the losing end. However, several wounds were inflicted by both sides. But Josephus said that Jews won the rock festival. Felix saw the quarrel turning into a war. He immediately told the Jews to desist. When they refused to obey his orders, he marched armed soldiers against them once more. Felix slew many Jews and took others prisoners, "and permitted his soldiers to plunder some of the houses of the citizens, which were full of riches." The Jews with moderate behavior and means asked for mercy. Felix then ordered his soldiers to withdraw.

Agrippa gave the high priesthood to Ismael, the son of Tabi. This appointment was grounds for new rivalry among the Jews who claimed holiness. There was more stone-throwing among rival Jewish groups. With the factions feuding, the high priests overran their authority by abusing the priests of power rank. The high priests demanded tithes due the priests on the threshing floors. The abuses were so intense that some priests starved because of lack of income.

Felix was relieved of his command by Nero, and Portius Festus succeeded him. Felix was accused by the Jews at Rome, and Nero was about to punish him when the Syrians arrived there. They had their thirty bags of gold, and bribed Nero's brother Pallas and his highly esteemed tutor Burrhus, who was secretary of his Greek epistles. Burrhus was authorized to draw up an epistle disfavoring the Jews and exonerating Felix.

Festus arrived in Judea to take command, while the land was overrun by thieves and arsonists. The Jews were angered by the epistle Burrhus dispatched in favor of Felix, and they became unruly once more. Judea was in turmoil. The Sicarii were more numerous now. They used small curved swords like the Roman *sicae* and the Persian *acinae*—a kind of sickle-looking weapon. Festus was incensed. He sent the infantry and cavalry against all persons suspected of disobedience. He used an infiltrator to promise the zealots deliverance from the Romans. They were to follow the informer into the forests to receive plans and information on strategic harassment. The Jews followed the infiltrator into the wilderness, where they were slaughtered, and he was sacrificed along with them.

Agrippa built a royal dining room in the palace, overlooking the Temple. His balcony gave him a complete surveillance of the area, and a bird's-eye view of the services, sacrifices, and transit throughout the Temple. The Jews promptly built a wall to block his view and the entertainment of his guests. Agrippa decided to demolish the Jewish wall of obstruction, but the Jews begged him to allow the wall to remain, as a matter of privacy. They also begged for time to arbitrate the demolition. He granted them permission to take the matter to Nero in Rome. The Jewish delegation went to Rome, even though Agrippa and Festus were displeased with their action.

Ismael, the high priest, and Helcias, keeper of the sacred treasures, had an audience with Nero. Poppea, Nero's wife, interceded on the Jews' behalf. The emperor decided in their favor: he let the wall stand. There was a catch-22, however, for the ten ambassadors were permitted to return to Judea, but Ismael and Helcias were detained as hostages. When the news reached the Holy Land, Agrippa promoted to the priesthood Joseph, called "Cabi," the son of Simeon, a former high priest.

Festus died after two years in power, and Nero sent Lucceius Albinus to Judea as procurator. In Judea, Albinus hurriedly discharged Joseph from the high priesthood, bestowing that honor on Ananaus, the son of Ananias. This father had also been the high priest, and so had been all of his five sons. Young Ananaus was a Sadducee[19] of bad temper and unusual arrogance.

Ananaus assembled the Sanhedrin of Jewish judges, for judgment. Albinus was away. So the high priest seized the opportunity to drag a "brother of Jesus, who was called Christ, whose name was James, and some others . . . and when he had formed an accusation against them as breakers of the law, he delivered them to be stoned." When the fair and just citizens protested to Agrippa about this rash judgment and execution, the king rebuked Ananaus the high priest.

Some Jewish citizens, unsatisfied with the rebuke, hastened to meet Albinus on a journey from Alexandria. They notified him of the executions and emphasized that it was unlawful for the high priest to order sentences of death without Roman authorization, and to assemble the Sanhedrin without his permission. Agrippa immediately demoted Ananaus—who had lasted in the high priesthood only three months—and made Jesus, the son of Danneus, high priest.

When Albinus returned to Jerusalem, he tried his best to keep the city calm without exercising force. Nevertheless, to achieve his objective, he killed many of the Sicarii who were arrested and found guilty. He only pardoned the high priest Ananias, whom he had promoted. Ananias was said to be a great hoarder of money.[20]

Ananias took advantage of this friendship by making substantial financial contributions to Albinus, and high priest Jesus. These bribes were obtained by Ananias' henchmen who went to the threshing-floors thrashing those who opposed them, and actually "took away the tithes that belong to the priests by violence." The extortioners did "not refrain from beating such as would not give these tithes to them." So the other high priests started following suit, and so did their servants. As a consequence, "some of the priests, that of old were wont to be supported with those tithes, died for want of food." Ananias' abuse of power, overlooked by Albinus and tempered with law-enforcing indifference or collusion, caused the people to seek relief. The people looked up to the Sicarii who raided the city by night. Just before the holy days began, the bandits kidnapped Eleazar the transcriber for the governor of the Temple. This hostage was none other than the son Ananaus the high priest. After he was bound and carried away, the ransom demanded was release of those prisoners taken from among the Sicarii ranks. Ananias was persuaded to contact Albinus and arrange the swap. Josephus declared that this yielding to Sicarii demands started a "great calamity."

The Sicarii began capturing Ananias' servants and keeping them hostage until all Sicarii members were released from prison. The fruits of greed had become poisonous to the government and the high priest. As the Sicarii increased in numbers, they increased in daring offenses. They overran the cities once more. This annoyed Agrippa, who extended the land boundaries of Cesarea Philippi and in honor of Nero, named it Neronias.

Agrippa (whose father—it was said—was of "Jewish stock")[21] built a huge, expensive theatre at Berytus. He adorned the city with several statues of himself and erected images made by foreigners. The moving of adornments from one area to another made the people angry.

In the meantime, Agrippa promoted Jesus, the son of Gamaliel to the high priesthood to succeed Jesus, the son of Danneus, whom Agrippa had demoted. This withdrawal caused animosity among Jews once more. Each faction hired hit men, but Ananias was more successful because he could hire more "knife men" to eliminate his enemies.

Agrippa's relatives, Costobarus and Saulus, joined the plundering and extorting, and employed guerilla tactics. Their harvest of fruits of greed added to the disorder. To make matters even worse, Albinus heard that Gessius Florus would soon succeed him. Albinus reacted by ordering a cover up. The hardened criminals were summarily executed, and prisoners held for misdemeanors had their charges dismissed. Through this amnesty, the country became more infested with thieves. Many of the prisoners released were already recidivists on minor charges.

During these times, when Judea approached the greatest Diaspora of her Hebrews and Jews, the Levites (the priestly tribe) made a request of the king. They wished permission—as the cantors of the Temple—to wear linen garments instead of wool and cotton. The priests made a similar request. Since part of this tribe conducted the priestly functions in the Temple and the Sanhedrin, composed of 71 ordained scholars was also included, it was politically advantageous to Agrippa to grant them their wish. The overhauling of the Temple had just been completed. It was considered the building of the Second Temple.

The last of the procurators was Gessius Florus (64-66 c.e.). He was sent by Nero, to succeed Albinus, as governor of Judea. His predecessors had been:

L. Coponius, ca. 6-9 c.e.
M. Ambibulus, ca. 9-12 c.e.
Annius Rufus, ca. 12-15 c.e.
Valerus Gratus, ca. 15-26 c.e.
Pontius Pilate, ca. 26-36 c.e
He used funds of the Temple's treasury to build up an aqueduct; executed Galilean militants without trials, mistreated the Samaritans, and was procurator when Jesus Christ was crucified. Pilate was recalled to Rome after the Samaritans protested vigorously, and were heard.

Marcellus, ca. 36-37 C.E.

Marullus, ca. 37-41 C.E.

He was in office when Caligula demanded to have his statues erected in the Temple. Marullus was called back to Rome when Herod Agrippa became King of Judea.

Cuspius Fadus, ca. 44-46 C.E.

Under Fadus, Thendas was encouraged by strange illusions to charismatically gather many people to follow him to the River Jordan. Thendas promised to divide the water, as a prophet of heavenly powers, and to let the people walk across. Fadus saved him embarrassment by intercepting the procession, killing the people, and beheading Thendas, the false prophet.

Tiberius Julius Alexander, ca. 46-48 C.E.

He executed the sons of Judah the Galilean.

Ventidius Cumanus, ca. 48-52 C.E.

This procurator massacred the Jews in Jerusalem, was indifferent when the Samaritans attacked them, and he was banished as a result of those actions.[22]

Antonius Felix, ca. 52-53-60 C.E.

Porcius Festus, ca. 60-62 C.E.

L. Albinus, ca. 62-64 C.E.

L. Gessius Florus, ca. 64-66 C.E.

Florus found Judea in misery, and maintained that status quo. His wife Cleopatra, who was a friend of Nero's wife Poppea, had influenced Nero's household in his appointment. Feeling secure in the governorship, Florus is said to have been even more ruthless than his predecessor Albinus. Florus' wife was said to be just as wicked as he. They meted out many unjust punishments to the citizens of Judea. Florus became a partner of the extortioners and a fence for the thieves. As a sideline, he accepted bribes with no attempts to conceal them, and showed no signs of compunction. His encouragement of criminal activities reached such proportions that many Jews fled their homes and preferred to live abroad rather than endure the abuses in their own country.

Queen Bernice, Agrippa's sister, visited Jerusalem on a religious pilgrimage. She saw the abuses and appealed to Florus. He ignored her and during a military onslaught on the people she barely saved her own life by ducking into the Temple in a split second. The Queen escaped the soldiers' wrath by being out of their reach; otherwise, she would have been attacked and beaten like any other citizen. Even some Jews, who were knighted in Rome by the emperor, found their titles ignored by Florus. The Jewish knights were assaulted and some of them were crucified.

Florus abused the Jews to such extent that, Josephus wrote, "it was Florus who compelled us to take up arms against the Romans." After the continued abuse became overbearing, the Jews felt that they might be better off dying all at once rather than being gradually ema- ciated through intolerance, and perhaps being eliminated should they delay.

REVOLUTION IN JUDEA; MASSACRE IN MASADA

Nero reigned twelve years; and Florus was appointed by him during the last two years of his tenure.

The Jews revolted against the Romans when they considered con- ditions intolerable, even though revolt might be unfavorable at that time. Florus had been tempting them to get cornered and come out fighting. The procurator felt that having a war would cover up his wrongdoings. A war against the Jews would allow him to charge them with challenging Roman authority and remove all possibilities of his being recalled to Rome and banished like Cumanus.

Florus plundered the Temple and took the resources from the sacred treasury. He pretended that money was needed by the emper- or to start projects. The people ridiculed Florus, and showed disgust with his avariciousness. A group of Jews passed a hat around, oth- ers threw coppers into it as though they were collecting alms for a beggar.

There was unrest in Cesarea Philippi, but Florus did not go there and fulfill his military duties. He marched his cavalry and infantry against the Jews instead. In addition to the Jews crucified by Florus, there were women and children slaughtered, and even babies in their mothers' arms. No one was passed up, and the number of indis- criminately murdered Jews reached over 3,600.

The people of Judea became incensed and their priests tried to keep them calm. Florus still tried to keep the war possibility alive by bringing in more troops, instead of trying to heed the offers for peace. He brought in more troops from Cesarea. These soldiers annoyed the people with their presence and behavior. King Agrippa sat back and watched. Florus knew that the Jews had stoned their only benefac- tor and were now unable to seek his assistance. Despite their pre- carious position, the people began resisting the treatment of the soldiers, and showing resentment to their attitude. They engaged the Romans on the outskirts of Jerusalem and suffered heavy casual- ties. The Romans had a taste of solid resistance, nonetheless, and had to start regrouping.

Florus went to the head of his troops and mounted another attack within the city limits. In this engagement, his soldiers were repulsed, and he was disappointed. Florus was beaten back to the palace walls before he could get back into the fortress of Antonia—connected to the Temple. It was no longer a question of chasing and beating Jews. He knew, from his casualties, that he had been in combat. The Jews stopped Florus by preventing him from reaching their Temple from his fortress. They cut an opening in the connecting passageway and left him checkmated. He felt defeat here, and backed away from open warfare in Jerusalem while he regrouped his forces and replanned his strategy. To keep the war obsession from completely fading away, Florus sent false reports to the Roman governor of Syria. He accused the Jews of inciting to riot, civil disobedience, and defiance of Roman authority. Hebrews and Jews were charged with violent attacks against soldiers and were supposedly insurgents instead of victims. To counteract his falsehoods, Jewish leaders, and Queen Bernice wrote many letters to Syria explaining Florus' misuse of Roman troops, his misconduct, and the abuse of citizens' rights.

Cestius was governor of Syria. He sent a tribune named Neapolitanus to investigate the unrest in Judea, the charges, and the countercharges. King Agrippa was returning from Alexandria when he met Neapolitanus in the suburbs near Jerusalem. They discussed the reports with accusations against Florus, and decided to follow Cestius' orders.

Neapolitanus was encouraged to survey the area and gather first-hand eyewitness accounts of the circumstances. In order to observe the situation without influence or pretense from the procurator Florus and his staff, Neapolitanus went around Judea without bodyguards. He tried to be inconspicuous by taking only one adjutant with him. He was also interested in testing the charges of disrespect for Roman officials. No one molested Neapolitanus or his bodyguard. He strolled through the marketplace, saw how the Roman soldiers had destroyed it, scrutinized the burnt-out houses and fire-bombed shops. No Jews accused or accosted him as he observed their losses. Their behavior made him conclude that the Jews were loyal to the Roman officials. The only person for whom they seemed to hold unbridled contempt was Florus. Neapolitanus called the citizenry to a meeting. He told the Jews that he admired their loyalty to Rome, and hoped they would try to live in peace. Then he returned to his superior officer—Cestius— in Syria to give an unbiased report.

After Neapolitanus left, the Jews and Hebrews beseeched Agrippa and the high priest to send a delegation to Nero with accusations against Florus. They felt that he had misused his authority, and was forcing them to unrestrained anger. King Agrippa felt the pulse of the city vibrating with wrath of its citizens. He was concerned about the temperature reaching a height that might cause uncontrollable reaction. Agrippa decided to act before the tension passed its normal degree.

He assembled the people, spoke about their problems, explained his concern, and begged for their cooperation. His sister Bernice listened from the roof of the palace for royal Hasmoneans. Agrippa explored the possibility of war through disobedience, the horrors entailed, sufferings endured, losses that would result, and the possibility of non-compensatory recovery which victims at the mercy of their conquerors usually suffer. He stressed the power of Rome, and the helplessness of those countries she conquered. Agrippa begged the Jews to be submissive and patient. He tried to show them that they could no longer be independent or self-ruling as a free-associated state of the Roman Empire. He reminded the Jews of Athens, Sparta, Macedonia, countries in Asia, Thrace, Illyria, Dalmatia, Gaul, Spain, Germany, and Britain of their control by Rome after previous defeats or annexation. Agrippa tried to convince the Hebrews and Jews that a war with Rome would cause irreparable destruction of the holy places, deaths and maiming of people, enslavement of those who survived, and ravaging of the land. In closing his remarks, he referred to the blessings of peace, which everyone should cherish, and which he would gladly enjoy sharing with them. However, if they chose war, he emphasized, they should not expect his support because he was a Roman soldier and citizen.

Agrippa stressed the fact that the Jews were already straining their relations with Rome by refusing to pay their taxes. Added to that act of war, they had cut down the passages connecting the Temple and Fort Antonia's lower fortress. These defiances, declared Agrippa, could be considered grounds for war. The people harkened and began rebuilding the passage. They even sent collectors to other villages for the purpose of hurriedly collecting the tributes due Rome. Agrippa, noticing their response to his advice, admonished them to be obedient to procurator Florus until he was recalled to Rome. The people became infuriated with that warning. They abused Agrippa, as if he were not the king, cursed and ranted that he should be banished from Jerusalem. Some dissidents were unreasonable and bold enough to throw stones at the man who had been pleading their cause. Agrippa realized these hotheads were becoming uncontrollable. He discontinued trying to reason with this rabble, withdrew to his kingdom, and began calculating their destruction. The Jews had insulted and assaulted their benefactor, causing other Roman authorities to justify Florus' mistreatment of them.

Some of the agitators, thirsty for war and bloodthirsty attacks on the Romans, followed up their violent misjudgment with an assault on the fortress at Masada. Florus was glad to see the Jews spinning a web of disaster by themselves. They subdued the Romans, slew those who resisted, and occupied the fort with a company of their

own disorganized regiments. In the meantime, some servants of the
Holy Temple in Jerusalem decided to refuse gifts and offerings donated by Gentiles and foreigners. As a result, no tributes were amassed
for the emperor or Rome. The high priests saw Rome being tempted
to declare war on Judea and allow Florus justification of brutality.
So they tried to discourage civil disobedience. And they pleaded with
their subordinate priests to renew the collections and ceremonial sacrifices they were accustomed to make for the Romans in the Temple.
But the insurgents contradicted that plea and convinced the Temple
priests that it was time to engage the Romans in a showdown. The
rebels wanted a contest where the winner would take all the spoils.
The conservatives were more practical. They considered the reactions
in Rome, as well as the local action that Florus or even Agrippa,
requesting an attack on the rabble-rousers before they could muster
enough sympathizers for a full scale revolution. Their petition amused
Florus, who had been planning to destroy them indiscriminately. He
pretended to be disinterested, while rejoicing at the Jews tripping
themselves by betraying their own people.

Agrippa heeded the request of the delegates, probably because he
was himself of Jewish heritage or perhaps because of the danger he
had foreseen. Agrippa had imagined the Jews losing Jerusalem and
the Romans destroying the Temple. He sent two thousand mounted
cavalrymen to Jerusalem to maintain order. This confrontation esca-
lated the already steaming cauldron of Jewish tempers. However, there
was some difference between the doves seeking coexistence with the
Romans and the hawks seeking war. The agitators clamored for war
and showed their discontent with disturbances that lasted seven days.

The eighth day of unrest was a feast day. The faithful members
of the religion brought firewood to the Temple to be burnt at the Holy
Altar. The rabble-rousers, and the hardened discontented citizens,
did not come to worship, they battled Agrippa's troops and forced
them out of the Upper City. The rabble then set the king's palace
afire, burnt the public archives with all records of debts to the Roman
treasury, and left Agrippa no palatial rooms in which to live. The poor
and needy citizens were relieved of debt with no records to dun them.
Being free from payment of debts, the poor looked upon the arson
favorably and began to empathize with the discontented citizens. This
increase in numbers caused some insurgents to become courageous
enough to attack the fortress of Antonia on the following day. For two
days they held it under siege, then they captured the fort, massacred
its troops, and set fire to the fortress. This victory gave the rebels
assurance that the Romans could be defeated.

These militiamen now moved on to take over the rest of Agrippa's
palace, where his soldiers had sought refuge. Some Jews who sympathized with the Romans, or feared their strength, were also seek-

ing sanctuary there. The rebels engaged the Romans in fierce combat which lasted all day and all night.

During this period, a zealot named Menahem hurried to Masada with a band of friends and followers.[23] This group burglarized the armory after forced entry and took off with weapons. Menahem and his companions had enough weapons for themselves and extra pieces for their sympathizers in Jerusalem. Upon arrival back in the Holy City, the thieves were welcomed like heroes, and Menahem like a king. He was gleefully put in charge of troops which reinforced those surrounding the palace. With fresh weapons, and forcefulness, the rebels battered the palace walls until they collapsed. The barracks were full of companies whose commander sought a moratorium for evacuation of his troops. The privilege to evacuators only. The other Romans left without sympathizers and felt isolated and embarrassed. They refused to plead for further consideration and withdrew to more secure battlements and inner-fortifications within the palace. From these towers and depths, the Romans decided to take their stand. Menahem and his men allowed the Roman troops to withdraw. But they suddenly charged those who did not scurry out fast enough. The Jews had now chalked up another victory.

The following day found Menahem being rejoiced as a conqueror and hailed as a king. Dressed as a king, he set out to meet his subjects. Jealousy among his followers, and dislike by his opposition— who considered his wearing of Agrippa's robe to be in bad taste—the people began grumbling. It was not long before they showed their dissatisfaction by stoning him. Menahem ran away and hid himself. His relative Eleazar, son of Yair, left Jerusalem and returned to Masada where he was still in command. Menahem tried to follow him, but was discovered by the doves, who still feared the Roman might. They pulled Menahem from his hiding place and dragged him through the streets to where he was killed.[24]

The palace siege continued until the Roman commander surrendered his arms and supplies in exchange for his men's lives. A treaty of safe conduct was settled and signed. But no sooner than the Romans laid down their swords and shields, the Jews surrounded them and put them to death. While the soldiers fell, the Roman commander agreed to convert to Judaism with circumcision for himself and a few of his men who also were afraid to die.

Jewish defiance had now reached its culmination. Rome had been pushed to the brink of war. Prudent Jews observed this reality and began mourning the day of reckoning throughout Jerusalem. It was feared that a brutal slaying of Romans on the Sabbath, when Jews should have been in the Temple worshipping, was one terrible deed which might be avenged by God or man. Whether God intervened or not, it was not long before Jews in Cesarea experienced equal genocide of more than twenty thousands of their coreligionists. Gentiles in Cesarea acted at the same time Jewish militants were slaughtering the defeated unarmed Romans. In less than one-half hour Jews were randomly attacked throughout the land. The Jews retaliated by killing all Syrians within reach. The Syrians responded by systematic elimination of helpless unarmed Jews. The vendettas spread from one Syrian city to another. Antioch, Damascus, Aleppo, Hamah, Dayr, and other cities saw Syrians spewing out vindictiveness against the Jews. "They slew them by the thousands." The anti-Jewish feeling spread from Antioch to Alexandria, where the news had traveled. Several Jews lived in the Delta of Alexandria, so when the Romans heard of disturbances there, two Roman legions were immediately sent in to restore order. The troops were told to kill, plunder, and burn if necessary. It was a military order like a blank check to murder. They cashed it! The result was that Roman soldiers became so uncontrollable and ruthless that Tamarin stated, "the district was drowned in the blood of 50,000 corpses."[25] Open season was declared upon Jews in all quarters, and hunters indeed set out to pursue them. The greatest Jew hunter was Cestius Gallus, governor of Syria. He saw a long-awaited opportunity to engage the resisters with full force. Cestius led his troops from Antioch and joined Agrippa. Selected crack troops were added from other legions. They included battalions of infantry and four squadrons of six cavalry detachments. Another 2,000 horsemen were added with 3,000 foot soldiers of the auxiliary corps. These additional troops were supplied by Agrippa, who combined forces with Cestius for the war to end all wars. To add to this overwhelming force, many archers were sent by Antiochus, the North Syrian king. With this combined Roman force, Jewish fortifications fell one after another, as the Romans approached Galilee. There in the training ground of most Jewish dissidents of the time, the Romans ran through the province and subdued the ill-prepared resistance forces forthwith. From Galilee, the combined armies marched to Jerusalem. They bivouacked at Gibeon, some six miles from the target area. It was time for the Feast of the Tabernacles—when thousands of Jews assemble in Jerusalem for the pilgrim festival which begins on Tishri Fifteenth and lasts seven days.[26] When the faithful Jews saw the Romans approaching their community in full battle gear, they abandoned their attendance for the feast, and hastened to arm themselves as best they could. The Jews rushed between the Roman troops in such confusion that the trampling Romans became disorganized. Roman ranks were broken by the Jews rushing to their arsenal and to the heights where they could secure an advantageous position above their enemies. Again, it was not long before there was a disagreement among the Jews. Cestius saw the commotion caused by disunity, and quickly attacked them. It was easy simply to chase

them all the way to Jerusalem. At the gates of the city, Cestius waited with his combined forces in a bivouac at Scopus, or "Lookout Hill,"
almost a mile from Jerusalem. The commander waited three days for
Jewish accession or intent to save the Temple, and themselves. But
the Jews were much too proud to surrender without a test. Cestius
advanced, entered Jerusalem, and entrenched his troops in front of
the Royal Palace. He started to push through the Temple and city
walls to quickly end the conflict. But he was diverted by his quartermaster and many of his cavalrymen. These officers had been bribed
by Florus—the ambitious and corrupt procurator. Cestius should
have pressed forward, says Josephus, and ended the war at once,
but he did not storm the walls. "He continued hand-to-hand combat
for five days before his troops actually reached the north side of the
Temple. Upon this ground, his Roman troops propped their shields
row behind row until it became a missile proof barrier called a tor-
toise." This protective roof caused the Jewish archers and stone
throwers consternation and frustration. Seeing the enemy entrenched
without possibility of being harmed, the Jews gave up and began running their separate ways, every man for himself. Some conservatives
attempted to open the city gates and allow the Romans to enter as
their protectors. It is said that at this point, Cestius could have ended
the war for the second time, but he did not seem anxious to take
Jerusalem and destroy the Temple. He pulled back his troops from
the city unscathed. The rebels took his retreat for defeat, and immediately attacked the Romans. The Jews managed to press on and kill
the rear guardsmen, surround the infantry, and destroy formations
on both flanks, causing Roman casualties. The rebels harassed the
Romans to an extent that the great Roman "phalanx" was of little use.
The Romans tried to maintain their phalanx by tightening ranks, but
the mistake had already been costly. With light armor and equipment, the Jews were able to tactically move in and out of the ranks
rapidly enough to confuse the Romans. Cestius and his men wavered
back to Gibeon under orders of retreat. He had lost 5,300 infantry,
and 480 cavalrymen. Among his losses were quite a few officers, supplies, as well as beasts of burden. The only animals saved were those
carrying missiles, the ones hitched to war machines. Despite his tactical elimination of hindrances, Cestius was almost wiped out by his
attackers, and was only able to escape without added loss when the
protective blanket of might concealed his retreat. The Romans,
Syrians, and other allies had suffered a staggering setback. So great
was their loss that the discomforting news had to be sent to Nero.

Cestius wrote to Nero blaming Florus for lack of cooperation and
the sabotaging of his operation. Nero responded by making Cestius
commander-in-chief, supported by generals Idumea, Jericho, and
Perea, the provinces of Thamnia, Gophna, and Acrabetta. Josephus,

son of Matthias, was put in command of the two (Upper and Lower) Galilees, and Gamala.

In the meantime, Jewish militiamen had triumphantly returned from Jerusalem. Their victory over the professional army afforded them the opportunity to recruit more sympathizers through verbal or physical persuasion. Plans were discussed and strategy for a mass offensive decided. Complete authority over municipal affairs was delegated to Joseph, son of Gorion, and Ananaus the high priest. These municipal officials were advised to raise the height of the city walls. Eleazer, son of Simon, had been the leader in dispossessing Cestius of his supplies and of his men's valuables. He was promoted to commander of Jewish forces. Eleazer was considered the hero who had defeated the great Roman governor Cestius.

Flavius Josephus arrived in Galilee and made his first order of public relations: "care to win the goodwill of the people." He feared that Galilee would be the target of the main Roman offensive— because the Romans always hated, and feared, Galileans for their militancy. Galileans were feared far and near—Jesus the Christ was also from Galilee when he was a young activist. Josephus had his men dug in. He fortified Jotapata, Bersabe, Japhna, Tarichaeae, and Tiberias as well as other areas. He raised an army of more than one hundred thousand young able-bodied men whom he equipped with old weapons which he managed to put together. Josephus organized his battalions, said he, in the Roman style, increasing his number of junior officers. He also created ranks for the soldiers, as non-commissioned officers, appointing over them commanders of ten men each, called decurions. For the hundreds, Josephus had centurions. He explained how his men were trained for war with an impression upon their minds of the disciplined corps organized and maintained within the Roman army. He explained why and how their regimentation had made them masters of much territory. After his pep talk, and orientation of recruits, Josephus was very much in command until an envious con man, John, Johanan the son of Levi, from the city of Gischala, became jealous of him. Josephus was commander-in-chief of an army with 60,000 infantrymen, 350 cavalrymen, 4,500 trained combat troops with experience in battle, and 600 hand-picked troopers of the elite corps. His troops were provided, supported, and supplied by their home towns.

When con man John came on the scene he hindered the war effort by organizing a body of 400 skilled, well-trained, and physically fit men. These rogues were led as highwaymen by John, whose purpose was to plunder Galilee. After collecting much booty from muggings and holdups, John, a liar and cheater, was now able to direct his energies to his main objective. He wanted the prestigious position of the people's general. John succeeded in persuading Josephus "to entrust him with the rebuilding of the walls of Gischala." After collecting enough money from the wealthy townspeople of Gischala, John was prepared to squeeze out Josephus and become general of the people's army. John guided his men in organized agitation, sabotage, and disruption of the normal processes of everyday living. Discreditable rumors were disseminated, aspersions were cast, and Josephus was accused of intent to betray the Jews for the Romans. Josephus' position as commander-in-chief was now in jeopardy. While leadership was in dispute, a band of young highwaymen began a new era of terror.

The robbers highjacked a caravan of silverware, 600 pieces of gold, and other personal effects belonging to King Agrippa and his sister Queen Bernice. The young hoodlums were unable to dispose of it on the open market or through a fence, without being detected, so they gave the stolen property to Josephus to stash. Josephus, in turn, gave the loot to someone else for safekeeping. He was deciding a way to return the property to its rightful owner. The thieves, fearful of double-cross by Josephus, accused him of squealing. Pretending that he had broken the code of honor existent among thieves, John agitated and gathered a mob. They attacked Josephus while he was asleep. His bodyguards scurried away before he could awaken from deep slumber. He was lucky enough to awaken moments before his house burned down. Josephus dashed out with ashes on his forehead, torn clothing, hands behind his back, and his sword dangling from his neck. He intended to trick the conspirators by appearing ready to accept the charges against him. When they allowed Josephus to plead his case, he pulled the Mark Anthony ruse used at Caesar's funeral. Instead of telling the crowd what they expected to hear, Josephus explained how far he was from returning the stolen property to the royal family, or keeping it for himself. He intended to use the proceeds to build walls for protection of the city of Tarichaeae, where the ramparts needed repairs, and the municipal treasury could not afford to pay for them. The people of Tarichaeae applauded, while the Gischala dissidents mumbled their dissatisfaction. The visitors were disappointed. They left Josephus, and turned on each other. He hurriedly reinforced his position with an added promise to repair and fortify all city walls with whatever funds the people would raise for those projects. He also pleaded with his fellowmen to unite against their common enemy, instead of conspiring against their leader.

Despite his dissatisfaction with this defeat, John was still undaunted. He tried to cause new ferment against Josephus in the city of Tiberias. To this end, he almost succeeded in assassinating Josephus, when the commander hurried to the city to speak to the citizens and expose the plot. Josephus made a narrow escape with two of his bodyguards by jumping from a nine-foot mound into a boat moored in the lake at the Sea of Galilee.

Josephus was now positive of John's rascality and determination to overthrow him. Confronted with this reality, the commander took forceful action against John, and his band of cutthroats. He broke up their gang and threatened to seize their relatives' property and whatever assets the criminals themselves might have, and to severely punish them if they did not discontinue their alliance, evil deeds, and association with John. Three thousand of John's cohorts dropped their weapons and immediately switched to Josephus' side. In a short while, the city of Tiberias rose up against Josephus for the second time. This time the opposition turned to King Agrippa for cooperation. The city gates were barred against Josephus, and he had to move swiftly. It was a Friday. With the Sabbath approaching, he would not have been able to maneuver on the following day. Most of his men were out foraging for food, so Josephus tactfully used 230 boats which floated on the lake. He manned each boat with only four sailors. Sailing ahead of the fleet, Josephus conned the people into surrendering without an engagement against seemingly overwhelming odds in his favor. With no more than seven armed guards, and many empty boats on the water, the entire population of Tiberias obeyed his directives because they feared his invisible force invading from the bay.

With all negative self-directed efforts abandoned, the Hebrews and Jews were now able to begin preparing for their war of wars. This last stand against the Romans required overhauling and assembling of war machines, missiles, suits of armor—that had to be forged—building of walls and drilling of recruits. The hustling and bustling seemed more like confusion than preparation, and Josephus felt overcome by a "feeling of doom and destruction."

During the commotion, Simon, son of Gioras, seized the opportunity to exploit and mistreat the rich members of the community. He recruited the unemployed and the loiterers. These vagabonds were taught to extort money from the merchants and hoarders. The leaders of Jerusalem sent angry vigilantes after him, but Simon refused to engage in combat. He withdrew his forces to the fortress at Masada, where he could dig in and reinforce his position.

By this time Nero was overwhelmed with news of rebellion in Judea. The Emperor of Rome could no longer rely on Agrippa, who was a Jewish sympathizer, and he could not depend on Florus who was busy robbing the Jews and the Roman treasury. So to prevent the idea of revolt from spreading to other Roman protectorates, he selected Titus Flavius Vespasian to deal with the problem. Vespasian (b. Dec. 30 A.D. 39; d. Sep. 13, 81), had proven himself an undefeated veteran against Germany and Britain where he conquered the Isle of Wight. These victories had made him consul (A.D. 51). Vespasian took command as troubleshooter after also having been pro consul in Africa (A.D. 66). He took over the divisions in Syria, while he sent his son, Titus, to Alexandria. Titus brought up his troops—the Fifteenth Legion—to meet Vespasian, who had crossed Hellespont, and continued on foot to Antioch—the capital of Syria at that time. Vespasian met Agrippa and his army attending guard here. Considering this territory secure, Vespasian continued to hike to Galilee, where the troublemakers were supposed to receive militant anti-Roman indoctrination. He met the people of the city of Sepphoris, who peacefully accepted occupation, and showed no intent to do battle. A Roman garrison was there. Its location was in the very heart of Jewish territory. A lagging cavalry detachment soon joined Vespasian, and an equally large infantry battalion accompanied the riders. From this strategic base, Vespasian began harassing the Jewish militia with sporadic attacks and retreats. These tactical approaches cost Josephus considerable loss of men and supplies. The Romans ravaged the surrounding areas of their centrally located and heavily fortified city of Sepphoris. They forced the Jews to take cover behind their own fortifications. Whenever the Jews ventured out to engage the enemy, the Romans repulsed them with overwhelming force. Josephus attempted a confrontation, but was beaten back. He had previously fortified Sepphoris so well, before the Romans occupied it, that he was defenseless against enemy entrenchment.

In strengthening their position, the Romans had Titus advance from Egypt with his Fifteenth Legion. These troops joined Vespasian's Fifth and Tenth. Father and son combined their legions, with the divisions and contingents recruited by the kings of the Roman protectorates. These forces now amounted to over sixty thousand combat troops. As if these were not sufficient, many servants were added—having been trained in basic military strategies on maneuvers and previous battles alongside their masters. When this impressive force paraded toward the Jews, in full battle dress and imperial formation, the sight of them was enough to scare away some of Josephus' men. The Romans, led by Vespasian, drew up in customary Roman order. The procession was headed by lightly armed auxiliary troops, with archers in the forefront as advance parties to scout and engage ambushers. Following these scouts were a heavily armed infantry battalion and a detachment of cavalrymen. Behind these divisions came the quartermaster corps, with tools for preparing bivouacs. Next in line came the engineers constructing and straightening curved roads, leveling surfaces, and chopping down trees. Then the commander and his generals approached, followed by their luggage, guarded by a well-armed mounted escort. Vespasian, his elite infantry and cavalry regiments, along with lancers, appeared wedged in between the cavalry company followed by mules carrying siege towers, battering rams, and war machines. They preceded the commanders and officers in front of the battle standards bearing the Roman eagle which represented each legion. After this horde came what was termed the "main body,"[27] shoulder-to-shoulder, marching as a solid column, six abreast. Behind this mass of humanity and equipment, the Jews had to endure the sight of servants and more auxiliary troops covered by a security rear guard composed of light and heavy infantry battalions, accompanied by a well-heeled cavalry regiment.

When Vespasian reached Galilee with this terrifying mass of humanity, the remaining insurgents had to reassure themselves of their undertaking. It seemed like survival through humility or extermination through determination. Josephus preferred to avoid the confrontation, particularly when some of his men became terrified and left their posts. He withdrew to Tiberias with his remaining flock, while he contemplated a truce rather than an engagement with this powerful enemy. Josephus sent to Jerusalem to inquire forthwith if the Jewish leaders there would be interested in suing for peace without delay. If they were determined to fight, he figured his besieged inmates were in deep trouble, and Jotapata unable to resist the battering pressures much longer. He decided to slip out and seek reinforcements. The people of Jotapata would not let him go. They felt that if he left, they might not see him again, so they begged Josephus to stay. The Romans now pushed up their most powerful battering rams into position and started banging the walls. The sides began shaking as if they would soon begin to give way. Josephus ordered sacks filled with chaff, and hung in front of the rams as bumpers. These cushions absorbed the bumps like shock absorbers. The Romans did not allow them to remain too long. Scythes were tied to the ends of long poles and used to cut down the sacks. The Romans attacked and were counterattacked. The battle seesawed until the Romans formed their phalanx and moved in like a solid human block, pushing the Jews back to the wall. Josephus ordered hot oil poured on them to loosen up their formation. Slippery herbs were also spread on the Roman bridges and gangplanks to make them slide. Many of them did lose footing and slid under their instruments and companions to become crushed.[28]

On the 47th day, the Roman earthworks (scaffolds) reached above the city walls. Roman scouts attacked the tired sentries that night, and by daybreak, they were inside the Jotapata walls slaughtering the Jews, even in caves and caverns. Only 1,200 women and children were spared, only to be captured as slaves or prisoners. Approximately 40,000 Jewish soldiers were killed, the city set aflame, and its walls flattened to the ground.

Some revolutionaries hid in caves and caverns, but most of them were found. Despite the diligent pursuit by Romans, Josephus and

40 of his aides-de-camp hid in a cave, deep enough to conceal them and with enough supplies to last them for a good while. These Jews were undetected for three whole days, even though Josephus crawled out at night to reconnoiter for an escape route.

The Romans had been searching the area for those three days. They found their quarry when Josephus' hideout was unexpectedly bargained over to them by a squealing woman of his own kind. She had been a Roman admirer, even though she had been captured and imprisoned by them. She sought her freedom through collaboration, and squealed on her people. With the informer rewarded, Vespasian sent one tribune after another to guarantee Josephus that no harm would befall him if he surrendered. The other Jews asked their leader to ignore Vespasian's offer. Vespasian resorted to sending tribune Nicanor, one of Josephus' old Roman cronies, to persuade him to give himself up. He was encouraged by the knowledge of a pardon from Vespasian without penalty. Josephus was told that Vespasian did not intend to seek revenge. While Nicanor was trying to convince Josephus of his safe passage and amnesty, other Romans were busy setting fires at the exits and entrances of most caves. They intended to smoke out the remaining cave dwellers who had eluded capture.

Josephus, who swore to have been a priest and a descendant of Levites of dark skin, stated that he had dreamt of the Roman victory. His consultation on the matter had descended from the Almighty. As a true servant, he declared, it had been impossible for him to disobey the Supreme Force—a Benefactor claimed by all men of the cloth. Tamarin related his skill in interpreting dreams and "reading the hidden meanings in Sacred Writings." Josephus also justified his surrender to the Romans by turning his "face to God in silent prayer," and swore that he had "willingly surrendered to the Romans, but I take thee witness that I go, not as a traitor, but as thy servant." No one was able to obtain affirmation or denial in the validity of his testimony, but the Jews did not readily accept Josephus' claims of being an interpreter of divine revelations and personal dispensations. They threatened to kill him. He was strongly suspected of cowardice and did not seem to feel any longer that the cause was greater than his life. They asked him the pertinent question all oppressed people should ask: "Are you so fearful for your life, Josephus, that you would rather live like a slave?" He responded by accusing them of unwillingness to listen to divine guidance and refusal to put their lives to the test. They then asked him to commit suicide rather than surrender. Josephus refused, and his men tried to run him through with their swords. Josephus fended them off, and reminded them he was still their commander. Thinking quickly, he suggested a lottery drawing to determine who would live or die. Josephus and one other man drew blank slips, and were allowed to live and survive the disadvantageous war. Josephus was escorted to Vespasian's headquarters, where the curious Roman officers assembled to see him. After sizing him up, some of them decided that he should be put to death, others commended him for his military prowess, and a few threatened revenge for their troops scalded with hot oil, crushed under feet or wheels, or shot with missiles. Josephus being young, and Titus also a youthful commander, they admired each other's ability. This admiration caused Titus to plead with his father (Vespasian) to save the young Jewish general, guarded with utmost diligence and his hands kept bound with equal cautiousness. This important prisoner was to be sent to Nero in Rome.

But when Josephus was brought face to face with the Roman commander-in-chief, he quickly notified Vespasian that he was not an ordinary prisoner of war, but a messenger of God, who had forgotten the outcome of the war. He had also foreseen that it would not be wise to have him sent to Nero, because Vespasian himself would soon become emperor of Rome. Vespasian was superstitious and feared Josephus might really be a prophet, so he sent Josephus fresh clothing and ordered special prisoner status and treatment extended to this messenger of God. Still, the prisoner was not released.

Vespasian withdrew his troops to Cesarea for a brief respite. He was suspicious of Josephus' ability to foresee events. Josephus took advantage of Vespasian's superstitious fears, and convinced his captor to set him free.

Other uprisings developed in Joppa, with pirates robbing merchant vessels along the coasts of Syria and Phoenicia as well. Vespasian did not hesitate to send troops after the pirates. The vandals withdrew and boarded their ships, but a storm—similar to the one that got Jonah thrown overboard—is said to have destroyed them all. "Four thousand and two hundred bodies were washed up on the beaches."

Sad tidings reached Jerusalem declaring Jotapata has fallen to the Romans. These words were said to have been doubted when they touched base in the minds of the populace. They had less credence when there was no eyewitness to confirm the report, and no one believed the great Jewish general could have been captured so quickly. When the news did reach home, in the minds of the Judeans, they were more eager to accept news that Josephus had perished than reports that the city had fallen and its commander was still alive. There were people mourning and lamenting for Josephus until it was confirmed that he had surrendered, and was not even wounded. Upon learning that Josephus was well treated, and even admired by the Romans, the Jews became furious enough to accuse him of treason, cowardice, and selfishness. Angry Jews revolted in Tiberias and Tarichaeae—two cities within Agrippa's kingdom. In Tiberias, the older people, resigned to Roman rule, remained passive; the younger people expressed their desires for self-determination and self-rule. These young Jews fought against Roman domination until they were oppressed for rebelliousness and were defeated because they lacked support. They retreated to Tarichaeae, when Vespasian occupied Tiberias, without resistance of any significance. Showing respect for Agrippa's territorial jurisdiction, Vespasian prevented looting in this city by his men. The Jews were now concentrated in Tarichaeae—a strategic area with sound fortifications, near to the shores of the Sea of Galilee. Built at the foot of craggy hills, and fortified with impregnable walls, Josephus had left only one opening to this city. That opening faced the Sea of Galilee.

Vespasian sent his troops to stand by, while his son Titus marched ahead with lead forces of 600, hand picked, cavalrymen. Finding it difficult to subdue the large number of Jewish forces dug into the city and around its ramparts, Titus sent for reinforcements. While waiting, Titus attacked once more, only to meet the same staunch resistance. He attempted once more and succeeded in breaking Jewish lines, trampling some militants, and spearing other Jews who were without protective shields or armor. Disorganization prevailed and he was able to take advantage of the scattered Jewish forces. Not being a well-disciplined army, and not having the popular support required, they were now open to defeat. The Jews of Tarichaeae had considered the revolutionaries troublemakers, from outside, who dared to confront their Roman masters. Their foolhardiness cost them dearly. Titus took advantage of their disunity, jumped on his horse, led his troops through the opening from the Sea of Galilee, and waded toward the scattered challengers. They were no longer a fighting force. With Titus within their walls, Jews were killed indiscriminately. There was no distinction made between peace loving doves or militant hawks. They were mutilated alike. Some of the Jewish citizens tried to escape by sea. These were pursued by Roman rafts forming a fleet which speared the renegades like fish and killed them to the last man. Those who reached the shore were also slain forthwith. It is written: "The whole lake was red with blood and covered with corpses, for not a man who had fled escaped."

When the wasting of Jewish lives was over, Vespasian separated the remaining hawks from the doves. The agitators were deported to Tiberias and promised safe conduct. However, it was only a few days before they discovered that the Romans had lied to them. These prisoners were ordered by Vespasian into a stadium where 1,200 old and crippled dissidents were slain. Six thousands of the young able-bodied men were sent to Nero in Rome. Some 34,000 prisoners were sent to Agrippa to be sold into slavery. Those remaining with Vespasian were immediately sold as slaves.

The overwhelming Roman display of military might at Tarichaeae caused most Galileans to discontinue their revolutionary struggle. Only a few militants, who had survived Jotapata's defeat, were still willing to carry on the fight. Two fortresses remained and refused to surrender. One was Gischala the other was Gamala.[29] Gamala was located on the other side of the Sea of Galilee and Mount Tabor. It sat on a hump shaped like a camel's back, on a rugged spur which descended from a precipitous mountaintop. Gamala declared there would be no surrender. Her inhabitants felt secure. Their position seemed invulnerable, and would have been if their army had been organized and mechanized. The Gamalians depended on their self-determination and hope to win their battle. They did not recognize physical power as the only reality. Vespasian established his bivouac in Tiberias before he marched to Gamala. He set up camps on the periphery overlooking the targeted area. Then his men received orders to build earthworks. While his men were hurriedly building, Vespasian brought his war machines with battering rams into position. He ordered the engineers to begin hammering away at the three impassable sides of Gamala. It was not long before the walls caved in. The Romans pressed onward, and got caught in a narrow-necked passage where their enemies pushed them back, as other Roman troops came up behind them. With the rear columns pressing onward, some Romans were forced to climb up to the roofs of the low Jewish houses. As they increased in numbers their added weight caused the roofs to cave in. Since the houses were built on a slope, many Romans got trapped when the lower foundations and supports gave away. One house collapsed in such a manner that other houses slid on it like dominoes. Some Romans were buried under the rubble, others were asphyxiated by the dust. Vespasian was almost trapped. His aides and his good physical condition saved him.

To confuse his enemy and rebuild morale, Vespasian sent part of his troops to Mount Tabor. These 600 horsemen immediately subdued that vulnerable citizenry. This cheap victory gave the Romans renewed confidence to return to the greater encounter.

Titus was not present at the battle of Gamala and became embarrassed when he learned how the greatest power in the world had almost been annihilated by disorganized, inferior combat forces. He mustered 200 cavalrymen and a company of infantrymen and advanced to settle Gamala's pitched hand-to-hand battle. The disorganized forces became terrified, and some of them grabbed their children and fled to higher ground. Vespasian saw an opportunity to advance, but was met by a hail of rocks and arrows from the Jews. Boulders were also rolled down on the Roman enemy; but with the winds of fate and nature blowing against the Jews, things changed. After gaining control of the situation for a good while "a storm arose, blowing full into the faces of the defenders." This stormy weather helped the Romans find their marks. At the same time, it blew in the Jews' faces forcing them to shoot their missiles against the wind, which blinded them to some degree. It was difficult for the Jews even to stand firmly on the sloping cliffs. Like a storm from the Bible, this phenomenon clouded the vision of the Gamalians, and screened the invaders' advance. Many Jews, refusing to be captured and sold into slavery, jumped with their families into the gaping ravines surrounding Gamala's heights. These ravines which had been dug for protection had now become graves.

There was another smaller town left unconquered. It was the town of Gischala. It was a small fortified town located in Upper Galilee. Many farmers lived here.[30] Josephus' rival, John, fortified this town. Recognized as a conman, he had steered his cronies toward encouraging the townspeople to defy the Romans, instead of pleading no contest.

Vespasian sent Titus to Gischala with a regiment of a thousand cavalry to subdue those in defiance. Titus considered the vulnerability of the town and the massacres that would result from an attack. He gave the citizens of Gischala a choice and awaited a reply—peace or war. John of Gischala deceivingly replied to Titus from the city walls suing for peace on condition. John informed Titus that he needed time to evacuate his troops or surrender. It was his Sabbath, a day on which Hebrew law forbade him to discuss war or to wage it. When Titus agreed, John and his agitators sneaked out of Gischala during the night and headed for Jerusalem. The next morning, Titus entered Gischala to conclude the pact, and was surprised to learn that he had been fooled. He immediately dispatched a company of cavalrymen to pursue John and his band of renegades. The cavalrymen did not catch up with them. Gischala became the last town of Galilee to surrender. Roman experience in combat with the Jews had made them aware of the fact that once Jewish frontlines are broken, panic sets in within the ranks.

John, who had not considered these weaknesses within the Jewish forces, arrived in Jerusalem and began boasting about his wittiness and Roman gullibility. He said the walls of Jerusalem were insurmountable, and the Romans could never come over them even with wings. John lied about his encounter with the Romans in Gischala, and fooled these people into believing the Romans had encountered great resistance in Galilee. Their war engines were supposed to have been worn out trying to destroy thin village walls in Gamala and in other Galilean strongholds, so these great Romans would be helpless when they faced Jerusalem's thick walls. Impetuous youths listened and enlisted. The older people foresaw doom. They were distressed. The skies seemed to be darkening with possibilities of gloom and mourning. Lamentations were heard among them. Their disagreement caused the Jews to begin fighting before the Romans had even set foot in Jerusalem. They were fighting among themselves. The doves and the hawks fought a death battle. Their ferocious vendettas caused the elimination of entire families, and the discontinuance of long-existing friendships. Finally, the young hawks defeated the old pacifist doves. A cloud of anarchy prevailed as many rogues pillaged the countryside and robbed crops, valuables and other personal effects. After the rampage subsided, these toughs united their gangs and headed for Jerusalem proper. The city was not governed by a strong administrator. It was further handicapped by a practice "which by ancient custom, admitted all of Jewish blood without question." That practice would have resulted unfavorably even if the country had not been ravished by internal instability and vandalism. Food was scarce and the existent supply could not meet the needs of the fighting men, let alone the vagrants and agitators. The wicked thieves began ravishing the country day and night. Armed robbery was frequent. It turned to unwarranted arrests of some prominent citizens, their accusation of collaborating with the enemy, confiscation of their properties, and execution without due process. The rogues increased their power politically and economically. Then the mob refused to recognize the authority of the high priesthood, an authority which had been inherited for generations. They ignored family tradition and rights, invaded the Temple, and like most hypocrites, called themselves the pious ones. The Temple was turned into their fortified headquarters. These gangsters became so abusive that one of the leading elders, Ananus, mobilized community forces for united action against the impious thieves.

The honest citizens attacked the rogues. Stone-throwing began and the skirmishes became more serious as the people became incensed. Community forces pressed the mobsters with such determination that the pious ones backed up farther and farther into the Temple. When they reached the inner court, the crooks barred the gates behind them. High priest Ananus gathered 6,000 armed men to guard the great entrances, especially where Boaz and Jachin stood.[31] Seeing an opportunity to profit from the disruption, John acted as if he were in sympathy with the high priest and the community he represented. At the same time, John played the role of double agent by secretly revealing the strategies planned by these people to the roguish Zealots every night.

John's encouragement caused the Zealots to send for the Idumeans to come to their aid. With reinforcements of their ranks, the crooks resorted to libel. They accused the legitimate high priest Ananus of being a Roman collaborator and therefore antagonistic to their cause. The Idumeans arrived in Jerusalem, seized Ananus, and killed him. With the Idumeans and Zealots uniting forces, robbery, burglary, and homicide increased. People were slaughtered mercilessly, false arrests were common occurrences, and freedom was only promised to persons who agreed to join the revolutionary forces. The decent young people refused to cooperate, and many young men chose death—which was the only alternative—rather than dishonorable behavior. When the respectable youth refused to join the wicked blood-thirsty Zealots, about 12,000 of them were butchered in cold blood. Meanwhile, the fratricide served to amuse the Romans; they even began to feel that their gods had favored them over the Jews. Vespasian's generals tried to encourage him to attack the Judeans while they fought among themselves, but the wise veteran persuaded them to be patient. He explained that the longer the Romans waited, the fewer Jews they would have to engage in battle. While the Romans obeyed his orders, the Jews convinced them that he was right. Vespasian's Jewish collaborators—anxious to save themselves—continually brought him information from nearby Jerusalem, and even from far away Masada, where the rogues were still pillaging the surrounding areas of the mountain fortress.

By this time, John was feeling strong enough to assume leadership of rebel forces. John selected a group of Zealots he felt would be loyal to him and formed his own band. But this new division only added to the confusion, and weakened the Jewish contingents.

Vespasian evacuated his bivouac and moved on to Jerusalem to begin mop-up operations, by advancing, upholstering, occupying, and fortifying Roman positions. He approached Peraea province, passed through its capital—Gadara—but found no resistance. The dissidents had disagreed with a local community leader intending to fight the invaders, and murdered him to maintain unconditional surrender to the enemy. These murderers had left the city before Vespasian's arrival. He sent some of his troops out of the province after them. When the Romans caught up with them, they killed many of them, and forced the survivors on to Jericho for refuge. The Roman pursuers continued their charge without relenting, and forced the Gadarans up to the River Jordan. Torrents of rain had not too long fallen, and the river was therefore impassable. Many Gadarans jumped into the Jordan, and others were killed on its banks. Numerous bodies floated in the river, and approximately 15,000 were washed down to the Dead Sea.

The people of Peraea were more cautious and prudent; they pulled down their walls themselves, and made their non-resistance obvious.

Vespasian, who had left for Gaul confident that Titus would continue and subdue the Judeans, was now anxious to return and conclude this chapter of rebellion throughout the Roman Empire. It was not long before he returned to northeast Africa, where the Hebrews and Jews seemed to be the greatest challengers of Roman domination. Vespasian attacked and defeated the Judeans and Idumeans on the outskirts, killing over 10,000 souls and capturing over 1,000 prisoners. When he moved into Jericho, the news must have preceded him, because he found the place almost deserted. Vespasian quickly set up camp around Jerusalem, with a bivouac at Adida. After occupying and fortifying these areas with numerous troops, supplies, and weapons, he advanced with cavalry regiments and infantry battalions upon the city of Gerasa (an ancient city of Transjordan). After capturing this city and subduing its weak forces, Vespasian burned it and razed its fortifications. This assault closed all escape routes from the main target city—Jerusalem.

In a short while, Nero died by his own hands, exclaiming, "What an artist the world is losing in me."[32]

Vespasian suspended his engagements to await the outcome of the political turmoil, and the nomination of Nero's successor. Servius Sulpicius Galba was called to the throne.

Galba (3 B.C.–A.D. 69) had been a distinguished politician, consul to Gaul, and military praetor. He was proclaimed emperor by his troops. After a few months, Marcus Salvius Otho became jealous of Galba and headed a rebellion against the new emperor. Vespasian suspended his war against Jerusalem, sent his son Titus to congratulate Galba, and awaited orders on the northeastern campaign. Agrippa joined Titus on the trip to Rome for the same purposes. But Otho—whose wife Poppaea Sabina had been Nero's mistress—joined the rebellion to oust Galba. Galba's administration, though short-lived, was parsimonious and honest. He was killed after a few months reign, and Otho declared himself emperor.

Marcus Salvius Otho (A.D. 32–A.D. 69) was soon defeated in war inside northern Italy, where he committed suicide. Upon receiving news of Otho's ascension to the throne, Titus had changed his mind about going to Rome and had detoured to Syria to join his father Vespasian instead. Agrippa kept on to Rome, where he soon learned of Otho's untimely death, whereupon his troops transferred their allegiance to Alus Vitellius (A.D. 15 –A.D. 69). Vitellius invaded Rome with his legions and those pledged to him. Galba had made him commander of the legions on the Lower Rhine in A.D. 68. With Galba's passing, Vitellius became emperor, with the help of the generals who favored him and aided him in defeating Otho. He was proclaimed emperor at Colonia Agrippiana, now Cologne.

With Titus and his father joining forces to vanquish the Hebrews and the Jews, the disunited factions hastened their own liquidation by continuing to fight among themselves. The Romans did not have to worry about them, because the recess caused by Jewish self-destruction allowed their enemies to repair equipment and heal their wounds.

Simon, son of Gioras, was now a general recruiting adventurers, mercenaries, bail-jumpers, servants, and vagabonds for his militia. Simon was a sturdy youth, and had become popular for his physical prowess and valiant deeds. However, his impetuosity was not all that he needed. He lacked knowledge of political intrigue to help shape his plans to defeat the schemes of John of Gischala. Simon left Masada, came down to the prairie and received many volunteers, who admired his successes in combat and his daring in jousts. The Zealots had not concerned themselves with Simon when he controlled the hills. When he emerged and extended his realm, however, they decided to cut him down like they had done Menahem, particularly after he began gathering a noticeable following. They started in a procession from Jerusalem to confront Simon and his followers. A confrontation ensued and Simon inflicted heavy casualties on his opponents. He forced the Zealots all the way back to the city walls. Nevertheless, he did not feel prepared enough to capture Jerusalem proper. Therefore, Simon detoured to the adjacent province of Idumea to meet approximately 25,000 Idumeans that were coming to reinforce the Zealots. The Idumeans battled with Simon's troops, at their border where he met them. The contest lasted an entire day without either side gaining a decisive victory. Simon withdrew and decided to use a different approach. He activated his intelligence network and accomplished through expert espionage and diplomacy what he had failed to gain through force. Idumea (Edom) fell without further bloodshed. Simon suddenly made a surprise attack and captured the small town of Hebron. He confiscated a considerable amount of corn, oil, and loot. Simon returned to Idumea as a conqueror, with his regular troops and 40,000 auxiliaries, and wreaked havoc on it, razed it to the ground, and burned some parts of the inner-occupied areas. All of Idumea's food and crops were either eaten or destroyed. Simon's forces grew to astounding numbers in a short time; the Zealots became afraid to challenge him in face-to-face combat, and began harassing his men with guerilla warfare and ambush. On one such expedition, Simon's wife and some of her attendants were abducted and held in Jerusalem. Simon led his troops to Jerusalem's walls and threatened to destroy all of its inhabitants if the hostages were not immediately released. The Zealots were so terrified, they immediately ordered the kidnappers to free Simon's wife and her entire retinue.

While the Jews and Hebrews were fighting each other and depleting their human and other resources, Vespasian and his men sat and observed. The commander had the Jewish rebellion to terminate, and the turmoil and instability in Rome to consider. Both of these situations afforded him an opportunity to become emperor, if he could control them now that he had won successful campaigns in the foreign protectorates of the empire. Vespasian left Cesarea to advance on Gophna and Acrabetta. His legions destroyed Upper Idumea, and marched on to Hebron (also called Kiriath Arba in the Bible), eighteen miles south of Jerusalem. Hebron was vulnerable and its inhabitants were soon liquidated; this ancient city (now in Jordan) was razed to the ground and burned. The only forts left now were Jerusalem, within reach; Masada, the stronghold under Eleazar— near the Dead Sea; Herodium, held by untrained rebels east of the Dead Sea; and Machaerus—another stronghold east of the Dead Sea. While Vespasian reconnoitered in Jerusalem, Simon continued to abuse the people of Idumea, causing groups of them to seek refuge in Jerusalem. In the meantime, John of Gischala and the Zealots were burglarizing the homes of wealthy Hebrews and Jews, murdering and torturing anyone who resisted or were disliked by them. Some inhabitants ran out of the city to escape these despots. But they ran from the frying pan and jumped into the fire. Upon reaching the outside, they would run into John of Gischala. His punishment was even harsher than the injustices meted inside. Fearing that these escapees were going to join the Roman enemies, John and his men would club and bludgeon the city dwellers to death. When the Idumeans realized John's unworthiness, they revolted against both him and the Zealots, then chased them into the Temple. John gathered his forces from all quarters and charged the Idumeans. Becoming confused, the Idumeans went to the high priests for advice. The priests, pretending to know the proper solution, advised the Idumeans to join forces with Simon and thereby rid themselves of John. Simon saw a good opportunity, and immediately consented to accept their offer. Simon did not hesitate to march through Jerusalem as protector and benefactor of the people and their cause. When the celebration had subsided, and Simon felt himself firmly established, he began acting like a dictator. It was the third year of the internecine wars, and Simon felt he had survived, even superseding the other leaders, as absolute ruler of Jerusalem. John and his Zealots were now locked up inside the Temple. It was not long before they became worried about their detention. The Zealots started to plan, but before they could implement their strategies, Simon attacked them. He broke their melancholy with an assault on the Temple. The citizens supported Simon's assault, but the Zealots and John were strong enough to repulse their adversaries. Simon's casualties were high. He lost many men because of their position. They had to storm the Temple's ramparts from below, and the Zealots peppered them with missiles from the higher position which gave advantage in aiming at the targets. However, Simon had such an overwhelming number of conscripts that his losses could be absorbed.

The Jews were not the only disunited people. The Romans were having their share of conspiracies, counterespionage, and military intrigues for another coup d' état. Aulus Vitellius was in Rome plundering the wealthy and murdering resistant victims, and legal defenders of civil and property rights. As emperor of Rome, Vitellius was known for his debauchery, extravagance, and incompetence. Flavius Sabinus, Vespasian's brother, was aware of Vitellius' weaknesses, and was certainly keeping his ear to the ground. Vitellius' government floundered, and Vespasian's brother must have informed him of the plot to converge all available Roman legions on the emperor's troops when notified to attack.

Vespasian returned to Cesarea after demolishing most Jewish fortresses of real consequence or menace. He now focused on Jerusalem as his main objective. Vespasian was angry, and perhaps also jealous of Vitellius' usurpation of the throne. Nevertheless, he exercised prudence and patience. The old warrior was far from Rome, and a hasty decision could very well be costly. Political as well as military support were of supreme importance in gaining the throne, and especially in retaining it. Vespasian's troops and their officers were not as patient as he. They did not hesitate to begin complaining and contemplating ways to revolt against Emperor Aulus Vitellius. They shouted, "Vespasian's claim to the Empire is better than that of Vitellius. Just as we are better soldiers then Vitellius' supporters."[33] It was not long before that kind of talk picked up momentum. The soldiers and officers started shouting the name of their commander as Emperor Vespasian. While they hailed him, Vespasian refused to display his anxiety in becoming emperor of the declining empire. He tried his best to concentrate on the task of quelling all rebellions in Judea. Vespasian's men continued to hail him as emperor, and he acceded to the honor to succeed Vitellius. His first official act as emperor was to secure the allegiance of Alexandria, Egypt, where Rome's granary was located. With this important source of food under his control, the people's demand for sustenance would definitely force Vitellius to fall into disfavor. There were also two Roman legions stationed in Alexandria and both showed willingness to join the veteran and his forces. Vespasian hurriedly sent dispatches to Tiberius Alexander, who was governor of Egypt, notifying him of his legionnaires' intent to make Vespasian go to the Roman throne. Tiberius Alexander read Vespasian's letter in the public square for all to hear. The letter requested all available support. Tiberius then asked his legions and all citizens of responsibility to cooperate by swearing to place Vespasian on the Roman throne. The people and the troops anxiously and joyously agreed to promote the commander-in-chief. Vespasian broadened his political base further by having one legion after another take the oath of allegiance to him. Then he began planning his chain of military command and control. In his recollections of implementation of procedures and promotions, Vespasian recalled

Josephus' prediction during Nero's reign that Vespasian himself would soon be the emperor of Rome, and his son also. Therefore, the emperor-to-be said, "It is disgraceful that one who prophesied my rise should still be in chains." Vespasian was superstitious and did not want evil to befall him because of mistreatment and ungratefulness to his seer. So he sent for Josephus, and freed him. Josephus was later given a command and he adopted the name of Vespasian's brother, "Flavius."

Armed with the necessary military and political support abroad, Vespasian made tentative appointments of governors for the provinces in the east, then hurried to Rome. His brother Flavius Sabinus was already making preparations to eliminate Vitellius in a battle for the throne. With Flavius approaching from one flank, Vespasian set up cavalry detachments, and infantry battalions to the other flank, while another legion sworn to him engaged Vitellius' forces on another front. Vitellius' engagement by overwhelming forces on the three fronts caused him to be defeated to a man. Feeling despondent, Vitellius started drinking. In his drunken stupor, he unconsciously staggered out of the palace. It was not long before he was nabbed by Vespasian's sympathizers and mercilessly murdered, after having reigned for only eight months. With Vespasian still abroad, the Roman populace was advised to allow Vespasian's younger son Domitian to represent his father as emperor until Vespasian returned to Rome. The Empire was now peaceful, rivalry abated, and the populace confident that Emperor Vespasian would stabilize politics and restore economic progress.

Actions and decisions reached the couriers who anxiously awaited all tidings. They hurried to Alexandria to inform Vespasian of their consensus. Feeling that Rome was secure and the Empire on the way to recovery, Vespasian now decided to direct his entire concern toward ending the disruptions throughout Judea. He summoned his son Titus and explained his decision to sail for Rome when spring arrived. Titus was to be commander-in-chief of all eastern operations. It was obvious that there would not be too much difficulty encountered in accomplishing a prompt victorious onslaught, because the Jews were already destroying most of their own forces. Titus accepted the command, and prepared to meet the challenge.

The first move by Titus came when he sailed up the Nile toward Cesarea. His army followed and approached the target as close as they could by water, then left their shuttle vessels, and proceeded across the desert on foot to the heart of Cesarea, where they mustered with the main military forces. Titus did not have to attack the Jews as quickly as he had anticipated, because they had already started eliminating themselves on a third front.

Eleazar, son of Simon who had cornered the Zealots in the Temple, revolted against his subaltern John of Gischala. This new army occupied the inner court of the Temple, erecting their battery of weapons on top of the Holy Gates. These soldiers on the Gates were not as numerous as the other two factions, but they were just as well or better armed with ammunition and stocked with supplies. John had more men, but he was vulnerable—being below his adversaries on top of the Gates. John tried to launch an offensive. He and his men stormed the Gates, but they were forced back by volleys of missiles. In the meantime, Simon, who occupied the Upper City and a sizable portion of the Lower City, took advantage of John's troops who were now in a crossfire from above and below. They fought back with all their might, repelling those foes on the ground with hand missiles, while engaging those above with war engines, catapults, and stone throwers. These weapons gave them cover and slowed down the javelin and other missile bombardment which rained down on them from the top of the Temple Gates. This repulsive stand prevented the hail of missiles from affecting John's men more severely, but many of those objects killed innocent passersby who simply had come to the Temple to worship and offer sacrifices at the well-known and venerated altar. The sanctuary became splattered with the blood of the sacrifices brought, as well as with the blood of those who brought them. The sacred place was stained with the blood of the innocent, the blessed, and the damned.

Titus assembled some divisions at Cesarea, while sending others to Jerusalem where he intended to rendezvous with other units. Not only did he have his own regiments, but those of his father Vespasian. Vespasian's units—composed of three legions—had seen action under him, defeating the Jews. The Twelfth legion, which had received its trouncing from the Jews when they were commanded by Cestius were on hand, and so were fresh allied troops from Egypt—commanded by Tiberius Alexander, Titus' dependable friend. These two commanders set out toward their objectives. Titus went through Samaria (Hebrew: Shomron), capital of the Northern Kingdom of Israel, on to Gophna, a city previously subdued by Vespasian. From Gophna Titus marched on to the "Valley of the Thorns" near the village of "Saul's Hill" (Gabath Saul), about three-and-a-half miles from Jerusalem. Titus decided to survey and plan approaches to the target area. He set out on his inspection tour with a patrol of approximately 600 specially selected cavalrymen, and trotted off to scout positions and concentrations of Jewish units. Whether he intended to instill fear in the Jews or to test their fighting ability, he was soon convinced that they were not afraid to fight or of Roman fame. The Jewish guerillas jumped Titus' guards, cutting them off from the main body, showering him with arrows and stones. Titus was not wearing his helmet or armor and should have been hit, but the Jews missed him. Acknowledging that he had to fight for his life, Titus wheeled his steed around and guided the mount into the ambushers head-on. He hacked his way through the guerillas, and got back to his main detachment of cavalry. This sample of Jewish capabilities caused Titus to move up to Scopus (Look Out Hill), the very next day. He pitched camp there and had a closer view of the city where the people could have defeated him if only they had not been fighting among themselves. Titus set up another campsite in the Mount of Olives,[34] beyond the Kidron Valley. When the Jews saw the Romans bearing down on them, they stopped fighting among themselves for the first time in a long while. They even attempted to join forces. They were beleaguered and had to consider the ring which the Romans had formed around their city. Roman soldiers began building defenses and strengthening attack command positions. These activities made the Jews hurriedly agree to merge their separate companies. With a tentative truce mutually accepted, some dissidents sat down with their weapons while others stood around their ramparts watching the Romans build assault platforms with logs, towers of timber, and portable parapets that would reach the height of Jerusalem's walls. Resigned to an imminent Roman attack, a company of Jews ran out of the city, fell upon the Roman engineers building the fortifications, and mutilated some of them. The eerie shouts of the attacking Jews consternated the Romans, and the element of surprise startled them even more. Furthermore, these Romans were unarmed. They had once again underestimated the courage of the Jews. The Romans scattered, and would have been wiped out if Titus, again, was not sharp-witted enough to come to their rescue. He and his unit managed to turn back the screaming Jews. The Jews retreated, and reentered their city; but it was not long before they renewed their squabbling.

On the day of Unleavened Bread, or Passover, Eleazar and his men opened the gates of the inner Temple just enough for worshippers to enter. John, a first rate deceiver, used the Passover's importance to the faithful as a means of entrapment. He armed some of his men with concealed weapons and sent them into the Temple disguised as worshippers. Once these hypocrites gained entrance into the Temple, they took off their costumes and pulled out their weapons. Some worshippers panicked. A stampede followed the beatings many persons were receiving from cudgels swung and lowered in their heads and bodies by John's men. Some worshippers were even run through or chopped with swords, others were trampled to death. John and his aides-de-camp agreed to transact a truce with the Zealots (who sought refuge in the inner recesses of the Temple) to end the unprofitable hostilities. An alliance was formed to resist and defeat Simon. The war was once again confined to two main factions—Zealots and Simonites.

During all this time, and lives wasted, Titus left Scopus and drew nearer to his beleaguered target. He selected crackerjack cavalry and infantrymen from among the legions, and put his engineers to work. The engineering corps began changing the surroundings. They chopped down trees and shrubbery to avoid ambush, filled all pot-holes, and knocked down fences and hedges. Even fruit trees were destroyed. Protruding rocks and tree stumps were scraped down to a dead level between Scopus and the monument to Herod. Titus then moved his bivouac closer to Jerusalem. He camped opposite the tower of Psephinus, very close to the area called "Serpents' Pool."

The Hebrew and Jewish forces were now reassembling the rem-nants of their fighting and human resources to determine their strength. To their amazement, their rolls still showed Simon with an army of 10,000 men, excluding his Idumean allies who numbered an additional 5,000 or more. John of Gischala had an army of 6,000 men. But the Zealots of Eleazar turned over an additional 2,400 men to John. The Jews seemed to have felt that with all these resources, it was time to renew the fighting among themselves. The Romans still continued to observe and enjoy the self-destruction of their adver-saries. The fratricidal war entertained the Jewish self-hatred, but it also drew chastisement nearer to them. Sensing their vulnerability, Titus finally decided it was time to take advantage of their disagree-ableness. He advanced some of his scouts toward the walls seeking out breakable sections and vulnerable spots for troop approaches. Titus settled for saturation near the tomb of John Hyrcanus, the for-mer high priest. That ground was lower, and so were the walls. Certain legions were ordered to fell trees and gather timber to build scaffolds. As soon as the Romans started building these earthworks (as they were called), the Jews realized the seriousness of the situa-tion and the precariousness of their position. They began darting out sporadically in desperate attempts to harass the Roman workers. They kept up their attacks day and night, but the Romans contin-ued to work on their assault platforms.

Titus wheeled his battering rams into position and began batter-ing Jerusalem's walls in three different locations. The noise from the areas pounded and sounded like thunder. The walls shook, and some people shuddered, but they did not give. Hebrews and Jews now decided to coordinate their efforts. The enemy was at the door and the hand of destruction was writing on their walls. They started throwing flaming torches at their Roman enemies, desperately trying to keep the battering rams from boring holes in the wall. At the time other platoons of Jews kept running out to attack the crews of the battering rams and the platform. Every time the flame-throwing groups assaulted the Romans, Titus would fight them off with the sentries of the guard patrols. The walls stood stoutly, and the rams had difficulty penetrating them. Adding to the Roman problems was the agility of the flame throwers. These Jews attacked and retreated so consistently and strategically that the Roman engineers backed away from their rams in confusion. The Jews set the battering equipment afire. Titus had to rush forward with some Alexandrian troops to hold the Jews at bay until his cavalry could reinforce them, rout the Jews, and save the entire Roman mechanized detachment from going up in flames.

Another lesson was learned. Titus immediately ordered his engineers to build three towers high enough to overshadow the Jewish ramparts and to expose the enemy to Roman javelin and stone throwers, archers, and artillery plates. This protective covering made them absolutely fire-proof, and too heavy to be overturned by the undernourished Jewish forces. With these towers overshadowing the Jews, and the missile throwers keeping them engaged, the battering rams were free to pound the walls. The Jews were bold and capable, but lacked sound military judgment. They did not boil water and oil to pour on the crews of the battering rams. The Jews allowed "Victor," their nickname for the most famous pounder to keep ramming with such persistence that the wall began to crack. Victor hailed for its continuous victories over supposedly impregnable walls, eventually knocked down a part of the outer wall. With this defensive third wall removed, Titus began to force his troops through the hole, while Victor continued to demolish the rest of this wall. As troops entered, Titus ordered concentration on the other two inner walls. In the meantime, he destroyed the northern part of the city. Fifteen days had been spent attacking and repelling the Judeans. The siege was now beginning to take effect, after another five days had passed, with the third wall partly demolished.

Titus ordered the battering of the second wall. Then he rushed some troops through the breach of the third wall. This narrow opening wended through the commercial district where textile manufacturers, artisans, metal workers, weavers, leather workers, and others had their stores, and workshops. The streets and alleys were narrow in this industrial and commercial center. The Romans were not familiar with the area or the city's layout. They charged in blindly to attack a hidden enemy head first. The Jewish forces allowed the conquerors to barge in until they had enough of them caught like troops in a mountain pass. The Romans were picked off like flies. They became so desperate in their futile attempts to confront the invisible enemy that Titus had to rescue them, bellowing retreat. While they scurried and backed away, he ordered the archers to cover them with arrows. The Jews, who knew the dens and shelters of the district, showed good strategy once more. The hole which Victor had opened for the Romans had become a pathway to death.

This successful withdrawal and attack was quite an accomplishment for the Jewish forces, but lack of food, and the piling up of dead bodies was beginning to take its devastating effect. There had been three days of siege and intermittent combat. On the fourth day, the Jews could no longer resist their enemy as they had in the past. The Romans sensed it and launched an all out offensive. They regained the wall and caused the Jews to back away. Titus took advantage and demolished the remaining northern portion of the third wall. Then he started the same operation on the second wall. After this advance, Titus decided to offer the Jews another opportunity to save their revered city and Temple. He postponed the siege; meanwhile the second wall exposed the Jews' weakening position. There was time to bury the dead, feed the hungry, and patch up the wounded. A simultaneous attempt was made to psyche the Jews into surrendering without further bloodshed.

Soldiers' payday arrived, and the department of disbursement followed Titus' orders. The officers were commanded to pay the men in the field. The poor besieged and exploited Jews, conned by Simon and John, were now able to see real wages paid for fighting a real war. The Jews lined up along the wall and the north side of the Temple. From the old wall they were able to view the Romans, already aware of Titus' intent to impress the impoverished Jewish fighters, parade to the treasury department officers. The Roman soldiers paraded in full battle dress with regalia. Each man collected his wage in a ceremonious manner—one unit at a time, the coins clinking. At the same time, the cavalry marched through in the same processional style. Horses and men were decorated with brass, silver, and gold. Their splendid array was enough to make the Jews look on with envy, and should have prompted them to encourage their leaders to sue for peace. Perhaps John and Simon would not have consented, nevertheless, because they pretended to be unimpressed. The Jews continued to stretch their necks to see the entire spectacle. Despite pre-planning and correct implementation by the treasury department, along with exemplary adherence to military orders, it still took four entire days to pay all legions. The Jews patiently observed the entire pageant, but still could not bring themselves to sue for peace. It was the fifth day after the penetration of Jerusalem. Refusing to waste more time or compassion on these obstinate Jews, Titus decided to assault and subdue the Upper City, and the Temple. Despite the Jews' obstinacy, Titus still hoped they would not compel him to destroy their Temple and crush them without mercy. He went as far as to send Josephus on a good will mission to persuade his countrymen.

Josephus, aware of the defeat that awaited the Jews and the defilement of the Temple that would be inevitable, tried to beseech his coreligionists to come to terms with the Romans. Alert to the uncertainty with which they would receive his implementation, and the hostility they would probably direct toward him, Josephus stayed out of their range. At this safe distance, he went around the wall reminding them in Hebrew of the discipline, strength, and mechanization of the Roman Army. He reminded them of their weaknesses, and pleaded with them to consider the odds against them. The Jews must have been ready to die for they jeered him. Josephus lectured them on past battles, and reminded them of the manner in which God had favored the enemy then and seemed to be helping the enemy again, instead of his "chosen people." With tears rolling down his cheeks, Josephus offered his mother, wife, and family to be sacrificed by the Jews, rather than see the city and Temple destroyed. A few Jews tried to listen, but their wicked and ambitious leaders would not harken. Those few who did pay heed were not allowed to go out to join Josephus. Consequently, the listeners sold their effects and swallowed the coins to prevent thieves from robbing them.

The scarcity of food became more and more ubiquitous in the beleaguered city. Self-centeredness also increased, as morality and shame decreased. "Wives would snatch food from husbands, children from fathers, and most pitiable of all—mothers from the very mouths of their babes."

As the population starved, Titus' well-fed men continued to construct more earthworks for escalation and invasion. They toiled for seventeen days despite continued harassment from Jewish missile-throwers on the ramparts. The war engines were brought into striking position. However, unknown to the Romans, John had made his men hollow out the ground under them, while he propped them up with planks and upright blocks. In the meantime, Simon's men kept harassing the Roman builders to distract people from surrendering. No one was able to enter or leave the city. The scarcity of food increased further and so did the demand. Hunger pains in the bellies of the unfortunate and deaths among the poor increased at the same terrible pace. Entire families perished by starvation.

With the alleys and narrow streets full of deceased senior citizens, half-dead youths and hungry suffering infants, the Romans waited for some sign of distress. Instead, the Jewish leaders arrogantly ignored the offers of peace, and the suffering of their people. Word reached Roman ears that children with swollen stomachs and adults as skinny as walking skeletons ambled along the streets or sat in doorways of stores and around the marketplace.

Still feeling compassion for the civilians, Titus tried to quicken the cessation of hostilities and suffering. With very few trees left, it was difficult for him to build more earthworks. Nevertheless, he ordered timber hewn and carted from ten miles away. In the meantime, Simon began accusing the men who had invited him to Jerusalem. He charged them with treason and sentenced them to immediate execution for conspiring with the Roman enemy. This was, seemingly, his best political solution to this sociomilitary problem. John, who could no longer extort funds from the physically and financially exhausted populace, transferred his greed to the Temple. He stole the holy vessels, the urns, bowls, salvers, and tables, and valuable ornaments sent by Caesar and his wife as offerings decades before John's time. The vessels and jewels were melted down to make transportable ingots. John justified his evil deeds by declaring that those who fought a godly war should be compensated with godly treasures which they justly earned. These wicked leaders showed no concern for their followers, who had reached such depths of hunger and despair that they had begun to eat garbage from the sewers and dumps. In the midst of this holocaust, some refugees made their way to the Roman camps. They informed them that their fellow Jews were dying at such an alarming rate that the poor were thrown over the walls to the tune of some 600,000. Those considered rich were almost as numerous as the poor. There was simply no food for anyone other than the immediate leaders and their cronies of the military echelon.

During 25 of these days of hardship in Jerusalem, the Romans had been building more earthworks. They had left Jerusalem clear of its parks, trees, and shrubbery for about ten miles. The area looked like a battleground. All pleasant scenery and suburban beautification were destroyed, and the earth was bruised from the trampling of feet and the dragging of equipment. The Romans moved up their freshly built earthworks. John and his Zealots looked on from the fortress of Antonia. It was not long before they began running out with torches to once again prevent the battering rams from demolishing other remaining walls. But this time they did not display the courage or determination shown in previous charges. Their lack of vitality made it evident that starvation was beginning to charge them a terrible price. There was also an obvious lack of cohesion and properly thought-out planning. The amount of attackers was insufficient, and their charges too sporadic to really chase the Romans away. Siege machinery was wheeled into place, despite feeble showers of rocks and other missiles, including pieces of iron, hurled by the dying Hebrews and Jews. The Romans pounded harder and harder, but the walls did not give in. Another group of engineer corpsmen pried the blocks with crowbars, but were only able to loosen up four stones.

To everyone's amazement, these same walls which resisted the pounding all day suddenly collapsed by themselves during the night. It seems that John had been busy extorting money and had forgotten to refill the tunnel he had dug under the walls to reach the earthworks and caused them to give way.

Four days after the wall had fallen, the Romans began preparing a commando-like operation. They had been momentarily satisfied when the wall fell, but were not joyous because there was, to their amazement, another wall behind that one. The Romans stealthily climbed to the top of the wall of the tower Antonia, where exhausted Jewish sentinels dozed after a hard day. In the meantime, other Romans were entering the tunnel dug by John to sink the earthworks. When the Jews, on top of the tower, discovered the enemy inside their walls, they ran to the Temple. They were surprised to learn that the Romans had entered the Temple from underground.

With the enemy on their home ground, the Jews and Hebrews made up their minds to take their stand. They stood side by side and fought the Romans toe to toe, like lions of Judah. Both John and Simon's followers found themselves face to face with the Roman foe, in spaces too close for missile launching or spear-throwing. It was a contest with swords. With the hand-to-hand combat and back-to-back support, it was sometimes difficult to determine who was foe or ally, if the uniform was torn off. Finally, Jewish manual skill out-lasted Roman mechanization and brute strength. The Romans began to waiver, and were forced to fall back. They had to be satisfied with reaching and gaining the fortress of Antonia.

At that point, Titus decided to demolish Antonia and use its stones to build a roadway for the entire Roman army to march up to the Temple. He received news that the perpetual ceremonies and sac-rifices were to be discontinued because of the war. Titus did not want religious ceremonies in the Temple to be discontinued on his account. Therefore, he sent Josephus to encourage the Jews to continue their religious devotions and practices. Josephus carried the appeal direct-ly to John and his Zealots. Titus' offer was delivered to the Zealots in Hebrew. Josephus hoped his condescension to meet his fellowmen with words of goodwill would soften John's heart and induce them to save the country and the Temple from disaster. John ignored Josephus' pleas and admonitions. He replied he "could never fear capture, since the city was God's." Josephus narrated a story of an old Jewish king who had voluntarily abandoned the Holy City when he felt his presence as ruler would cause it to fall into enemy hands and possibly be defiled. Josephus even reminded John that as a lead-er, he had not kept the City for God; and had he, "it is no disgrace to change your ways, even at a final moment." Josephus also promised amnesty negotiated with the Romans. When John refused to accept a good peace treaty, Titus himself came out of his tent and attempt-ed to convince John. Titus promised cessation of hostilities, salva-tion of the Temple, and amnesty for those who deserved it. John pretended that the enemy's offer of reconciliation was a sign of weak-ness rather than a proposal with pity, from a position of strength. The die were finally cast.

Roman forces were ordered to combat duty, in full battle array.

With little space in which to maneuver, only the elite corps was chosen for the front lines. The battle was begun during the night, while Jewish sentries and companies were tired and unprepared. Titus stood on the rampart to observe his commanders implementing planned tactical operations.

Romans and Jews dueled man to man, company against company. The Romans competed with one another for medals of honor and promotions. When the fighting subsided, however, there was no victory for either side to claim. During the combat with the Jews and Hebrews, Roman diggers and masons removed the better blocks and rocks from Antonia. As soon as those engineers completed the causeway to the Temple, battering rams were moved up to the western hall of the outer court within the Temple. At the same time other Roman companies battered the wall with their most powerful siege weapons. For six days they pounded the wall without success. Other engineers, who tried to disassemble the base of the Northern Gate, did not succeed either. Crowbars and engines were useless in attempts to dislodge parts of the Gate and the well built wall. When all attempts had failed, the Romans decided to climb the wall. They propped up ladders to reach the balconies and top of the wall. Some assault legions tried to have their standard bearers climb with their pennants and battle standards. The Jews snatched their standards and warded them off. Losing a standard was a dishonor to the combatant and a discredit to the Roman Empire. Consequently, the Romans defended their symbols stoutly. But the Jews grabbed those heroes-to-be as fast as they ascended. The Jews nabbed and clipped them until there were no more to be had.

Observing that trying to save the Temple was costing him men, Titus decided to set the main gates of the Temple afire. The fires blazed all day. The next day, Titus ordered his men to douse and smother the fires and prepare to attack. He conferred with his generals, while the troops fought the fires, and discussed preservation or destruction of the Temple. Some junior officers, in their impetuous youthful age, resolved that this Temple, like any other bastion that harbored and protected soldiers, should be destroyed. Most older and more conservative officers suggested that it be partly preserved, at the very least. The superior officers felt that the building would be a monument their empire could be proud to possess. Even though the young lieutenants exhorted that the Temple might be a "rallying point for the Jews as long as it stood," Titus, a seemingly God-fearing man, declared he "would not wreak vengeance on a building." He did not care if the Jews even used the edifice for military purposes. In addition, Titus said: "under no circumstance did he desire to burn down so magnificent an edifice."

While the Romans doused the fires, most Jews sat down in suspense, hunger, and fatigue. On the following day, these same Jewish fighters returned with their batteries of strength and courage very much recharged. They resumed their attack with renewed vigor, and routed the Romans. Titus had to call out his specially selected cavalrymen to hold off the oncoming Jews. Nevertheless, each time the Romans turned around to head back to their bivouac, the Jews would rush them. Titus realized he was facing a formidable enemy, and reached his breaking point. He decided to commit his entire army to an all-out invasion of the Temple on the following day.

Josephus knew that the Temple was destined to be destroyed on this day: the tenth of the month of Ab.[35] King Nebuchadnezzar of Babylon had burnt the First Temple on this same day of Ab 470 years and 6 months after the Canaanite population had been expelled by King David, the first Jewish king of Jerusalem.

Titus left the battleground for repose from the din and echoes of battle. In his absence a ferocious battle began between the Jews angered by the burning of the Temple Gates, and the Romans attempting to douse the fire. The Romans were chasing the Jews all the way up to the Sanctuary when a Roman soldier, acting on his own wicked initiative and hate for the Jews, grabbed a lighted torch, climbed up on the back of another soldier, and threw the flaming torch through a low golden door. This Dutch-shaped door led to the chambers surrounding the Holy of Holies. As the flames licked up the curtains, furniture, and wooden panels, a lament from the Judeans was heard. Their shrill cries, among the roars and laughter of the Romans, sounded like a lament from Greek criers who professionally scream and bawl at Greek funerals for a fee paid by relatives of the deceased. The Jews had finally realized that their magnificent and revered Temple was about to be consumed by flames, once more. They rushed to save the building or salvage whatever they could.

Titus had been reposing when a soldier rushed into his tent to inform him of the rising inferno in the Temple. Titus dashed out, half dressed, and rushed to order his men to put out the fire. His generals were close behind him, and their aides behind them. When this confused group reached the tumultuous crowd, Titus ordered with shouts and waving of his hands that the fire be put out. Those who came up behind him joined the melee, pretending not to have heard. These officers encouraged the soldiers ahead of them to throw more torches. When the flames began to spread through the Temple's chambers, panic went along with them. A stampede followed and many Romans who enjoyed playing with fire began running in different directions to avoid getting burnt. These arsonists ran into each other as well as the Jews who were now trying to save the Temple. There was pushing and punching and some arsonists, as well as firefighters, got trampled to death. Bodies piled up among the smoldering debris as people lost their balance and fell or got pushed over. Unintentional human sacrifices piled up before the altar, with streams of blood oozing down the stairs of the Holy of Holies. What started as a prank had become a disaster, and Roman lives helped pay the price. Titus, still concerned with saving the Temple, rushed inside with his generals to assess the damages and the possibilities of putting out the fire. The flames still had not reached the Inner Sanctum. Titus called on his troops to douse the fire. Hateful and greedy for the treasures in the Temple, the men ignored his command.

"The adversary hath spread out his hand upon all her pleasant things: for she hath seen that the heathen entered into her sanctuary."[36] The end of Jerusalem had come! It had not come through the forces of nature, but by the impetuosity of a Roman pagan. Titus ran to hold back his men, and an upstart threw a firebrand through the inner gate. Flames shot up through the Inner Sanctum with all its oil, corn, and incenses. Knowing all hopes of saving the Temple were lost, Titus and his generals left the scene. "Thus against the Roman leader's wishes, the Temple was set on fire."[37]

When the Romans saw their commanding officer depart, they knew it was time to start plundering. They rushed in to steal all they could carry, and murdered anyone who tried or might have attempted to stop them. As the fire increased its intensity, the hate turned to bitterness. But now, the Romans had the upper hand. They massacred priests, old men, women, and children, indiscriminately. The roars of the flames were heard mingling with the moans of the helpless citizens, who were whacked and hacked to pieces. War hoops from the legionnaires, and war cries of the Jewish warriors mixed with the screams of the innocent non-combatants, and the clanging of swords. Roman fury was unleashed without a merciful commander. The legionnaires had seen one building go up in flames, with little or no resistance or penalty. They now decided to go for broke. These Romans set other buildings afire by throwing a few more torches into the treasury chambers and other edifices. The remaining portico of the outer court lamentably was included. Here, 6,000 persons, most of them women, children, and the aged, who had sought shelter and refuge perished. Some of these distraught people burnt in the flames, others jumped to their deaths trying to escape the flames. No one is supposed to have survived that inferno. On the other hand, the mischievous rebels who caused all the unnecessary bloodshed and unwarranted deaths were still alive and fighting. They fought their way out of the Temple, it was left to the whim of the conquerors. These Romans marched in with their battle standards, placed them opposite the Eastern Gate, made sacrifices to their gods, and cheered and applauded their Titus as victor of the vanquished Jews.

Simon of Gioras, and John of Gischala sat beaten and deposed.

With their short-term kingdoms lost and their subjects diminished, these petty rulers requested a summit meeting with the opposition. Titus advised his men to keep their tempers under control and all weapons in their shields, while the armistice was under discussion. As conqueror, Titus was allowed to speak first. He asked John and Simon if they were content to see their country devastated and their people suffering because of their disregard for Roman might, and Jewish weakness. "However," said Titus, "if you throw down your arms and give yourselves up, I will grant you your lives." Simon and John responded that they had sworn never to surrender. All they requested, nonetheless, was permission to pass through the Roman lines with their wives and children. In addition, they promised to retire to the desert and leave Jerusalem to the Romans. Titus was angered at the nerve of his defeated enemies. They were making demands which should only be the right of victors, instead of the defeated making demands of their conquerors. Titus told the Jews they would get no further considerations. He warned them to prepare to defend themselves to the best of their ability. He added, that as conqueror, he intended to demand the respect and spoils due him. The remaining Jews were almost prisoners and could exact no terms. He therefore disregarded the Jewish leaders' request.

Shortly thereafter Titus ordered Jerusalem sacked and burned. Having no other escape route nearby, the Jewish militants headed for the King's Palace. They were hotly pursued by the Romans, who had already begun setting the Lower City afire.

Josephus, who had been hit on the head with a rock and knocked unconscious, on a similar mission went back to plead with the obstinate Simon and his crony John. He begged them to surrender, and allow the remaining part of the city of Jerusalem to be saved. He was castigated with more jeers and sneers. Some of the defenders regarded him as a traitor.

To conquer the Upper City, earthworks had to be brought into action. Engineers and other legionnaires worked on these projects for about eighteen days. After completion, these war machines were pushed up to knock down the sacred walls. When the Romans succeeded in demolishing the greater portion of this wall, the remnants of the Jewish forces took to the sewers for cover. They could no longer make a last stand and decided to hide out underground until the Romans had lost track of them and left. But Roman spies knew these underground passages, and told their masters about them.

Having reached the top of this last wall without losing a man, the Romans freely raised their standards of victory and dispersed, soon thereafter, to seek out the escapees. During their mop-up operations, the victors went through the streets, scoured the alleyways of the Upper City and the houses. Then they began burning houses, running their swords through their victims or chopping into them as they ran out of flaming shelters. By night time Jerusalem was lit up like torches in a city on a Roman holiday. The bodies of the dead reminded Titus of the horrors and he ordered a recession. Only armed persons or persons resisting arrest were to be killed. All obedient citizens were to be arrested and imprisoned. Rebels who had turned informants were to be executed. Squealers and militants shared the same fate.

The tallest and healthiest-looking young men were put in detention for embarkation to Rome. They were to be exhibited in the victory procession which went through the Gate of Triumph and the theatres after important campaigns and wars. Prisoners seventeen years of age or older were to be shipped to Egypt in chains if they were not selected for Rome. Quite a few men were trained to become gladiators, subject to fight wild animals and former brothers-in-arms. The total number of Jewish prisoners reached 97,000, and their war dead through starvation, pestilence, suicide, and combat amounted to one million.

The unscathed survivors of the war were, in spite of everything, the principal instigators of its unwarranted beginning, and its unnecessary continuation. Lack of food, discomfort, as well as discomfit, forced John and his followers to come out of hiding. Simon had been in a secret tunnel also. He tried to have experienced dredgers dig along the route of the old tunnels and try to extend them to reach under the wall to make good his escape. Simon's plan failed. He was captured and chained and along with the prisoners prepared for Titus' triumphant march into Rome.

Jerusalem, founded by the Canaanite ruler Melchi-Zedek—a man of peace and righteousness—was now in ruins, and her children in captivity. At the very beginning of Jewish history, the Canaanites had been defeated, and deported from their homeland by the Jews. Their powerful King David had led them to victory. But because of the blood on his hands, Jehovah denied him permission to build the Temple. Now Titus was at liberty to destroy it. Titus commanded his men to gut the city and demolish the Temple. Only a small portion of the wall was left, for sheltering the occupation forces. The highest towers were also left for sentries to observe and report all intruders. The rest of the area was leveled with the ground.

Jewish prisoners of war were used as gladiators in contests with ferocious animals or against their fellow captives in different parts of Syria and Cesarea. At the same time, Titus amused himself and his officers at the prisoners' expense. He took a long rest before he returned to Rome for the reception and laurels.

When Titus returned, the triumphal parade displayed John, Simon, and seven hundred more Jewish prisoners of the Judean War. They were weighed down with gold and silver wares, urns, menorahs, jewels, precious stones, ivory, Babylonian art pieces, tapestries, and other gifts which had been donated to the God of Israel through His Temple.

While Titus celebrated his victories, Lucius Bassus was sent to assume command of the remaining cities in the land of Judea. Bassus captured Herodium, where the remains of King Herod were buried, and quickly moved on to conquer Machaerus in 71 B.C.E.[38] This ancient stronghold east of the Dead Sea was fortified by Alexander Yannai, and destroyed by Gabinus (57-54 B.C.E.). Machaerus was rebuilt by Herod the Great to become a citadel and prison. The people of this citadel surrendered without bloodshed. The Romans could not satisfy their thirst for Jewish blood. Bassus obeyed Vespasian's orders and leased farmland to persons interested in farming. Eight hundred veterans from the wars settled on the land provided for Roman servants. Jews were ordered to pay taxes of two drachmas (basic Greek currency equal to 100 lepta or the exchange for one U.S. dollar) a head, each year. This was the tithe paid to the Temple before the wars. Bassus did not live long.

When Bassus died a natural death, Flavius Silva was made commander of the remaining territories of Judea—Masada being the first to have rebelled, now the last to be controlled.

Masada, a Zealot center, was under control of Eleazar. He was a descendant of an original Zealot. Eleazar ben Jair took command after Manahem was stabbed. He held Masada for seven years. Masada was built on a tremendous isolated rock surrounded by deep gorges. This fort could only be approached from two areas. It could be reached by ascending a winding road on the east, called the Snake Path, or the less difficult western side of the craggy mass. On the eastern side of Masada was the Dead Sea, and on the west a very steep path with seesaw curves and bumps. This fortress was erected by the High Priest Jonathan, a brother of Judas Maccabaeus, and named Masada. It was fortified by Alexander Yannai, rather than Jonathan, as it was previously thought. In Herod's time, the fortress was reinforced for impregnability. Herod encased the entire three-quarter mile of Masada's cragged peak with a wall of white stones at eighteen feet high and twelve feet wide. Along the walls were thirty-seven towers, each seventy-five feet high. They contained luxurious dwellings approached from a patio inside the wall. There were four more towers, each ninety feet high.

Herod's palace was built on the western slope beneath the walls protecting the crest looking toward the north. The palace had expensively decorated and well-furnished rooms and baths. Herod made an advanced irrigational system with reservoirs to keep an adequate supply of water and repositories to store large quantities of food to withstand a siege. Herod also cut a passage with a secret entrance from the palace to the crest. Persons using the passage could not be seen from the outside. The ruler was able to ascend and descend the summit without being a target for his enemies. Herod had so much stored there that when the Romans were ousted from Masada by Eleazar in 66 B.C.E., there remained a substantial amount of expensive food, corn, oil, seeds, dates, and dried fruits of different varieties. There was also wine and other beverages, all as edible and potable as the day they were stored. These supplies had been put there one hundred years earlier, and yet there was still a ten-year supply on hand. The climate produced by the high altitude of the area is considered the cause for their preservation. Herod had also fortified Masada during his Idumean reign. Herod feared Hasmoneans and kept enough weapons at Masada to adequately supply an army of 10,000 troops. There was also a large quantity of pig iron, brass, lead, and tools. Herod had Masada fortified like he had done Machaerus, because of the people's admiration for the Hasmoneans. He was also fearful of the Romans.

Antigonus caused Herod to run Rome, when the Parthians made Antigonus king, in 40 B.C.E. It was during his exile in Rome that Herod was appointed King of Judea by the Roman Senate. In the year 37 B.C.E. Herod returned to capture Judea, with the assistance of an overwhelming Roman force. After putting Antigonus to death, Herod married the granddaughter of the high priest Hyrcamus, Marianne, an Hasmonean. Herod obviously married her for political conveniences. When political conspiracies were suspected, Herod murdered his brother-in-law Aristobulus III, the last high priest. Then, for insurance he killed Marianne, their sons Alexander and Aristobulus, and in the end, his firstborn, Antipater.[39] Herod was also said to have been afraid of the Queen of Egypt—Cleopatra. She liked Judea, and wished to rule it as well. Like her predecessors, who had ruled the two Egypts, Cleopatra longed for the double crown of two lands. She begged Anthony, on more than one occasion, to get rid of Herod and to make her ruler of the Jewish kingdom.

Despite the provisions in food and armament at Masada, the Roman commander—Flavius Silva—managed to mount an earthwork near the White Cliff on Masada's western side. This area stretched out about 450 feet below the top, and could be a bivouac for an enemy. After surveying the Cliff, Silva built a wall around Masada, then dumped enough rocks and dirt to build up a solid ridge which reached 300 feet high. On the peak, Silva used huge stones to make a stoneway of 75 feet long, and just as wide. Then he built a 90-foot tower, which was covered with iron plates. Battering rams were moved into position, and quick-fire throwers were put into action.

The Jews were forced to withdraw from their ramparts the minute these engines were put into action. The battering rams kept ham-

mering at Masada's wall continually. Finally, the wall gave way and
the crest was exposed to the enemy. When the Romans attempted to
rush through the breach, they discovered a wooden wall built behind
it. This second wall was made of wooden beams crossed vertically,
and horizontally aligned to hold each other in place. The cross ties
were about twelve feet apart, with dirt packed between them to form
a bumper with a cushion. When battering rams pounded the beams,
they gave way instead of cracking like rocks or chipping like stones.
Since the wooden beams absorbed the pounding with resilience, Silva
considered setting them afire. With firebrands tossed at the beams,
it was not long before they caught fire. But a north wind soon blew
up with enough force to direct the heat and flames toward the
Romans. These Romans were fearful of their equipment catching fire,
and their Jewish rivals should have noticed that and attacked them.
But they started rejoicing instead. The wind suddenly changed to the
south, as if it had been guided by an omnipotent being. The force of
the wind seemed to show that these Jews were no longer "God's chosen." Masada's wooden beams were engulfed in flames. The Roman
enemy did not have to do battle any longer that night.

The next morning the Romans prepared for the final assault and
mop-up operations inside the compound. All through the night,
Roman sentries had kept vigil to prevent any Jews from leaving
Masada. But while the Romans planned their invasion, the Jews
planned their escape from Roman slaughter or enslavement. Knowing
that death was the only alternative to enslavement, Eleazar unfold-
ed his plan to deprive the Romans of their cheap glory. He explained
to the warriors how the Romans would inevitably defeat them in the
morning. Their wives and children would be captured. The Romans
would rape the wives and abuse the children. Word had reached
Masada relating the woes and humiliations suffered by captured
Jews, and the pleasures derived by the Romans who subjugated
them. Eleazar tried to convince his followers, in a most solemn, and
unvacillating manner. He said:

> Consider all those Jews in our own land who went to war with
> Rome. They had everything that could fire them with hopes of vic-
> tory! Arms, battlements, impregnable fortresses, and a spirit afraid
> of no dangers in the cause of liberty. Yet these were effective but
> for a brief season. After buoying us with hopes, they proved only
> the beginning of great disasters. Those men who fell in battle may
> be deemed lucky for they died defending liberty, not betraying it.

Eleazar told his congregation how hope had vanished, "So let us hasten to die honorably." He also told them to remember Masada was
the first to rebel against Rome, and now the last to refuse the Roman
offer to spare their lives. "Is anyone so blind that he will not see how

furious they will be when they take us alive?" Eleazar was not allowed to conclude his talk. Those Jews who had been undecided became overwhelmed with his description of the horrors that awaited them. Many warriors rushed to be among the first to show courage and be among the first to die rather than the last to stay alive and be enslaved. Men hugged their wives and children, kissing them with tears in their eyes. Then ten men were selected to be executioners of the plan. They killed all accounted for except themselves. Stores, wares, arms, and all other personal effects were set on fire. The husbands then embraced their wives lying beside their dead bodies. The warriors then cut their own throats, or had them cut for them. Lots were cast to decide the fate of the last ten, designating one to slit the throat of the others, and finally his own. They plunged their swords into their bellies, and fell beside their families. Men, women, and children amounted to 960 souls.

Eleazar and his Zealots perished believing they had all committed themselves, as promised. But, as fate usually has it, one old woman related to Eleazar did not kill herself. She escaped with five children.

At daybreak, the Romans charged for the final assault on the helpless Jews. Their assault was met with unexpected silence. No warriors met them, and the booty they anticipated was burning. There was utter disappointment for the Roman plunderers. Their sadistic appetites for Jewish blood were not satiated. One of them shouted to determine if anyone was alive, to explain this scene of consternation. The old lady heard their cries, and came out of hiding in the caverns. Josephus said she revealed how the defenders of Masada had cheated the conquerors through death by their own hands. Families lying in rows, with husbands clutching their wives, revealed the courage of a people brave enough to prefer death, by their own swords, rather than enslavement by others. So ended the Roman-Judean wars on May 2, 73 A.D. and thence began the motto *"Judea Capta!"* ("Judea captured!")[40]

With Judea captured, the temple built and rebuilt was now destroyed. This was the cost and effort put into the building of this temple built and overhauled—when necessary—to symbolize the determination to worship and continue to have faith in the Almighty God.

THE FIRST TEMPLE

In the fourth year of the reign of King Solomon, he began to build the Temple of the Lord. It was completed in the eleventh month of the Hebrew Year.

David fought many wars, killed many brave men, and even sent Uriah, one of his commanders, to the battlefront to be killed. He was denied the honor of building the Temple, because of Uriah's blood on his hands. After Uriah died, David took Uriah's wife Bathesheba to his bed. David took Bathesheba as his wife, and begat Solomon.

Solomon, the son of David and Bathesheba, was sent to Hiram, king of Tyre, as soon as he was appointed to build the Temple. Hiram had been David's friend in battle, and in peace. Therefore, Solomon asked Hiram to be his ally also. The king of Tyre sent Solomon 80,000 apprentices to be bearers of burden and hewers of log and stone. Another 70,000 men were sent as fellow craftsmen, while 3,303 master masons supervised. To plan and implement engineering and technical structural elevations, Solomon requested a man. Hiram sent Solomon the son of a woman famous as a daughter of Dan. This man's father had been a master metallurgist, carpenter, cabinetmaker, decorator, and mason. The man's mother was a widow, who named him Hiram Abiff, meaning "exalted brother."

The widow's son was filled with knowledge inherited from his deceased father, who was descended from the tribe of Naph'ta-li. Hiram Abiff cast two pillars of brass 18 cubits high (between 27 and 33 feet) and 12 cubits in diameter.[41] A chapiter or capital of molten brass was set on top of each column. After the foundations were laid, and the walls raised, the chapiters were decorated with brass wreaths and pomegranates. These pillars were raised with hollow centers. Those spaces were made to conceal documents and records. The right pillar, with its repository, was named Ja'chin and the left pillar, Boaz. On top of these two columns were brass lilies near the wreaths. They supported the front porch.

The Holy of Holies was made of cedar from the forests of Lebanon. The doors were carved with knops, knoblike ornaments, and blooming flowers. There was no stone visible in the Holy of Holies. And no hammering or clinging of metal was heard therein. Everything was measured and cut before being brought to the Temple. An oracle was prepared for the Ark of the Covenant. The altar was made of cedar and overlaid with gold. Chains of gold encasement were stretched across the entrance to the oracle. Within the oracle one could see two cherubim made of olive wood. Each cherub was ten cubits high. Their wings measured five cubits from the uttermost part to the innermost arch, while the longer part measured ten cubits. These also were overlaid with gold. All the walls within and without the First Temple were decorated with carved figures of cherubim and palm trees. On the floors, people walked on the cedar inlaid with gold within and without the oracle and the chamber that led to it. Doors, lintel, and jambs at the entrance were made of olive trees. On the ceilings there were heavy cedar beams.

Solomon had the inner court built with three rows of hewed stones.[42] He ordered Hiram to build a bowl ten cubits from one brim to the other. This basin had knops which had been cast in two rows to support and separate the worshippers when they washed in the bowl. Under the washbasin there were twelve oxen. Three bovines looked to the east, three to the west, three looked to the south, and the other three faced the north. This washbowl, or laver, was a hands-breath thick and "the brim thereof was wrought like the brim of a cup." It was also arranged to accommodate 2,000 bathers or worshippers; it was also decorated with lilies. Between the oxen there were ledges with lions and cherubim. Every base, under the ledges, had four brazen wheels with brass plates. The four corners had undersetters beneath the laver. There were also ten brass lavers with forty baths. Five bases were on the right side of the Temple, and five on the left. And the big basin with water, for the worshippers to wash, stood at the entrance to the holy chamber.

Hiram made the ladles and the basins used to dip and carry water for cleansing the hands and feet before passing into the chamber for worship. Those vessels were made of brass, but the table which held the shewbread[43] and the altar were made of gold. The incense burners, five candlesticks which stood on the right side and five on the left before the oracle, were all made of gold. Even the hinges of the door to the Holy of Holies were made of gold. The Ark of the Covenant was later brought in, with the two tablets of stone placed therein by Moses.

These were some of the artifacts, valuables, and architectural extravagances that Solomon provided for the First Temple of God.

THE SECOND TEMPLE

The First Temple was destroyed by Nebuchadnezzar in 585 B.C.E. It was rebuilt in 538–515 B.C.E. Major reconstructions were undertaken by Simon the Just, Judah the Maccabee, Simon the Hasmonean, and Herod the Great.

Herod is said to have built an extraordinary wall, which included the famous Western Wall. Herod undertook a more thorough reconstruction effort than any of his predecessors. His Herodian wall, surrounding the Temple hill, measured 913 by 1,515 by 1,050 feet. The enclosed area was developed by leveling the gap between the Tyropoeion and Kidron valleys. The Temple could be approached by different gates and reached by crossing four bridges. One bridge was located to the east, and the other to the west.

The Temple stood on Mount Moriah in Jerusalem, the Holy City. It was guarded by three well built walls which prevented approach. Therefore, only one battlement was erected there. The city was built on two hills opposite each other. The hills were divided by a hidden valley between them. On the higher hill was the Upper City, with a higher and steeper ridge. That sector was called Upper Agora or "marketplace." The other hill was called Acra, or citadel, where the Lower City was located. These two cities were made impassable by deep gorges and cliffs. There were three walls protecting Jerusalem and the Temple. The first wall was the oldest—built by King Solomon and his father David. The second wall encircled the northern part of the city. The third wall, with thirty-foot towers, was built by Marcus Julius, also called Herod Agrippa I (10 B.C.E.–44 C.E.). These towers were wide and high. The stones used for the towers were chipped and placed together with the same master masonry used in perfecting the stones sent to build the Temple. There were ninety of these towers, with a hundred yards between each of them. The towers surrounded the court with its internal porticoes, which were connected on the northwest by the Tower of Antonia. This royal portico was the largest of them all. It formed a basilica where money changers and merchants gathered to transact their business.

At the third wall was another important tower: Psephinus, with its octagonal shape. This tower was 105 feet high, allowing sightseers to view Arabia and the borders of Judea, all the way to the sea. The more recently erected towers were Hippicus—120 feet high—built and named by Herod for his friend. Phasel was another tower named for Herod's brother. A third tower was named for Herod's wife Marianne; her castle-tower was more extravagantly built and luxuriously furnished and decorated than any of the others.

Next to these towers was the king's palace. This structure was astonishingly beautiful and splendidly decorated. This palace-tower was completely surrounded by a 45-foot high wall. There were huge dining rooms with high ceilings, and bedrooms enough to sleep 100 guests.

The Women's Court in the east connected through the Nicanor Gate with the Court of the Israelites. It was adjacent to the Court of the Priests and the area of the general congregation arriving for holiday and holy-day worship. The Court of the Priests surrounded the Temple. It could only be entered by laity on occasions of sacrificial preparations or purposes. This court contained the chamber with the main altar. The main altar was located in the middle of the chambers used for rituals pertaining to sacrifices, ablutions, benedictions, and thanksgiving. A chamber of chipped stones was located nearby for the seating of the Sanhedrin and their court. The priests' quarters were also situated there.

The priests serving in the Temple were divided into 24 shifts. Levites assisted the priests. Musicians, cantors, and other assistants all had quarters. Doorkeepers, sweepers, and other maintenance personnel (*Nethanim*) also were housed there along with the *Shammim*[44] and Temple beadles. Some laymen assisted the priests in collecting first fruits from harvests, animals without blemishes or defects for slaughter or sacrifice, and ornaments to be blessed. There were also financial officers who collected tithes.

Built on solid rocks and soil at the top of the hill, the Temple was surrounded by steep cliffs. The foundations of the Temple were laid and raised from a depth of 450 feet or more. Sixty-foot blocks were laid at the base. Porticoes were built in double rows, supported by columns thirty-seven-and-a-half feet high and cut from a solid slab of pure white marble. The ceilings were paneled with cedar from Lebanon like the original Temple. The body was constructed with white stones and adorned with gold, under a roof of cedar wood. This Herodian-reconstructed Temple had nine gates leading to the inner chambers. They were completely encased in gold and silver, as were their lintels and jambs. A gate outside the sanctuary was made of Corinthian bronze, and said to be far more valuable than any gate plated or encased in silver or gold.

The Temple was located in the center of the City of Jerusalem. Twelve steps led to the entrance. The first gate was overlaid with gold, and so were the walls of the room it enclosed. Above that door hung golden vines and bunches of grapes as big as a five-foot man. There was a curtain made of Babylonian tapestry, embroidered with blue, scarlet, and purple linen. The blue represented the earth, the scarlet stood for fire, and the purple symbolized the sea.

The Sanctum Sanctorum (Hebrew, Quodesh) was 90 feet high and 90 feet long. It was empty and entered only by the high priest on the Day of Atonement. The lampstand, a table, and an incense altar were in the main chamber. A seven-lamp menorah represented the seven planets. The twelve signs of the Zodiac were represented by twelve unleavened loaves set on the table, symbolizing the months of the year. Thirteen fragrant spices gathered from Ophir and other lands expressed man's feeling that all things came from God and therefore belonged to God. In the interior of the Temple, there was a 30-foot section hidden from view by a curtain. It was an empty cubicle with windows, but was considered untouchable, inviolable, and unapproachable. It was venerated as the inner part of the Holy of Holies. There was an altar of brass twenty cubits wide and ten cubits high in the chamber for the congregants.

The foundation laid by King Solomon lasted until the second year of Vespasian's reign (A.D. 69–A.D. 79), 1,130 years, 7 months, and 15 days. From the date of its reconstruction, in the second year of the reign of Cyrus of Persia up to its destruction under Vespasian, the Temple had lasted 639 years and 45 days.

Titus destroyed the Temple 1,179 years after it had been demolished by the Babylonians. "From the city's first foundation until its final overthrow, the time elapsed was 2,177 years."[45]

NOTES

1. The Greeks called him Zeus and the Romans called him Jupiter and Jove, meaning King of the Gods.
2. Ish-Kishner Sulamith. *Jews to Remember* (New York: Hebrew Publishing Company, 1941), pp. 25-30.
3. Ibid.
4. *Golah*: Hebrew meaning exile, term applied collectively to the Jewish people outside Palestine (originally applied to Hebrews and Jews of Babylonia. *Tephutzot*: scattering of Jews to different places.
5. Series of verse were prophecies in Greek hexameters of pagan, Jewish, and Christian authorship, from second to fourth century B.C.E.
6. The word "ghetto" is a hybrid derived from the Italian *ghetto*, meaning to raise an uproar and *getto* meaning to cast metal. The Jewish ghetto was situated near the foundry, or hovel-ghetto area, of Venice, where Jews were forced to live in 1517.
7. Attilio Milano. (Firenze, Italia: Biblioteca Historica Italo-Judaica, 1954).
8. Attilio Milano. (Firenze, Italia: Biblioteca Historica Italo-Judaica, 1954).
9. Attilio Milano. *Storia degli Ebrei in Italia*, Giulio Einaudi Editore (Torino, Italia, 19-727, 1963).
Cecil Roth. *The History of the Jews of Italy* (Philadelphia, 1946).
Judah Pilch. *The Jewish Catastrophe In Europe* (New York: Crown Publishers—The American Association for Jewish Education, 1968).
Renzo De Felice. *Storia degli Ebrei italiani sotto il Fascismo* (Torino, Italia: Einaudi, 1961).
Umberto Tassuto. *Gli Ebrei a Firenze nell'eta' del Rinascimento* (Firenze, 1918).
10. Alexandria between Torino and Geneva.
11. Arnold J. Toynbee. *A Study of History* (London: Oxford University Press, 1961). vol. 12 Reconsiderations. pp. 499-500.
12. Caligula was given the nickname "Little Boot" by soldiers whom his father Germanicus had commanded as head of the Rhine Army. As a little boy, Caligula always wore military boots around the camp.
13. Agrippa I had ruled Caesarea, an annex of the province of Syria. He died suddenly while attending the games in Caesarea.
14. Josephus. *Antiquities of the Jews*, p. 593.
15. Encyclopaedia Britannica, 1968 ed. (Chicago University Press). vol.3 Josephus. *Antiquities of the Jews*, p. 359.
16. Samaritans of Sabastiya—Herod renamed it Sebaste (Greek for "Augusta") in honor of Augustus Caesar. The standard Jewish Encyclopedia p. 1646.
17. *Shiva* (Hebrew seven): The seven days of mourning following the burial of a relative. During this period, all ordinary labor is suspended. The mourners sit on low stools or the floor unshod; sexual intercourse is forbidden, and prayers are said.
18. Sicarii: "The knife men," from Latin Sicae. They carried daggers

beneath their garments, murdered political rivals or opponents desiring peace with the Romans. The best-known leaders were Menahem ben Jair and Eleazer Ben Jair—73 C.E.

19. Sadducee: member of a Jewish sect flourishing between first century B.C. and first century A.D.
20. Josephus. *The Works of Josephus*.
21. Alfred H. Tamarin. *Revolt in Judea: The Road to Masada* (New York: Galahad Books, 1968), p. 24.
22. The Samaritans (Hebrew *Shomronim*: in the Talmud *Kutin*) were people with their capital at Samaria. Originally called themselves *Bene Yisrael* or *Shomerim* (the "keepers" of the law). They were descended from the tribes of Ephraim and Manasseh (II Chronicles 34:9; Jeremiah 41:5) with an admixture of non-Israelite colonists (II Kings 17:24-41).
23. Herod had built the fort at Masada three years earlier. Alfred H. Tamarin, *Revolt in Judea: The Road to Masada* (New York: Galahad Books, 1968), p. 45.
24. Tamarin, *Revolt in Judea*.
25. Tamarin, *Revolt in Judea*, p. 45.
26. The eighth day is *Shemini Atzeret*, followed by *Simhat Torah*. The festival is also known as *hag* or hag—*ha-asiph*, "the festival of harvest."
27. Tamarin. *Revolt In Judea*, p. 57
28. Josephus. *Antiquities of the Jews*.
29. Gamal meant camel in the language of the region.
30. Gischala is the Arab village of El Jish, with a population of approximately 1,400 souls, mostly Maronites. It is five miles north of Safed, where one sees the ruins of two synagogues.
31. A possible imitation of these pillars is said to have been discovered in a Canaanite shrine excavated at Hazor. Standard *Jewish Encyclopedia*. p. 1007. However, the real parallel can be seen at the Grand Lodge of Luxor, in Egypt.
32. In the meantime a new militant emerged among the Jews. His name was Simon.
33. Josephus. *The Works of Josephus*, p. 791.
34. The Mount of Olives has three summits, one is occupied by the village of et-Tur (ancient Beth Phagi), the second by Victoria Augusta Hospice, and the third by Hebrew University. Mount Scopus, 2,684 feet, was called "The Ascent of the Olives."
35. Ab or Av: fifth month of the Hebrew religious calendar year, and eleventh of the civil year. Ab lasts thirty days and falls in July-August. Ab Ninth (*Tishal be-Av*) is a fast day to commemorate the destruction of the First and Second Temples. Av Fifteenth was a day of rejoicement during Second Temple times. Av Ninth is also a fast day, traditionally the anniversary of the fall of Betar (the last stronghold, 135 B.C.E.,) the expulsion from Spain in 1492, the memory of Bar Kokhbah, and other holocausts. The Book of Lamentations is read during the services.
36. The Lamentations of Jeremiah: Chapter 1:10.

37. Tamarin. *Revolt in Judea.*

38. *The Standard Jewish Encyclopedia.* (New York: Doubleday, 1959). p. 1278. Cicil Roth, Editor.

39. *The New Columbia Encyclopedia*, (New York: Columbia University Press, 1975) p. 890.

40. Josephus. *History of the Jewish War*, pp. 75-79.

41. A cubit: an ancient measure of about eighteen to twenty-two inches. Originally, the length of the arm from the tip of the middle finger to the elbow.

42. I Kings: 6:6.

43. Shewbread: unleavened bread displayed in the Temple. It was placed on the table, but it was not eaten by worshippers.

44. *Shammash*: Hebrew, meaning one serves, a synagogue beadle.

45. Tamarin. *Revolt in Judea*, p. 229.

CHAPTER 7

DIASPORA

Dispersion followed the destruction after the Romans destroyed the Temple and killed most of its instructors or priests. The black-skinned members of the priesthood ran back to Egypt where they had gained the knowledge of religion and the key to the mystery system. Others ran to Tehemu, or Libya, where masonry was practiced, and eastern Cyrenaica, Mumidia, or Algiers, and Tunisia.

The light, knowledge, still remained in the East. The high priests sensed the danger and cruelty of the invaders from the north, and decided to leave some of the secrets for the remaining black Hebrews in existence. They put the mysteries and their key into hieroglyphic, or picture writing, symbolic, and Phoenician script. Some historical data was also put into hieroglyphics.

The Egyptians had learned from the Cushites, and the Greeks had defeated the Egyptians and learned from them. Now the Romans had learned from the Greeks and were ready to be defeated by the Vandals who were more backward than they. The world sat on an edge of darkness penetrating from the dark north, where ignorance and cruelty flourished.

EUROPEANS STUDY AFRICA

Judaism and Christianity developed within Africa's borders. Around the world scholars agreed that historians' investigations would be dignified and truthful about worthy parts of man's relentless effort to discover whatever may be discoverable concerning the past, in order to understand his present and shape his future. Studies were therefore to have as their function, the responsibility of transmitting knowledge of the past as the memory or history of nations, the perpetuation of their deeds, their traditions, and even their mistakes. History was to show the aspirations and ideals of a nation even if that nation was no longer powerful enough to control news medias which disseminate historic information.

Around 1786, Constantin Francois de Cheeseboeuf Volney wrote a scholarly work on Africa. His paper, "Ruins of Empires," amazed European scholars and Americans—who were hardly recognized as a cultured entity at the time—to such an extent that it was soon translated from French to English. Volney stated that in Africa there once existed a people, now forgotten, who made discoveries in the arts and sciences while others were yet barbarians. He also declared that Africans were a race of men with sable skins and frizzled hair who founded, "on the study of the laws of Nature, those civil and religious systems which still govern the universe."[1] When the book was sent to the United States of North America, the translator tried to appease his racist countrymen by omitting these words. Some years later, Volney learned English and reread his book. He discovered that "truth had been surrendered to prejudice." Volney immediately requested that all future editions "contain the suppressed words or else the entire work be taken out of print."[2] A people without history had attempted to discredit those who civilized their progenitors by omission of facts.

Volney derived a certain pleasure from correcting an error, exposing a myth about black inferiority, and eliminating from the annals of history a most faulty hypothesis. His achievement became most valuable in clearing the ground for more accurate accounts in the dissemination of facts, which should have been the translator's original objective.

George Wells Parker, who also saw the Americans and some others trying to build cultural credits at the expense of Ethiopia and other ancient civilizations, proved that the Falashim and Ethiopia existed long before Europe and even Egypt. Parker explained Ethiopia's holding of the stage at the dawn of civilization. He showed how Ethiopia played the first role that "wooed civilization and gave birth to nations." Parker further declared: "Egypt was [Ethiopia's] firstborn and to Ur of the Chaldees she sent sons and daughters who scattered empires in Asia." It was further stated that Ethiopia built Phoenicia beside the beautiful Mediterranean, and in ships with purple sails sent her children to the blue Aegean to found Greece. Parker referred to Ethiopia as the marvel of men and the queen of history. "Troy was here," said he, "a burning city from whence swarthy Aeneas fled to later set the ferment for Rome." According to Parker, Ethiopia's admirable spirit called to Arabia, and out of the mystic deserts surged the black soldiers of Islam, who welded the world into a new empire that sang their songs of love from the shores of North Africa into the vales of Andalucia in Spain. Parker also documented contributions of Ethiopia in the areas of religion, art, literature, science, and civilization.

It is difficult for truth to overtake falsehood—paid for with large sums of money and academic accolades—even if the truth is based on facts and supported with indisputable evidence.

So-called scholars, and pseudohistorians who prefer to criticize "Black Jews and Black Muslims"—as Americans love to classify Africans—rather than educate them and encourage them to be more committed to their God and their country are playing with hatred. Hatred is fire, and the blacks have no more to lose. It might be better for all concerned if the facts are printed. Unity would be promoted through respect based on knowledge of the real contributors to what is called modern civilization. Promotion of bigotry through omission of historical facts and popularization of falsehood to justify non-existent racial superiority, only foments more dissension among Africans and Europeans. The establishment of a state in a part of Africa, and the usurpation of her culture will never legitimize any people's religious origin or cultural claims unless the invaders identify with an undeniable African origin. For if a hen has chickens in an oven, no claims under the sun will ever make them bread. And the Bible has shown: "The Gentiles are fearer"!

The Greeks who translated several Ethiopian documents revered and respected Africa, despite the fact that they later tried to burn all traces of those facts. Homer, nonetheless (born circa eighth century B.C.E.), Greek epic poet, wrote in his Iliad:

The sire of gods and all the ethereal train,
On the warm limit of the farthest main,
Now mix with mortals, nor disdain to grace
The feasts of Ethiopia's blameless race.

Herodotus, another famous Greek wrote ca. 404–CA. 420 B.C.E. of Ethiopians: " a wonderful race and the Hebrews paid them lofty tribute in their scriptures."

American historians, particularly many of Jewish origin, go to great lengths to prove that Africans were slaves on ancient monuments, and in ancient times. They often refer to Ralph Bunche, George Carver or other Americans, who have contributed much more as descendants of former slaves than they. Some Americans pay Uncle Toms to write about selected parts of history. One writer was paid handsomely to write a black "Roots." However, he never undertook to write a white "Roots," and neither did his masters. It should be common knowledge among those who call themselves historians that losing warriors were enslaved by their conquerors in Africa long before Europe became civilized or even recognized. In Africa, however, the slave was not chattel and could become free through accomplishment or consideration or passing of time. It should also be common knowledge to educated people that the Romans enslaved the Greeks who educated them, and the Greeks continued to educate the Romans even under bondage. It should also be well-known that the Romans only enslaved the Hebrews after the Egyptians had already enslaved and educated them. The Moors, from North Africa and Mauretania, enslaved the Christians after the battle of Guadalete in 711. Other Christians were under Moorish domination from the eighth century, when the Moors crossed the Straits of Gibraltar into Spain. The Christians, in turn, enslaved the Moors and Jews during the Reconquest. Many Jews were expelled from Spain in 1492 during the Spanish Inquisition. These Jews in turn financed many slave operations in Latin America and the United States.[3] As early as 1501, nine years after Columbus had come to America, slaves were transported by traders with the help of black navigators to Hispaniola (called Haiti and the Dominican Republic today). "These slaves were white—whether from Spain or North Africa—more often than black; for the black slaves, it was early found, were turbulent and hard to tame." Davidson, a legitimate white historian, discredited the old legend of African docility. Davidson wrote it was further stated by Ovando that during 1503, the Spanish governor of Hispaniola in his complaint to the Spanish Court declared "that fugitive Negro slaves among the Indians were teaching disobedience, and that it was impossible to recapture them."[4] Davidson also said 40 white girls were brought to be used in brothels in Santo Domingo.

Regardless of what so-called historians have depicted or may depict to prove racial superiority, indisputable evidence will emerge in pictures and writings with unquestionable evidence to prove that blacks were not the only slaves even in the United States. And the word "slave" comes from Slavonia, where it was used to describe the Croats, Serbs, and other Caucasians enslaved by their slavic counterparts even in Yugoslavia. On the other hand, we find historians such as Sir William Matthew Flinders Petrie, and some authentic historians using the word "Chemi" to describe Africans. They use it to mean Ethiopia, Ham, or Cham, "the land of the black people."

Edouard Henri Naville (1884–1926) stated in his report to the Royal Anthropological Institute, "(Egypt) belongs to a nation formed by an indigenous stock, of African origin, among which, settled conquerors coming from Arabia, from the same starting point as the Chaldeans." It was also emphasized at the conference that there existed "a certain similarity between Egypt and Babylon. The foreign element was not Semitic." The presentation concluded, "They belonged, like the natives, to the Hamitic stock."[5]

The purpose and scope of history has become more expansive and significant over the past decades. History now encompasses wars, economics, demography, politics, education, philosophy, and even religion. As a result, it is necessary to bear in mind the relationship between the purpose of a presentation and the sort of acceptance or rejection it might receive from those who review it. Assumptions and conclusions by different critics and literary analysts have caused this researcher to provide readers with extensive documentation on the origin and dispersion of the sons of Noah: Ham, Shem, and Japheth.

Naville explored the route of the Exodus for conformation or denial of historical statements written exaltedly in the Bible. Naville found the route existent, despite claims of inconsistencies by scholars, and others. He authenticated biblical references, and tried to eliminate doubt by copying and interpreting original inscriptions. Naville wrote: "Our tablet[6] says, in fact, that elephants were brought to the king from the coast of Africa."[7] The king of mention was Ptolemy Philadelphos, who sent several expeditions to that land for acquisition of goods that met his taste. He also used elephants for foreign exports in his trade encouraged along the Red Sea. Naville followed the route shown in the Bible, and found the Bitter Lakes. These lakes were mentioned by Strabo and Pliny in their historical accounts over a thousand years before Naville's existence. Naville also found "the canal near Bubastis, as we know from Herodotus," and the tablet of King Ptolemy was discovered: "Near the *naos* of Ismailiah was found the great tablet of Philadelphos, of which it is said in the inscription that the king ordered it to be erected before his father *Tum*, the great god of Succoth."

Succoth is a city east of the Jordan, in Palestine near the Jabbok River. It is the place where Jacob paused for a respite on his return to his native land. Gideon passed through Succoth in pursuit of the Midianites. It is the modern Tell Deir Alla of Jordan. Succoth is mentioned in Genesis 33: 17-20. Succoth is also the name of the "Feast of the Harvest." The three most ancient festivals of the Hebrews are *Succoth, Shabuoth,* and *Pesach,* or Passover.[8] The Europeans have difficulty pronouncing the African "th". They call it "Succos." There is also *Sukkot* meaning "Tabernacles" in Hebrew. A name for one of the pilgrim-festivals, which begins on *Tishri* 15, and lasts for seven days. On the eighth day *Shemini Atzeret* is celebrated, as part of the Diaspora (dispersion of the Hebrews). It is also mentioned in Exodus 23:16.[9]

Naville even found Goshen, where the Israelites settled. This name should be familiar to all Bible students. It is mentioned in the text as "the way of the land of the Philistines." In the fourth century the Christians traveled through Goshen and Succoth. The Romans called the area a hill in mid-valley, *"chivus modious in media valle".*[10] The Egyptians recorded the region as Etham. Their papyruses referred to it also as Atuna, Atima or Atma: "this land where the Israelites settled with good pasture to feed themselves and their cattle." They placed it near Tell el Maskhutah.[11]

Naville's discoveries were most significant in clearing up some doubts on the validity of the Bible as a source of history. European Jews often use the Bible to legitimize their claims of being "Semitic," Hebraic, or "God's Chosen." When Africans use the Bible as a source of reference, the Europeans and Americans discredit the study as "unscholarly, mythological, or plain sophistry." An observer referred to the Zionist-Semitic syndrome as "this problem that has caused so much worry to students who wish to give the African as little credit as possible."

Friedrich Ratzel (1844–1904) was a German geographer whose works were geared toward alignment with contemporary nineteenth century interest in evolution. He made serious studies of racial groups and compared them with European immigrants migrating to Mexico, and the United States. Like Naville, Ratzel concluded that there was definitely an African identity in original Hebrews. Ratzel stated, "What further contributes to make the Negro physiognomy less strange, and brings it nearer to our wonted conceptions, is that in many of its manifestations an approach to the Semitic type unmistakably emerges, such as one may often call Jewish in character." Ratzel was a pioneer in anthropogeography. He continually emphasized the importance of physical environment as a factor determining human activity and physiognomy. Ratzel's work was later cited by Hitler and other Nazis as a reference for determining non-Aryan features. During his time Ratzel also proved that the great Mesopotamian valley, now Iraq, Chaldea, Babylonia, and Assyria, have all divulged evidence of the African presence and rule there in ancient times. In Ratzel's long treatise, *Volkerkunde*, later translated to English as *The History of Mankind*, he made the ethnocentrics realize that the African had the torch of light in the east, and shared it with all men, including the hairy ones who came from the darkness in the north.[12] The African also shared his wealth and women with all men, it was part of his culture. The pale man had nothing but ice, and few small animals to feed off, and was glad to receive the two- and three-harvest crops which the African took to Europe by caravans and ships. The European, a hoarder by circumstances, was also wicked by nature due to the harsh climatic and other conditions of his native region. In our time we see the Europeans repay Africans with disdain and pretense of superiority. But his ingratitude will cause him to become more and more avaricious until he destroys himself. More amassing of wealth requiring more effective weaponry will guarantee his destruction.

Guiseppe Sergi, another impartial scholar from Universita di Roma, undertook a study on the origin of European civilizations, entitled *The Mediterranean Race*. After many investigations, Sergi concluded that after reviewing empirical studies and scientific analysis, weighing data gathered he found, "Until recent years the Greeks and Romans were regarded as Aryan, and then as aryanized people."

However, he disclaimed those views by replacing them with artifacts and documents unearthed. Then Sergi authoritively stated, "Today, although a few belated supporters of Aryanism still remain, it is becoming clear that the most ancient civilizations of the Mediterranean are not of Aryan origin."[13] Sergi caused Hitler to reorganize his structure of genetic advantages for racial superiority through Aryan ancestry. He proved that the Aryans were not of a culturally or even physically superior race. And Sergi concluded: "The Aryans were savages when they invaded Europe." Those brutes also destroyed a great part of the superior Neolithic civilization they encountered. The Aryans were said to be so backward that they could not have created the Greco-Latin civilization. This description fits Hitler perfectly. He was truly Aryan, if not by nature, certainly by desire and deeds. One only had to remember how destructive and cruel he was.[14]

Sergi strengthened his argument and validated his findings with a most poignant epitaph for the tombs of Aryan historians. He said in effect, that the primitive populations of Europe originated, without doubt, in Africa. Sergi said, "The basin of the Mediterranean was the principal center of movement when the African reached the center and north of Europe."

Sergi's findings proved that if someone professes to be a Semitic Jew or Hebrew, with claims to legitimacy which do not recognize original Hebrews and Arabs or Palestines as being of African origin, he or she must surely be a descendant of European converts or an "impostor," as Gamal Abd-an-Nasir called the Zionists.

More conclusive evidence was produced to clarify doubts of the origin of men, despite what they call themselves and what pretenses they make. Sir Arthur John Evans, keeper of the Ashmolean Museum of Oxford, England from 1884–1908, excavated in Crete—a part of the Grecian Empire. After finding three- and four-sided seals disclosing hieroglyphics and linear marks and scripts slightly different from those found in Egypt, Evans made studies in depth. His observations were, after intensive and painstaking searches, that the discoveries at Kaphala near the ancient ruins of Knossos, in the city of Minos contained several pieces among them that were neither Aryan or Semitic, but definitely African. The hair of the people amazed him. Although the flesh of the people on the artifacts was tinted a deep reddish brown, the hair of these Myceneans and Minoans was black and curly. Their lips were also somewhat full.[15] This discovery reminded Sir Arthur and other well informed scholars of Colerus—the Greek historian who continually said that even Socrates was a dark-skinned, thick-lipped Greek with unruly hair (according to Greek standards). Colerus described Socrates as having hair that was "black and wooly, with skin like unburnished brass."

FROM AFRICA TO AMERICA

In Schweitzer's *A History of the Jews,* we read that since the "proto schism" of the first century Jewish History has been ignored in the elementary, secondary, and higher educational institutions. He also stated that "Negro History. . . has not nearly the same richness of content or significance for the history of the Church, of the United States, or of Western civilization." The author of such unsupported generalizations shows popular ignorance existing among English-speaking so-called historians, particularly in the United States. These writers sometimes gain a high level of undeserved credibility, assumed by them or attributed to them by their benefactors and readers. One can often expect self-interest, prejudice, and distortion to filter into historical presentations. But falsehood can be more expected when history comes from an American writer. The information is unusually slanted to favor the personal or group interest of the writer.

History is the legacy of a people's past. It is inherited by those born free, and even some of those enslaved. This inheritance is an environmental naturalness, and almost innate knowledge the individual acquires from his immediate and past experiences as well as his ancestors. Therefore, the individual's behavior and development reflects the amount of pride his ancestors have instilled in him concerning his past and his heritage. One must then understand— instead of fostering prejudice—how spiritual ideas, religious preference, idealistic, or rationalistic elaborations still insistently surface among a people whose records were destroyed by vandals. One must also understand how despite enslavement of many of a people, others continued to transmit information from generation to generation despite beatings, tortures, and punishment for possession of even a book.

CATHOLICISM

In the first place, the history of the Catholic Church is based on the knowledge of Africans and the precepts of African religions. African popes and bishops laid the foundation of the Catholic and Christian churches.[16] The "Immaculate Conception" was painted on the walls of the Temple in Egypt five thousand years before the Christ was thought of. The earliest built statues of the Virgin Mary and the Christ in Europe, from as far north as Russia and as near as Rome, were black and of Negroid features. Even Saint Maurice, patron saint of the Holy Roman Germanic Empire (thirteenth to sixteenth centuries) was depicted as a black. It is obvious that Christianity received its beginnings from a people with a past more remote than the Hebrews. And the tenets, dogmas, vestments, and chants, for example, came to the Christians from Africa, by way of the Hebrews rather than the

Romans. Pagans had too many gods to have envisioned the monotheistic concepts that popularized Christianity, even with its Trinity popularized at the Ecumenical Councils and criticized by the Unitarians.

It was Pope Melciades, an African, who led Christianity to its ultimate triumph over the Roman Empire. And Saint Galasius, another African and the pope who succeeded Felix III in 492, a firm upholder of papal supremacy in the dispute between the Church and Emperor Anastasius, also African, during the struggle between Constantinople and Rome.[17] Rome made the Catholic Church white, and Ferdinand of Aragon and Isabel of Castille completed the task.

It then became easy to confuse Africans by calling their history "Negro history," and even to perpetuate hatred by confusing Americans (particularly the Jensens, Ku Klux Klanners, and the Nazi boy scouts) who have no culture or history and believe it all began with the scurvy ship called the "Mayflower." When African history is deliberately taken out of context and called Negro history, it is surreptitiously identified with enslavement of blacks while omitting enslavement of whites. Only fools, bigots, and programmed minds accept the term Negro. Every time the term is mentioned in Latin America, even to students at the lowest grade levels, the pupils laugh and say "We thought all Americans were the same!" The Catholic schools in Latin America taught one history, but that our people invented next to nothing.

So-called Negro history is a term recognized by North Americans. It can hold its own in terms of contributions to the United States or of Western civilization. One has only to be informed of the thousands of discoveries, inventions, and patents held by black scientists as well as inventions stolen by whites from their black underlings or coworkers, particularly in the United States. Those contributions include 300 discoveries from the peanut alone, including meal, instant coffee, paper, ink, shaving cream, and metal polish, and another 118 products from the sweet potato, including many cereals eaten by bigots, flour, syrup, starch, and linoleum. Dr. George Washington Carver gave most of his discoveries to civilization without making the millions he should have. Name one non-black who would have disdained money that much or cared for humanity half as much. The semaphores, traffic lights used all over the world, the gas masks used during World War I, the filament of Thomas Edison's electric bulb, shoe-stitching machines, the troller for the trolley car, and the many railroad-related inventions of Elijah McCoy were all invented by blacks. The blood plasma of World War II was developed by Dr. Charles Drew who, ironically, died because he was too dark to receive a blood transfusion in a white Chicago hospital. Even the camera/spectograph of Dr. George Carruthers recently took pictures of the moon.[18] If these are not enough to enrich any history, then some of the many books on black inventors and scientists should be mentioned to those unacquainted with history.

Even the development of Rome and the Catholic Church was so dependent on African prowess and intelligence that the pictures of the saints showed them as black. Even the Madonna in the inner chamber of the Vatican is black, as is the child. Saint Peter, the first Roman pope is black in art in la Basilica de San Pietro in Rome. The Christ and the Virgin Mary also are depicted as black in Poland, throughout the Catholic world and in many churches in Latin America. The Isis, Osiris, Horus concept was copied from Africa, and changed after the First Ecumenical Council of Nicea.[19] After this conference, Saint Jerome declared, "The whole world groaned, and marvelled at finding itself Arian" through Arians of Alexandria.[20] There was Potamon, Bishop of Heraclea in Egypt, who had lost an eye, Paphnutius, of the Upper Thebaid (Thebes), who had also lost an eye and was disabled in one knee, and several other Bishops of the Church from all over Africa and Asia (325 A.C.E.).

The Fourth Lateran Council, (1125) took care of Jewish rights and privileges, as well as black power and identity. There was the ablution of one and the abolition of the other. It should not be too difficult to see how one related to the other. Power within the Church left black hands and minds, and dark-skinned Hebrews' faces banned from sight on the streets during Holy Week. This ban, the Church said, was to protect the Jews and avoid riots. The Church considered that Jews showed no sorrow on Good Friday and therefore made a mockery of it. Converted Jews were said to be found, at times, observing their former religious practices (Passover) and only using Christianity for convenience.

Jews were, therefore, forbidden from holding public office in Catholic-dominated countries—according to the edict. Canon 69 of the Fourth Lateran Council promulgated, "It is most absurd that a blasphemer of Christ should exercise power over Christians." Canon 68 decreed that "Jews of either sex, in every province, and at all times, be distinguished in public from other people by a difference of dress." These canons led to the first banishment of Jews from England in 1290. And it was not until the days of Oliver Cromwell, archfoe of the Catholic Church and friend of the Free Mason-magician Manasseh ben Israel, rabbi of Amsterdam, that Jews were pardoned. Jews were also expelled from France in 1306, Saxony in 1349, Hungary in 1360, Belgium in 1370, Prague in 1380, Austria in 1420, the Netherlands in 1444, Spain in 1492, Portugal in 1498, Prussia in 1510, Naples and Sardinia in 1540, and Bavaria in 1551. Jews also were expelled from Sweden, and banned from there until 1782. Jews were made fearful of attempting to enter Denmark until the 1600s, and prohibited from seeking residence in Norway until 1815.[21] By this time they had intermarried and bleached themselves out to a large extent. In order to be accepted as pale-skinned Europeans, some Jews had even reproduced albinoes purposefully. But blackness came back to haunt the Jews atavistically. Many of their children were born with thick lips, big noses, and dark skins.

AFRICANS IN ROME

Pliny mentioned the Villa of Scipio Africanus made of Alexandrian marble and covered with Numidian plaster. Pliny said, "The first Scipio Africanus, [whose] ascendancy arising from his personal excellence, and the greatness of his renown, made him the object of much jealousy and destruction." Efforts to impeach Africanus were met with disdain. Knowing that other Romans were jealous of the power of people of color, Scipio Africanus ignored his rivals. He was finally left alone. Africans were so well respected in Rome that Marcus Aurelius said of Claudius Albinus, "who though Africa is his country, has little of the African in his genius and disposition."[22] Africans were often stereotyped as geniuses.

The overwhelming majority of dark-skinned people in the Roman enclaves included Septimus Severus, who claimed the throne of Rome and held it to A.D. 193. Roman Emperor Severus grew to like Roman literature, but he never lost his appetite and taste for African cooking,[23] he ordered imported foodstuff from Africa. Saul, or Paul, was a Roman citizen of Hebrew origin. Sextus Julius Africanus was a Christian traveler and historian of the third century. He was probably born at Aeolia Capitoline (Jerusalem). He died in Jerusalem.[24] Africanus was ambassador to Rome under Emperor Severus. Carcalla, another emperor of Rome (180 – c. 250), was of African and Syrian parentage. There were more than one hundred African bishops during the first century, when Christianity was established in Africa, and A.D. 256. The most distinguished figures were Tertulian and Cyprian, and the principal champion Augustine, bishop of Hippo Regius. The Thebaid of Egypt bears mention. He reappeared in Ireland and left such names as O'Dwyer, meaning the black one; Moore from blackamoor; and Carter from Carthaginians. Saint Maurice of Germany was a pure African. He commanded a Roman legion in Gaul (Switzerland) in 287 A.C.E. Maurice became sainted because he refused to attack Christians when ordered to do so by European Emperor Maximian Herculius.

Rogers shows illustrations of Saint Maurice with the German Eagle on his head as he appears in many German Cathedrals and museums. After 1,700 years Hitler, who was supposed to dislike people of color, took pictures with Saint Maurice's emblem on his head, and the *African* swastika as his symbol of power.[25]

Many Roman citizens of African descent composed a community known as *Africa Romana*. These Africans were usually very well educated. Many of them became professors, governors of Roman provinces, and generals. When the Church became introduced as part of the Empire, quite a few African-Romans became bishops. The Africans made significant contributions to Roman culture. These Roman citizens spoke Latin, lived in large luxurious villas, and were commuters to Carthage and other cities and towns of North Africa. Among these African-Romans resided Jews, Spaniards, and Italians, then disdained by some Romans.

Cyrenaica, with Benghasi, Al Marj, Darnak, and Tobruk as its chief cities, was a Roman port in East Libya. It bordered on the Mediterranean and many Jews lived there. In 155 A.C.E. the Jews rebelled against Rome. Roman might was exerted and the rebellion was soon crushed. The outcome caused all Jewish communities of the area to again disperse southward in two hordes. A number of Jews crossed the Bend of the Niger on to Senegal and Futa. These Jews encountered others whose diaspora was flowing westward via southern Morocco and Mauretania Adrar.

J. C. de Graft Johnson says:

> There is perhaps no group of people in the western Sudan who have more Jewish blood in them than the pastoral Fulani of Futa, who, by mixing with the people on the shore of Lake Chad, passed on their Jewish blood to the areas around Kanem and Bornu several centuries later.[26]

Henry Johnson observed the longhorn cattle of the Fulani. He commented, "The usual type of cattle belonging to the Fula is practically identical with that of ancient Egypt and modern Galaland and equatorial Africa. It is certain, however, that a considerable element of Egyptian Culture entered Negroid Africa by way of Darfur, Wadai, Lake Chad, and thence to the Upper Niger; and along this route the dominant type of longhorned cattle may have reached the Fula of West Africa."[27]

After the rebellion in Cyrenaica, the Church had great reaction and reactivation in Africa, particularly in the north. July 17, 180 A.C.E., saw the trial, sentencing, and execution of death penalties for the first martyrs of the Church in Africa. Twelve ancient fathers were executed—not in Rome or the western world—in Carthage, Africa. These Christians were natives of Numidia. The leader of these fervent believers, who did not imagine they were building a racist enclave, was none other than the African sister Perpetua.[28] Her brother Saturnius was among those executed for supporting the Church.

DeGraft Johnson wrote, "If you go to the place where the New Carthage once stood, (Tunisia) you will find still standing a chapel dedicated to Saint Perpetua, built with some of the pillars and stones from the Carthage of Hannibal's day."

During that era the Church had more African blood shed in its cause, more African leadership, culture, and loyalty from all African regions, than had Rome.

Another great African contributor was Quintus Septimus Flores Tertullianus—popularly known as Tertulian—born in Carthage, North Africa. Tertulian was the first of the Church's writers to make Latin the language of Christianity. His colleague in Christian endeavours—Cyprian—descended from a highly respected family of Carthage. Cyprian was a student of philosophy, and became professor of philosophy before he entered the Church to become Bishop of Carthage.

While these contemporaries of the African Emperor Septimus Severus were zealously involved in Christianity, the Roman Imperial Government was undergoing terrible struggles with inflation, corruption, and economic depression, and a compulsion to impose higher taxes on its poor, its working class, and the peasantry. As a result, taxes were more difficult to collect, and money lending was popular.

The Christ had been born during the reign of Augustus Caesar, and the world had not yet realized the impact his existence would later have on Jews and Romans. Many Christians were awaiting the second coming of their Messiah and did not realize the effect its delay would cause. Many early Christians admired martyrdom and even glorified death. Consequently, there were several Christians who deified Roman conscription for the armed forces and openly stated that the carrying of a sword was incompatible with their religion. Those preachings caused the army to lose enlisted personnel and possible recruits. Some Christians challenged secular laws with religious dogma and defied proclamations. Those Christians did not render unto the emperor the complete recognition of his laws. Quite a few believers of faith had forgotten their Master's teachings about rendering unto Caesar the things that are Caesar's, and unto God those things which are God's. However, some had not; after watching circumstances develop, these other Christians decided to be practical. They made convenient arrangements with the Imperial Government, and the government took advantage of the Christians' influence and services.

DeGraft Johnson explains in detail how the first record of an African being converted to Christianity came about. His name was Anthony. This twenty-year-old Egyptian sold all of his earthly possessions and withdrew to the Sahara to become father of the eremitic concept of hermitage. Most of his imitators were full-blooded Africans. From Meroe, the former capital of a Sudanese kingdom came another martyr of the Church. The Sudanese kingdom was on the Nile between Aswan, Egypt, and Khartoum. Meroe was in its glory and power during the seventh and sixth centuries B.C.E. This was circa the time of the Nubian Dynasty of Egypt, and a few decades after.

During this relevant period, the Sudanese kingdom boasted of a queen mother. Her official name was Queen Candace, and during her time, the Romans say that the English people were running around England, Scotland, and Wales in little clans, half naked.[29]

Nubia is located directly to the south of Egypt, between the Second Cataract, and the Fifth. It is an ancient country of North Africa between the Red Sea and the Sahara. "The people were of Negroid stock like the Bantus of today." A mixture of Hamitic and other African stock. The Numidians were from Numidia, roughly Algiers. They were the little black horsemen in Hanibal de la Barca's army, which went against Rome. The Numidian agility in the saddle drove thorns in the Roman cavalry's flanks. They rode and shot their arrows simultaneously. Where a rider looked, there went the arrow through the target.

The Blemmyes were another Negroid group which invaded Upper Egypt periodically. These Blemmyes, of more pronounced Hamitic origin than the Egyptians, occupied the area directly east of Nubia— commonly referred to as the Nubian desert. In the middle of the third century A.C.E., the Blemmyes conquered the kingdom around Meroe. They became a more direct threat to Egypt from this vantage point. Therefore, Emperor Diocletian (284–305) pulled Roman legions from the southern regions of the island of Philae, on the Nile, and brought in full blooded Africans from the western Nobadae desert to settle there. The Africans were to become a Roman buffer between the Blemmyes and the Egyptians intermixed with Romans and other invaders. The plot backfired and, ironically enough, the Nobadae became allied with the Blemmyes in the attempt to attack Egypt. Emperor Diocletian hurriedly sought a peace treaty. The treaty was obtained, but only lasted a year. The treaty contained a special clause which promoted a Nobadae visit to the temple of Isis at Philae. The Nobadae were soon converted to Christianity during the reign of Justinian (527–565 A.C.E.). Justinian is the Roman emperor credited with defeating the Vandals and bringing the African provinces back into the Roman Empire.

The first bishop appointed to Nobadae was Longinius (568 A.C.E.). He was so tactful that the emperors and empresses of Rome who had persecuted the Church in Africa ended up tolerating it there and later even in Rome. The acceptance of Christianity became not only an official state act, but the annexation of a new policy to maintain control over of the East and West.

In regard to monastic existence and abstinence, another African of note was the Egyptian Pachomius. He established the first Christian monastery on an island in the Nile on the Upper Thebaid. Monastic life became so popular in Egypt that it began to compete with Roman military arrogance, might, and opulence.

The natural kindness in Africans, coupled with their taste for opulence and leisure due to the richness of their African continent, was sure to attract Europeans. This is especially true after the Greeks visited Africa, had been treated with hospitality unknown in Europe, and had returned to tell the other barbarians that the Africans live like gods. Africans soon became tainted after becoming acquainted with the brutal, hateful, and naturally selfish Europeans. These people came from a continent with terribly cold winters and damp weather, where only one crop was produced per year. When they caught an animal, they had to eat a part of it and save the rest for the following day. In Africa, Latin America, and the West Indies, women still cook a fresh meal three times a day. It was only natural that these brutish people would want to use the Church to enslave Africans, usurp their land and exploit it as a source of providing their necessary sustenance to avoid starvation.

After a while, the Romans started fighting over Africa. Count Boniface, Roman Legate in Africa, invited the Vandals to come there and assist him in governing the five provinces in North Africa. Boniface was betraying Rome, and challenging her extended rule. This act was to offset rumors that Empress Placida was set to overthrow him. Saint Augustine, Bishop of Hippo, warned Boniface not to do so. Boniface's wife was a Vandal and must have influenced him or suggested the idea.

These Vandals were a Germanic people from North Jutland. They were forced out of their settlements in the Valley of the Oder about 5 A.C.E. Escaping more powerful barbarians than themselves, these Vandals moved southward through the Upper Danube, invaded Gaul (406), then moved on to northern Spain by way of the Pyrenees. The Vandals were pushed out by the Visigoths and went to live in southern Spain. Since the Franks, as allies of Rome, had refused the Vandals permission to settle in Gaul (409), they continued to fight with the Romans. Their aggression continued despite the fact that the Romans had given these Vandals, under Roman Emperor Honorius' hand, a signed peace treaty enabling them to settle on Spanish land. By 428, the Vandals developed maritime power and crossed into Africa in 429 A.C.E. By March 16, 455 A.C.E., Generic, the Vandal leader, arrived in Italy. They sacked, pillaged, and left it in ruins. Generic stole the golden roof of the Temple of Jupiter Capitolinus and the sacred vessels from Solomon's Temple at Jerusalem, once taken from Jerusalem by Titus. Publius, an Afro-Roman writer wrote, "These barbaric Vandals found Africa rich, pillaged her, and left her arid and desolate. Then they enslaved some of her people."[30]

NOTES

1. Constantin Francois de Chesseboeuf, Conte de Volney (France: *Voyage en Syrie et en Egypte*, 1787) His book was useful to Napolean during the general's Egyptian campaign.
2. George Wells Parker. *The Children of the Sun* (Baltimore, Maryland, P.O. Box 13414. Zone 21203: Black Classic Press, 1918).
3. William H. Prichard. "Blacks, Jews, and Negro Zionists: A Crisis in Negro Leadership" *Black Books Bulletin* (Chicago, Illinois: The Institute of Positive Education, 1977), pp. 18-23.
4. Basil Davidson. *Black Mother* (Toronto, Canada: Atlantic-Little Brown & Company, 1961), pp. 45-46.
5. Edouard Henri Naville. *The Origin of Egyptian Civilization* Washington, Government Printing Office, 1908.) pp. 18. "From the Smithsonain report for 1907, pp. 549-564."
6. Tablet: a new word for stelae. Stelae is used among scholars around the world. It means in Greek, "upright stone."
7. Edouard Henri Naville. *The Store-City of Pithom and the Route of the Exodus* (London, The offices of the Egypt Exploration fund. Asher & Co. 1903). Fourth Edition with 13 plates-2 maps.
8. *The New Columbia Encyclopaedia*— Edited by William H. Harris and Judith Levy (New York: Columbia University Press, 1975). p. 2644
9. Lillian S. Freehof and Lottie C. Bandman. *Flowers and Festivals of the Jewish Year* (New York: Hearthside Press, Inc., 1964).
10. Gamurrini. *"I misteri i gl'inni di S. Ilario"*, p. 10.
11. Edouard Henri Naville, *The Store-City of Pithom and the Route of the Exodus* , p. 28.
12. Friedrich Ratzel, *The History of Mankind* (Leipzig, University of Leipzig, 1886). Translated from the German original Volerkunde.
13. Guiseppe Sergi, *The Mediterranean Race: A Study of the Origin of the European Peoples* (New York: Scribner, 1901).
14. As crew members of the Dusseldorf, a German freighter which hired crews from Central America, before World War II, we saw Hitler at the Bundesrath at the Allotria, in Hamburg. He was not blond, even though he tried to breed blond, blue-eyed offspring.
15. Sir Arthur John Evans. *Cretan Pictographs and Prae-Phoenician Script* (Oxford, England: Royal Society of Antiquities, 1895).
16. African popes of Rome were: Victor (180–199 a.c.e.), Melciades (311–312), and Saint Galasius (496 a.c.e.) Rogers. *100 Amazing Facts About the Negro* (New York: Futuro Press, Inc. 1941), p. 9.
17. *Our Glorius Popes*: (Saint Benedict Center), The Slaves of the Immaculate Heart of Mary, Cambridge, Massachusetts, 1955).
18. Ivan Van Sertima. *Blacks in Science*, 1984. Carruthers and other blacks have been involved with NASA in various capacities for years.
19. Horus was stabbed before Christ with similar wounds—son of a virgin Isis.
20. Rogers. *100 Amazing Facts About the Negro*. After he exposed several mulattoes accepted as whites throughout the United States and Europe, including presidents and royalties, a woman offered Rogers a blank check if he would discontinue exposing myths.

21. The Slaves of the Immaculate Heart of Mary, *Our Glorious Popes* (Cambridge, Massachusetts, Saint Benedict Center, 1955).

22. William Roberts. *History of Letter Writing From the Earliest Period* (London: William Pickering Publishers, 1843), p. 281–364.

23. J.C. de Graft-Johnson, *African Glory: The Story of Vanished Negro Civilizations* (New York: Walker and Company, 1954).

24. *Encyclopaedia Britannica*, 15th edition. Vol. 1, p. 136.

25. Rogers, *100 Amazing Facts About the Negro,*

26. J.C. de Graft Johnson. *African Glory* (New York: Walker and Company 1954). pp.32-45. Professor of Economics at the University of Ghana. Dr. Johnson is a national of the Ghanian Republic.

27. Sir Henry Johnson. *The Nile Quest* (New York, 1903). Included in Joseph J. Williams. *Hebrewisms of West Africa From Nile to Niger* (From) *With the Jews* (New York, Biblo and Tannen, 1967). p.105.

28. Perpetua means continuous in Spanish, priest's housekeeper in Italian, and *perpetuo* in Latin means continual.

29. Barry Fell. *America B.C.* Ancient Settlers in the New World (New York: New York Times Book Company, 1978).
"Those who recall that Julius Caesar described the ancient Britons as mostly savages, wearing only iron torques about their necks, sometimes with the skin of a beast cast over their shoulders." Dr. Fell is a professor of anthropology at Harvard.

30. Here is another African, who lived, and wrote in Rome: Publius Terentius Afer (195–159 B.C.E.), and Terrence *Phormio The Brothers* was one of his works. It was translated by Frank O. Copley.

CHAPTER 8

ISLAM

Belisarius (ca. 505–565) was a Byzantine general, under Justinian, who governed African provinces. After suppressing the explosive Nika riot, with assistance from Narses at Constantinople, Belisarius routed the Vandals, captured their king (535 A.C.E.), and dislodged them from African soil.

Emperor Justinian, the champion of Christianity, was inevitably expected to meet in armed conflict against Chosroes I (the elder), king of Persia and defender of the Zoroastran religion. Afterward, Emperor Heraclius of Byzantium and Chosroes II of Persia (the son) also clashed in the early seventh century. But Chosroes II was shrewder and more tactical than his predecessor. Antioch, Damascus, and Jerusalem fell to Persian rule, while Chosroes' armies marched on to Chalcedon in Asia Minor. The occupation of Egypt was completed by 619 A.C.E. But the Persian domination was short-lived. A Roman army sent against them by Emperor Heraclius defeated the Persians at the Battle of Ninevah and expelled them from that area.

While Emperor Heraclius was in Syria restoring order, restructuring his government, and assigning military commands, he received a letter from the Roman outpost of Bastra, where it had been delivered south of Damascus. The letter meant nothing to Heraclius because it was written in Arabic, which was said to be "an obscure Semitic-desert language, so it had to be translated for Heraclius." The letter was signed by one who called himself "Mohammed the Prophet of God." The letter demanded that Emperor Heraclius acknowledge the One True God and serve Him. A similar letter was simultaneously sent to Kavadh, King of Persia, at Ctesiphon. The records state that Kavadh was so annoyed that he ripped up the letter and hastily dismissed the bearer.[1]

The fetus of Islam was maturing while seeking strength and nourishment from the most powerful world rulers of its time. The advent of Islam was at hand, and no one could conceive that by the end of Heraclius' reign, the Greek-reading historians in the West would soon find themselves with a suddenly obsolete Greek reading key, which had opened the doors to history for twelve centuries. The language of history had become Arabic, the once obscure Semitic-desert language.

Herodotus, Pliny, and other historians had used Greek. Cicero, Claudius, and those of their time wrote in Latin. But in the time of Caliph 'Abd-al-Malik (ca. 685–705 A.D.), Arabic had become the dominant language. Western historians were at a loss; they called it the "Dark Ages," but it was the West that was in darkness. They could not read Arabic, and anything the Western mind does not conceive is pretended to be "dark." Nevertheless, Arabic numbers, and civilization, soon overtook outdated Roman numerals and Christian obscurantism. Islamic and other histories were written and the Prophet Muhammad's[1] activities, unlike Jesus' were recorded and even included in prayer books.

The Prophet Muhammad was procreator of the Islamic infant and its teachings. Like most of the prophets of renown, he too had a vision. Ali Muhammad, son of ibn-al-Mutabib, was an Arab of the Kuraish tribe of western Arabia. His grandmother was Ethiopian. His wife Amiva was also of the Kuraish tribe. His father Abdallah died shortly after the boy was born in 571 A.C.E. Therefore, Ali Muhammad was brought up by his uncle Abu Talib. This was six years after the reign of Justinian. Some scholars place Muhammad's birthplace at Mecca, others give Medina. At the age of 24, Muhammad married a wealthy widow, Khadijah, much older than himself, and with whom he appears to have been truly in love. He had no other wife during her lifetime, and Khadija's daughter is the only child of note in his records. At age 40, the Prophet's interest in becoming a mullah,[2] and in mysticism, led him to his decision to be proclaimed the elected prophet of God, after Abraham and Christ.

Before the proclamation, Ali Muhammad had been a student of Hebrew rabbis at Mecca. His prophetic characteristics are said to have been "similar to those of the Hebrew prophets some twelve hundred years before him."[3] At that time, Mecca was the center of the pagan cult that had great fame throughout the Arab communities. The cult was built around the worshipping of a well-revered stone called El Ka'aba. This stone was a fallen meteorite and was worshipped along with a goddess named Allat. The Prophet envisioned Allat, El Ka'aba and Mecca, the center of the pagan cult, becoming interconnected. The female goddess became a male named "Allah," the stone became a relic to be visited, and a God like the Hebrew Yahweh or the Christian Jesus evolved.

It is recorded that the prophet of Allah "based his religion largely in the Hebrew Scriptures, some Christian ideas, and one or two ideas from the Zoroastrian faith of Persia." This religious admixture gave everyone connected with a major religion of the area and of the time some segment of ritual practice related to his original tenets.

Muhammad is also described as a likeable good-natured individual, and rather charismatic. He was also somewhat of a poet, but was not considered to be a learned man, even during those times. However, he did practice writing religious verses in rhyming couplets with enough repetition to allow his semiliterate congregants to readily memorize his poems. Muhammad was also able to befuddle the minds of the non-thinkers of his time by telling them the poems had been communicated to him from Allah through an angel. He claimed to have visions. An important vision was the one "in which he was taken up through the heavens to God and instructed in his mission."[4]

In the year 623 A.C.E., a year after the famous flight which Muhammad took from Mecca, he set up headquarters at the Palm Oasis of Medina. Muhammad was no longer a plain leader of raiding Arab bandits. He was now the leader of a new mystic religion. Nevertheless, some people of Mecca were not fully convinced that Muhammad's new religion would not be costly. They studied his prospectus for investment, in a trip to heaven, with logical scrutiny. But the Prophet was prepared to meet their challenges, spiritual needs, and economic demands with pragmatic solutions and with promises.

Mecca was already a prominent center, where pilgrims came to worship and merchants came to peddle their wares accumulated or manufactured through the year. A war ensued between Mecca and Medina. The pilgrims who came by the thousands to worship before the miraculous black stone El Ka'aba and to pray to the goddess Allat were tourists, in a way of speaking. They were like delegates at a convention. These pilgrims produced revenue for the government, profits for the merchants, and fees for the services of priests, government officials, and scribes who wrote for the illiterate. These scribes and merchants could not allow someone they called a bandit to share their profits, so they cried,"Muhammad must be caught and destroyed!" But the Prophet was cunning and daring. He arranged for Mecca to be maintained as the focus point of pilgrimages, and so it should be shared with his sect. Sound judgment and good planning allowed him to return to Mecca in 629 A.C.E. no longer a rascal, but the leader of a well-armed religious cult. He had escaped to his grandmother in Ethiopia, studied well, and returned with weapons both in his head and in his hands. Muhammad had learned what men learn to make other men follow them—like Moses, Christ, and others who came through the land of the Kings. The former wanderer who had sent letters to Emperor Heraclius of Byzantium, King of Persia, Kavadh and to Emperor Tai Tsung of China, just a year ago was now calling on these rulers of vast domains to worship the one true God, who was Allah, and had made Muhammad his Prophet. Muhammad prepared to make these and other rulers honor his words.

The Emperor of China had not only received Muhammad's letter with due consideration, but had followed the Prophet's instructions. Tai-Tsung had promptly allowed the Moslems to build a mosque at Canton. That masjid is well preserved and considered the oldest in the world.

Very few of the Prophet Muhammad's words were ever analyzed or criticized by his followers anywhere. The worst groups, however, were his last groups from the West and the East. These modern-day Muslim members are often dogmatic, erratic, and sporadic—not only in their knowledge of the facts, but in their fantasies and fanaticisms. They can hardly discuss the Prophet's true exploits, and the bizarre episodes entailed in Islamic history without undue emotionalism and savage physical threats. And they even attack each other, or people who write about Islam.

Hebrews were in Arabia before Ali Muhammad was born. In southwest Arabia, Yemen flourished with industry and general prosperity from c.750 B.C.E. to c.115 B.C.E. There was enmity between the Yemenites and the Abyssinians who repeatedly invaded resourceful Yemen. The Yemenites and the Abyssinians had a showdown when the Yemenites called on the Himyarites to repel the invasions of these Abyssinians, who were Christians. Nevertheless, the Himyarites failed to route the Abyssinians. The Abyssinians overpowered the defenders and a new kingdom was formed, called Yemen-Asir. The kingdom was part Hebraic and part Sabean.[5] The scholarly leader of this new Yemenite kingdom was Dnu-Nuwas, who became converted to the Hebrew religion. His Hebrew name was Joseph. The new monarch did not reign long because the Abyssinians renewed their assaults with support from Byzantine forces of Persia under Justinian I. This short-lived kingdom came to an abrupt end in 525 A.C.E. The Abyssinians' occupation was also of short duration. In 575 A.C.E., the Persians overran and assumed control of the land with their military might. The caravan route from north to south was dotted with settlements composed mostly of Hebrews. The whole Tihamah area was controlled by them.

Margolis and Marx informed us "Yathrib (the later Medina, the Prophet's City) was in all probability founded by [Hebrews]."[6]

The southern Arabs moved northward during the third century. Their Aus and Khazraj clans displaced the Hebrews at Al Madinah and turned them into subjugated residents rather than the successful burghers these Hebrews had been. This turning of the social tide and the pressure from the waves of power exercised by the Arabs, and the changes constantly brought about by rival factions, caused some Hebrews to adopt Arab names and customs. Hebrew poems of the time reflected Arab influence, but they often mentioned, in verse, the treacherous assassinations of the Hebrew chiefs and other heroes. The Arabs treated the Hebrews very much like the Jews are treating the Arabs today.

It is written that when Muhammad fled his native Mecca in 622 A.C.E. (the hegira), he was much concerned about one reversal in particular. The Hebrew people from whom Muhammad had learned so much were expected to follow his new version of their old religion. But most of them had totally ignored him and his emulated religion. They scorned "the confused utterances of the Arab prophet in all that pertained to Judaism."[7] What probably made the new religion seem unattractive was the Prophet's mere repetition of Hebrew teachings. Even his early religious practices were based on Hebrew teachings similar to Christianity of Christ himself who had been a Hebrew from the House of David. Ali Muhammad directed his prayers towards Jerusalem (*kibla*), and observed the great fast sanctified on the tenth day of *Tishri*, the Hebrew Day of Atonement (Yom Kippur).

Aware of his confusion and lack of erudition, the Prophet promptly decided to eliminate the learned Hebrews in his community. Furthermore, some Hebrews had been pedantically discrediting the arriving leader in debates with his supporters and firmest believers. As usual, the educated refused to be conned by functional illiterates. The Prophet allowed the Bene Israel to go unmolested for some time. He kept hoping that they would not have to be forced to join him. Muhammad, may Allah be gracious unto him, wished that the Hebrews would eventually become a segment of the Islamic community, but the years passed and that possibility faded. The Hebrews refused to give accreditation to the new religion. With no Hebrews among the Moslem chiefs of staff, and none in the Islamic hierarchy, with just a few in the lower echelons of the fighting forces, Muhammad said, "We shall spread Islam with fire, and the sword." Bekr, his disciple and commander-in-chief of the fighting forces, suggested that Islam discard its Hebraic liturgical penchants. The conclusion was a reversion to the goddess Allat and the Ka'aba-stone worship. The Day of Atonement was no longer observed. It was replaced by a month of Ramadan—a month-long fast.

Muhammad, the Prophet of Allah, was now ready to exemplify Arab vindictiveness. He attempted to massacre the entire Kaimuka community for refusing to join his religion. The Hebrews had deified themselves and said: "Thou wilt see that we are not men," but the Prophet had decided to make them dead men. After besieging their town for a fortnight, the Hebrews had to surrender when their Khazraj allies did not come to their rescue. However, they were fortunate enough to have the Khazraj leader Abdallah ibn Ubaiy plead with Muhammad to desist from annihilating the Kainuka men, women, and children. Muhammad sent these people into exile, and they went to Palestine. As usual, Muhammad kept the best arms and tools found among them before he sent the Kainuka on their way. Their properties were confiscated and their residences turned over to the fruitful members of Islam.

About one year later, the Prophet's army was severely defeated at the Battle of Uhud by the people of Mecca. The Prophet was among the wounded-in-action. The Hebrews were made the scapegoats, and false accusations were made charging them with schemes to end the Prophet's life. Knowledge of the plot, the accuser said, had come from the angel Gabriel. These Hebrews, indicted without tangible proof, were to be banished as undesirables. Banishment at that time meant parting with your most valuable possessions. After putting the Hebrew community under siege, Muhammad ordered all the date trees surrounding their fortress to very quickly be cut and left fruitless. The fortress-bound captives found themselves on the edge of starvation and therefore surrendered. These Hebrews were pleading for their lives when they were mercilessly massacred. Their women and children were sold to Bedouin tribesmen, and some found themselves being exchanged for arms, ammunition, and horses. Among the captives was a beautiful Hebrew woman named Rihana, whose husband had been among the six hundred men massacred. Rihana was selected to be a new trophy in Muhammad's collection of sex objects in his harem.[8]

According to Margolis and Marx, the Prophet stormed the Jewish settlement at Khaiba without provocation a year after the butchering of the six hundred. The Hebrews put up a strong resistance inside the fortress and outside its walls. But the Moslems attacked and attacked until one stronghold was subdued and then another. A Hebrew leader named Kinana was cruelly tortured to death. Kinana's beautiful wife, Sabia, a Hebrew woman, also was taken by Muhammad as an addition to his harem. But the Prophet of Allah had collected one sex object too many with Zainab, sister of the slain Hebrew leader Marhab. Zainab refused to cooperate with the Prophet and to avenge her brother's death seemed her only resolve. Zainab poisoned the Prophet's figs and other food. It is said, by some westerners, that her food poisoning was so effective that the Prophet Muhammad suffered from its effect through the years up to the day of his death.

Muhammad recruited followers and grew strong enough to become the controlling factor at Mecca, and in its surrounding areas. This power allowed the Prophet to divert most of his attention, during his last ten years, to the pursuit of happiness through polygyny. The man of God married concubines and wives.

Many of Muhammad's observers described his existence as one of a man with "a mixture of personal vanity, greed, cunning, self-deception, and quite a sincere religious passion." Muhammad's strongest attraction in Islam, it is said, is the perfect brotherhood and equality before God of all his believers, regardless of color, origin, or status.[9] Being himself dark-skinned, Ali Muhammad tried to protect the dark-skinned members of the faith. But his designs were altered shortly after the Moslems lost their war with Spain, and discrimination against blacks and other dark-skinned people began.

In the present-day Moslem world, the Egyptians hate the Palestinians and vice versa. They say to the Palestinians that all their troubles are due to them. Israeli agents imprisoned in Egypt wrote that while the Egyptians treated them as *baladiat* (fellow countrymen), being born in Egypt, they mistreated their fellow Moslems. "The prison also housed Sudanese, Syrians and Lebanese—who all hated one another." The Moslem Brotherhood hated their fellow Egyptians loyal to Nasir, at the time, and the guards hated their officers' faces when they approached them.[10]

After Muhammad died in 632 A.C.E., his disciple and friend Abu Bekr became Caliph. Bekr did not hesitate to attack and crush the Byzantine army, at the Battle of Faruk, a tributary of the Jordan River. Syria, Damascus, Palmyra, Antioch, Jerusalem, and other cities were captured by him. Enfeebled and ailing Emperor Heraclius could not defend his waning empire. Three years later (637 A.C.E.), the Persian general Rustam was engaged by the Arabs for three days' combat. Religious zeal, and determination, caused the Moslems to win that battle and push far into the western Turkestan. The Moslems pushed on, then turned eastward defeating all comers until they met face to face with the Chinese. They gained a foothold in northwest China, where there is still a large Moslem population. But they could not overrun the Chinese.

The Moslem conquest of Africa, it must be noted, was much more difficult than some writers admit. It was only after very difficult encounters, heavy losses, and many repulsions did the Moslems eventually occupy North Africa. It was from there that Islam was able to penetrate into Egypt.[11]

Moslem occupation of Africa made the Africans realize that Arab greed and callousness was no different from the insidious Vandals, Greeks, and Romans who had come to Africa before them. Therefore, the Africans decided to seek riddance of these barbaric fanatics. The North Africans united under the banner of Kuseila and defeated and killed the Moslem leader Oqbar-ben-Nafi in 682 A.C.E. Kuseila ruled as King of Mauretania for five years. Then in 699 the Arabs returned with overwhelming forces. They killed Kuseila, and defeated his army. His leadership of African resistance was not abandoned, however, and Kuseila was promptly replaced by a relative, a woman who became a credit to the legion, Queen Dahia-al-Kahina, [d.703/4] who skillfully led the Africans. During Queen Kahina's command, the Arabs were driven into Tripolitania. African historians state that she and all other queens of that period were Africans. The Jews state that she was a "Queen of Judaizing Berber tribes."[12]

The Arab general Hassan-bin-Numan captured Carthage, another part of North Africa. Queen Kahina rallied her force and eagerly awaited his return. When he arrived, she chased him and his Moslem forces out once more. Hassan regrouped his forces and returned to overwhelm the Queen. Kahina was cornered into a siege. She became desperate and ordered destruction of the fertile lands of Byzacene, hoping that lack of food and shelter would discourage the Arabs from their determination to capture her land and people. Her plans were misconceived and fatal. Her soil became infertile after salting and resulted in southern Tunisia becoming barren to this day. Furthermore, Kahina's plan did not deter the determined Arabs, it only deferred their insistence. They came back in 705 A.C.E. This time the Arabs killed Queen Kahina, the last African ruler of that area. Hassan became heir to her dominion. Queen Kahina was Hebrew and not a Christian, according to Professor De Graft Johnson of Ghana. She never gave up her faith. Like any good mother, however, she persuaded her sons to convert to Islam to save their lives later on. By being Moslems, Queen Kahina's older son was made chief ruler of his mother's domain after her death.

During and after Queen Kahina's defeat, several African chiefs converted to Islam. Among these chiefs was Tarik-ibn-Zarca. As general of the army, Tarik commanded Tangiers eight years after the Queen's death. He was also governor of Mauretania. Tarik sailed to Spain on two occasions. He built a garrison at the foot of Mons Calpe. The Africans named the fort after him in admiration of his great generalship: his name becoming Gebel Tarik. This hill of Tarik was later corrupted by the Spanish admixture of Arabic, Greek, and Roman words to become "Gibraltar." Tarik later became master of Spain.

"The conquest of Spain was an African conquest. They were Mohammedan Africans not Arabs," said Johnson, who also said that the Africans were the ones who defeated the Gothic kingdom of Spain. The Moslem conquest of Spain was an African and Arab accomplishment—a joint venture. But the Spaniards called them all Moors because the name Mauretania meant "the land of the Moors" in Roman times, when that part of northern Morocco and western Algeria near Numidia was under Roman dominion.

The Arab conquest of Egypt exempted converts from burdensome taxes. Egypt was conquered in 640 A.C.E., and Iran was subdued in 641. Records show 24,000 Christians renouncing Christianity there. Surely, there must have been Hebrews among them or near them.[13]

The mad Caliph of Egypt—Al Hakim—ordered all non-Moslems to wear black clothing during his reign. Three centuries later, Christians were ordered to wear blue and Hebrews were ordered to wear yellow. But despite all the edicts and oppression, Christianity and Judaism still survived in Egypt.

The eighth century, after the Christian era, experienced African-Arab domination from Algeciras, the seaport at the southern tip of Spain, to the Pyrenees frontier between France and Spain. The Moslems advanced and gained territory until France was penetrated. In France they were finally halted by Charles Martel in 732 A.C.E.

Of interest to historians is the fact that the Arab Dynasty in Spain was made up of Africans from Morocco, many Slavs, Austrians, and Germans. And the only free men among these converts and seekers of spoils were the Africans. The other warriors were all bought from Charlemagne and his successors as slaves. It was due to the large proportion of Africans from Morocco in the Moslem armies and the important roles they played that Shakespeare was interested in Othello as a Moor, and many English-speaking writers and people at court showed particular interest in the Blackamoor, as an added touch of class, in the European courts and boudoirs.

The Moslems reactivated so-called Greek classics—which the Greeks had copied from Africa, in Alexandria—stolen by Aristotle. The Moslems also promoted restoration of the museum at Alexandria and made it a research center for mathematics, sciences, and medicine. The outdated Roman numerals were replaced by Arabic numerals which we still use. The zero was added, and so were Arabic words such as alcohol, algebra, alchemy and camphor, to identify a few. The Moslems learned to make paper from the Chinese; mathematical innovations, and philosophical treatment in depth with metaphysics from the Indians, as well as the uses of alloys in metallurgical forging developed by the Africans.

The Moslems conquered people throughout the East and were educated by and learned from them. In the subsequent transformation of these people, their conversion to Islam was accomplished in one blow, but their acceptance of Islam's religious, artistic, and intellectual outlook was not accomplished any quicker than it had been by Christianity or Buddhism. It was a gradual process which took at least six centuries to accomplish. And even after all that time, it was not complete. Hebrew, Christian, and Zoroastrian believers still adhered to their doctrines in Moslem-dominated countries.

Islam won its battle for minds, like other missionary religions, by absorbing many of the elements in its converts' previous religions. In the case of Islam, as with other religions, the price of conversion was compromise. Islam also won a sociolinguistic battle. The Arabic language substituted Greek as the official language in those societies which were formerly ruled by the Roman Empire. The real society-language triumph came about in the area of literature. Sources of Islamic history are copious and date from Muhammad's lifetime onward. Most of them are said to be of unquestionable value—from the historians' point of view.

Muhammad did not make the mistake that Jesus made. The Islamic movement can be traced from period to period and, in some cases, from day to day. These records are all in Arabic. As a result, they befuddle the average western historian who had been researching the history of Southwest Asia and Egypt in Greek and Latin over a period of nearly 1,200 years.

After the Prophet's death, Abu Bekr, also known as Bakr, became the first Caliph (632–634). His short reign dealt with homogenizing tribes who had never been accustomed to a central authority controlling them from a power base far away. Muhammad's death caused four rival prophets to arise with intent to meet the needs and pleas of those self-ruling tribes. Bekr arose to meet their challenge. He was dealt with accordingly. Bekr declared Jihad wars which he waged not only to keep those already in check through continued indoctrination, but to convert other tribes and people as well. Bekr's next objective was to use the warlike temperament of the tribes, formerly used in internecine tribal raids, by channeling that uncontrollable urge into the invasion of other countries outside the Arabian peninsula and Arab communities. Bekr died in 634 A.C.E. Omar succeeded him and reigned until he was stopped in 644. He wrested Egypt and Syria from the Byzantine, Persia, and Iraq. He died one year before his armies reached the borders of India and China.

The only African country within reach of Egypt, even by way of the Sudan was Ethiopia. It was spared invasion, however, because Muhammad had promised never to challenge to war or attempt to destroy that land. He recognized and respected Ethiopia as the home of the first kings the world had ever known. Muhammad remembered his welcome there, in time of need, and joined the Africans in saying, "From Ethiopia came the King of Kings."

The Moslems recorded their conquests and showed that it was the African majority who conquered Spain with their great numbers. Islamic records also show that it was through Africa that the knowledge of China, India, and Arabia went to Europe where and when the whites were still savage vandals. The Africans were also the ones who protected Spain from attack by European despoilers, enabling learning to develop and emanate elsewhere.

The Hebrew and Christian religions, and Islam, all owe their origin and development to overwhelming African effort which they exploit up to this day.[14]

The Moslems were called Saracens by the Byzantine Empire (present day Turkey). Omar, the Byzantine Second Caliph, was at first hostile to Islam. He became converted by 618 and was adviser to Muhammad at that time. Omar was responsible for the selection of Abu Bekr—without opposition—for the position of first Caliph, in 632. He made Islam an imperial power after he himself succeeded Bekr, also unopposed, in 634. Omar is given credit for reopening the canals of Mesopotamia and the waterway from the Nile to the Red Sea. He was assassinated by a foreign slave. Omar was then succeeded by Uthman.

The Byzantine history shows the name Saracen defined as a term applied to Arabs and, by extension, Moslems in general. The name designated Arabs, Moors of Africa, and Seljuk Turks. Saracens were also popular.

Saracen conquests robbed the Roman Empire at Byzantium of Africa, and Syria. And it was with great difficulty, after years of confusion in Byzantium, that the Roman Empire held the frontier of Asia Minor, and bolstered against Saracen incursions.

The Moslems had a naval force which they used to invade Byzantium. Their sea power demanded a counterbalance. The Moslems knew that Byzantine rulers had only built a fleet when the Vandals went to Africa. At that time, the fifth century emperors of the Roman Empire did not have a fleet either east or west. And Justinian's make-shift Byzantine fleet was successful not because of its sea power, but rather by the declining conditions of the Vandal sea power at the time.

The Moslems or Saracens also made travel through Byzantium so difficult that well guarded sea routes became a necessity.

Steven Runciman, a Byzantine historian, says that Moslem sea power was also on the decline after 720 A.C.E. But Byzantine rulers carelessly allowed their naval force to continue its decline. That reduction of force was a costly mistake because around the ninth century, a Moslem fleet returned to the Byzantine waters to harass the Empire. The Saracens snatched Sicily and, even worse, Crete from the Roman Empire. Crete, it is said, became a base for pirate raids along the Aegean coasts.[15]

The Romans hurriedly rebuilt their Navy. That new Roman Navy was helpful, but it could not get back Sicily. It only recovered southern Italy for the Romans. However, Crete was finally recaptured after two futile attempts in 902 and 949.

Moslem sea power had waned by this time and Nicephorus was able to boast about Islamic command having ended. He used to shout, "I alone command the sea."

Constantine VII (913–959) then claimed the right to be supreme commander of the Straights of Gibraltar. But Byzantine sea power soon declined once more. This time, the Byzantine Empire was already rapidly declining.

The newly formed Empire resisted disintegration with integration, Immigrant Greeks, Hamites from Egypt and the Sudan, Semites from Syria, and other ethnic strains all united through intermarriage. Arcadius, a Spaniard, married a Goth, Eudoxia. And their son, Theodosius II, married a pure Hellene. Late in the seventh century, a Syrian was the Bishop of Rome, while Slavs—descendants of slaves—and Armenians existed in large numbers throughout the Mediterranean area. Narses, Justinian's great general of the sixth century, was an Armenian. During this period of racial admixture and demographic change, Byzantines went over to Islam, and Arabs went over to Christianity.[16]

NOTES

1. J.C. de Graft Johnson. *African Glory The Story of Vanished Civilizations* (New York: Walker and Company, 1954), p. 61.
2. *Mullah*: A Moslem religious leader; Turkish mullah and Persian mulla, from Arabic *mawla*, meaning "master."
3. J.C. de Graft Johnson. *African Glory*. pp. 31–61.
4. J.C. de Graft Johnson. *African Glory The Story of Vanished Civilizations* (New York: Walker and Company, 1954).
5. Josephus describes the Sabeans as descendants of Saba the oldest son of *Cush*. Josephus Flavius states that Ham of Cham, the father of Cush "Ham inhabited the country now called Judea, . . . and called it from his own name Canaan. . . Judadas, settled the Judadeans, a nation of the Western Ethiopians, and left them his name; as dis Sabas to the Sabeans."
   Josephus Flavius. *The Works of Flavius Josephus:* Antiquities of the Jews (Hartford, Connecticut: S.S. Scranton Company, 1917).
   At one time, Yemen was confused with another Arabic word meaning happiness. The name was popularized by European geographers as *Arabia Felix:* Happy or fortunate Arabia. At another time, the name comprised a much larger area.
   The people of Yemen are Arabs. "Most of those living on the Tihamah are of Arab and African stock. . . About 60% are Sunni Muslims, the rest are Zaidi Muslims." Columbia Encyclopedia.
6. Max L. Margolis and Alexander Marx. *A History of the Jewish People* (New York: A Temple Book Atheneum, Jewish Publication Society of America, 1973). pp.248-260.
7. Max L. Margolis and Marx. *A History of the Jewish People.* pp. 253–254.
8. Banu Kainuka: One of the three Jewish Tribes in Medina during Muhammad's times.
9. Ismael R. al Faruqi:*The Challenge of Islam*: Islamic Council of

Europe. "In a moment of high vision the prophet Muhammad said, 'All men are born Muslims (in the sense in which Islam is equated with *din al fitrah*), original religion' it is his [their] parents that Christianize him [them]." p. 94, 1978.

10. J.C. de Graft Johnson. *African Glory* (New York: Walker and Company 1954).

11. The *Standard Jewish Encyclopedia* states that Queen Kahina was a Berber.

12. *The American Heritage Dictionary of the* English Language (Boston: Houghton Mifflin Co. 1978). p.124, defines "Berber."
A member of several Moslem tribes of North Africa. . . The Afro-Asiatic languages of these tribes." There were no Moslems when Queen Kahina ruled North Africa. She was a Hebrew woman of black skin like the original Arabs and Hebrews of that region.

13. In the Sahara region of Morocco there are some Moslems who observe Hebrew rituals, kill their animals after that tradition, and will only reveal to Africans that they are descendants of original Hebrews. They are called Daggatun.

14. When Francisco Franco became Dictator of Spain in 1939, he brought in the Blackest Moroccans from Ceuta and Tetuan to be his honor guard. Salvador de Madriaga. Spain: *A Modern History*. J.C. de Graft Johnson.

15. Steven Runcinan. *Byzantine Civilization* (New York: The American Library, Inc., 1933) pp. 112-145.

16. Runcinan, pp. 112-145.3

CHAPTER 9

THE WANDERING JEWS

After the Greeks learned religion and philosophy from Africa, they hellenized it. They took Ethiopian gods like Ammon, worshipped at Ethiopia's ancient capital Meroe, and in Thebes, Egypt, and Libya. They called Ammon "Zeus." The Romans later called him Jupiter. Herodotus, Plutarch, and Diodorus all declare that Osiris left Ethiopia, invaded and civilized Egypt, placed his sister and spouse Isis on the throne with Hermes to assist her and to administer the government, while Hercules was put in command of the troops. The Greeks made Hermes, whom the Romans called Mercury, their messenger.

The people whom the Jews called Cushites, and the Greeks called Ethiopians, were thus named by the former because they descended from Cush, and the latter because of the beautiful bronze color of their skin.

The Ethiopian Queen Cambyses (525 B.C.E.) subjugated Egypt during the reign of the shepherd kings, called Hyksos, and the enslavement of the Hebrews.

In 334, Alexander the Great took over Persia's empire. Alexander's objective was to make all conquered nations adopt and maintain the same culture—Greek and Oriental fusion. Alexander built the city of Alexandria at Egypt and other new cities while he restored old ones. Alexandria was so beautiful and important that the Romans later built a city and named it *Alessandria fra Torino e Genova.*[1]

Alexander had confidence in the Jews as economic catalysts. He was not fearful of them as an enterprising people and therefore did not suppress or restrict them. Alexander did not conscript Jews as soldiers in order not to violate their Sabbath. But as soon as Alexander died, wars broke out among his generals seeking control and territorial expansion. Ptolemy took Egypt and Seleucus took the conquered lands of Asia.

Palestine was the battleground for these wars, and was therefore of importance to the first Ptolemy and the first Seleucus. Ptolemy got

Palestine and Seleucus desisted from further contests. However, Seleucus' descendants were more persistent than he. They never gave up their claim to the land, and a vendetta ensued. The Jews were caught in the middle and were attacked by Ptolemy's soldiers who got no resistance from them when they were attacked on the Sabbath. Ptolemy's soldiers then referred to the Jews as a foolish people who would not defend themselves on Saturdays.

The Jews then moved from Palestine toward the West rather than return to Babylonia in the East. They settled along the coasts of the Mediterranean, on the Greek island and on the coasts of the Black Sea. At this point their western Diaspora began. Many Hebrews were among these people from Judea. Far away from Hebrew traditions and language, these hybridized Canaanites began to study Greek and act like Greeks. They had left home speaking Hebrew or Aramaic and by the third generation they had intermingled with the charming Greek women and men to such an extent that they were unable to read Hebrew. In order to keep their Hebrew language and traditions alive, the converts and children of the Hellenists were sent to the Greek *Synagogues* to study Hebrew and maintain the teaching of Israel and Judea. The people of Canaan were Hebrews. Those from little Judea were called Jews.

Judea, the smaller of the two Hebrew kingdoms, had come to an end in 586 B.C.E. This catastrophe had probably made the Jews decide to come to Alexandria rather than return to ruin and desolation in Judea. Coming westward to Alexandria and later engaging in commerce with Roman-Byzantium, they became shipowners, silk manufacturers, and most of all physicians. Some Jews also held important positions in southern Italy, around Apulia and Calabria, where the people were dark-skinned despite miscegenation. Some Jews were date growers in Sicily a point near Africa, while others were regular farmers and goldsmiths. They became both thoroughly Hellenized and Latinized.

Alexandria was not the same under the Romans as it had been under the Greeks. There were lean and mean years and joyous and prosperous eras.

In Alexandria, there was a popular Roman orator named Apion, considered a philosopher and teacher by some pagans and a charlatan by others. In any case, he was a good agitator. Apion spread rumors against the Jews and caused the pagans and other Gentiles to attack the Jews. The rioters attacked the rich Jews who were isolated from the main community in their rich suburban homes. Over four hundred of them were robbed and their homes looted in August of 38 A.C.E.

The Jews were not cowards or patsies, and did not sing "We Shall

Overcome." They had clashed with these mobs before, for similar reasons, and had defended themselves well. That is perhaps the reason the mob only looted the isolated suburban communities. The Jews knew that it would not be advantageous to seek revenge at this time, so they sent a delegation to Rome. They wanted to explain their situation and seek redress. Philo was their representative. The Alexandrian pagans sent their delegates and deputies also.

Apion addressed the Roman emperor as a god whose statue was refused a place in the temple of the Jews in the winter of 39. They had also refused to allow a statue of Caligula to be erected, in the Temple of Jerusalem at Palestine in the summer of 40. The Jews tried to explain their tolerance and their grievances, but Caligula (12–41 A.C.E.) paid them little attention. Philo was asked a few unimportant questions and hardly allowed any time to answer. The Jews made one small gain, nonetheless. Flaccus, the Roman governor of Egypt who had tried to force them to put statues in their temples, was called back home to Rome. The Jews returned to Alexandria and bided their time for revenge. The pagans were expecting a vendetta and kept alert.

When Caligula (emperor from 37 to 41 A.C.E.) was assassinated by Cassius Chaerea, a tribune of the Praetorian Guard, at the Palatine games January 24, 41 A.C.E., the Jews suddenly picked up arms. They distributed weapons from their cache and made the gang war an even contest instead of the one-sided ordeal the pagans had put them through. Then some Jews began to roam once more.

THE ROAMING JEWS AND THE ROMANS

As the Jews dispersed through Europe, from the regions of the Hellenistic Diaspora, Jewish merchants from Italy followed them. These Italianized Jews carried their skills and trading acumen into northern Gaul, and along the Roman roads to the banks of the Rhine. In Roman Cologne, there was a Jewish colony established "before there were Germans."[2]

Many of the people who came in contact with these descendants of Hebrews became impressed with their moral standards, unrelenting confidence in their invisible God, and their metaphysical consciousness. This caused many pagans to become converted to the faith of the Hebrews, and some Hebrews proselytized. Numerous converts could not resist their old traditions and habits and became known as "God-worshippers."[3] They respected the Hebrews' commandments, but could not religiously maintain the fasts and other sacrifices demanding extensive hours of prayer and liturgical exercises. There were mixed marriages between Jews and Gentiles. And conversion was so widespread that the confessor of Emperor Louis the Pious converted to the Hebrew religion. This integration led to jealousy and antagonism among the people, and a violent reaction by the Roman Church. Expulsions were ordered and Jewish properties confiscated.

Charlemagne (742?–814 A.C.E.), emperor of the West (800–814), who sold slaves[4] of Austrian, Slavic, and German descent to the Moslems became the first Germanic king to defy the Church, maintaining his independence. This attitude favored the Jews. Charlemagne was a great crusader and champion of Christianity, but he still managed to crave enlightenment and rationalism that defied the Catholic Church's edicts. His beliefs gave him a lot in common with the Jews. He defied the Catholic Church's determination to prohibit Jews from owning land, employing Christian workers, or wearing distinctive clothing. As a result of his largess, Jews were able to become active in world trade and maintain commerce with African and Asian countries whose languages were usually familiar to them. Jewish merchants expanded their settlements and trading posts into newly acquired German areas such as Bavaria and Saxony. Jewish interaction with the East was exploited by Charlemagne who used them to intercede in his intercourse with the Caliph of Baghdad (797–802). The caliphate was later succeeded by the Fatimids in Africa after the fall of Baghdad. In the delegation sent to the Caliph of Baghdad, with Harum al-Rashid, was a guide and interpreter of Jewish descent. He was Isaac, the only survivor of a difficult three-year journey. When Isaac returned to Charlemagne, he aroused great interest and admiration. He brought back a tremendous gift from the Moslem Caliph to the Christian emperor. It was an elephant; the first animal of its kind and size to be seen in the West. This feat accomplished by a Jew and the importance of Jewish commercial success persisted unto the days of Charlemagne's son and successor, Louis the Pious (814–840 A.C.E.). Jews became so important that the busiest shopping and marketing day of Lyons changed from Saturday to a weekday.

The Jews became so popular that they expanded to distant towns and cities. Jewish communities were so prosperous that as late as 1084, just a few years before the First Crusade, the bishop of Speyer tried to improve the importance of his town by enticing Jews to come there and carry on their businesses. He wrote, as bishop and mayor of the town (Bürgermeister): "Desiring to make a town out of the village of Speyer, I thought to raise its dignity many times by getting Jews to settle there."[5] Jews and Christians became so friendly that when a town was attacked, the Jews joined the militia, bore arms, and defended it against its enemies. Jews dressed and acted like Christians. The intercourse of both groups bore little semblance to religious, ethnic, or other differences. It was inconceivable to most of the people that the neighborliness and camaraderie could ever see a violent end.

The Jews continued to flourish under Charlemagne's son Louis[6] (circa 814–840), until the twelfth century when Benjamin ben Jonah of Tudela, Spain, began his travels around the world. From the eighth to the twelfth centuries, Jews prospered culturally and economically. There were such notable scholars as Solomon ibn Gabirol (c. 1021–c. 1070 A.C.E.), known in Arabic writings as Avicebron, poet and philosopher who influenced Christian scholars; Moises ben Maimonides, known as *Rabbenu Moshe ben Maimom*, abbreviated RaMBaM, of Cordova, Spain (1135–1204), who lived in Fez, North Africa, practiced medicine, and taught Hebrew rationalism in his philosophic treatises till 1071; Yehudah Ha-Levi (1086–1140), Spanish poet and philosopher, who traveled up the Nile, and others.[7]

EUROPEANIZED JEWS

The people of the East known as Israelites or Hebrews, were now named after the smaller of the two kingdoms of Israel and Judea. Regardless of the name given to them, they came from the East; Europe is in the West, the Occident. Therefore, Europeans could not or cannot be Orientals or eastern people under any title, guise or given circumstances, even if Palestine was given to them.

When the eastern people arrived in the West, they came following in the footsteps of their Roman conquerors, like the West Indians followed the British to England or the Latin Americans followed the *Yanqui* or *Gringo* to the United States in recent times. There were Jewish settlements stretching from North Africa to Spain and Italy as far back as 160 B.C.E., and farther.

Judah the Maccabee[8] sought Roman assistance against the Syrians, after defeating them on successive occasions through his tactics of ambush, rapid changing of bivouacs, and night attacks. The Syrian forces were overwhelming his small army and he sent to the Romans for help. The Roman Senate did not send the desperate Jewish community supplies or troops, instead, a reply was sent stating that the Jews were now Roman allies and friends.

The Roman General Cneius Pompeius Magnus—Pompey (106–48 B.C.E.) rival of Julius Caesar—had conquered Palestine and taken a large number of Jewish prisoners of war to Rome in 63 B.C.E. and sold them as slaves. These Jews were freed later when their descendants became Roman citizens. Riots against Rome were fomented intermittently and more Jews were subsequently captured, and later freed, causing a considerable increase of the Jewish population in Rome. When the Romans advanced into Gaul, Jewish peddlers and established merchants followed the Roman armies into France and western Germany.

The Jews of southern Italy and Sicily found themselves going to Rome, Spain, or back to North Africa from whence their ancestors had traveled to the Mediterranean basin and elsewhere. In Spain, a

Roman-occupied peninsula, they were unmolested for a time, and acculturated their neighbors.

Many Romans visited the synagogues, observed the Sabbath, and intermarried with Jews. The Jewish women encouraged their Roman husbands to observe Judaic teachings and indoctrinated their children. The Jewish husbands, in turn, took their Roman wives to the synagogues. These customs were prevalent in France, Western Germany, and Spain.

In the meantime, many Jews had followed Yeshua—a Black Hebrew from the House of David—and were preaching Christianity.[9] In the competition between Judaism and Christianity, the Roman Emperor Constantine I saw a profitable opportunity in proclaiming Christianity a "permitted religion" and later the religion of the State. Soon after the Romans began regarding the pagans as barbarians and started accepting Judaism or Christianity. Many pagans accepted Judaism because it was older and had been the respected religion of Rome. Furthermore, the Jews were usually more educated than the Christians whose religion did not permit reading of the Scriptures, but had it read to them instead. Apart from that, Christianity had not really identified itself with traditions distinctively different from the old Hebrew rituals, attire or the simple burning of candles. The only outstanding feature with a marked difference was the sign of the cross, *il segno della croce*.

The Council of Nicea (325) decidedly separated Christians from Jews.[10] Arianism was promoted and Africanism demoted. The heretics were gaining in power and as a result *imbiancamento*, the process of bleaching the skin, or *emblanquecimiento*, as it was later called in Spain and Latin America, began.

Christians were no longer allowed to visit synagogues or intermarry with Jews. They were not to observe the Jewish Sabbath which was changed to Sunday instead. Jews were prohibited from eating *matzah*, unleavened bread.

As the fall and decline of Rome approached, the Barbarians rose and flourished. Rome became deserted, Vandals occupied North Africa, the Visigoths took Spain, the Franks overpowered France, and the Ostrogoths took Italy. The Barbarians formulated an admixture of paganism and Christianity and called it Arianism. All religions were respected and the Jews, in particular, were allowed to practice Judaism with protection against mob attacks. Alaric the Visigoth had sacked Rome, in the year 410, and left with most of the Temple vessels. When the Vandals came in 455 they took what was left of the Temple treasure to Carthage. Then twenty years later Odoacer and his troops, who had been mercenaries in the service of Rome, revolted and put a quick end to the western empire by defeating the Roman general Orestes at Piacenza. Odoacer occupied Ravenna (the West

Roman capital), and deposed East reluctantly recognized Odoacer's rule over Italy and granted him the title of Patrician. Then Zeno sent Theodoric the Great, King of the Ostrogoths, into Italy to oust Odoacer, his sons and chiefs of staff. They were invited to a banquet. Theodoric assassinated them, and made himself ruler of Italy. These changes enabled the Jews to quickly reestablish themselves and even become landowners of large estates.

The Christians started marrying Jews, again calling Jewish adherents to bless their soil and livestock, instead of priests, and having Jews arbitrate disputes as righteous and just arbitrators. These special recognitions and positions of authority caused jealousy. The Jews realized from previous experience that their prosperity would not last forever, so they began making preparations for that day.

The day came when the Gothic kingdom fell to the incursion of Justinian I, (483–565), Byzantine emperor from 527-565 A.C.E, who sent his generals Belisarius and Narses to overrun that kingdom.[11] The Jews of Naples helped their Gothic patrons and neighbors defend their city. They fought courageously, but lost in the end. Italy was captured in 555 A.C.E. An imperial lieutenant, *exarch*,[12] was put in command at Ravenna and the principal provinces were governed by Greek dukes under orders from the lieutenant-governor. The Code of Justinian was promulgated throughout Italy, replacing the laws of Theodoric. The Code of Justinian remained in force through all of Italy and the Island of Sicily. Jews were harshly treated and compelled to endure this treatment all through the Middle Ages, until the invasion of the Saracens from Arabia.

The Lombards (566–774) at first were Arian worshippers who later converted to Roman orthodoxy. They were unable to govern the entire peninsula; as several parts of Italy remained self-governing. With the emperor in a distant land and not immediately over there to subdue the populace, Rome became a target for the bishops. There was an opportunity to influence the people and set the stage for spiritual and psychological programming of western Europe and Rome.

Gregory I, known as Gregory the Great (540–604 A.C.E.),[13] neither empathized with Judaism nor sympathized with Jews. He felt that Judaism identified with a Jewish method of interpreting the Scriptures in a biased manner and that Jewish explanations and valid premises leading to conclusions against Christianity were nonsense. Gregory felt that the Jews were to be converted to Christianity by reason and persuasion. Converts were to be exposed to inducements, permitted to visit and worship in churches, befriended and protected. Converts were not to be criticized by other Jews or antagonized even by Christians. There was to be no exertion of force. If Jews were compelled to accept baptism, they would probably revert to their old superstitious and suspicious ways covertly or overtly. Gregory even felt that

214   The African Origin of Modern Judaism

Jews should be allowed to practice their own religion if they so choose, but that would prevent them from being able to acquire or possess Christian slaves or hire Christian workers. Any slaves held on Jewish-owned estates should be placed under a contract as tenants of the estate and share in the crops he produced or helped to produce. Gregory had Anglo-Saxon slaves of his own that he kept bound to all tasks, including meeting his personal needs.

The slaves of Gregory's time were usually acquired through their capture in war or purchase after a war. They were usually men and women, but at times even children. Agricultural tools were primitive and machinery unknown; many laborers were needed to farm large tracts of land. This necessity caused slavery to become a demand that was supplied even to the Church. Most armies preferred to sell the soldiers and families captured rather than kill them. The slaves, in turn, usually adopted their master's religion and customs. Slaves in Jewish households or on Jewish farmlands came under the Hebraic law that bound Jacob to his Uncle Laban's ranch for seven years.[14] Some slaves were freed as soon as they accepted Judaism. Gregory felt that these converts would cause a decrease in the population growth of the Church, or undermine its expansion. He decreed that Jews could not keep Christian slaves for more than three months. Jews could not proselytize among pagans or Christians.

According to the Catholics, the end of the great Roman Empire caused joy among them. For after that Empire had persecuted Christians for three hundred years and forced them underground to the catacombs, it fell to the Barbarians in 476 A.C.E.

But later, King Euric, of the Goths is recorded as having led a grievous persecution of Christians in Gaul. He beheaded those who did not convert to his "perverse pagan doctrine," cast priests into prison, blocked the doors of the holy churches with briars, "that only a few might enter and the Faith might pass into oblivion." Those developments saw Europe by the beginning of Pope Saint Gregory's century dominated by six barbarian nations. Catholicism was replaced by the cults of pagan Anglo-Saxons in Britain, pagan Franks in northern France, and Arian Visigoths in southern France and Spain, Arian Ostrogoths in Italy, Arian Vandals in North Africa, and Arian Burgundians in eastern France which "were more distasteful to God than sheer paganism."[15]

Pope Gregory once saw some Angles, while he was at the monastery of Saint Andrew's. The experience was of such importance to the Church that it was recorded in detail by the monks. It was recorded at that pope's famous meeting with English slaves, for the first time in his life. Gregory was on his way to the Roman Forum when he saw tall, blond youths being sold. He inquired from whence they had come.[16] The people replied to him "They are Angles." The pope then exclaimed "Angles, say rather they are angels."[17] The pope seemed to encourage the Roman onlookers to believe that pale-skinned slaves resembled angels as painted in the Sistine Chapel where Leonardo da Vinci painted frescoes with a white picture of Christ.

The papacy of Rome inherited new laws through its alliance with the Frankish kings. The Pope felt that the Franks would be bulwarks against the Lombards, just as the Lombards had formerly been used against the Greeks. The alliance was sealed with the coronation of Charlemagne, the Frankish king, at Rome in the year 800 A.C.E. The coronation ceremony was performed by Leo III, Bishop of Rome and vicar of Christ. Rome was again a center of importance in the orbit of the Holy Roman Empire. Nevertheless, the south of Italy remained under Byzantine rule.

By 827 A.C.E., Sicily was taken by the Saracens and held for more than two hundred years. In 982 Islamic Sicily was attacked by Emperor Otto II Holy Roman emperor (973–983) and Germanic king (961-83). The Saracens repelled his attack and routed his forces. Otto is said to have lost his horse in the battle, but was rescued by a faithful Jew, who gave the emperor his horse to escape capture. Saracen rule continued until 1061 when Roger I, invaded Messina.

Shortly thereafter, the entire island of Sicily was captured by Otto II. He was succeeded by Roger II (1101–1154), who united the mainland (acquired by his brother Robert Giscard) with the island of Sicily.

In 1130 A.C.E., Roger was crowned king of Sicily and Italy by the anti-pope Anacletus of[18] the Pierleoni family. The Pierleoni family was of Jewish descent, and the rumor spread near and far that a Jew was on the papal throne. Jewish consciousness was once again raised throughout the Italian communities and many Jews who had converted to Christianity returned to the Jewish fold. Tombstones then bore inscriptions in Hebrew rather than Latin or Greek. The community leaders were learned men, rabbis, who met at Venosa, a college or institution of higher learning called *yeshibah*.

Nevertheless, they continued to worship the Sun God of Africa, Amen-Ra. The Africans had forced the Hebrews to worship Amen-Ra while they were captives in Africa. Not being able to produce very much originality, the three main religions still worship that God up to this day. Hebrews or Jews, Catholics and Protestants all say, "Amen."[19]

THE IBERIAN

Prehistoric knowledge of Spain's chronology is based on Phoenician events and dates showing centuries of Punic penetration from Punic North Africa before the coming of Europeans.

Paleolithic cave paintings depict animals of the late quaternary geological period and engraved upon bones identified as remains of animals extinct for quite some time before the coming of the Greeks. The most well known of these relics is the discovery of Altamira[20] near Santander. The find was published by Edouard Cartailhac and an abbot, Henri Breuill [Monaco 1906]. Other sites where important discoveries were made are Hornos de la Peña, Pasiega and Castillo, Province of Santander; Basondo in the province of Biscay; Pindal, Buxu, as well as La Peña, Asturias, on the Iberian Peninsula. These paleolithic, decorated caverns are in the mountainous regions of the Pyrenees along the coastal hills beyond Santander. Some paintings are also found in France.

The Hispanic-Lusitanian Peninsula was named Iberia by ancient writers because of the Iberos people who migrated there from Oran, North Africa. They were, without doubt, of Hamitic origin. They apparently penetrated Spain since the aëneolithic period, 3000 B.C.E. This was before the Asiatic people left Asia for the Minoan Islands in 2000 B.C.E. to later become "Greeks," or the coming of the Celts to Iberia to produce the Celtiberians.

The Iberians were related to the Tartessians of Africa who also invaded Spain around the same era. The latter's presence is certified as being recorded toward the end of the so-called Bronze Age. One of the famous art pieces of the time is the famous *La Dama de Elche*.[21]

SPAIN

During the existence of the earliest representatives of mankind, men lived in caves throughout Europe. At the same time, other men more highly developed than they lived in huts, houses and in luxury. Around the glacial epoch there were only two "continents," so to speak. The two continents were Asia Major and Asia Minor. The area now known as Africa was Asia Major, long before America was even conceived of or even expected to exist. European cartographers, who came on the scene much later, tried to determine whether America was part of Asia Minor, since most of it had been covered with ice for a long time.

Africa had men and women wearing flowing robes and jewelry while the people of Europe were crawling around on their hands and knees and living in caves.[22] Some of the people who lived in caves have descendants who can be seen in that primitive condition up to the present time at Lumbreras and Granada, Spain. The people of North Africa (short, stocky, black and wooly-haired) were called Iberos and Igorots. They crossed from North Africa into Spain and were its first inhabitants.

The Spanish peninsula—as we know it now—then became *La Peninsula Iberica* (Iberian Peninsula).[23] These black people traveled to the Philippines and India as well.[24] These were the people who later amalgamated with the Greeks, Goths, Vandals, Celts, and Romans, as well as Phoenicians, Mauritanians and Carthaginians (later called Moors,) to become "Spaniards."

It must be emphasized that "Europe was then non-existent as a continent," let alone a civilized region.

The people known as Hebrews, later called Jews, did not arrive in Spain as a considerable number of immigrants until the Diaspora circa 64 B.C.E., under Herod the Idumean. This was during the time of the Hebrews Second Commonwealth, 316 B.C.E. to 70 A.C.E., their age of recognizable literary achievement. During this era Ezra sifted through Cushitic and Egyptian manuscripts to produce a work of letters, events, and laws called the *Book of Jubilees*, beginning with a creation and ending with the tales of Mount Sinai.

The Hebrews desisted from worshipping idols and made the God of Israel the most powerful God on earth and in the heavens. The golden calves, copied from the Cushites and Egyptians before they began worshipping one Amen-Ra or other (monotheistic deity), were no longer worshipped, and neither were Baal and other Babylonian gods such as Sabaoth.

After the desecration, destruction and burning of the Temple at Jerusalem by Titus Flavius Sabinus Vespasianus (39–81 A.C.E.), Roman emperor from 79 to 81 A.C.E., Jews dispersed to North Africa, Spain, Italy, and India. Pompey's conquest of Jerusalem had already caused numerous captives to be led through Rome in the victory procession, as proof of his accomplishments. The victorious generals sold their captives into slavery. Those Jews who became Romans by citizenship were soon freed, nonetheless. However, many of them refused to perform services on the Sabbath and were submitted to harsh punishments. These scattered Jews were mostly peasants, artisans, and a few scholars. But after being uprooted and shifted about, they soon found themselves in the midst of Arab conquests that made them prosperous in the great mercantile society established by the Moslems. They quickly became merchants, traders, businessmen and professionals. They enjoyed the symbiosis of Moslems and Jews.

Opportunities for Jews in Palestine dwindled to almost nothing of consequence through restrictions by the Romans and the commercial control of the Gentiles. Ships sailed, from Alexandria across the Mediterranean to Rome, laden with cereals (wheat and barley), berseem,[25] beans, onions, incense, dyes, and spices from caravans arriving from in and overland.

Spain, noted for its wine, food and minerals became a competitor. The ports of Cadiz, Barcelona, and Malaga, the oldest seaport on the Mediterranean, busily exported barrels of olives and olive oil, brandy, and wine. It was not long before the Jews became participants in the commercial traffic.

The Goths and Romans had not been the last conquerors of Spain. The Arabs and North Africans had been sitting in the wings watching the drama unfold. When their opportunity came, eight centuries of Arab domination had to be reckoned with.

At the beginning of the eighth century (702–709 A.C.E.), the Arab Viceroy in North Africa—Musa ibn Nusair—was incited by Count Julian, governor of Ceuta and Andalusia. Julian and the sons of Visgothic King Witiza were to attack Spain. The Moslems immediately crossed the straits of what is now known as Gibraltar, entered Spain and defeated the Goths. A notable African, General Tarik, defeated the Spaniards at the battle of Guadalete in 711 A.C.E.[26] After that astounding feat, Don Pelayo, first king of Asturias—a mountainlike region in the north where the Spaniards had taken refuge—won the famous battle of Covadonga in 719. The decisive battle set the stage for the wars of reconquest between Spaniards and Moors that lasted almost eight centuries.

Under Moorish rule, Cordoba became the capital city and cultural center of Spain. There were Moorish palaces, mosques, open courts and halls of architectural splendor built. There were the Alcazar in Sevilla, the Alhambra of Granada, and the Gardens of Valencia and Murcia. Jewish artisans and smiths participated in the constructions and decorations. They were cunning enough to put Jewish stars of David or seals of Solomon (that can be seen interspersed among designs on tiles and projects there, up to today). The Jews enjoyed freedom with the Moors until the latter were expelled in 1492.

The defeat of the Moors was not an easy victory. The Spaniards still remember the astounding defeat of their greatest hero, Don Rodrigo de Bivar, el Cid Campeador. He was forced to shed tears[27] after his defeat in 1086 A.C.E. by Yusuf, a king from Upper Senegal. Yusuf crossed the Straits of Gibraltar with only fifteen thousand men, mostly "pure blacks."[28]

During Moorish domination, Spain flourished. She had been blossoming from the Middle Ages up to these Islamic times. Sevilla, Granada, Toledo, and Cordoba, the capital, became centers of culture with courts and masjids in Cordoba leading the way in elegance unequaled by any other cities of that time.

In 719, Jews had no longer been restricted to money-lending and tax-collecting. Moorish culture and Hebrew culture were side by side. Jewish education was reorganized and some Jews became educators, public officials, clerks, horse and mule traders, jugglers, and lion tamers.[29] Many Jews received the title of Don in Portugal and Spain. A number of them were so opulent that King John II of Portugal remarked, "We notice Jewish cavaliers, mounted on richly caparisoned horses and mules, in fine cloaks, cassocks, silk doublets, closed hoods, and with gilt swords."

A few Jews went to Lazcano and were either absorbed by the Vascos, or forced out before the reconquest, perhaps during that period. The little town of Lazcano was always a Catholic stronghold.[30]

After the reconquest, many Jews went to Holland. The emigration from Spain started in 1421.[31] Saint Vincent Ferrer and the Chancellor of Castile were anti-Semitic. Jews and Arabs were still pretty dark-skinned, so they were equally disliked. Anti-Moorish laws forced Hebrews and Moors to wear badges of identification on their outer garments. Systematic expulsions from Spain began in Andalusia in 1481, Sevilla, in 1483, and from Cordoba, Saragossa, Alarán and Teruel in 1486.

Isabella I, or Isabel la Católica (1451–1504), queen of Castile, and Ferdinand II, or Fernando de Aragón, married and united their kingdoms, proving the unquestionable benefit of unity. They conquered the Islamic armies after forcing the Moors into a position of being under siege in the last Moorish stronghold at Granada, in April 1490. These Catholic monarchs surrounded Granada, besieging the Islamic troops for many months after many hard-fought battles. The Moors anxiously awaited reinforcements from Africa without success. They too, like Hanibal de la Barca of Carthage before them, had been abandoned by their African compatriots at home. In the end, hunger and hopelessness forced their surrender on 2 January 1492. This was the capitulation of the last Islamic army in Spain. The banner with the Catholic Cross, emblem of the Crusaders, was raised over the Alhambra as slowly as the Islamic Crescent slid down the pole in front of it. The dark-skinned Moorish King Boabil, walked to the mounted pale-skinned Ferdinand to offer the symbol of surrender.[32]

This defeat led to the Christian decrees that gave Hitler a basis for his condemnation and sentencing of Jews to death. Hitler felt that they were racially and ethnically inferior to Aryans.

Martin Sagrera associates Hitler's assumptions with the Alphonsine decree of Spain which condemned the act of coitus between Jews and others under a penalty of death for the Jewish partner. Sagrera also points out that in recent times, the farmers of Mallorca disrobed Jewish boys they found unprotected, to see if they had tails. This famous ethnologist claims that all Hitler did was to follow the precedent set by the Spaniards. Sagrera explains that Heinrich Himmler visited Spain, he was received with all official honors. When asked about the Jews, Himmler replied that all he was doing was following the old norms of being "socially sanitary."[33]

The destruction of Moorish rule and cultural influence did not only destroy racial respect and mutual admiration among the two prominent religious groups and so-called races, but it brought about another cause for suppression of black or dark-skinned people. Moorish warlike potential had been so devastating to the light-skinned Crusaders that the fear of blacks has continued to this day and become one of the basic causes of racial prejudice.

Ramon Menendez Pidal, the most outstanding writer of Spanish classics wrote: "It is pretended by the Christians that the medieval tolerance of Spain proved superiority but facts show the contrary. Arab civilization was thereby more tolerant and much more civilized." Pidal also stated, "It was the Arab who taught the barbaric Spanish Christian to admit his black blood."[34]

The culture of the Moors of North Africa was superior to that of Europeans in Spain; it gave the Spaniards a knowledge of making soap, how to bathe with it, and to wear Moorish garments that the Spaniards called *calzoncillos* and *camisetas*, undershorts and undershirts.

Moorish military failure and Christian success still endured an absorption of Moorish culture and values by Europeans. It also caused many pretenses to surface. Some of these attitudes followed the Spaniards to Hispanic America. Racial complexities continued into the eighteenth century and later.

Sagrera shows where in 1743, a father Gilij, of the Catholic Church, considered the exploitation of the dark-skinned Indians and blacks, and the saying in Buenos Aires that "I am white is like saying I am a gentleman." Miguel Hesse also wrote during the same period: "in this part of the New World those who come from Spain, in other words the Whites are held up as nobles....[35] It is also a sort of special nobility in Spain to not be descended from Jews or Moors; in America, the white skin more or less decides the class a man occupies in society."[36]

Sagrera also related how someone in a town or city would have an argument with another "gentleman" of that place, who has a title. It is common to hear the former say to the latter, "*pues que, ¿cree usted ser más blanco que yo?*"37 The lack of character or honesty in the individual was compensated for or equated with his whiteness or excused by his autojustification based on cutaneous pallor.

These sayings led to a psychological surrendering of self-esteem by the Africans and Indians of pure stock who began to try to escape their origin. They did not want to be identified with their origins. They shunned or even resented their autochthonous origin or culture and substituted it with a white consciousness. The naturals or natives, as they were designated, tried to escape by discriminating against their own relatives and countrymen. The conclusion, therefrom, is: racism in Latin America is nothing but, first, escapism from one's African-Indo-European ancestry; second, the "rabi blancos" midgets; and third, they have an inferiority complex.

Those escapists are psychologically ambivalent and quite unaware of their ancient history and the heroic deeds of their noble progenitors. Even in Brazil, the so-called intellectuals have not been able to acknowledge that there are no superior races, only superior individuals. Richard Jackson refers to them as *Indoblanquinegros Blanquinegrindios and negrindoblancos*.[38]

Isabella and Ferdinand were not the real financial backers of the Spaniard, Christopher Columbus' first expedition to the New World. "Jews were the real backers of Columbus." Misters Santangel Sanchez and Abraham Senior, his bankers, received the letter from Columbus (when he wrote from America), instead of good Queen Isabella.

Columbus' family name was Colon, derived from *colonista*, meaning colonist in English. His family escaped from Spain during the Inquisition and settled in Genova, Italy. Cristobal Colon (as he is called in Spanish), spoke Italian poorly, but he was fluent in Spanish.[39] His family resided in the colonia guidea of Italy, known as *il ghetto*. These facts can be gathered from his ship's log.

Kahler indicates, "Jews had a major part in the expeditions of Columbus, in which they promoted, financed and actively participated. Columbus' Jewish interpreter, Luis de Torres, a linguist, was the first European on these expeditions to step upon American soil." Kahler, understandably, did not mention Estevanico, Columbus' black navigator. He did state, however, that Columbus was a "Jewish Marrano."[40]

Torres was credited by Ish Kishor in *Jewish Survival* as having named the big birds he saw in America "tukki" from whence the etymon led to "turkey."

The negative actions of one persecuted minority member or group against another minority invariably leads to repression of the person or persons initiating the actions, according to the laws of retribution. Jews, who persecute blacks should definitely reflect on this thought. This type of negative action was the cause, or at least one of the causes, of the Inquisitions of Spain and elsewhere.

Non-Christians were disliked for converting Christians to other religions and for refusing to convert to Christianity. Consequently, King Henry IV—half brother of Alfonso and Isabel of Castile (1425–1474)—enforced the restrictions upon Jews according to laws the Catholic Church had long sought to impose on non-believers. The Jews accelerated the rigid enforcement of these horrible laws through their own misjudgment. They killed a fellow Jew who was a royal tax collector well favored by the Spanish court. This victim of their fratricidal misdeed was Joseph Pichon. He probably deserved that fate because of the betrayal of his own people whom he also often exploited in favor of the Christians. His treasonable acts caused his Jewish community to consider him a spy and traitor, who should be eliminated at any cost.

However, the shedding of his blood soon caused the flowing of the blood of his fellow Jews. It caused reflection on past experiences.

The arrival of the year 1391 had seen Jews experiencing a line similar to the one drawn by Hernan Cortez on Mexican shores, when some Spaniards among his followers wanted to return to Spain and abandon the Conquest of America. Cortez drew a line in the sand encouraging one faction to follow him to glory by standing on his side of the line, or going on the opposite side to perish. The ships were burnt behind him, leaving the crew members an offer they could not resist.

On Ash Wednesday, March 15, and June 4, 1391, Jews were given the option of staying on one side of the invisible line of demarcation as Jews or crossing over to the opposite side as Christians. The ultimatum being death if they refused the cross. Become Christians and live or remain Jews and die! Mobs broke into Jewish communities of Cordoba, Sevilla, Toledo, and Granada, and stormed synagogues offering them conversion or death. Ferrand Martinez, archdeacon of Ecija, frenziedly agitated against alleged Jewish conversions of Christians and the illegal construction of synagogues in the domain of the Catholic diocese. Martinez pursued Jewish communities even in Castile and Aragón after he had upset the diocese of Sevilla. In the Jewish quarter of Sevilla, governor Juan Alfonso de Guzman, and the alcalde who was his relative, Alvar Perez de Guzman, had two leaders of the mobs seized and whipped in the public square. This pro-Jewish act angered the mobs.

The Christians could not understand that the Jews were also Spaniards, like themselves, who simply had a different religion. There were rumors that Jews had horns and were only religious when they worshipped money. Mobs surrounded the Jewish quarters. The regency acted swiftly in trying to avert violence. Their swiftness did not help very much. Lawlessness and dastardly acts of cruelty followed the coward gangs. Jewish residences and businesses were set afire. Four thousand Jews of all ages and both sexes were killed.

At Ecija and Carmona, the Jewish barrios were burnt to the ground. Dead bodies were heaped up in the streets. Prisoners and passersby were forced to drag the bodies out of the synagogues and dwellings.

The slaughter at Toledo took place on June 20, the fast day of Tammuz seventeenth. One of the victims was Judah, the son of Jehiel, who rather than die by Christian hands, cut the throats of his mother, his wife, and his children before killing himself. Several fearful people survived by accepting Christianity. Two of the rich converts were Samuel Abravallo and Joseph Abarim who were hurriedly baptized and protected for a sizeable fee.

But in Valencia, two hundred and fifty Jews were liquidated on

July 9,1391. The tidal wave of carnage swept across Spain and reached Barcelona on August 5th. The first attack left one hundred casualties. Hundreds of Jews fled to the citadel and took refuge there. The authorities tried to protect them, but the mob broke into the *fortaleza* and killed more than three hundred persons. One of the victims was the son of Hasdai Crescas who was in the city registrar's office awaiting a permit to get married. Some eleven thousand Jews are said to have been baptized by the clergy on that day. The wanton homicides continued for approximately three months.

The Jews who sought refuge in Islamic territory or resided there were the only ones spared. The "bear (Edom)" and the "wild ass (Ishmael"[41] were no longer Jewish enemies. Their enemies were now the charging papal bulls. The waves of persecution engulfed the island of Mallorca, where hundreds of Jews were massacred in the city of Palma, on August 2.

After the riots began to cause national disequilibrium, the government of Spain and its local *municipios* decided to halt the acts of terror. However, it was not before similar mob violence occurred in Catalonia and Gerona. Lerida was also affected with the thirst for Jewish blood. Most Jews in Gerona preferred death to conversion.

In Aragón, the Jews delayed their fate with huge *mordidas*, bribes, to officials and their stooges. In Portugal, extreme persecutions were avoided through the influence of the head Rabbi Moses Navarro who interceded to protect his flock from the butchers.

The amount of Jewish-owned property destroyed, and businesses lost, put several workers formerly employed by Jews on the streets with the mass of unemployed citizens. The Jewish yarn and leather factories were damaged, and thousands of Christians were in need of the income they took home from Jewish payrolls. Even the churches and cloisters, dependent on rates and taxes paid by the Jews, were now suffering economic depression. Many Christians began to reconsider, others continued to hold their grudges without compunction.

The question which remained was whether to exterminate the Jews or extirpate their Judaism. In 1411 Vincent Ferrer, a Dominican monk, initiated riots by inciting the rabble and forcing his way into synagogues with a cross in one hand and a Torah in the other. Ferrer offered Jews the cross or death, burrowing paths to conversion, but the mobs that decided to follow him offered only death, and had weapons to make their victims accept the threats. Several Jews converted on the spot. Some of the affluent Jews who were converted Christians acted against those who were not. One of these was a famous turncoat named Solomon ha-Levi, a wealthy and erudite Jew who had been a rabbi in the province of Burgos, in northern Spain.

Ha-Levi adopted Christianity and claimed that his salvation would come from that end. His aggression against his own group was seemingly based on his possession of like qualities, beliefs, and knowledge of the Judaic teachings. Whether his self-hate was based on real or imaginary justification of Christian misdeeds, Ha-Levi attended Christian theological seminaries and was soon made archbishop of the Catholic apostate. Ha-Levi's devotion to his new faith enabled him to be quickly promoted to the governing religious hierarchy of Castile, where he very soon became a close friend of Pedro de Luna of Aragón, also known as the anti-Pope Benedict XIII. Identification with the oppressor—a form of mental surrender—was the adjustment made by this Ha-Levi. He was so fanatically adherent to his new-found religion that he preached against Judaism and often had those Jews who did not harken, rounded up and punished.

Joshua Lorki was another turncoat Jew. He had been a student of Rabbi Ha-Levi at one of the synagogues. As a Christian, Lorki became as fanatic as his former rabbi, who was now an archbishop. This team of Solomon Ha-Levi (later known as Paul of Burgos) and Joshua Lorki (popularly known as de Lorca, born at Lorca, España— Joshua ben Joseph Ibn Vives), jointly spread enough anti-Jewish propaganda to cause Jews to suffer more than they ordinarily would have. As a convert to Christianity, under the name of Geronimo de Santa Fé, Lorki was physician to the anti-Pope Benedict XIII, a position that enabled him to take active part in frenzied anti-Jewish propaganda which led to the Disputation of Tortosa. Christianity found many Jews for Jesus at that time. The Church received more assistance than expected or solicited. As a result, Christian leaders actually found more credence and logical-hypothetical arguments with well-explained value judgments to outweigh Judaism. A panel was formed to settle the question of which religion surpassed the other in the proper knowledge of God, had Him on its side, and could unquestionably profess to receive all messages and blessings emanating from that omnipotent and ubiquitous force. This organized dispute was called *The Tortosa Disputation.*

Judaism found a good Jew in Hasdai Ben Abraham Crescas (c.1340–c.1410), a philosopher and Crown Rabbi of Aragón. He and a fellow student at the school of Nissim, in Gerona, defended Jewish teachings with rigor and wisdom. Crescas had lost his son in the massacres of 1391 and therefore dedicated himself to the regaining of apostates. His writings produced a famous work in Hebrew translation known as *Or Adonai—"La Luz de Nuestro Señor."*[42] The uprisings of 1391 caused him to leave Spain hurriedly and seek refuge in Algiers, North Africa. His absence was a great loss to his community. Crescas descended from a family of scholars and would have been a great debater in the Tortosa Disputation. As a leading rabbi, at Saragossa, his preachings exposed the logical inadequacies of the entire system of Greek philosophy. He criticized Aristotle's system of physics and applied talmudic arguments to Aristotle's studies with clear logic and unquestionably valid conclusions. Crescas proved that there was no direct relation between the truth and the validity of Aristotle's conclusions. He numbered eight dogmas, "the denial of which entails renunciation of Judaism."[43] Jews should believe, he insisted, that the word was created from naught by divine will at a given time; immortality of the soul; retribution; the resurrection of the dead; immutability of the Torah; its perpetual obligatoriness which cannot be abrogated in the supremacy of Moses as prophet above those that preceded or followed him; inspiration inherent in the priest's Urim and Thummim; and the Messianic redemption.[44]

Crescas proved to the world that so-called Greek theology as proclaimed by Aristotle with Aristotle's two doctrines: 1) theology showing purpose and design in nature as the work of a supreme intelligence was debatable; and, 2) the Unmoved Mover was not an Aristotelian concept with unquestionable premise. This and other discoveries led other thinkers to conclude that most of the concepts credited to Greek philosophy could be pursued to the creation story attributed to the Egyptians before them.[45]

THE TORTOSA DISPUTATION

Tortosa, a city in northern Spain, had Jewish settlements dating as far back in Spanish history as the Roman Period. In 1413, Benedict XIII, who was not considered the legitimate pope because of his professed anti-pope position, ordered Jewish scholars to represent their community by demonstrating their Talmud and Hebrew literature's validity if compared with the truth of Christian doctrine. The Jews pondered and hesitated to accept the challenge. They feared compulsion and bias in a debate where they would be forced to exercise restraint in their expostulation of convincing arguments. The Jewish scholars declined the invitation and found themselves threatened with fines, imprisonment, and expulsion from Spain if they did not appear. Disobedience was mentioned and the Jews capitulated. The disputation was held in the city of Tortosa in February 1413. It dragged on for sixty-nine sessions, lasting over twenty-one months into November 12, 1414. The last session was transferred to la fortaleza de San Mateo.[46]

The converted Christian Joshua Lorki started the debate in favor of Christianity. Vidal Beneveniste represented the Jews—with a long discourse in Latin—reinforced by Zerachiah Levi, Astrue Levi, Joseph Albo, and others. There were twenty-three Jewish orators in all. Benedict presided with his court of archbishops, bishops, abbots, and knights. He stated at the opening session, "The truth of the Christian religion is above contention." The debate was often interrupted and the pope intermittently exerted physical and psychological pressure on the Jews to apostasize. The coercion caused many conversions during and after the disputation. When the disputation and its suspense were over, as expected the decision was a thunderbolt in favor of Christian dogma, with strong condemnation of the Talmud. The Jewish communities were thenceforth forbidden to study any *halakhot*.[47] Several other anti-Jewish laws were proclaimed by the anti-pope, and the government of Castile ratified them.

During the Tortosa debates, one of the most important questions was, "Did the Messiah come and was he realized in Jesus?" Like most well thinking Jews, Joseph Albo disciple of Crescas, stated that one may still be considered a Jew even though he accepts, with others, that creation was preceded by primeval matter. Albo wrote a dissertation on "dogmas," completed in 1428. He believed that a future prophet might come forth to save humanity and declare the law abrogated. Nevertheless, that prophet's teachings would have to be authenticated, as in the case of Moses, by a preponderant majority consensus of all Israel.

THE INQUISITION

The original name, the Inquisition, was derived from the Latin verb *inquiro*, meaning "inquire into." During the first three centuries of Christianity—before the twelfth century—heretics exclusively were spiritually excommunicated from the Church. When the emperors became Christian, Arian emperors persecuted the Christians and Christian emperors pursued and persecuted the Arians. Then Theodosius I the Great made Christianity the established religion—in the fourth century—and heretics became enemies of the state and laws enacted against them. The leaders of the Church opposed state intervention. Nevertheless, Optatus of Milevis defended the death penalty whereby Circumcellions (North Africans attacked Catholics in the Donatists' cause).

Priscillian, bishop of Avila, was the first heretic to be executed in 395. Saint John Chrysostom appealed, saying, "Let both the wheat and the weeds grow together until the harvest." Around 1000, nevertheless, the doctrine called the Cathari in France Albigenses began to spread throughout Europe. By 1022, Robert II of France had thirteen heretics burned at Orleans, while the Emperor Henry III had some people hanged at Goslar in 1051.

The First Lateran Council to be held in the West was held at Lateran Palace, Rome in 1123. The Second Council was convened in 1139 as the tenth ecumenical council of the Roman Catholic Church. This Council was held in the same place, and was intended to allow Pope Innocent III to heal the wounds left by the schism of the anti-Pope Anacletus II (d. 1138) and to condemn the theories of Arnold Brescia.

The Third and Fourth Lateran Councils, 1179 and 1212, led to decrees of death penalties, as well. Intermittent reprieves and condemnations continued under different rulers and popes. The Early Inquisition was later concerned with deliberate obstinacy of baptized Christians against encouraging others to also baptize.

Jews and Moslems were only subject to the Inquisition if they tried to convert Christians. Then came the Medieval Inquisition where the extreme penalty of death was applied to St. Joan of Arc, John Huss, and Girolano Savonarola. The Medieval Inquisition had left its scar on the Iberian Peninsula during the thirteenth century. The struggle against the Moslems had kept the Christians occupied and somewhat united in their faith. But the world of anti-Christians was still festering underneath the body of the land. As the reconquest became more and more possible, the desire for religious unity became more and more fervent. The Jews seemed to be the only obstacle obstructing the path to unity.

As stated before, Henry III of Castile and Léon began pressuring the flourishing and influential Jews, in the fourteenth century. He wanted them to convert. It was felt that the secretly worshipping Jews were more of a threat than those who openly professed their religion.

After a period of sporadic physical attacks and continuous psychological torture through persecutions, Jews began to worry. Their fears and doubts were soon removed by stark reality. The nightmares had not been unfounded dreams, and the dreads proved to be more factual than they had imagined. Some natives felt that it was humanly profitable to be kind and courteous to the Spanish nationals. Other members of the Jewish merchant class felt like many throughout America today, that boldness would combat bigotry and intolerance would not reach uncontrollable proportions. They exploited their customers and considered their non-Jewish competitors insignificant. Conversions decreased, neo-Christians secretly crept back into the synagogues, or homes of friends, where they could worship and identify with the Omnipotent. They identified with their traditions instead of a triumvirate, saints, idols, the cross, and a life with its rewards after death.

The Christians became aware of the loyalty and devotion to Judaism rekindling like a lamp in the darkness receiving more fuel after it had almost flickered out. The clergy was informed and the accusations of disloyalty to Christian teachings and beliefs were claimed. The rabbis were consulted and requested to cooperate by desisting from encouraging or even allowing former Jews to enter their temples. The penalty was death if the names of reconverts were not submitted to the representatives of the Church and the government. The rabbis would not comply. They had compunctions about informing on their brothers and sisters. At the same time, converted

Christians felt pressures of dislike, distrust, and hatefulness from the Christians, by birth, who called themselves *Catolicos apostolicos romanos*, Roman apostolic Catholic. These latter referred to the converted Jews as *Marranos*, meaning pigs. The converts were accused of enjoying privileges that should rightfully be reserved for Christians by birth. As Christians, many Jews were now disliked for enjoying equal opportunities and rights. The greatest resentment held against Jews was their prominence in politics and economics. Christians, by birth, felt threatened by converts.

Spanish policemen, noted for appointments through patronage rather than qualification or education, were an ignorant minority with major physical force. They initiated sporadic unlawful arrests, and riots broke out against converted Christians who resisted rather than against known Jews. The rich Marranos were bigger targets than small Jewish worshippers. Looting and persecution were directed at the rich mercantile class. A promise to discontinue hiring Marranos to hold public office was exacted from the government. This promise was soon annulled due to lack of enforcement and its encouragement of Christian persecution of fellow Christians—all children of the same Jew, Jesus Christ. Some restrictions were legislated, however, limiting the converted Christians to certain occupations and designated levels of governmental positions. The limitations were soon appealed by Christian Jews who felt they had been less restricted socially and professionally when they worshipped Torah and Talmud than now that they were Christians. Furthermore, many Christians were not as fervently Catholic and as sincerely patriotic as they—the Christian Jews. Quite a few of them had accepted Christianity not just for the sake of maintaining their career or political position, but perhaps out of a deep conviction of true belief or a profound desire to be totally accepted as Spaniards. They also cherished their social acceptance in the upper strata. Their grievances were heeded, their charges investigated and found well founded and well documented. As a result of the investigations, some Jews who had been unscrupulously or unjustly discharged from important positions were reinstated. This special treatment aroused jealousy. Charges of disloyalty to the new faith were made and unscrupulously hurled at the neophytes. Various members of Catholic communities, and the priesthood, especially monks, began to recommend an inquisition. The Inquisition meant "Holy Office" or ecclesiastical tribunal of "heresy" to be conducted by the Dominican friars.

One of the first manifestations of this inquisition was visible in Castile when the Marrano tax collectors were mandated to make their Jewish neighbors contribute one million *maravedis* for defense of the Spanish frontier. But some Jews were well treated.

It is important to mention that during the reigns of Henry IV of

Castile (1454–1474) and John II of Aragón (1458–1479) each monarch employed Jewish physicians. Jacob Ibn Nuñez was even named chief rabbi under Henry of Castile, and Abiathar Ibn Crescas, who restored King John's vision through two expert surgical operations, were held in high esteem. Before that, Abraham Cresques—a Majorcan cartographer who died in 1387—had helped Henry the Navigator (1394–1460) with his maps and compasses. Cresques was the maker of the famous Catalan Atlas, which was sent to the king of France as a present, and is now treasured in the Bibliotheque nationale in Paris. Cresques' son, Judah, assisted his father and became patronizingly known as the "map Jew." Judah was later compelled to accept Christianity (for advantage or survival in 1391), with his name changed to Jayme Ribes. Judah later served the king of Portugal as Jacomo de Majorca, director of the nautical observatory of Sagres. The good deeds of Jews led to a recess from persecution, and the Marranos recuperated some losses while others were actually successful.

Then in 1467, there was a riot in Castile. Jews were killed and several Jewish homes burned. In 1469, clamor was heard for anti-Jewish restrictions, legislation or enforcement of old decrees. In 1470, when Ferdinand and Isabella joined their hands and kingdoms through marriage, her Jewish courtier and loyal servant Abraham Senior reconciled a dispute between the queen and her brother, Henry. Isabella showed her gratitude to Senior by bestowing an annual pension on him of one hundred *maravedis* for life—an act of apparent good Judeo-Christian friendship. Also in 1470 in Valladolid, however, there was a bloodbath of Jewish victims. The sanguineous acts of terror even engulfed some Marranos who were friends of Isabella and members of her entourage.

New Christians and other Jews saw a number of their kin killed or arrested and sentenced to death at the gallows in 1471. Imposed penalties were inflicted on Jews by the bishop of Segovia, Juan Arias Davila, the son of Diego, a new Christian. This attack on Jews by Marrano-Jews caused many Jews to be slain and others to hurry abroad. At Cordoba, Bishop Peter formed a society called the Christian Brotherhood (*la Hermandad Cristiana*). The society adamantly excluded all new Christians. March 1473 came in with the "Ides of March" and the bad fortune it bore in the case and times of Shakespeare's Julius Caesar. A procession was held in commemoration of the Brotherhood. After the parade, rumors circulated that a girl of a Marrano family had willfully thrown dirty water from a window spattering and desecrating the image of the sacred Virgin Mary.

This accusation activated the seething undercurrent of hatred that had been temporarily at low tide. Turbulence began. The current gained momentum and force as tales were added to the accusation, and a riot broke out. The mob attacked residences of all wealthy

Marranos, and set them afire. Alonao Fernandez de Aguilar, whose wife descended from a prominent Marrano family, ordered troops to repel the mobs. During the confrontation of mobs and troops, a mob leader was killed. Aguilar was charged with the slaying. That damaging charge gave the rioters a tangible motive for redeploying forces against Jews and any Christians who came to their defense or rescue. The mob armed itself with weapons and reinforced its ranks with outlaws to confront the authorities and Jews. Plundering was a reward, and massacre an attraction. The turmoil lasted three whole days. The news left Cordoba for other cities. At Jaen the *aguacil* (constable), attempting to protect the Jews was killed in a church. By 1474, the attack on Marranos had gained enough momentum to reach Segovia where Jewish bodies were heaped up in the streets like piles of rubbish. Alcalde Andreas de Cabrera became concerned and intervened to save the Marranos from being annihilated.

King Henry IV (1425–1474), king of Castile and Leon, died and Isabella ascended the throne of Castile in 1474. Henry's daughter, Juana la Beltraneja, was rejected by Castilian nobles as heiress to the throne. Henry had first designated his half brother, Alfonso, but he died in 1468. His sudden death forced Henry to name Isabella successor. After Isabella married Ferninand of Aragón in 1469, Henry again recognized Juana la Beltraneja as heiress to the throne, but his wishes were overruled by Castilian nobles.

Isabella's reign saw bishops opposed to the Inquisition because it intruded into people's personal lives, held secret investigations behind closed doors, and tenaciously pursued and persecuted persons considered nonaligned with the state religion or disloyal to it. The Inquisition also divested bishops of their authority and operated independently of the legally established government. However, the Inquisition was revived under a Papal Bull on November 1, 1478. It was supposedly intended to deal solely with royal control primarily concerned with the persecution of Marranos (converted Jews secretly practicing their old faith). Ferdinand had just defeated the Portuguese at the battle of Toro in 1476, and the confiscation of Jewish property would do well to increase his and Isabella's financial powers, strengthening them in their struggle to subdue the feudal opposition. So Isabella reluctantly consented to subduing the feudal opposition.

The first inquisitors were appointed by Tomás de Torquemada (1420–1498), a Dominican monk who had been Isabella's confessor when she was a young girl. This circumstance was unfortunate for Jews. The year 1480 bore the unfavorable tale of an embarrassing moment where a group of opulent Jews were surprised at a *seder* on the first night of Passover. They were summarily accused of treason and brought to trial. Queen Isabella of Castile, wife of Ferdinand of

Aragón, considered a most pious Christian, tried to be just to all Spaniards. She even had Jewish members in her court. Upon hearing of the Passover incident, the queen began to distrust converts, nevertheless, she tried to be just and merciful. She was inveigled by her former confessor not only to mistrust Jews, but to be stern with them. Isabella yielded to pressure and made her consent an act by finally signing a decree.

The Inquisition began at Sevilla, where sentiment was divided about its good or evil results. Some Christians felt pity for the accused, others did not. The majority of the people upheld justification of the Inquisition but many members of the noble and privileged classes rejected it because of their own marriages to Marranos. Nevertheless, the more the pressure was applied by the inquisitors, the more the in-laws of the Marranos abandoned them to save their own Gentile necks. Rich and politically influential Marranos resisted with bribes and intrigues, but they were betrayed, their plots exposed, and their efforts readily suppressed. Approximately eight thousand Marranos from Sevilla, Cordoba, and Toledo fled to Cadiz. The governor of the province, Rodrigo Ponce de Leon, was anxious to protect these Jews, but de Leon was pressured by the inquisitors and forced to extradite them back to Sevilla. There were so many Marranos rounded up that their trials had to be moved to a much larger court. The castle of Triana, near Sevilla, was selected for the occasion.

The Pope, who had been hesitant about accepting methods of the "Holy Office," or Inquisition, reluctantly consented after being severely pressured. An *Auto Da Fe,* Act of Faith, was officially held on February 6, 1481.[48] Punishment was to be meted out to heads of government and the Church and to new Christians. The Marranos opposed the decree with all of their resources and outside forces they could muster, but to no avail. The opportunity for rival merchants to enrich themselves with Jewish markets and the opportunity for the Royal treasury to be replenished were too tempting. So despite desperate Jewish effort, the Inquisition reached Aragón.

Six men and six women were burned at the stake, or *quemadero* (burner), in one instance. Over three hundred Jewish persons perished, and eighty were condemned to death or incarceration. The eighty survived and were sent to prison, but the wealth and property of all accused persons was confiscated and added to the Royal treasury.

Tomãs de Torquemada (1420-1498) was the inquisitor general. The first inquisitors appointed by Torquemada were Dominican monks Miguel de Murillo and Juan de San Martin. They were assisted by Juan Ruiz de Molina and Diego Merlo, who were appointed as first inquisitors of Sevilla. This extension made the Inquisition more national, except for Malaga and Granada, Moorish-held provinces. The court centralized control over punishments to be executed in

Castile and elsewhere. The power of the Church was subdued. On October 17, 1483, Tomás de Torquemada[49] was appointed Inquisitor General de Aragón, Catalonia, and Valencia along with Castile, which he already controlled. Torture chambers were put into full operation.

Thousands of Jews were tortured, lynched, and burned alive. The Auto Da Fe was read in the public square with the inquisitors sitting in the *kiosco*.[50] Spectators looked on from rooftops, balconies, windows, and park benches, where they tried to look over each others' shoulders. The upper class and the nobility were dressed in fashionable attire of the day and sat near the spectacle, beside a scaffold and a pulpit built for the occasion. The procession usually began at the fort or castle where the prisoners were crammed, then proceeded to the square while church bells knelled their funeral dirges. Priests and monks led with the cross held high, while acolytes and members of the government and Church hierarchy followed. The crippled, underfed and disheveled Marranos often followed, hobbling along with the soldiers at their heels. Each condemned soul was forced to hold a candle, while dressed in a tunic which determined the seriousness of blasphemy, heresy, or treachery for which he or she had been accused and condemned. A confessor preached a long sermon and the sentences were penance, flogging, confiscation of property, or execution. Those condemned to death were handed over to the civil court. The Catholic Apostolic Roman Church upheld the Commandment no *mataras!* Thou shalt not kill! The Church could not condone wanton murder. Another irony was the inquisitor's final plea to those condemned to die; condemned Jews were asked whether they had worshipped Judaism secretly, repented, and now recognized the Catholic Roman Church as their true and only salvation. The ones who answered yes were the first strangled by the executioners. Their dead bodies were placed beside their living fellow worshippers who sat on the platform with their legs drawn up close to their cheeks or standing huddled together like bundles of wheat. A member of the ruling class, sometimes the king, would set fire to bundles of sticks to begin the cremation. The crowds would cheer while the church bells tolled mournfully. Some Jews would groan or scream while others chanted *Shema' Israel, Adonai Elohenu, Adonai Ehad!* Hear, Oh Israel, the Lord is One, the Lord our God is One! Jews who admitted only part of their guilt as charged, were put on the rack, an instrument of torture with a wooden frame supporting a mechanical device or man-powered wheel to which the prisoner was tied and stretched as the ropes tied to his arms and legs tightened until his hands or legs were pulled out of their sockets. Once the victim gave a total confession he or she was immediately condemned to death or sentenced to life imprisonment.

The month of May 1485 saw the courts of the Inquisition transferred from Villa Real to Toledo Province. An abortive attack was made against the inquisitors but it was not well planned and supported. The rebellion was ruthlessly suppressed, with its surviving participants strangled or hanged. A similar development occurred on August 10, 1486, where five men, a city official included, and fifteen women from the upper social class were liquidated. A couple of years later, priests and friars were accused by people who simply did not like them or their lifestyle, or considered them rivals for promotions or special considerations. The accused were often divested of their ranks and rights and even burned at the stake with the Marranos.

Torquemada was allowed to become so powerful that after the Inquisition gained full recognition he began consideration of other methods of elimination. He proposed expulsion. To test its effectiveness, he ordered the expulsion of Juan Arias Davila of Segovia and Pedro de Aranda of Calahorra of Logroño Province, two bishops of Jewish descent. Davila fought his case by appealing to Rome directly and was exonerated. De Aranda was not as fortunate, being guilty as charged, stripped of his authority, and sentenced to life imprisonment where he died incarcerated near the Vatican.

Alfonso de la Caballeria, the vice-chancellor, was suspected of active participation in the murder of Peter Arbues, canon at Sargosa and inquisitor for Aragón. Arbues had been assassinated in his church. The persons suspected of heading that plot had their hands lopped off and their heads and limbs chopped up. Alfonso was therefore considered a Jewish sympathizer. He appealed his case to Rome and was reinstated as a good Catholic. He helplessly witnessed his grandmother's grave vandalized, her remains exhumed and burned along with those of other Jews. His wife, whom he divorced to marry a Christian, was also compelled to wear the *sanbenito* without his being able to intercede in her behalf.[51] Many other Marranos were married to Christians, two of Alfonso's daughters among them. There had been so much intermarriage that even the Spanish nobility could no longer boast of *limpieza de sangre*, meaning cleansing the blood of impurities from non-Christians. The Christians did not consider the Moors, that were very much amalgamated with them, as a virulent threat because the Moors were warriors, and conquerors. When they lost power—the only reality—they too were discriminated.

Many persons involved in the boasting about pure Christian blood were part Jewish, and merely alienated themselves from their Jewish antecedents—like those now clearing themselves of their African origin through intermarriage to whiter mates to claim to be Semitic through abandoned or never-existent Semitic ancestry.

The Moors, married to Spaniards or lived with them unmarried. Their offspring were called *Moriscos*, the equivalent of *marrano*, though not as degrading. It simply meant Moorish, while marrano is literally a pig. Faced with conversion, death, or banishment, the Moors also accepted mass conversion to Christianity. With the reconquest completed, and the desire for religious unity more preponderant only Christians were totally safe at times. But it was the Jews who seemed to be the real threat to Christian unity. That idea became an obsession throughout the Iberian Peninsula. And with Spaniards being the tale-bearers they are, it helped to hasten Jewish banishment.

Jewish banishment was a blessing in disguise. It was their roundabout way to escape admission of guilt that forced them to wear a yellow cross on their outer garments, suffer imprisonment, confiscation of property, or both. It also meant Jews no longer had to face the inquisitor and the nine to fifty clerics and laymen he consulted about their fate. Life imprisonment was a common penalty imposed on those who confessed on the rack but escaped death.

JEWISH EXPULSION FROM SPAIN

In 1487, a special war tax was levied on Jewish and Moslem families in Castile. Fourteen Jewish families are said to have been there at that time. With the Moslem failure to hold and defend Malaga—due to treachery by some of their troops—it fell in the month of August. The entire population was captured by the Christians and subjected to slavery. Four hundred and fifty Jews were fortunate enough to be ransomed from among the captured by their coreligionists, and transported to Africa. The Spaniards were friendly to the Jews because the Moors had subjugated Christians in Granada, the Moorish capital, in southern Andalusia. The fall of this last Moslem stronghold in southern Spain in November 1491 caused the Christian kingdom to become united. This meant that Ferdinand and Isabella no longer had to worry about their frontier with Africa. It also meant religious institutionalization would become a reality; the cross would now become the only national emblem, and all non-Christians could be severely dealt with, without fear of reprisal from the Africans or Moors.

Ferdinand and Isabella had been considering expulsion of Jews with some hesitancy. Pope Innocent VIII (1432–1492) also was reluctant to affirm expulsion of such industrious and productive citizens. But Tomas de Torquemada was resolute. He rekindled the flames of the fire spread earlier about six Marranos and five Jews killing a Christian child by the name of La Guardia, as a sacrifice in Jewish ceremonies. There was supposed to be a star witness. He turned out to be Yuce Franco, considered by his community members to have been mentally underdeveloped. It was said that a priest who disguised himself as a rabbi learned about the crime through Franco's confession. The accused persons were hurriedly burned alive, and the entire story exposed as a concocted tale to expedite the expulsion of Jews.

The *Registro Civil* of the province showed no such child in the registry of births, and the records of the *pesquisidor* (coroner) showed no such death. Nevertheless, tempers flared and the thirst for blood was once again aroused in the throat of the terribly hateful beast called anti-Semitism.

Inquisitor Torquemada—an expert propagandist—exploited that tale, and disseminated the charges and punishments inflicted on the accused. The news was spread throughout the Iberian Peninsula. On March 30, 1492, "heathens", or non-Christians and Christians received the edict from the fort at the Alhambra in Granada, proclaiming no Jew or Moslem should be considered a legally constituted resident in the United Kingdom of Castile and Aragón or the Islands of Sardinia and Sicilia—Aragónese territorial possessions.

The Medieval Inquisition had served an important purpose in Christian Spain during the thirteenth century, but the war against the Moslems had kept the Spaniards occupied and preoccupied. This Moslem-Christian struggle helped to strengthen Spanish faith in Christianity. With the war of the reconquest won, it was now impossible to convince Christians that God was not on their side and that whatever measures they undertook were not just.

The centuries of Moslem domination and partial reign had allowed Jewish communities to flourish throughout Spain. They had multiplied in numbers and risen in influence, despite the anti-Semitism imposed on them from time to time. The African origin of the Iberians, the Moslems, many of whom had come from Mauritania, and the Hebrews, had helped to maintain considerable cooperation and coexistence. Harsh pressures were not brought to bear on the Jews until the time of Henry III of Castile and León (1390–1406). At that time, they were forced to convert or perish. Now it was conversion or banishment. The edict of March 31, 1492 gave Jews an ultimatum: conversion by baptism or exile. It was assumed that once the Spanish-Jewish problem was settled, there would be more time to deal with the Spanish-Moslem and Protestant question in 1502. Islam was not too great a threat. Moslems were not as aggressive in politics, business, and education as were Jews and therefore less progressive.

The Spanish Inquisition, as mentioned before, was not designed to harass Jews as much as it had been designated to ferret out converted Jews, *Marranos*, who practiced *Judaismo* secretly, or Moslems, *Moriscos*, who converted to Christianity but secretly worshipped Islam. It was also for intensive control and penalizing of Christians who permitted this mockery of Christian baptism. Several priests and bishops were judged. Catholics did not escape the tentacles of the Inquisition. It must be noted that Ignatius Loyola was arrested twice on suspicion of heresy and the Archbishop of Toledo, Dominican Bartolemé de Carranza (q.v.), was imprisoned for almost seventeen years. The

Inquisition was rigorously practiced as late as the sixteenth century, under the dark-skinned, wooly-haired King Phillip II (1527–1598).

As public testimonies were heard at these solemn gatherings—most ceremonies took place on Sundays—it was learned that Jews in the upper strata exerted more power than had been anticipated. It was therefore proposed that expelling them and their Moslem counterparts would make conversion of those remaining easier. The inquisitors and the Church agreed unhesitatingly that the best solution to the Marrano, non-Marrano, Morisco, and non-Morisco problem was separation of the baptized converts from non-Christian relatives and friends.

Expulsion began, but many Jews were sickly, too old, or too young to travel under the existing forms of transportation, lacking comfort and basic sanitary conditions necessary to safely accommodate such an exodus. Furthermore, some of these Jews had been in Spain for generations. Their questions were: where to go, to whom, and with what? Which countries would accept Semites—with the Inquisition spreading to other lands—and which relatives and friends would receive them, and how much funds would they have to finance a trip and start life anew? It was suggested by the rabbis that a last desperate effort be made in the form of an appeal to the queen and king.

A caucus was held and a delegation selected. Abraham Senior and Isaac Abravanel, two Jews who had served the crown loyally, were chosen to represent the Jewish community. They requested an *audiencia* (audience) with Ferdinand and Isabella. Abravanel[52] had labored for years keeping the financial matters of Spain's treasury well balanced, thereby contributing greatly to the Moslem defeat. Senior, the chief rabbi, had kept the Jewish congregations in a sphere where sound Judeo-Christian interaction revolved, discouraged reconversion or at least did not proselytize. As loyal Spaniards and *servidores de la corte real* (servants of the Royal Court), these Jews were well appreciated and respected. They appeared before the monarchs with a bag of gold and money. One writer said that the eloquence of the Jews and the logical explanations that supported their pleas made the queen consider leniency. At the same time, the bag of gold and money seemed to attract the king from a fair exchange or collateral point of view. Just before a final agreement was reached, the unrelenting Grand Inquisitor Tomás de Torquemada—who had been informed by his spies—stormed into the court, placed a crucifix beside the bag of ransom, pointed to the image of Jesus on the cross and said, "Here he is; sell him." Queen Isabella felt strong compunctions though Ferdinand did not seem to share her religious guilt. The deal was called off anyway and the Jews were destined to be sent abroad. "Abraham Senior, like so many of his kind, unwilling to make final sacrifice for the sake of his religion, thereupon became converted to Christianity."[53] Isaac Abravanel, a more faithful and true human being, seemed to have reasoned that of two contradictory propositions, one had to be true (loyalty and sincerity) and the other false (disloyalty and hypocrisy). Abravanel cast his lot with his Jewish brethren, preferring exile to glory and resisting the tempting offers of his king and queen—to make an exception in his case—and holding steadfastly to his religious beliefs. The monarchs offered Abravanel permission to remain in Spain as a passive Jew abiding by Christian laws and practices.

CRISTOBAL COLON

It is important to mention Columbus more extensively because of the preponderant effect this voyage had on the world. While the Jews were being hustled onto the ships for their departure from Spain, the man known to Italians as Cristoforo Colombo, and to the English-speaking people as Christopher Columbus—claimed by the Jews, the Italians, and Spaniards—set sail from Palos near Sevilla. It was August 2, 1492, when Columbus left the piers, and passed by the ships on which the Jewish exiles were embarking for unknown lands. He recorded the exodus in his log. Columbus had been financed by many prominent Jews directly and indirectly through monies donated or confiscated from them. Some of his sailors were Marranos, as a result, and others Africans.

Columbus sailed with three small ships: *La Niña, Pinta y Santa Maria*. One of his pilots was an African named Nuflo de Olano, who was also a navigator, the other pilot was Alonso Niño, and the navigator was Estevanico, also of African origin. Columbus mentioned them repeatedly in his "Descubrimiento de la Mar del Sur."[54]

The diary of Christopher Columbus also mentions that a substantial loan had been made to him by a Jew named Luis de Santangel, chancellor of the royal household and controller general of Aragon. Santangel hoped a new home could be found for persecuted Jews. Gabriel Sanchez, the chief treasurer of Aragon and other Marranos also patronized Columbus. One of the reasons for their interest might have been the fact that among the explorers there were Jewish relatives such as Alonso de la Calle, Rodrigo Sanchez, the ship's doctor Bernal, the surgeon Marco, and Luis de Torres, a baptized Christian. Torres was a student of Oriental languages. Because Columbus thought he would find the Indies in India, Torres was hired as the interpreter.

The African traders visiting the Americas told Columbus that they were called Indies.[55]

Columbus' second voyage was said to be also largely financed from the Jewish fortunes and properties confiscated by the monarchs. On this voyage merchants and navigators of Portugal were consulted. Many Jews had fled there.

JEWS IN PORTUGAL

Portugal was closer to Spain than other lands admitting Jews. Furthermore, the language and customs were similar to Spanish cultural traits and practices. John II, the perfect, of Portugal was willing to extend temporary asylum to the ousted Jews. The wealthy Jews, who were able to pay attractive bribes to Portuguese authorities and the tradesmen needed for their expertise were allowed permanent residence status. Other poorer Jews were to be permitted temporary asylum until they received acceptance from another country willing to admit them. Therefore, most of the refugees preferred to stop off in Portugal rather than travel farther to unknown lands. Consequently, the Castillian and Aragonese residents decided on Portugal. The totally poor were excluded. To add to their misery, transportation was insufficient. Ships were small and few. This and financial hardship as well caused many Jews to be left back in Spain to be forced to accept Christianity or to be sold into slavery.

Before leaving Toledo, Jews were told to surrender all their communal and some personal property to the municipal authorities on agreement that the cemeteries would be preserved. Being of African tradition, the Hebrews felt that the souls of the ancestors usually hovered near their bodies, and should not be disturbed unnecessarily or desecrated and be forced to wander about the earth. More than one hundred and fifty thousand refugees were now forced to struggle along the highways toward the seaports for embarkation to Portugal, North Africa, or Turkey, without having to worry about their dead. About twelve thousand Jews fled Aragon and Catalonia into Navarro, but Ferdinand insisted that John the Perfect deport them. Some exiles like Isaac Abravanel escaped to Naples. He could not venture into Portugal because he had fled there after the death of Alfonso V, father of John II. John had accused Abravanel of abetting the conspiracy of the Duke of Braganza against the throne. Under Alfonso V, Abravanel had been the royal treasurer, continuing under John. After he was accused, his valuable library and assets were confiscated by John II, and Abravanel barely escaped death by going to Castile in 1483.

Jews from the southern provinces of Spain embarked for the North African coast; but only some of them were allowed to land. Many of the other Jewish exiles embarked in search of a new world and one of their vessels passed Columbus' little fleet without knowing that they were both en route to the New World. Twenty vessels were met off the North African coast of Fez by pirates, who attempted to enslave the refuges as human cargo. While the negotiations for ransom was in progress, the captain of the refugee ship put to sea with the hostages and sailed back toward Spain. The homeless Jews ran into a storm that sank three vessels and washed up the others on the Spanish coast. In despair, five hundred survivors embraced the Catholic religion as haven of refuge for the persecuted. The other despondent, but devout, survivors preferred to seek refuge in Fez and Portugal. Those arriving at Fez were permitted to land. It was not long, however, before ill fate caught up with them again. Fire and pestilence consumed and killed over twenty thousand faithful worshippers.

Some of the roving vessels that booked the refugees charged them exorbitant passage; in many cases, the ship's master heartlessly heaved the low-paying passengers over the port or starboard side of the vessel before reaching port. There was scuttlebutt that the fugitives had swallowed jewels and gold coins. This rumor caused greedy sailors to begin knifing and ripping open thousands of passengers' bowels in search of swallowed treasure. Brigands searched among the mutilated remains before they were cast overboard. Some Jews were offered refuge in Genova, Italy, if they would be willing to be baptized. Many took refuge at Corfu, Candia, and other Greek islands instead. The ships' masters sold quite a few of their passengers as slaves or human cargo unable to pay adequate passage. Other Jews came to the rescue, and quite a few were ransomed from this terrible fate. Those Jewish deportees fortunate enough to push on to the shores of the Ottoman dominions were received with a hearty welcome. Ottoman-Turkish Sultan Bayazid II (c. 1447–1512), elder son of the Sultan Mohammed II, rejoiced at the misjudgment of the Spaniards. He felt that Spain had debilitated herself and strengthened Turkey by expelling industrious people.

At Portugal, there was neither joyous welcome nor benign neglect. State councilors and native Jews were unwilling to receive the few refugees. Fear and selfishness prevailed over brotherhood and sympathy. Thirty of the richest immigrant families were permitted to settle in Oporto after their rabbi, Isaac Aboab, the last Jewish scholar of Castile, interceded on their behalf. Six hundred other families, able to pay a tax of one hundred *crusados* each, were also allowed to sandbag their permission. Many skilled in the manufacturing of munitions, were needed and therefore granted permanent residence, if they paid a poll tax of four *crusados*. The remaining majority received permission to remain eight months, if a poll tax of eight *crusados* was paid while they prepared to set sail for another country willing to accept them. Many months of delay ensued and finally ships were rigged. The refugees met untold hardships at sea for the vessels were hardly seaworthy. Those Jews left ashore were sold as slaves and their infants pulled away from their arms to be sent to San Thome— near Nigeria and Cameroon—where King John had already deported great numbers of African Jews in 1483 and 1484.[56]

Manoel I (1495–1521), cousin, brother-in-law, and successor of John II, ascended the throne of Portugal and was favorably inclined toward Jews. He made Abraham Zacuto, the pupil of Aboab, his astrolabe technician and astronomer. Zacuto advised Vasco de Gama, and enabled the explorer to venture out on the discovery of Cape of Good Hope through the guidance of an astrolabe he perfected. Manoel I was aware of the prosperity brought about by his new subjects and became ambitious. He decided to marry the eldest daughter of Isabella and Ferdinand of Spain, whose husband, Portuguese Prince Alfonso, had died. The Catholic monarch consented to the marriage under one condition: in order to become heir to the Spanish kingdom through this marriage, Manoel I would have to get rid of all non-Christians on Portuguese soil through baptism or expulsion. It was a difficult decision for the Portuguese suitor to make. The Jews had made his small kingdom prosperous, but this marriage could make it greater. The bishop of Portugal, Ferdinand Continho, advised the king against forced baptisms. Manoel ordered the Jews to leave on a certain date, then he issued contradicting orders to the Portuguese police force.

On Sunday, the first day of Passover, March 19, 1497, all Jewish youths up to twenty-five years of age were dragged out of their homes and forcibly baptized. Some parents stifled their children with their last embrace, others threw their offspring into wells and later killed themselves. Some parents, unwilling to separate from their children, followed them to the Church and underwent baptism as a family.

Manoel I had hoped to detain the parents and retain them permanently in Portugal. He zoomed in on the remaining Jews with the same threat, but they began preparations to leave instead. The king became desperate and resorted to yet another trick. Manoel ordered the departing Jews to assemble at the Port of Lisbon to embark there. Twenty thousand Jews were assembled. He detained them until the set date passed, herded them together like aimless animals, refused them food and beverage for several days, then ushered them into government offices. Finally, Manoel sent the Jews word that they were now King Manoel's slaves to be dealt with according to his wishes or whims. Then he sent them a converted fellow Jew of the royal court, with other converted leaders including a Jew from the royal entourage who was a sextant of the Catholic Church. The Catholics persuaded the Jews to convert to Christianity. When this attempt showed marked futility, the king ordered use of force. The Jews were dragged to the baptismal font and forcibly baptized. Only a small number of the twenty thousand was able to escape baptism. Among those who escaped was Abraham Zacuto, who later became rabbi in Jerusalem; Isaac, son of Joseph Karo, the uncle of Joseph Karo of Safed, the codifier, and a few other faithful. A small number of Jews protested openly; among them was Rabbi Simon Maimi. King Manoel decided to use this rabbi as an example for the protestors. Rabbi Maimi was buried alive up to his neck. Maimi refused to convert and died after seven days. His handful of followers who resisted, were then allowed to depart for Africa.

The converted Christians appealed to Pope Alexander VI for protection. The Pope recognized that it might be unpopular to pursue an inquisition in Portugal at that time, and requested that King Manoel use less physical force and more religious persuasion. By May 30, 1497, there was a *rescriptho* (rescript) which allowed the Jews a respite from persecution for about twenty years. Some of them could not forget or forgive, and sought their earliest opportunity to leave Portugal for Africa, Italy, and Turkey. By April 1499, a decree was issued forbidding Jews to leave Portugal without royal permission. There was a riot in April 1506, in which the Jews were again victimized. Over two thousand of them were slain secretly. The king then allowed all Jews who wished to leave the country permission to leave Portugal with all their effects.

Beginning in 1521, emigration was once again forbidden. John III, the fortunate (1521–1557), son of Manoel I, ascended the throne of Portugal. The Marranos were again subjected to persecutions and injunctions against emigration. In 1531, the Inquisition was proclaimed.

The Portuguese Inquisition was considered busier than the Spanish Inquisition because on trial were the descendants of the Spanish Marranos who had been most insistent upon maintaining their old Hebrew religion. Quite a few Marranos were forced to flee Portugal.

Under Sebastian (1554–1578), grandson and successor of John III, the Jews were granted free departure at a cost of two hundred and fifty thousand ducats. It was rather impossible for all of them to depart. As a result, there is still a settlement of Marrano descendants in Portugal with some knowledge of their African-Hebrew origin.

NOTES

1. Alexandria between Torino and Genova.
2. Enrich Kahler. *A History of Jews*, p. 74.
3. Kahler, p. 74.
4. Kahler. p. 90.
5. Kahler. p. 313.
6. Charlemagne insisted that the Baghdad scholar Machir come to Narbonne to found the first Talmudic school of southern France.
7. Sulamith Ish-Kishor. *Jews to Remember* (New York: Hebrew Publishing Company, 1941).

8. Ish-Kishor, pp. 58-59.
9. Yosef ben-Jochannan, *Black Man of the Nile* (New York: Alkebu-lan Books Associates, 1972) p. 376. *Yeshua*, the Hebrew name meaning Joshua, was joined with the Greek name *Kristos* or *Cristos* to make Jesus Christ. The same name in Hindi is Krishna: meaning "the black one." *The American Heritage College Dictionary of the English Language* (Boston: Houghton Mifflin Company, 1978).
10. Ben-Jochannan, p. 70.
11. Ben-Jochannan, p. 79.
12. Exarch: general or governor—in charge—of an outlying province.
13. Gregory I — administrative, liturgical and moral reformer. Gregorian Chant attributed to him. *Encyopedia Britannica:* 1987 Vol. 5, p. 477.
14. Genesis 29:18.
15. The Slaves of the Immaculate Heart of Mary, *Our Glorious Popes.* (Cambridge Massachusetts: Saint Benedict Center, 1955). pp. 34-35.
16. Ibid
17. If Pope Gregory was amazed by the paleness of the color of the Saxons, and the blondness of their hair, it is obvious that the Romans were not pale-skinned, blond people.
18. Erich Kahler, "Jewish financiers and personal physicians, and one pope, Anacletus II, even came from the Jewish family of Pierleoni." The Jews Among the Nations (New York: Frederick Ungar Publishing Co. 1970) p. 51.
19. George G.M. James, "How the African Continent Gave Its Culture to the Western World." *Stolen Legacy* (San Francisco: Julian Richardson Associates, Reprint 1976).
20. M. Romera-Navarro. *Historia de España* (Boston, Massachusetts: D.C. Heath and Company, 1932).
21. Ministerio de Informacion y Turismo, España, 1975.
22. Carleton S. Coon. *The Origin of Races* (New York: Alfred A. Knopf, 1967). p. 474.
23. M. Romera-Navarro, Chapter II, p. 6. The cited text was translated by the author.
24. Carleton S. Coon. See plate 17, illustration of Negrita-native, Luzon, Philippines—an extensive study of man's origin.
25. *Berseem*: Egyptian clover, of the legume family, grown and used as a forage crop.
26. John M. Pittaro and Alexander Green. *Segundo Curso Progresando.* (Boston, Massachusetts: D.C. Heath and Company, 1960), p. 72.
27. Cesar Barja. *Libras y Autores Clasicos* (New York: Las Americas Publishing Company, 1964).
28. Rogers. *100 Amazing Facts About the Negro,* p. 10.
29. Stephen Birmingham. *The Grandees* American Sephardic Elite (New York: harper & Row Publishers, 1971), p. 38.
30. Jose Maria Auzmendi Aguirre. *Historia del Pueblo de Lazcano* (San Sebastian: Graficas Izarra-Pena y Goni, Mayo, 1970). A little town north of Beassin, about two kilometers from villa Franca de Ordiza.
31. *The Grandees.*
32. *Ibid.*

33. Martin Sagrera. Racismos en la America "Latina" (La Valle 1208 Seccion 10, Buenos Aires: Editora Astrea, Rodolfo Hnos, 1974). Translated by the author. pp. 77–78

34. Menendez Pidah. *Origenes del Españon* 1953

35. Most of those "Conquistadors" were semi-literate Spaniards—adventurers and undesirables from Spain.

36. Martin Sagrera, p. 102.

37. "So what, do you think you're more white than I?

38. Richard L. Jackson. *The Black Image in Latin American Literature* (Albuquerque, New Mexico: University of New Mexico Press, 1976). Jackson defines Latin American and Spanish escapism as purely the "sum of prejudices, myths, and collective attitudes of a given group." Jackson did not apply it to Jews, who are the subjects of this investigation.

39. Erich Kahler

40. *Marrano:* hog in Spanish, used pejoratively to classify a pork eater or filthy person.

41. Edomites, descendants of Esau; reddish-skinned people who suppressed Israel; name of an oppressive people in the Talmud. Ishmael, eldest son of Abraham by an Egyptian handmaid, Hagar. Traditionally, the ancestor of the Arab Moslem people.

42. "The Light of the Lord."

43. Max L. Margolis and Alexander Mars. *A History of the Jewish People* (New York: A Temple Book Atheneum, Jewish Publication Society of America, 1973), p. 452.

44. Max L. Margolis and Alexander Marx, p. 452.

45. George G.M. James, pp. 164–184.

46. The fortress of Saint Matthew.

47. *Halakhot:* collection of oral laws in accepted traditions existent before the Mishna was written. It embraces percepts not found in the written law. It is the legal part of the Midrash.

48. The Medieval name was *sermo generalis,* (meaning general sermon).

49. *Antorcha* means torch in Spanish. Torce means a loop or chain around one's neck. *Quemada* means a burn. Notice the connections between the surname of a child that became a hangman and the path he blazed in human history.

50. *kiosco:* a large gazebo or kiosk, an open summerhouse-type structure found in Spanish and Latin American cities, especially the parks where the heart of the city and municipal offices are located.

51. *Sanbenito:* a penitential garment Jews were ordered to wear at the Auto Da Fe tribunals on their day of judgment or before. At the trial, the degree of non-adherence to Christian doctrine could be determined by the color of the tunic worn.

52. Isaac Abravanel (1437–1508): served as treasurer to Alfonso V of Portugal, fled to Spain (1483) to escape charges of conspiracy. Served Ferdinand and Isabella, left Spain and joined the court of Naples, Italy.

53. Solomon Grayzel. *A History of the Jews* (Philadelphia: The Jewish Publication Society of America 5707–1947), p. 415.

54. Lord Kingsborough: *Antiquities of Mexico*, Volume VI, p. 291.
55. David C. Cook. *Black America Yesterday and Today* (Elgin, Illinois: David C. Cook Publishing Company, [area 60120] 1969).
56. Jose V. Malcioln. *How the Hebrews Became Jews* (New York: U.B. Productions, 1978).

CHAPTER 10

THE JEWS
AMONG EUROPEANS

After the Diaspora—a Greek word meaning dispersion since classical times and applied to Hebrews settled outside of Palestine—we are forced to revert to the period of the close of the First Temple.

The First Temple was firmly and splendidly built by King Solomon (965–926 B.C.E.). It was known for its luxurious decorations. After its completion (965 B.C.E.), Solomon made it a shrine for the Ark of the Covenant, with a place for the sacred vessels and offerings, a hall, and an inner sanctum, the Holy of Holies. The Temple measured $113^3/_4$ by $32^1/_2$ feet; the hall was $16^1/_4$ by $32^1/_2$ feet, the shrine measured 65 by $32^1/_2$ feet, and the Holy of Holies $32^1/_2$ by $32^1/_2$ feet. This First Temple was situated to extend from East to West. The important worship was performed in the shrine, where those allowed to enter came by way of the great hall (hekhal) through two huge internal cedar doors. The Holy of Holies (devir) contained the Ark and was only entered by the High Priest once a year on Yom Kippur. It had a raised floor and no window. The Temple was built of hewn stone, masonry laced with beams, and cedarwood. The two columns Boaz and Jachin stood at the entrance to the great hall. Solomon's Temple was a popular center of worship, where multitudes of worshippers came to atone, sacrifice, and hold conferences. All adult Hebrew males were required to pay a tithe of a half-shekel toward repairs and maintenance of the Temple. They were also expected to attend the three Pilgrimage Festivals: Passover, Pentecost, and Feast of Tabernacles. There were eight gates, such as the Nicanor's Gate, the last gate through which only Hebrew men could pass, and the Susa (Shushan)[1] Gate which led to the Court of the Gentiles. This great Temple built by Solomon was erected by Phoenicians[2] skilled in wood carving and architecture.

Solomon's Temple was raided on many occasions. The vessels

were often despoiled by conquerors or taken as tribute. However, the Temple was never demolished until the time of Nebuchadnezzar in 586 B.C.E. It was rebuilt from 538 to 515. This overhaul was called the Second Temple. Major reconstructions were later carried out under Simon the Just, Judah the Maccabee, Simon the Hasmonean, and Herod I the Great (73 B.C.E.– 4 B.C.E.), king of Judea, son of Antipater the Idumean and his Nabatean wife Cypros.[3]

Gerard Israel and Jacque Lebar state that the Law received on Mount Sinai and placed in the Holy of Holies in Solomon's Temple was lost when Nebuchadnezzar's soldiers burned and sacked the Temple, destroyed and profaned the Ark of the Covenant and other sacred treasures. These writers also state that Zerubbabel was of the line of David. What they did not mention was the fact that anyone of the line of David had to be of African ethnicity. They also mentioned that Herod's wife Marianne was dark, tall, and delicate. But these men did not show that no European Jews existed at that time. Furthermore, the woman they describe did not have thick ankles like European women are wont to have, in many cases. She displayed the features of the Falashas or other non-Europeans of her time. There were only some red-skinned people called Edomites among the Semites.[4] They would probably be called mulattoes today. But more important is Israel and Zebar's statement concerning Zerubbabel's rebuilding of the Temple in 520 B.C.E. They state, with some authority, that Zerubbabel returned from exile in Babylon and "no longer had anything to put in the Holy of Holies."[5] They are right, he had nothing to put in the Inner Sanctum. Why? The Ethiopians stole the Ark while Babylonians amalgamated with leprous pale-skinned tribes, causing the original Hebrews to keep the Laws, according to Leviticus 13:13, 19:19, and even 15:19, which explain the beginning of white people's evolution in the East. The original unamalgamated Hebrews of Ethiopia Falashim kept the Ark of the Covenant and buried it at Axum, Ethiopia.

Hebrew settlements became important during the overthrow of the Kingdom of Judah, sixth century B.C.E. At that time, large deportations were enforced by Babylonian conquerors. When the banishments subsided, it is very possible that the majority of the exiled Jews did not return to Palestine. They were scattered, as stated in the Book of Esther, throughout the 127 provinces of the then existing Persian Empire. "The Elephantine papyri illustrate the vitality of the Jewish colony in Egypt in the fifth century B.C.E.," states the *Jewish Encyclopedia*.

Elephantine was an ancient island fortress on the Egyptian-Ethiopian frontier, on the Nile opposite Aswan, c. 590 B.C.E.[6] During this epoch, there were also Hebrew kingdoms in Yemen. Christopher

Wren tells of a rock-studded landscape discovered at Dhofar Yemen. He mentioned farmers plowing with their camels and discovering stones and artifacts that reveal the ancient past. The wind-beaten area bears such names as Jebel Yahudia, which means "Mountain of the Jews," and Jebel Shamer Yuharish, the name of an old king of the Himyarite dynasty.

The Himyarites were a Hamitic-Semitic people. Their language is similar to Ethiopic or Amharic. The end of the Himyarites came in 115 B.C. They lasted until 525 A.D. when they were defeated by the Ethiopians, who were later driven out by the Persians.[7] The word Hamitic tells of the African origin of people, regardless of what modern historians pretend. Before the Himxariles and after the Persians came Alexander the Great (356–323 B.C.E.). This Macedonian king entered Judea in 332 B.C.E. He was at the height of his military career and invited Aristotle to come to Africa and obtain Ethiopian-Egyptian ideas later labeled "Greek Philosophy" throughout the world.[8]

The cultural unification of the total eastern Mediterranean began through the conquests of Alexander. The Egyptian community was rapidly developing and had extended itself westward into Cyrene. At the time, Ethiopia was declining. Deportations, misplacements, and colonizations extended the boundaries of so-called Hebrew settlements. Hebrews and Jews were found all throughout Syria and Asia Minor. During that period, they penetrated into Greece and up to Rome. This community was numerically substantial during the time of Caesar and Augustus. More immigrants came after the destruction of Jerusalem by Titus, Roman emperor (79–81), after a five-month siege in 70 A.C.E. Diasporas, however, were not the dominant reason for the rapid growth of Jewish settlements in Europe. There were other more significant reasons. One of them was the writing of a Bible by the Hebrews.

A Bible, copied from the Egyptians, who had copied from the Ethiopians before them, gave the Hebrews undue credit. The Ethiopians were the people who organized the first proselytizing religion. The Hebrews emulated the Egyptians and claimed not only a mission but a blessing of "Chosen people!" They proclaimed responsibility not only for the salvation of their own tribes, but for all people of the world. It was truly a religion with enough dynamism to cause awe and jealousy. The religion was one that proclaimed identity with a God so powerful they did not need other gods to help him with fertilization, birth, crops, seasons, or wars. This God was omnipotent. A people associated with a God that powerful had to be feared, and their God had to be tested. With fear breeding distrust and perhaps hate, the Christians decided to get a black Hebrew prophet Jesus (Yeshua) to help them. Then they added a Holy Ghost. Why shouldn't the Hebrews be tested at that point? The Hebrews were flourishing in Babylonia intellectually and economically when Palestine was weakening. This historical development repeated itself centuries later when Spanish Jewish settlements and communities along the Rhine came to the foreground just as Babylonian leadership was declining. Hebrew tradition was abolished by the Romans when they spitefully built a temple on the spot where the First Temple of Solomon stood in Palestine, Africa.

Spanish Jewry, an admixture of converted and non-converted believers, was dissolved through conversions and expulsions of many undecided persons. It probably became obvious to them that taking on European characteristics, superficially and culturally, would be advantageous. We must, therefore, conclude that the reason to take on a European physical appearance was tempting to Hebrews and made them become "white Jews" to overcome color prejudice. They surely felt that whiteness would save them from persecutions, since they could easily pass for their oppressors, through acculturation and integration. From the fourteenth to the present century, the Spanish word to describe this phenomenon has been *"emblanquec-imiento,"* for "whitening." Hebrews rose from insignificance to prominence in Poland, Germany, and elsewhere. However, they did not foresee the Nazi terror behind the gas chambers they were helping white supremacy to build through their significance as consultants in these countries and their prominence in world affairs. The Spaniards, Italians, and Blacks also practiced avoiding marrying darker countrymen. Dances at Howard University and Hampton Institute in the U. S. had only light-skinned students or very prominent blacks up to 1950.

POLAND

Poland must be mentioned because of its role played in the transition of African Hebrews to European Jews.

Arthur Koestler, a well-recognized writer, said that "during the Middle Ages, the majority of those who professed the Judaic faith were Khazars." Koestler declared that "a substantial part of this majority went to Poland, Lithuania, Hungary and the Balkans, where they founded that Eastern Jewish community which in its turn became the dominant majority of world Jewry." Koestler, himself an Hungarian Jew, went on to say that even if the original core of that European community "was diluted and augmented by immigrants from other regions, its predominantly Khazar-Turkish derivation appears to be supported by strong evidence, and should at least be regarded as a theory worth serious discussion."[9]

As early as 966, Poland found itself under the control of the emperors of Germany, and under the spiritual rule of Germany's bishops. The bishops represented the Roman See with impartiality, however, and the interaction between Poland and Germany stimulated commerce. Impartiality, in particular, attracted Jews—as most of them had now become—and there was an influx of Jewish merchants and settlers leaving Germany for Poland. An expulsion after the first Crusade (1096) also forced Jews to seek refuge in Poland. The Crusaders attacked the Jews of Prague and forcibly converted them to Christianity. The Bohemian Jews immediately began rushing to Poland to avoid the ruthless Christian throngs.

The Bohemian Prince Vratislav robbed the refugees of most property and valuables they possessed, but even that abuse did not deter their flight. They left Bohemia in 1098. That plunder and other injustices caused a steady flow of Jewish people to emanate from around the Rhine and Danube provinces streaming into Poland, as the Crusaders pushed onward from 1146 to 1147 and in 1196. The refugees sought shelter in the provinces of Cracow, Posen, Kalish, and Silesia near the Austrian-German border.

The fission between Christians and Jews began in the second half of the twelfth century, when Poland fell apart. The dislike showed itself more vividly when several feudal principalities or "appanages," (districts) were formed. The most important of these being: Great Poland in the northwest, with the leading cities of Posen and Kalish; Little Poland in the southwest, with Cracow and Lublin; and Red Russia in the south.

Old Prince Mechislav III, in his anxiety to enforce laws to protect individual rights, issued strict injunctions in 1173 forbidding all forms of violence against Jews, especially by Christian scholars. Persons found guilty of abusing Jewish civil rights were to be fined heavily. The Jews farmed, and minted the coins of Great and Little Poland. They even struck coins with names of the ruling princes in Hebrew.[10] Jewish intelligentsia was at its height. Rabbai Eliezer, a contemporary Bohemian, wrote that having no scholars of their own, in his Tosafist school, numerous Jewish scholars were brought in from Germany. Those German scholars brought "a German dialect which subsequently developed into the Polish Jewish jargon, or Yiddish."[11]

Under Casimir, Polish kings ruled over all the principalities into which Poland had been divided, and Casimir had added more protection for the Jews (1333–1370). Jewish civil rights had been bolstered with the added political insurance coverage, because a few years later there was the epidemic known as the Black Death. This epidemic (1348–1349) raised a rumor in Savoy, Germany, that the Jews had poisoned the wells and caused the disease. The rumors reached Poland and there were a number of attacks on Jews there, but not as disastrous as it had been in Germany. Jews ran from Germany into Poland in significantly large numbers. This immigration was larger than previous ones. There were numerous expulsions of Jews from German cities, numbering about three hundred fifty, while those in sixty large, and one hundred fifty small communities were exterminated. Poland was the nearest place of refuge and they flocked there.

Casimir the Great, it was rumored, behaved favorably toward the Jews because of his infatuation and admiration for the Jewish maiden, Estherka, the daughter of a tailor in his community. She is supposed to have overwhelmed the king with her charm and affection to the extent that in 1356, he abandoned his former lover for her. Estherka lived in the palace of Lobzovo near Cracow and bore the loving king two daughters. The girls, it is said, were brought up by their mother in the Jewish faith and the two sons were educated as Christians. The sons later became the progenitors of several noble heirs to the throne. Their mother was killed, despite her relationship, during the reign of Louis of Hungary, who succeeded Casimir (1370–1382). Louis did not reign long, but he managed to persecute the Jews before his term ended. His persecutions were not too harsh, and it was not until the reign of the Polish King Vladislav Yaghello (1386–1434) that the Jews were really resubjected to harsh treatment.

Having been converted from paganism to Catholicism, Yaghello became somewhat fanatic as a Catholic. He forced the Lithuanians to follow his example of adherence to the new faith with the ardor of a true convert. He often yielded to the influence of the Church's officials as well.[12] His predecessors like Boleslav of Kalish, surnamed the Pious, ruler of the province named Great Poland, had been the cause of the Jews coming to Poland. Jewish immigration was then considered important for the economic development and the cultural enrichment of an underdeveloped Poland. The native Slav population suffered no inconveniences from the immigrants who had brought them a higher civilization.

The Christians and Christian-German immigrants organized everyone they could into guilds to monopolize artisanship. Jews were soon prevented from obtaining farming concessions and were limited to leasing farming estates to Christians, operating salt mines, money lending and custom duties collection. Despite the Christian opposition, Jews still managed to penetrate the economic periphery of the country. An added advantage of theirs was their academic advancement over the Christians in the thirteenth and fourteenth centuries. Polish culture was yet incomparable with that of other western countries. Coming from Germany with decidedly higher intellectual and industrial knowledge than the Poles caused the Jews to be feared not only by the Poles but by the Germans as well. The Christians also resented the special considerations extended the Jews by Yaghello's predecessors. There became only two fixed socioeconomic classes: the owners of the soil and the tillers of the soil. The Jews, therefore, became a "third estate," pioneering in trade, finance, and the professions. Temporal powers of the same state officials had been influenced by their economic needs causing a promotion of Jewish existence in Poland on more or less rational material and civil foundations. Nevertheless, the ecclesiastic authorities were more inspired and dominated by their spiritual ideals of the Roman Church than the love of their national development. This warped determination caused them to generate their energies toward removing the Jews from general participation in the country's development. Jews were thenceforth segregated from the Christian population and alleged to be injurious to Catholics and their unquestionable adherence without experience of Bible reading. The popularized Church Council of Breslau, convened in 1266 by the Papal Legate, Guido, was revived. During that period Guido had introduced to his fellow clergymen in the oldest Polish diocese of Gnesen the canonical laws that included statutes against Jews. Jews had been decreed to sell houses they owned in the Christian quarter within the shortest time possible. Jews locked themselves up when Christian processions marched through the streets. Christians were prohibited from buying meat from Jews who might poison them. The ancient canonical promulgations also forbade Jews to hire Christian servants, nursery-maids, and nurses. Jews were barred from collecting custom duties and other government revenues. A Jew living with a Christian woman unlawfully was liable to be publicly whipped and permanently banished from the town.

By 1279 the Church Council had convened in Buda (Ofen), Hungary. That Council ratified the clause known as the "Jewish sign," supplementing that edict with other adverse clauses. Jews were to be forced to wear a ring of red cloth sewn on the upper left side of their outer garments. A Jew appearing on the streets without that sign was to be considered a vagrant, and no Christian was permitted to legally transact business with him. A similar sign, saffron in color, was to be worn by "Saracens and Ishmaelites," names given the Moslems. The laws also affected Christians of the Greek Orthodox persuasion to some extent. Jews were also told to wear a peculiarly shaped hat, with a horn-like shield (*cornutum pileum*) to identify them among Christians. Any Jew caught without this headpiece was subject to punishment in accordance with the law of the country where he was charged.

Christians were forbidden to invite Jews to dine, drink, dance, or celebrate with them at merrymaking functions, under penalty of ecumenical sanction or excommunication from the Church. Catholicism had not reached complete control over Poland as yet, so the laws were not strictly enforced. Christian intolerance reached its zenith, and the first really significant persecutions of Jews in Poland began in 1399. The Christians charged the Jews of Posen with having bribed a poor Christian woman into stealing three consecrated wafers from the local Dominican church, stabbing the hosts, then throwing them into a pit. To coincide with the old concept of vendetta, "Blood for blood shed!" a rumor was spread to incite the community. The talk was that blood spurted from the pierced wafers in confirmation of the Eucharist dogma. Other miracles were ascribed to the three holy wafers and in a few hours the charges had been so magnified that tempers flared, and justice was demanded. The archbishop of Posen heard of the alleged blasphemy and instituted punitive proceedings against the Jews. The rabbi of Posen, thirteen elders of the Jewish community, and the woman charged with the theft of the holy wafers became targets of reprisals. After hours of torture and interrogation, "they were all tied to pillars and roasted alive on a slow fire (1399)."[13] The Jews of Posen, were soon subjected to an "eternal" fine to be paid to the Dominican church annually. The fine was enforced up to the eighteenth century.

CONFLICT BETWEEN CASIMIR IV AND CLERGY

Casimir IV, third king of the Yaghello dynasty, reigned 1447–1492. He was concerned with the ideas of humanistic practices pursued during his reign by other countries. Like a wise ruler, he decided to safeguard the rights of all his subjects, regardless of their religious beliefs. As Grand Duke of Lithuania, Casimir followed the policies of Vitovt who reigned over Lithuania before him. He proclaimed protection for Rabanite and Karaite Jews according to law. Jews were therefore employed by the government as tax-farmers to assist in augmenting the revenues of his state treasury. The clergy was advised to refrain from dictating to the crown.

Casimir IV made a state visit to Posen in 1447. While he was there a fire broke out and raged for some time before it could be controlled. The Charter which Casimir the Great had bestowed upon the Jews was destroyed by the fire. A Jewish delegation composed of members from Posen and other Jewish communities petitioned Casimir IV to restore the old pledge on the basis of copies made and safeguarded over the years. Casimir readily consented. About one year later, the Church held a great Council at Basle where Casimir IV protested against the canonical laws reissued by the Council of Kalish for Poland and the whole Catholic world. Casimir countermanded that edict with his own Charter of 1453. The monarch's charter permitted Jews to associate with Christians, and exempted them from the jurisdiction of the ecclesiastic courts. These special privileges soon caused reactions by the Church and the jealous anti-Jewish feelings it encouraged with its policies.

The Archbishop of Cracow, Cardinal Zbignyev Oleshnitzki, openly defied the king. He criticized Casimir IV for granting safety to the Jews and referred to the charter as a proclamation "to the injury and insult of the holy faith." Oleshnitzki also threatened the king in a letter in which he referred to the famous Jew hater, the Papal Legate Capistrano, who was in Poland on a visit from Germany.

Capistrano had come to Poland with his scourge of the Jews that had been effective in Germany. The campaign against the Jews began with the two allies Oleshnitzki and Capistrano. The former called the Jews heretics (or *Hussites*) and the latter preached in the marketplace that the king should revoke the "godless" Jewish privileges. Capistrano also said that if the king did not curtail these acts of due process, he (the king) would be scourged with the "tortures of hell and terrible misfortunes for the country." The king tried to ignore him and the other anti-Jewish elements but, Poland was at war with a semi-religious, semi-military organization called the Teutonic Order. Therefore, after the first defeat suffered by Polish troops in the war of September 1454, the clergy boasted that God was chastising the country because of the king's sympathy toward the Jews and his disregard for the Church. That charge made the king capitulate to the nobility and the Church. As a result, November 1454 saw the servants of the king disclaiming the statute of advantages law. All former Jewish privileges were rescinded as "being equally opposed to Divine right and earthly laws."

The Christians went on to say that "it is not meant that infidels should enjoy greater advantages than the worshippers of our Lord Christ, and slaves should have no right to occupy a better position than sons."[14]

The Varta Statutes of 1423 and other old anti-Jewish laws were all reinforced. It was not long before several Jews were attacked and robbed. In 1463, an army of Polish volunteers passed through Lemberg and Cracow on their way to Hungary to fight the Turks. This unorganized army made up of monks, students, peasantry, and indebted noblemen attacked the Jews on the third day of Easter week, looted their homes and shops, and massacred approximately thirty Jewish persons. Casimir IV was disturbed with the lawlessness and fined the magistrate for the disorders. Nevertheless, similar misfortunes were suffered by Jews in other cities.[15]

Casimir IV continued to protect the Jews, despite the clergy's nonviolent opposition. However, upon his death the kingdom was divided among his sons. The first Polish Ghetto was then established under his son John Albrecht. To add to Jewish woes, there was a large fire in the Polish capital of Cracow in 1494. The mob took control of the Jewish part of the city. There was plundering and pillaging of Jewish shops and homes. The Jews were living in different parts of the city, and therefore quite defenseless. The king gave orders that they all move together in Kazimiezh, on the outskirts of Cracow.[16]

John Albrecht's rule of Poland was a contrast to that of his brother Alexander who ruled Lithuania as Grand Duke. In 1492, Alexander reaffirmed the charter of his father, Casimir IV, according to the Magdeburg Law, adding other privileges. He also paid the Jews a part of the funds that they had received under his father that had later been denied.

In 1495, the Grand Duke Alexander had a complete change of heart. His reversal contained a statute that ordered the expulsion of all Jews from Lithuania. It was difficult to determine whether the reversal was due to the expulsion of Jews from Spain, pressure from the Church, or Alexander's intent to confiscate Jewish assets, renege on debts owed them, and thereby bolster his treasury. Alexander confiscated all immovable properties of the deported Jews in the districts of Grodno, Brest, Lutzk, and Troki. He later distributed some of the property to the local Christians. The expelled Jews hurried to the Crimea (Kaffa), but the majority of them accepted an offer of John Albrecht, who permitted them to settle in the neighboring Polish cities.

In 1501, Alexander I accepted the crown of Poland as an extension (1501–1505), a few years after his brother's death. He permitted the reentry of Jews into Lithuania and their former homes. They recovered some of their houses, estates, synagogues, and cemeteries (1503).

The beginning of the fourteenth century had seen Polish Jews become recognizable as economic and social entities. They had also become an independent spiritual body. At the same time, other Jews were migrating to Turkey from Spain and Portugal. The Ghettos, of Germany and Austria, were overcrowded causing Jews from those areas to come into Lithuania, Poland, and most of the Slavonian east. During that period, the Reformation of the Catholic Church and Protestantism was keeping the Church so occupied that the Jewish question was unimportant. A large Diaspora center emerged in eastern Europe as a result, particularly in Turkey and Poland. The Sephardim, or dark-skinned Jews, were now approaching their cultural decline, "lapsing into Asiatic stupor," as Dubnov called it. On the other hand, the fair-skinned, blond-haired Ashkenazim, of Poland, were beginning their historic development, having absorbed or maintained the original Hebrew culture. "The mission of the Sephardim was a memory of the past; that of the Ashkenazim was a hope for the future."

It was now an era of Jewish intensity and autonomy comparable to medieval Babylonia and Spain during the Golden Age. The continuous colonization of Slavonian territory by Jews emigrating from

Germany, having started in the Middle Ages, transformed Poland from a colony to a Jewish metropolis. The poorer Jews engaged in land tenure and farming, retail trade, money lending, and other commerce. They also collected state liquor taxes in Lithuania and Poland. The really rich merchants exported agricultural products from Poland to Austria, Moldavo-Wallachia, and Turkey. The Catholics observed with jealous subtlety and remorse, but bided their time.

Then the Jesuits began to show their resentment. They noticed that the Jews were favored by two powers within the state: royalty and the big Shlakhta.[17] The Jesuits turned to the opposing faction for support: the clergy and the burghers. In the case of royalty, the exchequer was well provided for through regular and irregular imposts on Jewish importers and exporters. The kings also derived personal benefits from the commercial transactions of these industrious subjects. The Jewish tax-farmers paid large sums in advance for the lease of the state revenues and custom duties collections, and the tenure of royal civil services. Jewish contractors and tenants often became the financial agents of the kings due to their ability to advance large sums of money to secure the positions they preferred. Those opportunities were so continuously monopolized by Jews that it caused the magistrates representing municipal governments to force certain local restrictions on Jews in the acquisition of real estate, trading rights, and handicraft manufacturing and distribution. The trade unions also incited mobs to attack the Jews from time to time.

The sixteenth century found Jews under the liberal regime of Sigsmund I (1467–1548) as king of Poland from 1506–1548. This son of Casimir IV, who succeeded his brother Alexander I, had some difficulty. Sigsmund I encountered obstacles in consolidating his domestic power to be able to ward off external challenges menacing Poland. The 1505 enactment of Alexander's *Nihil Novi*, which forbade the kings to enact laws without approval of the Diet, seriously handicapped Sigsmund I.

The Jews were now fully restored the properties and rights lost at the end of the fifteenth century. Alexander Yaghello, the same Lithuanian Grand Duke who had chased them away in 1495, had called them back as soon as he ascended the throne in Poland after his brother's death.

The cooperation between Lithuania and Poland made the Jews more popular, especially because the royal budget depended on their efforts and proficiency. They settled near the castles and localities they previously occupied. One of the well-known royal financiers under Alexander was a wealthy fellow named Yosko.[18] King Alexander favored Yosko and his employees by placing them as dignitaries under the direct jurisdiction of the court. But the king had already safeguarded Christian economic development with Boleslav's old charter, *Ad cautelam defensionis contra Judaeos.*[19]

Sigsmund I, Yaghello King of Poland and Grand Duke of Lithuania was more considerate toward the Jews. Sigsmund I was a devout Catholic who despite his spiritual preference was free of religious bigotry. He also proclaimed that equal justice should be meted out to the rich and poor alike.

In Lithuania Michael Yosefovich, a Jew from Brest-Litovsk, was made intermittent grand ducal treasurer. He paid local officials and all debts accrued by his royal master. Sigsmund appointed Yosefovich to serve as "senior," a term used to identify the official with the most seniority. This official was given extended powers which entailed the right to confer directly with the king in all important Jewish matters, dispensing justice to his coreligionists, and in accordance with Jewish laws. Yaghello also made Yosefovich's brother, Abraham Yosefovitch a civil servant of Smolensk. Yosefovich then propelled his brother to the high rank of Chancellor of the Lithuanian Exchequer. However, he was more eager to defend the rights, privileges, and financial interests of Jews than of his brother Abraham, who soon became a high Polish noble who took his offspring along with him into the domain of the Gentile way of living and believing.[20]

At that time, Jews were not distinguishable from Christians in customs, appearance, and language as they would become in later years. Some of them had black hair and black skin, to whom the Germans referred as *schwartze.* These were descended from Khazars. Ishtakhri, the Arab geographer, referred to them in his writings as "swarthy verging on deep black as if they were a kind of Indian." These Jews Koestler called "Kara-Khazars," or black Khazars, and the pale-faced ones he called "Ak-Khazars," meaning colorless.[21]

The Jewish communities of Brest, Grodno, Pinsk, and Troki, "the last consisting principally of Karaites," had a municipality of their own. These were important Jewish centers in the Duchy where Jews enjoyed considerable autonomy. Rabbi Mendel Frank of Brest received extensive administrative and judicial authority, which included the right to impose the *herem*[22] and other penalties upon the uncooperative members of the Jewish community of 1531. In the large cities of Poland proper, Jewish existence was not so pleasant. The commercial life of Jews in Poland was on a higher level than in Lithuania nonetheless. Jews competed with Christians enterprises and took advantage of the autonomy granted the estates through the Magdeburg Law. But the Christians were dissatisfied and prepared to clip the wings of the soaring Jews. Christians were particularly ready to aggravate social unrest in Posen, Cracow and Lemberg, the three provinces of Great Poland, Little Poland, and Red Russia.

Jews were prohibited the right to display merchandise in stores or transact business outside their Jewish quarter. The Jews protested to the king, who in 1517 warned the authorities of Posen about harsh and unjust treatment against their competitors. The Christian merchants retorted that Jews had been allowed preference to the extent of being in control of the best businesses, locations, and even the stalls in the markets where only Christian merchants (mostly Germans) had been the prominent proprietors. They further added that there were on a per capita basis more Christians than Jews in the area. Jewish predominance might therefore induce Catholics to stray or begin proselytizing among the Christian majority. "The reference to religion used as a cloak for commercial greed did not fail to impress the devout Sigsmund."[23] He prohibited the Jews from having businesses at the marketplace in 1520. Jews also were banned from buying food and other merchandise before Christian fellow citizens completed their purchases and left the counters. Later on Jews were barred from Posen after they began entering that city in large numbers.

The king ordered that no houses be sold to Jews without permission of the *Kahal*[24] elders. In 1523 Jews were forbidden to build new houses in Christian neighborhoods. The same laws were enforced in Lemberg. No Jews were allowed to sell cloth in Red Russia Podolia, unless there was a fair in town. Their transactions in horned cattle could not exceed two thousand heads per year.

In 1521, the Piotrkov Diet enacted a law limiting the trade of Lemberg Jews to the following four articles: furs, wax, cloth, and cattle on the hoof. The magistrates of Posen, Lemberg, and Cracow exchanged ideas on Jewish economic control. There were anti-Jewish riots and physical confrontations to prevent Jewish expansion in Posen and Brest-Kuyansk, a former Polish province on the left bank of the Vistula. The inhabitants protested to King Sigsmund, who issued a decree condemning the riots with a threat of the death penalty and confiscation of property. To guarantee Jewish rights and equal opportunity, Sigsmund commanded the burghers of Cracow to deposit ten thousand gulden with the exchequer as insurance guaranteeing safety and maintaining order in their cities. Burgomasters, Aldermen, and trade union leaders were told by the king that all differences with the Jews should be contested through due process of law, rather than violence or force with or without arms. The Christians of the Polish regime switched their tactical offensive to one of extortion, over which the king could have no control.

Sigsmund's second wife, Queen Bona Sforza, was said to have been an avaricious Italian princess who sold offices of the state to the highest bidder. Her favorite courtier was Peter Kmita, Voyevoda of Cracow and Marshall of the Crown. It is said that he "managed to accept bribes simultaneously from the Jewish and the Christian merchants. . . by promising to defend their interests before the Diet or the King."

In the fourth decade of the sixteenth century, there were heated debates at the Polish Diets, and deputies of various regions received the anti-Jewish instructions. The controlling Polish Diet was the Shlakhta, despite the fact that there was divisiveness. The big Shlakhta, comprised of magnates, owners of huge estates and whole towns, were more favorable toward their Jewish communities. They employed Jews as farmers and revenue collectors. But the small Shlakhta of struggling squires joined forces with the burghers who had always been hostile to the Jews. As usual, these alliances allowed the clergy once again to attack Jews for being a threat to the Catholic religion.

The Piotrkov Diet of 1538 saw anti-Jewish protests at their peak. The Diet adopted a constitution with a separate Jewish clause brandishing the iron rules of the old canonical laws. The clause stated, "those who manage our revenue must unconditionally be members of the landed nobility, and persons professing the Christian faith."[25] Another emphatic statement was, "no Jews shall be intrusted with the collection of revenues of any kind."[26] Jews had no right to engage in business within any locality unless he or she had special permission from the king or through authorized agreement from the magistrates. In the villages there was no trade permitted except pawnbroking and money-lending, which was restricted to a selected few. Jews were all supposed to replace their badges of identification that they had discarded. Stars of David were to be replaced on outer garments to make them distinguishable from Christians. Exception was made in the favor of travelers and Jews of Lithuania.

It is said that the clergy instigated discrimination because of insecurity caused by the initial success of the Reformation in Poland. The Church feared that Judaism might overpower Christianity through its support for "Anti-Trinitarianism" which was becoming popular among thinkers of that era. Religious fear of challenges regarding the dogma of the Holy Trinity, instilled fear—without true cause—among the residents of Cracow. There was hysteria everywhere.

Catherine Zaleshovska, the 80-year-old Catholic wife of an alderman, was charged with denying the fundamental dogmas of Christianity, secretly converting, and later publicly professing Jewish beliefs. The Bishop of Cracow, Peter Gramrat, made several attempts to debrief her so that she could be born again. His efforts were futile. In the presence of canons and collegiates assembled at her inquiry, "she was asked whether she believed in Almighty God, the Creator of heaven and earth." Her reply was, "I believe in God." When asked the question, "Do you believe in His only begotten Son, Jesus Christ, who was conceived by the Holy Ghost?" She answered, "The Lord God has neither wife or son, nor does he need them." For being sensible enough to know that no mammal can produce an offspring without mating for continuance of the species—an elementary biological fact, . . "the unfortunate woman was burned at the stake on the marketplace of Cracow, 1539." Zaleshovska's concluding remarks were even more poignant in their logic and consistent with sound reasoning that a Polish writer, Lucas Gurnitz, recorded the entire speech. She is quoted as saying, in summary, "For sons are needed by those who die, but God is eternal, and since He was not born, it is impossible that he should die. It is we whom He considers His sons, and His sons are those who walk in His paths." The hypocrites who questioned the apostate woman were said to have explained quite a bit to her, but every time she was asked the biological question, "Do you believe in His only begotten Son, Jesus Christ, who was conceived by the Holy Ghost?" she became more obstinate. She contended that God is omnipotent and does not need a son to do a father's job. After being in jail for a few days, "She went to her death without any fear." The charge was blasphemy. [27]

During these times, there was undercurrent hysteria enforced with gossip. The rumor was, "many Christians are embracing the Jewish faith and after becoming circumcised, they flee to Lithuania where they are sheltered by the Jewish community there." These rumors led to investigations. Finding no evidence to substantiate the charges, the authorities discontinued the inquiries after many months. Shortly after the scuttlebutt subsided, the Lithuanian Jews found themselves slapped with a more serious charge. They were accused of leaving the country in large numbers, due to the consent of the sultan of Turkey who was supposed to be sheltering Christians converted to Judaism. It was even announced that some circumcised Christians of minor and adult ages had already crossed the Moldavian frontier. King Sigsmund ordered another investigation to determine whether the Jews were actually doublecrossing him or not. Acts of violence and looting followed the charges. The Jews attempted to forestall homicidal acts by sending an *ad hoc* delegation to the King. They were also concerned about Sigsmund beginning to heed the accusations and to withdraw his protection of them. Those who composed the delegation were Jews from Brest, Grodno, and other Lithuanian communities. They reassured the King that the charges were false rumors, that they were loyal to their country, and did not intend to emigrate to Turkey. They also swore that there were no attempts to proselytize among Christians, and that they were unjustly insulted, abused, and robbed. The Jews also explained to King Sigsmund the loss of revenue those investigations had cost the country's economy through lack of trade in their commercial districts. Their grievances were all founded on the basis of investigations made and events that provided evidence to clear them. The King promised to ignore further charges based on suspicions and lacking in evidence. A special charter was granted to the Jews in 1540 as a form of civil rights protection.

This proclamation did not make the Catholics discontinue their hatred for the Jews. They attacked them with libelous publications such as *De stupendis erroribus Judaeorum* Stupendous Errors of the Jews,1541, *De sanctis interfectis a Judaeis*, Concerning the Holy People 1543, and other condemnations. To add more agitation to public indecision, the Church Synod of 1542 gathered in Piotrkov and issued a constitution requiring that non-Jewish community members become aware of the abundance of Jews driven out of neighboring countries coming in to overcrowd Poland. Christians were told to be prepared to resist conversion because Jews combined holiness with ungodliness. Gnesen was the seat of the Primate, with Cracow as its capital. Therefore, the diocese of Gnesen was considered the most important in having its quota of Jews reduced.

Jews were not to be permitted to buy homes from Christians. "Those already bought to be returned to their former owners." Jews were prohibited from living in areas where they had never resided before. A new section was added to the old laws. It said there were to be no new synagogues erected in Cracow. Those already built were to be demolished, and old ones could not be repaired. The old laws regarding outer garments with special identification were added, along with seven other clauses about trade on Catholic holidays and holy days.

Sigsmund II, or Sigsmund Augustus (1548–1572) was the successor of Sigsmund I and the last of the Yaghello Dynasty to rule Poland. He continued the old statutes of Casimir IV with its principles of liberalism for all Poles. Sigsmund Augustus enacted a law similar to his father's guaranteeing impartial court proceedings to Jews living in the royal cities and villages. This protection did not extend to Jews living on the estate of nobles or townships owned by them. To enjoy royal privileges in 1549 the chosen few had to begin paying the king a special Jewish head-tax.

The ugly head of controversy began to rise again when rivalry between the royalty and the big Shlakhtas began. They fought for control of all free enterprises. The conflict between Jews, the third estate, and burghers also came into focus once more. In cities such as Cracow and Posen, compacts were designed to safeguard the limits of the ghetto; the Jews had no legal right to live outside of the line. In Posen they were not allowed to increase the number of homes they owned above a quota of forty-nine. This restriction forced them to build houses with several floors. In other cities, including Warsaw, the magistracies were allowed to maintain the privilege called *de non tolerandis Judaeis*, which meant the right to not tolerate Jews coming into an area not previously occupied by them. It also meant keeping them off limits in main thoroughfares or avenues, confining them to a restricted area, and banning them from transacting business outside the ghetto. Some Jewish merchants were allowed to come out on business days and remain for a few days, provided they procured the proper permits. Sigismund Augustus still attempted to secure equal rights for Jews in most Polish cities. In some instances, he tried to go as far as forbidding market-day shopping on Saturdays in order to protect Jewish businessmen who did not labor on the Sabbath. All the Polish estates abided by the laws of the king with but one exception, the Catholic enclave.

Around 1556, the Papal Nuncio, Lippomano, arrived from Rome to agitate religious zeal among the Polish Catholics. Rumor was soon circulating that a woman in Sokhachev named Dorothy Lazhetzka had sold her wafer received at holy communion to her Jewish neighbors. The wafer was said to have been stabbed by the "infidels" until it bled. Three Jews were charged with sacrilege and imprisoned along with Dorothy Lazhentzka. The Bishop of Khelm pressed charges. These prisoners were put on the rack and later sentenced to death. When the King heard the unfortunate news, he ordered a stay of the capital punishment. The clergy hurried the execution of the verdict instead of delaying it and the accused blasphemers were burned at the stake. Before dying, these sacrificed lambs made this statement:

> We have never stabbed the host; because we do not believe that the host is the Divine body (*nos enim nequaquam credimas hostiae inesse Die corpus*): knowing that God has no body nor blood. We believe, as did our forefathers; that the Messiah is not God, but his messenger. We also know from experience that there can be no blood in flour.[28]

The protests of these monotheists were silenced by the executioner who hurriedly stuffed the mouths of the alleged criminals with torches.

During Sigsmund Augustus' reign the Calvinists and the extreme right wing of the Reformation Movement rejected the Eucharist Dogma of communion wafer being the actual body of Christ and the wine being his blood. Perhaps some of these Christians had learned that 4,000 years ago, before Judaism or Christianity, the Mary and Jesus story had already been told and used in Africa as Isis and the infant Horus. They might have even learned that the infant's birth date had been merely changed from August 25 to December 25.[29]

Sigsmund said that he was shocked by this hideous villainy. He was also disgusted enough to expostulate, "nor am I sufficiently devoid of common sense to believe that there could be any blood in the host."

The Papal Nuncio Lippomano, who seemed to derive some psychological pleasure and physiological release from Jewish persecution, did not consider repercussions. Like the Euro-Americans who discriminate against people of color without due cause, he and his followers aroused indignation in the Protestants. However, anti-Jewish sentiment overshadowed all protective action and the Diets of 1562 and 1565 reissued the old anti-Jewish constitution of 1538. There was more pillaging, rioting, and requirements of special attire for Jews. In Bielesk in 1564, a Jew was charged with killing a Christian girl. He screamed innocence from the steps of the scaffold but no one harkened to his pleas.

LITHUANIA

The "Lithuanian Statute" was promulgated in 1566. It extended a new feature to Tartars and others [infidels.] It curbed most of their former privileges. And introduced a new form of xenophobia to them. Lithuania had another special feature worth mention here. It is a case which shows more proselytism or conversion of non-Jews despite the tortures anticipated by persons of that religious preference. This case is recorded as that of the Righteous Proselyte.[30]

A Polish nobleman, Count Valentin Potocki, and his friend Zaremba left Poland for Paris during the early part of the eighteenth century. In spite of the hostility and intolerance meted out to Jews at the time, they vowed to each other to convert to Judaism. Potocki and Zaremba met in Paris some time later and became very close friends. Potocki went to Rome to assure himself of his determination and whether he had the right to adopt the Jewish fate.

Zaremba returned to Poland, where he married a rich nobleman's daughter. A few years later, his conscience is supposed to have reminded him of the vow he had made with Potocki to convert to Judaism. Therefore, he took his wife and their young son on a trip to Koenigsberg, caught a ship and sailed to Amsterdam, where all three members of the family were accepted as converted Jews.

According to Israel Cohen, the author of *The Jews of Vilna*, "nothing is known of a subsequent meeting of Potocki and Zaremba," Anyway, the "discovery of the 'righteous proselyte' by the Polish authorities was due to a comparatively trivial incident." Potocki was studying the Talmud in the *Bet-ha-Midrash*, or house for study of the true laws in the Bible, at Ilye, a townlet some miles away from Vilna. Potocki was disturbed by a small boy who made noises that kept him from concentrating. He shushed the child, but the youngster refused to be quiet or go play outside. The boy is described as having been impudent as well. Potocki, not having learned the tolerance of Jews, grabbed the boy by an ear and put him out of the study room. In rebuking the brat, Potocki is supposed to have said a boy who misbehaves like that cannot be a real Jewish child and should probably be baptized later. Converts seem somehow to often become more faithful than those born into a faith. The Jewish expression, in such cases is "You're a better Jew than I am" or "he is a better Jew than we." The boy is said to have immediately run to his father's tailor shop, told his father the story and probably added some of his own words to make his accusation convincing. The father was so indignant at the discrediting remarks and the reflection cast on his religious fidelity— by a convert, no less—he hurried to the local squire and betrayed the righteous proselyte. When Potocki heard of the tailor's charges, he fled to a village inn a few miles away. The innkeeper was afraid to be charged as an accomplice if he should hide Potocki, so he turned him over to the squire's deputies. They immediately handcuffed Potocki and took him back to Vilna.

The authorities tortured Potocki supposedly to have him return to Christianity. It is said that neither the tortures nor the pleadings of his family could make him revert to Christianity. Legend states that Potocki's mother obtained a pardon either from the King or the Pope, but when the document reached the prison—as often occurred—it was too late. A good Jew, Leiser Zhiskes, succeeded in bribing the executioner to receive Potocki's ashes. Zhiskes was beardless—according to the writings—and dressed in Christian clothing as a disguise to avoid detection. The other Jews of that community felt unsure of the public's reaction and remained indoors that day.

The "elected period" when kings were chosen by popular vote, saw Shalkhta members elect in 1574 the French Prince Henry of Valois, who instigated the murder of Saint Bartholomew. That election alarmed the Jews and liberal Poles, who anticipated a reprisal from the clergy. Their fears were soon diminished when Henry fled Poland after only a few months. He went back to France and accepted the French crown as soon as he had learned of the death of his brother, Charles IV. The polish throne was then won by Stephen Batory, the brave and enlightened Hungarian Duke who won the election by popular vote.

The "Union of Lublin" concluded between Lithuania and Poland was to provide closer administrative and legislative cooperation between the two countries. However, the constitutional legislation for both parts of the republic affected the conditions of the Lithuanian Jews. Several injustices were permitted, and physical abuses against them were reactivated.

With Sigsmund Augustus II, the last of the Yaghello Dynasty died in 1572, Batory introduced ideas and intervened to enforce those ideas designed to protect Jewish civil rights in Posen. Batory disregarded the draconian regulations promulgated by the city fathers who competed with the Jewish merchants and allowed the latter to rent business places all over the city. Jews were also permitted to establish businesses and rent premises and even transact sales on Christian holy days and holidays. Batory's benevolence was sure to arouse resentment in the holy Christian sector where it was felt that the Christians were God's chosen. Repercussions came three short months after the enactment and posting of his protective laws. The Jewish quarter of Posen was attacked, their property looted, picked over, and the rest destroyed. Several Jews were killed. The pretext used to justify the rioting and wanton murders was that some Jews had prevented a Jewish man from meeting his wife while he was at the point "of accepting baptism." Dubnov says that in reality, the Christian merchants did not want to face their Jewish competitors on an equal basis.

Batory fined the Posen magistrates heavily for having allowed the Catholic backlash to have gotten out of hand. Nevertheless, the fines were soon revoked after the magistrates declared under oath that they had not known of the plot.

Catholic reaction became so forceful that even Batory had to yield to the powerful Jesuits attacks led by Peter Skarga and others. Batory surrendered management of the academy to the Jesuits, just as the Indians were psychologically compelled to do in Latin America, during the days of the Spanish conquest. The Jesuits took charge in Vilna and extended their schools from there to other parts of Poland. Batory did not foresee "all the evil, darkness, and intolerance" of these pretentious tyrants. Jesuits controlled the seats of "learning and monopolized the education of the ruling as well as the middle classes."[31]

SIGMUND III AND VLADISLAV IV

It is said that Jesuit control over Polish educational development increased during this period. Consequently, the urge to convert Jews to Christianity also increased. Parallel was Jewish resistance to conversion. The Polish political system and governmental practices made it difficult for any structural plan to obtain and maintain absolute control operationally or otherwise. No one system could even control influentially. The politicians of the period were said to boast "Poland subsists on disorders." Therefore, the golden liberty of the Shalakhta gradually deteriorated and became a total carving instrument with which the upper classes carved up and oppressed the middle classes; the oppression led to anarchy. A single member of the Diet could use the *Liberum veto* to override a decision of the entire assembly. Dubnov and other observers said that continued dissension among the states was preferable to monarchic absolutism similar to the concentration of power existent in Western Europe at that time. Otherwise, Poland might have been like Spain under Phillip II and the Inquisition with its autocratic hangmen exercising their calling.

Polish magnates were said to be engaged in amusement or the rhetorical sessions of the national and provincial assemblies where politics was a pleasurable affair in a clubhouse setting rather than in a dependable legislature where policies were formulated and effective laws enacted to benefit human existence. The politicians were, in effect, absentee landlords and they acted accordingly. Jewish tax-collectors were, therefore, greatly needed to collect rents and administer the affairs of these nobles in their respective towns and townships. These collectors, called "arendars,"[32] collected income from dairy farms, mills, distilleries, liquor vendors, and other businessmen. Even Sigsmund III, subjected to Jesuit pressure, found himself obligated to protect his Jewish revenue collectors. But the hostility of the burgher class, made up mostly of Germans, was relentless in its anti-Jewish efforts. Their mobs often attacked the Jewish sector under the protective guise of rightful exercise of the "lawful" persecution right proclaimed by the magistrates and trading unions. Jewish tradesmen were thus limited to trade exclusively with Jewish customers.

A muralist employed to paint a mural on the walls of the Posen town hall sketched Jewish subjects in ridiculous and offensive poses. The caricatures were carrying large sacks of money, had big noses, beards,and black hair. Most of them wore yarmelkes. The painting amused the populace but they aroused the activists and incited them to riot against the Jews.

This interpolation is an aside to show how Jews later meted out the same treatment to persons of color in N.Y. This exact treatment of character assassination was meted out to the ex-Deputy Chancellor, Bernard Gifford of the Board of Education of New York when he ran against a Jewish candidate for an elected office. The pious Jews characterized the Chancellor as an ape despite the fact that Europeans have more body hair than original people, Africans or Mongols.

Atrocities against Jews in Poland, Lithuania, and Russia were so frequent that one would need several volumes to cover each incident. However, this particular incident attracts interest because there was a repetitious trend that occurred in the past, producing negative results and disastrous consequences to the sycophants.

The Jews of eastern Europe joined the Poles to combat the Greek Orthodox Cossacks. The Jews of America today join the Judeo-Christian alliance in a Zionist-Papal agreement that will encourage Jewish capital investments but merely tolerate Jewish presence until the purpose has been served.

Jesuit Michinski wrote a pamphlet which charged Jews with every disdainful act that men commit, including treachery, robbery, swindling, witchcraft, murder, and sacrilege. This "scurrilous pamphlet," as it was called, beseeched the deputies of the Polish Diet to treat the Jews as they had been treated in Spain, France, England, and elsewhere. It recommended that Jews be expelled and their properties confiscated. The accusations were directed at the rich Jews, more particularly, who lived in Cracow. As a result, there was another riot; more Jews were bruised, abused, and used.

Vladislav IV was confirmed successor of Sigsmund III in 1633. He hurriedly granted Jewish merchants freedom in export trade and protection against unwarranted attacks. In order to appease the Gentiles simultaneously, Vladislav IV forbade building of new synagogues and cemeteries by the Jews without a royal license or permit. In many cases he would make the Jews a favorable proposition and later rescind his own orders. In 1642 Vladislav authorized Cracow's Jews to engage in export and import trade without fear. Then two months later he revoked the permission when the Christian merchants of Cracow lobbied with complaints.

In 1643, the Warsaw Diet witnessed riots in Vilna, Brest, and in other cities, which forced it to form a price-control system. A law was set compelling merchants to take a public oath that kept their profits at a limit. The price index was put at a fixed price allowing 7 percent profit for Christians called *incola*, 5 percent for foreign merchants called *advena*, and only 3 percent in the sales made by Jews *regarded as infidels*.[33]

Jews were continually charged with murders of little children, the bleeding of a monk, and Polish doctors even claimed that Jewish physicians were poisoning good Catholics with minor ailments. In the case of a missing boy, although no evidence was found to implicate the Jews, they were still held on suspicion and tortured on the rack. Despite the fact that they did not confess to the crime, these Jews were executed. Their bodies were cut into pieces and hung on poles at the crossroads. The monks of Lenchitza were credited with this horror and they preached about it with zeal, placed a sign and picture of the martyred boy in their church. Libelous accusations were attached with details of his murder by the suspects. The credulous and superstitious Catholic community filed into the church in droves to see the "juvenile saint." This pageant served their purpose, "swelling the revenues of the Bernardine church," an apparent hustle well planned by the holy monks. Similar abuses are now perpetrated aginst blacks and Hispanics in the U.S.A.

Another classic conversion occurred when Peter Yurkevich was accused of stealing some church vessels. Peter was interrogated on the rack. He told his interrogators that a Jewish tailor named Jacob Gzheslik had persuaded him to steal a host. Since this Jewish tailor could not be found, Yurkevich was the only suspect left to pay the piper. His tune just before his execution was, "I have stolen no sacraments from any church." He confessed this to the priest, and later repeated the same words to an official committee of inquisitors.

Yurkevich also informed them that during his former depositions, he had said the first time he met Judge Belza, the honorable magistrate advised him as follows: "Depose that you have stolen the sacraments and sold them to the Jews. You will suffer no harm from it, while we shall have a weapon wherewith to expel the Jews from Cracow." Peter had hoped to gain his freedom by lying for the prosecution. He lamented and repeated, "and I did as I had been told!" Yurkevich was executed and probably woke up in another world realizing that the more religious people tend to be, and the more pious bishops and priests pretend to be, the less they should be trusted. After Yurkevich's conviction, he was burned at the stake and anti-Jewish riots were encouraged by the holy monks. Forty Jews were seized, dragged from their ghetto, and thrown in the river. "Seven men were drowned, while the others saved themselves by promising to embrace Christianity" (May 1637).

Toward the end of the sixteenth century, Warsaw was chosen to become the Polish capital, replacing Cracow. The Polish kings moved their residences to Warsaw and Jews were permitted only short visits to the capital.

Instruction became a problem for Jews, especially at the elementary and secondary levels. Jewish children enrolled in public schools were compelled to stand during classes, while their Polish counterparts were seated. Jewish parents decided to send their children to *heders* (private Jewish schools). The curriculum at the heders was based on the Bible in the original form and a Judeo-German translation as well. Some heders also taught Hebrew grammar, Talmudic studies, and mathematics. Students were then exposed to the *Jüdisch-Deutsch* Jewish-German which filtered in from Germany to Poland and Lithuania. It was not until the seventeenth century that the dialect of Polish-Lithuanian Jewry began to separate itself from the *Jüdisch Deutsch* spoken by the German Ashkenazis to form the base of *Yiddish*. Higher education was obtained through the Yeshivas or sacred places attached to the synagogues. Students were taught the Talmud and other religious devotions. Despite fervent insistence on Jewish studies, it is mentioned that students often strayed to pursue secular studies such as exact sciences and so-called Aristotelian philosophy. Rabbi Solomon Luria, the great rabbinical authority of the sixteenth century attested, "I, myself have seen the prayer of Aristotle copied in the prayer-books of the *bahurs*."[34] Dubnov concluded that the "expression indicates in all likelihood, that among the books of yeshibah students some `contraband' was occasionally discovered, in the shape of manuscripts of philosophic content." That writer was not aware that those yeshivah students were merely plagiarizing Aristotle like he had plagiarized Africans before him.

Aristotle had no philosophy. George M. James wrote, "The Greeks were not the authors of Greek Philosophy, the true authors were people of North Africa, commonly called the Egyptians.[35] Aristotle took possession of the Royal Library and carried off a large quantity of scientific books from which he copied African thoughts. These were the texts copied and used by Greeks from African scholars. Jewish students then copied from the Greeks.

Jewish girls were treated differently, in accordance with Jewish law. Their education was not compulsory, and there were no *heders* for them. Girls received instruction in prayers, preparing meals, and lighting candles. Very few girls were taught Hebrew. They studied the *Jüdisch Deutch*. No women of outstanding academic achievement were recorded in Poland or Lithuania. Hebrew law was written and rewritten with new interpretations and European laws added. "Rabbinic Judaism [was] superimposed upon Talmudic Judaism." The mass of religious ore, accumulated over the centuries, dominated the minds of the educated Jews, making Poland a second Babylonia.

There were debates between two great rabbis of the time: Luria, who gravitated toward the Cabals, and Iserles, who leaned toward philosophy. Luria argued that the wisdom of the "uncircumcised Aristotle" could not be of benefit to Jews. Iserles tried to convince the listeners that many points of view in the Cabala were not in agreement with concepts in the Talmud, "and that mysticism was more dangerous to faith than a moderate philosophy." Talmudic and Rabbinic science of law absorbed the best mental energies of Polish Jewry. The only exceptions—it is assumed—were the physicians who, because of their training in a different discipline, studied applied sciences at the universities of that period. Most of those physicians were originally born in Spain and exiled in 1492, or born in Italy.

The Italian physicians were graduates of the Catholic University of Padova, a town in Veneto, northern Italy. Many of these doctors attended to the Polish kings. Isaac Hispanicus was Albrecht and Alexander's physician. Solomon Ashkenazi was physician and diplomat at the court of the Turkish Sultan Selim II, and also attended Sigsmund Augustus. Solomon Calahora attended Stephen Batory. By the sixteenth century, however, these foreign-born Jews encountered professional competition from local doctors who traveled to Italy's school of medicine as well. The Italian registrars enrolled the Jewish students as *Hebraei Poloni* in the national register, *registro nazionale*. Jews were not considered equal with other students. Italian laws in 1654, for example, stated, "not to mar the memory of so many celebrated men by the name of an infidel."

Jewish religious development in Poland during the sixteenth century encountered rivalry by the Reformation and rationalistic sects with radical anti-religious penchants. The closest group or the group with tenets most similar to Judaism was the Anti-Trinitarians also called Socinians, who were organized by Faustus Socinus. These faithful followers believed that Jesus was not divine and that there was no trinity. They said they recognized and respected the Gospel, but considered virgin births and other myths emphatically puerile with dogmatic ideologies.

Notable Trinitarian leaders were the theologian Simon Budny of Vilna and Martin Chekhovich of Lublin. Catholic clergymen classified these leaders as "Judaizers" or semi-Jews. These nicknames made the Anti-Trinitarians uneasy and anxious to prove that their religious preference and divergence had no relationship to Judaism. To eradicate all doubts, written or spoken, they organized forums to debate the issue with rabbis. They strongly felt that debates would provide an opportunity to expose Jewish falsehoods. Chekhovich arranged debates on logic "with genuine as well as pseudo Jews."

The Jews were able to resist economic competition and social oppression through their influence in Polish government circles or through a "firmly organized scheme of self government." Nevertheless, the struggle between Poles and Jews, Christian and Jewish estates, Church and Synagogue, was more intense and complicated on the southeastern border provinces of Poland known as the Ukraina. The entire region comprised of provinces, namely Kiev,[36] Poltava, Chernigov, parts of Podolia and Volhynia, which were under the political domination of the Polish king and the economic control of Polish magnates. Enormous estates were owned by Polish landlords who had many villages inhabited by Russian peasants. Feudal Polish owners looked at the Russian peasants with disdain and pejoratively nicknamed them Khlops.[37] The peasants had a different religion and were from a strange country (Russia), considered backward and barbaric. Their religion was Greek Orthodox and the Poles, particularly the Catholic clergy, named it a "religion of *Khlops* ignorant enough to be an easy target for Catholic conversion." They lived in a secluded neighborhood apart from the Russians—who depended on them for survival—and communicated with them only through Jewish *arendars* who collected the rent and taxes paid by the Khlops. . . This relationship led to the philosophic adage *cause* and *effect*. The cause was oppression through exploitation and segregation, the effect became revenge through pride and dissatisfaction.

OPPRESSED BECOME OPPRESSORS

The South Russians were politically and economically dependent on the Poles. Despite their poverty, however, they refused to be submissive beasts of burden. Their ignorance helped to make them more hateful and intolerant. The closeness of the New Russian steppes and

Khanate of the Crimea (seat of the Khan) added more to their deplorable condition because of its geographical position. Hordes of Tatars found them vulnerable to constant raids in those eastern provinces of Poland. The raids were so frequent that the Ukraina population organized a defense league of Cossacks to ward off the intruders. The Polish government encouraged the Cossacks through approval and cooperation of the starostas, local governors. These defense leagues were to protect those defenseless borders of the Polish Empire prone to repeated attacks. That was how the Vigilantes began. They soon augmented in numbers, increased in weaponry, and swelled with military pride. Pretty soon, the Ukrainian Cossackdom, a semi-military, semi-agricultural peasant class, became a fighting force to be reckoned with. It was autonomous and selected a self-appointed (hetman)[38] leader.

In addition to the Ukrainians' Cossack league accountable to the Polish government to some extent, there was another group of Zaporozhian Cossacks that lived beyond the Falls of Dnieper in the steppes of New Russia. This latter group was accountable to no government. Its paramilitary organization frequently raided the Turks and often engaged the Tatars of the Crimea in warfare, just to keep in practice. The Zaporozhian Cossack defense league attracted many Khlops from Ukraina. It offered them a free, unrestricted military life preferable "to the dreary existence of laboring slaves." There were also knightly contests, jousts, and exploits that proved courage and rank. This league was considered a semi-barbarous Tatar group. It practiced the Greek Orthodox faith, was of Russian origin, and had a considerable admixture of Mongolian blood respected by all. The Ukrainian and Zaporozhian Cossacks recognized each other, were both admired and respected as a national guard that had pride in ethnic origin, and hope for freedom from abuse and exploitation by the Polish landlords, their administrators and collectors.

Like the Mafia or *Mano nera* (Black Hand) in its inception no one foresaw any danger in the Cossacks' defense leagues. The leagues were for the defense of the oppressed.[39] No one feared them even after many warnings of even the impressive appearance in 1637 of a new Cossack leader, Pavluk. He came from the province of Poltava beyond the Falls, inciting revolt, and advising the peasants to free themselves from the pans, (lords) and Jews. Several synagogues were destroyed and approximately two hundred Jews were killed. After engaging in that preliminary maneuver with no military resistance, the Hetman withdrew and trained his troops for the real extermination of *Lakhs*[40] and Jews. The Cossacks returned for their combat mop up all-out effort in 1648. This annihilation began a history of pogroms for Eastern European Jews. It was inflicted on them by Southern Russians and it continued to the beginning of the twentieth century.

During the spring of 1648, while King Vladislav IV was still monarch of Poland, a Cossack leader named Bogdan Chmielnicki (1593–1657),* came from the town of Chigrin in the province of Kiev. He started his rebellion in the Ukraina and behind the Dnieper Falls. According to accounts given, he became enraged after learning that the chief of his village had pillaged his tent, carried off his wife, and flogged their son to death. Chmielnicki called the Ukrainian Cossacks to arms. They hurriedly made him their hetman and gave him authority to coordinate forces with the Zaporozhian Cossacks. Upon arrival in the region beyond the Dnieper Falls, he organized battalions and formed an alliance with the Khan of the Crimea, and negotiated a treaty which included sending a large contingent of troops made up of Tatars. These troops were mustered to assist him in his rebellion against the ruling class.

During the month of April 1648, the triple alliance of the two Cossacks and the Tatars rode down from the Falls of the Dnieper to the Ukraina borders. They defeated the Polish regular army under two well-known commanding officers, Potozki and Kalinovski. The important battles were in the vicinity of Yellow Waters and Korsum. This defeat of the Poles gave immeasurable confidence to the entire contingent of peasants who had been seeking a messiah to bring them salvation from oppression.

This situation is historically parallel with the Mexican Revolution. A Mexican peasant, Demetrio Macias, had been resisting abuses by local landowners around 1916. The federal troops came after him, entered his hut, and a few of them abused his wife. Macias killed most of those, organized his neighboring farmers, and went on a rampage which made him a colonel when he met Pancho Villa's troops, and other revolutionary forces. Before the revolution was over towns like Tacambaro and others saw men and women's heads, arms, and legs cut off with machetes or blown off with machine guns. The Cossacks and the Mexicans had such a similar experience that the interpolation showed cause and effect relevance.

Russian peasants and city servants left their masters' homes and estates, after killing them and their Jewish rent and tax collectors. Thousands of Jews were slaughtered in Pereyaslav, Piryatin, Lokhvitz, Kiev, and Lubny. The only Jews allowed to live, when discovered, were those who converted to the Greek Orthodox religion. Many Jews ran to the Tatar camps and surrendered as prisoners of war, hoping to be sold as slaves in Turkey rather than be barbarously killed by the Cossacks.

King Vladislav IV died in May 1648 and internal dissension added to the consternation of the persecuted Jews and the despised Poles. There was anarchy for about six months. Rebellions spread throughout Ukraina, extended to Volynia and Podolia. Squads of Cossacks and mobs of Russian peasants, led by Chmielnicki's subalterns, his Zaporozhian Cossack allies, their underlings and those of the Tatars, spread out in all directions. The battle cry was "exterminate Poles and Jews." A Russian historian is quoted as saying:

> Killing was accompanied by barbarous tortures; the victims were flayed alive, split asunder, clubbed to death, roasted on coals, or scalded with boiling water. Even infants, at the breast, were not spared. The most terrible cruelty, however, was shown toward the Jews . . . and the slightest pity shown toward them was looked upon as treason. Scrolls of the Law were taken out of the synagogues by the Cossacks, who danced on them while drinking whiskey. After this dancing, Jews were laid down upon the scrolls and butchered without mercy . . . Thousands of Jewish women were thrown into wells, or buried alive.[41]

Jewish historians of the time told an even more gruesome story. They related the sadism of the Cossacks as being inhuman because the Cossacks enjoyed torturing their victims rather than killing them forthwith. "They cut off their hands and feet, split the children asunder, 'fish-like,' or roasted them on fire. They opened the bowels of women, inserted live cats, and then sewed up the wounds." The Cossacks seemed to enjoy their unbridled bestiality like intoxicated savages enjoying a psycho-sexual release from these frightful tortures of which the Tatars themselves were never capable.

Also tragic was the fate of some Jews who in the hope of escaping those abuses sought refuge in the neighboring town of Niemirov in Podolia. Chmielnicki dispatched a contingent of Cossacks, under the command of a Zaporozhian officer named Gania, to ferret them out. The Cossacks stormed Niemirov, but the thousands of valiant Jews repelled them. Finding it difficult to overpower the entrenched defenders of their last hope of survival, the Cossacks devised a trick. They raised Polish banners, suggesting the approach of a Polish army contingent requesting entry to protect the Jews. The desperate besieged souls opened the gates on June 10, 1648, Sivan 20 of the Jewish calendar. The Cossacks joined forces with the local Russians, entered the city, attacked the Jews, massacred the males, raped the females of all ages, and took some of the women as hostages. Most of these women were spared to be baptized and married Cossacks and peasants of the Greek Orthodox faith.

One victim, a beautiful Jewess, kidnapped and forced to marry a Cossack, fooled him into considering her mystical. She told him that bullets could not harm her because her spell would cause them to bounce off her body's invisible shield. She induced her lover to test her metaphysical powers. Anxious to trigger his pistol, and curious to know the extent of her powers, he fired and she dropped dead.

Another Jewish girl was on the way to marry a Cossack. While the wedding procession marched across a bridge on the way to the church the bride climbed the wall, jumped into the water, and drowned herself. Six thousand Jews are said to have perished in Niemirov.

Jews who escaped the Cossacks, outside of Niemirov, and elsewhere, ran to fortified Tulchyn in Podolia of the Ukraina to seek refuge. Instead they were betrayed. A large number of Cossack cavalrymen and peasants besieged a fortress with several hundred Poles and approximately fifteen hundred Jews inside. The Jews and Poles made a sworn pact to stick together and defend themselves to the end. The Jews took to the ramparts and defended its walls stoutly for quite some time. Considering it impossible to make a breach in the wall, the Cossacks reverted to the old basic philosophy of confidence through egotism . . . "Thou man, look for thyself." . . They promised the Poles that no harm would come to them if they simply turned over the Jews, the only enemy pursued. The Poles, who did not like the Jews too much either, fell for the ruse. They quickly surrendered the Jews who had just been their allies. The Poles were looking out for themselves, but had not thought about the French proverb which says, "The same knife that sticks the lamb, sticks the calf."[42] The Polish leaders handed over the Jews to save themselves and their own. The Jews, who outnumbered the Poles by this time, suspected them of the treason. They decided that they should turn on the Poles and eliminate them before concentrating on the Cossacks outside. Their religious *Rosh-Yeshibah*, or Dean of the seminary, pleaded with them to leave the Polish leaders to God, otherwise Jews all over Poland might very well become despised for attacking Polish sympathizers.

After the city surrendered to the Cossacks, all Jewish captives were marched into a garden about fifty yards away. They were offered the choice of coming under a banner raised for those who wished to be baptized; those who refused would be killed. The rabbis preached religious fidelity and its rewards. No Jew went under the banner to become a Christian. The Cossacks immediately began to slaughter them like sheep. Shortly after the Polish traitors, who had doublecrossed these Jews, found themselves stuck with the same fate. A different band of Cossacks attacked the same fortress of Tulchyn, only a few days after the sad Jewish experience. The Cossacks might have been sent by the other band that dealt with the Poles; because they slaughtered the Poles, and even killed Chetvertinski, the Polish leader who had made the deal to hand over the Jews. "Treachery [was] avenged [by] treachery."

The entire summer and autumn of 1648 saw Jews massacred by the thousands. Those who were not murdered were taken into captivity by the Tatars. Individual cases are too numerous to mention here. At least two four-hundred-page volumes would be required to record all of the massacres and Jewish expulsions that were so frequent in that part of civilized Europe.

Polish troops, under Count Jerennah Vishniovetzki, subdued the Cossacks and rebellious peasants on a few battle fronts. He retaliated with the same cruelty the Cossacks had inflicted on the Poles and Jews. Receiving no reinforcement from other regular Polish battalions, for mopping up or deployment, he was soon overwhelmed by Cossack and peasant forces.

Chmielnicki marched at the head of his troops to Lemberg and besieged that Red Russian capital after pillaging the suburbs and terrifying its people. His troops failed to enter the capital because of its defiant resistance. He then offered to lift the siege if the Jews were surrendered to him, along with their possessions. The magistrates retorted that the Jews were subjects of the King and entitled to his protection. A heavy ransom was paid to him—most of which was contributed by the Jews. Chmielnicki withdrew his troops and headed for Warsaw. An election was in process at the capital and John Casimir, a brother of Vladislav IV, was crowned.

Having been a Primate of Gnesen and Cardinal (1648–1668), the King negotiated a peace treaty with the rebel leader but could not meet Khmelnitzki's exacting demands. Talks, for a negotiated peace were broken off and the battle began. The Polish troops were defeated and an agreement ratified banning Jews from Cossack territory, and the usual demands added. King Casimir permitted baptized Jews to return to their original faith and Jewish wives who had married Greek Orthodox Cossacks for survival were allowed to return to their families.

RUSSIANS AND SWEDES IN POLAND

After these horrible experiences, a treaty was signed. The Polish government was dissatisfied with the terms in the treaty and ignored them. As a result, civil war broke out in 1651. The Polish government called up the militia, with an added detachment of one thousand Jewish troops. This time the Cossacks were overpowered and Chmielnicki signed the Treaty of Byelaya Tzerkov in September 1651. The treaty rejected many Cossack demands and it restored some Jewish privileges, including their right to live in the Greek Orthodox portion of the Ukraina. Bogdan Chmielnicki was dissatisfied with the treaty and formed an alliance with Russian Tzar Alexis Michaelovich in 1654. The Greek part of Ukraina was made an autonomous province, under the name of Little Russia, of the Muscovite Empire. That same year the Russian army and its allies invaded White Russia and Lithuania to clash with the southern and northern Scythians.[43] The unified forces of Muscovites and Cossacks cost Jews their property and lives.

In 1655 the Jews that were not killed by Zaporozhian Cossacks were forcibly baptized or sent to Pakov, Novgorod, and Kazan, Polish provinces on the Vistula and the San River which had been spared the barbaric attacks of the Cossacks and Muscovites, where they faced a new enemy. They faced the Swedes, who were considered the third enemy of Poland.

Swedish King Charles Gustav made Polish cities capitulate like falling dominoes. The old Polish capital, Cracow, and other big cities like the new capital, Warsaw, also fell. Polish King John Casimir fled to Silesia for his life. The political disagreement among the Poles helped to cause sub-Chancellor Radziejevski to treacherously invite the Swedes into Poland.

The Swedes were welcomed and supported by the Protestants and the Calvinists. The Jews were caught in the middle. When the Swedes started withdrawing their forces, the persecution of the Jews began. They were not molested by the Swedes and were therefore charged with having collaborated with the enemy.

General Charnetzki massacred Jews in Great and Little Poland "to save the country from the invader." Rabbis were slaughtered, women violated, and only those willing to become Catholics were allowed to survive. Charnetzki cowardly vented his wrath on the unarmed Jews as the warring Swedes abandoned ruined Poland. From 1648 to 1658 there were from four to five hundred thousand Jews killed in approximately seven hundred Jewish communities. Quite a few Jews fled to other parts of Europe and to Asia. "Jewish refugees or prisoners of war, who had fled from Poland or had been carried off by the Tatars, and ransomed by their brethren," could be met almost everywhere. In the meantime, Jewish persecutions and executions continued intermittently. There was even an attempt, at the Diet of 1740, to enslave them outrightly.

The nobility submitted a resolution demanding that Jews living on Shlakhta estates be "recognized as the `hereditary subjects' of the owners of those estates." What saved the Jews from becoming total-ly enslaved? The Polish government refused to lose the Jewish head-tax which would go to the landowners bank accounts rather than to the Royal Treasury.

The Tatars often took the Jews as slaves because their Jewish coreligionists usually paid their cost of manumission. The Cossacks, however, preferred to kill them outright.

JUDEO-CHRISTIAN COEXISTENCE

The Catholics and their die-hard members of Synods have always persecuted the Jews because of their belief that the Sanhedrin con-demned Christ to death. Catholics it was said have never been open-minded enough to investigate whether Christ planned his own death—in order to be saved by a miracle, but could not be reached with the antidote quickly enough to counteract the poison as preplanned or not.

Hugh J. Schoenfield wrote how "Jesus had now to prepare for the most difficult and dangerous part of his present mission."[44] And Schoenfield explains how Jewish history of the previous decades had shown that a Messiah, one man rather than multitudes with women and children, could die to relieve Hebrews and Jews from continued persecutions. With the fervor of a new convert and the ambition of a young prophet, Yeshua decided to be that man. Schoenfield stated how Yeshua's plans demanded the utmost caution, and the most careful organization and timing." Everything Yeshua, or Jesus, requested from the Judeans had been granted.

> There was no hitch. The man with the water-pot was at the rendezvous. All was made ready, and in the evening Jesus came with the twelve to their destination. The circumstances had made it impossible for Judas to notify the council in advance where Jesus was. Such incidents as this are extremely revealing, because they illustrate the generalship of Jesus and furnish concrete examples of the devices to which he was prepared to resort to accomplish his ends.[45]

At no time does Schoenfield say that Yeshua should not be respected as a great prophet, planner, or leader. After studying his plans and the manner in which they were implemented, and the greatness his name achieved after his death, praises were given. The author said, "When given the value they merit, they compel us to look at him with new eyes and a different kind of respect." Schoenfield also states, "There were fourteen, not thirteen persons, who reclined at the table for the paschal meal."

Schoenfield seemed to say in some general form, that most Christians have never considered Christ's last words, "Father, Father, forgive them for they know not what they do!" That statement should, at least, signify that if any people were guilty for Yesus Kristos' death, it should at least be time for them to be forgiven.

Catholic hatred of Jews can be traced back to the Middle Ages from whence it penetrated down to the Synod of Lovich in 1720. A resolution was passed emphasizing that Jews should nowhere dare build new synagogues or repair old ones. The idea being to allow temples to decay to the ground or to be burned down from time to time. In that manner, Jewish places of worship would gradually become unavailable, forcing the Jews to accept the next alternative, become Christianized. The Synod of Plolok repeated the medieval maxim which declared that Jews were only tolerated in Christian countries to serve as a "reminder of the tortures of Christ and, by their enslaved and miserable position, as an example of the just chastisement inflicted by God upon the infidels."

In Sandomir from 1698 to 1710 there were inquisitions by the Church, and many innocent persons were executed. A Christian woman threw her illegitimate child's dead body into the yard of a Jewish leader named Berek. He was accused of the act. The case went through court after court. The lower court had no adjudication because it lacked evidence. The case was dismissed. The Christians took it to a higher court. A priest, Stephen Zhukhovski, brought additional charges, published a book full of allegations, and made the people of Sandomir feel that murder of Christian children was a part of Jewish rituals. There was another such false accusation made in Posen in 1736; then one in Zaslav in 1747. These trials were all conducted with tortures and interrogations endemic to the methods employed at inquisitions by inquisitors. The trials were often held in the Supreme Tribunal of Lublin, and the cunning priests always made sure that they ended with executions.

To encourage and secure executions, Father Zhukhovski and his clique used a converted Jew, Seranovich, who claimed to be a rabbi of Brest, to write a book and to testify against Jews at the Sandomir trials. Seranovich titled the book, *Exposure of the Jewish Ceremonies before God and the World*, published in 1716. Seranovich claimed "that Jews use Christian blood" to smear the doors of Christians, in religious ceremonies. Seranovich also stated that Jews put an egg, given to newlyweds during the marriage ceremony as a pledge for a human sacrifice to be made, and the matzoh eaten at Passover were also smeared with Christian blood. So many unjustifiable deaths of rabbis and their congregants persisted that the Jewish community of Posen was driven to affirmative action. They appealed to the decency and conscience of King Augustus III, who had the cases transferred to a special commission composed of royal officials. No admission of guilt was exacted from the Jews, since the charges were all trumped up and the evidence fabricated. Nevertheless, the judgment was held firmly until the Jewish bankers of Vienna threatened to exert pressure on Augustus' unstable economy. The surviving suspects were then freed after having served four years of unwarranted incarceration.[46]

In the spring of 1747, a body was found under the melting snow. At the same time near the area where the body was discovered some Jews happened to be celebrating the circumcision of a Jewish infant whose father was the innkeeper. Since someone was guilty of the crime, the people celebrating the circumcision were indicted. Their accuser was a peasant, who incidentally or intentionally passed by the inn, saw the guests eating and drinking, and jealously or maliciously informed the authorities that the Jews had been praying, eating, and amusing themselves all through the past evening into daybreak. The Bernardine monks of Zaslav—where the incident occurred—associated the circumcision with ritual murder. Some of the suspects were placed on an iron pale that slowly sliced their bodies and gave them a slow torturous end. Others had their skin cut off in strips, their hearts cut out, and their hands and feet cut off and nailed to the gallows.

There were so many cases of Jews being accused of murders that they did not commit that affirmative action was again taken. The Jews sent a delegation to Rome to plead their case before Pope Benedict XIV. The delegate entrusted his petition to Cardinal Giovanni Ganganelli who later became Pope Clement XIV. Ganganelli, Pope from 1769–1777, considered the charges false and the trials blatant miscarriages of justice. He sent an alternate to Polish Prime Minister Bruhl stating that the Roman Tribunal of the "Holy Inquisition" petitioned protection for Jacob Selek, the petitioner, upon his return to Poland. The Cardinal found no validity to the accusations that "Jews need human blood for the preparation of unleavened bread." A brief period of relief followed until the partition of Poland. There were still intermittent charges of ritual murder.

King Augustus tried to appease the Christians by reissuing laws previously decreed by his predecessors. The Diet of 1768 reactivated laws that allowed Jews to engage in commerce only with permission from the magistrates. At the same time, the Russians on the right of the Dnieper, still under the sovereignty of Poland, were effecting agitations against Poles and Jews.

The Khlops who had followed Bogdan Chmielnicki organized themselves into platoons of *Haidamacks*.[47] They occupied themselves with looting estates of nobles and plundering Jewish residential and business areas. After destroying many towns and villages in the provinces of Kiev, Volhynia, and Pudolia, slaying pans (peasants) and Jews, the *haidamacks* became well organized by 1768.

After most of the Jews were eliminated, the *haidamacks* attacked the Polish churches with cannon fire in the same manner they had attacked the Jewish synagogues: blowing away the doors with cannon fodder then rushing in and slaughtering the fearful, panicky refugees. Approximately twenty thousand Poles and Jews were assassinated at the Massacre of Uman.

FIRST PARTITION OF POLAND

The first partition of Poland became an act of record in 1773. The provinces on the Polish border were selfishly partitioned by three neighboring expansionist countries, namely: Russia, Austria, and Prussia. Russia received the southwestern part, which included a large part of White Russia. Austria took possession of the southwestern region, with Galicia and a length of Podolia. Prussia grabbed Pomerania and a portion of Great Poland. Two and a quarter million Jews were dispersed.

This dispersion of Polish Jews caused a deterioration of Jewish intellectualism. The rabbis were no longer well prepared like their forerunners, Solomon Luria, Moses Isserles, Mordecai Jaffe, and Meir of Lublin. Sermons and liturgical writings were composed of Haggadic and Cabalistic quotations, often misinterpreted. The secret writings of Ari and his school of mystics became famously acknowledged for "gruesome stories" full of assumptions and accounts of life after death were dogmatically accepted.[48] Handwritten manuscripts even told tales, like Dante's *Inferno*, of sinners in hell, the transmigration of souls, and the meanderings of demons. Some of the stories were incredibly puerile, others seemed based on mere superstitions. After dissemination of these Cabalistic stories and their arguments against Talmudic concepts and precepts, Jews began to seek deeper spiritual satisfaction and more plausible reasons for their continuous persecutions and executions. Those anxieties led to a messianic hope. A savior was continuously prayed for.

SABBATISM

Continued differences of opinion led to the development of a movement among Cabalist worshippers which became known as the Sabbatian Movement. The schism began with Sabbatai Zevi around 1648. The movement developed rapidly and appealed to the spiritual needs of an extensive part of the Polish Jewish populace. Jewish minds in Poland were said to have been mystically oriented and therefore quite open to new beliefs promising spiritual and physical reliefs. With the numerous massacres of Jews in 1648, Ukrainian Jews were desperate for a messianic appearance.

Sabbatai Zevi's appearance, on the scene of Smyrna, drew recognizable attention. Thousands of Jews who had escaped death by surrendering to the Tatars were now in Turkey where they had been taken as slaves. Most of them were later ransomed by fellow Jews. Many of them were Orientals. They considered themselves and the destruction of the great Jewish center of Poland accursed. Their feelings caused them to hope for messianic salvation, regardless of its legitimacy. They were not as pragmatic as their European-Ashkenazi counterparts, many of whom did not join in praying for a Messiah.

Sabbatai roamed through Turkey, Palestine, and Egypt, convincing Jews of his Messianic mission. Polish Jews were not responsive. However, Jews of other nationalities responded so fervently that they fasted, and often denied their children food during those periods of self-denial. Some of the fanatic members gave up their homes and worldly goods, took baths in ponds partly frozen during the winter season, while they recited a recently composed prayer.

A contemporary writer wrote that "faint-hearted and destitute Christians, hearing the stories of the miracles performed by the false Messiah and beholding the boundless arrogance of the Jews began to doubt Christ."

The Sabbatian movement extended from the North all the way South to far away White Russia. A monastic chronicler of the time said that on the church walls of Moghilev, lying on the Dnieper, were mysteriously appearing graffiti inscriptions, "proclaiming the Jewish Messiah 'Sapsai'."

Delegations arrived from many outlying Jewish communities to visit Sabbatai's residence in Abydos, near Constantinople. There were so many bodies that they often resembled a pilgrimage to Mecca. Sabbatai's residence was called Castle of Splendor. Even the Polish Jews sent a delegation to observe and document the legitimacy of Sabbatai's messianic claims. David Halevi's son was a member of the Polish group. He and Joel Sirkis, the grandson of another highly respected Jewish intellectual, were impressed with Sabbatai's eloquence. The self-proclaimed Messiah sent a letter and a new hand made shirt to the aging Rabbi Halevi by his son. The instructions in the letter advised the doting old man to wear the shirt and recite these words whenever he wore it: "May thy youth be renewed like that of the eagle!"

A delegate named Nehemiah Cohen, who had predicted the coming of the Messiah, was a staunch defender of the Cabala. This belief gave him something in common with Sabbatai. The latter tried to capitalize on that commonality by enclosing a postscript to Halevi's letter requesting that the prophet, a forerunner of the Messiah be hurriedly sent to him. Dubnov wrote humorously, "The omniscient Messiah failed to foresee that this invitation spelled ruin for him." Nehemiah was enthusiastically involved in Cabalistic studies that seemingly did not proclaim Sabbatai as the Messiah. He debated Sabbatai so accurately that the dispute lasted three days. Nehemiah refused to accept Sabbatai as the truly expected Messiah, and went a step further. He reported Sabbatai to the Turkish authorities in Adrianople as an imposter fostering a new religious preference. The false Messiah was arrested. Seeing a way out, Sabbatai pretended to convert to Islam by putting on a turban and conning the Sultan. Even though news of Sabbatai's religious switching or conversion reached Poland, many of his followers refused to abandon him. They continually waited for miracles to occur. When Sabbatai died, as all Messiahs do, Poland became susceptible to the mystical messianic transformation which was spreading through Western Europe at that time. Prophets and pseudo-Messiahs sprung up like mushrooms. They often came from among Cabalist students or some other poor working-class group.

Toward the seventeenth century, a semi-literate Lithuanian Jew named Zadok decided to stop being an innkeeper and become a prophet. He started prophesying that the Messiah would appear in 1695. During the same period, an apparently more sincere Cabalist appeared. This one was Cabalist Hayim Malakh, who had been exposed to the Sabbatian movement in Turkey, where he lived in Saloniki. Malakh returned to Poland and confused the Jews a little bit more. He preached that Sabbatai Zevi was the Messiah. He even protected the Israelites in the desert for forty years before taking them to the boundaries of the Promised Land as stated in the Scriptures. His astounding convincer was a prediction that Sabbatai would rise from the dead and redeem the suffering believers in 1706. That date was exactly forty years after his conversion to Sabbatism. Malakh's false testimonies were successfully propagated and accepted among the ignorant masses of Podolia and Galicia. Malakh was speedily joined by another self-appointed prophet called Judah Hasid, who came from Shidlovitz.[49]

HASIDIM FROM POLAND

Judah Hasid studied practical Cabala in Italy. He returned to his native Poland and began imitating studious Polish scholars while initiating youthful students into his cult of hidden wisdom. His emphasis on esoteric powers, unknown to the West, made his movement arouse curiosity that swelled its ranks very rapidly. The cult was soon consolidated into a special faithful group which called itself "The Pious Ones," or *Hasidim*. The congregation of "Pious Ones" became a sect that practiced ascetic behavior, made public confessions called "testimonials," and confessed their sins with interjections of mystical prayers they inculcated into the Orthodox liturgy that came out of Africa. Hasid was joined by another young man named Hayyim Malakh as the forerunner from Turkey. Malakh and his Sabbatians helped to swell the ranks of the newly self-appointed Hasid. This union popularized the teachings of Judah Hasid to the extent that the word became *Hasidim*.

These mystics grew so rapidly that they alarmed the Orthodox Jewish rabbinate. The Orthodox Jews persecuted the new sect through fear and suspicion. During the days of persecution, the Hasidic leaders spread a thick veil of promised salvation through mass migration to Palestine. Once the believers arrived in the Holy Land, they would be on the spot to welcome in triumph the approaching Messiah.

Many Jews were impressed with the promises, which turned out to be just that. The first months of the year 1700 saw a pilgrimage of one hundred and twenty pious souls starting their journey under the joint leadership of Judah Hasid and Hayyim Malakh. The emigrants traveled in groups via Germany, Austria, and Italy. They stopped in various cities, where their leaders dressed in the manner of penitent sinners in white shrouds, and made some impressions. Preachers continuously made convincing speeches and sermons proclaiming the expectation of a speedy arrival of the Messiah. The poorer class and the women were overwhelmed with admiration for the rigorous manner in which Hasid denied himself common pleasures, and they therefore exalted him. They were convinced that he was the Messiah. The Polish Jews were also admired by other Jews anxious to visit the Holy Land, to escape persecution by the Christians, and to be in Jerusalem as they had daily prayed for and hoped to realize. The number of pilgrims grew to over thirteen hundred. One group of believers under Hayyim Malakh was assisted by charitable contributions received from Jews in Vienna. They went on to Constantinople. Another group, led by Judah Hasid, went toward Palestine by way of Venice, where some rich Jews lived. Several disappointments were suffered along the way and several believers died or were left behind. Only approximately one thousand persons were said to have reached Jerusalem. The Pious Ones encountered great disappointments when they reached the Promised Land. To add to their woes Hasid the pious died shortly upon arrival in the Holy Land. His believers had to live off charity from the residents, while existing one on top of the other in a courtyard. The permanent residents of Jerusalem also were poor. These depended on their European relatives and friends for assistance, in the manner of goods they could sell or for financial aid. They were in no condition to be able to rescue the destitute newcomers. Disillusioned after the hardships and discouraged after awaiting the Messiah in vain, some Pious Ones joined the sectarians of "Turkish Sabbatians, who posed as Mohammedans." The others returned to Poland, much disgusted but still trusting. They mystified people who believed them with very tall tales of spiritual development and revelations. "Others, in their despair, let themselves be persuaded by German missionaries to embrace Christianity."[50]

These people were confused Europeans seeking salvation through eastern religious teachings understood and known only by Cushites, Egyptians, and their African offspring. They did not understand the original African Mysteries systems and therefore ended up believing in a Messiah rather than a Supreme Being.

Hayyim Malakh, the other leader of the pilgrims who survived Judah Hasid, remained in Jerusalem. His followers worshipped in the way the Sabbatians did. They danced before wooden images in their secret meeting places. Hayyim was considered a dangerous heretic and forced to leave Jerusalem. He went through Turkey maintaining contact with sectarian groups as he went along. He was later exiled by the Orthodox rabbis of Constantinople, and forced to return to his native Poland. Home again, Hayyim Malakh disseminated his religious propaganda in Podolia and Galicia until he died in 1720.

The falsehood of the coming of a Messiah, who never arrived, and the inconsistency of the leaders through their changing sectarian practices, and even conversion to other religions whenever suitable, still did not discourage the *Hasidim*. They merged with other Jewish out groups, met secretly, proselytized, and increased in numbers. In Galicia and Podolia, the Galicianos and Podolianos were nicknamed the "Secret Sabbatians," after their leader Sabbatai Zevi. They were popularly called "Shabsitvinnikes" or the abbreviation,"Shebsen."

These Sabbatians ignored many ceremonies, such as the Ninth of Ab, because it fell on Sabbatai's birthday. They changed the Holy Day of *Ab*, a day of mourning, to a day of festivity. The Sabbatians' cult contained elements of asceticism as well as libertinism. Some of the Shebsen submitted to repentance, self-torture and mourning for Zion. A considerable number of them indulged in debauchery and other excesses. The Orthodox rabbis considered these Shebsen heretics and dangerous to the existence of Orthodox Hebrew religious practices and worship. They decided to take action against the Shebsen. The summer of 1762 saw a number of rabbis come from various communities to a convention at Lemberg. After serious deliberations and orthodox ritual activities, they proclaimed the herem[51] against all Sabbatians who failed to renounce the Sabbatian religious preference and return to orthodox practices, within a limited period.

The ruling was somewhat successful, but some sectarians held fast to their hope in their faith and the coming of a Messiah. Many of them continued to confess their sins and make penance publicly. It was said that in most cases, the Shebsen tenaciously held to their beliefs. Their obstinacy compelled the rabbis to decree another herem against them, as heretics, in 1725. This new act of excommunication held every Jew responsible for reporting to the rabbinical authorities any names of persons or secret organizations of Sabbatians. Several communities were contacted by the rabbis, and charges were made from the *bimahs*[52] in the synagogues. Sabbatians still met secretly in the hidden recesses of homes in Podolia and Galicia. No punishment was severe enough to make them relinquish clinging to Messianic devotion. They were said to finally diminish into a dangerous movement known as Frankism.

The Frankist sect came about through Jacob Frank who was born in a part of Podolia. Frank's father, Judah Leib, was a member of the Jewish clergy, among whom "all kinds of perverted mystical practices and notions were particularly in vogue." Judah Leib was suspected of Sabbatism and expelled from the Podolian community' where he had served as rabbi and preacher. His son, Jacob, was born and reared in Wallachia, where Judah settled after his expulsion from Podolia. The boy was raised in an environment saturated with Messianic longings, varied superstitious beliefs, and moral laxity. Jacob Frank did not like to study, and was therefore semi-literate. He worked as a clerk in a shop when he lived with his parents. He later became a traveling salesman, selling jewelry and trinkets in towns and villages. Frank also traveled to neighboring Turkey where he sold merchandise in Smyrna and Saloniki, two popular meeting places of Sabbatians. It is here that the Turkish Sabbatian worshippers named him Frank or *frenk*, a designation applied in the East to all Europeans. From 1752 to 1755, he alternated his living quarters between Smyrna and Saloniki, where he was exposed to the Sabbatian "symbolic semi-Mohammedan cult." Frank received his thoughts of relieving the oppressed members of the cult, in Turkey, but decided to return to Poland where he could protectively exercise his calling. His supposed call from the unknown was obviously—like it still is with some religious leaders up to present times—a good excuse for avoiding a good day's work. It was also a good reason for pretending to be a leader without making the sacrifice of becoming academically prepared. Certain rabbis studied assiduously and became qualified scholars. It was only natural that they would disdain a charlatan like Frank, who made his messianic pretenses without preparation. Furthermore, his appearance among the Shebsen was sudden and unsubstantiated of superhuman achievement. The only unusual elements in his pretenses were some additional doctrines he had picked up in Turkey. They encompassed religious mysteries centered around the Sabbatian Trinity consisting of "God, the Messiah, and a female hypostasis of God, the Shekinah." Frank had himself regarded as the second person of the Trinity, and as a reincarnation of Sabbatai Zevi. He was nominated S.S., meaning literally "holy sir," but the Poles interpreted it as the "Holy Lord."

A fair was held in Lantzkorona where Frank and his male and female congregants gathered at an inn to celebrate a mystical service. They sang hymns and excited themselves to a frenzy, dancing ecstatically and merrymaking. Some inquisitive outsiders peered at them through the windows, and reported seeing them dancing around a naked woman, who might have represented the Shekinah, or *Matronitha*, the third person of the Trinity.[53]

The Orthodox Jews were not accustomed to the Sabbatians immoral behavior. It disgusted them to the extent that they informed the Polish police of a Turkish national arousing the people and promoting a new religion. "The gay company was arrested." Frank was deported to Turkey, and his followers were turned over to the rabbis and the Kahal authorities in 1756.

A convention of rabbis was held in the town of Satanov, Podolia.

Several men and women from the Sabbatian sect appeared to confess their sins and repent for having strayed from the orthodox path. They admitted committing behavior not only embarrassing and sinful, but intended to undermine the Orthodox Jewish religion and to disrespect its moral principles.

The persecuted Podolians of the sect were encouraged by their leaders to resort to receive counsel. Their leaders requested an audience with the Catholic Bishop Dembovski in the city of Kamenetz-Podolsk. The sectarian leaders declared that their sect rejected the teachings of the Talmud, even considered it false and harmful to all concerned. Their faith and beliefs were in the Zohar, the sacred book of the Cabala. They believed that God was one in three persons, of whom the Messianic redeemer, Sabbatai Zevi or Jacob Frank in reincarnation, was one.

Bishop Dembovski ordered publication of the ambiguous confessions of the anti-Talmudists, or Zoharists as they called themselves, and promoted a religious discussion between the Frankists and the rabbis. The Bishop ordered the Podolian rabbis to send orators to participate in the debate or be punished by heavy fines and the burning of the Talmud for non-attendance. The rabbis attended the debate held in Kamenetz in the summer of 1757. Bishop Dembovski and other Catholics moderated the debate that lasted seven days. Certain parts of the Talmud's *Haggadah* were disputed and considered peculiar. The Frankist recited those parts and assessed them as blasphemous. The orthodox rabbis felt sensitive about the issue and refused to defend the sacred writings extensively. They preferred to avoid the interpretation of certain dogmas in the presence of Gentiles. Another disadvantage suffered by the rabbis was their inability to speak the Polish language extensively, or at least well. The bishop concentrated on that weakness and concluded that the Talmudists had lost the debate. A fine was imposed on the rabbis for having insulted the sectarians. The Bishop immediately ordered all copies of the Talmud seized and burned. Fate came to the rescue of the Orthodox Jews, however, when Dembovski died in November of the same year the harassment began, 1759. The sectarians lost their defender and were again sought after by the Kahal authorities.[54] Once again, the sectarians confessed their disloyalty to the Jewish religion as well as its fundamental principles of morality and respect for chastity. Most women admitted committing adultery and sensual excesses that they justified with mystical speculation. After evidences were presented and analyzed, a Sanhedrin or conference of rabbis met in Brody as the Council of the Four Lands. The old rabbis proclaimed a strict herem against those sectarians who had failed to repent. Contact with those degenerates was also forbidden.

The sectarians felt that Jacob Frank could be very helpful, so they sent to Turkey for him. Frank returned to Podolia with a new religious outlook. He planned a tactical maneuver to permanently end orthodox persecution by elimination of the Orthodox Jews. Frank reactivated the old accusation of ritual murder by Jews using Christians for sacrifices. His accusations caused quite a few Jews to get killed.

The Frankists negotiated with Primate Lubinski and Papal Nuncio Sierra of the Polish Catholic Church in the same year of Bishop Dembovski's death (1759). The bargaining force offered by the sectarians was a proposal of mass conversion of Jews to Catholicism, like their leader Sabbatai Zevi had one year earlier when he converted to Islam. Some Catholic clergymen were skeptical and hesitated to believe the sectarians. Canon Milowski was anxious to have the proselytes, and boasted that he held them above suspicion. He convinced the Catholic hierarchy that this was a great opportunity they should not spurn. The orthodox rabbis protested, and the issue was up for debate. Eleven sessions were held during the months of July and August of 1759. Milowski presided as moderator of the panels— sympathizing with the respective converts all along. Solomon Shorr, Leib Krysa, and several Catholic theologians defended the dogma of their church. They presented seven theses as grounds for their arguments. Six interwoven parts of a written text explained the Messianic theory and dogma of a fallacious Trinity. These treaties were selected as the themes for discussion. The seventh treated thesis asserted that the "Talmud considers the use of Christian blood obligatory." The discussion of the first six was minimal. The rabbis were reluctant to offend the Christians. In some cases, the rabbis feared refutation of certain Christian dogmatic views. In the case of the seventh, however, the charge of ritual murder was strongly refuted and condemned as a false, malicious charge conjured by the Frankists or enemies of their own people.

As soon as the disputes were concluded, the sectarians were summoned to prove their devotion to Christianity. Frankist baptisms were performed en masse. The Polish nobility assisted the clergy in the performance of the rituals, acting as godfathers and giving their names to the neophytes, whom they admitted to their ranks as nobles. Between 1759 and 1760, 514 men and women were converted in Lemberg alone. Leib Krysa and Solomon Shorr were among the converts.

Frank rode through Lemberg in a carriage drawn by six horses, escorted by a large bodyguard. He was pompously adorned and doubly baptized in Lemberg and Warsaw. At the Polish capital Frank requested that King Augustus III be his godfather. The King agreed and the conversion of the sectarian leader to Catholicism was performed with grandeur before the royal family and court retinue in November 1759. Frank's Christian name was Joseph.

The Polish clergy still remained wary of the neophytes. They were even more concerned about Frank's opulence and the reverence paid him by his followers who addressed him as "Holy Lord." The Catholic hierarchy sent out spies who soon informed them that the sectarians still regarded Frank as their Messiah and had merely converted to Christianity for security. The accusations led to the arrest of Frank in January 1760. He was arrested in Warsaw, through orders from the upper echelon of the Church, cross examined and indicted for treason. The testimonies or defensive arguments presented by his disciples and his interpretations of the Sabbatian Trinity, were revelations too astonishing for the clergy and only helped to convince the tribunal of his guilt. Frank was found guilty of deception, sentenced to imprisonment in the citadel of Chenstokhov, and detained in that monastery for thirteen years. The Frankists continued to worship their Holy Lord, with even more fervor. He became a martyr. His followers entered Chenstokhov's citadel, settled close to Franks' cell, gathering as near as the law would permit them, and referred to his cell as being at "the gates of Rome." They compared Frank's incarceration to that of Sabbatai Zevi, who had been imprisoned in the castle of Abydos, near the capital of Turkey. Frank inspired his worshippers with sermons of the persuasion that their only salvation depended on the "holy religion of Edom."[55]

The first partition of Poland ended Frank's imprisonment. He was freed by the commander of the Russian troops when they occupied the Chenstokhov fortress around the end of 1772. Frank renewed associations with his family and followers, stayed in Warsaw only for a short period, and promptly left Poland for Brina, Moravia in 1773.

Frank was later heard from when he appeared in Western Europe. In predominantly Catholic-dominated Austria, he took on the role of Christian missionary leader among the Jews. He gained admiration and acceptance at the Court of Vienna, but his past reputation soon caught up with him. His previous incarceration caused him disfavor which made him end up on all international passports as *personna non grata*. Frank fled to Offenbach, near Frankfort, Germany. He soon ennobled himself with the title Baron of Offenbach. The former Messiah was assisted by his daughter, Eve, who carried on as Holy Lady, in their luxurious mansion. She was, however, unable to hold the sect together after his death in 1791. Bankrupt and dunned by her creditors, she died in Offenbach in 1816.

HASIDIM AND ISRAEL BAAL SHEM TOV

The Hasidic preference found its substance in the Cabala, the mystic and messianic dialectics and doctrine of Sabbatism. This new Doctrine of Piety began as a product of obscure Podolian Jewry with Israel Baal-Shem-Tob, abbreviated Besht, who was born about 1700 to the people on the border of Podolia and Wallachia, the son of a poor Jewish family. His parents died at an early period of his existence, and he was reared by the townspeople who sent him to a heder to study the Talmud. Talmudic studies did not interest him and his attitude made his teachers consider him a poor student and reveler who wasted a lot of valuable time daydreaming. Israel Baal-Shem-Tob was also a truant who was often seen in the forest just idling his time away. At the age of twelve, he was faced with the need to survive through his own efforts. Besht made himself a *behelfer*, or Hebrew tutor, who was later promoted to a synagogue beadle. He slept during the day and prayed or pretended to pray at the synagogue at night, when he was not reading religious books. His contemporaries considered him a maniac or an eccentric He avidly studied the Cabala and the "Ari manuscripts," which taught the art of performing miracles through Cabalistic incantations. At the age of twenty, Besht settled in Brody, a principal city of Galicia, where he married the sister of a well-known Cabalist rabbi, Gershon Kutover. The rabbi tried to interest him in the Talmud but found him incapable of absorbing the teachings. Kutover advised Israel to leave Brody. The dependent brother-in-law heeded and left with his wife for a village between the towns of Kuty and Kosono. From there, Besht often traveled to the nearby Carpathian Mountains, where he fasted and prayed to himself.

The hopeful prophet barely eked out a living by digging clay in the mountains and having his wife carry it to market in the city. "According to Hasidic legend, Israel Besht led this life for seven years." This is the period when he is supposed to have received his calling. When his metaphysical studies in the Carpathian Mountains were sufficiently advanced, Besht lived in the Galician town of Tlusta where he filled a minor ecclesiastic position as *melammed, shoshet* and cantor of a synagogue. "He was universally regarded as an ignoramus, no one being aware of his innermost cravings." Upon reaching the age of thirty-six, Besht decided on proclaiming inspiration from above "as the Hasidim believe." His time had come to reveal himself to the world. Besht "began to practice as a Baal-Shem, i.e., as a magician and Cabalist."[56] He was now supposed to be able to cure diseases through incantations, amulets, (*kameoth*) and herbs with medicinal substances. *Baal-Shem* was not unusual among Polish Jews of that time.

Like other Messiahs before him, Besht saw an opportunity to exploit ignorance and faithfulness. He went from one town or village to another through Volhynia and Podolia, curing patients with herbs and incantations. His patients were not just Jews. Many peasants and even some pans had great faith in magical healing. Besht became widely known as a miracle-worker, and was nicknamed the "good Baal-Shem." The Jewish people are said to have considered him above the ordinary conjurer because of his righteousness and saintliness. People would often call on him to forecast their futures. As a fortune-teller, Besht would open the *Zohar* at random, and make predictions according to his interpretation of the sayings on that page of the holy book. His healing consultations involved herbs, incantations, and prayers. But he would also fall into ecstasy and violent gesticulations while diagnosing a case. These unusual behaviors made him even more popular as a warm-hearted healer. It also allowed him to get close enough to his neighbors to learn their spiritual and other needs, as well as their personal problems.

Besht soon graduated from a spiritual healer to a religious teacher. He taught his followers that true salvation was not attained through the teachings of the Talmud, but from sincere devotion to God through simple, unrelentless prayer offered fervently with faith. He even tried to convince the learned men of his time with arguments selected from the Cabala. Besht did not practice the ascetic form of Cabalistic laws that demanded of the Jew a mournful frame of mind, to kill the lusts of one's flesh, and strive to attain expiation of sin for acceleration of the coming of the Messiah. He accepted, instead, that Cabala which tries to establish an intimate communion between man and God, nourishing the human soul through belief in the goodness of God and his willingness to comfort the poor, persecuted, and suffering adherents. Besht insisted that ordinary man—imbued with plain faith, ability to pray fervently in all sincerity and blind hope—was nearer to God than the formally educated scholar who spent a lifetime studying the Talmud. This simplified form of Judaism appealed to the Jewish masses and even attracted those scholars dissatisfied with the rigors of Talmudic studies and the ascetic demands in the Cabala from the school of Ari.

Around 1740 Besht reduced his profile as sorcerer and miracle worker and increased his potential as a full-fledged religious teacher. He gathered disciples and followers, initiated them into his new religious order, taught them its doctrine and mysteries, not through systematic exposition, but through cliches and parables. Like the Christian Messiah, he left nothing in writing, but the Pious Ones inherited his parables and sayings fostered by his nearest disciples from their memories. They memorized two fundamental ideas from their Doctrine of Piety, or the Hasidim of Besht, namely, the idea of pantheism, through the omnipresence of God, and a concept of interaction between the lower and upper worlds. Besht formally stated:

> It is necessary for man constantly to bear in mind that God is with
> him always and everywhere; that He is, so to speak, the finest kind
> of matter, which is poured out everywhere; that He is the master
> of all that happens in the Universe . . . Let man realize that when

he looks at things material he beholds in reality the Divine coun-
tenance, which is present everywhere. Keeping this in mind, man
will find it possible to serve the Lord at all times, even in trifles.[57]

Contrary to the fundamental precepts of the Practical Cabala, Besht
insisted that excessive fasting, killing of the flesh, and general ascetic
restrictions are injurious and sinful, therefore, a lively and cheerful
way of life is more acceptable to God. The Pious, or *Hasid*, should
serve God not only through the ritual services held, but in his everyday thinking as he performs his activities. This constant communion
with God may allow man to attain the gift of clairvoyance, prophecy,
and miracle performance. "The righteous or *Tzaddik* is the person
who keeps the precepts of Hasidism most consistently. His function
as mediator between man and God, is supposed to make the Tzaddik
a holy person revered by other Jews, and looked up to as God's messenger and favorite."

After Besht's death, Hasidic propaganda was given authentica-
tion by an erudite scholar named Baer (1760-1772). Baer managed
to convince a large number of Talmudic scholars that the principles
of Tzaddikism was a hope for the masses who, instead of rational
beliefs in truths, preferred to put their blind faith in the human expo-
nents of these truths based on miraculous powers promised in the
teachings of the Tzaddiks. Another disciple, Jacob Joseph Cohen,
was the first rabbi to attempt a literary exposition of the principles
of Hasidism.

Cohen, who had been fired from his rabbinate because of his
devotion to Hasidism, was persecuted by his rabbinical colleagues.
Receiving protection from Besht, Cohen decided to support and honor
the deceased Besht with a published collection of the latter's sayings
titled, *Toldoth Ya'kob Yoseph*.[58] In his treatise, Cohen attacked the
Talmudists as arrogant pseudo-scholars. He also stated that the attitude of the scholars toward the masses was one of contempt for their
lack of education. The scholars' religious practices and knowledge,
he felt, was limited to book learning. Their image of being empirical-
ly aware was false. Cohen's book became the foundation of Hasidic
literature, differing in content and form not only from the rabbinical
literature, but from the earliest Cabalistic literature as well. The
Hasidim adopted the Cabalistic prayer book of Ari, which differed
from the accepted liturgy through numerous textual alterations and
transpositions. They changed the time limit of morning prayer, the
ritual of the slaughtering of animals, and some congregants dressed
themselves in white on the Sabbath. "The Hasidim engaged in drinking, merry making and boisterousness, which was in accord with
Besht's philosophy of a cheerful disposition."[59]

The boundless veneration of the Tzaddiks made leader worship the most noted trait of the Hasidim. The appearance of a miracle-working Tzaddik in a neighborhood would often be cause enough for rumors to lead to mass conversion, particularly if someone was actually or accidentally healed. A good guess or prediction, and even a good diagnosis of a malady, would also trigger mass conversion. Men who wished to resolve the sterility of their wives, and women who hoped to be cured of an illness, received advice, had their fortunes told and even received love potions to make their lovers react positively. The home of the Tzaddiks were often overcrowded.

The principal branches of Hasidim were two, one in Poland and Ukraina, the other in Lithuania and White Russia. The leader of the largest group was Emielech of Lizno and Galicia. Then there were Levi Itzhok of Berdychev, Nohum of Chernobyl, and Borukh of Tulchyn, a grandson of Besht. Emielech preached that the first duty of the Hasid was to revere the Tzaddik as "a middleman between Israel and God." The Hasid is therefore compelled to have blind faith in the Tzaddik, treat him as his benefactor, and contribute toward the Tzaddik's financial support. The Tzaddik should not work. He must be able to devote himself entirely to worshipping God and thereby becoming a blessing to mankind. This profitable calling of the Tzaddik became hereditary, passing from father to son and grandson. Petty dynasties of Tzaddiks sprang up all around. Soul-saving became lucrative.

Hasidism reached its peak in 1770 and flourished despite rabbinical attacks of the orthodox Jews. In 1781, however, the government of Grodno appealed to all Jewish communities to exert much disciplinary force against "the dishonorable followers of Besht, the destroyers of Israel." All orthodox Jews were asked to isolate the Hasidim socially, avoid them as infidels, avoid contact with them, especially burying their dead.

The opposing group calls itself *Mithnagim*, Protestants. They harassed the Hasidim, and persecuted them even with prosecution in the courts as dangerous schismatics. One of these pious Hasidic leaders was the "pious fraud" Solomon Maimon (1754–1800).

Maimon was born in Lithuania, near Nesviah, where he received Talmudic studies as an orthodox Jew. At the age of twelve he was married off by his parents, according to old customs. From the Talmudic sphere of thought he went on to the Cabala, then to the religious philosophy of Moises Maimonides and other medieval Jewish rationalists. Maimon's environment did not provide the intellectual stimulus he sought, so he moved to Germany in 1771. Having left his family behind, he was able to seek secular education in Königsberg, then Berlin, Posen, Hamburg and Breslau. After enduring hardships and financial difficulties, he met Mendelssohn and his disciples in Berlin. Maimon absorbed German science, literature, and philosophy avidly. His preference centered on Kantian transcendentalism. Maimon's exposure to critical philosophy was antithetical to his earlier experience as a religious Lithuanian Jew of an academically underdeveloped background. The free thinking of philosophers and secular scholars rocked the foundations of his dogmatic pyramid based on religious tenets. Those pragmatic ideas filled his mind with skepticism and disbelief. He began to deny religion and morality and the infallibility he had previously attributed to them. This neophyte became so zealous in his philosophic undertakings that he advanced beyond Kant's reasoning on transcendentalism. Maimon published *A Tentative Investigation of Transcendental Philosophy* in German, and followed up that book with more writings on metaphysics and logic. After reading Maimon's first book, Kant remarked that no one among his contradictors had "grasped the essence of my system as profoundly as Maimon."[60] Kant also felt this student was one of the few men "endowed with so refined and penetrating a mind in questions so abstract and complex."

The Talmud humbled man, but the Kabbalah ennobled him. A part of the Talmud reads thusly:

> Whence come you? From a fetid drop. Whither go you? To a place of dust, defilement and worms. And before whom are you some day to vindicate yourself and give account of your actions? Before the King of Kings, before the Holy One Whose name be praised!

The Kabbalah contradicts:

> Man is both the summary and the highest expression of Creation; hence, he was not created until the sixth day. As soon as man appeared, everything was completed, the higher world as well as the lower, for all is summed up in man; he unites all form . . . He is also above all, the image of God, considered in the totality of His infinite attributes. Man is the divine presence on Earth.

Kant criticized those philosophers. He taught Maimon and other thinkers that David Hume had awakened him from his dogmatic slumber and put him on the road to becoming the critical philosopher. Kant considered himself a synthesis of the Leibnitz-Wolffian rationalism and Humean skepticism. He went on to state that morality requires belief in the existence of God, freedom, and immortality, for without the existence of those abstractions there would be no morality defense argument.

Maimon was considered a fraud by the Hasidim because he became a pragmatist, whose reasoning advanced beyond dogmatic rationalism.

The Hasidim became a strong united component of Judaism. In modern times they do not keep pictures or photographs of any prophet or other revered person. They do not go to cinemas or theaters, and they only dance among themselves. A Hasidic Jew does not kiss any woman other than his own wife. That wife is picked for him through a contract agreed upon between the groom's parents and the parents of his wife-to-be. The marriage is usually contracted before adolescence.

The most recent thinker of prominence among the Hasidim was Martin Buber. Born in Vienna, he preached that Israel knows itself to be "addressed" by the Divine and to "respond" and to "listen and obey."

The philosophic basis for Hasidim is the Cabala. It concerns itself with the cosmos and its relation to man. Hasidim was primarily concerned with morality and religion. God or the *Shekinah* incorporates all creation, including animal, vegetable, mineral, and human life. Evil is merely a cover for good, and all evil will eventually turn into good.

Buber has retold the Hasidim anecdotes, "God is both the matter and the form of the universe." Another saying is, "The material form of intelligence, represented by the twenty-two letters of the alphabet, is also the form of all that is, for, beyond man, the universe and time, nothing but the infinite can be conceived." The most popularly used cliche is, "Purity of heart is more pleasing to God than learning."

The term Hasidim was applied to three different movements at three distinct times. The first Hasidim, also called Assideans or Hasideans, were an ancient Jewish sect which developed between 300 B.C.E. and 175 B.C.E. They were more rigidly adherent to Judaism than the Hebrews and Jews, who became influenced by Greeks. During the twelfth and thirteenth centuries, a second Hasidim arose in Germany as the Hasidei Ashkenaz. They were influenced by Saadia ben Joseph who referred them to his belief in mystical and messianic involvement. After that introduction, the third movement was that of Israel Baal Shem Tov.

RUSSIAN PREJUDICE AGAINST JEWS

During the sixteenth century the Empire of Muscovy had been curtained off from Western Europe by what was called the Byzantine Wall. The Jews had been considered dangerous magicians and seducers since the conversion of some Christians by Sabbatai Zevi. Most crimes were relegated to the Jews. The ambassador of the Muscovite Grand Duke Basil III, situated in Rome, informed the Italian scholar Paolo Giovio that "The Muscovite people dread no one more than the Jews, and do not admit them into their borders." Jewish merchants were permitted to visit from Poland and Lithuania to the border fringes of Smolensk. They were not extended permanent residence, however, despite petitions submitted for adjustment of emigration status. Jews would still sneak into Moscow occasionally since it was the capital city. Whenever they were caught, the Russians would punish them.

Tzar Ivan the Terrible had rejected the Polish King Sigsmund Augustus' charter as far back as 1550. Ivan did not want Jews transacting business in Russia. In 1563 Ivan sent Russian troops to occupy the city of Polotzk on the Russian border. This Tzar had also ordered all resident Jews to convert to the Greek Orthodox faith or be drowned in the Dvina that flows northwest to Dvina Bay and southwest to Riga. With the Poles, Ivan simply took them captive and demolished their churches. He did not waste time with them. By 1613, a considerable number of Jews had penetrated Russia despite Ivan's efforts. Forty years later in 1654 Tzar Alexis Michaelovich took allied Russian troops with the Cossacks and occupied White Russia, Lithuania, and Ukraina. Surprised by the number of Jews populating cities without their permission or knowledge, the allied forces decided to avenge the murder of Christ. Jews were immediately barred from Greek Orthodox Russia, some murdered in Vilna and Moghilev, with a few survivors expelled after the confiscation of most of their goods and properties. In Vitebsk Jews were held as prisoners of war, others were assaulted and their properties plundered or confiscated. Those held prisoner were deported to the central provinces of Russia and soon extended themselves all the way to Siberia. The merchants formed a colony, began selling cloth, obtained a "red ticket" to visit the capital and had to be forced out of Moscow in 1676. Their conditions worsened under Peter the Great, who said, "I prefer to see in our midst nations professing Mohammedanism and paganism rather than Jews. They are rogues and cheats. It is my endeavor to eradicate evil and not to multiple it."[61]

By 1727, however, Catherine I (1683?–1727) of peasant origin from Livonia, found that some Jews were becoming powerful and rich. She issued an *ukase*[62] for the deportation of Borukh Leibov, who had become rich enough to build a synagogue in the village of Zverovich. The local priest was afraid of losing his flock, and members of the Holy Synod had protested to Saint Petersburg in his behalf. Jews were expelled to Poland and prohibited from carrying gold and silver abroad. They were forced to exchange their money for copper coins before leaving the unpromised land.

Disagreement between the authorities of the central government led to protests by the Little Russian Cossacks. Hetman Daniel Apostle sent a petition to Saint Petersburg requesting travel for Jewish salesmen to the Little Russian fairs because of their commercial usefulness. Emperor Peter II, who was still a minor, had a permission granted through a ukase issued on advice by the Supreme Secret

Council in 1728. Jews previously deported were now granted the right to visit fairs and sell merchandise once more. The flood of favors and privileges soon stopped flowing, and muddy banks of cruel repressions were used as dams instead. One of the incidents which occurred struck at the core of Judeo-Christian social relations. It came about through the well-known tax farmer of Smolensk, Leibov. He continued to cross the Polish-Russian frontier despite his deportation. During one of his visits to Moscow, Borukh struck up an acquaintance with Alexander Voznitzin, a retired navy captain who had studied the Bible with a Jewish friend. Realizing that biblical teachings were more in tune with the concept of the One God, rather than the concept of the Trinity and idol or saint worship in the Greek Orthodox dogmas, Voznitzin decided to convert to Judaism. Knowing the dangers and consequences involved in such a decision, the new Jew went to a small town named Dubrovna, where Leibov's son lived. Voznitzin was circumcised, there was a ceremony performed, and everyone was satisfied. His conversion to Judaism circulated through rumors, causing the neophyte and his converter to be summarily arrested and taken to Saint Petersburg to face the Chancellor for Secret Inquisitional Affairs. Captain Voznitzin and Leibov were both put on the rack to confess their criminal acts. The former for "blasphemous words against the Holy Church," the latter for having "deliberately seduced" a lamb of the Greek Orthodox flock. Added to Borukh's charges was an accusation that he had insulted the local Russian Pope Abramius by establishing a Jewish synagogue in the village of Zverovich a few years earlier. The *auto da fe* (authority of faith) was executed, in the presence of a large crowd of spectators gathered at the Saint Petersburg public square on July 15, 1738. Hatred of Jews was rekindled through this conversion and the murders and plundering were simultaneously reactivated. There was a respite through the war with Turkey. Then, in 1740 Empress Anna Ivanovna (1693–1740), issued an ukase expelling Jews.

During the reign of Elizabeth Petrovna (1741–1761), an empress who devoted a lot of her time to court balls and church services, persecution of non-Orthodox Greek Church adherents became intensified. Moslems were fined, as pagan nationals of the East who could be exempt only if they accepted the state religion. To dampen the spirit of converts to Islam and to suppress Muhammadan propaganda, orders were issued to demolish mosques in villages of the Government of Kazan and Astrakhan. Destruction of mosques ceased only when fear of Turkish reprisals were considered. There were rumors that the news would reach those countries in which Greek Orthodox lived in the midst of Muhammadans, and churches existing there would be equally destroyed. Jews, living in the border provinces received like treatment. "They were expelled with one hand

and pushed into the doors of the church with the other."

In Poland in 1772 there was deterioration in the socioeconomic and political ridges of the entire country. To solve the internal chaos, the cause had to be found. The Jewish problem was considered the primordial cause of the chaos. Two solutions were suggested. The first one was lined with repressive measures and saturated with hate. The second was padded with special privileges for those considered nobility or clergy. The liberalism in the latter was fostered through compulsory enlightenment cherished by Austrian Emperor Joseph II. There was a famous Chancellor Andreas Zamoiski who supported the first edict, granting Jews right of residence in specifically designated areas and limiting them to temporary visits in places such as markets and fairs. The second edict proposed, supported by Butrymovich and Chatzki of the Diet, was more liberal. It did not insist that Jews could only visit their coreligionists in the presence of Christians or those converted should be moved from their old communities. Zamoiski feared that the Jews were forming a state within a state, and wanted them therefore to speak Polish instead of Yiddish.

By 1789 there was the uproar of a French Revolution resounding through Europe. The Jews were adding to their own woes by fanning the flames of Hasidim. There was an emergence of two factions among them: Hasidim and Mithnagdim. The Jewish plutocracy exploited their ignorant and hard-working masses just like the Polish pans (land owners) abused their poor. The plutocrats administered to the needs of the rich and overtaxed the poor. There was enough dissatisfaction to bring about a split in Vilna, the Lithuanian capital, between the aristocratic rabbinical party, headed by Samuel Vogdorovich (son of Avigdor) and the Kahal Party). As we have often seen during the oppression of a group, a champion of the poor arrived in the person of Simeon Volfovich. This savior defended the Jewish poor and prevented further abuse against them by obtaining an "iron letter" from King Stanislav Augustus. The letter guaranteed protection against persecution, violation of personal and property rights of the individual as well as the community, "which the tyranny of the Kahal had brought to the verge of ruin." His defense of the downtrodden Jews angered the Kahal authorities, and Simeon Volfovich was inscribed in the "black book," excommunicated with the *herem*, and sent to prison through collaboration of the Voyevoda and the tyrannical Kahal members who in 1788 exploited their own people

The first year of the French Revolution was simultaneous with the Polish reform. Those proposed reforms promoted "useful pursuits among the Jews, such as agriculture and handicrafts, and to remove them from the obnoxious liquor traffic." Yiddish dialect was to be abandoned and the Polish language used in its place and taught in the schools. Hebrew books were not to be imported from abroad, and no distinctive clothing was to be required. Butrynovich added that Jews were not to be recruited to military services until "enlightenment had transformed them into patriots ready to serve their fatherland." Butrynovich was forced at least to contemplate a pamphlet written in Polish by Rabbi Hirsch Yosefovich of Khelm. This pamphlet, *Reflections Concerning the Plans of Transforming the Polish Jews into Useful Citizens of the Country*, gave Butrynovich credit for enlightening and wishing the Jews well but it expressed amazement at the fact that even cultured men engaged in making generalizations and blanket condemnation of a people.

By March 1790 incorporated artisans, mostly tailors and furriers, promised at the steps of the town hall to murder all Jews if the magistracy did not expel them from Warsaw. The following day Jewish artisans and street peddlers were ordered to leave the city. Only merchants in stores or warehouses were allowed to remain.

On May 16, 1790 there was a riot, which began when a man named Fox met a Jewish tailor on the street carrying a piece of material under his arm. Fox tried to wrest the cloth from the tailor but the man held on to his goods and fought him off. Fox shouted and attracted a crowd to whom it was told that Jews had killed a Christian tailor. The mob attacked Jews on Tlowatzkria Street but were resisted. They rushed other more vulnerable Jewish residences instead. There the mob looted private homes, stores, and warehouses of valuables while discarding raw materials or throwing them into wells. The municipal guards approached to disperse them but were met with a hail of stones and bricks. Only a detachment of cavalry and infantry soldiers were able to disperse the rioters and restore order. A severe administrative measure was then proclaimed to maintain order and prevent further incidents of a similar nature. The marshals and guards used rods to punish all Jewish peddlers or artisans found on the street with goods, then expelled them.

In 1793 Poland was partitioned between Russia and Prussia. Russia annexed Volhynia and a part of the province of Kiev, Podolia, and Minsk. Prussia took the other part of Great Poland (Kalish, Plotzk). Hundreds of thousands of Jews were taken out of Polish jurisdiction and legal domain.

The Revolution of 1794 was nurtured. A Polish leader of the protesters, Thaddeus Kosciusko (1746–1817), attracted several followers with his commitment to liberty and equal treatment for all citizens.

Kosciusko had fought in the American Revolution after his military and academic training in France and Poland. Having experienced revolutionary causes and effects in Paris and New York, Kosciusko was aware of the value of freedom and the cost. He knew that no free country could survive and prosper for long without equal civil rights and privileges for all of its citizens. The prolonged siege of Warsaw by the Russians proved him right during the summer and autumn of 1794. All Poles were forced to become obligated to the defense of their capital city.

The Jews who had just recently been attacked and banned from the capital volunteered and fought in the trenches shoulder to shoulder with their former persecutors. After a while they decided to form a Jewish legion under Berek Yoselovich.[63]

Yoselovich had worked for a high noble, the Bishop of Vilna, Masalski. They had often traveled to different countries abroad, mostly to Paris, where Yoselovich had learned French language and customs. Therefore, the spirit of liberty and equality was not foreign to him. Realizing that many of his Jewish and Polish countrymen were subdued and subjected to the whims of those who held them hostage, Berek decided to join Kosciusko. Yoselovich and Aaronovich requested permission from Kosciusko to form a special regiment of light cavalry composed of Jewish volunteers. The commander-in-chief granted their request for such a company. The Jewish soldiers fought valiantly until their regiment was finally defeated by superior Russian horsemen. Yoselovich fled with General Zayonchek; Kosciusko was captured by the Russians. Yoselovich and Aaronovich went to Austria, where Yoselovich was arrested. He managed to escape, and went on to France.

The third partition of Poland in 1795 was another historical event. Twelve years later, Napoleon I took away the province of Great Poland from Prussia and turned it into the Duchy of Warsaw, a small Polish commonwealth under the rule of the Saxon King Frederick Augustus III, a grandson of Augustus II, the last Polish King of the Saxon Dynasty (1807). Two years later in 1809, Napoleon defeated Austria, took her Polish dominions, and added them to the Duchy of Warsaw.

Jews hoped the Napoleonic Code, introduced to the French lawmakers would benefit them. The French Minister Champagny hated Jews, however, and ignored them completely. Outstanding Jews began to file petitions until the Duke interceded in their behalf. On October 17, 1808, a decree was issued stating that the inhabitants of Varsovia professing the Mosaic religion should be barred for ten years from enjoying political rights.

The reign of Catherine II (1772–1796) saw Russian population swell through the large acquisition of Jewish citizens from White Russia. What was to be done with the unwelcome heritage bequeathed by Poland? There were two suggestions, one was to give them communal autonomy, the other was to restrict them to designated areas where some were burghers and artisans. A *Gubernator*, the equivalent of French *government* or English governor, was put on each border town and village. Jewish homes were often requisitioned

to house these officials and for other municipal purposes. Jewish lit-
igants lost whenever they challenged a Christian in court. Their lack
of fluency in the Russian language was also a liability. It was not long
before the first territorial ghetto of White Russia was established by
law; its purpose was to relocate the Jewish population taken from
Poland.

The same ukase that designated the areas of Jewish residences
also determined the amount of taxes to be imposed on them. The tax
did not relieve them from military service or special assessment
demanded in the ukases of 1794 or 1796.

Interestingly enough, the Karaites' sect (which rejected Oral Law,
ethics, metaphysics, and Hanukkah) were protected by Count Zubov,
the Governor General of New Russia. The Karaites did not have to
pay the double tax. This handful of Karaites, who lived apart from
other Jewish communities for centuries, were considered by the
Russians as being more desirable than the spiritual Zionists.[64]

Under Catherine II, however, the Jews made some improvement.
The pejorative term *Zhyd*—a Slavic translation of the Latin *Judaeus*
—was substituted with *Yevrey* (Hebrew) as a Russian linguistic
improvement.

The Polish magnates who kept many slaves on their estates found
it convenient to blame bad crops and poverty on the Yevrey rather
than climatic conditions or deprivation. Jewish tavern-keepers were
often blamed by the nobles for selling their liquor to the peasants on
credit, causing them to become irresponsible alcoholics unable to
work.

Under Alexander I, Jews were allowed in 1892 to open a cemetery in Saint Petersburg. The Jewish Constitution of 1804 allowed
them to open their own schools as well. Three languages were permitted for secular enlightenment: Russian, Polish, or German. Jewish
children were to leave for state-operated schools at the age of twelve.

The Holy Synod sent out instructions to the Greek Orthodox clergy notifying the Russian people that Napoleon was a pseudo-Messiah
and an enemy of the Church, but a friend of the Jews. The Church
seemed afraid that Napoleon might unite the Jews through his permission of the Great *Synhedrin** to function in France on February
9, and March 9, 1807. He had also permitted the Jews to build synagogues in France and to set up a central Jewish communal administration.

On July 7 and July 9, 1807, the Peace of Tilsit was concluded
and an *entente cordiale* established between Napoleon and Alexander
I. Russia was no longer afraid of Napoleon Bonaparte's intrigues or
the contacts between Russian Jews and the Parisian *Synhedrin*.
Bureaucratic consideration for Jewish rights diminished and the final
date for their expulsion was fixed for January 1, 1808.

300 The African Origin of Modern Judaism

On October 19, 1807, the Tzar issued an ukase of rigid measures to be enforced against the protected Jews. Jews who did not leave Russia willingly were ejected forcibly. They were driven like cattle into the townlets and cities, where they were left dispersed around the public squares in open air. The manner in which the expulsion was executed was said to have been ferocious.

The war of 1812 saw Napoleon supported by the Poles, who expected restoration of their annexed territories. The Jews had to decide whether they would support their French benefactor or tolerate Russian abuses. The flexible Hasidic leaders made overtures to Alexander, and were given preferential treatment in Russia. The Russian government seized the opportunity to inveigle those Jews to become farmers on the big estates, but the Jews refused. They preferred to sell liquor to the Russian peasants who did the farming.

Some time after 1780, the Jews were accorded the unusual privilege of taking active part in the city government, exercising voting rights and occupying magistrate and municipal courts. Russian lawmakers felt that the Jews would now cherish their Russian nationality and abandon Kahal inclinations. The coalition between Jews and Christians did not materialize because the Jews encountered strong opposition from the insecure Christian aldermen and members of the bar who kept the Jews in a minority. That move kept the doors closed to Jewish entry into municipal administrative positions. Complaints to the higher authorities went unheeded, even in Saint Petersburg. The Russians and the Poles especially sensed that the opportunities given to Jews were, in fact, a lack of consideration for Christian rights and chartered privileges. It was not long before the authorities were forced to recognize their dissatisfaction and begin limiting the placement of Jewish magistrates even in predominantly Jewish sectors with a Jewish majority vote. The two Lithuanian governments, now under Russia after the third partition of Poland in 1795, suspended the law permitting Jews to occupy offices in the magistracies. When the Senatorial ukase authorizing Jews to fill available positions in municipal government reached Vilna, the local authorities had to ignore it through pressure from the Christian community which showed its religious prejudice and hatred in written and vociferous verbal protests to the burghers and then directly to Alexander I. The Christians of Kovno protested in a similar manner. They referred to the "sacred crucifix" with its agonizing figure by placing it on the table of the court for the taking of oaths before testimony could be accepted in a judicial case. The people of Kovno felt that the Jews would be mocking their sacred beliefs if they refused to testify on the crucifix rather than the Bible. Their strong argument was that Christians entering the sacred court of justice could find a Jew on the bench as his superior if Jews were permitted to continue holding administrative positions, and might well act contrary to "reason of class and religion."

The continued disagreement between Jewish religious sects did not help their cause. Hasidim and Rabbinim were continually at opposite ends of the Jewish yardstick; but by 1796 the tide began to turn. The Hasidim now outnumbered Orthodox believers scattered between Russia, Austria, and Prussia. There was mention of a significant coincidence in dates: the first partition of Poland taking place in 1772, the same year of the schism of Judaism or first declaration against Hasidism. The year of the third partition of Poland, 1796, also ran parallel with the second emphatic declaration by the same rabbinate which completed the schism. The interval between the dates is said to have allowed the Hasidim to have gained numerically. This numerical gain helped the rift to become serious enough to require government intervention. Hasidic dominance of the religious scenes extended to the Russian southwest provinces of Volhynia, Kiev, and Podolia. In the Northwest they were merely holding a minority position against the rabbinate in White Russia, which had been under Russian control for over twenty years, causing it to be cut off from Poland. The disputes became endless. There were Kahals, Hasidim, Tzaddiks, and Mithnagdim, or Protestants, involved in the disputes. Only in Lithuania did the Hasidim fail to gain control. There and elsewhere rabbis, like Elijah Gaon accused the Hasidim of being an illegal secret organization. Consequently, it was only in Karlin on the outskirts of Pinsk, that the Hasidim had synagogues and Tzaddiks.

In order to gain strength against the charges made by Gaon, with his signature of the epistle, the Hasidim made charges of various classifications to legitimize themselves and discredit orthodoxy. The aged Gaon was compelled to publish his treatise months before the Hasidic Shneor Zalman, head of White Russian Hasidim published their anti-rabbinate propaganda. The Gaon died in the fall of 1797, about a year after his last publication exposing the Hasidim as "heretics." The Jewish people of Vilna went into mourning for him. In the meantime, the local Hasidim were said to have "indulged in a gay drinking bout, to celebrate the deliverance of the sect from its principal enemy." Their dignified demonstration was discredited by their behavior on the day of the Gaon's funeral. Hasidic intolerance and vindictiveness reached such levels of disrespect that it was credited with having raised "indignation throughout the community." Their behavior stirred the Kahal elders to take an oath, at the Gaon's grave site, to exert corrective measures against the entire Hasidic community. The next day, the elders met and planned the repressive measures to be exerted against the undesirable sect. Resolution of a new herem for excommunication was passed. A five man committee of elders was appointed to deal with the heretics.

The Prosecutor-General in Saint Petersburg (Lopukhin) was sent a denunciation against the leader of the Karliner Hasidic sect, Zalman Borukhovich and his followers in Lithuania. Acting in the name of the Tzar, Lupukhin ordered the local authorities to arrest Borukhovich in the early autumn of 1798. He was picked up in the townlet of Lozno; twenty-two of his disciples, found in Lithuania, were also apprehended. As head of the Hasidim, Borukhovich was hurriedly sent to Saint Petersburg under guard of a strong convoy. His incriminated disciples remained in Vilna under arrest.

Borukhovich was arraigned before the "Secret Expedition," a legal arm which dealt with political crimes. His long indictment charged him with being "founder of a harmful religious sect, which had changed the order of divine service among Jews," disseminating pernicious ideas, and collecting funds for mysterious purposes in Palestine. Borukhovich replied to the accusations in a detailed and eloquently written account. His response was translated into Russian. The language he used was so impressive that Tzar Paul I immediately issued an order to have him and his followers released. However, the Prosecutor-General told the local authorities to keep him under surveillance.

It was now the Hasidim's time to make their move. The Kahal elders had fostered a case against them that had reached its high point of interest and was no longer of concern to the public. The Hasidim bought off the officials of Vilna with *bakhshish* and gained their sympathy. With this feat accomplished, they lodged their complaint against the Kahal Committee of Five in the first month of 1779. The Hasidim charged that the elders abused their power and even embezzled public funds. Several elders were removed from their positions and sent to prison. When the government requested Jewish leaders to represent their community, the Hasidim hurriedly filled the vacancy or selected rabbis sympathetic to their sect and its persuasions. Charges and countercharges between the two sects became so common that the first years of Russian rule in Lithuania saw some of the most vicious informers come to the surface or go undercover to destroy their own Jewish kin.

Avigdor Haimovich of Pinsk, lost his flock and a sizeable income. After dragging his persecutors and their Hasidic sect to court unsuccessfully, Haimovich charged the Hasidic community with fomenting Sabbatism and popularizing a "pernicious and dangerous organization." Tzar Paul rearrested Borukhovich who again wrote an elaborate response in Hebrew and was again released on probation.

When Paul's reign was abruptly ended with the palace revolution that put Alexander I on the throne, the senate dismissed the case and Alexander acquitted Tzaddick Borukhovich. Hasidism and Rabbinism were both sensibly allowed to flourish side by side in

Poland. The men learned Judaism and the women worked their hands cooking, laundering, and sewing. Everyone was proud of this form of religious worship, except those Jews who had visited or lived in Germany. They were arrogant as they still are even to this day in Israel.

The *Berliner*, or "new men", was the name applied to those persons who wore modern clothing fashioned with a Parisian veneer. From Germany came the *avant garde* dressed in short German coat, with neither earlocks, beards nor religious observance. Here was the type of Jew that reminds one of those who considered themselves so German in the 1940s that Hitler had to convince them they were Jewish when they continued their insistence on being *Ich bin ein deutscher.* "*I am a German*," And Hitler ranted "*Du bist ein Jude*" "You are a Jew."

The new men spoke fluent German, the language of the land. They disdained most Jewish folkways and traditional inclinations but they upheld the name of Moses Mendelssohn (1729–1786), a student of philosophy and wrote pre-Kantian ethics, who was cultured enough to have spoken Latin, French, and English as well as his native German. By the nineteenth century the contact between Poland and Prussia began to show "enlightenment, *kultur*." The Jewish "dandy" appeared on the streets of Poland and the long-coated Hasid was said to timidly step off the sidewalk to make way for the short-coated German fellow who wore the symbol of *kultur*.

Napoleon had made the Duchy of Warsaw an entity. Now, in the years between 1807 and 1812, Warsaw saw itself sustaining the promenades of Parisian dandies. They claimed equal recognition with the German short coats because of their modern dress, cultured behavior, "moral" conduct, and linguistic ability. In their attempt to accept the transformation in significant proportions, an appeal was made to the rustic Polish brethren. It read as follows:

> How long will you continue to speak a corrupt German dialect "Yiddish" instead of the language of your country, the Polish? How many misfortunes might have been averted by your forefathers, had they been able to express themselves adequately in the Polish tongue before the magnates and kings! Take a group of a hundred Jews in Germany, and you will find that either all or most of them can speak to the magnates and rulers, but in Poland, scarcely five or ten out of a hundred are capable of doing so.*

Other pamphlets appeared on cultural and linguistic improvement. Among them was one which stated that the name "Judean hath become an object of ridicule." It was written by Lev Alexandrovich Nyevakhovich, who admired Mendelssohn and Lessing. Nyevakhovich wrote:

> While the hearts of all European nations have drawn near-
> er to one another, the Jewish people still finds itself despised.
> I feel the full weight of this torment. I appeal to all who have
> sympathy and compassion. Why do you sentence my entire
> people to contempt? Thus waileth sadly the daughter of
> Judah, wiping her tears, sighing and yet uncomforted.

Shortly after publication of the "*the Wailing*," Nyevakhovich converted to Christianity. Like most opportunists who take on the role of
their oppressors, he and his patron Abraham Peretz, who had become
bankrupt by military contracts in the War of 1812, joined the many
Jewish converts of the baptism fad that was very popular in those
times. Both men were well accepted and their offspring given high
positions in the Russian government.

The last days of Alexander I (1815–1825) saw a form of mixed tendencies. There was benevolent paternalism and yet there were also
severe restrictions.

During the first half of Nicholas I's reign (1826–1840) there was
the subjection of Jews, through lectures as military enlightenment,
to conscription at an early age. They were dragged away from their
homes as early as the age of twelve. These Jewish recruits were subjected to austere disciplinary training, rigid barrack orientation and
confinement accompanied by compulsory religious assimilation.
There was said to be endless correctional and educational process-
ing to revive medieval, inquisitional-type punishments for entire
communities, when military service was rejected by nonconformists
who saw it used as a form of de-Judaization.

Nicholas I is supposed to have traveled through Russia as a youth
in 1816. When the Tzar saw Jews for the first time (on this trip for
educational development), they made such an impression on him that
Nicholas I recorded his reaction in a diary:

> The ruin of the peasants of these provinces are the Zhydos. As
> property-holders, they are here second in importance to the land-
> ed nobility. By their commercial pursuits they drain the strength
> of the hapless White Russian people . . . They are everything here;
> merchants, contractors, saloon-keepers, mill owners, ferry-hold-
> ers, artisans . . . They are regular leeches, and suck these unfor-
> tunate governments to the point of exhaustion. It is a matter of
> surprise that in 1812 they displayed exemplary loyalty to us and
> assisted us wherever they could at the risk of their lives.

Nicholas I looked upon the Jews as transient residents whose patriotism seemed attached to an ulterior motive: getting rich quickly and
emigrating to their own promised land. He felt that they were too well
treated, and even exempted from taxation by Alexander I. Nicholas I

was determined to enforce taxation on them. He also imposed a civil duty obligation on the Jews, although they had no civil rights. Their Russian military service under him was to be educational and disciplinary. Their commercial proclivities were to be changed in the barracks. Instead of being in a store or factory, they would now be in a school or plant that produced not merchandise, but a new generation of Russian-oriented Jews. They were to be religiously disoriented and Christianized.

In 1829 a special statute of military service was drafted for Jews. The Tzar's brother, Grand Duke Constantine, received the draft in Warsaw. It was sent to him for further suggestions and approval. Senator Nicholas Novosiltzen felt that the rigid orders in the memorandum might cause undesired repercussions, and that those laws were harsh and should be "slowly `prepared for such a radical transformation.'" The contents of the mandate reached the Jewish leaders shortly after, and they immediately moved their defense machinery into position. Jewish delegates were promptly sent to Saint Petersburg and Warsaw to complain, appeal, and seek relief from the deposition. Many negotiations were made and deals were transacted with the nobility and high-ranking officials. There was a rumor that huge bribes had been offered to Novosiltzen and several other officials to desensitize the command. The scuttlebutt caused the Tzar to act without suggestions from Novosiltzen. The Tzar ordered the Minister of the Interior and the Chief of the General Staff to submit the ukase of compulsory military service for Jews directly to him for his signature. The enactment was signed by Tzar Nicholas on August 26, 1827.

There was rapid juvenile conscription. Recruitment entailed enlistment for a twenty-five-year period. The basic training and accomplishments of Jews during military service was to be communicated to their families. The news was supposed to motivate the families to be more useful and efficient in their economic, administrative, and social development. Jewish parents wept. Mothers suffered, and pleaded, but their pleas only made the Tzar more heartless. To equalize military duties, he insisted that ninety-five clauses, with supplementary instructions, be issued. One instruction was, "The general laws and institutions are not valid in the case of the Jews." Another law stipulated that the years of basic training were not included in the term of active service, which started at the age of eighteen. This clause, ninety, added another six years of enlistment to the Jewish soldiers' induction. "Children born of soldiers were the property of the Military Department."

There were relief provisions. A volunteer could serve in the place of a recruited soldier, but the volunteer also had to be a Jew. Persons exempted from military service were merchants with membership in a guild, artisans affiliated with trade unions, mechanics, factory workers, agricultural workers, rabbis, and those few Jews who had graduated from a Russian academic institution. Those fortunate enough to be exempted did not escape entirely. They were forced to pay recruiting money which amounted to one thousand rubles per recruit.

The recruit should be inducted with great solemnity. He was to be dressed in his *tallith* (prayer shawl) and *kittel* (shroud), with philateries wound around his arm and forehead. This demand was indeed a mockery of the Hebrew religion because people of other faiths were not forced to wear rosaries, crosses, etc. From the time of Peter the Great there was mockery of the Russian's own Orthodox Christianity. Therefore, the order to execute this ritual in the synagogue, as the place of induction, should not have surprised the Jews.[65] Nevertheless, many of them were astonished. The recruit was supposed to stand in front of the Ark with candles burning, while a *shofar* (ram's horn) was blown as the recruit recited an endless fear-oriented oath. Those conscripted soldiers were only permitted to stop over at Christian homes while making their furlough before leaving for camp.

The inductees were called cantonists. Some of them were dragged away from their parents at the age of six. Those who ran away were often recaptured and sent to be kept in confinement until their physical examination had been received at the induction center. Their detention would continue until they had been assigned to an outlying post.

Hertzen, a famous Russian writer of the time, says that he interviewed an officer with a company of Jewish youngsters between eight and nine years of age. The officer gave the reporter this account: "The officer that turned them over to me told me they were an awful nuisance." A third of them died during the hike "and half of them would not get to their destination" . . . "the boys of twelve or thirteen managed, somehow, to stand up, but the little ones of eight and ten," did not make it. They had been forced to march no less than thirty or forty miles on rations of crackers and water only. Those youngsters who survived were taken to basic training by non-commissioned officers to be reeducated. The juvenile corps permitted those soldiers who accepted conversion to be baptized and they got sent to bed. Those who refused to become Christians were fed cabbage soup prepared with lard, pork, or salted fish, and forbidden to drink water. The thirst would often make the children agree to conversion. The stubborn non-conformists were left to die or to be taken from the barracks into the military hospital where they were "released by a kind of death."

In this Russia, where houses were mostly made of wood or logs, there were several rivers running through the villages. These rivers were often used as waterways to escape the muddy roads where carts and coaches got stuck in the spring or rainy seasons and uncomfortably dusty in the summer. In the winter they were feet deep in snow and usually too cold to traverse. It is said that after a parade to one of these rivers in Kazan, where the Tzar himself had come to visit and review the training of the cantonists, a strange thing happened. After the parade to the riverbank to be baptized, the Jewish cantonists were briefed orally by their officers. When the Orthodox priests gave the manual command, the Jewish boys were to reply in the military manner and execute the order. This they did by shouting "Aye, aye!" as they dived into the water. When they had not surfaced for some time, swimmers were sent in after them. It was discovered that the cantonists had committed mass suicide. Other recruits did not get the same opportunity or publicity. Different companies were quietly tortured in the guardhouses, barracks, and military hospitals. The fate of any Jewish recruit between the ages of eighteen and twenty-five was even more gruesome than that of some cantonists. The adult was forced to spend his twenty-five years of service in some village away from his wife and extended family. Many of these soldiers were ridiculed for their inability to speak Russian or adapt to military orientation and harshness or be able to eat *trefa*.

As the compulsory enlightenment shone with undue oppression, the brutality increased. The Russian government attempted to seek improvement in its method of handling Jews. Sergius Uvarov and other leading statesmen contemplated certain methods used by the reactionary governments of Prussia and Austria in solving their Jewish problem. Jewish determination to worship in their particular way was considered fanatical and distinct from the ways of the Russian Orthodox Church. Therefore, the Russian government issued an enlightenment ukase on April 20, 1843. That law declared that all Jews living within Russia should consider themselves granted two years in which they should sell their homes and leave the country. The French, German, and English language newspapers criticized the order and called Russia "New Spain." Several foreign communities in Germany, America, and elsewhere petitioned the Russian government for reconsideration.

Tzar Nicholas I was consulted while visiting England, and diplomatic as well as notable high ranking persons requested his intervention on behalf of the unfortunate Jews. The Tzar and his court might have ignored the pleas, but after careful consideration it was concluded that several cities would be deserted, large sums of revenues lost, and foreign sympathy lost as well.

The Russian Ministry sought an alternative. It classified Jews within Russia's borders under two categories, "useful" and "useless." The useless ones were the masses without employment, the artisans, tradesmen, and burghers of small earning power or no income. Merchants, artisans with membership in the guild, trade unionists, independent farmers and burghers with fixed income were considered "useful." The latter paid more taxes.

In 1846 Sir Moses Montefiore, a Jewish philanthropist of London, set out with the recognition of Queen Victoria to petition the Russian Ministers to have mercy on the Jews. Montefiore had become famous through his defense of the Jewish cause in Turkey during 1840. There had been a ritual murder trial at Damascus, and Montefiore had been successful in having the Turks acquit the condemned. The Tzar received him and listened to his suggestions as a matter of protocol. However, nothing was actually done to ameliorate the Jewish condition. Montefiore's personal recommendation from Queen Victoria was supposed to have been pregnant with hope but it bore no fruit. Mitigation of the harsh laws was not achieved and communal autonomy was never restored to the Jewish quarter.

At the same time, another prominent Jew, a wealthy merchant from Marseille named Isaac Altaras, went to Russia with a proposal to relocate a certain number of Jews to Algiers. That territory had just been subjected to French colonization. Altaras assured the Russian authorities that the French government was willing to give the Jews immediate permanent resident status in the North African region. Transportation costs were guaranteed by the Rothschild Bank of Paris. A fixed ransom was promptly demanded for each Jewish emigrant. After serious consideration, the Tzar waived the ransom in October 1846. Despite the hopefulness which pervaded diplomatic circles in Russia and elsewhere, no Jews left Russia and Altaras left that country suddenly, after the transactions had seemed so favorable. Jewish rescue operations considered salvation for the unfortunate was called a scheme by the Russians, which had been discovered in time.

It was not long before the Jewish people took note that their Russian compatriots were strongly urged to keep them at a safe distance. Russian writers depicted the Jew as one who bore "the well defined features of an inhuman fiend." Aleksander Sergeevich Pushkin is said to have presented the "despised Jew" of the street in comparison to the figure of "the venerable old man reading the Bible under the shelter of the night" in a "Black Shawl." Another writer of the same period, Thaddeus Bulgarin, stereotyped the Jew in his novel *Ivan Vyzhigin* as a Lithuanian Jew named Movsha (Moses) who represented "the embodiment of all mortal sins."[66] Bulgarin's novel did not remain a bestseller for long, but by the time it was forgotten its pejorative effects had already taken root in mental soil unreasonably permeated with hate for the Russian Jew.

The last years of Nicholas I saw the "assortment" of the Jews become a purposeful evil. They were forced to register as soon as the law was decreed in guilds and estates to which whey were assigned. If that operation failed, the government would assume implementation of the "assortment." It would separate Jews not engaged in productive labor from others making social and economic contributions. The former would be classified burdensome to society and be subject to various restrictions. All Jews were divided into five categories: merchants, agriculturalists, artisans, settled burghers, and unsettled burghers. The first three categories were composed of Jews enrolled in guilds and estates. Settled burghers were those Jews engaged in the "burgher trade" (selling city positions). The remaining majority or proletariat was classified as "unsettled burghers." This unsettled mass, unprovided with social assistance of any kind, was subjected to compulsory military draft enforced with harsh penalties for evasion. That mass was branded and despised as outcasts. After April 1, 1852, Jews of the four tolerated categories were ordered to show a certificate of enrollment in a settled occupation or be summoned in the fifth category by local authorities. With a limited period allowed, many Jews found themselves unable to procure the required documents. The cutoff date was suspended until the autumn of 1852, but even then the "assortment" had not been significantly achieved. The police inspectors' routine inspections with intent to sentence these "parasites" to forced labor, was averted by fate when the Crimean War erupted in 1853, in which Russia found herself pitted against Turkey, England, France, and Sardinia after occupying the Turkish vassal states of Maldive and Walachia. Russia was too occupied externally to worry about the Jewish assortment at home. The Jews were temporarily relieved of the *razryaden*,[67] as it was unpopularly called.

Before the thirty-year Crimean War, however, Jewish women had been forbidden to shave their heads (in April 1851), according to marriage custom. No *sheitell*, or wig, babushka, or handkerchief were to be worn on the heads of the brides. A married woman of the Jewish faith guilty of shaving her head was liable to a fine of five rubles.[68] Jewish women were raided intermittently, taken to the police stations where their kerchiefs or other head covering, especially wigs, were removed to see if they still had their own hair. In some villages, the men in long coats were hauled to the stations and their coats cut by the cops in the midst of laughter and related jokes. The Hasidim resisted, and the joy of coat-cutting persisted for quite some time. Nicholas I was determined to make the Jews assimilate or at least look like Christians; and was especially hard on the men who were more conspicuous. He admired the pretty women and had his men pursue them.

Families were robbed of both a young father and tender sons. To evade this atrocious military obligation, several men mutilated themselves or disappeared like other Russians had done during the conscription of Peter the Great, when he intended to fight the Swedes.

Able-bodied Jewish men were novelties when one was found. Apart from men beyond the draft age or physically handicapped, no men could be found who might be drafted into the armed forces. Some of the able-bodied males fled to neighboring countries or smaller unpopulated areas. Those in hiding were hunted like wild animals. Others simply "chopped off their fingers or toes, damaged their eyesight, and perpetrated every conceivable form of maiming themselves to escape military service which was in effect penal servitude." A contemporary observer wrote, "The most tenderhearted mother would place the finger of her beloved son under the kitchen knife of a home-bred quack surgeon."

With these machinations, justifiable as they might be, a hardship was created for the entire national Jewish population. Most Jewish quarters on Russian soil could not meet the quota imposed on them. They simply had too many maimed male citizens. To reimpress the seriousness of his demand, the Tzar issued orders demanding three men of the minimum age of twenty from each delinquent sector, one more recruit and two thousand rebels for every draft dodger belonging to that community. One year later, a decree was issued ordering the capture of fugitives evading the draft. They were to be flogged and enlisted; the communities wherein they were found were to be heavily fined. A relative harboring a draft dodger who had not reported for duty on his appointed date was to be taken in his place. Any Jew caught in another city without a passport could be arrested and forced into the service as a substitute for a recruit absent without leave. "The `captive' regardless of age, was made a soldier, and the captor was given a receipt for one recruit." A bounty hunt began.

The official captors hired by the Kahal elders were no longer the only human trackers. Several private bounty hunters sought a substitute to serve in his place or his relative's place. Furthermore, he could obtain a "penny by selling his recruiting receipt." Hordes of Jewish bandits arose all over the country. They "infested the roads and the inns, and by trickery or force made the travellers part with their passports and then dragged them to the recruiting stations." Jews are said to have sunken to such levels of degradation that their fellow Jews became such beasts of prey most of them were soon afraid of budging an inch from their native cities. The suspicion and frustration grew to such proportions that everyone suspected a passerby of being a captor or a bandit.[69]

The Crimean War had the Russians so confused that they spared no subjects in acquiring targets for the battle practice against the well-trained English and French armies. Russian cannon fodder sacrificed to the enemy for the honor of Russia, was conscripted from all inner and outer recesses of the country. Even Tatars were used. Battalion after battalion was sacrificed after recruitment to meet the needs of the thirty-year conflict. Thousands of Jewish servicemen were among the maimed and slaughtered troops. History had repeated itself.

During the thirty years of intermittent wars between Charles XII of Sweden and Peter the Great, the Russians complained of the recruitment. One said, "The village is weighed down with furnishing roubles and half roubles and horses' [sic] carts and there is no rest for us peasants. He has forced us all into service, he has seized upon our people and peasants for recruits . . . He even goes into the service himself."[70]

Alexander II (1818–1881), came to power in 1855 as a successor of Nicholas I. He had been active during the Crimean War from 1853 to 1856. Alexander set about seeking peace in Paris while instituting an era of "Great Reforms." Certain Jews charged with the usual ritual murders were even set free. Considering the time ripe for redress, the Committee on Jewish Affairs petitioned for the Tzar's intervention on behalf of their fellowmen unjustly conscripted as penal and captive recruits. The Russian armed forces released the soldier children (cantonists) who had survived the harshness and horrors of war.

With the children returned to their homes, and the Jewish condition relieved, several Jews began moving to the interior. This centrifugal force became so intense that the Tzar himself had to put a stop to it. He vetoed proposals to extend Jewish privileges and expand their residential limits. Nevertheless, Alexander II encouraged offers of financial aid to converts embracing Christianity. The law of 1864 decreed, nonetheless, that there should be no stipends paid to converts serving in the armed forces. The law was soon repealed with reduction of sentences for "criminal offenders who embrace Christianity during the inquiry." Although acculturation was supposedly more advantageous than a religious preference, many Jewish youths still preferred the *yeshibahs* and sought refuge in them.

The rabbinical students often came from the poor masses who felt the force of the draft. One year later all Jewish sectors were ordered only to accept graduates of the rabbinical Crown Schools or Russian secular academic institutions as official rabbis. In case of insufficiency, educated Jews from Germany were to be invited.

The law also extended to Poland. Then, in 1859, the *Warsaw Gazette* published an article branding Jews as foreigners. Jewish patriots in Poland, including a reputable convert, Kronenberg the banker, protested. The article was referred to as anti-Semitic, but by this time the Jews had amalgamated so much they were no longer Semitic. They were Hasidic and labeled themselves tacitly European.

More charges were printed, and other rebuttals appeared in the Polish press and the radical periodicals of Polish exiles abroad. A pamphlet was even circulated by historian Joachim Lelewel of Brussels, who still lamented over Poland's unfair treatment of Jews during 1831. At that time, Jews had volunteered to serve the fatherland under Polish dictator Khlopitzki. He rejected them, declaring they had no civil rights and therefore could not serve in the Polish Army.

A revolution which penetrated Poland from 1860 to 1863 demanded so much manpower, however, that a half million Jews were eventually involved. Ostracized rejects categorized as second, or no-class citizens were then in the forefront with Polish patriots of Galicia defending the fatherland. The Jews of Warsaw were also involved. They fully participated in all protest marches and demonstrations against the oppressors during 1860 to 1861. Many of those Jews died from Cossack target practice and trampling. In honor of the unarmed dead shot down in the protests, Jewish mourners and clergy marched to the funerals together with their Catholic counterparts. Lamentable and inflammatory eulogies were delivered in churches and synagogues simultaneously. Some Jews also attended services of their comrades at the churches where expressions of tolerance and brotherhood was preached. Some Poles even reminded Jews of the anti-Jewish position hatemongers of the Polish establishment had maintained. All Catholic churches were later closed in protest against Russian military attacks inside them. Rabbis and elders followed by closing synagogues as well.

On May 24, 1862 Alexander II signed an ukase permitting acquisition of immovable property on manorial estates where peasants had improved their lot from serfs to tenants. Jews could also settle without restrictions and appear in court as witnesses or defendants with equal rights in all proceedings. This ukase was entitled the "Act of Emancipation." Emancipation continued until 1870 when Alexander I visited the Kingdom of Poland and saw a large number of Hasidim in long black coats and earlocks. "The Tzar repelled by this spectacle," ordered the Polish governors to prohibit Jews wearing "the ugly costumes and earlocks." This insistence of maintaining an eastern custom in the West led to the declaration of "differences in dress is yet far from leading to the goal pursued by the Government." It was further interpreted by some Russians as a "hostile attitude of the Jewish communities toward Christians." The Council of State further declared that the Jews were "a secluded religious and civil caste or, one might say, a state in a state." One dissatisfaction led to another, and the stage was set for the action that followed.

Odessa, known as the granary of the South, enjoyed a successful business climate activated by Jewish and Greek merchants. Competition was keen, particularly in the marketing of corn, and jealousy ensued. Greek merchants began firing their pistols to celebrate Easter in front of their churches. Their churches were in the Jewish sector. It was therefore easy to surmise that the Jews would sooner or later show some resentment. In 1871 the Greeks prearranged their pistol-firing to irk the Jews. Seeing no physical resistance, the Greeks decided to spread a rumor. They exclaimed that some Jews had stolen a cross from a church fence and stoned their sacred place of worship. By Palm Sunday, March 28, the attack on Jews, their houses, and businesses was in motion. Lootings and beatings picked up momentum as the Russians joined the harvesting of unprotected valuables sown by Jewish labor and planted in their homes and shops. Many houses were made of wood, making arson easy to undertake and desecration of temples tempting. All sins were committed in the presence of policemen and militiamen who stood by and watched without enforcing the law. When the Jewish leaders sought redress from the officers, they were astonished to be told that the rioting was begun by the Jews.

Numerous pogroms followed until 1891. In that year the Jews who had already been ordered to put their Hebrew surnames on all signs of shops and stores they owned, had to make sure all names were exactly the same as those in their passports. The object was to promote ridicule and encourage isolation. During this subtle boycott, Europe was assured that Jews were well treated in Russia. The ordinance was secretly promulgated and did not receive publicity or press coverage. Jewish awareness of the cruel intent and purpose of the signs induced them to print their names in small letters. This tactical defense caused Governor Gresser of Saint Petersburg to design a drawing and demand that the letter be copied and conspicuously placed in all stores according to his enlarged size.

In Moscow, Jewish survival was more precarious. On February 14, 1896, the governor-general of Moscow lost his position to a brother of the Tzar named Grand Duke Sergius. Had Peter the Great still been alive, he would have probably beheaded Grand Duke Sergius.[71] It had been common knowledge, throughout Russia that this governor-general would be selected because of his strong desire to transfer the Imperial capital of Russia from Saint Petersburg back to Moscow. That act was to symbolize the return home to the old Muscovite political ideals. In order to accomplish his aim, it was considered progressive to rid the capital of its undesired occupants. Jewish residents numbered about thirty thousand. They became undesirables because of their religious preference, customs, distinct costumes, and business acumen. Their financial independence had earned them the name "Jewish capitalists." Moscow's burgomaster, Alexeyev, described by the townspeople as an ignorant merchant with an eye for graft and illegal transactions, anxiously embraced the opportunity to expel his Jewish competitors. Owing Jewish banker Lazarus Polakov a large sum of money, Alexeyev was eager in his efforts to expel the Jews from Moscow. He encouraged the forming of a council with the benign consent of the Holy Synod, Pobyedonostev, and an inquisition was initiated.

The first news of the expulsion proclamation reached Jewish ears during the first day of Passover services. While the worshippers thronged the synagogues for blessings, they received the accursed news. The terrifying tidings was whispered among congregants who could now only pray more fervently or begin to wonder if God had forsaken them. It was March 29, 1891, and the imperial ukase had proclaimed the long-feared expulsion of Jews from the reestablished capital at Moscow. This horrible edict was published, and its date of imperial order was March 28, one day less for the deportees to prepare for their departure. Following that discomforting edict was another ukase the next day. It demanded preparation for acceptance of relocation assignments to designated areas, and immediate departure. The first persons affected were illegal and semi-legal Jews residing in the suburbs or Moscow proper. They were promptly raided by the Cossack general Yurkovski, police commissioner-in-chief, who attacked by night. His target population was in Zaryadye, where most illegal Jews resided in Glebov yard, a former Moscow ghetto.

Policemen and firemen surrounded the houses while the disrobed and pajama-clad Jews were awakened and hauled off to the police stations. Women and children were spared. Everyone was kept in unsanitary prison cells for a day or more until they had signed a pledge promising to leave the city at once. Other victims were taken to an edge of the city in prison vehicles or patrol wagons commonly used for criminals. Many families hid themselves in whorehouses, cemeteries, and other places away from their homes. These unfortunate souls feared mistreatment and arrest by the police. Others walked or rode all night. The cold Russian weather was just as insidious as the pursuers, it did not let up. Purging continued for a month before Grand Duke Sergius made his grand entry into Moscow.

The Duke was soon followed by the Tzar, who passed through his capital on his way to the Crimea. A Jewish soldier petitioned the Tzar for recognition as a veteran of foreign wars. He received a prompt and unexpected reply. It was an order demanding his immediate arrest and deportation.

Tzar Alexander II issued special considerations for privileged Jews under the ukase of 1859 to 1865. That order permitted them to live outside the "Pale Settlement." It was not long before they were sought out and monitored by jealous members of the secret police. By February 1891, the governor of Saint Petersburg began examining their status to determine what artisan or commercial activities they

pursued. When April came around, it was learned that the first wave
of expelled Moscovites had reached the shores of Berlin, Paris, and
London. Teletypes and newspapers related the plight of the Jews who
had contributed much to Russia's commercial and financial development.

It was even mentioned that Peter Shafirov—a Jew—had been Vice
Chancellor under Peter the Great when Russia was one of the most
backward countries in the eighteenth century.[72] His and other contributions were ignored, however, until Alphonse de Rothschild, head
of the outstanding financial firm of Paris, refused to control or consent toward a floating loan of a half billion francs transacted by Russia
at the time. Rothschild's protest, through financial pressure, caused
great concern. It came when France and Russia were shuttling diplo-
mats in preparation for celebration of a long-sought Franco-Russian
alliance.

News of the Jewish expulsion from Moscow also reached the ears
of an American with a Jewish-sounding name. William Henry
Harrison (1773–1841), the ninth president of the United States. In a
message to Congress, the President expressed concern for the harsh
treatment of "the Hebrews in Russia," and the "probable effects of the
Russian expulsions upon America."[73] The Congress of the United
States reacted in a forceful resolution sent to the Tzar.

Russia's Jew-hating authorities were up in arms. They condemned the foreign Jewish financiers for using devious methods of
economic pressure. Anyhow, as a result pogroms were discontinued
for some time, and expulsions were temporarily discontinued.

On September 29, 1891, there was an attack on Jewish merchants
in the City of Starodub. Russian merchants had been honing their
hatred for Jewish competitors and longing for an opportunity to slash
their Yiddish success. Gladkov, a Russian politician who hated foreigners, had a law decreed banning business on Sundays and
Christian holidays. His ordinance was intended to ruin Jewish merchants who would have to close their shops on the numerous Greek
Orthodox holidays, including Sundays, as well as their own Jewish
Orthodox holidays, holy days, and Sabbath. The Jews appealed to
Governor Chernigov who agreed to let their stores remain open from
noon until six o'clock on Christian holidays. His decision kept the
Jewish merchants from remaining closed twice as many days as their
competitors, but it upset the agitators and they reacted with force.

On a Sunday, a day before Yom Kippur, the Jews opened up for
the few hours permitted. They were quickly set upon by a paid mob.
Looting and destruction began. Some Jews quickly closed their doors.
The action moved to the homes of the Jews. Furniture was destroyed,
mattresses torn open in search of hidden loot, and premises set afire
after being vandalized. Losses were said to have run into many mil-

lions. With this unexpected event on kol-nidre, the eve of Yom Kippur, it was impossible for Jews to dare attend synagogues on their highest Holy Day. Many helpless victims spent the night in a field outside of the city where they shivered and watched their businesses and homes shoot up in flames like undesired fireworks.

Those acts of purposeful evil gave the Russian government a black eye, and it tried to save face. They played down the attacks by allowing it as little publicity as possible. Then, in a short while, Russia began transactions with Argentina through a German Jewish millionaire philanthropist, Baron Maurice Hirsch, for gradual transfer of three million Jews to that Latin American country.

Hirsch's millions of dollars fell into the hands of those who encouraged Jewish schools in Galicia, Poland, through the Austrian government. In March 1891, Hirsch began to purchase land in Argentina. It was a good investment for at the same time Jews were hurriedly emigrating from Russia to North and South America, as well as to Palestine. Hirsch sent an Englishman, Arnold White, to Saint Petersburg as his representative. White was a member of the British Parliament. He strongly disliked foreign emigration to England where those barren isles could hardly provide enough employment for their own inhabitants. In transacting the migration, certain Russian officials derided the Jews, referring to them as thieves, usurpers, and parasites. Hirsch's proposal for emigration of three million Jews was discussed with the Russian Minister of the Interior and other officials. Upon his return to London, after having visited Jews in Moscow, Kiev, Berychev, Odessa, and Kherson, and agricultural colonies in South Russia, Hirsch reported Russian prospects fit for undertaking agricultural responsibilities in the land of the Pampas. After matters were discussed with Kirsch at great length, White was sent back to Russia to organize the Jewish transfer of 3,250,000 Jews in lots of 25,000. When all preparations were concluded, and Jews were uprooted with some voluntarily hurrying to Berlin, Hamburg, Antwerp, and London pleading to be sent to the United States or Argentina, the huge sums of money previously discussed became a mere trifle. After this reduction of funds, only 2,500 of the suggested 25,000 refugees actually left Russia during that first year. Argentina received approximately six thousand Jews between 1892 and 1894. Most of the others were discovered heading for Canada and the United States.

On October 20, 1894, Alexander III (1845–1894) died. He had been in power from the time of his father's assassination in 1881. Alexander's limited intelligence and education made him one of the most repressive human forces of the Russian enlightenment. He increased police powers, tightened control on education, subjected national minorities to russification and persecuted all religious groups, especially the group called Zhyds. While the Tzar's cortege was carried to Saint Petersburg on a train to Yalta, Jewish refugees from Yalta were escorted on a nearby track taking them toward the area of relocation designated for them as the Pale Settlement. Alexander III was succeeded by his son, Nicholas II, who continued his policies and failed to a great extent because, like his father, he did not obtain knowledge of fundamental issues affecting or benefiting his national structure. Branches of his Russian economy, their composition, and sources were not properly studied.

Nicholas II did not learn the depth and intricacies of economic integration and interaction between the Jews and their social environment at the local and countrywide level. He yielded to ethnic discrimination, religious persecution, and xenophobia; three malignant diseases that gnaw out a country's heart, even if the death is slow in coming. Nicholas II failed to be a great Tzar like Peter the Great. He was more successful than Peter, however, in becoming the Tzar of Russia.

JEWS IN GERMANY UNDER THE GERMANS

Hendrik William Van Loon (1882–1944) stated the following remarks about Hitler's superhuman race and its supposedly Nordic origin, "At an unknown date, the Germanic tribes had left their old home in Asia." He also made it quite clear how during that era, "the noble torch of learning and art which had illuminated the world of the Egyptians and Greeks and the Romans was burning very low." Loon did not mention the Greeks at this time, but they too came out of Asia around 3000 B.C.

When the small tribe of Germanic shepherds left their homes along the River Danube, it is said that they "did not amount to very much, were very ill-mannered, and lived like pigs."[74] They even "threw the bodies of their enemies to their dogs." This Germanic backwardness existed after the Egyptian pyramids were already over a thousand years old. And at that time African civilization had reached its peak in some parts of Africa and was beggining to experience decline.

The Germanic tribes were said to have also had "very little respect for other people's rights, and they killed natives of the Greek peninsula." These people called themselves "Helenes after Hellen, the son of Deucalion and Pyrrha."

About 1000 B.C., these bellicose tribes began migrating from northern Europe to the region now called Germany. They roamed from place to place, farming and hunting. Around 100 B.C.E., these tribes moved south to the Rhine and Danube Rivers, along the border of Rome.

The Romans called this tribal group Germani. But there were Teutons, Cimbri, Franks, Goths, and Vandals among them. Their great ethnic complex became a basic stock for the modern people of Sweden, Norway, Denmark, Iceland, Germany, Austria, Switzerland, Northern Italy, the Netherlands, Belgium, Luxembourg, North and Central France, Lowland Scotland, and England. The Germans divided into many people by the seventh century B.C.E. A Greek navigator first saw them in Norway and Jutland in the fourth century B.C.E.

The Germani historical recognition began with the Romans recording them in the first century B.C.E. In A.D. 9, Rome tried to conquer Germania or Germany, but the warlike tribes crushed the Romans.

the Teutons and Cimbri were the first Germanic tribes to be historically classified. They joined their neighbors called Ambrones. It was at this point that they wandered through Europe and ended up giving the world a group of Teutonic languages, including Scandinavian and Germanic tongues, Dutch and Flemish of Belgium and the Netherlands.

The Teutons and their German counterparts were said to have run around England in half-naked clans. They struck their women with clubs and raped them to consummate conjugal unity or marriage. The brides were usually stolen from another tribe with more or better-looking women. The Romans are credited with having civilized the Teutons. The Romans gave them their alphabet. The English had no written form of phonetic significance. They used ideographic characters called runes. Teutonic history was transmitted orally. Their history was not written like that of the Jews even during migration.

JEWISH IMMIGRATION

In much later years, Maximilian I took the title of Roman Emperor-elect (1493–1519). At that time, European Jewry was ahead of other religious denominations. Palestinian, Polish, and Russian Jews followed the esoteric studies with mysteriousness.

When the Jews arrived in Germany they did not call themselves Semitic. They called themselves, after hurried acculturation, Hebrews. And in some cases, they called themselves Germans, and practiced more German mannerisms than the Germans themselves. The only time the word Semitic was used was at times of persecution. But the German and Italian Jews found themselves restricted by the European impediment called ghetto, traced to the Hebrew word get meaning divorce.[75] For several hundred years the Church had been trying to keep Jews separated from Christians.

The Lateran Councils of 1179 and 1215 decided to segregate Jews from Gentiles, and the custom was continued sometimes more and at other times less. "Il geto" became the walled-in residential and restricted area specifically designated for Jews in Venice in 1517. The idea came from Spain and Portugal and later became popular in Germany. The term ghetto, as used by the Germans was not limited to the areas in which Jews lived.

The term when used by the Germans also applied to the entire "Jewish Question." The Third Reich and its power Wehrmacht considered the Jewish people with a vigorous religious and cultural life a threat from which Germans had to be protected. The Reich considered that the determination of these people to survive and to achieve despite obstacles placed before them because of their maintenance of a Jewish identity was most menacing. They had to have some ulterior motive. That motive, the Germans believed, was world domination through economic control. Apart from the fundamental preoccupation, the Jews were identified as a Jewish Problem because they identified with a foreign state which did not exist visibly at the time.

The Nazis kept hearing the Jews pray "Jerusalem next year. I hope to awaken in Jerusalem tomorrow," and so on. They felt that the Jews had a separate alliance. They seemed to be a part of Germany, but also separate. The Jews were therefore considered a threat to the economic, political and sociocultural future of the established Third Reich.

Hitler became Chancellor of Germany in 1933. He succeeded semi-senile Paul Von Hindenburg (1847–1934). Hindenburg and Ludendorf had jointly ruled Germany, and overrun countries as Hitler did when he came to power. When Hindenburg was sure of *Deutschland uber alles* (Germany over all) he moved against France in World War I. But America and Britain helped to stop Hindenburg in accord with the Treaty of Versailles. Hindenburg was not tried when his co-ruler Ludendorf resigned in 1918. And the special German court never tried or attempted to indict him as a war criminal for his daring acts in World War I. Hindenburg consequently lived to become the figurehead who gave Hitler the keys to the German Reich.

Hitler did not hesitate to start preparations for World War II. Along with Hitler were the German nationalists, Alfred Hugenberg and Franz von Papen, who created the Nazi dictatorship. The new German war, political and propaganda machines were built on German illusion of a master race based on Aryanism. This pseudo-linguistic term or label, like some others, was a part of the Nazi dictatorship propaganda weaponry. It gained popular use as the dictatorship gathered momentum. It was used against the Jews like white is used against people of color, Semite is used against Palestinians, and the "blond-Aryan" is used against others.[76]

The Nazis began to build their anti-Jewish campaign step by step. By April 1, 1933, the S.A. Storm Troopers of the struggle for power promoted a boycott against Jews throughout Germany. After no objections were heard from within or without Germany, the Nazis' Reichstag passed the "Law for the Restoration of a Professional Civil Service" ousting Jews and rehiring Germans. It was now April 7, 1933, and protests had still not been forthcoming from any of the super powers. England was trying to appease the Nazis by sending Neville Chamberlain to seek concessions from them with his umbrella, and the United States was busy cornering world markets to ease her depressed economy. The Nazi Civil Service law restored positions to Germans and forced non-Aryan civil servants to retire early. Many Jews still did not believe that they were considered non-whites. They stayed on in Germany.

Hitler noticed no rebukes from public opinion polls and grabbed the opportunity to hurriedly enforce accepted and ratified Nurenburg Laws. Just as in the Middle Ages, Jews were again banned from marrying Gentiles, having sexual relations with them, voting as citizens, and holding government positions. Almost a million persons were deprived of their civil rights. Professional people lost their professorships, medical, dental, and legal practices, and scientific right to research and declare findings. Jewish intellectuals were stagnated.

By 1937 over one hundred and eighteen thousand Jews had left the fatherland. These Jews had managed to leave while the world was romancing Hitler and his Nazi regime as they made money from the World Olympic Games of 1936.

Between 1933 and 1942 the Nazis established many agencies to deal with the Jewish Problem. There were libraries, institutes, information, and publishing centers geared toward indoctrination. Leaflets were distributed, pamphlets were printed and disseminated, posters were made and posted to alert the Greater German public to the invisible menace. The Germans were to deal with this Jewish menace. The Nazis knew that the original Hebrew was not Teutonic, Germanic, Aryan, or the like. Therefore, to prove Jewish inferiority, and that of persons who spoke and read Hebrew, a Teutonic superman was created.

This inferiorization process, through the imagined superiorization of Aryans, was a psychological ambivalence of powerful design. It made the Germans feel that they had been exploited and deprived of official and professional practice by an inferior people, in their own fatherland. But the Jews did nothing to prove that Africa had civilization and culture which the Greeks copied and exported to Europe. They still hung onto their German nationality, displayed their medals won helping Germany in World War I and in peacetime. They fell easy prey to the Nazis. They actually helped by propagandizing blondness, and participating in that process. They married non-Jews who were supposed to be blond. But paleness was not enough for Hitler's *Judenrein* (freedom from, or cleansing of Jews).

"The Nazis built upon the past. They did not begin a development of anti-Semitism; they completed it." The Nazis banned intermarriages of Germans and Jews, punishing the Germans even in Poland. They were wise to the Jewish solution, and decided to keep them apart from the blondes. Jews could not sell or rent real estate, hire Gentile servants, hold public office, eat with Christians, or go about with a Star of David patch on their garments.

The Germans had lost World War I and signed the humiliating Treaty of Versailles in 1919. By April 1920, they had formed the Nazi Party. By 1923 dissatisfaction with the costly inflation and economic depression in the fatherland, the Germans had become victims of depression. Many people were unemployed and someone had to be blamed. Some Jews were well off and able to loan money. When their German and other clients could not repay their loans, the collateral was confiscated. Properties were sold, jewelry and other valuables were impounded, or kept outright. By 1933 the Nazis began blaming the Jews for Nazi insufficiency. The Jews were even blamed for Germany's defeat in World War I.

There were 525,000 Jews in Germany at the rise of the Nazi regime in 1933. At the time the Nazis had laid the groundwork for decreeing all Jews "foreigners and uninvited guests of the nation."[77] All Jews who had emigrated to Germany since 1914 were to be expelled. The expulsion became progressive. Jews were supposed to add the surnames "Israel" or "Sarah" to their regular names. They were not allowed to play Bach, Beethoven, or Mozart. Jews could not shop in certain pharmacies, butcher shops, bakeries, and dairies, which had signs on their doors or windows stating "Jews not admitted." They could not stay in hotels, even overnight, because signs read, "Jews strictly forbidden in this town." Some signs read "Jews enter this place at their own risk."

In 1938 Jews of Germany began sharing their misfortunes with their coreligionists elsewhere. No one had attempted to crush Hitler, so he took Austria and Czechoslovakia that year. By September 1, 1939, the Treaty of Versailles which had made Gdansk or Danzig free from Prussian rule was not enforced by the Allies. Hitler stepped in and took Danzig. Nazi terror was spreading so rapidly that between 1933 and 1939, more than fifty thousand Jews had committed suicide.

In the meantime, the deportation of Jews increased between 1939 and 1941 to these invaded countries. The Sudetes were taken from Poland. These mountain ranges of the Sudetenland were annexed to Germany while the people were Germanized. After Nazi propaganda had been well disseminated abroad, the general approval of the Nurenburg Law for the Protection of the State was enforced. German blood and German honor were to be rigidly protected against Jews.

To fulfill this measure a most heinous crime was committed on October 28, 1938. While the allied governments were still trying to avoid World War II, the Polish government invalidated all passports of Polish nationals abroad. The Nazis must have anticipated this act because the Gestapo, German State Police, immediately began deporting from Germany Jews of Polish nationality or origin. The Gestapo arrested Polish Jews, packed them into trains and trucks which carried them to the Polish border and dumped them there. When the Jewish refugees alighted from the trains and trucks, they were chased across the Polish fields toward the towns.

On November 20, 1938, about a month later, the Nazis received an excuse for wholesale abuse of Jews. A young Jewish fellow named Hershel Gryszpan assassinated Nazi official Ernst von Rath in Paris. Hershel's parents had been expelled from Germany with the October victims. The Nazis took advantage of Hershel's impetuosity. They initiated a real pogrom. This massacre lasted only twenty-four hours, but it took its toll. Although it was shorter than the old pogroms, hundreds of synagogues went up in flames, many Jewish homes were raided and their occupants abused before being led to concentration camps. Businesses were looted, destroyed, and set afire. To top it off, the German Government demanded a collective fine of one billion marks from the Jewish community.

Edward Crankshaw declares that a plan was soon devised by a Nazi officer named Reinhard Heydrich to avenge the assassination of Von Rath. A police action was disguised as a popular riot aggravated by Jews. That pogrom was named the Crystal Night, or *Kristallnacht*. Its memories left many German Jews anxious to forget their hopes of survival in Deutschland. Some managed to escape. They amounted to 290,000 from 1933 to 1939. But a larger number was forced to remain in their fatherland.

In September 1939, World War II progressed. Nazi tanks, their air force with lightning, or *blitzkrieg*, and paratroopers added Denmark and Norway to the countries overrun by Hitler. The Polish Jews numbering three-and-a-half million found themselves trapped.

The Austrian annexation witnessed three thousand suicides in Vienna alone within two months. Now Holland had fallen to the Nazis. Belgium followed with France close behind. All of these territories had sheltered Jews. The Nazis told them there was a Jewish Problem subject to certain laws imposed by the Third Reich. The solution to this problem involved putting Jews in ghettos, assigning them to forced labor camps and factories, freezing their bank accounts, and turning over their businesses and factories to Aryans. Slavs, Gypsies, and other undesirables in occupied countries were also subject to these laws.

Heinrich Himmler appointed Reinhard Heydrich the chief of the

Gestapo. Implementation of the Jewish elimination policy was received from the commanding officer. The orders included deportations to the Lublin reservation in southeastern Poland, or to Madagascar. There was a plan to transport undesirables to the Madagascar Plan.

Adolf Eichmann was chief of the Gestapo's Jewish Section. He was in charge of transportation. At first, Eichmann pretended to be complying with Jewish requests to be transferred to ghetto areas of their choice. But he ended up sending them to concentration camps instead, with most of them going to extermination camps. However, by 1940 seventy-eight thousand Jewish deportees had been relocated in the Lublin district, on top of the forty thousand residents already there.

Heydrich was deeply committed to deportation and acquisition of bribes in immense sums passed from rich Jews into Gestapo hands. Heydrich was therefore slow in activating the Action Groups to murder Czechs en masse. He simply wanted to maintain the fear established by the Gestapo in the killing of intellectuals and leaders. But Hitler by then had decided on the "Final Solution,"[78] the murder of Jews.

By the time the war had begun with Russia, the Madagascar Plan had been abandoned. There was no room for a mass concentration camp on that overcrowded island. As a result, between June and October 1941, Group Commander S.S. Major General Stahlecker signed a document claiming elimination for 167 Jews, 4,000 Communists, and 748 lunatics. The lunatics were described as either Jews or Gentiles, but there were retarded and physically handicapped persons among them.

Heydrich was experienced in handling Jews. He had notified the Gestapo of what was to take place on *Kristallnacht*. Mueller was to execute the order, while Heydrich dined nearby. The plan was so well executed that Heydrich even saw one of the nearby synagogues go up in flames while he dined. But Heydrich did not know how well Mueller enjoyed arson. This subaltern ordered underlings to do more than was expected of them. Heydrich was therefore able to report to Goering on November 11, 1939 that 20,000 Jewish persons were arrested, 191 synagogues, and 171 apartment houses burned to the ground, while 815 shops were looted and destroyed. The report was revised on the following day. It read, "Thirty-six Jews had been killed" along with seven thousand five hundred more.

The ordinances of September 25, and December 18, 1939 had proclaimed all Jews between fourteen and sixty years of age to be forced to labor for the benefit of the fatherland. Those laws were not enforced in 1941. There were fifty-one labor camps installed in the District of Lublin alone. The largest camp was located in Belzec. In these camps, were boys of ten and old men of seventy years of age, weakened by hunger, incessant work, and insults between beatings which caused them to work until they dropped dead. Most of the workers considered that the better or harder they worked, the greater would be their chances for survival. But they were duped.

Despite the sufferings in the labor camps and other places of employment, a "life permit" was a certificate which enabled the bread-winner, usually the father, to obtain a supposed guarantee of the safety of his wife and children. This certificate was only given to work-ers. The holder of a "life permit" could also get wind of the new decrees ordering transportation to unknown destinations.

Ohlendorf testified at the Nurenburg trials that between June 1941 and June 1942, ninety thousand people had been "liquidated" by the Eisatzkommandos not far from Russia. The invasion of Russia, on June 22, 1941, caused the Final Solution to become top priority. Jews and other Russian victims of war were to be eliminated. The decision for implementation of the Final Solution was decided at the Wansee Conference in January 1942. Jews were collected on a daily basis and transported to death camps. The Action Groups were in charge of "liquidations because famine was threatening and there was a great housing shortage."[79]

In the same year, 1942, there was similar activity in Paris. There was a case of 4,051 Jewish children seized with their parents during the unforgettable Paris roundup of July. Approximately seven thou-sand children and adults were crowded into the uncomfortable spaces of the Velodróme d'Hiver. They were given no food for five days, and the only water available came from a single street hydrant. There were ten toilets to service the seven thousand souls. Many of the women were pregnant; and quite a few of them gave birth. Some of the peo-ple screamed until they lost their minds, and thirty of them died of fear, cardiac arrests and the like. In the meantime, S.S. Captain Roethke and Knochen discussed the fate of the children without urgency. The Vichy officials were involved. So on the fifth day the mothers were taken away and their children left behind. While the mothers were on their way to the gas chambers on the other side of Europe, D'Arquier, the Vichy chief officer, argued that the children should be spared and sent to French orphanages. But Knochen and Roethke insisted that the children should also be eliminated. The only obstacle to the solution was transportation. Before the officials could begin to worry, word came from the chief of the Gestapo's Jewish Section in charge of transportation. He was none other than Adolf Eichmann. Eichmann cabled from Berlin saying that enough transportation had been arranged for the 4,051 children to be brought to Auschwitz. The children were dragged away from their parents, and placed in the care of other sick children and old detainees hardly able to care for themselves. They were all carted off to the transit camp at Drancy, where the French railhead to Auschwitz was located. From Drancy, the victims were hauled off to their deaths; three hundred to four hundred at a time.

Jews were transported to their places of execution, which was usually an anti-tank ditch dug for their burial or a gas truck. They were transported to their execution in trucks, trains and gas vans. The gas vans had arrived in 1942 because Knochen, Ohlendorf, and other heads had decided on more expeditiously humane methods of elimination.

In explaining the use of death vans Ohlendorf said, "The general concept was," through the mechanical construction, that "when the motor was started up, gasses were conducted into the van, causing death in ten to fifteen minutes." After that, said Ohlendorf at his trial, "The vans were loaded with the victims and driven to the place of burial." This site was usually the same place where the mass executions were carried out.[80] At the mass execution sites, dug near the railroad tracks, "certain functions of the body had taken place, leaving the corpses lying in filth." The trip by train lasted several days, and the victims were obviously too weak to contain themselves when evidence pointed to imminent death. The experience of anxiety and fear of the unknown is also said to have caused many victims severe mental shock. There was no food given to the human cargo during the trip. There was overcrowding, with no sanitary facilities for passengers destined to be executed en masse. Whenever the victims showed resistance or panic, the Commandos were forced to restore order violently. In order to carry out the liquidation in an orderly fashion it was necessary, for example, to resort to beatings. The Germans used rifle butts, officers' dog whips, and their fists.

Auschwitz, Belsec, Treblinka, Wolzek, and other extermination centers were infamous. But the territory of Slutzk, in White Russia, saw German police officers and Lithuanian partisans drag Jews and other people out of their homes, herd them together and shoot them on the streets. The police looted Jewish and Gentile homes. "Anything of use, such as boots, leather, cloth, gold, and other valuables were taken away." Watches were torn off people's wrists, and rings pulled off their fingers in the most brutal manner, right on the streets. But there was still more bestial treatment awaiting these poor souls in the concentration camps.

EXTERMINATION EXPEDITIONS

At the beginning of the Nazi planning, there had been about fifty concentration camps. Along with those mentioned before, there was Dachau near Munich, Buchenwald near Weimar, and Sachsenhausen near Berlin. By 1942, the Einsatzgruppen determined that there were more Jews than they could kill by just shooting them. At Auschwitz the governor said to his staff, "We cannot shoot or poison three and a half million Jews." Then he added, "but we shall nevertheless be able to take measures which will lead somehow to their annihilation." The German word was Vernachtungslager, or extermination. The camps were originally planned for the elimination and imprisonment of anti-Nazi or anti-Hitler dissidents and Communists until the Third Reich decided to rid the Polish government of Jews. However, once Russia had been invaded along with other countries of large Jewish populations, Heydrich had to appoint Goblocnik to liquidate Polish Jews or overextend himself. So he cowardly ordered liquidation of Polish Jews beginning in 1939. To expedite matters, crematories were built at Auschwitz.

Here the famous Dr. Joseph Mengele performed his experiments with human guinea pigs he carefully selected. As a result, he was nicknamed the "Selector." Mengele is said in literature of the Holocaust to have ordered a sign made which ordered the lining up of new arrivals. There were two lines formed. One on the left was for the crippled, the aged, and women with children under fourteen. The other line on the right side was for able-bodied men and women fit to work or serve where needed. The sick, disabled, too old to walk, and those considered off-balance mentally were packed into Red Cross vans. When the trains pulled away from Auschwitz, the left column fell in step behind them—five abreast—as they departed. S.S. guards were in the lead, on the sides and rear of the Jews. The right column would remain for a while at Auschwitz. In a few moments, the Jewish displaced persons who left in the vans, cars or trucks, as well as those who marched through the gates, would all begin to get a whiff of the stench coming from the crematorium. Once inside the gates it became obvious that they were trapped and doomed to die.

Goebbels wrote in his diary, on March 27, 1942, that "Beginning with Lublin, the Jews in the General Government are now being evacuated eastward." He also wrote: "The procedure is pretty barbaric and is not to be described here more definitely." Goebbels also stated that much of his satisfaction as an official came from learning that "Not much will remain of the Jews. About sixty percent of them will have to be liquidated." Goebbels even served notice that only about forty percent could be used for forced labor. That forty percent came from the right hand column set aside for Dr. Mengele after each overcrowded train arrival. It was stated at Nurenburg that the doctor "was present at the arrival of every train."

ADMINISTRATION

Inside the concentration camps and liquidation centers, there were S.S. and S.A. guards.[81] At the top of them stood Rudolf Hess, whom

Himmler had promoted to Commandant at Auschwitz—the largest extermination camp. Under the Nazi echelons were the elders, camp clerks, chiefs of labor statistics and distribution records, and the kapos (heads). Some elders were used as camp clerks. The chiefs of labor statistics separated the blocks in the camps of *stalags* (barracks), with their wooden bunks about twenty-eight inches between each tier. One inmate was stacked beside and above the other in a twenty-four-inch width of sleeping space. Each block was supervised by an elder chosen from among the inmates. The block clerks kept records for the elders who could not retain all events and decrees. Then, the kapos were labor enforcers under the kapo-in-chief, who was usually a German prisoner serving time for a non-political offense. As the camp population increased, certain Jews were also made kapos.[82] The kapos were generally chosen by the Germans. He had to be a selfish person, ready to act like his masters and willing to brutalize his fellow prisoners in order to be considered capable of his dirty job. After being bossy and sometimes bestial for three or four months, the kapo's reward was sudden death. He was sent to the crematorium and replaced by another short-term kapo. Nevertheless, this short-lived position had to be filled.

Hess had a remarkable record at Auschwitz, but he was outdone by S.S. Major Christian Wirth who was given credit for having the best record of gassings. Wirth was camp commander at Treblinka. His rank was *Kriminal Kommisar*. As Chief of the death camps organization in Poland, and administrator of Treblinka, Wirth's technique for success was using peer pressure. He gave Jews authority over their fellow Jews and vested interest in the spoils. Jews handled the gassing and were allowed to plunder the corpses, especially for gold from their teeth. Some Jewish trustees became rich quickly. Not knowing how long they might live, these trustees squandered their loot in festivals. An S.S. witness at Nurenburg told an amazing tale of a wedding near Lublin. the witness related how Wirth's special Jewish *Kommandos* gave a most lavish banquet at a reception given with money taken from the corpses of their fellow Jews.

RESISTANCE

While some Jews conformed or adjusted to their circumstances, others resisted and planned open revolt. As early as 1942, Mordecai Anielewicz explored the idea of organized resistance. The twenty-three-year old youth, born in Warsaw during 1919, undertook various missions for the Jewish underground resistance movement. By January 1943, Mordecai had assumed command of a Jewish uprising and made resistance a stern reality. By May 8, 1943, four of his young friends joined him in wiring the bunker office of the German General Staff where the staff died. Anielewicz and eighty other underground fighters were later trapped. The Germans tossed grenades into their bunkers and demolished the youth.

On August 1, 1943, the German Security Police and the S.S. warned the "Geto Yedies" through the *Ghetto News* that many Jews had been arrested with saboteurs or brigadiers among them. The Jews were reminded that their representative had promised to discourage armed protest or other demonstrations of discontent. Therefore, all Jews were to be collectively held responsible for any disobedience. The news also stated, "it is your duty to yourself and to the ghetto to inform German authorities of any suspicious actions which might endanger the lives of the entire ghetto population, and the ghetto itself."

With the death toll reaching more than 1,750,000 Jews killed in two years, the area of Majdanek was credited with having delivered up more than one and a half million of them. The death camps served their purpose, but shootings were still carried out in Lithuania, Latvia, White Russia, and Ukraina. The policemen of these cities collaborated with the Germans as auxiliaries in the mass slaughtering of Jews. One distressing scene reported is the shooting of sixty thousand Jews on an island in the Dvina near Riga. Twenty thousand Jewish persons were also shot in Lutsk, thirty-two thousand in Sarny, sixty thousand in Kiev and Dnepropetrovsk, with twenty-five thousand mowed down by machine-gun rapid-fire in Odessa. There was one case of unforgettable resistance which should have started earlier.

This case of historic defense took place in the Warsaw Ghetto. On July 22, 1942, all Jews of Warsaw wrestled with mental anguish when they were remanded to the death camps, regardless of sex or age. Since they were not allowed to venture out of the high concrete walls of the ghetto and its limited space, the Jews had been hibernating and dying of typhus and starvation. About forty-five hundred of these ghetto-restricted victims died from day to day. By September 1942, half of the population was dead. In April 1943, more Jews were to be moved in. The Jews rebelled against that unjustified abuse. The S.S. responded with artillery fire, heavily armed S.S. troops were reinforced by German and Polish policemen.

On April 18, *Kol nidre*, or Passover eve, saw the encounter of greatest amazement to the Nazis accustomed to having everyone afraid of them. The ghetto residents had been continually smuggling arms into the compound to await the confrontation. Everyone was prepared to meet the Nazis in the final confrontation. Men and women of all ages, boys and girls all wielded machine guns and homemade hand grenades. Tanks were forced to back up or stand back, and troops were forced to join them. The Nazis cowardly hid behind their tanks as shields and found themselves resisted until early May. At that time the repelled troops and police force which joined them finally succeeded in firebombing the ghetto. Underground forces hid in the basements and underground passages of buildings, but they were eventually flushed out. There were about twenty thousand huddled together in different blocks and sent off to death camps where they could no longer resist oppression and starvation.

The world had heard rumors about Nazi cruelty, but no one had imagined it to be as stark a reality as it was. When the Allied troops invaded German death camps and saw the crematoriums, gas chambers, and the emaciated condition of the victims, the world became aware. Only then was the gruesomeness of the criminal acts of the Nazi regime viewed at the level of inhumanity they reached. The bestiality of the Nazis was only comparable to the enormous inhumanity committed against Africans during slavery where more than three hundred million innocent people were deprived of their rights.

Another form of resistance was sought through correspondence. In 1930 Generalissimo Francisco Franco of Spain who had been friendly toward the Jews, invited them to return to Spain. Franco knew what was going to happen to Jews in Germany and tried to save as many as he could without endangering his relationship with Germany or exposing himself. He went a little further in one little-known incident. During the height of the Second World War, on January 8, 1944, Franco made a personal call to Hitler regarding Jewish prisoners held at Bergen-Belsen's concentration camp. Many of these Jews were Sephardics from Greece, and they were economically well off when they were arrested. Hitler responded to Franco by releasing 1,242 Jews who were sent to Spain.

The Spanish Constitution of 1869 was then made null and void, tolerance was proclaimed, and Jewish rights reinstituted through a new Constitution.

When the Bergen-Belsen Jews arrived, Franco met them in person at the Spanish border. They complained that the Germans had kept their properties and had confiscated their valuables. Franco made another call to Hitler. The German leader had their monies and transportable possessions sent to them.[83]

The New York Times of December 17, 1968, datelined Madrid showed that four-hundred and seventy-six years after King Ferdinand and good Queen Isabella had ordered Jews expelled from Spain in 1492, the Spanish government had now declared that the order was void. The Times showed that Franco, who continually helped Jews, was altruistic and could have been a Jew himself. In any case, Jewish persons can now reside in Spain legally without fear of being constitutionally deported. Jews can also own property. Many Jews still left for the Americas despite Franco's great assistance, and valuable offers.

NOTES

1. Susa or Shushan was the capital of Elam. The Elamites were a mighty black people of Persia, c. 2900 B.C.E. They conquered Babylon. In the Bible, Esther, the Hebrew, sought favor of King Ahaserus of Persia and Ethiopia. J.A. Rogers, *100 Amazing Facts About the Negro*, p. 4.
2. Phoenicians. People of Tunisia, descendants of Canaan; their relics show their Nubian neighbors on glassware. *The New Columbia Encyclopedia*, Columbia University Press, 1975. pp. 2435, 2711.
3. Nabateans. People of Arab origin who occupied Edom in the sixth century B.C.E. The Edomites were descendants of Esau, a red-skinned people. *Standard Jewish Encyclopedia*. pp. 1803-1806.
4. *Ibid.*
5. Gerard Israel and Jacques Lebar, *When Jerusalem Burned*, (New York: William Morrow & company, Inc. 1978), p. 23.
   Frances Cress Welsing., *The Isis Papers* (Chicago: Third World Press), 1991.
   Jose V. Malcioln. *How the Hebrews Became Jews*, (New york, Universal Brotherhood Press, 1978).
6. Elephantine. Ancient name of an island fortress on the Egyptian-Ethiopian border, on the Nile opposite Aswan c. 590 B.C.E. *The Standard Jewish Encyclopedia* (New York: Doubleday, Inc., 1959) pp. 556, 1938.
7. Christopher Wren, "A Rich Jewish Kingdom in Ancient Arabia," New York Times, July 6, 1980. p. 8-E.
8. George G.M. James, p. 21.
9. Koestler. *The Thirteenth Tribe* p. 151.
10. S.M. Dubnov. *History of the Jews in Russia and Poland*, vol. 1. (Philadelphia: The Jewish Publication Society of America, 1976), p. 43.
11. S.M. Dubnov, p. 43.
12. Solomon Grayzel. *A History of the Jews*, pp. 448-449.
13. S.M. Dubnov, p. 55.
14. S.M. Dubnov, p. 63.
15. Dr. Vladimir Bychakov—former professor of pathology at the University of Moscow, presently at Einstein College of Medicine in the United States—stated, "We [Jews] were easily identifiable because we were most of us darker than the Gentiles."
16. The correct Polish name is *Kazimierz*, meaning Casimir the Great, after whom the town was officially named.
17. *Shlakhta:* Big Shlakhta referred to magnates, owners of big estates and whole towns—members of the Polish Diets. Little Shlakhta: struggling squires seeking positions in civil and state services—subservient to the burghers and hateful to Jews.
18. *Yosko* is the popular Polish form of the Hebrew name Joseph.
19. Toward caution and defense against Jews.
20. Dubnov, p. 73.
21. Koestler, p. 20.
22. *Herem:* Hebrew meaning to ban, boycott, excommunicate.

23. Dubnov, p. 75.
24. *Kahal:* Hebrew. Congregation of Jews known as *kahal kadosh.* Holy Congregation among Ashkenazim. It is colloquially called kehillah or k:k: meaning Jewish community with rights to taxation and responsibility for organized Jewish communities in East Europe.
25. Dubnov, p. 75.
26. Dubnov, p. 75.
27. Dubnov, p. 79-80.
28. Dubnov, p. 86.
29. Ben-Jochannan, *Black Man of the Nile,* p. 200.
30. Israel Cohen. *History of Jews in Vilna* (Philadelphia, Pennsylvania, The Jewish Publication Society of America, 5704-1943), pp. 484-485.
31. How history repeats itself in diverse forms. Some Gentiles are now saying that Jews are now accused of controlling and monopolizing education in New York. One group of students referred to New York University as "Jew York University."
32. *Arendar* or *arendator* was derived from medieval Latin *arrendare* to rent. The Yiddish translation was abbreviated to *randor,* meaning a "village Jew."
33. Semen Dubnov: *History of the Jews in Russia and Poland 1916–1920.*
34. *Bahur.* Hebrew term for young man—used in the Bible to indicate a selected combatant. In rabbinic literature and the common vernacular, it referred to an unmarried male. In the Middle Ages, it meant an advanced yeshibah student: In Yiddish (*yeshiveh bokhur*).
35. George M. James, p. 127: Alexander gave him money to buy the large number of books to which his name has been attached; but at the same time fails to tell us when, where and from whom Aristotle bought the books.
36. Kiev. This city was captured by the Lithuanians in 1320, and remained, with the union of Lithuania and Poland as a part of the Polish Empire until 1654, when it was ceded to Muscovy along with the province of Little Russia.
37. Khlops. "The Poles looked upon the Russian populace as an inferior race, which belonged more to Asia than to Europe." Dubnov, p. 140.
38. *Hetman.* Derived from the German *Hauptmann,* a word meaning "chief" or "leading man."
39. The Jewish Defense League attacked a Black Panther Branch Office occupied by one man who gathered old clothing and distributed it to the poor people of Harlem, at 121st Street and Seventh Avenue. They fire-bombed the place and sprayed it with machine-gun fire while the policemen stood on rooftops with rifles protecting them in the late 1970s. This interpolation shows how oppressed often become oppressors.
40. *Lakhs.* A contemptuous word or nickname for a Pole, hence Polak or "Polack" in English.
*   Bogdan Chmielnicki (Polish) or Khmolnitsky (Ukranian) (1593-1657) Cossack leader. "In 1648 he headed the rising of the Cossacks and

Ukranians against Polish landowners, the Catholic clergy and the
Jews." *The Standard Jewish Encyclopedia:* Cecil Roth, B. Litt., M.A.,
Ph. D. Editor in Chief, Doubleday & Co. Garden City, NY. 1959.

41. S. M. Dubnov. *History of the Jews in Russia and Poland,* 1920.
42. Le couteau qui coup l'agneau coup le loup.
43. Schythians. A people who moved from Asia to southern Russia dur-
    ing the seventh and eighth centuries, B.C.E.
44. Hugh J. Schoenfield. *The Passover Plot* (New York: Bantam Books,
    Inc., 1967).
45. Hugh J. Schoenfield. *The Passover Plot* (New York: Bantam Books,
    Inc. 1967), 0. 132.
46. S. M. Dubnov, pp. 172–176.
47. *Haidamacks.* A word of uncertain origin meaning "rebel" or "rioter."
48. Ari. Isaac Ben Solomon was known as Ari, an abbreviation of his
    popular title, "Ashkenazi." He was born in Jerusalem (1534–1573),
    and was educated in Egypt. He was a Palestinian Kabbalist. He
    became famous because of his ascetic way of life and saintly pre-
    tenses known throughout Safed in 1570. His identifications of
    ancient graves in Galilee honored him with a sanctity which has
    continued among Orthodox Jews up to the present. *Standard Jewish
    Encyclopedia,* p. 1230.
49. The two names were not clearly distinguishable in Hebrew. The first
    name is Sydloweic in Polish, the site near Radom, the second is
    Siedice, not far from Warsaw.
50. Dubnov.
51. *Herem.* Hebrew excommunication.
52. *Bimah.* A dais or altar from which the Ashkenazim read the Torah.
53. *Matronitha.* A word coined, by the Turkish Sabbatians, from the
    Spanish word madrina, Godmother, or *madrona,* big mother. Most of
    the Turkish Jews were originally from Spain and spoke Judeo-
    Spanish or Ladino.
54. Kahal. (Hebrew). An Ashkenazi congregation, generally known as
    kahal kadosh (Holy Congregation) sometimes abbreviated as
    k.k.=*kehillah.* In Eastern Europe the term was applied to the orga-
    nized Jewish community members with autonomous rights and
    responsibilities for taxation. It was abandoned in the nineteenth
    century.
55. Edomite. They were a red hairy people from Edom (Idumea) in
    Southeast Palestine. They traditionally hated the Israelites descend-
    ed from Jacob with dark skin. The Edomites are said to be descen-
    dants of Esau who lost his birthright for "a mess of pottage" to his
    dark skinned brother, Jacob, whose name became Israel, father of
    the twelve tribes.
56. Baal-Shem. Master of the Name. Dubnov, pp. 223–224.
57. Dubnov.
58. *History of Jacob Joseph.* Considered "a clever allusion to the Hebrew
    text of Genesis 37."
59. Besht might have learned this axiom from Imhotep, the father of
    architecture and medicine, who said "Eat drink and be merry for

tomorrow we die!" He lived circa 2340 B.C.E. Yosef ben-Jochannan, *Black Man of the Nile* (New York: Alkebu-lan Books, 1970) p. 110.

60. Immanuel Kant. (1724–1804), German philosopher; author of *Critique of Pure Reason.* The critical philosophy sets forth the doctrine of *a priori* knowledge: man experiences the material world through sense perception, but its form is determined by the mind alone.

61. Dubnov, p. 247.

62. *Ukase.* Pronounced *ookaz* and meaning edict.

63. Berek or Berko. Polish form of the Jewish name Baer. *Yoselovich:* Polish for son of Yosel or Joseph.

64. Karaites. Jewish sect which rejected the Oral Law given to Moses, analyzed and interpreted by others. They originated in the eighth century in and around Persia where the disciplines of the Babylonian gaonate (spiritual leader) were rejected. They interpreted the Bible literally, and deduced their own interpretation of the Oral and Written laws.

* Synhedrin: Religious Executive Council for interpreting Jewish tenets and laws.

* Hebrew periodical Ha-Meassof ("The Collector") published in Berlin in the late 1700s.

65. Robert K. Massie. *Peter the Great: His Life and World* (New York: Ballantine Books—a division of Random House, 1980). In 1609, The Bacchanals of autumn reached a peak in the carnival before Lent. The Mock-synod marched in mock-solemn procession to honor the god Bacchus. Peter derived great pleasure from imitating the Churchmen by dressing his soldiers as bishops and priests of the Orthodox Church.

66. Massie, p. 760. Aleksandr Sergeevich Pushkin was the maternal grandson of a black man from Ethiopia named Ibrahim (or Abraham) Hannibal (1799–1838). Peter the Great made him General of Artillery. Pushkin wrote several novels and poems, some of which became operas, and a novel about his grandfather, Hannibal, titled, *The Negro of Peter the Great.*

67. *Ach, a tzore, a gzeire mit die razryaden.* "Alas! What misfortune and persecution there is in the assortment."

68. Hasidic women are prohibited from looking in mirrors and must avoid kissing any men other than their husbands; and they shave their heads to be unattractive to men. The Czar demanded the wedding night with the bride if he wanted her.

69. Dubnov, p. 149.

70. Massie, p. 390.

71. Massie, p. 384. "When Saint Petersburg was rising, Peter ordered a new road, fifteen hundred miles long, between the new city and the old capital of Moscow."
Massie, p. 603. "The iron will of a single man, the skills of hundreds of foreign architects and artisans, and the labor of hundreds of Russian workers created a city which admiring visitors later described as the 'Venice of the North' and the 'Babylon of the

Snows.' " In 1712, there was no decree issued on the subject, nevertheless, Saint Petersburg became capital of Russia. "Autocratic government centered on the Tzar and the Tzar preferred Saint Petersburg."

72. Massie, p. 387. Peter Shafirov became Russia's first Baron in 1710. His parents came from Smolensk near Poland. He spoke Western languages, including Latin, like his father who had been a translator. Shafirov's father had worked in the Russian Foreign Office after having converted to Orthodoxy.

73. Dubnov, pp. 408-410.

74. The first wave of settlers came by sea from Asia to Greece not later than 3000 B.C. The Greeks were Minoans, "a people still in a neolithic stone age stage, with tools made of stone and obsidian found on the island of Melos." *Encyclopaedia Britannica* (Chicago, 1966).
Hendrik Willem van Loon. *The Story of Mankind* (U.S.A. Liverright, 1962), p. 155.

75. Grayzel, p. 474.

76. Ariana or Aryana both used as the general name for the eastern provinces of the Persian Empire. Arianism was used in the Unitarian church. It came from Arius and Eusibius of Nicomedia. As a priest in Alexandria, Arius taught (ca.318) that Jesus was a supernatural creature, neither equal or eternal like god. Aryanism came from a Sanskrit noble term used to designate Indo-European language, race, family, principally Iranians and Hindus. It has nothing to do with "blonds." *The New Columbia Encyclopaedia.* "Our Glorious Popes," pp. 25-161.

77. Paul Hilberg. *The Destruction of European Jews* (Chicago: Quadrangle Books. 1961), p. 4.
Alexander S. Kohanski. *Jewish Life in Europe Between the Two Wars (1919-1939)* (New York: American Association for Jewish Education, 1968), pp. 51-53.

78. Edward Crankshaw. *Gestapo* (New York: Viking Press, Inc. 1957), p. 114.

79. Crankshaw, pp. 126-128.

80. Crankshaw, pp. 126-128. Note: Some of these people survived. When they arrived in Israel, years later, they became some of the biggest racists humanity had ever seen. They criticized Yemenite and Moroccan Jews and classified them as being of a backward, non-Germanic cultural background.

81. S.S. Abbreviation of the German word *Schutzstaffer*, meaning protection squads. S.A. Abbreviation for the German *Sturmabteilung*, meaning notorious "brown shirts" or Storm Troopers to fight Hitler's enemies.

82. Capo, in Italian, means head or head man. The Germans used the "K" for the "C."

83. Stephen Birmingham. *The Grandees.* Franco means Frank: a common Jewish name of Marrano possibility.

CHAPTER 11

THE JEWS
AMONG AMERICANS

It has been mentioned in more than one language that soon after the Mongolians and other Asians came through the Bering Straits to the land called America, the Africans came across them in their voyages. It has also been discovered, through studies and records, that after the Africans came the Celts.[1] About a thousand years later, the Spaniards, the Jews, and more Africans arrived.

There was Juan Garrido, a free man born in Angola, the first black to set foot in Puerto Rico with Ponce de Leon. He later went on to Mexico with Hernan Cortes and taught the Mexicans how to plant wheat. They had only known about corn. Luis Torres was a Jew who also came to the New World with the Spaniards. He tried to use Hebrew with the Indians who did not know Spanish, and thought they were a lost tribe of Israel. He was on Columbus' flagship.[2] Many persons, particularly from America pretend that blacks came here only as slaves.

The Spanish venture to the New World is said to have been financed by Queen Isabel la Católica and Fernando de Aragón, (their names in Spanish), (Isabella the Catholic and Ferdinand of Aragon). But H.P. Adams is quoted as having commented, "Not jewels, but Jews were the real financial basis of the first expedition of Columbus."[3]

It was also said that Don Abraham Senior of Castile—where Isabella ruled—invited Ferdinand to his house to court Isabella there. He was what is called an *alcahuete* in Spanish, and a *Shathan* in Hebrew, or a *Shatchen* in Yiddish, a matchmaker.

Along with the Jews of Portugal and Spain heading for America, there were other groups. These other Sephardic groups were from Turkey, where there were blacks, the Balkans, North Africa, and other parts of Asia Minor. Many of them spoke Spanish and some of their descendants still do. These Jewish refugees are said by Stephen Birmingham to have spent the first generation of their emigration struggling to emerge "from the ghetto of New York's Lower East Side." Once emergence was accomplished, the struggling Sephardim soon became "the ultimate snobs, who treated all Jews of lesser vintage with utter disdain."[4] But one of the real reasons for that Sephardic arrogance was not mentioned in Birmingham's work.[5] The Sephardim were almost racially ("Semitically") pure. They had not intermarried as much as they now do. They were dark-skinned, had less European syphilitic, hemophiliac, and other diseases from that continent. And they had no skin cancer problems due to sitting in the sun and over-baking themselves. They had natural color and did not look like ghosts when they had no rouge and lipstick or other artificial skin-coloring needed for pale faces. The Sephardim were also very much more acquainted with laws against uncleanliness. They did not cohabitate with their wives during the menstrual period. They heed-ed the law which causes the Falashas to isolate their women during the menstrual cycle and causes them to live in separate huts. That law among others made the Sephardim able to resent the Germanic and Khazaric Ashkenazim "not only [as] upstarts but usurpers," of the Hebrew religion.

Nevertheless, the German peasants were determined to dominate and rule Judaic circles as Germanic people are often viciously and brutally accustomed doing. So, the Ashkenazim set out to be, and are, the leaders of discriminating forces against the Sephardim and other descendants of Hebrews in Israel and throughout the Jewish-Zionist world. Their heartlessness can be felt throughout most Jewish institutions, and their policies. At Yeshiva University in New York City, where Sephardic celebrations were held with invitations extend-ed to the black Hebrew communities, the Ashkenazi community now makes them feel unwanted; and the members of this horrible group of bigots look at the blacks with disdain. Their attitudes have been of such racist magnitude that most black Hebrews now avoid them when possible, and Judaism as well.

The concept of *Zehut Avot*, otherwise known as ancestral merit, was highly regarded through inheritance among the Sephardim. It is now dying out, even in Ethiopia where the Falashas are continually starved to death, forced to amalgamate or be killed outright. One of the main causes for the death of ancestral merit in some areas is absorption through intermarriage. Low European morals, and prac-tices cause children to disregard their parents, moral traditional obli-gations, and common courtesies, which Westerners attribute to a generation gap, or some such nonsense. There are also more and more Christians intermarrying with Sephardim.

Since Spain and Portugal are near Africa, the cradle of civilization, any religious or culturally ethnic designs coming out of North
Africa or Canaan had to be more enlightened than whatever would
later come out of the Dark North. Furthermore, the Moors of
Mauritania, North Africa, and Arabia (who taught the Spaniards to
take baths, make soap, wear underwear, build libraries, beautiful
mosques and other artistic architecture, and use alchemy) had to be
more advanced than the Germanic Vandals, Goths, and Visigoths
who only destroyed Europe, and even defiled the Temple of Solomon
in Jerusalem. The Sephardim knew those historical and illuminat-
ing facts. That is why they were proud and discriminating. They also
knew that the Falashim, Moors, and Sephardim were and are the
Semites, if such animals do exist. Therefore, no pale-faced person
could be classified as Semitic unless that person was the product of
intermarriage or amalgamation. The Sephardim also remained aloof
from other Jews met in the New World because they heard the
Ashkenazim speak an unknown tongue. This linguistic variety was
described as a "heavy Teutonic language such as an ugly abominable
garble of German and Hebrew, called Yiddish, instead of 'musicao
lyrical' Spanish and Portuguese." It was even pointed out that the
Ashkenazim had "large awkward-looking noses." Their speech was
considered like their appearance. These Ashkenazim were considered
crude, lacking in refinement, and having to burn themselves in the
sun to obtain the olive-skinned Spanish face.   The Sephardic
Grandees also boasted that to make matters worse for their Germanic
tribesmen, they had come from places where it was a disgrace to be
a Jew. On the other hand, the Sephardim descended from lands
where for a while to be a Jew had been to be a knight in shining
armor, a duke, duchess or "the King's physician—the proudest thing
a man could be."[6] However, it was noted that some Sephardim were
so "dark-skinned that they became shoeshine men in Los Angeles."
    The Jews became involved in the American struggle for indepen-
dence from Great Britain to such an extent that one Haym Solomon
is said to have raised a loan for George Washington to pay his troops
and provide supplies for their maintenance. Presidents Jefferson,
Madison, and Monroe were all aided by this Jew named Solomon at
one time or another when they were short of cash. But this prominent citizen was not a Sephardi. He is recorded as being born in
Poland. Some historians claim that Haym Solomon's loans to the
United States government are questionable. It seems that he did not
document them, but made gentlemen's agreements instead of
demanding promissory notes. Nevertheless, Solomon shares a statue with George Washington and Robert Morris (1734–1806) in
Chicago.[7] Morris was a member of several committees in Congress,
and was particularly "important in obtaining munitions and other

supplies, and in borrowing money to finance George Washington's Army."

Another early American involved in the history of United States Treasury disbursement and stability was a West Indian from Nevis named Alexander Hamilton. He is mentioned as the witness to a case of "intermarriage" between a Sephardi and a Goyim or Gentile. Hamilton, himself a mulatto, is said to have noticed that despite the mother's sophistication and orthodoxym, her intolerance was surprisingly pronounced. This religious Sephardi mother was overwrought with grief when her son, David, married Margaret Evans of Philadelphia, barely six months after his sister had married to De Lancey, (later spelled Delancey), a member of a family of political leaders and merchants during colonial times. David's Jewish mother is said to have died "convinced that she had been a failure as a parent." Haym Solomon's wife was related to the deceased mother, who was a member of the Frank family. Quite a few of the Sephardim were accused of marrying Christians and breaking old Hebrew traditions in the New World. This marrying of whiter-skin partners was practiced all over the world where prejudice existed. It started among Jews in Russia and Spain after the Sicilians started it in Italy with the black Romans intermarrying.

BLACK INFERIORIZATION AND WHITE SUPERIORIZATION

The Moors lost their power and being black, were no longer popular. After the Moors had come out of Mauritania, North Africa, and Arabia, the Iberian became the Celtiberian from his admixture with Celts— a barbaric people who were familiar with iron. The Moors used the zero, made alcohol, used starch in their clothing—made from cassava roots from Africa—tried chemical experiments, built buildings of magnificence, and even taught the Spaniards to fight the bull. During their occupation of Spain, the Jews worked and enjoyed freedom. The Jews engaged in different trades, became master masons, tilers, and the like. In setting the tiles and finishing surfaces, the Jews made engravements of small Stars of David on their constructions or the projects on which they worked. Such symbols may be found in Alhambra, Sevilla, and Cordova. They are usually in corners and near the edges of walls or floors. The Courtyard of Lions in Granada shows those trademarks made by artisans of that era.

Since there are no lions in Spain, or in the lands of the Celts, Romans, Vandals, and other invaders of the Iberian Peninsula, we know that there was an African presence in Spain expressing ruling power and physical strength through that royal symbol. The only lions the Romans ever saw were taken from Africa to Rome for the savage gladiatorial contests between man and beast. So when the dark-skinned Moorish King Boabdil the Young Arab moved on foot toward the mounted Ferdinand of Spain and his bride Isabella to offer these pale-skinned monarchs the symbol of capitulation—after losing the last war and relinquishing seven hundred years of Moorish rule—the end had come for "Black Power."

It is reasonable to assume that after the end of Islamic rule in Spain, the Jews, Indians, Africans, and Asians would have members of their group emulating the conquerors. After all, most losers usually imitate winners, for power is a reality. The blacks had lost control, so those dark-skinned Jews who came to America had to meet some prejudice from their lighter-skinned counterparts imitating the Spaniards who had kicked them all out. Everyone who had some power looked for someone worse off than himself to look down on. That is why the Sephardim discriminated against their less-cultured brethren. But the powerful Dutch people of New Amsterdam discriminated against all Jews hailing from an imaginary country which had no warships, army, or government to defend them.

In September 1653, Peter Stuyvesant, himself a foreigner, did not want to grant Jews permanent residence in New York City. Stuyvesant came from Curaçao where he was governor for the Netherlands. He was Director General of the Dutch Municipal Government in New York. Stuyvesant referred to the Jews as being "people with their customary usury and deceitful trading with Christians." He requested that the deaconry isolate them. Stuyvesant also condemned the Jews as "sorcerers, ritual murderers of children, poisoners of wells, killers of Christ." He was narrow-mindedly intolerant to certain religious groups, most especially the Quakers. However, when Stuyvesant wrote to the West India Company's head office in Amsterdam, the directors informed him that he was to grant asylum to the Jews. One reason for the positive decision was the number of wealthy Jews among the Dutch company's shareholders.

The Dutch settlers sought their revenge in another manner. They did not allow the Jews complete religious freedom or civil rights. Jews could not practice trades or engage in retail businesses. And they were forced to live under those restrictions until the British captured New Amsterdam. When it became a British colony, the area was named after the Duke of York. At that time, the only sign of a Jewish presence on the island of Manhattan was a Jewish cemetery plot permitted in 1656.*

British arrival in 1664 gave the Jews undocumented freedom. But in the 1700s New York's Jewish settlers were able to begin using their artisan skills and engage in retail trade. By 1717 a dark-skinned Jew named Daniel Gómez was able to trade with the Indians. The Indians trusted Gómez because they had been trading with Africans since the fourteenth century and had never been robbed or threatened with enslavement.

Around 1750 Jews from Central Europe joined the Sephardim and spread out to live in places like Philadelphia, Pennsylvania; Charleston, South Carolina; Savannah, Georgia; New Orleans, Louisiana; and Mobile, Alabama. Other Jews were inhabiting the northern seaboard.

Birmingham mentions a "Free Woman of Color", Ellen Wilson, who had a house purchased for her in New Orleans by Judah Touro, who was nicknamed "Strange Man," because he adored her. Apart from the house, there was also $4,100 left for this same Wilson woman who never claimed the inheritance. More striking, however, is the fact that Touro's appointed executor was a black man named Pierre Andre Destrac Cazenove. At the time of Touro's death in 1790, young Cazenove was reported worth some $20,000, quite a bit of money for a black man who worked as a clerk in the prejudiced antebellum South. Cazenove also was credited with the operation of a funeral parlor and livery stable after Touro's death, and was worth $100,000 or more.[8] His family was conveniently classified as "Quadroon—Creoles, more properly now called colored persons."[9]

Birmingham expressed Jewish power continuously, and answered a question asked by insecure and uninformed persons, "Why do Jews have so much power?" The answer becomes: If the Blacks in the U.S.A. were as well educated (per capita) as the Blacks in Barbados, Curaçao, Aruba, and even Panama are, and as well organized as the Jews, through group awareness, and as self-determined to be their brother's keeper sharing their wealth and providing legal aid and protection, they would have the same question asked about them. Then, the Jews have bleached themselves out, and managed to pass for whites enabling them to be in a position to help others. The blacks have not been able to pass for whites in the Christian world to help their own, and many blacks have turned around and enslaved their relatives or mistreated them as niggers, while they— as whites—were really the worst niggers who have existed on this planet.[10]

From 1881 to 1910, nearly eighteen million immigrants arrived in the United States. They were Italians, Slovaks, Croats, Poles, Rumanians, Greeks, Hungarians and, Jews, with some Jews coming as members of the other groups as well. The new immigrants crowded the manufacturing and mining centers of New York, Detroit, Chicago, Pittsburgh, Buffalo, and Cleveland. They brought their linguistic varieties, cultures, customs, prejudices, religions, and other practices with them. Each group followed its language and cultural baggage (such as regionalisms and nuances) and helped form an ethnic community of its own. The overcrowded neighborhoods began swelling with competition for jobs. This experience engendered hostility and prejudices based on jealously and fear. The differences in language also became a factor in general misunderstanding. Very often an old-timer and citizen would say to a newcomer, speaking a foreign tongue, "This is America, speak English!"

The newcomers were hungry and anxious to become rich, so they worked longer hours for lower wages. That attitude did not make them popular in labor circles. Trade unions came into the labor market. Each group formed its own union. The Sons of Italy cornered masonry and bricklaying while other members became peddlers. The Hungarians cooked; the Jews sewed clothes and hats and peddled wares. Everyone took a piece of the labor market. The Germans sewed up the clothing industry with their United Garment Workers Union and the Hatters Union. The Jews formed their United Hebrew Trades Union in 1888, to counteract prejudices from the other groups.

Prejudice and competition continued and twenty-five years later, the Amalgamated Clothing Workers Union broke away from the United Garment Workers. This split is said to have reflected the unabating tension which grew among Jewish and non-Jewish workers in the men's clothing industry.[11]

The Jewish and Gentile unions developed mutual hostility, even in the hat workers' locals. That dissension grew to such proportions that it lasted thirty years, and took a few more to peter out. It was after that battle that the two hatters' unions came together in 1934. The old-timers and newcomers finally learned that through unity they would have greater bargaining power.

The Jewish unions in the garment trades are said to have helped to shape trade unionism in America, also helping acculturation. However, the European Jews were too radical for Samuel Gompers—an English Jew who was afraid that the Russian Jewish socialists of the time would jeopardize smoothly organized, and well-functioning unions of the era. There was fear of German philosophical thought, French political slogans, and English economic theories taking over with ulterior motives. However, all these unions kept out blacks and identifiable Italians.

As a result of these developments in the United States and Jewish identity with the political left, the Catholics supported the conservatives and the political right. The Catholics somehow felt that Christians had the right to govern. And the Jews felt that they could not expect right judgments from the wrong people who had denied them their civil rights in Europe. A point in support of that fact is Davidowicz' 1977 tale of Rabbi Don Berish Meisel's, who was elected to the Austrian Assembly in 1848. The spiritual leader was from Cracow, Poland, and should have voted with the Polish bloc. He voted with the left instead. When Rabbi Meisels voted with the left, the assembly's president asked him, incredulously, How could an Orthodox Rabbi support the left? Rabbi Meisel is said to have replied, *Wir Juden haben keine Rechte*, meaning We Jews have no right. The Jews, like other people mistreated and disenfranchised, were forced to lean to the left in Europe. To escape the political battles and organized labor's hassles, many Jews became peddlers wherever they found themselves. Peddling is the retailing of wares, fruits, vegetables, and sundry goods bought at one price and sold at a profit on the street or going from one place to the other as a means of survival. During the persecutions in Europe, the Jews who could not own property or land estates earned their living by lending money or peddling. In America, the Italians peddled most of the vegetables and fruits in the early times. But the Jews peddled most of the wares, household goods, haberdashery and lingerie items, textiles, grains, and manufactured goods. Some Jews rode horses and carts, ringing bells to collect old rags, furniture, newspapers, and other junk.

Sephardic peddlers were noticed in the United States as early as 1665.[12] Records of licenses to peddlers in Pennsylvania show one out of eighteen licenses was extended to a Jewish peddler in 1771. Five out of forty-nine were said to have been in business in 1772, and four out of twenty-seven peddlers were Jewish in 1773. There was trade in cutlery, textiles, and cotton goods, with calico and flannel in great demand. Snuff, and other sundry goods were also bartered for skins and furs gathered by Indians and trappers, many of them French.

Jews are said to have settled far West after 1865. In Cincinnati peddlers were recorded as having increased from a handful in 1818 to 3,300 in 1850. Peddlers followed the Gold Rush to San Francisco and Sacramento to ply their trade to miners and communities founded in the mining towns. One of those pioneer peddlers was Levi Strauss, the manufacturer of original blue jeans. The Goldwater department stores of Arizona were founded by a peddler named Meyer Guggenheim who began his career in the West. The successful peddlers of New York were the Seligman family, Adam Gimbel, Moses, Caesar Cone, and Nathan Strauss.[13]

On the East Coast, the Sephardim had built the first synagogue on Manhattan island and in North America. It was named Shearith Israel; the original structure no longer stands. Nevertheless, one of the most opulent Sephardic synagogues stands in its place. Out of this Spanish and Portuguese synagogue at 8 West Seventeenth Street and Central Park West, in New York also came a Rhode Island synagogue built by the supporters of Shearith Israel.

By the beginning of the nineteenth century, Jewish life was still one of Sephardic dominance. Central and Eastern European Ashkenazim began trickling in among the Orthodox veteran settlers. There were no organized Jewish educational institutions of learning or brotherhood; each group survived as best it could. And there were also no outstanding rabbis to educate the people regarding the dangers of prejudices now forgotten. Every well-fed person was an American; arrogant, self-centered, and scornful of poor refugees invading the turf. A group of Askenazim in Charleston, South Carolina, petitioned its elders for modification of the liturgy and sermons. There was a petition to have the prayers said in English, the official language of the country. The plea was considered too unorthodox and therefore rejected. The Sephardim had again disdained the Ashkenazim.

In 1815 the Sephardim and other Jewish communities combined totaled three thousand Jews in the United States. Most of these Jews were members of the seven Jewish congregations in the country, each dominated by Sephardim. By 1840 the Jewish population of the United States had jumped to approximately fifteen thousand. Most of these additional Jews came from Central Europe and were German speaking. Keller said that there had been a number of German-Jewish families scattered among the Sephardic communities throughout America, but only when this mass immigration began in the nineteenth century did the German Jews become recognizable as a challenge to Sephardic domination. This large number of German Jews made a decisive change in the fabric of Jewish community life in the United States.

In 1827 the German, or Ashkenazi, Jewish group within the New York Shearith Israel congregation bolted from the group to form a congregation of its own ilk. The Askenazim named themselves *B'nai Jeshrum*, a group which is still existent. By 1838, the Hebrew Sunday school came into operation in Philadelphia. It was instituted by Rebecca Gratz who came from a German-Jewish family. With the German Jews arriving and sending for their relatives, there came a desire for innovation. German Protestantism and liberalism found its expression in a Reform Movement which led to Reform Judaism wherever Yiddish was popular.

In July 1846 the Rabbi Isaac Meyer Wise (1819–1900) arrived in the United States. There were three Reform congregations by then. The Charleston, South Carolina congregation which first bolted from Sephardic Orthodox control in 1824; the Baltimore group; and a New York group which had followed. The New York group was Temple Emanu–El, now relocated to a different site. It was and still is one of the largest Reform congregations in the United States. Wise, who had been active in the modernization process sweeping Europe during that time, was a writer in Jewish philosophical, historical, and playwriting circles. He became very popular in the United States.

With the pale-faced Ashkenazim gaining control, the Jews no longer needed the dark-skinned identity they had adored and arrogantly displayed during Moorish rule in Spain and early arrival in America. Their ancestors had been in eminent positions, and Sephardic olive and dark skin color and features had been status symbols in the past. Now the blond peasants were taking over and outnumbering the Sephardim.

B'nai B'rith, the international Jewish organization, was formed in 1843, the Hebrew Union College was founded in Cincinnati 1875, and power was extended. By 1886 a rabbinical school called the Jewish Theological Seminary of America was founded in New York City to contradict Reform tenets and practices within religious Jewish networks.

The beginning of the twentieth century saw another movement in the religious arena called the Conservative Movement. At that time, waves of Jewish immigrants flooded the United States. "By 1910, the Jewish population of the United States was larger than that of any other country in the world." And the newcomers joined the old Askenazim to form the largest Jewish community in the country. It was founded in New York City. These people were mostly from Germany, Poland, and adjacent countries where Jews were being persecuted. They were considered Nordic people, they spoke Yiddish and received contempt from the older American population which now had someone poorer to look down on. The new immigrants were considered poor in manners, hygiene, and capital. They were criticized, resented, and disdained by all Americans. But of all the immigrants, the Jews were discriminated against for being Jews more than for being poor or dirty.

> The impact of this resentment was felt with particular sensitivity by the old German-Jewish families, all the more so because many of them, in the innermost recesses of their hearts, had shared in this attitude toward other people to some extent.14

The descendants of these people are the racists now propagating hatred against Arabs, blacks, and Sepharadim of dark skin in Israel, South Africa, the United States, and the world over. One of their principal organizations is "The Jewish Defense League." Their specialty is attacking blacks in New York and Arabs in Beirut and Israel.

ZIONISM

Until the 1930s, Zionism had very little recognition in the United States. But after Winston Churchill—First Lord of England's Admiralty—ordered studies for the production of acetone from chestnuts, Israel was brought into focus. As the story goes, Churchill asked

Chaim Weizmann (1874–1952), what he would like as compensation for his services to England. Weizmann is said to have replied "A homeland for my people."

Weizmann had been an active professor of biochemistry at the University of Manchester, England, from 1903. In the 1940s England sorely needed acetone as part of her war production. With acetone, old airplanes could be cleaned and many British guns did not have to be rebuilt, they could be overhauled. Weizmann discovered that chestnuts could provide acetone, a volatile liquid which could be used as a solvent for other liquids and remove paint and grease from metal and other surfaces. The British Navy was glad to have it. As a result of Weizmann's discovery and Churchill's promise to reward him, the Balfour Declaration was issued in November 1917.

The Declaration said: "His Majesty's Government view with favor the establishment in Palestine of a national home for the Jewish people." It was sent by British Foreign Secretary Arthur Balfour (1848–1930) to Lord Lionel Walter Rothschild in a letter. When it was made public, the Declaration impressed the whole world. Most Jews in the United States were in favor of a Jewish homeland. However, there was a small segment, mostly Hasidim, against the proposal. Jewish leaders from around the world began visiting the United States to seek support for the proposal.

On July 24, 1918, a cornerstone was laid outside the gates of Jerusalem. In 1920 the Zionist Conference was held in London and Chaim Weizmann was elected President of the World Zionist Organization. On July 1, 1920, Sir Herbert Samuel—a Jewish former British Cabinet Minister—was appointed the first British High Commissioner of Palestine. The League of Nations gave Britain a mandate over Palestine in 1922.

The Arabs protested the mandate, but they were ignored. Realizing that the Europeans had moved in on them like they had done the Indians throughout America, the Arabs began acts of violence in protest. It was not long before the Arabs, who were a preponderant majority, found themselves becoming a minority among the waves of immigrants to Israel from 1919 to 1923. During that time, thirty-five thousand Eastern European Jews had entered Palestine. Jews then constituted almost one-third of the total population of Palestine, their numbers having increased from 150,000 to 400,000 between 1928 and 1937.[15]

The English realized that the Arabs were literally losing ground. Therefore, Samuel (the High Commissioner of Britain) tried to gain Arab confidence with reassurance. Samuel appointed an Arab mayor for Jerusalem's interfaith community. Then he made Emin el Huseini chief of all the Arabs in Palestine. The Jews were upset and felt that they had been given less than they had expected. The lands were sold to the Arabs, but the Jews said that the Arabs did not plant or till the lands. The Jews worked the semi-arid lands they were given and encouraged others to come and share their lots.

By 1928 more than one hundred thousand more Jewish immigrants arrived. In 1929 they began building the port of Haifa for shipping potassium and bromide salts to be produced near the Dead Sea.

Realizing that they had missed great opportunities for industrialization and expansion, the Arabs began to attack the Jews while they worked. One hundred thirty-three Jews were killed in 1931, their businesses and houses destroyed, and unprotected Jewish villages ravaged. As a result, a few Americans tried to keep the refugees from coming to the U.S. as an alternative homeland.

Geneticists Osborn of Columbia University, Brigham, and others encouraged the United States Congress to pass an Immigration Restriction Act of 1924. This Act was to prevent Jewish immigrants trying to escape Europe, from entering the United States. They had been classified by the IQ tests as being possessed of an order of intelligence far inferior to that of the Nordics born in the United States.[16] It was estimated that "The legal quotas, and continuing eugenical propaganda, barred up to six million southern, central and eastern Europeans between 1924 and the outbreak of World War II."

Numerous German Jews began entering Palestine along with those from Eastern Europe. By 1933 there were 220,000 Jews in the country.

The Arabs were really flustered by this time. They called a general strike. Mobs were gathered to attack Jews and to begin grouping in Jaffa. Germany and Italy furnished Syria and Iraq with arms, supplies, and funds to suppress the Jews. Britain still tried to avoid a clash with the Axis powers, so she commissioned that Palestine be partitioned. Britain's promise did not appease the Arabs, who had already tasted blood. They continued their hostilities against the Jews, even in the presence of armed British troops.

A White Paper was issued on May 17, 1939 under Neville Chamberlain, prime Minister of England. The paper set a quota of fifteen thousand Jews to be permitted into Palestine each year. Furthermore, the White Paper declared that England had not intended to have a Jewish state in Palestine. To everyone's amazement, Winston Churchill came to the Jews' rescue once more. Churchill denounced the White Paper in the House of Commons, as a "break of a solemn obligation."

A Zionist Congress met in Geneva in August 1939. It voted to denounce the White Paper and requested admission of a hundred thousand more Jews into Palestine. On August 24, 1939, while Chamberlain was trying to negotiate peace with German's warlords, Hitler said, "He who wishes to take chestnuts out of the fire for others surely shall be burned!" At approximately the same time, Weizmann said to the British—one week before the Germans marched into Poland—"Your cause is our cause and your struggle is our struggle."

Then the war started. Jewish organizations chartered vessels and secretly loaded them with refugees bound for Palestine. Those old tubs taken out of mothballs were called coffin ships. Unseaworthy, they were over-ballasted with human cargo. They were often stopped by British naval vessels and forced into Cypress or Mauritius. On one occasion, England is said to have even "vetoed a rescue operation involving some twenty thousand Polish children." But the refugees kept up their attempts to run the British blockade. In 1940 the Patria blew up in Haifa's harbor; two hundred and fifty-two persons were unaccounted for. In 1942 the Struma sank off Istanbul on its way from Rumania. There was an explosion, probably caused by a burnt out boiler. Seven hundred and sixty-eight souls went down with that vessel.

In the meantime, a lawyer named Menachem Begin joined other persons who formed a terrorist organization called *Irgun Zwai'i Le'umi*, meaning National Military Organization. These Jews bombed the British installations, robbed their armories, and eventually forced the British to leave the land. In the meantime, the Arabs backed off. They would often become terrified when the terrorists' Le'umi were mentioned.*

One hundred and thirty thousand Jews volunteered to serve in the British Army. But Palestine's Jews were not permitted absolute confidence and freedom in restricted areas for some time. In 1944 the Axis powers caused great concern among the Allies. The Palestine Jews were then allowed to form a Brigade under a blue-and-white flag with a Star of David in its center.

The Le'umi continued harassing the British soldiers in Israel to no end. They sabotaged them until the King David Hotel, the British Headquarters and administration building in Jerusalem, was rocked with explosive detonations which caused part of it to crumble July 22, 1946. Ninety British officials, Arabs, and some civilian Jews were killed.* Seventy persons were also wounded. The Arabs began infiltrating Le'umi territory. This caused other Jews to form a group called Haganah—a type of vigilante organization. The British did not like the Haganah any more than the Le'umi and classified them as illegal. They were often disarmed, their weapons confiscated, and their freedom fighters put in prisons. The Le'umi often rescued Haganah fighters, fought the Arabs, and performed sabotages which the Haganah leaders disdained.

Then in 1947, after years of attempting to maintain peace between the Arabs and the Jewish territorists at the expense of British soldiers' lives, the British government turned over the Palestine Mandate to the United Nations. In the summer of 1947, an American of color, Ralph Johnson Bunche (1904–1971), who had helped formulate the United Nations' Charter went to Palestine. He was accompanied by a special United Nations Commission on Palestine (UNSCOP). The United Nations Commission partitioned Palestine into a Jewish and an Arab national state, with Jerusalem and Bethlehem under international jurisdiction.[17] On May 14, 1948, David Ben-Gurion proclaimed *Medina Israel*, or a State of Israel, at midnight in Tel Aviv, just before the last British troops and their High Commissioner left Palestine.

The next day the Arabs declared war on the infant State of Israel. Five Arab armies invaded Israel from different sides. Egypt from the south, the Arab Legion from the east, Transjordanian allies included, Syria, Lebanon, Iraq and Saudi Arabia from the north. These troops were joined by other forces from the Sudan and North Africa. With this overwhelming force, the Arabs proclaimed that the war would end within a week. But the Saudis had no missiles then. American airplanes and modern weapons in Israeli hands stretched the war into a month. After a month of fiercer fighting than the Arabs had anticipated, they sought peace on June 11, 1948.[18] The special envoy of the United Nations, Conte Folke Bernadote, recognized the peace. Hundreds of thousands of Arabs fled their homes to enter Syria, Transjordan, and the Egyptian-occupied Gaza Strip as refugees. On July 22, 1948, Jordan and Israel signed an agreement making Jerusalem a no-man's-land.[19] By 1949 there were approximately 940,000 Palestinian-Arab refugees dispersed around the Arab territories.

JEWS OF MEXICO

After the Spanish Inquisition in Spain and Portugal, Jews scattered far and wide; some of them scurried away among Hernan Cortes' conquerors. They were found with Cortes when he captured Mexico in 1521. That was 133 years before the first Jews arrived in New Amsterdam in 1654. These Jews were Hernando Alonso and his brother (whose name is unknown), Gonzalez de Morales, and another Marrano (whose name also is unknown). The records show Alonso becoming successful in Mexico, but also becoming the first person to be caught in the extended arms of the Inquisition. Alonso was "burned at the stake in Mexico City for practicing Jewish rites." His brother and de Morales were punished in the same manner.

Alonso and de Morales were ship's carpenters. They were credited with building the thirteen bridges which Cortes used to attack Montezuma's palace in the middle of Lake Tenochitlan. Rewarded with land on which they raised cattle, Alonso became envied. Having fled the Inquisition in Spain and Portugal, and having become Christians, they had no problems for some time and probably felt secure enough to practice their true beliefs secretly. In any event, their new-found brothers in Christ still killed them to acquire their riches. They were required to prove Catholic ancestry for four preceding generations, and they could not.

After the conquest of 1521, many Jews invaded the shores of New Spain (Latin America). These "New Christians often ignored Jewish tradition or practiced a Judaism that resembled that of no other group within Judaism."[20] There was said to have been more Jews than Catholics among the Spaniards in 1550. Therefore, there were bound to be some Jews still practicing the old religion, despite the risks and their consequences.

Bernard Postal found that the archives of Jewish history during the Mexican colonial period of 1521 to 1821 can be found among the documents of the Inquisition. These documents are in the Mexican *Archivo Nacional Antigua*. There were supposed to be 1,553 volumes. *Indice del Ramo de la Inquisicion* consists of thirteen volumes which have the names of all Jews or New Christians suspected of being Jews and compelled to appear before the Holy Office of the Inquisition. Some of the suspects were also listed as being disinterred for inquest from their graves.

The words of the Inquisition show Marranos recorded because of their practices of circumcision, regarding the Almighty as One, worshipping on the Sabbath, observing dietary laws, and even raising funds for their coreligionists in Palestine. Judging from these records, one might easily assume that the Jewish problem began in New Spain when certain Jews went from one town to another instructing New Christians and reminding old Jews of the Torah. Many Jews were recorded as jewelers, tailors, shoemakers, doctors, merchants, and tradespeople dealing in goods from China.

El Libro, de Judio, or *The Book of the Jew,* was published by Ricardo Osado in 1647. This book showed New Christians holding high posts in the Mexican government of New Spain. It served as a guide in the use of Mayan herbs, medicinal potions and tonics, as well as the different diseases of that time. Osado was a Marrano from Italy who had converted to Christianity. Another famous New Christian was Don Luis de Carvajal y de la Cueva. Carvajal was bruised by the Inquisition despite his fame as a hero who had conquered the area known as Nuevo Reino de Leon, and governed about one hundred thousand square miles from Tampico, Mexico, to what is now San Antonio, Texas. Carvajal had a Jewish maternal grandmother, a sister, brother-in-law, and nephew who were all secret Jews. Carvajal's nephew had the same name, but was called Luis de Carvajal el Mozo. The added name meant Junior. It appears on more than four hundred printed pages in the records of the Mexican Inquisition.

The younger Carvajal came from Spain to join his uncle. The older

Carvajal resisted his nephew's efforts to Judaize him. Nevertheless, the uncle was tried and imprisoned for not informing the authorities of his relatives' religious practices. The younger Carvajal and his family burned at the stake in 1585. Between 1577 and 1586 the Inquisition tried sixty-three Judaizers in Mexico. One New Christian was freed, thirty-eight repented publicly, renounced their heresy, were deprived of their possessions, and sent to prison. Another fourteen New Christians were burnt in effigy, and ten were burnt at the stake after being strangled with an iron collar tightened by a bolt, called *el garrote*. However, of the 1,500 persons convicted by the Inquisition in Mexico for being Judaizers, less than 100 died at the stake; and only 270 were imprisoned, compared with Spain, 2,000, and Portugal, about 1,000.

When Mexico became independent in 1821, the cells of the Inquisition were opened. The last prisoner found alive was recorded to be a Jew, who had been imprisoned since 1795. Despite the severe penalties for non-Catholic religious practices, Jews had kept risking death and imprisonment in migrating to Mexico. They seemed to feel that the Inquisition there was less cruel and severe than the trials in Spain and Portugal. Most of the commerce of New Spain was credited to them. They were said to have left Mexico City for Monterrey in the mid-seventeenth century, while others changed their names and went to more unpopulated areas to settle safely among the Indians. The Indians were less anxious to rob them of their property under the guise of religious persecution.

Two Mexican Presidents were considered descendants of New Christians. One was Porfirio Diaz (1830–1915), and the other was Francisco Indalecio Madero (1873–1913), president from 1911–1913. Diego Rivera, the famous muralist, also was a descendant of New Christians.

From the middle of the seventeenth century there was a noticeable decline in Inquisitional persecution of New Christians. The focus was directed toward preventing independence.

One outstanding *independentista* was a priest named Miguel Hidalgo y Costilla (1753–1811). This mulatto was the champion of Mexico's War of Independence (1810–1811). Hidalgo was charged with being a Judaizer. When captured he was shot to death on orders from the court of the Inquisition in 1811. Hidalgo was parish priest of the village of Dolores. The heroic battlecry for independence is still called *el grito de Dolores*, the cry of Dolores.

AFTER MEXICAN INDEPENDENCE

There were only a few Jews left in Mexico when independence began in 1821. These Jews were mostly traders from the West Indies, agents of European mining companies, and representatives of the

Goldschmidt banking house of London. The English bank floated Mexico's first foreign loan. Between 1835 and 1850 Jews came to Mexico from England, France, Belgium, and Germany. Among these immigrants were a statistician, mapmaker, educator, railroad contractor, and a publisher named Isidor Epstein. He published and edited a newspaper in German and was considered a liberal and leading citizen for more than forty years in varied occupations. Another paper, the *London Jewish Chronicle* mentioned one hundred Jews residing in Mexico City. Forty of that number are said to have rented a room to conduct High Holy services on the Day of Atonement. The service had been disguised as a Masonic meeting. Another service was held for Rosh Hashanah at the home of one Nathan Dorsen, a representative of the Rothschilds. The Yom Kippur services which followed were held at the home of Bernard Wiener.

Another prominent Jew of that time was Marcus Otterburg. He had migrated to Milwaukee, Wisconsin, in the 1840s, and became a leader of the Republican Party. After being appointed United States Consul to Mexico, by Abraham Lincoln in 1861, Otterburg played an heroic role. He protected American citizens during the militancy which preceded the French invasion of Mexico under Austrian Archduke Maximilian. Napoleon III had Maximilian go to Mexico to subdue Benito Juarez, the Mexican revolutionary leader.

Maximilian (1832–1867) and his wife Carlotta had no real knowledge of Mexico, its political development, or its people. They could not even speak the language. They found most Mexicans hostile to them as foreign emperor and empress. The United States was also hostile to them because Napoleon had violated the Monroe Doctrine. The United States was sympathetic to Juarez, but was involved in her own Civil War. As soon as the Civil War was over, however, pressures caused Napoleon III to withdraw the French troops (1866–1867). Empress Carlotta went to Napoleon and pleaded for more support. She also visited the Pope and explained the precariousness of the Emperor Maximilian's position in a hostile foreign land. Her pleas were not heeded.

Marcus Otterburg was then the United States Consul in Mexico, and attempted to save Maximilian's life. As a friend of the revolutionary leader and the aspiring emperor as well, Otterburg tried, but was ignored because he was not an ambassador pleni-potentiary. Maximilian was forced in front of a firing squad as soon as he was captured. On June 21, 1867, Otterburg received his appointment as United States Ambassador to Mexico. President Andrew Johnson had made the appointment only forty-eight hours after Maximilian had been liquidated.

AFTER MAXIMILIAN

After the 1849 California gold rush, there was a Baja, California, gold rush in 1881. Many Jews were anxiously prospecting among the miners, investors, and speculators. One of the mining engineers was David Goldbaum, the son of a German mining engineer. Among the Mexican residents was another Jew named Max Bernstein, who opened a flour mill [21] and speculated in real estate.

Even though there were only a few Jews in Mexico between 1875 and 1900, the Jews there published their first newspaper called El Sabado Secreto, *The Secret Sabbath*. The newspaper's editor and publisher was Francisco Rivas Pulcerver, a descendant of converted New Christians. Pulcerver taught Greek and other classical languages at the national Preparatory School. He also edited a Spanish journal called *La Luz del Sabado*, meaning The Sabbath Light. This paper was dedicated to the Sephardic Jews of Spain and Portugal and their offsprings. Pulcerver's works contained many Hebrew words and cliches. He also published a novel, *La Higa del Judio*, meaning The Daughter of the Jew, that started as a popular newspaper serial before it was published in book form.

From 1871 to 1891, the Jews of Tzarist Russia were persecuted and robbed of their property. Many were also killed. To escape those pogroms, the chief rabbi of Austria published a letter in the *London Jewish Chronicle* suggesting a Jewish migration to Mexico. Pulcerver supported the idea. In the 1890s Jacob H. Schiff, an American banker and philanthropist, and Baron Maurice de Hirsch, the French railroad builder, joined forces. Hirsch invested millions of dollars in various efforts to settle Russian refugees in Mexico. President Diaz offered free land to the Russian Jews, but they never left Russia.

The Jewish Territorial Organization scouted around the world for a homeland for Russian Jews. Its members sought a possibility of settling some Jews in Mexico. By the time a decision was reached, the government of Mexico had changed and the new government would not consider the Jewish appeal. A Mexican organization formed in 1921 attempted to have a petition addressed in favor of Jewish migration.* After some attempts to be heard President Alvaro Obregon finally met with them. In 1924 President Plutarco Elias agreed to accept Jewish immigration to Mexico.

Some Russian Jews, along with others from Lebanon, Damascus, Syria, Greece, Bulgaria, Turkey, Serbia, and some Arab-speaking countries took advantage of the Mexican offer. Before World War I, there were Jewish immigrants from Poland and the Balkans. The Sephardic Ladino-speaking community was now outnumbered by their Yiddish-speaking counterparts from Eastern Europe.

By 1937 a quota system was put into law. Jewish immigrants

from Rumania and Poland were limited to one hundred a year. From 1943 to 1944 there were several hundred Jews from Europe admitted to Mexico. The Arabic-speaking community established its synagogue in Colonia Condesa, Mexico City. They had begun holding services in their homes in 1901. And in 1920, President Madero had permitted the Sephardic Jews to build Monte Sinai Synagogue, considered the first temple to be built in Mexico. The first Jewish cemetery opened in 1911 was no longer the only one. There are now about ten synagogues for Sephardics, Litvaks, Galicianos, the large Arab-speaking community, and others. However, there is a Central Committee, and the Centro Deportivo Israelita Mexico are two centers where all Jewish communities come together for celebrations or serious matters affecting all Jews or Israel.

The Jews of El Paso, Texas, raised funds under the leadership of Rabbi Martin Zelonka in the 1920s. Those funds were to help needy Sephardic Jews attempting to organize *Beneficiencia Alianza Monte Sinai*, the Mount Sinai Beneficient Alliance. More than eight thousand Jews were brought to El Paso from Eastern Europe. Being poor and unskilled, many of them had difficulty earning a living under the low Mexican wage scale. B'nai B'rith opened a Mexican branch in 1924. That agency soon provided *gimilis haysin*, Yiddish for small interest-free loans. The new arrivals acquired merchandise and equipment which enabled them to begin trade and commerce. The B'nai B'rith also opened a Banco Mercantile which served Jewish peddlers and small stores. In 1931 a Jewish Chamber of Commerce was established by the Ashkenazim. Many of the new arrivals who worked as peddlers carried sundry goods to tenants' doors, others carried clothing and utensils across Mexico to outlying towns and faraway villages. Many Jews opened furniture stores and clothing stores or factories in Mexico City. Some rented small stalls in the markets. After a while, foreign peddlers were forced to give up their stalls in the municipal markets and allow Mexicans preference. When this law came into effect, Jews opened sweat shop factories where poor Mexicans manufactured clothing, household goods, and furniture.

Jewish merchants and peddlers introduced Mexican farmers, workers, and housewives to the purchasing of shoes, hosiery, and clothing on installments. By the 1940s, Jewish businessmen and industrialists had become recognizable in such industries as building materials, iron, steel, textiles, banking, import-export and jewelry. By 1970 Jewish salesmen traveled all over Mexico; from Mexico City to Veracruz and the Yucatan peninsula. The Jewish industries have enabled the Mexicans to discontinue their dependence on foreign importations of textiles and other goods. Jews also entered professional fields and civil service occupations. Very few of them have become laborers because of the low wages paid in Mexico.

JEWS OF MEXICO TODAY

There are now twenty-two synagogues in the Mexican Republic. About fifteen of them are in Mexico City proper; the others are scattered throughout the country. The state legally owns the land sites and buildings occupied by religious institutions. That law went into effect when Benito Juarez became president of Mexico. The Catholic Church was all powerful, paid no taxes to the government, and its priests were immune under Mexican law. The Church owned most of the resourceful land, and its secret agents were always waiting in the shadows to foment trouble for any political leader who attempted to reduce its control of national policies.[22] There are also ten Jewish schools. Jewish children receive elementary education; but no religious instruction is permitted in the classrooms. There are also two public schools built and supplied by the Jewish communities in Mexico City. One is the Albert Einstein Preparatory School, donated in 1948, and the other is *Estado de Israel*, donated in the 1950s.

In 1977 the Jewish population was 38,000, with 35,000 living in Mexico City. Other cities, with sizeable populations are Monterrey, with 750 souls; Guadalajara, 750; Tijuana, 350; Cuernavaca,400; and Tampico,100. Other Jewish communities have smaller numbers, like Ciudad Juarez,75; Veracruz, 50; Nuevo Laredo, 65; Puebla, 50; Nogales,25; Torreon,50; Acapulco, 35; Oaxaca,10; Cocula,10. Other Jews are scattered throughout principal cities and other towns of the 29 Mexican states unrecorded. The 35,000 Jews living in Mexico City are an admixture of approximately 1,000 United States citizens; nine hundred of German descent or Austrian origin, 600 from Hungary; 4,000 from Syria (2,500 from Damascus and 1,500 from Aleppo); 10,000 from Turkey, Greece, Lebanon, Bulgaria, Yugoslavia; 19,000 from Poland and Rumania.[23] When people are persecuted they often seek refuge among other disadvantaged groups. The Jews are no exception. During the days of the Spanish Inquisition in Mexico, several Jews escaped from the Spaniards to seek refuge among the Mexicans. As a result, there was a 600 percent increase recorded in Mexico's census for the decade 1950 to 1960. There was considerable confusion and dismay until Raphael Patai, a prominent American anthropologist, discovered the statistical error. The cause had been ethnological and denominational. Mexican census takers had computed data which showed Jews numbering 15,574 in 1950, and jumping to 100,750 in 1960. There had been no significant Jewish immigration to Mexico during the period and, therefore, the increase was unjustifiable. Jews entering the country during the period should have been recorded at less than thirty percent normal increase.

Patai discovered that an evangelical Christian sect, Iglesia de Dios Universal Israelita, was the cause. The members of the Universal

Israelite Church of God numbered about 100,750 in 1960. The mystery of Jewish increase in numbers while there had only been a trickle of Jews admitted for that period was cleared up. Statistical data showed Universal Church members numbering twenty thousand families in 1960, as compared to only a few hundred in 1950. They had listed their religion as "Israelita" for the census takers.

The Mexican government's Census Bureau only recognizes three religious groups. They are first and foremost, the Catholics, then the Protestants, and finally the Israelites. Moslems are called *Musulmanes*, and given very little official recognition. Unlike the Moors of Spain in older times, Islam and the Moslems of Latin America are no direct threat to the Roman Catholic hierarchy. The 60,000 Christians of the "Christian Universal Church of God Israelite" erroneously counted as Jews, would as Christians receive more consideration than a religious group of either the Jews or Moslems. Jews are still considered by some Mexican people to be strange, sacreligious persons with horns, who do not believe in Christ and his Virgin Mother.

Despite superficial differences, Enrique Luis Tabaxas, a noted anthropologist, claimed that the original Mayan and Aztecs of Mexico were descendants of the ancient Hebrew tribes who landed on the Mexican coast thousands of years ago. Tabaxas based his theory on a study of Mexican rocks with carvings which he said contained Hebrew characters. In contradiction, Seymour Liebman, an "authority on Mexican Jewish History calls the stories about 'Indian Jews' a 'confused mixture of myths, legends, distorted history and wishful thinking.'" This last statement expresses arrogance and maliciousness. People coming out of Europe claiming inheritance of an African religion have no more right to be considered Jews or descendants of Jewish tribes than the Indians from Asia originally. Furthermore, ancient Hebrews were dark-skinned. The Gentiles are fairer. These authorities are the wishful thinkers who cause Jews to be hated the world over. They fail to realize that people who give others refuge resent having the refugees turn around and insult them. When a people proclaim themselves "God's chosen," and deny that identity to those who have had to give them a chance to live, hatefulness is sure to be their portion.*

Quite a few descendants of Jews, and others born elsewhere, have become successful Mexican citizens. Rumanian-born Roberto Haberman organized producers and consumers of farm products in 1917. Haberman even wrote the Constitution of the State of Yucatan, founded a school of social work, and was chief administrator of the department of foreign languages in the Ministry of Education. He was sent to the United States under Mexico's first labor administration as a special commissioner from the Department of Industry,

Commerce and Labor.

Another Jew of renown was Frank Tannenbaun, an American educator and economist, who had earned his Ph.D. with a dissertation on Mexican land reform. Tannenbaun later made important economic surveys for the Mexican government. Mexico's first national anthem is also credited to a foreign-born citizen, Henry Hartz, a Vienna-born musician is the composer of that famous piece. Marcos Moshinsky, born of Polish immigrant parents, is one of Mexico's nuclear scientists. He won the national award of the Academy for Scientific Research in 1961. Marcos was the first Jewish member of the society and taught science at the Universidad Nacional Autonoma de Mexico. Anita Brenner, the daughter of a foreign-born Jew, was recognized as an authority on pre-Spanish art, and also worked for the National Autonomous University of Mexico. Brenner also completed some art surveys for the University.

A Mexican stamp was issued honoring Arturo Rosenbleuth, a Jew born in Mexico of a Hungarian father. Rosenbleuth taught and practiced neurology and psychiatry in Mexico City from 1927 to 1930. He later became chief administrator of the department of physiology and pharmacology at the national Cardiological Institute of Mexico. In 1960 Rosenbleuth was appointed director of the Center of Investigation and Advanced Study of the National Polytechnic Institute. Rosenbleuth's brother, Emilio, is also a recognized scientist.

Rosenweig Dias led the Mexican delegation to the first United Nations General Assembly. Dias also represented Mexico as a diplomat to El Salvador, Sweden, Venezuela, and France. Benito Berlin, a noted economist and politician was Mexican ambassador to Denmark and Israel. Emilio O. Rabasa, a former Foreign Minister of Mexico, had a Jewish mother whose maiden name was Mishkin. Under Jewish law, he would be considered a Jew.

Sidney Franklin was a matador born in Brooklyn, New York. He was the first American bullfighter to perform anywhere. Franklin fought in the Plaza Mexico arena in 1923 at the age of eighteen.

The Sourasky brothers were born in Poland. Both Leon and Elias Sourasky arrived in Mexico in 1917 and became successful bankers. As philanthropists, they award a Sourasky Prize every year to the best creative achievement in the arts, letters, and sciences. The Sourasky award is equivalent to the Nobel Prize. Edouard Weinfeld cited the ten volumes of the Jewish Encyclopedia published in Spanish in 1951.

Jews have made significant contributions to Mexican progress. Some have even joined the Mexican officers' corps, despite Mexican xenophobic tendencies and psychological ambivalence.

JEWS OF THE WEST INDIES AND THE CARIBBEAN

The Jews who did not come to the United States or Mexico went to the West Indies and the Caribbean Islands and to South and Central America. Many of those Jews became plantation owners, exploited the people of the islands, and made their wealth from sugar, tobacco, and human traffic. Baron and Kahan document that in the Americas:

> Until 1730, the Dutch West India Company maintained a monopoly on the importation of slaves into all the Dutch colonies in the Americas, but Jews appear to have been among the major retailers of slaves in Dutch Brazil (1630–54), because Jews possessed ready money and were willing to trade slaves for sugar . . . On the North American mainland, a number of Jews were active participants in the infamous triangular trade, which brought slaves from Africa to the West Indies, where they were exchanged for molasses which was in turn taken to New England and converted into rum for sale in Africa.[24]

Those people were wicked, to be sure. They ignored Nehemiah's words, "Yet now our flesh is as the flesh of our brethren, our children as their children; and, lo, we bring into bondage our sons and our daughters to be servants."[25]

After Cuba, Santo Domingo, Trinidad and Tobago, and Puerto Rico were freed from Spanish tyranny in 1898, Jews settled in those countries in recognizable numbers. Those Eastern European Jews escaping the Balkan Wars before World War I, and the dissolution of the Turkish Empire after that war, sought refuge in the United States or the West Indies and the Caribbean. Jews also came to the Islands from Russia and Germany. They often intended to use the islands as a way station to the United States.

ARUBA

Aruba is a leeward island. It had a population of 64,106 in 1985. There are about four hundred Jews there. The capital of Aruba is Oranjestad, where Jews first settled around 1563. The Dutch West India Company could not make much profit off the barren island with its scarcity of potable water. In the mid-eighteenth century, the Dutch began renting the land to private individuals. The first Jew to file an application for land was Moses de Salomo Levy Maduro from Curaçao, who had arrived with a wife and six children in 1754. Other Jews and families shifted in and out of Aruba until 1860. Some Maduros ended up in Panama. Other small numbers of Jews left Curaçao for Aruba in the 1790s. But it was not until the 1850s that a small quantity of gold was found there, and the Aruba Phosphate Mining Company became popular. Jamaicans and other West Indians went to Aruba, and Jews joined them as investors, but not as settlers.

During the 1920s, a few immigrants trickled in from Holland, Syria, Egypt, and Surinam (Dutch Guiana). These Jews followed the 1929 opening of the Lago Oil Refining Corporation which handled crude oil from neighboring Venezuela. Some Jews started as laborers and later expanded into small businesses.

By 1946 there were enough Jews to form a *Minyan* for prayer, and organize a Hebrew school and a social center. In 1962 they opened a synagogue designed by Morris Lapidus, who also was the architect of the Aruba Caribbean Hotel.

BAHAMAS

This independent member of the British Commonwealth had a population of 240,000 in 1982. The British named it Watling's Island in 1620. And the Spaniards, who were glad to see the first sight of land, followed Columbus in calling it San Salvador. When Columbus landed there on October 12, 1492, his Jewish interpreter Luis de Torres spoke to the Indians.

Nathan Simpson of New York had a trading station in the Bahamas during the 1720s. Jacob and Moses Franks of London were in a syndicate which supplied Nassau's British garrison, before the American Revolution. Another Moses Franks was attorney general of the seven hundred islands during the eighteenth century. Very few Jews are said to have settled in the Bahamas until after World War II.

There was a Jewish cemetery in Nassau in the 1800s, and in 1917 a record of the Pan American Union listed a Miss Amalia Dorothy de Frees, member of a prominent London family, as the only Jew. The names in the old cemetery are Sephardic, but today the Jewish community of Freeport and other areas are predominantly Ashkenazic.

Stern and Postal declared that after World War I, eight to ten Jewish families from England, Poland, and Russia settled in Nassau. Their numbers increased to approximately forty families in Nassau and one hundred more in Freeport. The major migration began in the 1950s when British and American tourists hurried to the attractive gambling casinos. Real estate developers, hoteliers, and bankers followed, with accountants and business people supplying their demands. The Nassau community is now composed mostly of Jewish business and professional men from the United States, England, Canada, Ireland, and South Africa.

Jewish religious services were occasionally held in private homes or in hotels. Some residents often traveled to Florida to observe Rosh Hashanah (The Jewish New Year) and Yom Kippur (The Day of Atonement). In 1965 the Nassau Hebrew Congregation was organized under the guidance of Hal Hoffer and his nephews, Rubin and Jack

Bott, who own department stores. A synagogue with a seating capacity of fifty to accommodate the worshippers opened in the Hoffer Building. The congregation did not have a permanent rabbi at the time. This Conservative group brought in a cantor and rabbi from Florida for High Holy Days. Marcel Urbach from Switzerland acted as religious leader during the rest of the year. Daily services usually required at least ten male adult Jews to form the communal group (Minyan). To compliment this requirement, most of the worshippers are usually Jewish tourists to whom a hearty welcome is extended, even if they are Jews of color.[26]

BARBADOS

Barbados is an independent island in the windward West Indies, northeast of Venezuela. The population was 253,000 in 1981. The capital is Bridgetown. Jews are not recorded in the annals of Barbados until after 1654, when Peter Stuyvesant would not grant them permanent residence in New Amsterdam (New York City). In that year, Jews left Recife, Brazil, in a group intending to flee to Amsterdam. When the refugees learned that Oliver Cromwell had opened British possessions to Jews, they applied for permission and were allowed to disembark in Barbados. The Mercado family was among the early settlers. Their tombstones are evidence of that record in the cemetery. As noted, Aaron de Mercado was buried in 1660, and said to have been the second Jew laid to rest in that tropical island then called Little England. His relative, David Raphael de Marcado, who passed on twenty-five years after Aaron, left money for a marble tombstone to be put on his grave and for a wall to be built around the graveyard.

The first Mercado settlers were joined by Lewis Dias, alias Jeshrun Mendes, who had escaped to Amsterdam, Holland and Recife, back to Amsterdam, then to Barbados. Here he became the principal organizer of Congregation Nidhe Israel, meaning The Scattered of Israel. In 1678 Eliau Lopez, a Marrano born in Malaga, Spain, in 1648 became their rabbi. Eliau had been a disciple of the Rabbi Isaac Aboab de Fonseca, the former rabbi of Recife. Lopez had also been a teacher in Abraham Mercado's home in Amsterdam. Rabbi Eliau Lopez officiated at Nidhe Israel for fifteen years. He ended his career in Curaçao.

By 1680 more than three hundred Jews resided in Barbados. At least three of them had large plantations. Jews often commuted from that island to the United States, where they had business connections and relations. Mordecai Campbell and Moses Pacheco had established a Jewish community on Rhode Island, but Joseph Bueno de Mesquita[27] was established in New York with his aging father. In 1862, Mesquita purchased the oldest existent cemetery in North America, at Chatam Square in New York City. The next year his father Benjamin died and was buried there, in the second oldest grave in Manhattan.

The route from Barbados to the United States mainland was often traversed by Jews in both directions. The cemetery in Barbados shows the grave of Moses Hayim Nahamias. *The Tourist Guide* shows that "he was the same man involved in tobacco litigation in Yorktown, Virginia, 1658." Nehemias was the first Jew to live in that state. In another case it was suggested that despite family claims, the will and tombstone of Jacob or Rodriguez Marques, deceased in 1725, was not Isaac Marks' father. Marks was said to have been born on Long Island and was not a progenitor of Bernard Baruch, the financier and government economist in World War I.

In Saint James' Parish, Speightstown, Jews had their second most populated area in Barbados. Speightstown had a branch synagogue called Semach David, meaning Offshoot of David. According to accounts given, that synagogue was destroyed in 1739. It seems that a family named Lopez had a hearty wedding reception. A young Gentile named Burnet, who pretended to be the governor's son, complained of a headache. A family member with a good heart, directed Burnet to the bride's father's home to lie down. The bride's father learned that the uninvited guest was an impostor. He gathered a group of Jews to help him search Burnet, whom he had accused of stealing. The Gentile was citywise and made such a noise that a mob of neighbors came to his rescue. With their bad tempers, and their love for a good fight, the Bajans (a pet name for Barbadians) scared the Jews and made them flee. With their fury unabated, the Bajans tore down Speightstown's synagogue.

In Saint Michael's parish, Bridgetown, the capital, the Jews had their largest community. The Bridgetown synagogue was destroyed in a hurricane in 1831. The decreasing Jewish population raised funds and overhauled the synagogue two years later.

Sugar prices declined in 1832 when slaves were emancipated. Emigration of Jews soon followed. Pretty soon there were only seventeen Jewish men, women, and children participating in Barbados. They were the total Jewish population. E.S. Daniels was the *Shammash*.[28] He opened the synagogue every Sabbath and was often the only worshipper there.[29] Daniels died in 1905. Jewish leadership was continued by two brothers named Baeza. They disposed of the cemetery and synagogue. The synagogue's beautiful wrought iron chandeliers became decorations of an outside porch at Delaware's DuPont Winterthur Museum.

A young Barbadian Gentile barrister named Eustace Maxwell Shilstone attempted to purchase the property in 1908. He had visited the synagogue as a child and had felt some reverence for it. Furthermore, he had seen his neighbors buried in the cemetery. Baeza overlooked Shilstone and sold the properties to a Mr.

Hutchinson instead, who turned the synagogue into office space. Hutchinson then turned the cemetery into garages, after turning the tombstones and mounds into rubble and level ground. Shilstone confronted Hutchinson and warned him that the dead should be respected and that no good would come of desecrating the cemetery and the temple. The Bajan curse which was put on Hutchinson might or might not have hexed Hutchinson; the poor fellow had a stroke before long, withered away and died.

New European refugees arrived in Barbados. They saw Shilstone trying to salvage whatever he could of the old cemetery. He put it in perpetual trust in the deeds of Barbados. After teaching himself Hebrew, Spanish, and Portuguese, Shilstone got on his knees and copied down 374 epitaphs on Jewish graves. They were published by the Jewish Historical Society of England in 1955 and by the American Jewish Historical Society the subsequent year, under the title Jewish Monumental Inscriptions in Barbados. Shilstone also recovered items from the abandoned synagogue and placed them on exhibition in the Barbados Museum. Afterwards, Shilstone obtained permission from the Barbadian Government to undertake recent burials of Jews in the old Jewish cemetery. As a result, recent gravestones may be seen there. In order to preserve those tombstones from tropical vegetation, some were dug out and placed into the cemetery walls with plaster. Quite a few were thus damaged and the process had to be discontinued.

Between the 1930s and 1940s, Barbados was admitting a recognizable number of Jews. They were mostly from Eastern Europe. After World War II the Jewish community found itself enjoying continued sunshine, beautiful beaches with clear water, and almost-white sand, and a Jewish community center. The Ashkenazi majority formed an Orthodox congregation named Share Tzedek, or Gates of Righteousness. That group is now decreasing in numbers. Most of the second and third generation leave Barbados for higher education in the United States. They often get educated and married and seldom return to the island. The cemetery has therefore been abandoned by the younger people. Many of them lack interest in traditions and often intermarry with Gentiles to become part of the power structure at home or abroad.

Postal and Stern conclude that the history of Barbadian Jews now shows:

> The arrival of Black Jews—natives of Barbados who became Jews during their working years in New York and have returned to their island to establish a Bridgetown synagogue known as Congregation Zion House of Israel.[30]

What these writers failed to mention is the fact that many of the refugees who were given shelter in Barbados were also allowed to

have Bajan women whom they kept on the side. Those Jewish men
became the negligent fathers of the dark-skinned Mendes, Lindo,
Blackman, Angus, Maduro, Henriquez, and other Jewish people all
over the West Indies and Latin America. Most of those poor women
raised their children with very little assistance from their pious
fathers. Naturally, the children were more concerned with survival
than being interested in ethnic or religious traditions. But once their
primary needs were met, they, too, began searching for satisfaction
of their cultural needs and spiritual guidance on a higher plane than
the one where Christians lynch others for having a different skin color
or non-Protestant affiliation. Moreover, the Romans took a Jew and
Romanized Him. So why shouldn't the Barbadians of color seek and
practice an African religion which Judaizes them? And why should
someone seek to worship the Son, when he can worship the Father?
And, after all, most people want to be God's chosen people!

CUBA

Cuba, with its 8,553,395 population, including the Isle of Pines and
adjacent isles, and its capital Havana lies ninety miles south of Key
West, Florida. Cuba has resources such as sugar, tobacco, nickel,
manganese, gold, lead, zinc, limestone, oil, gypsum, salt, and sul-
phur. Her multiple natural elements easily make her self-sufficient.
Cuba's Jewish population is only about two thousand, most of whom
live in Havana.

The first Jews who arrived in the Pearl of the Antilles, *La Perla de
Las Antillas*, went there with Christopher Columbus' ships. They were
the Marranos Luis de Torres and Alonso de Calle. Those men were
sent as interpreters to speak to the Indians and inquire if there were
any kings or cities in Cuba. The interpreters did not find any kings
and they could not speak the language, but they discovered tobacco. Torres stayed in Cuba to become a tobacco planter, exploit Indian
men, and use Indian women. He is considered the first Jewish set-
tler in the Western Hemisphere.

Other Marrano Jews, escaping three Inquisitions, followed Torres
to the newly discovered Cuban paradise. The Spaniards later sent
Hernando Alonso with a fleet of warships in 1511. These crew members later helped Hernan Cortes build the ships he used to conquer
Mexico. Alonso is said to have introduced sugar cane to Cuba. He
was later killed at the stake for heresy in Mexico. Alonso died without realizing that Cuba and India would become the two largest producers of sugar from cane.

Other Marranos were also killed at the stake for religious practices. After 1783 Cuba's Inquisition ended. However, the religious
laws were not totally discontinued until 1823. At that time, public
worship by non-Catholics was still punishable until Cuba became

independent from Spain in 1898. Despite Spanish religious persecution, Jewish merchants from Newport, Rhode Island; Philadelphia;
New York; Curaçao; Jamaica; and the Virgin Islands traded with Cuba
throughout the eighteenth century. When slavery was abolished, and
blacks refused to continue working in the fields, Chinese coolies were
brought in as field hands.

The Marranos began disappearing as a special group, but some
of their descendants remained on the island. They boasted of their
Grandee origin by being of Sephardic aristocracy or ancestry. In 1869
a popular actress named Delores de Dios-Porta received publicity for
having confessed her Jewish ancestry by refusing to accept the sacra-
ment offered to her on her death bed in Paris. Her refusal led to the
discovery.

Among the earliest Cuban freedom fighters, there was one Juan
Elias, credited with having organized an underground movement in
Santiago in the 1820s. That Jew is also credited with having served
under Simon Bolivar of Venezuela, and Jose Marti, the Cuban patri-
ot. Marti, himself, is charged with having adopted quite a few progressive ideas from Jewish labor leaders while he worked in New York
as a journalist among the cigar makers. In his effort to attain Cuban
independence from Spain, Marti is reported to have requested support from many Florida Jews.

Jews were also recorded among the 266 American seamen killed
on the U.S.S. Maine when that battleship exploded. The master of
the ship, Captain Charles Sigsbee, said he had been sent to Cuba to
protect American lives and properties (February 1898). The ship blew
up mysteriously in Cuban waters. The Secretary of the United States
Naval Board which investigated the mishap attributed the combus-
tion to mechanical failure and miscalculation in the ship's engine
room. The Naval admiral who conducted the investigation was Adolph
Marix, the first Jewish admiral of the United States Navy. Very strong
protestation of United States Annexation of Cuba came from U.S.
Senator Isidor Raynor, a Jew representing the State of Maryland.

After the Spanish-American War, Jews remained in Cuba with
other aliens who had served there. Those Jews became planters,
industrialists, and businessmen. One of them was a former American
sergeant, Frank Steinhardt. He built the first streetcar which ran in
Havana. A few Sephardic Jews, from North Africa and other parts of
the Near East, began drifting in. After the nineteen hundred Jews
came to Cuba steadily during the Balkan Wars of 1910 to 1913. One
of these Jews, from Turkey, was Maurice Soriano, who introduced
moving pictures to Cuba.

However, the history of the Jews in Cuba might really have begun
in the 1900s. Jews from the United States, particularly Florida, went
to Cuba in significant numbers at that time. In 1904 they opened the

United Hebrew Congregation and the Union Hebrew Shevet Ahim was composed. Its members were from Mexico, Syria, and Turkey. They were almost all Sephardic. After World War I there was an unsupported rumor that visas were more easily obtainable in Cuba for the trip to the United States. The rumor about easily obtainable visas caused twelve thousand poor Polish and Rumanian Jews to hurry to Cuba. They came steadily from 1924 to 1925. These Jews became very enterprising and caused several new industries to develop in Cuba. They received small loans from the Jewish Committee for Cuba, organized in the United States. Then in 1933 several thousand refugees came in from Austria and Nazi Germany. Cuba admitted these Jews as temporary residents. They had intended to use Cuba as a springboard to the United States.

Before the 1930s, American Sephardic and Ashkenazic Jews in Cuba segregated their synagogues and communal centers. The first synagogue was a Reform synagogue opened in 1906 by Americans. The second synagogue was a 1914 Sephardic one. It had a Colegio Herzl added to it for Jewish children. The Ashkenazi had their first synagogue, called Adath Israel, which opened in 1924.

Jewish immigration to Cuba slowed down due to changes in government in 1947. By 1957 there were approximately eleven thousand Jews in Cuba. Eight percent of those immigrants lived in Havana. About two hundred fifty of the Jewish immigrants left for Israel. Cuba had two Jewish periodicals at that time, *Havaner Lebn*, a Yiddish weekly newspaper, and *Israelita*, a Spanish monthly newspaper.

Fidel Castro came to power in 1959 after the revolution. Two years after the struggle for liberation from Batista's regime, the Jewish population of Cuba declined to about five thousand. Around 1971 exit visas for emigration were discontinued, but Jews left as tourists and the Jewish population declined to about fifteen hundred. Most of the Jews went to Florida along with Cuban political exiles and refugees. Others went to Puerto Rico, Israel, or to Latin American countries.

Castro's government has not affected Jews adversely as a group. Jews are treated like all other Cuban citizens who support the revolutionary policies and endure the sacrifices demanded. Castro seems to appreciate the fact that Jews contributed to his revolutionary efforts. Many young Cuban-born Sephardim and Ashkenazim were early Castro supporters. They were with his troops when Castro triumphantly marched into Havana in 1959. Jewish young men and women wore their *Mezuzahs* and Stars of David (Mogen David) along with their revolutionary emblems. Castro's revolutionary Minister of Communications was twenty-nine-year-old Enrique Oltuski, whose Jewish immigrant parents owned a shoe factory in Santa Clara. Manuel Novygrod, of Polish parents, was Castro's twenty-two-year-old Charge d'Affaires in Canada. Maximo Bergman, also of immigrant parents, led the pro-Castro revolutionary youth movement at the Havana University. In contrast, Jose Egozi, of Sephardic parents, living in Miami, joined the 2506th Brigade in the doomed Bay of Pigs invasion. Egozi was captured, along with the other Cubans of that counterrevolutionary movement, and imprisoned for eighteen months.

All five synagogues which existed before the revolutionary government came to power still have services. Government agencies often rent synagogue recreational facilities for concerts, theatrical presentations, moving picture shows, and other social gatherings. The Cuban government makes kosher meat available to two kosher butcher shops—said to be the only free enterprise in Cuba. The community's ritual slaughterer of kosher prepared animals and the superintendent of the Jewish cemetery are both government employees. All cemeteries are nationalized. The annual commemoration of the Holocaust victims of Nazi Germany's death camps is still held at the cemetery without impediment. At that site, Jews still view a cake of soap made from the remains of victims from an extermination camp. It is kept on view as a memorial.

Jewish meals can be obtained from a couple of restaurants. However, meat is rationed so very few people can overeat. To meet dietary needs, especially for High Holy Days and holidays, the Canadian Jewish Congress sends kosher products to Cuba. This practice is a recently implemented effort.

The Jewish Communists or sympathizers who remained in Cuba find themselves on the lower echelons of government administration and the armed forces. They occupy minor public offices. Nevertheless, George Altschuler was vice rector at University of Havana. Eduardo Davidson of Baracoa, the son of an Irish Jew, was a leading figure in Cuban music in 1976. Some of those Jews who remained attend Passover and other Jewish holidays and Holy Days. They get an opportunity to share the imported Matzos and follow the prayers.

Although it is believed that the Arab states pressure Cuba to discontinue relations with Israel, Castro still permits the Jews religious freedom and equal rights. All the government seems to expect from them is that they do not engage in counterrevolutionary activities. Cuba is so neutral in the Arab-Israeli dispute that Union Sionista (The Zionist Union) is located next door to the *Sociedad Club Arabe* (Arab Club Society. A similar situation exists in Mexico. Foreign people on the host country's soil are not allowed to bring their political differences into the country. They are guests and must act accordingly. Cuba does not tolerate abuse of privileges it extends. Furthermore, Israel was among the first nations which recognized the Castro government. And Cuba was the only country in the Communist orbit which recognized the Jews' right to worship openly. Cuban volunteers helped the Israeli army fight the War of Independence. Cuba's ambassador to Israel was Ricardo Subirana y Lobo in 1976. Lobo supported Castro before independence was won. Israel maintains diplomatic relations with Cuba; her legation is in Havana (1976–1993). And Cuba has a consulate in Israel (1993). Israeli technicians have visited Cuba and advised Cuban cattlemen of ways to improve their cattle breeding and livestock, citrus fruits, and other agricultural products.

With the harmonious relations existing between these two countries, a coordinating committee of Jewish organizations has been permitted. It coordinates communal activities. Charitableness is one of the committee's important functions. Nearly thirteen percent of the impoverished community depends on charity. Jewish merchants and manufacturers who lost their businesses to government expropriation depend on the organization. Jews who have been unable to leave Cuba receive a government compensation and old-age pension.

With the decrease of the Jewish population, two of Cuba's Jewish schools had to be closed when their enrollment dropped to less than one hundred pupils. The third largest school, Colegio Autonomo del Centro Israelita (Autonomous School of the Israelite Center) lost its self-governance and became nationalized. It is now called Albert Einstein School. All Jewish children whose parents remained in Havana attend that school.

CURAÇAO

Curaçao is the largest of the six autonomous islands of the Netherlands Antilles in the Dutch West Indies. Curaçao's population was 162,362 in 1981. Willemstadt (or William's City) is the capital of the Netherlands Antilles, which also includes the islands of Bonaire, Aruba, Saba, Saint Eustatius, and the southern half of Saint Martin.

Curaçao lies thirty-eight miles north of Venezuela. She has some shipbuilding, manufacturing of tiles, paints, and cement. However, the country's largest income is derived from her oil refineries. She has some of the largest oil plants in the world, and refines oil from Lake Maracaibo of Venezuela, one of the largest oil producers of the world.

Curaçao is one of the most important islands to Jewish historians and traditionalists. There were Jews there three hundred years ago. The descendants of those Jews, and even the newcomers, proudly show visitors their little wooden synagogue and boast about its aged existence. Historic Mikve Israel synagogue was a jumping-off point from which cantors and rabbis left to go and establish other Jewish communities abroad. Financial aid also left Curaçao's small community to assist "struggling young North American congregations." Curaçao's synagogue and cemetery are claimed to be the oldest Jewish shrines in the Western Hemisphere. When the United States came together in 1776, tiny Curaçao already had two thousand Jews, more than could have been found in all thirteen original states.

A Dutch fleet captured this little island from the Spaniards in July 1634. The interpreter of the naval vessel was a Portuguese Marrano convert to Christianity. He was Samuel Cohen, who had lived in Brazil in the 1620s where he had studied Dutch, Portuguese, Spanish, and a few Indian dialects. He had searched for gold in Curaçao unsuccessfully. In his fit of disappointment, Cohen had returned to Amsterdam. When he left, at least one Marrano is thought to have remained in Curaçao. That islander is felt to have been Julio de Araujo, who later went on to Mexico.

In 1651 the Dutch West India Company invited immigrants to settle in Curaçao. Joao de Yilan, also a Portuguese Marrano by birth, lived in Amsterdam. He signed a contract to escort fifty Jewish settlers to Curaçao. Only twelve persons actually arrived. Finding the land as arid as it was, the Jews considered it agriculturally unproductive and left. When the Dutch lost Recife to the Portuguese five years later, Isaac da Costa established Curaçao's first permanent Jewish settlement.

Even though Yilan and the first settlers might have worshipped in their homes, the people of Curaçao feel that the official synagogue and its Mikveh Israel congregation date back to 1659. The new arrivals on the island seem to have followed the practices of the old congregations they left in Amsterdam. Because Mikveh Israel's leaders enacted *hascamot*, (approval) there was dissatisfaction among the communicants. These were regulations which governed the life of each Jew as well as his obedience to the secular laws of the country in which he lived.[31] These laws were enforced for the two hundred years that followed; disobedience was punished by suspension. By 1674 the Jewish community of Curaçao had become large and economically solvent. They sent to Amsterdam for an *haham* (wise man or rabbi). This scholar was none other than Josiau Pardo, whose father and grandfather had been rabbis in Amsterdam. After serving here for nine years, Rabbi Pardo left Curaçao for Port Royal, Jamaica. It is supposed that he died there in the 1962 earthquake which shook up that island and others nearby.

We are told that when the Portuguese navigators began raiding the African coast in 1440, Curaçao became involved in the triangular trade. She had also been involved in the enslavement of Indians. Curaçao's Jewish community rose rapidly. There were about two thousand souls there by the 1770s. Many Jews were forced to go to Curaçao because of unfavorable French laws in Martinique and Guiana, where black slavery was also practiced. At the same time, every ship coming in from Holland brought Jewish passengers eager to become rich at any cost. With their basic needs met, the newcomers converted some houses into places of worship. The congregation of

Mikveh Israel-Emanuel built its first synagogue in 1703.

By 1730 the Jewish community had outgrown the pews in the synagogue. A collection was made for a new Temple. The town wall, which had been built along the present Columbusstraat (Columbus Street) had to be demolished, and a stream behind it was filled in with dumped land to provide the needed space. Community members bought some of this man-made land developed for expansion. A big contract was signed with a builder brought in from Holland, and the construction began. On the first day of Passover 1732, the present structure was consecrated and opened to worshippers.

The wooden floor of the synagogue was covered with sand. The congregants wanted to remind the old and acquaint the new generation with the manner in which they had to muffle the sounds of their footsteps when they held secret prayer meetings in countries where Jews were not permitted to worship their God. This tradition created varied interpretations over the years. One interpretation is that the sand symbolizes the desert through which the Children of Israel passed to reach the Promised Land. Another belief is it reminds us of God's promise to our forefather, Abraham, in Genesis Chapter 22. That promise states, "I will make your descendants as numerous as the sands of the sea." The sand is also said to remind us that Jews survived even when tossed about like sand in the seas, uprooted from soils by the winds of the ruthless, and rolled to and from by the waves of history. Some people say, however, "the sand serves as an easily available carpet over a bare plank floor, so worship is not disturbed." Some of the sand was shipped in from Jerusalem up to 1880. Mixing the imported sand with the sand from Curaçao symbolized Curaçao's close ties with the Holy Land from as early as 1671.

Some bitter feuds developed among Curaçao's Jewish factions in the early years. Some disagreements were considered social, others economic, or religious. The governor of the island was asked to arbitrate matters in quite a few instances, or to make decisions. Amsterdam's Jewish authorities were also called in from time to time to make decisions for the Curaçao factions.

After the dedication of the beautiful Mikveh* Israel-Emanuel synagogue, the Jews living across the canal in the Ostraband section organized their own *Neve Shalom*, or Dwelling of Peace. This new temple became the focal point of factional rebellion against the Mikveh Israel congregants and their orthodoxy. Another synagogue was built in 1746. It lasted until 1817, when it had to be abandoned through the relocation of most Jews to other parts of the community.

In 1863, some dissidents opposed incumbent Rabbi Chumacheiro, a Sephardi of Portuguese origin. The group of dissenters formed a society called *El Porvenir*, The Future. Their purpose was to reform the tenets and liberalize their way of life. *El Porvenir's* members published a periodical, "The Future." Its purpose was to criticize its enemies or critics against reformation. The schism produced Dutch Reform Congregation Emanu-el. This name was similar to New York's largest Reform temple.

In 1962 the Mikveh Israel congregation employed Rabbi Simeon Maslin for their Hebrew Union College. Rabbi Maslin found the seven hundred fifty Jews of Curaçao divided into three congregations. Mikveh Israel was Sephardic Orthodox; Emanuel, Sephardic Reform; and Shaare Tsedek an Ashkenazi Orthodox group composed mostly of recent arrivals from Eastern Europe. The new immigrants first organized themselves as a club then purchased a house which they converted into a temple in 1959. Rabbi Maslin organized a B'nai B'rith chapter as a cultural bridge for the entire seven hundred fifty or more Jewish residents of Curaçao. Maslin then encouraged the leaders of Mikveh Israel, and Emanu-el to reunite under the reunification plan.

Jews were actively involved in Curaçao's economic development. Some of them controlled trade in many freeport stores, dominated the professions, and participated in other activities of socioeconomic growth. "Numerous Sephardim can trace their families through the entire Jewish history of Curaçao."[32] As recorded here, some Jews left other areas for the Dominican Republic.

DOMINICAN REPUBLIC

The Dominican Republic is located approximately five hundred miles southeast of Florida, with Cuba to its west and Puerto Rico to its east. The Dominican Republic occupies two-thirds of the eastern part of the island of Hispaniola, while Haiti occupies the other poorer one-third.

The capital of the Dominican Republic is Santo Domingo. Under dictator, Rafael Leonidas Trujillo, the capital became Cuidad Trujillo. The population is about 4,012,000, of which in 1980 about seven-hundred fifty were Jews. The national resources of value are sugar, gold, tobacco, rice, coffee, and agriculture.

In 1938 when Jews from Nazi Germany and Austria sought refuge, the Dominican Republic was the only country to offer them unrestricted asylum. A home was discussed for Jews at the Evian Conference on the Geneva Lake near France, 1938. President Franklin Delano Roosevelt inquired about ways to rescue the Jewish refugees without a homeland. Representatives of thirty-one nations turned their backs on the Jews. Trujillo surprised the world by announcing that he would accept as much as one hundred thousand Jewish refugees into his country.

Trujillo kept his word, and reinforced his promise with a donation of twenty-six thousand acres at Sosua, on the northern coast of the Dominican Republic. That town, about two hundred miles from

Santo Domingo was formerly owned by the United Fruit Company and valued at $100 million. Trujillo also gave the Jews two additional tracts of land, totaling 53,000 acres.

In the spring of 1939 a team of land experts were sent to survey the land and test its soil. The agronomists declared it was arable land of good quality. The American Jewish Joint Committee organized the Dominican Republic Settlement Association (DORSA). On February 21, 1940, DORSA signed a contract with the Dominican government. The agreement included waiving all taxes for the Sosua Jews. The Dominican Congress ratified the contract and the Jews were allowed to bring in tools and equipment duty free. They were also promised religious freedom.

The first settlers arrived on May 10, 1940, the day Hitler invaded Belgium and the Netherlands. There were twenty-seven men, ten women, and one child among the settlers. Other settlers began coming in. By November 1941, the Jewish immigrants had increased to 413. The highest number of Jewish immigrants reached was 670. Each refugee was allotted seventy acres, ten cows, and a small amount of cash. The money came from the then existent American Society for Jewish Farm Settlement in Russia.

The majority of the settlers had been professionals or white collar workers in Europe. They had no farming experience or artisan skills. The Jewish DORSA organized their projects, and spent some $3 million on transportation, land improvement, roads, housing, and maintenance. It took some time for the newcomers to become self-sufficient. After their projects developed, the settlers owned a cooperative dairy complex, farm areas, cattle, and trucks. Later on these Jews established their own hospital, school, synagogue, and radio station. Alfredo Rosenzwieg, the managing director of the settlement, was later elected to the Dominican Senate in 1951.

By the mid 1950s the Jewish refugees are said to have changed plans. "Sosua began losing its young people to Puerto Rico [the gateway to the United States], the United States and Israel." Some of the older people followed. By 1966 the Jewish population was down to fifty-six families totaling about two hundred persons. At present, there are supposedly even fewer Jews in the Dominican Republic. From 1959 to 1960, when Sosua was declining, the government of the Dominican Republic issued two postage stamps introducing the Jewish colony and its people to the world. By that time, the yellow paint on the synagogue was fading and its congregants were still leaving the Dominican Republic for greener pastures. The only symbol of the community which remained undiminished was its Star of David on the front door. Even Moses Arnoldi, the colony's last religious leader, had left.

The Jews of Sosua were incorrectly recorded as the first Jews to have migrated to the Dominican Republic. But other historic data show that they had been preceded by others 448 years before. The first Jews were said to have landed in 1492 when Columbus called the island Hispaniola. The Marrano who interpreted for Columbus, Luis de Torres, tied the ship to a tree trunk for Columbus to land. The tree trunk to which the ship was moored is still preserved in Santo Domingo's cathedral, along with other Spanish relics, including ashes believed to be from Columbus' cremation.

Some historians believe that Marranos settled in "Santo Domingo during the reign of Columbus' son Diego, who governed the island from 1509 to 1520." A record is said to show one Marrano being burned at the stake by the Inquisition of the 1520s. But no document has been found to substantiate the claim. However, a descendant of a Marrano is mentioned as having become Minister of Finance toward the end of the nineteen century. Postal and Stern wrote about General Marchena as that Marrano. They also stated:

> Among the white descendants of the early Spanish colonists, many claim marrano ancestry, and some even treasure an old mezuzah or menorah to prove their claim.[33]

The same writers state that the oldest existing Jewish community in Santo Domingo began with a few Jews from Curaçao who settled there in the nineteenth century. About 1890 those few were joined by Russian Jews escaping Tzarist imperialism.

In 1917 several Jewish families arrived in Santo Domingo from the Virgin Islands. Among them was Wolf Paiewonski, whose relative later became a governor of the Virgin Islands. A Pan American Union report of 1917 recorded thirty-seven Jews living in the Dominican Republic. Most of them "it is said, had married native women and were rearing their children Catholics." Other Jewish families reached Santo Domingo from Cuba in 1933, when Cuba's President Machado and his henchmen were overthrown.

The growing Jewish congregation of Santo Domingo was known as Kahal Adas Israel before the Sosua colony was founded. Between 1939 and 1948, the congregants published a weekly newspaper in Spanish, Yiddish, and German, called *Diario del Sabado*, translated Sabbath or Saturday Diary. Their religious mentor was Fritz Steinmetz. Disagreement between the German speakers and their Yiddish-speaking brethren caused the organization of a new group to come into existence. This one was called *Centro Israelita*, translated Israeli Center. Their feud continued until 1957 when Trujillo sponsored an entirely new synagogue with marble and mahogany built at his expense. Forty Jewish families were counted in Santo Domingo, twelve in Puerto Plata, and two in Romana, at that time.

The total Jewish population of the Dominican Republic is estimated at 350 souls. Most of those Jews, living in the capital city, are listed as merchants by occupation; only a few of them are professionals.

JAMAICA

The political status of the island of Jamaica is classified as Independent Dominion in the British Commonwealth. The population of Jamaica in 1993 was less than 2,000,000. This island lies south of Cuba and west of Haiti. Jamaica is the second largest island in the Caribbean after Cuba and Hispaniola. The capital of Jamaica is Kingston, 550 miles south of Florida. Jamaica produces sugar, bauxite, tobacco, and other farm products.

The ethnic composition of the Jamaican community, at large, is somewhat different from the other islands studied here. In Cuba, the people are of predominantly Spanish, African, Taino Indians, and Chinese ancestry who were sent there to cut the cane after black and Indian slavery was abolished with independence. The Cubans pretend otherwise, but the facts are unquestionable. In the Dominican Republic, they are predominantly African, Indian and Spanish. The Haitians on the same island are mostly African, with some French. But the Jamaicans next door have an African, Hindu, Chinese, and Hebrew admixture. Nevertheless, the Jewish population of today is approximately 600, with most of them living in Kingston.[34] There are also some Lebanese, Hindus, and Syrians living near the Jews. The Hindus were brought in to cultivate the sugar cane after the black slaves were freed and refused to work.

The first Jews of record arrived in Jamaica during 1655. However, in 1868, Hill, a census taker, recorded illegal entries of Jews under pretense of not being Jews, and legal entries under the guise of being Christians.[35] The Jews are said to have begun arriving in Jamaica thirty-six years after Columbus landed there, about 1530. The Spanish governor de Cordoba in the 1590s, "may have been related to one of the island's earliest Jewish settlers."

During the British snatching of Jamaica from the Spaniards, about half of the foreigners on the island were considered Marranos escaping the Portuguese Inquisition. The Spaniards had killed the Arawak Indians and dominated the Island under Columbus' son. Now Admiral William Pen and Robert Venables had captured the island and subdued the Spaniards. However, it was not until 1670 that Jamaica was formally ceded to the British. A Marrano resident of Jamaica is heralded with having guided the British fleet into Kingston. He was Captain Campoe Sabbatha. He sailed up to the capital of Saint Jago de la Vega on May 16, 1655, for the bombardment and capture of that area now called Spanish Town. Another Marrano Jew or Sephardi of record is Acosta—a British supply master who arranged the terms of the Spanish surrender. The Spaniards were all ordered to leave Jamaica immediately after they surrendered. Only the Marranos were permitted to remain.

The British were more liberal with the Jews, and allowed them to worship as they chose. The Jews became British subjects under Oliver Cromwell's petitions which in 1660 became law under Charles II. In 1680 the Sephardim saw other Jews arrive from Brazil, France, Holland, and England. A large number of the new arrivals were Ashkenazim. The first Jewish community of influential numbers developed and multiplied in Port Royal, where prosperity had been brought by Sir Henry Morgan and other buccaneers.

The rapid success of Jewish settlers engaged in commerce after the British occupation caused much disagreement with the Christian merchants. The non-Jews requested the expulsion of all Jews in 1671. Even though the island's governor, Sir Thomas Lynch, commended the Jews for courageous combat against the buccaneers, the Christian traders repeated their petition for expulsion of the Jews in 1681. When that attempt failed, the Christians repetitioned.

Aware of the role Jews were playing in the sugar, molasses, rum, vanilla, slave, and intercolonial trade, the British attempted to protect the Jews of Jamaica. In 1699 the King of England advised the Earl of Jersey, Governor of Jamaica, to "treat the Jews gently, that they not be obliged to bear arms on their Sabbath or other solemn feasts unless it be when the enemy is near."

The Jews received special consideration from the British. They were the first British subjects in the entire United Kingdom to gain complete political equality and religious freedom denied other Jews outside of Jamaica. Catholics, and other Jews in the United Kingdom were barred from voting or holding public office. Those privileges were reserved for Anglicans until 1831. The instigator in the effort to obtain Jewish rights was Moses Delgado, a descendant of the first Jewish settlers in Jamaica.

Once the Jamaican Jews achieved political equality, the yearning was over and action began. Jews assumed important positions in the island's political and cultural life. In 1835 Alex Andre Bravo became the first Jew elected to the Colonial Assembly. Bravo saw Daniel Hart join him the next year. Hart was the first slave owner to free Jamaican slaves before slavery was outlawed in 1834. In 1837 and 1838 Jacob Sanguinetti and Samuel Barnett also joined the Assembly. By 1849, eight of the forty-seven members of the Jamaican Assembly, including its speaker C.M. Morales, were Jews. The Assembly adjourned on Yom Kippur out of respect for Jewish tradition and adherent members.

Jews made history in Jamaica even before these men arrived. The Hunt's Bay burial ground is considered the oldest burial ground for

Jews and others. The cemetery was first dug in the 1660s. The oldest dated grave shows 1672. The site was restored in 1936.

The first synagogue built in Jamaica, Kahal Kodosh Neve Tsedek, The Holy Congregation, the Abode of Righteousness, was erected in Port Royal. It was completed just sixteen years before an earthquake hit Jamaica in 1692. (The deed of this synagogue is now on view among the documents in the British Museum of London, England.) This synagogue was one of the topics in a letter written on the day of the earthquake, June 7, 1692. The letter was addressed to the master of University College, Oxford. Part of the correspondence reads as follows: "I turned into Ye Jewes Street, in order to get home, when their synagogue fell by my side." The temple was rebuilt and it functioned until a terrible fire devastated the town in 1815. The surviving Jews moved away to Kingston and Spanish Town.

Jews had also lived in Spanish Town before 1815. The synagogues appear to have been opened by Sephardim in 1704 and Ashkenazim in 1706. When Spanish Town became unpopular, the Sephardim moved to Kingston and erected a synagogue there in 1750. The Ashkenazim later built their synagogue in Kingston in 1789.

Jamaica's first rabbi was Josiah Pardo, who is believed to have arrived there from Curaçao in 1683. Later, Isaac Karigal, who preached in the Touro Synagogue of Newport, Rhode Island, arrived in 1771. Touro had been the first cantor of the Touro Synagogue when it opened in 1763. He headed to Jamaica in 1780 when the British captured Newport.

Kahal Kodesh Neveh Shalom and Mikveh Israel, the two synagogues for the Spanish Town community, were merged in 1844. They functioned until 1872, when Jamaica's capital was switched from Spanish Town to Kingston. The two synagogues were damaged in a 1907 earthquake. As Kingston developed, a new Ashkenazi synagogue was built in 1837. The Jamaica House of Assembly and the Kingston Corporation donated 1,070 pounds respectively for that project. But the two synagogues later caught fire and burned to the ground in 1882. After the fire, efforts toward merging the Sephardim and Ashkenazim temples caused disagreements which led to the formation of a third synagogue. This one was called Amalgamated Congregation of Israelites, founded in 1885. The older congregations, K.K. Shangar Hashamyim of the Sephardim and K.K. Share Yosher, rebuilt their temples and merged in 1900, they were again both flattened by the 1907 earthquake. The Amalgamated Congregation rebuilt its damaged synagogue on its original Duke Street site in 1911. Ten years later, the Ashkenazim joined the renamed United Congregation of Israelites, often called the Duke Street Synagogue. This congregation is credited with uniting all the present-day Jews of Jamaica.

A fourth Jewish community gathered in Montego Bay, Jamaica, in 1845. They built a Sephardic synagogue. By the early twentieth century, very few Jews remained to maintain the temple and the building was abandoned. The rabbi of the Montego Bay synagogue, during the 1850s, was one Abraham Pereira Mendes. His two sons, Frederick and Henry, followed in his footsteps and became noted rabbis in the United States.

The Jamaican newspaper, *Daily Gleaner*, was founded in 1835 by Jacob Cordova. Cordova and his brother Phineas planned and surveyed for the development of the city of Waco, Texas. The Cordovas' granduncle Joshua served as the religious leader of the Sephardic communities in Port Royal, Spanish Town, and Kingston for more than forty years. His tenure ended with his death in 1792. Jewish influence is proven by the Hebrew calendar and Hebrew letters in Jamaican almanacs of that era.

The Sephardim and Ashkenazim communities kept separate synagogues, cemeteries, and social activities. Until the late nineteenth century, intermarriage between the two groups "was considered as bad as marrying out of the faith."[36] Sephardic Jews, usually of non-converted Jewish stock, felt so superior to the central European converted stock that intermarriage was considered a loss or disfavor on the part of the Sephardic partner:

> Thus, the marriage of Dr. Lewis Ashenheim, an Ashkenaz who held the first M.D. [degree] awarded a Jew by a Scottish university, when he arrived in Jamaica in 1841, to Eliza de Cordova, daughter of the island's most prominent Sephardic family, caused great excitement.37

Ashenheim's grandson, Sir Neville Noel Ashenheim, became a member of the Jamaica Senate in 1976. Neville was part of the cabinet which negotiated Jamaican independence from Great Britain in 1962. He was then made Jamaica's first ambassador to the United States and one of the composers of that island's constitution. Sir Neville also became chief stockholder of the Jamaican *Daily Gleaner* and a trustee of the board of Jamaica College.

The present Jewish community of Jamaica is about eight hundred souls, most of them living in Kingston, with Montego Bay following. Some of those persons are said to be descended of Sephardic families from Syria. Others are of Ashkenazi families which took refuge from unstable political situations or unfavorable circumstances and climate in countries such as Egypt, Cuba, the United States, and Britain.

One recent mayor of Kingston was Eli Matalon, of Syrian origin. The Matalon brothers are credited with having done much for

Jamaica and its Jewish community. They built part of Kingston's harbor and large, new middle-and lower-income housing projects. Aaron Matalon was president of Jamaica's Manufacturers Association, honorary consul of Israel, and representative of the People's National Party of the Jamaican Senate.

A well-known business firm in Jamaica is the House of Myers, producers of world-famous Myers Rum. The Myers and the de Cordovas are related. Horace Myers was in the legislature in Kingston and served as president of the Jamaica Chamber of Commerce. Altamont da Costa of another leading Jamaican family served in the Legislative Council, and as Mayor of Kingston. He was a judge, and was named Jamaica's first citizen in 1926.

Jamaica's Jews are recognized as contributors of coastal vessels to the British Naval Command during World War II. Sir Neville Ashenheim coordinated a Jewish community relations and German Refugee fund which financed one thousand Jewish refugees forced out of London and Gibraltar. They came to Jamaica during the war. Wooden barracks were built for these Jews on the campus of the Jamaica University of the West Indies. Another relief committee was set up in the 1960s. This committee served Jews coming to the United States from Cuba.

Several cemeteries, the Duke Street Synagogue, and a Jewish institute were founded and maintained through Henry Silverman, who retired from public duties of great responsibility in 1965. Hillel Academy, a multi-racial non-denominational day school was established by the Rabbi Bernard Hooker. That academy supports a women's Zionist organization and a B'nai B'rith lodge. The Shaare Shalom Synagogue contains the seventeenth and eighteenth century relics of the synagogues Jews owned at that time. Records of documents, inscriptions, and epitaphs are evidence of the Jewish presence in Jamaica from 1920 to 1941. Jacob Andrade compiled those memorabilia after twenty years of research and acquisition. The Andrade family claimed to have lived in Jamaica for generations, dating back three hundred years.

PUERTO RICO

Puerto Rico is also called *Estado Libre Asociado* (Free Associated State). This Commonwealth is neither a state of the United States nor a republic. It has a population of almost two and one-half million—an average of 664 persons per square mile.[38] Of that number, about 3,500 are Jews. Some of these Jews float between Puerto Rico and the United States. Puerto Rico is located 1,000 miles southeast of Miami, Florida, with Haiti to the west, the Virgin Islands to the east, the Atlantic Ocean pounding its northern coast, while its southernmost shores are washed by the quieter waters of the Caribbean Sea. This island has some sugar cane, tobacco, and coffee.

Unlike the other islands, Puerto Rico has no revered synagogue or cemetery for Jews of olden times. But it has the largest Jewish population in the area in modern times.

When Columbus landed after his second voyage in 1493, Marranos accompanied him once more. There were also Africans on this voyage. The Africans had been visiting these shores and were familiar with the coastlines. Some writers feel that Jews settled in Puerto Rico as early as 1519.[39]

> The Spanish ships brought men of every sort to the New World. There were soldiers, who conquered the native people and defended Spanish claims to land. There were priests, who came to bring the Christian religion to the people called Indians. There were daring men, who came because they loved adventure. And always there were men who came to seek their fortunes, for treasure was discovered in the New World.[40]

The reason for believing that Jews settled with the early Spaniards and Africans stems from the fact that there are old Catholic families in Puerto Rico, who light candles on Friday evenings, "but with no recollection as to their meaning or origin." The tradition of lighting Sabbath candles allowed these Catholics to be considered as possible descendants of Jews. However, the practicing of Jewish religious liturgy and rites by Africans and Indians did not allow these dark-skinned persons to be given the same acknowledgment. Non-Europeans who practice any form of Judaism are usually classified (with hostile disdain) as converts or adopters. That behavior with its psychological ambivalence of practicing brotherhood while denying brotherly love, leads some to believe strongly that the racists are the converts and adopters.

Jewish presence in Puerto Rico gained significance during the Spanish American War. It was felt that when the Spaniards occupied Puerto Rico prior to 1898, the fear and recollection of the Inquisition moved thousands of Jewish immigrants to volunteer to help the United States defeat Spain. Some Jews rode with Teddy Roosevelt's "Rough Riders," and quite a few of them received medals for meritorious service.

The first Jewish congregation of Puerto Rico is said to have been informal, and short-lived. The group was organized by Rabbi Adolph Spiegel, who served with an American regiment at Ponce in 1899. Spiegel held Rosh Hashanah and other services in a telephone exchange building from 1899 to 1905. Lieutenant Colonel Noah Sheppard, who went to Puerto Rico as an Army sergeant in the Spanish American War, stayed after his retirement. Sheppard married a local woman after his war years and became an early leader of the Puerto Rican Jewish community.

From 1900 to the early 1920s, there were transient Jews arriving in Puerto Rico and leaving. Only a few seemed to settle permanently. The Charles Gans family of Connecticut went there and opened a cigar factory in 1899. Milton Farber and Nathaniel Nameron were other early settlers. Some East European Jews who did not gain legal admittance to the United States remained in Puerto Rico to await legal entry. After learning Spanish, however, some of them stayed in Puerto Rico and became owners of a chain of department stores. Simon Benus and Aaron Levine were among them.

An organized Jewish community was not recognizable in Puerto Rico until World War II. Nevertheless, individual Jews made their contributions to Puerto Rican history from 1900 to 1935.

The Island made progress as soon as Spain ceded it to the United States. United States President McKinley named Leo Stanton Rowe the codifier of laws for the acquired territory called Puerto Rico. Rowe later became director general of the Pan American Union. Jacob Hollander, professor of economics at Johns Hopkins University, organized Puerto Rico's revenue system and became its first treasurer. Louis Sulzbacher, who encouraged American citizenship for Puerto Ricans was a Justice of Puerto Rico's first supreme court, who encouraged American citizenship for the Puerto Ricans. Adolph Wolf—another Jew—succeeded Sulzbacher.

Associated with the University of Rio Piedras was Julius Matz, who administered the insular experimental pathology laboratory of Rio Piedras for many years. Joseph Jacobs, who helped to develop Puerto Rico's earliest irrigation system, was an engineer with the United States Reclamation Service. William Hoffman and Charee Weiss were medical doctors who spent several years fighting, researching, and documenting tropical diseases. During Franklin Delano Roosevelt's administration, A. Cecil Snyder served as United States Attorney for Puerto Rico. Snyder later became Chief Justice of the United States Territorial Supreme Court. Robert Zold, considered a prominent Zionist, was Attorney General in Puerto Rico during the Wilson administration. Max Goldman directed the Puerto Rican government's Tax Exempt Board. David Helfield is now dean of the Law School at University of Rio Piedras.

A Pan-American Union trade report of 1917 listed only six Jewish families in Puerto Rico when Weiss had a Passover Seder in his home in 1927. There were only twenty-six known Jewish families then. Most of them were Americans, a few French Jews from other Caribbean islands among the group, and a few families from Cuba. These Jews were mostly unable to hold services for lack of a Minyan. As a result, they did not have a permanent congregation.

By 1942 the number of Jewish families increased in Puerto Rico.

The thirty-eight families then existent formed an organization called the Social Services League. The name of the league was later changed to the Jewish Community of Puerto Rico when thousands of American troops landed there in 1941 and 1942. Jewish chaplains joined the Puerto Rican Jews giving the islanders kosher foods, appurtenances, and professional expertise in traditional practices.

In 1942 the Puerto Rican Government formed an organization to promote industrial development, officially named the Economic Development Administration. The Spanish-speaking people called it *Fomento*— a word meaning development or promotion.

Milton Farber, one of the early settlers, became chairman of the National Jewish Welfare Board Armed Services Committee. It supported the Jewish servicemen and rabbis in uniform. His wife became president of Puerto Rico's chapter of Hadassah, founded in 1945 as the organization's first overseas unit. Then there were chaplains like Rabbi Levy Becker and Rabbi Bertram Pollans, who coordinated Jewish servicemen and civilians in cultural and social activities which led to present-day Jewish community interaction.

After World War II, Muñoz Marin, the first Puerto Rican governor of Puerto Rico, promoted industrial expansion fostered by American capital. Corporations and big industries were offered tax exemptions under Operation Bootstraps. Several young Americans of Jewish origin followed the boom as merchants, engineers, scientists, administrators, teachers, and investors. Factories were built and production began. Their curious relatives and friends then visited Puerto Rico as tourists.

The Puerto Ricans were also interested in bringing tourists to Puerto Rico. The climate and beaches made it an ideal place for tourists. But Puerto Rico had few modern hotels and no one wanted to invest in building good hotels; Cuba had the tourist trade. Teodoro Moscoso, a Gentile interested in bringing tourists and factories to his country, felt that one good hotel would attract tourists and start a trend. His agency (*Fomento*) built a fine modern hotel in San Juan for $7,200,000 and leased it to the Hilton Chain. Tourists flocked to the Caribe Hilton completed in the late fifties. Other hotels were soon built along the beaches at San Juan.

Castro had come to power and rejected United States foreign policy. More tourist trade detoured from Cuba to Puerto Rico. Jews from Cuba and other Spanish-speaking areas migrated to Puerto Rico, a laboratory or land yearning for technicians and experts, capital and vision.

When World War II ended and the chaplains left the island, regular services and Sabbath observance were held in a rented loft in San Juan under the guidance of Aron Levin and Simon Benus. The first Hebrew school was opened in 1952. On July 25, 1952, Puerto

Rico became a Commonwealth of the United States. And until 1955 the Jewish community on the island found its religious guidance directed by part-time Jewish chaplains stationed at Ramey Air Force Base and the Roosevelt Roads Naval Station. Rabbi Nathan Witkin, the field director in the Panama Canal Zone also helped conduct traditional observance.

In 1953 the Puerto Rican Jewish community purchased an old mission, formerly owned by a Nazi sympathizer which was turned into a Jewish Community Center with Shaare Tzedek as its synagogue. The congregants were Conservatives. In 1964 a B'nai B'rith lodge was organized by the group and the first cemetery for Jewish bodies on the island became consecrated. Another congregation, the Reform Temple Beth Shalom, was founded in 1967, the second Jewish group organized in Puerto Rico. They conducted a religious school, supported several Jewish youth corps, and coordinated annual campaigns for the United Jewish Appeal. The Beth Shalom congregants and sympathizers also conducted drives for the sales of Israel's Bonds.

THE VIRGIN ISLANDS

The Virgin Islands are United States Territories. The three principal islands are Saint Thomas, Saint Croix, and Saint John. The other islands total one hundred, including the British Virgin Islands of Tortula, Anegada, and Virgin Gorda. The population of Saint Thomas and its counterparts numbered approximately 138,000 in 1993. These islands are located forty miles east of Puerto Rico, and strategically situated along the approach to the Panama Canal. In 1917, these islands were purchased from Denmark by the United States for $25,000,000 because of their strategic position.

SAINT THOMAS

The capital of Saint Thomas is Charlotte Amalie. Before the United States purchased its portion of the Virgin Islands from Denmark, many Jewish families left the islands for Santo Domingo. They spoke Spanish and the Dominican government was easier to deal with. The Jewish portion of the present population is, therefore, a meager two hundred or so. The Saint Thomas Hebrew congregation called their synagogue Beracha V. Sholom V' Gemilath Chasdim. The name meant, Blessing and Peace and Acts of Piety. Their Reform movement identified them with Union of American Hebrew congregations in the United States. In 1833 a building was erected to replace one destroyed by a hurricane. The writers Postal and Stern did not give more data. They stated that more information would be available from the Virgin Islands' Public Library.

The Virgin Islands have no large deposits of natural resources as do Cuba and Jamaica. The people of Saint Thomas depend mostly on tourism and shipping. American citizens and residents with permanent status are allowed to purchase duty-free goods imported to the islands from various parts of the world.

SAINT CROIX

The island of Saint Croix is the largest of the United States Virgin Islands. Its capital is Christiansted. Saint Croix is located forty miles southeast of Saint Thomas.

The Jewish population there is numbered at about forty souls according to a local Jewish resident. The Jews of Saint Croix are not congregationally oriented and they meet only occasionally.

The United States Virgin Islands have had Jewish, black, and white governors. A Jewish cemetery may be found in Saint Croix's western suburb, beside the Moravian Cemetery of Christiansted. It shows tombstone engravements with epitaphs dated from 1779 to 1862.

Unlike other islands, the Virgin Islands have Jewish families and cemeteries dating back to the seventh century. Jewish traders and merchants seem to have arrived there for residence from Holland and Brazil shortly after the islands were settled by the Dutch in the 1650s. Saint Thomas, more populated than the others, passed to the Danish West India Company in 1671; Saint John was claimed by Denmark in 1683; and Saint Croix was purchased from France by the Danes in 1733. The islands became a Danish colony in 1754.

Saint Thomas and Saint John were governed from 1684 to 1686 in the name of the king of Denmark by a Jewish soldier of fortune named Gabriel Milan. He is said to have belonged to a prominent Marrano family. However, Milan was a rascal whose incompetence, dishonesty, and brutality led to his being recalled to Copenhagen, tried, and hanged.

Saint Croix had also rescued and maintained Jews in the late seventeenth century. However, there was no recognition of a considerable Jewish community there until 1733, when France ceded Saint Croix to Denmark. Emanuel Voss, a Danish-Jewish trader, relayed word of the French secession of Saint Croix to Denmark to the governor of French Martinique. By 1760, a small congregation was formed at Christiansted, Saint Croix. Six years later the small group opened a synagogue. Moses Benjamin, a Saint Croix merchant, received kosher meat ordered from New York. The Saint Croix congregation disintegrated about 1800.

Saint Thomas' permanent Jewish community is supposed to have come into existence after British Admiral Rodney raided Saint Eustatius Island. Rodney looted that island in 1781 because the residents had been supplying arms, ammunition, and food to the

American colonies during the Revolutionary War against Britain. The Jewish merchants and shippers were said to leave Saint Thomas and resettle in Saint Croix.

Denmark was neutral, so Saint Thomas' excellent harbor and its valuable geographical position made it important to the sea rovers. As a result, Saint Thomas prospered as a free port, with dry docks for repairs, and a repository for cargo in transit. Ships from Jamaica, other islands, and the United States stopped there, unloaded, exchanged, or picked up cargo. They also put in for supplies and water.

Existing records indicate that the first synagogue in Charlotte Amalie was built in 1796. However, there are suspicions that an earlier Jewish group might have existed in Saint Thomas before 1796.

There were only nine Jews with families recorded up to 1801. In that year the Jewish population of these islands rose steadily from the lower figure to twenty families in 1803. That number increased to sixty-four in 1824 to more than eight hundred Jewish families in the area by 1850. During that period, Jews accounted for almost half of the Virgin Islands' white residents.   When the steamship era declined, the islands' economy dropped with it. Conditions worsened when a cholera epidemic and a cyclone combined their evil forces in 1837 to kill 3,000 people.* The two disastrous experiences upset an already depressed population. The Jewish chandlers, brokers, traders, importers, and shopkeepers began drifting away. The planters followed them. By 1890 the Virgin Islands' Census Bureau reported only one hundred forty Jews contacted. In 1917, when the United States purchased the islands, there were only forty Jews found. So few whites were there that the "rabbi was the only authorized clergyman available to bless the transfer of the islands."

The synagogue built in 1796 was destroyed by fire in 1804. Nevertheless, it was rebuilt in 1812, enlarged in 1823, and overhauled in 1831—after being burnt out on two suspicious occasions. The present synagogue in Charlotte Amalie is the only one of recognized use in the modern Virgin Islands. This synagogue was dedicated in 1833 on the same site of the original building.

The old synagogue might have been witness to those American patriots and revolutionaries who visited the Virgin Islands in her olden days. Because the older Saint Thomas cemetery shows gravestones of the parents and grandparents of those trafficking there and remaining to enjoy eternal rest on the island. Among them are two generations of the progenitors of Camille Pissaro, a famous French impressionist painter who was born in Saint Thomas in 1800. This older cemetery also bears the remains of David Yulee's ancestors. Yulee was the first Jew elected to the United States Senate—from Florida—in 1845. And Joseph Benjamin, who became Secretary of

State for the U. S. Confederacy, was also born in Saint Thomas. The coming and going of Jews created the need for a synagogue. The Saint Thomas synagogue was saved from being destroyed like the one of Saint Croix because of Moses D. Sasso, who kept the congregation alive even when it had reduced in numbers to merely six Sephardic families. One of the remaining congregants was Morris Fidanque de Castro, who was born in Panama. Fidanque was a career civil service employee who became commissioner of finance, cabinet member, and secretary to the governor of the Virgin Islands. Later on, this same Fidanque became Governor of the Virgin Islands under President Harry Truman in 1950.

Sasso (another Sephardic name very popular in Panama) was born in the Virgin Islands of parents whose ancestry dates back two hundred years. Sasso served the congregants of his native Saint Thomas from 1914 to 1965. Rabbi Sasso's predecessor was Rabbi David Cardoze who served the Jewish community of Saint Thomas from 1887 up to his death in 1914 at the age of ninety. "Sasso had left Saint Thomas for Panama but he returned to marry Cardoze's granddaughter and to succeed him at his request." Under Sasso's guidance, the Saint Thomas' synagogue slowly abandoned the Sephardic liturgical practices to become a Reform congregation following the island's renaissance during and after World War II. Sasso's followers were all Reform rabbis from the United States, where early reformers at Temple Emanu-El in New York had tried Torah reading and other reform practices of the Leipzig Synod of 1871.

The Synod had proposed shortening the readings of Torah, partial or full translation of the text, meaningful reading with explanations without chanting, and abandonment of the practice of saying a personal blessing (*mi she berakh*) in behalf of those called up to read the Law on the *bimah*, or pulpit.[41]

The first Jews to come to the Virgin Islands from Eastern Europe were said to be members of the Levine and Paiewonsky families. They arrived from Lithuania in the 1880s about the time that Manuel Joel of Breslau arrived in New York. Rabbi Joel had been one of the two debaters at the Synod in Leipzig. He later went to New York's Temple Emanu-El to support Zionism and promote Reform Judaism.[42]

The Levines opened a dry goods store where Isaac Paiewonsky worked as a boy at the age of fourteen. After some years, Paiewonsky branched out into different businesses which contributed much toward the revival of Saint Thomas' economy. Papa Paie, as he was called, was the father of Ralph and Isidor Paiewonsky. He built up his family business to such an extent that they became leaders in the island's economy and its cultural and political life. The Paiewonskys assisted in founding the College of the Virgin Islands in 1962. This family in 1964 also organized the B'nai B'rith Lodge called

Cardoze and Sasso in honor of those two rabbis.

Ralph Paiewonsky was appointed Territorial Governor by President John F. Kennedy in 1961, after several terms in the island's legislature. He was the first local-born person of European parentage to be made governor of the Virgin Islands. Paiewonsky was reappointed by President Lyndon B. Johnson in 1965. He soon encouraged tourism to the islands and spurred remarkable economic recovery and social progress. In addition, Isidor Paiewonsky was mentioned as having written a history of Jewish life in the Virgin Islands.

About two hundred families now reside in Saint Thomas, with a small number living in Saint Croix. Most of these *Yehudim* came from the United States after World War II. Most of these Jews are teachers, government officials, dentists, doctors, and lawyers. However, one-third of them operate hotels, souvenir shops, rum distilleries, bottle manufacturing plants, factories, and real estate offices.

A few members of Sephardic families have survived. They keep in contact with mainland and other island Jews or those in Panama. Some popular residents of the Virgin Islands are Herman Wouk the author, who orders kosher food from New York by plane, and Maurice Petit, a former superintendent of the West India Cable Company, who also is the founder of the Saint Thomas Botanical Gardens. A famous family that has been forgotten is the Gabriel Milan clan. Milan came from Hamburg and was governor of the Virgin Islands from 1684 to 1687. Some Jews who did not go to the Caribbean islands went to Bermuda, nearer to the U. S. A.

BERMUDA

Bermuda, or Great Bermuda, is a British Crown colony located 500 miles east of Cape Hatteras, North Carolina, and 675 miles southeast of New York. It comprises 300 coral rocks, islets, and islands of which some 20 are inhabited. Other smaller secondary islands are Somerset, Ireland, and Saint George. The beaches are excellent and the people are as sunny as the climate.

Bermuda is small with a population of 52,700 persons in 1990. About ten of that number are Jews. There were Jews in Bermuda's capital city Hamilton as early as the seventeenth century. Records show a syndicate headed by Moses and Jacob Franks as the largest purveyors of supplies to Bermuda's British troops during the two decades preceding the American Revolution. Then, in the twentieth century President Franklin D. Roosevelt convened a Bermuda Conference to consider methods of rescuing Jews trapped by Nazi occupations. A number of Allied nations sent representatives to Bermuda from April 19 to April 30, 1943. The proceedings were kept secret, but no feasible suggestions were made and no concrete results obtained.[43]

World War II saw the United States lease air and naval bases from Bermuda in 1940. The Jewish employees, in civil service and military agencies, organized their Jewish community. Services were held and burials were sporadically conducted at the United States Air Force chapel. The rabbis were usually visiting Jewish chaplains from mainland United States. Jewish tourist were also recognizable participants.

It is said that although no Jewish community ever established permanent settlement in Bermuda, many Jews have been there as tourists since the post World War II tourist boom. Most popular hotels in Bermuda will provide Jewish guests with kosher meals for *kashrut* observance or vegetarian dishes if they are requested.

GUADELOUPE AND MARTINIQUE

Guadeloupe is a French overseas possession. Its capital is Basse Terre. Guadeloupe's population was approximately 326,000 in 1994. Its island group is comprised of Grand Terre and the dependencies of Marie-Galante and Les Saintes to the south of Guadeloupe proper.

Guadeloupe is located 110 miles north of Martinique. The people speak French and a patois, an admixture of French and an African dialect. After Columbus landed in 1493, Guadeloupe was occupied briefly by Spaniards. They did not remain after 1604. The French who shared the island with the Caribs and Spaniards came in full force in 1635.*

Although this island might have had early Jewish residents, no permanent settlement was recorded for them until the arrival of Jewish refugees from Recife, Brazil in 1654. Benjamin da Costa d'Andrade was among those pioneers.

By 1676, a synagogue was erected in Martinique. That year, Andrade went to Amsterdam and brought back a Torah from the Amsterdam Synagogue. The 1680 census shows eighty Jews in Martinique. Three years later, that number is supposed to have increased. They went to and from Martinique, but no permanent group of Jews established residence in the sister island of Guadeloupe or on Martinique.

The island of Martinique is found in the midst of a chain of islands which extend from the United States Virgin Islands to the Venezuelan coastline. Martinque is approximately 375 miles southeast of Saint Thomas. The capital of Martinique is Fort-de-France. The total population was 343,000 souls in 1994.

Sugar cane was introduced to Martinique from Brazil in 1654. In 1946 Martinique became a department of France after being blockaded by the United States Navy from 1943 to 1946. The Martinicans had supported the Vichy pro-Nazi regime after France collapsed in

World War II. But the United States' blockade forced the islanders to change their allegiance and support France under General deGaulle instead of the Vichy Regime under Marshal Henri Philippe Petain.

The synagogue which was built by the Jews did not gather any momentum. The island was controlled by Jesuits, who engaged in banking and soul-saving of the merchants and other islanders of the Catholic faith. The Jews found some protection, however, when King Louis XIV's comptroller general of finances, Jean Baptiste Colbert, came to their rescue in 1665. Colbert (1619–1683) encouraged colonial trade and felt that Jews were good businessmen. As a result, the Jews of Martinique were protected for a little while.

An anti-Jewish governor was appointed for Martinique by the French. With Colbert's power weakening in France, the Jews began to find themselves pushed back once more. They abandoned the island in considerable numbers in 1683 when Colbert died. Two years later, the Jesuits succeeded in passing a Black Code Law which prohibited Jews from obtaining permanent residence in French territories or colonies. Jews, who passed through Guadeloupe and Martinique after 1683, are an unrecorded group. (Postal and Stern, 1976).

A few Jews are in Martinique's new capital (Fort-de-France) now. They claim that most Jewish historical data, monuments, and relics were destroyed when Mount Peles erupted in 1902 and ruined the old capital, Saint Pierre. Earthquakes and tropical vegetation is said to have also covered and rotted whatever relics and data or objects which might be helpful in a study of Jewish settlers.

HAITI

The island of Hispaniola is shared by Haiti and the Dominican Republic. Since 1697, the western one-third of Hispaniola has been separated from its Spanish-speaking neighbor. Haiti has no gold like Santo Domingo, just a little bauxite, cotton, sugar, sisal, and spiny lobsters which are exported to the United States. This country was handed over to the French by the Spaniards in 1697. One hundred years later, Haiti's Africans revolted against their French exploiters. During that time, the Americans had gotten rid of their British exploiters, and the French peasants had also revolted against tyranny in France. Those two historical experiences inspired the Haitians to seek independence also.

Haiti is an independent republic located seven hundred miles southeast of Miami, Florida. Her population was approximately 5,000,000 in 1994. Of that number only a handful are Jews. But many Jews left offspring there who are not counted as Jews.

The first Jews to reach Haiti are said to have been Marranos who arrived there in the early sixteenth century. They landed at Cape

Haitian, the old capital. The current capital is Port-au-Prince. A record of a Marrano named Juan Sanchez is shown at the library of Port au Prince explaining a special license granted to him in 1502 to ship horses and grain to Haiti.

Even with the 1683 Black Code prohibiting trade by Jews in French colonies, Jewish traders could be seen in almost every Haitian port. The Gradis family of Bordeaux were outfitters of French settlements in Canada. The Mendes family were considered their competitors. The latter operated trade posts in Haiti beginning in the 1750s. The Du Pass clan is said to have operated plantations. Abraham Sarzedas from Bordeaux, later of Charleston, South Carolina, was called Haitian agent for important Jewish merchants from Newport, Rhode Island, around 1764 to 1774. Among the merchants were Jacob Rodriguez Rivera and Aaron Lopez. A tax list dated January 1675 shows twenty-nine Jewish families in Cape Haitian. Another eight families were widely scattered throughout other areas. It is possible that a congregation might have been assembled at some point during that time, but evidence is unavailable.

A Jewish planter of record was Jacob Toussaint. There has been "speculation on his relationship to Haiti's great Black liberator, Pierre Domingue Toussaint L'Ouverture."[44]

The African revolt of the 1790s shattered and scattered the Jewish community in Haiti. The rebels were not all black. Some of them were white, and others were Creoles (French and African) or mulattoes (Spanish and African, Jewish and African, and whatever European and African). Very very few Europeans brought women with them; that is why Europe decided to furnish strumpets for America even from prisons. Nevertheless, most people who write history research superficially, and garnish their works with the same old cliches about enslavement being endemic to blacks. They seek to justify bigotry rather than reveal facts.[45]

Another book of reference mentioned the revolutionaries of Haiti as "blacks (the descendants of African slaves) who still follow West African cultural patterns."[46] It is of greatest importance to state, in passing, that Hispaniola (Haiti and Santo Domingo) is the island where the first slaves were landed in America. However, it is yet more important to note the fact that those slaves were not black. They were white, and they were women—prostitutes to be sure. These whores were dropped in Canada, Haiti, and the United States at different times in history. The first slaves came as early "as 1501, only nine years after the first voyage of Columbus." Blacks were not thought about with importance until 1510.

Davidson states: "These slaves were white—whether from Spain or North Africa—more often than Black, for the Black slaves, it was early found, were turbulent and hard to tame." Some historian contradicts the pseudochroniclers whose works are steeped in insecurity. Some writers, who are bigots, have an irrepressible urge to continually distort the facts in order to superiorize themselves and inferiorize others. Davidson exposed them by declaring, "How poor grounded in fact was the legend of 'African docility.'"[47]

A Soria family is credited with a hair raising tale of escape from prison during the slave uprising in Haiti. It is said that a black leader who recognized Aaron Soria as a merchant saved him from possible liquidation or interminable incarceration. Jews who were able to leave Haiti, fled to other lands. Those who could not leave, fled to the interior. A few are said to have "found their ways to the town of Jeremie, where today's Blacks frequently claim Jewish descent."

The 150 or more Jews now residing in Haiti are believed to be mostly in the capital city of Port-au-Prince. However, they are no longer considered an organized group. They are classified as offspring of Jews who came from Syria and the Balkans. Their progenitors immigrated to Haiti early in this century. Other later arrivals came from Egypt, Eastern Europe and Germany and some have intermarried with blacks.

An American novelist, named Herbert Gold, went to gather information for a novel. "He found Black Haitians of Jewish descent." Gold also "met an anti-semite named Cohen who advertised kosher wine imported from the United States." Gold even met a French Jew named Calman who had run to Haiti to escape Nazi terror. There was also mention of a Russian Jew named Lazareff in a mountaintop home. Lazareff had a Haitian wife and a good library at home. An old tailor, named Schneider (which means tailor in German), was also interviewed in 1969. The tailor was referred to as a person who spoke French with a heavy Yiddish accent. Schneider died. It was also written "Gold attended Schnieder's funeral in Jacmal, where a voodoo ceremony was conducted by his Black children."[48]

Israel is credited by Fischer with sending experts to Haiti to teach fish hatching and tomato cultivation to the Haitians. Kurt Fischer, the former chairman of the Haitian Tourist Bureau, is now living in San Juan. He assembled all available documents and relics he could find relating to Haitian Jewish presence. A voodoo cup, given to Fischer by Haitians, turned out to be a *Kiddush* cup with a Hebrew inscription—made in Dublin in 1788. The Israeli Consul General is mentioned as having "taken a lively interest in Haitian Jewish history."

SAINT KITTS-NEVIS AND ANGUILLA

Saint Kitts-Nevis and Anguilla were discovered by Columbus in 1493. Saint Kitts was named after Columbus' Saint Christopher. Nevis was derived from nieves, meaning snow in Spanish (St. Kitts is the nickname of the island Saint Christopher.) But the British began arriving at St. Kitts in 1623. French settlers came to Nevis two years later. British settlers arrived in 1628, and the Treaty of Paris of 1783 award-ed the islands to Britain. These islands were part of the colonies of the Leeward Islands until 1967, when they became a self-governing state in association with Great Britain.

Nevis is the home of the brilliant lawyer Alexander Hamilton (1755–1804) who formed the United States Coast Guard. He was a Secretary of the Treasury under George Washington, after a heroic military career, and was a member of the Continental Congress. This mulatto—like so many other people who have been conveniently clas-sified as white—helped to show how Hebrews became Jews through miscegenation. The people of color in Nevis, and the descendants of Hamilton recount tales of his mulatto mother and Scottish father.*

Nevis is part of the independent state of Saint Kitts-Nevis; its cap-ital is Basseterre. Anguilla is still a colony of Great Britain. The chief settlement on Nevis, however, is Charlestown, Hamilton's birthplace. The population of Nevis was about 46,000 in 1987; she lies 175 miles southeast of Saint Thomas.

Of the quarter of a million people living on these islands, only a handful are Jews. But Jews were considered part of the inhabitants as far back as 1670. At that time, the British separated the admin-istration of the Leeward Islands from Barbados and other Windward Islands. With the increase of sugar taxes in Barbados, many people migrated to up-and-coming Nevis.

In Nevis, there were only five heads of Jewish families from 1677 to 1678. But by the 1800s there were enough Jews in Nevis to form a congregation and have a synagogue. These Jews became active par-ticipants in the enslavement of blacks. Charlestown was a busy slave market and way station. By 1724, Jews were considered one fourth of Charlestown's white population—according to an observant Anglican minister's report. Existing tombstones in the Jewish ceme-tery date from 1679 to 1768. A hurricane might have caused the Jews to abandon Nevis in 1772.

One of the most popular Jews on the island of Nevis was Roland Gideon (1654–1722). Gideon was a Sephardi born in England of Portuguese ancestry. Gideon and his brothers, Samson and Abraham, sought their fortune in Barbados, but did not succeed there. He then tried Boston from 1674 to 1675, trading in tobacco and other com-modities. In 1680, Gideon sailed from Barbados to Antigua, and from there on to Nevis. He returned to Barbados and married Bathesheba on August 8, 1684. When she died, Gideon honored his deceased wife with a well-decorated tombstone elaborately carved in Hebrew and English. He returned to Barbados and then went on to England where he remarried. He died in England as a wealthy man and a leader of the Sephardic community. Gideon's son Samson (1699–1762) became a financial consultant to George II, king of England.

Rabbi Malcolm Stern, coauthor of *American Airlines Tourist Guide*, visited Nevis in 1957. The island was celebrating the two hundredth anniversary of the birth of its famed native son, Hamilton, who helped to organize the government of the United States in its infancy. Stern and others learned that Hamilton had a house there which was almost in ruins before it was rescued by the United States and made a museum. The Sterns also learned that Hamilton had been an illegitimate son. As a result of the union between a Black mother and a white father, Hamilton "was denied admission to the Anglican school and consequently received his elementary education in the synagogue." After learning some of the history of Nevis, as handed down through oral tradition and relics to his relatives from Nevis, clues were followed. Stern and his wife sought the synagogue. The husband wrote that they found an almost unidentifiable structure. The old *schule* was dilapidated, and totally abandoned, even though it was located adjacent to the island's power station off the main road at the south end of Charlestown. There was a path from it called "The Jews' Walk" which led to the burial ground, a weeded area covered with wild grasses. The Sterns checked the ground and were able to record sixteen tombstones with relative inscriptions. As a result, an article was written and published the following year, in 1970. It gained some interest. A Philadelphia attorney and his wife (Robert and Florence Abrahams) then visited Nevis. The couple liked the island and bought a ruined sugar plantation which they converted into a vacation home. With the assistance of concerned visitors and the cooperation of the Nevis Government, the Sterns have restored the Jewish burial ground and built a protective wall around it. This cemetery was rededicated with proper Jewish ceremonies on February 25, 1972.

The Abrahams are considered the only Jews now residing on the island of Nevis. Their plantation is called "Morning Star" and is located in Fig Tree Parish, about three miles from Charlestown. Morning Star is also the site of the Nelson Museum, a remarkable collection of Lord Horatio Nelson's effects and utilities. Lord Nelson was the British Naval hero who defeated Napoleon Bonaparte in 1798. Nelson married a widow named Frances Nesbit in Nevis in 1787. They were married in Fig Tree Parish Church. He is revered there as a native son. Queen Elizabeth and her husband Prince Phillip are recorded as visitors to the Nelson Museum in 1966. Many Jews visit this museum although Nelson was not Jewish.

SAINT MARTIN/SINT MAARTEN

Saint Martin is an island almost equally divided between the Dutch and the French. It is located 120 miles east-southeast of Saint Thomas. The population is split, and so are the capitals. The Dutch have the southern portion of Maarten with a capital named Philipsburg; it has a population of 5,061. Marigot is the capital of the French part of the island; population, 6,881. The people of Saint Martin speak Dutch, French, and English.

In 1648, this island was divided between the Dutch and French through a strange method. The territorial division came about after two sailors (one Dutch and one French) were set ashore at a certain place and ordered by their ambassadors to walk in opposite directions along Saint Martin's coastline until they met each other face to face. The Frenchman walked toward the north and the Dutchman walked southward. The purpose was to have them meet at the dividing line. Now the Dutch have about half the island, and the French have the other half. The faster walker covered more ground.

The Dutch portion has had Jewish residents intermittently since the eighteenth century. British Admiral Rodney was a pirate who raided Saint Eustatius and brought away a number of Jews from there. They built a community and a synagogue with authorization from Amsterdam's Jewish center and the Dutch government.

A Dutch traveler who visited Saint Martin/Sint Maarten in 1828 remarked that by that time the synagogue had become a weed-strewn rubble heap on the south side of Achterstraat, or Backstreet. It was suggested that a hurricane had destroyed the synagogue and circumstances had caused the Jewish community to abandon the island of Saint Martin.

Today, a few Jews are numbered among the merchants of Philipsburg. These persons maintain Curaçao stores which sell Dutch treats and souvenirs, import kosher foods and distribute those products among tourists and hotels which use them.

SAINT EUSTATIUS

Saint Eustatius is one of the three islands of the Leeward Netherlands Antilles. Its capital is Oranjestad. The population is eight hundred.

Saint Eustatius, or Statia, is located 130 miles southeast of Saint Thomas. The official language is Dutch. During the American Revolution, Saint Eustatius was the single most important port of supply for the colonial army of the United States. It is also recognized "the first place to salute the Stars and Stripes."

Jews were on this island as early as 1660. They continued arriving slowly until 1709 when there was a French incursion which pushed out many settlers. Some of the ousted people returned because of the profitable opportunities in Oranjestad's harbor. Merchant ships from the nearby Spanish, French, Danish, and Dutch speaking islands all used to put in at rich Saint Eustatius. She had rich soil and her sea location was good for transit and storage.

A New Yorker, Isaac Naftali, was one of Saint Eustacius' busiest merchants in 1720. But a census taken some years after only showed twenty-one Jews on the island. They were six men, four women, five boys, and six girls. Then in 1730 the leaders of the Amsterdam synagogue pressured the powerful Dutch West India Company—in which rich Jews owned shares—to encourage Saint Eustatius' governor to allow Jews "freedom of religion and trade and that no difference whatsoever be shown between Christians and those of the aforementioned Nation." Jews were also excused from guard duty on the Sabbath. As the Jewish population multiplied, the governor was often called on to settle the problems of his growing Jewish community of Ashkenazim and Sephardim, Orthodox and Reform members.

By 1737 the community needed a decent and appropriate place to worship. Salomon de Leon appealed to the Curaçao congregation in the Ostraband section of Curaçao. They responded with a gift of a Sefer Torah, Pentateuch scroll with the Five Books of Moses, and other useful items. The synagogue was built the following year and the congregation of Saint Eustatius was named Honen Dakim, meaning Kind to the Poor in Hebrew. Four year later, a French invasion menaced Saint Eustatius. Panic set in and many Jews scampered away from this island onto Curaçao carrying with them most of the synagogue's portable ornaments. However, the objects were returned home in 1744.

The Jews of Saint Eustatius were Sephardim from Holland and Curaçao. These Jews attracted others from Bohemia, France, England, Germany, Jamaica, New York, Rhode Island, Saint Kitts, and Surinam. Some of these settlers were of Spanish or Portuguese origin. Some of their traditions were different. Those differences led to arguments which had to be adjudicated by Jewish and government authorities in Amsterdam.

Joseph Buzaglo de Paz (1701–1761) was one of the most prosperous settlers in business on Saint Eustatius. The inscription on his tombstone is legible. He rests in the Jewish cemetery under this epitaph of his legendary achievements as a shrewd businessman. It reads:

> Prosecuted [sic] all his days
> Envey'd to the grave
> In spite of false friends
> Is praised by the grave . . .

These explicit words can be compared with those of twenty-one other legible tombstones at grave sites in the cemetery near Oranjestad. This graveyard is dated c. 1730. The oldest visible inscription is marked 1742, and the most recent engraving is dated 1843.

An earthquake destroyed the synagogue on August 31, 1772, but the Saint Eustatius congregation rebuilt it with contributions from the New York and Curaçao congregations in about three months after the disaster.

Substantial trade with the young American states or British colonies increased during the Revolutionary War. And at the end of 1780, Britain declared war on Holland because of the contraband trade which the island maintained with the American colonies. Shortly after British Admiral Rodney captured Saint Eustatius and demanded to meet the merchants and to check their merchandise. After confiscating their goods at gunpoint, Rodney picked out about two hundred fifty Jews, told his soldiers to search them, and mugged them of eight thousand dollars, in cash. After that holdup, Rodney sent a boatload of Jewish men to Saint Kitts, and another load to Antigua. The women and children were left abandoned and destitute before they were banished. The Jews sent a letter to Rodney, inquiring of the cause for their banishment. They could not determine if it was because of their religion or if they had committed some criminal offense. The letter of complaint reached the Admiralty. Rodney's superior contemplated the charges, and Lord Edmund Burke tried to have Parliament rebuke Rodney. Burke referred to a British Loyalist Jew, Jacob Pollock, as a British supporter. Pollock, his brother-in-law Isaac Hart and their family were driven out of Newport, Rhode Island, by the American colonials. The family sought refuge on Long Island when Isaac Hart was killed. Pollock, a victim of American expulsion, escaped the enemy to arrive in Saint Eustatius only to be mistreated by the British forces with whom he had sympathized.

Nine months after Rodney had attacked the island and occupied it, the French bombarded Saint Eustatius and captured it. The Jews from there were allowed to return. They prospered once more until around 1795 when business slackened and they became attracted to Saint Thomas and other islands. By 1850 there was almost no trace of Jews on Saint Eustatius, or of their having been there, except in the cemetery.

Around 1976, there was only one Jewish family recognized in Saint Eustatius. The children, made out of wedlock with local women, were not taken into account.

TRINIDAD AND TOBAGO

The capital of Trinidad is Port of Spain. The name implies that the Spaniards also landed there. A few Jews are numbered among the merchants who settled in Trinidad from Surinam, Dutch Guiana, in the 1660s, when Trinidad and Tobago were both in the Spanish dominion.

Trinidad is located seven miles north of the Orinoco River Delta of Venezuela. Her population amounted to appoximately 1,200,000 in 1993. She is a member of the Commonwealth of Nations of the

West Indies. Trinidad was raided by the Dutch in 1640 after Columbus had been there in 1498. Later, the French occupied Trinidad from 1666 to 1690, but none settled there after no precious metals were found. The island was later raided by the British sailors as well and captured in 1797, receiving formal title in 1802. Tobago had been settled by the British since 1616; but the Carib Indians drove them off. Trinidad became independent in 1962.

Tobago is twenty-one miles northeast of Trinidad. The major natural resources of these two islands are oil, asphalt, and sugar cane.

Sephardic traders were among the inhabitants when the British took possession of Trinidad and Tobago between 1797 and 1818. Nevertheless, no evidence of a Jewish presence is available. The names of Pereira, De Lima, Henriques, Acosta, Gomez, Sion, Senior, and Lasada are Sephardic names. However, none of the people with these names on their shop windows admitted to Jewish identity to the researchers. Furthermore, there was no evidence of a Jewish presence in either Trinidad or Tobago in recognizable numbers in 1989.

Trinidad is recorded as the appendix of the diocese of Cuba, where the Inquisition reached out to grab Jews and torture them until the early nineteenth century. Postal and Stern also stated that in 1900, the thirty-one Jews residing in Trinidad were all government employees, or British civil servants, or representatives of British firms. A Jew, Sir Nathaniel Nathan was an associate justice of Trinidad's Supreme Court from 1893 to 1900, and Chief Justice from 1900 to 1903. "A Pan American Union Report of 1917 showed not a single Jew in Trinidad or Tobago" at that time.

Nevertheless, a few families from Syria and the Balkans had lived in Port of Spain before World War I. Trinidad became a place of rescue for two thousand Jews, just the same, during the mid-1930s. They went there escaping Nazi terror in Germany and Austria.

When World War I started, the German and Austrian Jews were detained as enemy aliens and no persons from Axis countries were admitted to Trinidad or Tobago. Toward the end of 1949 persons who obtained visas for other countries were released from the detention center and allowed to leave. About one hundred families left. They had arrived when Hitler had begun mistreating and exterminating Jews, so it was obvious that they were not possible spies or enemy aliens sympathetic to the Nazi cause. When the United States opened naval bases in Trinidad in 1941, American Jews were in those areas as servicemen and supervisors of civilian war support occupations.

After World War II some Jews stayed in Trinidad. Among them were Mr. and Mrs. Hans Stecher, the Chimon Ber Averbonkh family, and a few others. Stecher arrived penniless in 1938. His wife now owns a chain of retail stores. These persons "represent the Zionist movement on the islands and all Stecher stores display the flag of Israel."

The Averbonkhs came to Trinidad in 1933. They began with a tiny clothing store and later expanded into real estate development. It is stated that the Averbonkhs came to Trinidad when a male worshipper was needed to complete the Minyan of ten males required to make up the quorum for a religious synagogue service.

Averbonkh's housing development was expanded with dumped land poured into swamps outside Port of Spain. Most of the streets were named after such Zionists as Theodore Herzl, Chaim Weitzman, Jonas Stalk, and Albert Einstein. Only three streets are named for Trinidadians. After Averbonkh passed away his wife and Mrs. Stecher became leaders of the Zionist organization he had led for years. These two women also conducted the Women's International Zionist Organization, "maintaining close contact with the Israeli ambassador to Venezuela."

The only Jewish congregation or Jewish Religious Society of Trinidad and Tobago was organized in 1938. In 1950 these members opened a synagogue and remodeled a house in Port of Spain. At one point that congregation reached above two hundred affiliated families. They then planned to build a house. But their population began to decline. By 1939 they numbered one hundred twenty instead of two hundred families. And by 1971, only fifteen families were left. As a result, the plans to build a synagogue were abandoned. However, a trust fund was established to provide continuous maintenance of the Jewish cemetery in Trinidad, consecrated in 1940. At present, most of the Jews of Trinidad live in Port of Spain and San Fernando.

When Trinidad became independent in 1962, its first Prime Minister, Eric Williams—who had been a former United Nations researcher—visited Israel. Williams requested technical advice and assistance from the older state. He felt that Jews and Americans of color had something in common. Furthermore, there seemed to be an established friendship between Jews and Trinidadians for some time. There is even a legend about the first chief of police in Trinidad having been Jewish. Consequently, Trinidadian policemen wear Mogen Davids (Stars of David) or six-point badges on their uniforms and pocket shields.

PANAMA

The Republic of Panama had a capital city when the United States was still a wilderness in 1516. Panama is not an island; it is an isthmus. This Latin American country is shaped like the letter "S", and it joins two larger portions of land. Panama is divided by the Canal and the Panama Canal Zone along the Canal. On the north, Panama borders with Costa Rica in Central America; on the south it borders with Colombia, South America.

Compared to other Latin American countries, Panama is under-populated. Her population was 1,700,000 in 1994 in an area of 29,209 square miles. Like New York City, Panama is the crossroads of the world. People have gone to Panama from all parts of the world. Many of these visitors and residents have been Jews, Americans, and even Arabs. Some people went there in transit, some went to seek their fortune, and others were contracted to work on the Canal. Immigrants who went to Panama and remained are the progenitors of the multi-ethnic existence of Panamanian *criollos, mestizos, fules*, and Negroes of today. Very few Panamanians exist without a black, Indian or pale-skinned grandfather or grandmother. That admixture has caused Panama to have had two black presidents, many half-Indian presidents and some pale-faced presidents who looked like people called white.[49]

Among the immigrants who went to Panama and remained there was a unique minority. They were called Judios. In 1876 there was official awareness of their presence as a group in Panama. A small number of Sephardic Jews of Spanish and Portuguese origin emigrated to Panama. It was said that other Jews had wandered through the Caribbean islands and finally landed at Panama before this group. However, this is the group of record.

Valencia, while relating their history, mentioned that the word Sephardi comes from the ancient word, *Sepharad*,* in the Bible and means the Iberian Peninsula. Valencia also mentions that numerous families emigrated from the Holy Land farther East, settling in Babylon and other parts of Asia Minor. He continues, "and others to the West that is, towards what is today Spain, Portugal, and Southern France." There is a little shortsightedness here in this hypothesis, because the people of Turkey, Syria, China, and other parts of the East also have many Sephardim among them. It is true that Hebrews came from Spain and Portugal in the 1490s, but Hebrews also left Nehardea and Palestine in 425 B.C. and as late as 70 A.D. Some left this Northeast African port and headed for Libya, Egypt, Ethiopia, and other parts of Africa, while others headed to Europe or the vicinity nearby Africa called Portugal and Spain, as well as hillside France near the Pyrenees. Valencia must have heard the old cliché which says El Africa empieza en los Pirineos.[50] "Africa begins in the Pyrenees". This cliché does not encompass but does relate to those Hebrews who went in other directions and reached East and West Africa, Asia, and even Europe. Some remained in those areas, while others moved on to the Caribbean islands and even to the United States, Panama, and South America. Then there are those Hebrews of Egyptian, Syrian, and Moroccan origin, for example, who are not Ashkenazim or Falashim. Therefore, those outcasts are of the only tribal designation exclusively held. With only three tribal designations, Falashim, Sephardim, and Ashkenazim, those Hebrews or Jews who are not Falashim or Ashkenazim must be Sephardim.

Valencia recognizes that Hebrews expelled from Iberia went to Salonica, Alexandria, Naples, Venice, and the possessions of the Turkish Empire where they were well received. He also repeated the Jewish experience under Sultan Bayazed who opened his doors widely to the Jews and said, "Call Ferdinand a wise monarch, but he impoverished his empire to enrich mine."

Hebrews expelled from Spain and Portugal eventually reached such places as Brazil, Saint Thomas, Curaçao, and other Caribbean islands. They adapted to their environment, learned English, bought and sold black and white slaves like their masters and rulers did. These were the customs of the Dutch masters and the French rulers. Valencia says, "The Jews treated the slaves in a most humane way. Often, they provided them with an education and respected their rest."[51] He goes on to show how unlike the Protestant Pilgrims, the Jews never sold nor bought a mother without her children. The Jews are also credited with freeing older slaves and emancipating others for considerate reasons. Some of these platitudes might be true, but they might also be false. Then, they might very well be made up because of compunctions. In any case, it is often said that God never forgave Pharoah Rameses II for having enslaved the Israelites. Did he forgive the Jews for having enslaved people of color?

Valencia also mentioned that Simon Bolivar found support for his revolution among the Jews of Curaçao. Bolivar lost the Battle of Puerto Cabello in 1812 and was routed. He found refuge in the home of a Jew, Abraham de Meza, in Otrabanda.[52] Letters and diaries of the Liberator revealed assistance extended to Bolivar's sister by Mordechay Ricardo on the Island of Jamaica in 1815. Venezuela and Colombia both received support and protection from their Jewish communities during the struggle for independence from Spain.

Fidanque says that Bolivar wrote his now-documented letter to a gentleman in Jamaica, West Indies, requesting assistance in liberating Colombia and Venezuela in September 1815. Bolivar told his benefactor-to-be, "the American colonies now fighting for their emancipation will in the end be successful." Then he explained how the common language bond of the Americans of the North might help them become monarchies and republics. Bolivar did not envision the colonies becoming United States, he did imagine, nonetheless, "How beautiful if the Isthmus of Panamá could be for us, what Corinth was for the Greeks!" Bolivar often compared the Isthmus of Corinth and its canal to Panama. He hoped that an eminent congress of all the republics, kingdoms, and empires could meet at Panama to discuss and decide the difficult problems of war and peace "with nations of the three other parts of the world."

The idea of an interoceanic waterway across Panama to join the

Atlantic and Pacific oceans for passage was thought of as far back as the fourth voyage of Christopher Columbus. When he explored Almirante Bay, the Chiriqui Lagoon, and the Portobelo Harbor, as well as the Nicaraguan and Costa Rican coastlines, Columbus had sought a strait to carry him to the Far East. Balboa also searched for the same strait when he met the Indians who showed him the Pacific Ocean on September 1, 1513.[53]

The early nineteenth century saw the world contemplating an interoceanic canal to discontinue transiting the Isthmus of Panama through forty-seven or more miles of jungle with inconveniences and dangers. There were robbers, heavy rains, mud slides, snakes and other animals in the bushes.

Alexander Von Humboldt wrote about his travels through Central America. In his journal, Humboldt logged nine possible sites for a canal excavation. But Panama was not mentioned. He had not considered Panama as a worthwhile possibility for a canal.

On the other hand, Simon Bolivar was interested in Panama and worried about the threat of a canal being built in Nicaragua. So before calling the Pan-American Congress at Panama in 1825, Bolivar appealed to England for financial and technical sponsorship in the construction of a Panama canal. He also wanted to protect the young Latin American nations from reprisals by Spain and the probable takeover of an interoceanic canal project by one or more powerful nations. England rejected both Bolivar and his plan. Other oceanic routes were sought.

In 1522, Gil Gonzalez Davila discovered Nicaragua Lake. The competition for acceptance of a route began between Panama and Nicaragua. The Nicaraguans courted British and American investors for an interoceanic canal through Nicaragua. The concession was given to The Central American-United States Atlantic Pacific Company. The project failed to begin, however, when the contractors could not raise enough funds to start excavating.

In desperation, Colombia renegotiated with England, France, Holland, and the United States. She failed once more and did not get sponsored in building the Isthmian Canal. In 1835, the Congress of the Republic of Colombia issued a charter to the adventurous Baron Thierry. Thierry held a conference with Jewish businessmen Augustin Solomon and Sylvan Joly de Sabla and four others to form a syndicate on the French Island of Guadeloupe. Solomon and Sabla made several trips to Panama to promote the canal project during the following ten years.

Sabla became well known in real estate circles as a realtor in the City of Panama. Sabla's name also appears on file at the Balboa Library, in connection with the Thierry-Solomon theory for an interoceanic canal through Panama.[54]

Washington is said to have considered the Thierry-Solomon idea because "President Jackson suddenly appointed Colonel Charles Biddle of Philadelphia to survey the state of Nicaragua and the Isthmus of Panama that same year (1833)." Biddle advised Washington against the Nicaraguan canal, without even visiting Nicaragua. He visited Panama, but also condemned the idea of a suitable route across the Isthmus. Biddle suggested the use of shallow steamboats from the town of Chagres to Cruces, then further travel by railroad from Cruces to Panama instead of by canal. During his stay in Panama, Biddle joined a group of Panamanians who organized called itself *Los Amigos del Pais* (Friends of the Country). The group encouraged Biddle to set up a private syndicate which would operate a combined steamboat and railroad trip across the Isthmus. These conveyances would shuttle passengers and their cargo from the Pacific Ocean to the Atlantic Ocean and vice versa. The concession was requested from the Colombian government in 1837. A financial depression came about in the United States at the time, and the syndicate dissolved without a concession.

In 1825 William Wheelwright of Massachusetts visited Panama and explored the Pacific area between the Bayano and the Chiriqui rivers. He declared that his surveying had shown that "the Chagres to Panama City route was the one that offers the greatest natural advantage connecting the oceans." His recommendation encouraged the beginning of the Pacific Steam Navigation Company which operated ships between Panama, Lima, Peru, and Valparaiso, Chili.

On March 30, 1838, the Congress of Nueva Granada approved a contract for a Jew named Augustin Solomon et Compagnie to operate a canal across the Isthmus of Panama, a railroad or highway as well. The canal was to run sixty years after completion, and the highway privilege would be for only forty years after construction. Solomon's corporation represented France's interest in the canal from 1838 to 1848. During those ten years the Chancellor of the French Embassy in Panama wrote to the rulers of France that the "keys of the world are here, but the name of Señor Solomon does not seem to be sufficiently Christian to qualify him for the role of guardian of Saint Peter's."[55] This remark and other similar snide remarks about Jews caused Solomon's corporation to become unpopular in Panama and Colombia. Finally, the Colombian Congress declared all transit concessions to Solomon et Compagnie terminated in June 1842. The Solomon grant was specifically discontinued. Solomon appealed to Francis Gizot, who represented him before the French Ministry in Paris. He requested application of diplomatic pressure on Colombia to honor his treaty. The Colombian government filed a countersuit demanding a guarantee of neutrality in canal dealings with France, England, and the United States before considering a new loan and the concessions of a canal by the French, English, and Colombian governments.

France considered the project and sent an engineer named Napoleon Gabriella to Panama for a detailed study of interoceanic canal possibilities on that isthmus. The French engineer spent several months in Panama and recommended to the French home office a 3.3-mile tunnel, divided by thirty to forty lock gates.

The French vacillated and Gabriella's idea was never executed. That hesitation caused Solomon to eventually abandon the canal idea. Anyway, Solomon managed to hold onto the railroad concession, and in 1845, untiring Solomon opened the Panama Company. He soon obtained a contract from the Colombian government through his agent and legal counsel Mateo Klein. In 1874 Solomon was to build and operate a Trans-Isthmian Railroad to be completed within six to eight years under a ninety-nine year concession. Without warning, outbreaks of violence erupted in Europe about 1848. Those revolutions caused European investors to refuse funds to new entrepreneurs undertaking new businesses with great risks. Without European capital Solomon could not deposit the $600,000 francs demanded as a security bond. The Colombian Congress then declared Solomon's contract breached through inability to fulfill the demand. This failure ended the first Jewish attempt to build an interoceanic canal in Panama.

Valencia says that Jewish contributions were hidden from public records and news media:

> The curtain of silence that surrounds this early Jewish involvement with an interoceanic canal and railroad across the Isthmus of Panama is a typical example of the general practice of historians of omitting any reference to Jewish contributions to civilization, or involvement in the arts and science, philosophical or educational fields since the split between the Jews and the Christian Church occurred some nineteen hundred years ago.

Truer words never written. The same can be said for people of color in the United States, and for those in Panama. A case in point was the fear of blacks to the extent that former President Demetrio Lakas saw Dr. Beecher sent to prison on the orders of Commander Omar Herrera Torrijos because of Beecher's intellectual prominence. The educator went to England, where he was so well received that the Panamanians sent for him and honored him upon his return.

Apart from the French, we find the British also diplomatically active in Panama from 1825 to 1848. In 1831 Captain George Peacock, the skipper of the H.M.S. *Hyacinth*, landed at the foot of San Lorenzo after anchoring his corvette at Chagres. Peacock made a personal journey on foot and paddle boat across the Isthmus. He surveyed a canal route parallel to the present Panama Canal route.

In 1842 the Royal Mail Steam Packet Company started a passenger, mail, and cargo transportation service between England and the West Indies. In 1845 that company investigated possibilities of a transisthmian route to connect the West Coast ships of South America from Panama to Valparaiso, Chile, with those from England to the West Indies. W.B. Liot recommended a highway from Portobelo to Panama City. His administrators listened, and in 1846 a monthly passenger, freight, and mail service was begun by the Royal Mail Line. The ships ran from London to the West Indies, on to Panama. In the meantime, minor repairs were made on the once-abandoned and run-down Cruces Trail. The Royal Mail built up a canoe and mule transport service for commuters shuttling from Chagres to Panama City, via Las Cruces. This pathway later became a highway for forty-niners during their rush to California for gold.

In 1846 Jewish presence in Panama became significant. That year saw the Royal Mail extend its West Indian steamship service to Panama. This development enabled Jews to arrive in Panama from Saint Thomas (Danish West Indies at the time), and from Jamaica (British West Indies at that time). Later on, these Jews were accompanied by other members of their faith from the Caribbean Islands—including Curaçao (Dutch West Indies)—and even Europe. These different groups coalesced to form the Kol Shearith Israel Burial Society of Panama on May 14, 1876. This society eventually became Congregation Kol Shearith Israel of Panama.

When these Jews arrived in Panama, many of them had come from Saint Thomas, where from 1800 to about 1867, that island had been the center of commerce for Europeans, Americans, and Caribbean people in general. Saint Thomas was considered the clearinghouse for nations at war. This was the time of Napoleon, and agents came from different places to purchase coal, provisions, and ammunition for ships during the British-American War of 1812. When the Civil War later broke out, Saint Thomas was also a haven for Southern privateers attempting to run the Union blockade of Southern ports.

Between 1827 and 1838 Panama received very little administrative direction or financial support from Colombia. Consequently, Panamanian politicians and a group named Los Amigos del Pais (Friends of the Country) encouraged the provinces of Veraguas and Panama to secede from Colombian rule and its Nueva Granada Confederation. These two provinces formed a *State of the Isthmus*. They remained independent until they decided to be reinstated in 1841. Hubert Henning was aware of the situation and is supposed to have said, "Panama grew and evolved as a result of Colombian indifference and abandonment."

Colombian irresponsibility and neglect caused the stage to be set for Panamanian independence. John Stevens, an American, was sent to Panama by the United States government. Stephens was supposed to report on canal routes explored. He never reported his findings and the plans for another canal route was ignored for another fifty years. Then came the Californa gold rush requiring a fast route to the West Coast.

The Gold Rush

An American named John Marshall discovered gold at Sutter Creek, California, on January 24, 1848. Several adventurers followed Marshall in monthly shiploads to California, by way of Panama. This rush of eager forty-niners (the nickname for those rushing to California in 1849) was followed by prostitutes and prospectors from Latin America, Europe, and elsewhere.

The Colombian Treaty for a canal was in the hopper, but the Colombian offer was more demanding than the United States Congress had expected. Therefore, Congress authorized the Secretary of the Navy to make a contract with a private company to carry mail from Panama to Oregon, on March 3, 1847. Soon after, another contract was awarded to transport United States mail from New York and New Orleans to the Chagres town at the mouth of the Chagres River enroute to Panama City by land across the Isthmus. On the West Coast, the mail would be collected by the Pacific Mail Steamship Company which shuttled between Panama and Oregon making ports of call at Monterey and San Francisco, California. The United States Service competed with the British Royal Mail Service from Liverpool to Panama. It connected a Chagres River-Cruces Trail across the Isthmus to the Pacific Steam Navigation Service from Panama to Valparaiso, Chile, and back.

A contract was awarded on April 20, 1847 to the United States Mail Steamship Line with a yearly subsidy of $290,000 for the Atlantic Service. This contract included a service from New York to Chagres by way of New Orleans, Charleston, Savannah, and Havana every fifteen days. By May 4, 1847, the United States Navy gave another contract of a $199,000 yearly subsidy to A. Harris for the Pacific service to San Francisco and Oregon. Harris gave the contract to Henry Aspinwall of New York, who had already planned a railroad across the Isthmus. About one year later, Mr. Aspinwall and his associates organized the Pacific Mail Steamship Company. The Pacific Mail contracted for three paddle-wheel steamers, the *California*, the *Oregon*, and the *Panama*. Each steamer averaged 1,000 to 1,100 tons of capacity and was capable of carrying mail sacks, freight, and two hundred passengers aboard.

The *California* left New York eight months after the gold discovery at Sutter Creek, but there were still no forty-niners on board. The *California* reached Rio de Janeiro on November 2, 1848, then sailed through the Straits of Magellan on December 7, 1848. She arrived in Callao, Peru, where seventeen first class and eighty steerage passengers of Peruvian nationality boarded her, bound for California.

When the *California* arrived in Panama on January 4, 1849, her agents, Jewish and Gentile, were confronted with over 178 eager passengers willing to pay any amount for a fast trip to the gold fields of California. To make matters more complicated, other passengers arrived aboard the S.S. *Falcon* at the Atlantic U.S. Mail Line Service, which sailed from New York with only twenty-nine California-bound passengers, but picked up 178 more in New Orleans. Three other vessels had also left California-bound passengers in Panama. These passengers, in transit, now totaled more than five hundred. The Americans vented their wrath against the California Port Steward, agents, and the Peruvian passengers. They insisted that the Peruvian passengers be pulled off, and those cabins given to them. Among them was one General Persifor Smith of the United States Army, on his way to assume command in California. The General threatened to prevent the Peruvians from making the trip. Good General Smith promised to use force if necessary. The agents stood their ground and the Peruvians remained on board for the trip to California.

William Nelson (born in Scotland) represented the Panama Railroad Company. He was also the American Consul in Panama. Nelson had been in partnership with Zacharisson when the *California* landed in Panama with the Peruvians aboard and had to leave the Americans stranded. It was the time when the gunboat diplomacy was feared, and Americans made other nationalities tremble when they said "I am an American!" To add insult to injury, American General Smith threatened the ship's agents (Nelson and Zachrisson), but the consul and his partner stood their ground. They defended the Indians against the posse. Ignoring the General's rank did not help. So, the Americans decided to make these defiant foreigners pay. They demanded the replacement of Nelson. The Americans protested and pleaded for a new American consul. The protest was followed by a resolution stating, "We consider the American Consul in this post unworthy of his station." Then a petition followed in the form of a query. It read "Where is the American Consul? Why is he always out of sight when the interest of Americans require protection?" The cry was heard in Washington, D.C., and Nelson was replaced by a new United States Consul, Amos B. Corwine.

Corwine soon reported to Washington that Nueva Granada was unable to govern Panama properly. He requested United States military intervention and occupation of Panama. Corwine's charges were partly true, because Granada had ignored Panama to such an extent that there were highwaymen, cutthroats, and desperadoes attacking people at will. It was difficult to cross the Isthmus, particularly at night. Nelson had sent to the United States for an ex-Texas Ranger, named Ran Runnels, to patrol the areas. The Colombian authorities were still so irresponsible and lax in maintaining order that one night in January 1852, Runnels and his deputies had to round up the worst elements among the highwaymen and desperadoes overrunning the Isthmus. The hoodlums were sentenced to be hanged from trees, Texas-style. Runnels' swift United States marshall-type justice brought swift results. Law and order was maintained on the Chagres River trails and throughout the country. But Panama was slipping out of Colombia's control and becoming supervised and administrated by the American-owned Panama Railroad Line. It was Granada's negligence which allowed Corwine to start sending for United States troops to invade Panama anytime there was the slightest misunderstanding involving United States citizens. The former Consul Nelson had been a catalyst in United States military intervention in Panama's affairs. He had also respected Panamanian territorial rights as well as Colombian sovereignty. He did not practice battleship diplomacy. But Corwine now showed United States might against Colombia's incompetence and weakness, and Panama's dependence. Hatred developed and there was a showdown.

The so-called watermelon incident erupted on April 15, 1856, and was classified as a war. An American, Jack Oliver, fired a shot at a Panamanian who demanded a few extra cents for a penny's worth of watermelon bought by Oliver. This pistol-packing ruffian soon learned from a local ruffian that Panamanians are neither tired of living nor afraid of dying. They just didn't die alone! A riot followed Oliver's shot. When the gunsmoke had cleared, fifteen Americans were found dead and sixteen wounded. The riot was only ended when Ran Runnels intervened with his posse. Corwine recommended that Panama be occupied under a clause of the 1846–1848 treaty with Colombia. Therein, the United States "guaranteed the neutrality of the Isthmus," to safeguard continued transit and prevent European intervention in Panama. The same clause was cited against Colombia in 1903, when Panama was encouraged to become independent of that nation. United States troops came into Panama, and the barefooted Colombian troops were chased back to their trains by the United States Marines. In the meantime, the United States battleships lurked in the harbor. A Colombian gunboat fired and a poor Chinese man was hit by a shell which landed in his shop. The Chinese was Wong King Yee, and the gunboat was the *Bogota*.

During these times, the Jews kept coming to Panama from different parts of the Caribbean area, and elsewhere. Some came from Jamaica and Saint Thomas, others from Curaçao. Their differences in worshipping on the Sabbath showed signs of varied practices in the rituals, and mispronunciations of the Hebrew words. These differences often caused disagreement. Many of the believers were undergraduates or semiliterates, and were therefore often more anxious to prove how much more they knew than to be tolerant enough to accept the fact that regional differences exist even within the same ethnic group. There was much criticism of the Ashkenazi method of praying and chanting, and so on. This should have been understood because one method was Oriental and the other Occidental. The Ashkenazim pretended to be better than the Sephardim because of their Germanic cultural patterns. The Sephardim pretended to be better than the Ashkenazim because they were closer to the sociolinguistic original Hebrew practices. The chants and prayers were different. So were the spoken words. The Sephardim spoke Ladino as their second language and the Ashkenazim spoke Yiddish. Since pretenses do not alter facts, the Sephardic pronunciation of original writings from North Africa taken into Europe for centuries had to be different. They were affected by transportation, translation, and accommodation. But with a larger land area and population than Saint Thomas and Curaçao, the Jews became more and more tolerant in Panama. The different sects learned to compromise.

Valencia mentions the Maduros of Curaçao, who went there from Holland. They later found their way into Panama. One outstanding member of that family was George Maduro, who was born in Curaçao in 1916. He studied at the Leyden Law School and was trapped in Holland when the Germans invaded that country in 1940. George Maduro joined the Dutch Army and was captured when the Dutch surrendered. He was taken to the concentration camp at Saarbrucken and later transferred to Dachau, where he died on February 5, 1945. In 1946 the Dutch government honored George Maduro posthumously. His name was called and the Fourth Class Cross of the Military Order of King William I was awarded to Maduro's family in his honor.

Many other people came to Panama with their religious beliefs. It was good to be in a country which did not believe in the Inquisition and permitted people to practice religions other than the Catholic-Apostolic dogmatic faith. These non-Jews were attracted to the natural beauty of this tropical isthmus. Panama had not been overwhelmed with North American progress, banditry and overdevelopment. One of these visitors wrote in the *Panama Star:*

There is not in the whole range of this most beautiful country so desirable a place as Coconut Grove.

Nature seems to have been decorating and supplying it with its

vast abundance of fruits, springs, and rural establishments—
abundant shade and fresh air are not the last of its luxuries.

Mr. Middleton, the writer of the enchantments of Coconut Grove,
must have found more delight there than the fruits and the air. He
must have found even more pleasure when he read his countrymen's
advertisement which appeared in the same *Panamá Star* on January
4, 1851. The article read:

> "Twelve good strong and healthy American Irish females to wash
> and iron. To good women, the most liberal, urgent, permanent
> employment will be assured. Clark & Company."

Coconut Grove was the red-light district where the prostitutes strolled
under the abundant shade mentioned by Middleton. Some strumpets walked the streets, while others remained in their rooms and
hooked the Johns who went into them. Since many fortune hunters
were in Panama, with very few English-speaking women available,
these Irish females met the needs of the settlers, transients, prospectors, and other male inhabitants in Panama. Another article measured the next progressive contribution made by cultured Americans
residing in Panamá at that time. This article read:

> Our friend, Dunmerford, has just received a large supply of fire arms
> of the most approved American invention and construction. Among
> them may be found an extensive assortment of six (6) shooters.

Sephardic and Ashkenazic Jews continued settling in Panama during this period. The *Panamá Star* mentioned Sephardim settling on
the Isthmus in 1848 and promptly engaging in businesses of different sorts. Jews were in banking, merchandising, and ships' chan-
dlery. Quite a few of them were Sephardim from Jamaica and other
Caribbean areas. On the other hand, the Ashkenazis were mostly
direct from Europe.

Among the Caribbean Jews who came to Panama from Saint
Thomas, and Jamaica, after the hurricane, tidal wave and cholera
epidemic of Saint Thomas in 1866 and 1868 were many who intended to remain there. Others simply wanted to raise a stake or substantial bankroll and move on. However, most West Indian Jews
arrived with the intent to found a homeland and plant their roots
where people spoke English, as they did, and Spanish as well.

As time went by, the official language of Panama became Spanish,
under President Arnulfe Arais Madrid, in 1941. So, even the prayers
of Kol Shearith Israel were changed to that language.

Fidanque declares that the Jews who migrated from Curaçao to
Saint Thomas (c.1805–1835) later scattered themselves between three
continents, Europe, North America, and South America. While seek-

ing homelands, these Jews were caught in the draft of winds blowing religious, political, social, and economic changes which swept the old and new worlds. The French Revolution, the American Revolution, and the Latin American Revolution were all gusting forth like whirlwinds. As a result the Jews found themselves in the middle of an age of enlightenment.

The Jews of Panama contemplated the times' developments and decided that Panama was a homeland. On July 18, 1876, a Jewish cemetery was consecrated in Panama. The cemetery was opened next to the Catholic cemetery, and it was "presented to the Jews by Mr. William Nelson, Esquire, of Guatemala." During the ceremony, a few of Lord Byron's lines were quoted. They read:

> Tribes of the Wandering Foot and Weary Breast,
> Where shall ye flee away, and be at rest?
> The Wild Dove hath her nest, the Fox his Cave,
> Mankind their Country, Israel but the Grave.

Among the Jews who came from Saint Thomas in the 1800s was Rabbi E.N. Martinez. Although he lived in Panama for a short period and returned to Saint Thomas, his monumental efforts were recorded there. Another name of record is Henry Ehrman, a Jew from Alsace-Lorraine, France, who arrived in Panama accidentally. Ehrman was on his way to the United States to live in the South. On his way, the ship wrecked off Cuba. Ehrman ended up in Panama and never moved on to the United States. The name of Brandon, or Brandao, the Portuguese version, is recorded among the earliest emigrants from Portugal to Jamaica by way of Bordeau, France. Among them was Jorge Vaz Brandao, who became a rabbi at Acombra, Portugal, where he led the Marrano Jews. Brandao was put to death at the stake, following an *auto-da-fe* judgment in Lisbon May 5, 1624.

"The firm of Isaac Brandon & Brothers was an important factor in the movement for (Panama's) independence in 1903." Brandon's firm supplied the Panamanian revolutionaries with funds for the undertaking.

The First Synagogue
The first synagogue built on the Isthmus of Panama was built by the Colon congregation, forty-seven miles away from Panama City. The Kaal Kadesh Yangakob Congregation of this smaller city 47 miles away (one hour and a half by train or bus now), gave the Jews of Panama City a shock on April 13, 1913. It was ten years since the Canal construction had begun, and yet this smaller congregation was able to invite the larger Kol Shearith Israel group to the inauguration of their synagogue in Colon. This Kaal Kadesh Congregation even offered to pay half the fare for the larger group to attend the affair.

The Panama group declined the invitation, but promptly began getting organized to form a group which would at least worship regularly. A place was rented, because there was no available economic reserve to build a synagogue. A school fund was created and a committee appointed to make plans for a Sabbath School. Yom Kippur services were held at a Masonic Temple, and dues were collected with the understanding that funds would be set aside for the building of a temple.

The City of Colón

Let us digress for a moment to explore the sociopolitical and economic conditions of Colón during the early times. That area was first named Aspinwall by the directors of the Panama Railroad Company for authoritative decisions and administration. Being the principal port for cargo and passenger embarkation, its economy boomed. Colón was similar to Hong Kong, Singapore, Shanghai, and San Francisco. People flocked there from all parts of the world. Of all the nationalities and races which went there, the most important and prominent in numbers were the black West Indians. They did the dirty work on the Canal, lived in the mosquito-infested areas, and outsurvived the Spaniards, Chinese, Irish, and other laborers who tried to work in the ditches. Some West Indians worked as carpenters, masons, artisans, engineers, and architects.[56]

Colon bustled with businesses to serve the wage earners, cargo handlers, passengers embarking and disembarking, and the Army, Navy, and railroad personnel. The Panama Canal workers and the merchants called it The Gold Coast.

The West Indians formed a benevolent society, held social affairs, and developed burial security fund systems. The Sephardic Jews also formed societies like those they had kept in the West Indies and elsewhere. The people on the Atlantic side (Colón and Cristobal) were mostly English-speaking. On the Pacific side (Ancon and Balboa) there were more Spaniards and Hispanics (people of Indian and Spanish or African and Spanish descent.) But while Panama City was Panamanian, Colón was another colonial enclave like the Canal Zone existing separately and apart from the rest of Panama. The West Indian Jews were at home in Colón because they were shielded by the Protestant West Indians, other denominations, and the Salvation Army among the missionaries trying to save the souls of sinners in the midst of temptation. In Panama City, on the other hand, the Jews had to maintain a low profile because they were correlated with foreign influence or intent to dominate native existence.

Fidanque says that the Jews of Colón were enjoying more latitude at the time, were more numerous in Colón and therefore more able to open a synagogue without fear of the Spanish-speaking elements becoming hostile. However, after sixty years of planning, and anxiety, Kal Shearith Israel (A Voice of the Remnant of Israel) opened the doors of its newly built temple in Panama.[57] And on the evening of September 7, 1935, the first wedding ceremony was held in that synagogue. It is important to mention that despite the institutionalization of Judaism and the unification of Jews of different backgrounds, the Jews of Panama remember the prayer which instructs Jews to pray for the leaders of the country in which they sojourn, reside, or were born. Jews are also taught to be law-abiding, respectful at all times, and willing to assist whenever capable. These instructions encouraged the Jews of Panama to become involved culturally and politically in the Panamanian system to the extent that without relinquishing their Jewish traditions and faith, this group contributed to the independence and continued progress of the Republic of Panama.

By 1935 Ashkenazi Jews started arriving in Panama in significant numbers. Before that, there were only a "few European Jews in Panama." Toward the end of the 1940s, the steamship *Jana Salem* was expected to dock at the port of Cristobal, Canal Zone, with twelve hundred refugees aboard—on their way to Israel. These Jews were fleeing the Communist take-over in China. Among those Jews were two hundred Christians. Most of these passengers were said to have been terribly depressed after having lost their personal properties and valuables through confiscation.

It was Kol Shearith Israel's time to show its worth. The ladies' auxiliary acquired assistance for the needy passengers from churches and even from poor people who heard their appeal. Dozens of cans of powdered milk were received along with other food from the churches in the Canal Zone. The ladies of the Jewish auxiliary wore white arm bands with the Star of David on them. When the three truckloads of food collected arrived at the Cristobal piers, the ladies of Kol Shearith Israel met Catholics, nuns, and priests waiting to join them. The Christians put on the Star of David arm bands, and aprons, and began to help distribute the food, take the sick passengers to medical clinics in Colón, and also to attend to two newly born babies. One infant was Jewish and the other one was Christian—an equitable distribution of nature.

The Kol Shearith congregation trotted back and forth, and returned from Colón exhausted. They were very pleased, however, because of their acts of kindness. One member, Mrs. Abadi, suddenly realized that her overcoat was missing. She had worn it because of a persistent cold she had been trying to get rid of. She gasped, "My overcoat! Where is my overcoat, Bertha?" Bertha replied, "Oh, was it yours? I gave it to someone that was feeling cold on the ship."

This same congregation was active in maintaining friendly relations and family interactions with non-Jewish Panamanians. As a result, Panama's United Nations Delegates—one of whom was Jewish—were some of the first to cast affirmative votes for the establishment of a Jewish homeland—Medina Israel. Shortly after Israel gained independence, the Arabs attacked her.

The United States avoided direct intervention for certain convenience, and the Kol Shearith congregation saw the need for their diplomatic involvement. The spokesman convinced the United States Armed Forces Bureau of the need to transfer airplanes to the Government of Panama for Israel. These aircrafts were the first ones to arrive in Israel. They slowed down the Arab assaults and prevented invasion. Those planes arrived in Israel with the Panamanian flag painted on one of their sides. But despite those sacrifices, the Valencia paper stated:

> Zionism provoked an ideological conflict in our congregation, that has always felt great affinity towards Panama and is profoundly rooted in this land. Zionism has not been subjected to criticism or spurred on debates here, as it has happened, for example, in the United States, but our Congregation does not feel politically vinculated to Israel, nor do we accept the determinant that the only way for Jewish people is to immigrate to Israel.

The Jewish community of Panama continues to support Israel spiritually, morally, and materially. Their intent is said to be, "promoting the highest ideals of Judaism and humanity." In order to foster those ideals, the Kol Shearith Israel Congregation was formed one hundred years ago as a burial society.[58] Shearith's first Jewish Cemetery of Panama was designed to provide a resting place for its deceased members in accordance with the tenets of the Hebrew faith.

The Hebrew religion and culture are associated with life. Death is considered an evil, because it is unavoidable, very mysterious and leaves no options. These observations are reasons why Jewish communities refer to their cemeteries as *Beth Hayim*, or House of Life. And when one drinks a toast, the glasses are raised to the words *Le Hayim*, meaning "To Life!" The kaddish, or prayer, for those dear ones no longer with us has a praise to God, who is trusted in spite of one's grief. The unavoidableness of death is above human comprehension, and the mysteries of the spiritual world more extraordinary than might be perceived. Therefore, there is no speculation about a life after death, compensation for good deeds or castigation for evil ones (reward or punishment) are measured here and now.

In the Panamanian Hebrew home, traditional values are stressed day after day. Great emphasis is placed on scholastic achievement as well as religious tradition. One's parents keep repeating that knowledge is power. Hebrew fathers do not encourage their children to steal at any cost and expect forgiveness in heaven, even after having taken someone's life. And a child is not taught that someone can die for him or her. Every child learns that if he commits an evil deed, he will pay for it right here on earth. He is not encouraged to believe that by donating money from his organized crime to the temple, he will be absolved. If a person does good, he or she will reap good fruits. If he does evil, retribution is sure; either he or she will pay or the children will. And anyone who lives must surely die. No one can die for another. If someone could, one would live forever. If a ransom had been paid for one, eternal life would exist for the asking.

Some groups are taught individuality. The individual says, "I'm looking out for me, man!" Or, "I'm looking out for number one." It may be a witty-sounding quote, but it is empty, and has no value. This type of person helps no one, and no one helps him or her. The egotist is an easy target for exploitation, destruction, and miseducation.

Among Hebrews and Jews from Europe, there is *Haish garan.* This saying means that each person steers not only his individual destiny, but is responsible for assisting the needy members of his fraternity or group. He or she is also responsible for fostering the progress of his or her group.

NOTES

1. Barry Fell. *America B.C.* (New York: Simon & Schuster, 1976) p. 17.
   Ivan Von Sertima. *They Came Before Columbus* (New York: Random House, 1977).
2. Salo Baron, Arcadius Kahan, et al. *Economic History of the Jews.* (New York: Schocken Books, 1975), pp. 214-215.
3. Federico Ribes Tovar. *A Chronological History of Puerto Rico* (New York: Plus Ultra Educational Publishers, Inc., 1973) p. 19.
4. Stephen Birmingham. *The Grandees* (New York: Harper Rowe Publishers. 1971)
5. *Sephardic* Jew from Spain, Portugal, etc. *Ashkenazi.* German or Central European Jew. The /im/ ending in Hebrew, denotes plural.
6. Birmingham, p. 230.
7. Werner Keller, *Diaspora,* The Post Biblical History of the Jews (New York: Harcourt Brace World Inc., 1969) p. 468.
   William Harris and Judith S. Levey. *The New Columbia Encyclopaedia* (New York: Columbia University Press, 1975), p. 1836. Birmingham, p. 201.
* "First Shearith Graveyard" was located on James Place in Chinatown. Used between 1683–1828.
8. Birmingham. *The Grandees.*
9. These immigrants and their descendants coined the name *colored,* but if you look among ten white people sitting on a bus, you will notice that they are colored. No three of them will have the same pale color.
10. As for the white niggers. J.A. Rogers distinctly name a few of them.

Presidents of the United States were included. See J.A. Rogers. *The Five Negro Presidents*, U.S.A. (New York, Empire Book Store, 200 West 125th Street, New York 10027).

11. Lucy S. Davidowicz. *The Jewish Presence*. Essays on Identity and History (New York: Holt Rhinehart and Winston 1944-1977) pp. 118-120.

12. Baron, pp. 263-265.

13. Baron, pp. 263-265.

14. Keller.

15. Keesing's Research Report, *The Arab Israeli Conflict* (new York Charles Schribner's Sons, 1968).

16. Stephen Jay Gould. *The Mismeasure of Man*. (New York: W.W. Norton, 1981) pp. 231-233.

* *Encyclopedia Britannica*, P. 42, *Encyclopedia Judica*, Vol 8, Tome 1469, with picture of hotel.

17. Keesing's Research Report, *The Arab Israeli Conflict* (New York: Scribner's 1968), p. 3.

18. Keesing's Research Report.

19. The Ethiopian Hebrews of New York City's Harlem community contributed and solicited funds from blacks of all religious persuasions. Some Jewish and other teachers of Public School 207 on 117th Street, near Lenox Avenue, also contributed. The collection was initiated by Madam Konate, her mother, and Professor Jose V. Malcioln. The proceeds were handed over to Dr. Maurice Blond at 11 West 42nd Street, 14th floor. These funds were to help Israel in her war against the Arabs in 1973, the Yom Kippur War. Therefore African Hebrews contributed funds and even fought Israeli Goños, proving they have supported Jews in peace and war.

20. Bernard Postal. *Mexico*. American Airlines Tourist's Guide to Jewish History. 1980.

21. Juan Garrido was a free Negro and one of the forty-two passengers on Ponce de Leon's ship." Garrido was born in Angola, and lived in Sevilla many years. "It is also claimed that he followed Hernan Cortes to Mexico and was the first man to plant wheat in that region." Federico Ribes Tovar. *A Chronological History of Puerto Rico* (New York: Plus Ultra Educational Publishers, 1973), p. 19.

* PRI: Partido Revolacionario Institucional.

22. Postal.

23. Ronald Syme. *Juarez: The Founder of Modern Mexico* (New York: William Morrow and Company, Inc. 1972).

* Frances Cress Welsing. *The Isis Papers* (Third World Press, 1991). p. 228

24. Salo W. Baron, Arcadium Kahan & others (edited by Nachum Gross). *Economic History of the Jews* (New York: Schocken Books, 1975) pp. 273-274.

25. Nehemiah 2:5.

26. Postal and Stern, p. 15.

27. *Mesquita* means mosque in Spanish.

28. *Shammash*. Hebrew word for temple beedle or caretaker.

29. Jewish men had children with Black women, but seldom educated them academically or religiously.
30. Postal and Stern.
31. *Haskamah.* Hebrew "approval" name given among Sephardim to a communal regulation. Authorization sometimes prefixed to Hebrew books. The regulation came into effect after the decision of the Synod of Ferrara, Italy in 1554 that Hebrew books should be approved by the local Jewish authorities to avoid difficulty with the Church. Now pronounced *ascama,* plural *ascamot.*
* Mikveh means collection.
32. Postal and Stern.
33. Postal and Stern.
34. Postal and Stern.
35. Bernard Postal and Malcolm Stern (1976). M.M. Carley, Jamaica (1963). R. W. Palmer. *The Jamaican Economy* (1968).
36. Postal & Stern, *Tourist's Guide.*
37. Postal & Stern.
38. Edna McGuire. *Puerto Rico: Bridge to Freedom* (New York: The Macmillan Company, 1963), p. 7.
39. Van Sertima. *They Came Before Columbus.*
40. McGuire, p. 24-25.
* Smithsonian Institute Report 1867.
41. *Bimah* is the Hebrew word for a raised place in the synagogue. The Torah is read from a desk-like lectern there. the Ashkenazim also called it *almemar* or *alemor* derived from Arabic *alminbar,* meaning platform. These words came into general use in the Middle Ages throughout Southern Europe. The Sephardim were not familiar with them and used the word *tebah,* instead. *Tebah* is box, in Hebrew.
42. W. Gunther Plaut. *The Rise of Reform Judaism.* A Sourcebook of its European Origins (New York: World Union for Progressive Judaism, Ltd. 1963), pp. 178-180.
43. Bermuda Conference: Cecil Roth. *The Standard Jewish Encyclopedia* (New York: Doubleday & Company, Inc., 1959) p. 286.
* *Encyclopedia Britannica* 1994, Vol. 5.
44. Postal and Stern, p. 80.
45. Basil Davidson. *Black Mother: The Years of African Slave Trade* (Boston: Little, Brown and Company, 1964), pp. 45-47. Davidson shows the first slaves arriving at Hispañiola. "These slaves were white — whether from Spain or North Africa." Hispañiola today is Haiti and the Dominican Republic.
46. William Harris and Judith S. Levey. *The New Columbia Encyclopaedia* (New York: Columbia University Press, 1975) p. 1175.
47. Davidson. *Black Mother.*
48. The ceremony performed at Schneider's funeral leaves some doubt as to whether he'll end up in a Jewish heaven or an African paradise.
* The scuttlebutt is that Aaron Burr insulted Hamilton with a perjorative term about his ancestry. The insult led to the dual which cost Hamilton his life. My stepfather and relations were born and raised in Nevis.

49. The two black presidents were Dr. Carlos A. Mendoza (1910) and Don Tomás Gabriel Duque (1928).
* Ralph Delima Valencia, co-author, *A Hundred Years of Jewish Life in Panama* 1876–1976.
50. It might be interesting to note that Israel is called "Middle East," and Spain and Portugal are not called mid-Africa and Europe. The Iberians are called ancient people descended from "Caucasians." But these Sepharads and other Hispanics are mostly dark-skinned or at least dark-haired people.
Navarro says (1932) that the Iberians, an ancient African people came from North Africa. He makes more sense because Spain and Portugal are nearer to Africa than to the Caucasus. And the languages of Spain and Portugal have no Slavic words. Furthermore, there is no sociolinguistic connections between Slavic, North African and Hispanic people.
51. Ralph De Lima Valencia and E. Alvin Fidanque. *Kol Shearith Israel: A Hundred Years of Jewish Life in Panama, 1876-1976* (Panama: IGMAR, S.A. 1977) pp. 1-3.
52. Valencia, p. 43-150.
53. The oldest son of Chief Comogre was disgusted by the greed of the Spaniards for precious metals. He declared that he would lead them to a land on the other side of the mountain which was so rich in gold they would become sated with gold and silver. Helen Delpar. *Encyclopedia of Latin America* (Panama: McGraw Hill Book Company, Inc. 1977).
54. The Balboa Library also shows the name of two black engineers who worked on the Panama Canal construction. They were John W. English and L.M. Crooks. They were so good at their craft that when they fired even a white person, he would go to Goethals (the U.S. Chief engineer) only to be told that their word stood. They were from the island of Jamaica.
55. It is obvious that the French Chancellor had never been to the Vatican to see the color of the real Saint Peter, who was not only a Jew, but a black Hebrew.
56. Valencia & Fidanque.
57. The words *Kal* and *Kol* are used interchangeably. The "a" is the form used by African and Afro-European Hebrews, namely Sephardim and Falashim; the "o" pronunciation comes with the Ashkenazim who pronounce "a" like "o" and "i" like "y," etc.
58. Valencia, p. 237.

CHAPTER 12

THE BENE ISRAEL

OF INDIA

The population of Israel's kingdom was decimated by the Assyrians in 722 B.C.E. The Kingdom of Judah was eliminated by neo-Babylonians in 586 B.C.E. There was no Jewish state from 135 a.c.e. to 1948 after the Babylonian exile.

European history had not begun in all seriousness until the eleventh century B.C.E. However, for that beginning, the Greeks got credit for civilizing the world. The Romans received credit for conquering it and the Africans got discredited for letting the world slip away from them.[1]

The Greeks were not able to absorb the barbarians peacefully. Their unconquered enemies joined with Carthage and the Etruscans to expel them and stop Greek colonization. The Greeks had urbanized and educated the Khazars, and many of their words even infiltrated other languages. One of those languages was Hellenized Hebrew, popular among converted Jews seeking acceptance.

With the kingdom of Israel and Judah discounted for centuries, Jewish History became isolated from some of its tribes called "Lost Tribes." They were considered lost either because no one wanted to include dark-skinned people's history in the mainstream of Judaism, or because the people were too proud to buckle their knees to those who came after them and now arrogantly pretend to be ahead of them.

Therefore, when one speaks of Hebrews or Jews, the picture which develops in the poorly informed listener's mind (especially one who has not visited Northeast Africa or Israel) is an image of a pale-faced person of European ancestry. The same picture comes into focus in the mind of the listener who hears the words: Semitic, Oriental, or Indo-Aryan people. By the way, those terms are not worth a bag of beans. They are all pseudolinguistic. For the man on the street, I mean that those words are all nonsense terms or false names.

The word "Semitic" comes from Latin; it means a path. Oriental means someone from the Orient, not Europe. And Wolfram Eberhard depicts the original Oriental as blacks with slanted eyes. Eberhard is German. There are also *los moros*, the short black people of the Philippines up to today. And a black General Tanaka invaded Japan in the fourth century A.C.E. (After the Christian Era). In that same area where some people are called Indo-Aryan, the Dravidians were originally black people of South and Central India, as well as North Ceylon. The so-called Aryans were migratory pale-faced Europeans, who had no written language or recognizable culture. They were not white.[2] There are no white people. Sheets and shirts are white. However, there are genuine black people. These are sometimes so black, from the melanin in their skin, that they appear blue when the sun shines on them. These are facts that should be taught in order to stop inadequate so-called whites pretending to be better than other people more self-achieving than they, merely on the basis of a weak color that has to be reinforced with sunbaths and blood transfusions to counteract the various blood diseases which caused the pale color to begin with. Most racists are people trying to cover up personal inadequacy. A self-assured person does not have to pretend to be better than someone else under normal circumstances. That's why traveling helps one see and learn more and more real facts about people.

Those who have visited Asia, and seen the descendants of Dravidians in India or in Guiana (South America near Brazil), living in houses on stilts in swamps, Mongols in China, igorots, aetos, or negritos of the Philippines, and so on, know the truth about the origin of so-called races.[3] Those who have not had the opportunity to travel, but have read, know that the aristocrats of Australia are descended from the thief of the Great Train Robbery in England, the convicts sent to that small continent, and the prostitutes rounded up in England and sent there to procreate for the Crown in the Australian colony. The readers will have also read that those criminals called ladies and gentlemen are wantonly killing off the original black people of that continent while they call them aborigines.

As a result of the amalgamation of races, we hear about Jews of India, and look for a pale-faced syphilitic-looking individual, who has to sit in the sun to roast like a pig to become brown. The Jews of India are not white. They are people of color—a cinnamon color. And those whose parents interacted indiscriminately vary from cinnamon to buff. When the Dravidians were met by the incoming Aryans, the Dravidians were called *Daysus*, which meant goat-nosed or noseless. The descendants of these people are still in India and elsewhere under different names.

India has another group of uncommonly known people, the Jews of India. Benjamin Israel informs us that "there have been small communities of Jews settled on the western coast of India since the tenth and eleventh centuries." Other writers inform us that the Jews of India arrived after the Romans destroyed the Second Temple in 70 a.c.e. In any case, we now know that the Bene Israel are descendants of Hebrews because they say so, believe so, and continuously act so. Consequently, they do not need any self-appointed European Messiah of occupied Israel to make them Israelites.

Benjamin Israel put their declaration rather lucidly and matter-of-factly when he wrote:

> The Jews of the anti-Semitic caricaturist shares his hooked-nose [dark skin], thick lips and curly hair with numbers of people without a drop of Jewish blood in their veins, and millions of Jews have none of these features, still less all three in combination.[4]

The Jews who supposedly came out of the tribes of Benjamin and Judah, with Jerusalem as its capital, constituted the Kingdom of Judah. But after the Diaspora, many members of the tribe of Judah and Israel went south to Ethiopia. The area inhabited by the other ten tribes incorporated the part known as Israel, with Samaria as its capital. This latter part was named after Jacob, a son of Abraham, who had a vision in which his name was changed by God from Jacob to Israel.

The Indians, properly called Bene Israel or Children of Israel, contend that after the Kingdom of Israel was conquered by the Assyrians in 85 A.C.E., the inhabitants were lost to history. Some people remained behind and slid away from their religion. Those few backsliders, the unfaithful, are considered ancestors of the Samaritans who presently "survive as a very small community on the west bank of the Jordan."

The Kingdom of Judah, conquered by the Babylonians in 586 B.C.E. saw the descendants of Judah and Benjamin come to be known as Jews (from the word Judah) who practice a religion called Judaism.

With the other tribes being considered lost to history, the Falashim who call themselves Bene Israel and the largest Hebrew or Jewish community of India, also called Bene Israel, must be part of the larger kingdom.

The first mention of Jews in regard to India is recorded in the Book of Esther in the Bible. The Bene Israel's history in India is dated 586 B.C.E. That history involves the Persian King Xerxes (A-has-u-e-rus), who had Jews rally their forces and defend themselves. Jews were dispersed through his 127 provinces, from India unto Ethiopia. At that time, the Persian Empire extended all the way to Baluchistan, regarded as part of India. That area is now split between Pakistan and Iran. After two centuries passed, Judah was in turn captured by the Babylonians in 586 B.C.E. Most of its inhabitants were then deported.

Benjamin Israel states that "the ten tribes which constituted the kingdom of Israel disappeared from history, their common name of Israelites or Bene Israel was retained solely by the largest Jewish community in India." Israel obviously had not read about the Falashas of Ethiopia. They too had been treated like the black sheep of the family. Benjamin did notice, however, that, curiously enough, the name Israel was adopted by Muslim tribes in Afghanistan and elsewhere is Asia. He said one "occasionally comes across Indian Muslims with the surname Israel."

Another version of oral tradition, published by Kehimar in 1937 states as follows. The arrival of the Bene Israel to India was about 175 B.C.E. They fled from Galilee to escape oppression by the Greek autocrat Antiochus Ephiphanes.

The Bene Israel then maintained a couple of reasons for identifying themselves with the Lost Tribes:

> Because they had never called themselves Jews, and because they had no knowledge of the feasts adopted after the destruction of the First Temple by the Babylonians, or of the festival of Hanukkah instituted even later, until they were introduced to the legendary David Rahabi, a European.

The Bene Israel's arrival is also correlated with the assumption that Solomon's sailors were of the tribes of Asher and Zebulun, two tribes also considered lost. A ship from their fleet is said to have traveled to India in search of apes, peacocks, and ivory. Solomon's headquarters was in northeast Africa, which explains the dark complexion, and black-skin members among the Indian Bene Israel. Solomon's fleet was supposedly headed for the ancient port of Sopara (identified by Indian scholars as Ophir, twenty miles north of Bombay). At that spot, they were blown off course. The crew was shipwrecked at Navagon farther down the coast. The survivors of Solomon's sailors became progenitors of the Indian Bene Israel.

Another version of the history is that the Bene Israel landed at Cheul or Chemul (pronounced tsemvul), which is presumed to have been the "Silulu" or "Timonla" mentioned by Ptolemy and other geographers. In biblical and Buddhist writings this land appears as Chamula. The Chinese refer to Chemul in their language as Tchi-mo-lo. In Arabic, we read the name as "Saimur" or "Jaimur." This ancient port of Ophir or Sopara is now called Penanda. Having lost its popularity and necessity, as well as some land through soil erosion, Chemul is now located between Bombay and Alibag. The sea around it has withdrawn, due to silting of the inlet, causing present Penanda to be approximately two miles away from its ancient location which experienced the Portuguese conquest.

This historic version also relates that seven men and women who escaped Titus' persecution, after the destruction of the Second Temple, survived a shipwreck from Palestine to India. The bodies of their former shipmates who drowned were washed ashore. Seven couples recovered the dead and buried them in two mounds. The mass graves were called *Tumuli*. One mound is for females and their children, and the other for the male members of the unfortunate group. That village is situated near the town of Alibag, now named Nangoan meaning new village. The fourteen survivors raised large families, which increased their numbers proportionately and rapidly. In time, they fanned out through villages leading to the Konkan area.

These Bene Israel engaged in oil pressing, as a means of earning a decent living. The result was their being called *Shanwar Telis*, meaning Saturday oilmen (Cujarati Language of Bombay).[5]

There is still another version of the Bene Israel's arrival in India. This story is the best of all. The story says that Bene Israelites arrived about the second century C.E., escaping Roman persecution. The sociolinguistic evidence points up that after calculating the dates, analyzing the language they spoke, and the way they acted, there had to be some connection between these Hebrews or Israelites and those of the diasporas.

It is difficult or almost impossible to determine whether the Bene Israel or the Cochinim of Cochin, India, are the older settlers in India. There seems to be no existing records to declare which group arrived first, the Bombay group or the Cochin. However, people are just beginning to become aware of a Jewish presence on the western coast of India from as early as the tenth or eleventh centuries (1000 B.C.E. to 70 C.E.). The evidence gathered has supported the theory that there is some link between these people and the original Hebrews who by all records were predominantly dark-skinned people. What is definitely proven is that the Cochinim came to India from different countries which included Egypt, Syria, Turkey, Iran, Iraq, Palestine, Spain, and even Germany. Their dark skin caused them to stand out as sore thumbs and their strange religion made them even more conspicuous in Christian, and even Moslem, lands of certain areas. They arrived in India at different intervals. There is no movement recorded for the Bene Israel in the same pattern over any period of years. Just as important, is the Cochin presence being encountered by Marco Polo as far back as 1293. There are also earlier documentations of a Cochinim contact with Jews in Israel and Egypt. And the kind of information gathered by Benjamin Israel through an Indian-Christian historian maintains that there were some Jews settled both in Malabar and in the Konkan region of Maharasthra before 50 C.E.

or 55 C.E. The Cochinim were also visited by the well-known traveler Benjamin of Tudela in 1167. He remarked that the Cochinim numbered "several thousand Israelites dark like the other inhabitants."

RELIGIOUS SURVIVAL

The writings of the early Catholic Church fathers are supposed to
show two apostles sent to India to convert the Jews to Christianity.
One was Saint Thomas who went to Malabar and is supposed to have
converted the Syrians. The other saint was Saint Bartholomew. Those
two missionaries are considered to have settled near one of those
communities.

One of the first evangelistic actions by the Protestants was under-
taken by Dr. Wilson of the Scottish Presbyterian Church around
1819. That mission undertook translations of Biblical passages from
English into Marathi as one of its principal functions. The Mission's
Dr. Wilson received credit for introducing Hebrew into the curricu-
lum designed for the Bombay University. In 1827, the Presbyterian
Mission established a Hebrew School at Alibag in the Kolaba District.
The initial attendance was about thirty pupils. The instructors were
Jewish.

The influence of the missionaries was reported to be predomi-
nant. However, by 1829 there were one hundred thirty Jewish
instructors in seventeen schools owned and operated by the American
Mission. Seven of those schools were on Bombay Island and the other
ten in the Kolaba District.

By the middle of the nineteenth century, missionary influences
began to wane with missionary schools decreasing in primary education. In the secondary schools the missionaries limited themselves
to secular education, and conversion attempts subsided. There was
a rebellion in 1857, and the British Government feared Christian
influence in the quest for equal rights. Consequently, all grants for
school aid were tightly monitored and guidelines rigidly prescribed.

The interesting phase of the Bene Israel's history is the chapter
relating how the Christian missionaries did not only teach the Jews
English, but also taught them Hebrew. It seems that before the coming of the Christians, the Bene Israel had studied with the Cochinim
and learned as much as they possibly could about Judaism. But their
knowledge of Hebrew was limited either because the Cochinim themselves did not know that much or because the importance of Hebrew
was a low priority.

The Church of England later sent missionaries to India around
the tail end of the conversion period. Those Christians were the most
aggressive evangelists who landed there. The Scottish and American
missionaries are mentioned as altruistic when compared to the hawk-
ers who went out of their jurisdiction to attack what they considered

"the errors of Rabbinic Judaism." but the Bene Israel had learned enough from the Cochinim to be able to resist and reject psychological pressure from those pressing evangelists trying to lead them to conversion. The Bene Israel really upset the missionaries when they refused to accept the divinity of Christ.

At the end of the seventeenth century, the Bene Israel community was concentrated along the coastal strip of almost one thousand miles—a little south of Bombay. The region was governed by hereditary Maratha admirals called Angreas. They were in part under another Maratha feudal chieftain. The chief ruled Pant Sechiv of Bhor, and partly under the Moslem Nawab of Janjira. The British East India Company only held the Island of Bombay. And the Bene Israel who were Anglophiles are thought to have begun enlisting in the British Army way back in 1754.

BENE ISRAEL AS SOLDIERS

The Bene Israel of India joined the British India Company's marine and infantry forces as early as 1755, when the company acquired a depot called Fort Victoria on the mainland. The fort was also used as a recruiting station for the Bombay Army. That army was later expanded to a fighting force large enough to defend Bombay and powerful enough to attack the mainland for colonial and territorial expansion. By the middle of the nineteenth century, the Bombay Army had enlisted many Bene Israel privates and attacked the Marathas, Mysore, and the various princelings in coastal Karnatak. "The Bene Israel began enlisting in substantial numbers, often under the `caste' name of Israel."[6] It is at this time, says Benjamin Israel, that Bene Israel detachments had served in the army and navy of the Marathas before going over to the British Army where the treatment, wages, and formal training was more professionally and convincingly organized.

The Bene Israel's enlisted men rose to higher ranks than other Indian groups because of their numbers and academic skills. But the British soon began curtailing their privileges, and keeping their officers at a level termed Subed, or major, or native Commandant. This rank was used as the equivalent of Sergeant Major in the regular British regiments. With British discrimination against Indians in their own country, it was not until 1918 that a few Royal Commissions were grudgingly granted to Indians—Bene Israel included. And it was not until World War II, when the British were hard pressed by the Japanese and Germans that the Bene Israel renewed their interest in military service. At that time, one of them rose to the rank of vice-admiral, one to major-general, and even a Baghdadi Jewish lieutenant-general was put in command.

There was need to further colonize India and to send foreign troops to colonial China after the Opium Wars. "The British were anxious to recruit reliable soldiers into their native regiments."[7] Some of the Bene Israel who enlisted in the new army had served under Konkan potentates before the coming of the British. Jews had also served under the local princes in the Malabar area of India. In some instances it had been necessary for the princes to postpone a battle because their Jewish troops would not engage the enemy on a Sabbath.

There was only nineteen percent of the Bene Israel males in the army between the late nineteenth and twentieth centuries. Nevertheless, more than a half of that small number were promoted to officers' rank in the native military Bombay Presidency which covered most of northwest India.

There were Bene Israelis who even fought in Persia, Afghanistan, China, and Ethiopia. Barber explains their record for bravery and loyalty was considered extraordinary. The occupation and acquisition of Seringapatam in 1799 was supported by Samuel Ezekiel Khurrilkar, the boldest attacker in the Twelfth Native Infantry. Subadar Major Ellojee Davidjee Israel (1799–1826) of the Seventh Native Infantry was awarded a special silver medal and clasp for valor. About 1830, Subadar Daniel ben Israel of the Sixteenth Native Infantry received a special gold medal for bravery. Many Bene Israel served the British for decades and quite a few of them were promoted to positions of command in the British Armed Forces. According to Kehimkar, hundreds of decorations were awarded to Bene Israel enlisted men who contributed while being identified by their Jewish names translated into Marathi, with surnames which carry the suffixes of the villages in which they were born and recorded. The citations awarded to the Bene Israel for valor fill the pages of thirty sides in Kehimkar's book.[8] Those awards were received from the latter half of the eighteenth century on toward the end of the nineteenth century.

Sirdar Bahadur Haskeljee Savlikar served with the British for forty-two years. He was commended by all of his field officers as "First class on account of his long, arduous and loyal service." Moosaji Israel provided the earliest information regarding oncoming Indian revelation of their countrymen's rebellion against British domination. There were so many Bene Israel regulars and officers serving with the British forces that an Indian once said, "the Bene Israel in the army were like corks in water; they simply had to come to the top. There was no help for them when in 1891, Lord Roberts introduced the caste system into the army." Regiments were then grouped by caste, with each regiment having officers of its own caste. The possibility of promotion was then phased out. The Bene Israel started boycotting the British Armed Forces between 1896 and 1947.

Before the caste system was introduced some Bene Israel had risen to the rank of native Commandant—in charge of a battalion.

Quite a few of them had sacrificed their lives in the Mysore and Maratha Wars of the 1778 and 1780 duration. During the second Mysore War (1780–1784) several Bene Israel troops of the British East India Company were captured and imprisoned by the Sultan's Moslem army. The Bene Israel were released because they were protected by Mahoma in the Koran. Tipo, a Moslem high ranking officer, met them.

"Tipo's mother had begged him to spare the lives of the Children of Israel. The most celebrated of those children was Samuel Ezekicl—known in Marathi as Samuel Hasajee Divepar. He enlisted in the British-supported army in 1750. He rose through the ranks to native Commandant of the Sixth Battalion, under General Matthew of the Second Mysore War. Divepar is the fellow who had built the synagogue after his release. Other Bene Israel died in the Sekh, Persian, and Afghan wars in the early nineteenth century. More of the Bene Israel also died in the Indian Rebellion of 1857, and in the Saukin and Sondan wars at the end of the nineteenth century."*

The Bene Israel served the British well. But even though a few were given their due recognition, they were still considered a unique lot among Indians, and even among Jews. They were always involved in the armed forces of their country, but were still always regarded as the oil pressers of Kolaba District. That is the portion of the Konkan in which most of them resided, and were commonly addressed as *teli*, the Marathi caste name for oil pressers. They were never addressed as Bene Israel, their true and deserving Hebrew name. As recently as 1935 to 1944, the name was still used, and a Bene Israel physician of prominence and recognizable skill was still popularly addressed as the teli doctor.[9]

BENE ISRAEL PEOPLE

It appears that the Konkan did not have original indigenous Hindu telis, and it was only recently that India's Hindu telis migrated to the Konkan area from the interior of the country. So it is possible that for some time, the only telis in the Konkan area were the Bene Israel.

Like good Hebrews, the Bene Israel educated their children to the best of their knowledge and ability. That effort produced artisans, professionals, semi-professionals, and both male and female government civil servants, and male construction workers in Bombay. Some women worked in stores and offices. They did not stay at home like the Hindu and Moslem middle-class women, who were mostly illiterate. The Bene Israel entered different branches of government, business, and manufacturing. Since seed oil pressing had ceased to be a lucrative business by the eighteenth century, they branched out into several other occupations. Those Bene Israel probably became distinguished from the Hindu telis because even though the demand for oil abated, they still owned most of the scant number of oil pressers remaining in India.

When the Bene Israel increased in numbers on the mainland and in Bombay City, their movement was ordered controlled. A Bene Israel Kaji was recognized by the authorities as the *macadam*, or community leader.

In the Kolaba District, the Bene Israel lived in different villages. Their surnames were taken from those villages as other Indians' names were. There were names such as Penkar, Divekar, Pajpurkar, Ashtamkar, Talkar, and Nagavkar. The suffixes of these names came from *kar*—the suffix on the name of the village.

Benjamin Israel suggested that a marking of the locations of the villages could be found on a map. Those markings would support the Bene Israel's argument that they entered India through Navagon where two ancient mounds might be seen. These mounds are in the Bene Israel cemetery. They are frequently mentioned and revered as the mounds covering the graves where the shipwrecked survivors buried their dead relatives and coreligionists, who drowned escaping persecution.

The first Hazans came from Cochin, where most Jews knew Hebrew. The Bene Israel learned from them and were later able to occupy those positions. The Kajis gradually lost power until they were totally powerless, about 1890. Their lack of academic preparation in legal, secular and religious matters was their downfall.

Many Bene Israel also worked as cartmen, small plot farmers, shopkeepers, artisans, especially carpenters and painters, as well as clerks. Quite a few of them were timber, grain, and grass salesmen. Many Bene Israel even participated in technology. One could find them in almost every industry and profession. That is why the Bene Israel are often considered to be more affluent than their Hindu and Moslem compatriots.

Many Bene Israel looked just like other Indians. Up to the beginning of the twentieth century, most Bene Israel dressed very much like their neighbors in the towns and villages where they lived. The women wore and continue to wear saris. But they did not wear the *kunkoo*, or red mark, on their foreheads. Many men wore *peyoth* side burns, and observed the Sabbath, Jewish holidays, holy days and rituals, but, always ignored idols.

In modern times, the Bene Israel wear whatever styles and apparel are worn around them. The men wear European and American suits and trousers in the cities and towns, while the women wear jeans, skirts, dresses and saris. But unlike most parts of India, one sees more girls in Bombay wearing jeans, skirts, blouses, and dresses. This is a popular seaport. There are also more Christians there than in other parts of India. Nevertheless, many Bene Israel women and girls still wear *saris* because of its light weight, silky fabrics, and loose fitting. It is also very cool. Some Bene Israel women also wear *parsi* and Moslem outfits.*

A story is told of a little fellow who attended services at a certain synagogue for the first time. The temple was in a large town where the people were very cosmopolitan. Upon seeing them in their varied costumes, the little boy asked his mother, "How is it, mother, that in this synagogue there are Hindus and Muslims, Parsis and Europeans as well as Jews?" The child confirmed the fact that Jews cannot be judged even by the way they dress in certain areas or certain times.

BENE ISRAEL WOMEN

The Bene Israel women have been called the torch-bearers of their Israelite religion and ethics. They traditionally maintain records of the various feasts and fast days. These women are always ready to prepare for those feasts, and share the family hardships without murmur or intolerance. They have never ceased maintaining the family and traditions with economy and prudence as well as diligence.

When Dr. Wilson started his schools in the Kolaba District, "With the object of spreading Christian education among the Bene Israel, girls are said to have joined in disproportionately large numbers." Later on, when these girls became mothers, they in turn encouraged their daughters also to become educated even at the expense of their being missed at home for domestic chores. The mothers did the housekeeping and cooking. That sacrifice allowed the Bene Israel women to be among the first Indian women liberated and academically prepared.

The Bene Israel girls are said to have comprised one-third of the student body in Dr. Wilson's school in the 1820s. At that time, illiteracy was common, not only among women, but among well-respected men as well. A story is told of an old man who used to harass girls on their way to the high school for Indian girls in Rasta's Peth—a Bene Israel residential area of Poona. The old man had been a truant as a youth during the latter part of the nineteenth century. Therefore, he thought that girls with higher education training would only develop into blue-stocking gals and fail to become good housewives and mothers. The old gentleman told Moses that most of the girls he had harassed in his youth were now settled down, married, and become excellent mothers. "They had brought up highly educated children; both boys and girls and they themselves were now highly placed and respected parents, both in and out of the community." Those results led to the opening of another school. An Organization for Rehabilitation and Training (ORT) Girls' School was opened to young Bene Israel females in 1970, at Bombay. The boys also have their ORT School.

426 The African Origin of Modern Judaism

Many Bene Israel women had to live alone, however, because of the lack of men, and especially educated men, in India. Others had to marry functional illiterates, semiliterates, merchants, or tradesmen with incomes, in order to avoid becoming old maids. Nevertheless, tradition has helped the women maintain happy and resourceful families. They believe in education and give their children the best academic preparation they are able to afford.

Even in present times, the Bene Israel women are the providers of the sumptuous dinners, with succulent meats and other delicately prepared Indian foods for *Purim*, the *Pesach seder*, and other holiday feasts. They also act as hostesses, secretaries, writers, and publishers in New York. One Bene Israel's researcher is Brenda Joseph.[10]

Girls' involvement is even more prevalent among Bene Israel parents now. This acceptability is due to the women's liberation movement's impression throughout the world. The popularity of a woman as Prime Minister of India (Indira Ghandi), and a woman at the helm of the British Kingdom (Margaret Thatcher) has also given impetus to greater respect for women's ability and rights, even among women of non-Hebrew religions.

The Bene Israel mother begins her Sabbath cooking on Fridays, about 2:00 P.M. and completes her chores by 5:00 P.M. Any other duties to be presently or later performed on Friday after sundown or on the Sabbath are relegated to a Gentile servant, or abandoned until Saturday evening or Sunday morning. After the cooking, the mother takes the children to Friday evening services, beginning at sunset and lasting for approximately one hour. At the closing of the services, a *kiddush* is repeated by a rabbi or a *Hazan* for the blessing of the synagogue. Saturday morning prayers begin at 6:30 A.M., and the mother has to have her husband's shirt and underwear ready. The early morning services, from 6:30 to about 8:30, are usually attended by men. The women only attend on High Holy Days or New Year's Day. Then they sit in the gallery and observe the ceremonies until the service ends. These women usually return to the synagogue with the entire family at 3:00 P.M. The evening services are similar to the morning services, where the Torah is read. But this service is an hour or so shorter. When it ends, lamps are lit by the *Shamash*, or beadle. A plate is placed on the *teba*, or reading desk, where the reader holds one of the two glasses on it. He repeats a blessing, then tastes the juice, and shares the rest poured out to the other members of the congregation present. Then he recites *Veyit*, a *Mishna* that explains thirty-nine principles of occupations prohibited on the Sabbath Day, which is to be kept holy with no manner of work performed.

The active participation of Bene Israel mothers in civil affairs helped bring about a branch of the Mazgoan School which was inaugurated in the Israel Moholla of Bombay in 1902. Children unable to travel to the old primary school attended there until 1929. At present, children are few, and no religiously controlled schools of consequence exist.

The Bene Israel School had some dedicated teachers worth mention here. One of them, in particular, is Miss Reuben. Her attentiveness to student needs, and her dedication to her profession is most remarkable. She paid particular attention to the Kala, or darkskinned students. She instilled pride in those children, by teaching them that "Even the great King David was a Kala."[11]

BENE ISRAEL CUSTOMS AND TRADITIONS

It is said that the Jews of India are like most Jews or Hebrews elsewhere. They are education oriented. Their first publication of record was a Hebrew prayer and song book published in Marathi. Then there was publication of the liturgy, special prayers for fasts and feasts. There was even a translation of Marathi into Hebrew, and a Hebrew grammar book *The Rudiments of Hebrew Grammar*, published by John Wilson in 1832.

About eight years later, a Bene Israel published a book of prayers used by the Sephardic orthodox group printed in 1840. That same year Shalom Sharabi—probably a Cochin—published a book followed by an edition of Shiroth-Hebrew in lithograph press with songs for prayers, festivals, and ceremonies from Obidiah Jhakkai. In 1845, David Judah Ashkenazi published a Hebrew calendar covering five hundred years, while Haeem Isaac Galsukar published an *Illustrated Haggadah*. Then, in 1856, the Bene Israel Benevolent Society published its book and a four-hundred-year Hebrew calendar. At that time, funds were solicited in the book called, *Suggestions for Charity to the Poor*. That book solicited assistance for the orphans of the Bene Israel community.

During that period of literary awareness, about 1856, some Hebrew quotations were translated into Marathi. They were published by an author who simply called himself G.K. No other original publications dated between 1840 and 1856 could be located.

In any case, from 1858 to 1920, various literary works were published. Among them was a translation of the Old Testament, the Liturgy, a novel in two parts called, *Gul and Sanobar*, and a book titled, *Wonders of the World*, and other works. In the Bombay, Poona, and nearby libraries, the Old Books Collection revealed works by Bene Israelis according to their surnames. And the *Bene Israel Annual and Year Book*, published by Miss Reuben in 1920, made it clear that between 1842 and 1915 a considerable number of writings in Marathi and Hebrew were published by Bene Israel authors. Benjamin Samson Ashtamker headed the list of writers with thirty-two published works. Ashtamker was also credited with being the first person to perform the Kirtan.

The first Bene Israel newspaper was the *Or Emeth*, meaning *The Light of Truth*. It first appeared in Marathi about 1877. The *Or Emeth* was edited by Aaron Samson Ashtamker, a younger brother of the author, and Kirtanker mentioned before. This newspaper was followed by other periodicals which had names such as *Teruvvah, The Lamp of Judaism, The Bene Israel*, and *The Friend of Israel*. These were merely a few of many other published works.

Then it seems that while the Ashtamker brothers insisted on publishing Marathi writings, other authors were also busy maintaining publications in that language. However, in 1916, the Anglo-Marathi monthlies began circulation in that area.

When the Jewish publications in Marathi were discontinued in 1970 due to decreased circulation, the Bene Israel began losing consciousness of their roots. They also began failing to find exposure to any other Hebrew or Jewish culture publicly advertised.

Barber claimed in 1981 that journals with contemporary events were printed in English or Marathi. And English was still the language published in 1971. The last publication, being the *Maccabi*, which stayed on press from 1946 until 1971.

COMMUNITY DEVELOPMENT

The Bene Israel community held its first conference in December 1917. That act was considered the first movement in communal consciousness. That conference was acclaimed as an outstanding achievement for India. For the first time, members were said to have debated social, educational, and financial problems of the Bene Israel community at large. They struggled with means of survival, illiteracy, poverty, and discussed erecting a home for the aged and homeless, a sanatorium, as well as schools.

The ways and means committee of the conference discussed ways to obtain funds and methods of beneficial disbursement for those funds. Between 1917 and 1937, there were fifteen conferences held with delegates from interconnected areas. Many proposals were discussed, discarded, and implemented. In the end, the desired effect was obtained from two of them. A home for the destitute was proposed and realized and an orphanage was opened. Donations from charitable people and organizations were received, and said to have been well distributed to the needy. The sick were also well cared for.

The conference also resulted in the establishment of a Hebrew Cooperative Credit Society and a few cooperative stores. The stores were not successful and had to be phased out after a short period of time. The Credit Society became a sort of credit union after awhile and provided small-business and personal loans which kept the poor members of the Bene Israel community from being devoured by loan sharks or big banks with high interest loans.

Barber declared that the oldest recorded Bene Israel community institution was a Benevolent Society founded in 1853. Haeem Kehamkar, a historian, was the founder. The purpose of that society was to render assistance to the needy Bene Israel. Another popular Bene Israel Mandal was founded and operated by the famous Dr. Jerusha Jacob Jhirad in 1913, "for the social, educational and economic uplift of women."

There were other groups formed to encourage participation in national sports and in oral communication. A couple of these organizations were The Israelite League and the Jewish Sporting Club. They were founded between 1900 and 1913. In 1905, E.S. Baker founded a Saint John Ambulance Brigade, Jewish Division, Overseas Section. Other friendships were formed intermittently, but they all faded out when the Bene Israel population started leaving India for Israel, Canada, and the United States most of all.

Poona still has a Jewish Welfare Association which gives financial aid to indigent Bene Israel up to the present time. That association and the Jewish Club in Bombay were the only two Bene Israel benevolent societies encountered in the research of Barber (1979). In Karachi, which became a part of Pakistan after the partition of 1947, there were six groups similar to those in Bombay. Barber could not find out, however, if those groups were still in existence. Only a few Bene Israel continue to live in Karachi.

Some of those who have left Poona recall childhood experiences there with reverence and longing. Elizabeth Naidu, a member of Bene Israel wrote in *Kol Bina* about the Succoth Shaloma Synagogue there.[12] She stated how "Poona at that time was teeming with Bene Israels. Every second house had a Mezuzza." The festivals would begin from the month of *Elul*, which precedes the month of Tishri. The Rosh Hashanah, or New Year, comes in Tishri. Rosh meaning head and Shanah meaning year. The new year would be celebrated for two days.

Inquiries have revealed that there are no *Havurah Kaddish* to be found in that area now.[13] The reason being, the continuous exodus of Bene Israel to the United States, Israel and other parts of the world. Consequently, it is difficult for synagogue members to raise a Minyan during most of the year. There is a cemetery, however, and the few Bene Israel left there have burial sites staked out. Those sites were provided by the public assistance boards of the synagogue.

BENE ISRAEL OF DISTINCTION

The government of India has made awards to three Bene Israel for outstanding achievements. They were Jerusha Jacob Jhirad, a gynecologist and social benefactor for the indigent (1966); David Abraham

Cheulkar[14] an actor in Indian movies (1969); and Reuben David Dandekar, for outstanding efforts and originality as a zoo curator (1975). These awards were called *Padma Shri* and were awarded by the Indian government on India's independence day. It is the highest honor of national appreciation given by the State of India for outstanding effort in different fields of endeavor. Other Bene Israel accomplished fame by being chief justices, physicians, attorneys, writers, poets, publishers, mayors of Bombay, and chief administrators in government. One Bene Israel even became a well-respected cricket umpire of the India Panel of Umpires. *The Kol Bina Bulletin* of New York mentioned that in 1949, Ayro Levi, the first Israeli Immigration Officer of India, organized an aliya group. It consisted of forty boys and girls trained in Eli Kadoorie School of Mazgaon in Bombay. These children were sent to Israel in 1950. Since then, the Bene Israelis have advanced to such positions as pilots, professors, teachers, army officers, air hostesses, engineers, union leaders, and politicians. The Bene Israelis have even run on their own party slate during a recent election in Israel. They succeeded in electing three candidates under their SHILUV banner (meaning integration) in 1984.

American Jews have taken a keen interest in the history of the Hebrews of India. They have been showing and researching their heritage even in the Judah L. Magnes Museum (2911 Russell St., Berkeley, California) where an exhibit entitled "The Jews of India" attracted wide public attention.[15]

Another book on the history of Jews and Hebrews was written by Benjamin Israel of India. Its title is "The Bene Israel of India–Sangam."

It is now thirty-five years since Bene Israelis began settling in Israel. Today, they number over 30,000. But of the 650,000 villages in India, only about 110 are considered formerly or presently occupied by Bene Israelis. The Bene Israel women all have children or are part of families with children.

In the cities where there are hospitals or midwifery, Jewish mothers find similarities between their religious customs and those of the Hindu and Moslem mothers.

RELIGIOUS AND HOLIDAY OBSERVANCE

The Bene Israel believe that the soul departs from the body when one is sound asleep, and returns to the body when one awakens. Like the Rosecrucians, the Bene Israel also feel that one should thank God for the privilege of being able to reflect and meditate.

Upon awakening, the Bene Israel does not mention the name of God until their hands and faces have been washed at the beginning of the day. After a warm bath, the morning prayers are repeated along with the *Shema Israel*.

Rosh Hashanah is the day of remembrance and reckoning for the harvest of our deeds. It is on this first day of the New Year that the sessions of the Great Heavenly Father's Tribunal begins. The Bene Israel then go before Him, on his throne of judgment, with prayers and supplications that He might temper justice with mercy on all creatures. On that day, the Book of Life is opened and on Yom Kippur—the Day of Atonement—the judgment is sealed. On this day, is recalled the proclamation of Prophet Nehemiah to the Hebrews and Jews of Jerusalem:

This day is holy unto the Lord your God, mourn not nor weep. Go eat rich dainties and drink sweet drinks, send portions to him who has nothing ready, for this day is holy to our Lord, Grieve not, for the joy of the Lord is your strength.

The *Haath-Boshee*, the Kiss of Peace, has been preserved by the Bene Israel from ancient times. This greeting is used at the conclusion of services in the synagogue and on festive occasions in the home or elsewhere. It is a Marathi word, meaning a kiss transmitted by hand.

Jhirad (1984) stated that perhaps the best description of this greeting was given by the Rev. J. Henry Lord in a book published by the Mission Press, Kholapur, India, in 1907. It was entitled, *The Jews of India and the Far East.** The Haath Boshee is said to emanate from the chief minister, who bestows it on the elders nearest to him. Then it passes through the congregation with each individual seeking it from his senior or superior. The arms are extended with the hands flattened out, and in the position of thumbs being uppermost, the person approached takes the hand between his own similarly held. The junior then probably places his remaining hand on the outside of one of those of the person already holding his other hand. The hands of each are then simultaneously released and each one immediately passes the tips of his fingers which have touched those of his neighbor to his mouth, and kisses them. He then moves on to receive the same from or to bestow the same on another, and so on, till all persons in the synagogue have saluted one another. Two or three minutes may be spent in the process. A movement is going on all through the synagogue, and a distinctly audible sound of the lips is heard throughout the hall until all have finished. The Jews of Cochim also use this greeting.

According to Lord (1907), this greeting is identical to the greeting of the early Christians who called it the Kiss of Peace. The custom appears among the Jews of Persia also, especially those of Kurdistan. It is popular among the Syrian Christians in South India who trace their origin to the first century when Saint Thomas went to India.

The Haath Boshee is so distinctive that it should not be confused with imitations used by Hindus and Moslems. "It is a misnomer to describe the Haath Boshee as an Indian mode of greeting, for no other Indian people use it."[16]

It was also pointed out that religion and education went hand in hand among the Bene Israel. Therefore, in order to meet sound academic needs of students, the affluent members of the community formed an association in 1875. The organization was headed by H.S. Kehimkar and was named "The Bene Israel Benevolent Society for Promoting Education." It was started with a primary school which became inadequate to meet the school population's needs in a very short while.

Kehimkar then appealed to the Anglo-Jewish Association of London, most of the synagogues, and the Indian government. The English people and others from neighboring countries responded with their contributions. A larger school was immediately built and named The Israelite School in 1886. Classes which had been held in a rented house in the slums were now housed here. A minimum tuition was charged; by 1892, the school expanded to include a coed high school with preparatory courses to enable students to enter higher learning institutions like the Bombay University. In 1896 Kehimkar and other community developers bought another building in Mozgoan.

NOTES

1. Hendrik Van Loon, The Story of Mankind (U.S.A. Liveright Publishing Corp. 1962), p. 57.
2. Raymond James, The News World Newspaper (New York, 1979).
3. Benjamin J. Israel. The Jews of India (New Delhi: Interfaith Jewish Welfare Association, 1982).
    Ezekiel Barber. The Bene Israel of India: Images and Reality (Washington, DC: University Press of America, 1981).
4. Israel.
5. Ezekiel Barber. The Bene Israel of India (Washington, D.C.: University Press of America, 1981).
6. Israel.
7. Barber.
8. Haeem S. Kehimkar. The History of the Bene Israel (In Marathi) (Bombay: Prakesh Company, 1927).
*   Kehimkar.
9. Israel.
*   Parsis came from Persia originally. They are called fire worshippers.
10. Mikhtav Shelanu, "Our Letter" (Organ of the Jewish Welfare Association) Poona, India., Vol. No. 1 3-1984 c/o Moses Mapgaonkar. Sahney Sujjan Pk. Poona, India 411 040.
11. A Kala is a black descendant of the Dravidians or other people of African origin who migrated to India.
12. Kol Bina News. The Bulletin of Congregation Bina. An organization of

Indian Jewry settled in North America. New York: September 1984. Vol. IV, No. 1.

13. *Havurah Kaddisha.* Hebrew and Aramaic title applied to "sacred society" for visiting the sick, and making charitable donations and even burying the dead. Among Sephardim, it's called *Hesed ve-Emet* also, meaning "kindness and truth." Genesis 47:29.

14. Cheuklar is a surname meaning, "from the village of Cheul."

15. *KOL BINA.* The bulletin of Congregation Bina, an organized group of dark-skinned Hebrews settled in North America. New York, September 1984, Vol. IV, No. 1.

* The book was reprinted in 1976 by the Greenwood Publishers of Westport, Conn.

16. Elijah E. Jhirad. The Haath Boshee: The Kiss of Peace (article) Kol Bima bulletin of Congregation Bina. New York 1984. vol. IV, No. 1.

CHAPTER 13

THE TRIBAL JEWS OF NORTHEAST INDIA

In 1948 V.L. Benjamin stated that through the breaking up of the Kaifeng community in China, many Chinese and other Jews fled for their lives along the rivers, streams, and mountain ranges. The routes taken by these refugees dispersed them in boats toward the south going to IndoChina. As a result, the Manipur Jews or Northeast Indian Tribal Jews are claimants of descent from the refugees who fled in that direction. Some members are also said to have found shelter in the well-known valley of the cave.

Benjamin emphasized:

> Our aims and objects are to strengthen Judaism to live, act and die as what we are the same of one of the tribes.Hence, we are neither to be neglected [sic] nor to be regarded by our brothers who are in Yisrael.

The tribal Jews of Manipur claim to descend from the tribes of Manasseh, the son of Joseph and the father of Machir.[1] Machir's brother was Ashriel. The half tribe is said to have been led into captivity in Assyria, 722 B.C.

The twelve tribes are supposed to have descended from the Jacob tree. Isaac was Jacob's father, and Abraham was the father of Isaac. Jacob's twelve sons were Reuben, Simeon, Levi, Judah, Isaker, Jebulin, Joseph, Benjamin, Dan, Naphtali, Gad, and Asher from whom came forth the nations. These tribes are said to have lived in Canaan or Palestine quite peacefully under kings like Saul, David, Solomon and his son Rehoboam.

When Rehoboam ascended the throne of Israel he appointed young men of his age rather than accept the old wise men of his father's court. Those elders then sought support among ten tribes. The other tribes, Judah and Benjamin's houses, supported the young courtiers. The ten tribes then moved northward where they called the land Samaria. They called themselves Israel. Rehoboam and the two tribes then called themselves Judah and named their capital Jerusalem. The Jews lived under kings such as Pekah, Hosea and Jeroboam.

An Assyrian invasion of 722 B.C.E. caused the dispersion of the ten tribes which lived in Samaria. They were led into captivity in Assyria under wicked King Shalmanezar.[2] The Israelites are said to have experienced merciless treatment under that tyrant. He deported some and put others under Halah, Habor, and Hara routes toward the River Gozan. Others were sent to Medes. Later, Manasseh's half tribe was also brought into Halah, Medes, and Persia.

In 457 B.C.E. the tribes had been under kings Darius and Cyrus of Media and Persia. In 331 B.C.E. Alexander the Great of Macedonia defeated the Persian monarch Darius at Arbella and annexed Afghanistan and India. The Persian Jews began migrating to Afghanistan or Pakhtoon where they lived among the Moslems and Pakhthus. By 200 B.C.E. the Jews had become slaves and servants engaged in sheepherding and other menial tasks. The twelve tribes built stone dwellings for their masters, and offered animal sacrifices to the gods of their masters. Some of those Hebrews became Moslems after being pressured by members of Islam. As a result of these dispersions and conversions, many of those Hebrews or Israelites lost their knowledge of Hebrew and their traditions. The ones who lost the customs became known as a "Nomadic tribe of the Semitic speaking peoples. They choose to live in hills rather than live in towns."[3] However, according to Josephus, these Jews held onto their scrolls and prayer shawls and practiced the tenets under the guidance of the priests and elders who maintained the Laws and practiced them secretly.

KAIFENG, CHINA

The remaining members of the tribes, said Benjamin, left Afghanistan through the Hindu Cush[4] Valley and moved farther east. They then crossed the rivers and climbed mountains in the hilly region of Tibet, on to the border of China. Those Hebrews moved through China until they reached Central China. At that point, they crossed the Wei-river and arrived at *Kaifeng* also known as *Kaifung* or *Laifang*. The tribes established a colony there in 231 A.D., remaining in peace for many years. But the Mongols came in 1287 and the Hebrews had to flee elsewhere. Some surrendered to the Chinese king as hostages and servants for protection. But they paid a price. They had to give up their religion and identity. Furthermore, many of them intermarried with Gentiles, changed their names, and found themselves living mainly in the caves of the rocks and the hilly region. The local people began calling those refugees cave dwellers, mountaineers, or hillmen. The names Hebrew, Israelite, or Jew was no longer heard. They ignored their origin for fear of being detected as different in customs or ethnicity.

One group is said to have reached IndoChina where they also became cave dwellers in caves that had been mentioned to them by their progenitors who had sojourned there two generations before. This group is one of those which kept their scroll and parchment. They supposedly hung on to them until the prince of China drove them out of the caves. At this time, they lost their Torah, which had been secured until the beginning of the nineteenth century.

During their sojourn in the caves, their sustenance depended mostly on fruits and their raiment was made of animal skins. They lived as hermits and no longer maintained the Day of Atonement, and other days of rest and worship as important as the Sabbath. However, the Jews of China kept their parchment scrolls.

THE PARCHMENT

A special family was usually selected to protect the Parchment. According to Benjamin, this family's identity was treacherously disclosed and the hiding place publicly exposed. The Chinese prince and his army immediately drove out the Hebrews because of their religious practices. Those who wished to remain adopted Taoism, the popular Chinese religion of that time. Another version is that the Chinese could not read the Hebrew scrolls and therefore ripped them up and burned them. But some Jews said that the scrolls were buried and never recovered.

The priesthood, which had been preserved until the beginning of the nineteenth century, was ended by the Christian missionaries from Great Britain and the United States (1854–1910). The Christians are blamed for throwing out the vessels of the temples, burning the temples and other materials consumed by the fires they set. The Christian priesthood did not entail guiding the worshipers to read the Law for themselves. So the Jews could no longer discuss the Law or its interpretations.

BURMA

The wanderers, chased by the Chinese prince, found themselves migrating toward the West. They passed through Burma, after leaving Chinlung to Manipul, now called Burma. The Israelites were passed through Thailand (Siam), Kale Valley, Mount Kennedy, the Natchuang ranges, and Shan to reach Burma. Here, the refugees found the Irrowdy River and followed it almost up to the city of

Mandalay, where there was a small village named Aupatuang. Chinlung was the chief of the village and he allowed the Israelites to settle there. They were then forced to build the palace of Burma for the king. It was made of teakwoods, for there were no other materials available. That palace was later destroyed by war.

Later, there were agreeable terms for the refugees, but a great famine soon added to their plight, spreading throughout Mandalay and Aupatuang. The refugees had to seek food elsewhere. They found the Chindwin River after a sound exploration of the area. They followed Chindwin until they reached Kalenyo. The tribe remained here for quite a number of years. Some members went on toward Chin Hills and Khampat Valley.

In central Burma, the Israelites were called *Luse* but the natives called them *Kachin*. *Lu* means tribe or of the ten lost tribes, and *se* means ten. The natives also called the Israelites *Chin Lusi*, meaning Ark carriers, and carriers of the ten tribes and Commandments. It was felt that these Israelites had carried an Ark with them from IndoChina and elsewhere, like the *Chin-Cholkar* of Bombay. *Chin Cholkar* means coming from China in Bangla, although they sometimes spoke *Chin*, which is a language of IndoChina.

During the eighteenth century, some of the Jews from Kalemyo, Khampat Valley, migrated to Manipur and the Mizo District, as it is now called. The recorders claim that these Hebrews were originally from China rather than from India. However, the rituals and practices they exercised were adopted from their surroundings. Circumcision no longer took place among these people, and they no longer possessed a Torah. They lived like Moslems, Christians, and Pagans.

MARRIAGE

The Hebrews were mistreated in the Burma, IndoChina and China regions. Nevertheless, they received freedom of movement and some opportunity to worship and earn a decent living. They began to intermarry with Indians according to Indian customs, but interjected some Hebrew customs in their religious practices.

The parents of the bride and bridegroom had equal authority in making marital decisions. The agreements were settled in the presence of a priest. The priesthood was and still is inherited. The ceremonies are valid even if there is only one witness on each side. Marriage to distant relatives and persons of other religious persuasions is now prohibited. The eldest son must be engaged to his maternal uncle's daughter as soon as he reaches adolescence. The marriages are performed by priests as elders.

The eldest son also inherits his father's estates and properties when his father passes. The dead man's brother is committed to marry his sister-in-law as soon as his brother dies. And the first son born to this couple must be named after the deceased husband to keep his name alive.

Adultery was not condoned among these people; neither was divorce permitted. The husbands' extramarital affairs were and are still considered, to some extent, to be a male spreading his oats. But if a wife was caught breaking the marital vows, she would be expelled from the village. Women could not participate in the affairs of men. And no woman was permitted to wear men's clothing. No woman could have power equal to that of a man or over her husband.

When someone became terminally ill, the priest was called in for the final benediction. The priest cut the throat of the lamb or other animals brought for sacrifices. If a male patient died, he would be immediately put on pyre, doused with kerosene, and burned to ashes. If the deceased were a female, she would be buried in the bowels of the earth to reproduce. Newborn babies were brought to the priests after eight days on the planet to be blessed and then circumcised.

During the year, at least three feast days were celebrated. One was *Chap Chor Kist* or *Hun Juneh Kut* or *Mim Kut or Chang thah kut* and *Pawlkut*.

The basis of religion in Burma around the early 1900s was said to be based on ancestor worship and animism. The people believed in pantheism. They worshipped trees, fruits, fairies, rivers. Then Christianity was introduced by William Peyer in 1834 A.D. When the Israelites arrived, they began adopting some pantheistic beliefs to avoid being conspicuously different. Then the Christians discovered the Hebrews and began teaching them Christianity. More Christians came from America in 1910. Then the Hebrew-Israelites began practicing Judaism once more. They realized how much the Christians had copied from the original Law, and Christ, who himself was a Hebrew and not a Christian. The local people turned hostile to the Israelites.

TEN LOST TRIBES

The Ten Lost Tribes are known to speak different dialects, depending on the area they inhabited. They were scattered among Gentile nations throughout Medea and Persia. But Josephus and other chroniclers said that some of them held out against conversion. These tribes celebrated interesting customs, practiced their inherited traditions, and kept Torah, nonetheless. Those practices caused them to be called Jews like the Jews practicing the same religion throughout the Roman Empire.

JUDAH JEWS, ISRAEL HEBREWS

Although the words Jews and Hebrews, or Israelites, are used indiscriminately, the general consensus among well-informed members of the religion is that a majority of converts to the Judaic faith came from among the tribes of Judah and Benjamin and were scattered mostly among the Ashkenazim of Europe. We studied the captivity of the Jews and their subjection to temptations in Babylon under Nebuchadnezzar. The Jews were there in 600 B.C.. After seventy years of subjection in Babylon all the Jews and some Hebrews returned to Jerusalem to continue their prayers and offerings in the Temple. The Jews were again forced into captivity by Titus when the Romans ruled the area of Judea and elsewhere. The Ten Tribes of Israel, which constituted the northern kingdom during the biblical period, were also taken into captivity, but by the Assyrians in 721–715 B.C. The act assumed great importance among Jews and Hebrews because it had been prophesied (e.g., Ezekiel 37:16). Through those times, the Jews and Hebrews became lumped together as Wandering Jews. These two tribes were really not lost, but rather displaced.

After being captives under Assyrian King Shalmanzar in 722 B.C., the Israelites were later dispersed among the Medes and Persians, as well as other Gentile nations. The Israelites were misplaced for seven hundred years and considered lost. During that time, many of them became converted to Christianity or were simply assimilated. Those assimilated worshipped idols, along with their God of Israel. Some became Jews for Jesus, and preached that Jesus was the Messiah. But most of the Chinese, Mongolian, Indian Jews and Hebrews remained loyal to the religion of their forefathers. These wandering people became known as "Nomadic people or Tribes of the Semitic speaking peoples." The consistent believers in Hebrew Laws were later called *Kuchis,* the wandering people whose descendants had at last arrived at Manipur in 1830. The word meant people of color.

NOTES

1. I Chronicles 7:14.
2. I Chronicles 5:26. II Kings 18:1-11.
3. V.L. Benjamin. The Tribal Jews of the Far North East. (Manipur, India: Beyth Sholom Prayer Hall, 1948) p. 6.
4. Kush or Cush is also the name of Ethiopia, which was also called Koch.
5. Christopher S. Wren. The New York Times, Tuesday May 18, 1982, p. A-2.
6. Wren, The New York Times.
7. All Hebrew words, except Youtai which is Chinese.

CHAPTER 14

THE CHINESE HEBREWS

The Israelites who left Canaan went out in different directions after the Babylonian exile or Hebrew *galut bavel*. Many Hebrews went to China and elsewhere. But the most remarkable group of the dispersed communities was the community of Kai-Feng-Fu in central China, south of the Yellow River. Kai-Feng-Fu existed and still remains, in part, to this day. It only became unpopular after the nineteenth century. Some of those Hebrews had come from Persia in connection with silk trading. Others had come directly from Babylonia.

Christian missionaries reaching the Far East in the seventeenth century reported seeing these Hebrews. These Hebrews resembled the Chinese people among whom they lived, but they observed their own Hebrew traditions and religion. The chroniclers state that these persons reached China during the Han Dynasty of Liu Pang, 220 A.D. One of the recorders was Josephus and another was Soliman of Andalusia, Spain. Pearl S. Buck also wrote the novel *Peony*, about a Chinese family's struggle to maintain its Hebrew identity in isolation.

Many Chinese Hebrews were absorbed through intermarriage, sociolinguistic interaction, writing the seven thousand graphic Chinese characters, and wearing the same style clothing. Like the Hebrews and Jews of India, the Chinese Hebrews worshipped with some similarity to their neighbors who in China practiced Confucianism. As a result, their neighbors did not consider them too different and treated them as countrymen of the Chinese nation.

Now that the people were good to the Hebrews, nature became unfavorable to them. There was a flood. It washed away part of the synagogue and left it heavily damaged in 1642. The synagogue was later rebuilt by a Mandarin, Chao Yng Cheng, in 1652. The new temple was built like other temples of the Confucian architectural style. This synagogue later fell into decay as the older Chinese Hebrews died out and their offspring dropped the practices in the nineteenth century.

Many Chinese Hebrew prayer books were lost in the flood. That loss caused the community to lose some interest in the religion. As a result, quite a few youngsters did not learn to read Hebrew. The Hebrew manuscripts which survived seemed to be copied after Chinese calligraphic style. However, the manuscripts have provided knowledge of the Chinese Hebrews' and non-Hebrews' interlinguistic connections. The ordinary person called their Chinese-Hebrew neighbors the people who pluck out the sinew (meaning they demanded well founded explanations plucked out of dogmas).

Then in 1982, more was learned about the Chinese Hebrews. Reporter Christopher S. Wren saw remnants of the Kaifeng-Fu community still living there. He stated, in a *New York Times* article, that the people were now called by their neighbors, "the Moslems of the blue caps."[5] These descendants of the ancient Hebrews no longer wear yarmelkes but still maintain some knowledge of Hebrew traditions passed on to them through oral tradition of teaching the young recorded or non-recorded history.

The site of the old synagogue is said to have turned into a garbage dump until the Communists built a hospital on the site in 1953. Some stone tablets were found with indications of a Hebrew presence there in earlier times. These relics can be seen in a local museum warehouse where they are stored. "The fragile old Torahs were spirited off [by European collectors] to museums abroad on the pretext of confirming their authenticity."[6]

UNITED STATES TOURISTS VISIT

In 1982 ten Americans of Jewish origin went through the dusty streets of a Kaifeng alley still called Nanzuejing Hutong, or South, trying to find clues or the cemetery where a prayer remembrance of Kaddish could be said for the departed ones. New York Times reporter Wren named a 59-year-old local official who stated that he was a descendant of the Hebrews of China. The man was quoted as saying, "Our ancestors came here from Arab Jerusalem and settled down. It is already nine hundred years."

A Chinese-Hebrew scholar is said to have placed the Hebrew presence of Kaifeng-Fu at a much earlier period. The scholar, Pan Guangdan, dated the migration as second century B.C.E. He also mentioned that smaller groups of Hebrews settled in nine other cities throughout China. The heavier concentration was in Hangzhou and Canton. Different Hebrew descendants interviewed related interweaving stories which proved their knowledge of the Pentateuch and the early prophets of the Old Testament.

OTHER LEGENDARY DETAILS

A Chinese gentleman, named Zhao, informed visitors that the Hebrews first migrated to India when they lived there for eleven hun-

The Chinese Hebrews   443

dred years before moving to China. They were supposed to have lived in the Cochin-Hebrews' area now called Bombay. From Cochin, the Hebrews sailed on to China, about the eleventh century. Other Hebrews also arrived form Persia to settle in China.

The Chinese Hebrews are regarded as having arrived in China during the Song Dynasty. They went to offer cotton materials to the emperor. Zhao is also said to have learned, from his progenitors and other Hebrew elders, as is customary that, "In that period, China was quite developed in silk, but its cotton cloth `industry' was backward." Another legend states that the Hebrews went there to trade. But Mr. Zhao felt that, "if they were only traders, the government would not have let them settle in Kaifeng, which was then the capital of China."

The Song emperor, it seems, invited the Hebrews to Kaifeng-Fu and bestowed seven Chinese names on their clans. They only numbered about one thousand, but soon enough, some of them rose to become bankers and merchants of prominence and occupied positions of prominence during the fourteenth and fifteenth centuries.

One oldtimer remembers his parents having cakes and dainties without salt or yeast during a certain time of the year. His family did not eat pork and definitely would not raise pigs. The Chinese of Hebrew origin also recalled flying kites with friends at a site commonly known as the place where the Jewish mosque once stood. And they distinctly recollected how, after the destruction of the synagogue, the timbers were carted away and sold to an old congregation which owned a mosque not too far away.

The Chinese also had heard of a place, named Israel, and that Jews were going there with some great purpose. They also heard of Hitler and his woeful deeds. They had also heard of the consequences of World War II, and the affect it had on minorities one way or the other. But, they had not considered themselves an ethnic minority. These Chinese Hebrews interviewed had outgrown the need for a distinct language, cultural difference, and religious ethnocentricity. The state controls birth registration and citizenship preparation. Therefore, it was considered that there could be no need for a rabbi or *mohel* to perform circumcisions. One of the interviewed members proudly declared that in China, all ethnic groups enjoy equal status. So, there was really no advantage in being a *mashullah*, or promoter of Hebrew orthodoxy. However, one young lady claimed, with apparent pride, that when she fills out forms or state questionnaires, she lists herself as *Youtai*, meaning Jewish. No one seemed interested in becoming a *Halutz*, or pioneer, in Israel.[7]

Some writers, including this researcher, met other Chinese Hebrews in Shanghai and Kowloon across from Hong Kong in Canton province.

EPILOGUE

This researcher was once purchasing some materials from a Chinese-looking merchant who was closing early on a Friday afternoon. The merchant did not have certain pieces at the shop and asked [the customer] to come to his home to pick up the selected pieces. The merchant stressed, however, that the pickup be made before dusk. He thought that the insistence on promptness was rather unusual, in China, and might have insinuated fearfulness because of neighborhood dangers. Perhaps there were burglars there like in Shanghai where youngsters grabbed your hat and if you chased them into an alley, you came back out without your outer clothing and wearing just your underwear. But this danger did not exist under British-controlled territories, such as Hong Kong, Kowloon, or Portuguese Macao. Then, there was the thought of the delay because of rickshaw traffic, or the delay in getting across the Canton (Pearl) River by ferry back to Hong Kong.

The visitor was anxious. When the visitor, from New York City, arrived at the merchant's home, a servant opened the door. It was a quiet residential area with no apparent dangerous threats, but dusk had begun to fall. The master and his family were at the table having Sabbath eve supper. The master got up and stretched forth his hand. But there was something unusual or unexpected about him. He was dressed in a Yarmelke and a *tallith gadol*, or full-size prayer shawl.

The visitor was offered supper, as is customary in the East, where the host shares wine and breaks bread with the stranger within his gates. The stranger put his hat back on his head and curiously accepted the invitation to share wine and bread along with the prayer for *lahem* and *ha gafen*. Then, the prayers started *Baruch Atah Adonai Elohenu Melek Haolam*. It meant Blessed be God, King of the. The Chinese merchant seemed astonished, and I was also somewhat amazed. Then it came to mind that the old Jews which visited my grandmother's home used to say, in Yiddish, "Der yid ist in der ganze Welt." The Jew is in the whole world.

This event occurred on one of the many visits made to China by this researcher on the S.S. President Cleveland and S.S. President Monroe, from 1948 to 1949.

This researcher was then told of families living in China and still practicing the Hebrew tradition which began in northeast Africa and not in Europe as most Ashkenazis pretend. But, the Communists were marching down from the hills under Mo Chack Tung whom the westerners called Mao Ze dong. They were chanting:

Chilai put yin jo no ta di yan mun.
Wao mundi hi yo
Chook sin chandi chan sin.
Chun wop min ehow toliao.
Chow mun wundi chandi chan sing

Chilai, Chilai, Chilai!
Go wun man chong yee sing
Mo Chack tick yandi pao foo.
Chin Chan! Chin Chan! Chin Chan, Chan.

Onward to victory
With our hands and bodies
We will build the New China
We will march over the dead
bodies of the fallen.

Onward Onward Onward
We will be victorious
We will triumph
Forward, Forward, Forward.

The Chinese were jubilant, but the British soldiers and sailors were worried. A street walker said to a British sailor, "You will no longer be able to insult our people. The Communists will show you.

At that time, many Chinese would crouch or sit on their legs, along the sidewalks. The British used to come along and chase them or kick them out of the way. The Chinese, who were usually doped up while begging *cumshaw*, would scurry over to the wall of the building where they were begging or loafing. But, the Communists came down, detoxified them once or twice and then eliminated them if they did not cease the habit. Soon, there were no more idlers, and the British were saying, "I beg your pardon, old chap," instead of pushing and showing unchallenged authority.

The question with which we are now confronted is, "Will Judaism survive in China?"

INDEX

Benjamin Israel of India, 417,
    427, 430, 432
Benjamin of Tudela, 56, 106,
    211, 420
Benjamin, Moses, 381
Benjamin, V. L., 435, 440
Bennett, Lerone, 68, 83
Benus, Simon, 378-379
Beracha V. Sholom V, 380
Berbers, 68-69
Bergen-Belsen Jews, 329
Bergman, Maximo, 364
Bering Straits, 335
Berkeley, 430
Berko, 333
Berlin, 291, 315-316, 324-325,
    333, 356
Bermuda Conference, 384, 413
Bermuda, 384-385, 413
Bernal, 237
Bernardine, 266, 278
Bernstein, Max, 352
Bersabe, 133
Berseem, 217, 242
Berychev, 316
Berytus, 124
Besht, Israel, 287-288
Bet Din, 64-65
Bet-ha-Midrash, 262
Beta Israelites, 57
Betar, 172
Bethlehem, 348
Beyth Sholom Prayer Hall, 440
Bible Dictionary, 15, 39, 80
Biblioteca Historica Italo-
    Judaica, 171
Bibliotheque, 229
Biblo, 101, 191
Biddle, 399
Biddle, Colonel Charles of
    Philadelphia, 399
Big Shlakhta, 255, 258, 330
Bilingual Education An
    International Sociological
    Perspective, 83
Bimah, 332, 383, 413
Birmingham, 88, 101, 242, 334,
    336, 340, 411
Birmingham, Stephen, 88, 101,

242, 334, 336, 411
Biscay, 216
Bishop Dembovski, 285-286
Bishop of Carthage, 187
Bishop of Heraclea, 184
Bishop of Hippo, 185, 189
Bishop of Rome, 204, 215
Bishop of Vilna, 298
Bishop Peter, 229, 258
Bishops, 182, 184-186, 213,
    225, 230, 233, 235, 267, 333
Bismarck, 93-94
Bitter Lakes, 179
Bivar, 218
Black Africans, 69
Black Code Law, 386
Black Culture, 79
Black Death, 249
Black Europeans, 69
Black Haitians of Jewish, 388
Black Hand, 270
Black Hebrew, 4, 75, 79, 205,
    212, 247, 336, 414
Black Jews, 23, 43, 67-68, 82,
    84, 91, 102, 177, 361
Black Khazars, 102, 256
Black Muslims, 67, 177
Black Panther Branch Office, 331
Black Power, 184, 338-339
Black Sea, 72, 96, 99, 111, 208
Black Shawl, 308
Blackamoor, 185, 201
Blackest Moroccans, 205
Blemmyes, 188
Blond, Dr. Maurice, 412
Blum, 92
Board of Education of New York,
    265
Boaz, 118, 143, 167, 245
Bodner, Frederick, 79
Boers, 69, 89
Boethus, 117
Bogota, 404
Bohemia, 85, 249, 392
Boleslav of Kalish, 250
Bolivar, 363, 397-398
Bolivar, Simon of Venezuela, 363
Bombay Army, 421
Bombay City, 424

King Solomon, 22, 54, 166, 169-
170, 245
King Stanislav Augustus, 296
King Taharka, 33, 45
King Vittirio Emanuele III, 108
King Vladislav IV, 271
King, Rodney, 83
Kingdom of Ethiopia, 15, 50
Kingdom of Israel, 66, 150, 415,
417-418
Kingdom of Italy, 108
Kingdom of Judah, 1, 66, 103,
246, 415, 417
Kingdom of Naples, 107
Kingdom of Poland, 312
Kingdom of Sardinia, 107
Kingston Corporation, 374
Kir, 78
Kiriath Arba, 147
Kirsch, 316
Kirtan, 428
Kirtanker, 428
Kish, 44
Kiss of Peace, 431, 433
Kitchener, 24
KITTIM, 72
Klinger, 41
Kmita, Peter, 257
Knochen, 324-325
Knopf, 81, 242
Knossos, 181
Koch, 15, 440
Koenigsberg, 262
Koestler, 82, 84, 94-95, 101-102,
248, 256, 330
Koestler, Arthur, 82, 101-102,
248
Kohanski, Alexander S., 334
Kol Bina News, 433
Kol Bina, 429-430, 433
Kol Shearith Israel Burial Society
of Panama, 401
Kol Shearith Israel Congregation,
401, 410
Kol Shearith Israel, 401, 406-
407, 409-410, 414
Kol Shearith, 401, 406-407, 409-
410, 414
Kolaba District, 420, 423-425

Kon-Tiki, 25
Konfu, 45
Königsberg, 291
Konkan, 419, 422-423
Konta, 28
Koran, 10, 37, 51, 66, 100, 423
Korea, 40
Korosko, 30
Korsum, 271
Kosciusko, 297-298
Kosciusko, Thaddeus, 297
Kosono, 288
Kovno, 300
Kowloon, 90, 443-444
Koyra, 28
Krefen, 45
Kriminal Kommisar, 327
Krishna, 83, 242
Kristallnacht, 322-323
Kristos, 242, 276
Kronenberg, 311
Ku Klux Klan, 59, 69, 109
Kucha, 28
Kuchis, 440
Kuera, 28
Kullo, 28
Kuraish, 194
Kurdistan, 431
Kuseila, 199-200
Kush, 15, 440
Kushitic, 25
Kutover, 288
Kuty, 288
Kuwait, 83
La Dama, 216
La Guardia, 234
La Higa, 352
La Luz, 224, 352
La Niña, 237
La Peña, 216
La Peninsula Iberica, 216
La Perla, 362
La Valle, 242
Labor Zionist, 110
Labor, 48, 87, 110, 261, 309,
313, 322-324, 326-327, 333,
341-342, 355-356, 363
Labour of Egypt, 39
Ladino, 332, 405

Menkaure, 45
Mercado, 359
Mercado, Abraham, 359
Merchants, 25, 86-87, 99, 135,
    169, 195, 209-211, 217, 231,
    237, 249, 255, 257, 261,
    263-264, 266, 293-294, 297,
    304-305, 308-309, 312-313,
    315, 338, 349, 353, 363,
    366, 372-373, 379, 381-382,
    386-387, 391-393, 408, 426,
    443
Mercury, 110, 207
Merlin, 10
Meshech, 18, 72
Mesopotamia, 2, 10, 32, 39, 41,
    72-73, 98, 203
Mesquita, 359, 412
Mesquita27, 359
Mesraim, 15, 39
Mesre, 15, 39
Messiah of Socialist Dialectism,
    94
Messiahs, 280, 288
Messianic, 225, 279-280, 283-
    287, 293
Messina, 215
Mexican Archivo Nacional
    Antigua, 349
Mexican Inquisition, 349
Mexican Jewish History, 355
Mexican Republic, 354
Mexican Revolution, 271
Mexicans, 271, 335, 351, 353-
    354
Meza, 397
Mezuzahs, 364
Miami, 365, 376, 386
Micah, 55
Michigan, 11, 81, 83
Middle East, 6, 31, 88, 105, 414
Middle Road, 83
Middlesex, 101
Middleton, 406
Middleton, Mr., 406
Midian, 4, 67
Midianites, 4, 179
Midrash, 243
Miguel, 220, 231, 350

Mikveh Israel-Emanuel, 368
Milan, 108, 381, 384
Milan, Gabriel, 381, 384
Military Department, 305
Military Order of King William I,
    405
Milowski, 286
Milwaukee, 351
Mim Kut, 439
Minister of Communications, 364
Minister of England, 92, 346
Minister of Finance, 371
Ministerio, 242
Ministry of Education, 15, 19,
    83, 355
Minoan Islands, 216
Minoans, 181, 334
Minos, 181
Minsk, 297
Minyan, 358-359, 378, 395, 429
Miriam, 8
Mishkin, 356
Mishna, 243, 426
Misr, 15
Misraim, 39
Mission Press, 431
Mithnagdim, 296, 301
Mithnagim, 291
Mizo District, 438
Mizraim, 50, 66, 72
Mo Chack Tung, 444
Moab, 90
Moabites, 90
Modigliani, 108, 110
Modigliani, Amadeo, 110
Moghilev, 280, 294
Mohammed II, Sultan, 239
Mohammed-Gerad, 24, 26
Mohammedan Africans, 200
Mohammedanism, 294
Mohammedans, 26, 282
Moholla, Israel of Bombay, 427
Moises Maimonides, 94, 211, 291
Moldavian, 259
Moldavo-Wallachia, 255
Molina, 231
Momigliano, Professore Arnoldo,
    110
Monaco, 216

Nangoan, 419
Nanzuejing Hutong, 442
Nao, 28
Napata, 21, 23, 25
Naphtali, 435
NAPHTURIM, 73
Naples, 107, 184, 213, 238, 243, 397
Napoleon Bonaparte, 299, 390
Napoleon Gabriella, 400
Napoleon I, 47, 298-299
Napoleon III, 351
Napoleonic Code, 298
Narbonne, 241
Narcosis, 62
Narses, 193, 204, 213
NASA, 190
Nashville, 11, 82
Nasir, 48, 70, 199
Nassau Hebrew Congregation, 358
Nassau, 358
Nassay, David, 86
Natal, 89
Natchuang, 437
Nathan Dorsen, 351
Nathan, Sir Nathaniel, 394
National Autonomous University of Mexico, 356
National Jewish Welfare Board Armed Services Committee, 379
National Military Organization, 347
National Party, 376
National Polytechnic Institute, 356
Native Americans, 43, 95
Naturalization Service, 77
Navagon, 418, 424
Navarre, 106
Navarro, 223, 238, 414
Navarro, Rabbi Moses, 223
Navigator, 25, 221, 229, 237, 318
Naville, 178-180, 190
Naville, Edouard Henri, 178, 190
Navy, 41, 108, 203, 295, 345, 363, 385, 402, 408, 421

Nazi Germany, 70, 364-365, 369, 394
Nazi Party, 69, 321
Nazism, 70
Neanderthal, 7
Neapolitanus, 127
Nebuchadnezzar, 1, 48, 52, 159, 168, 246, 440
Nefertiti, 36, 42
Negative Commandments, 37
Negative Confession, 36
Negrita-native, 242
Negro History, 24, 83, 182-183
Negro Leadership, 84, 190
Negro Zionists, 77, 84, 190
Negroes, 58, 60-61, 67, 396
Negus of Ethiopia, 38, 53
Negus, 15, 38, 53-54
Nehardea, 396
Nehemiah, 280, 357, 412, 431
Nehemias, 360
Nelson Museum, 390
Nelson, Consul, 403-404
Nelson, Lord Horatio, 390
Nelson, Mr. William, 407
Nelson, William, 403, 407
Neolithic, 181, 334
Nero Claudius Drusus Germanicus, 115
Neronias, 123
Nesbit, Frances, 390
Nesviah, 291
Nethanim, 169
Netherlands Antilles, 366, 391
Neus Dionysius, 42
Neve Shalom, 368
Neville, 320, 346, 375-376
Nevins, Albert C., 80
Nevis Government, 390
New Amsterdam, 339, 348, 359
New Carthage, 18, 186
New China, 445
New Christians, 87, 229, 231, 349-350, 352
New Delhi, 432
New England, 357, 392
New European, 80, 190, 268, 361, 413
New Flower, 15